More praise for *The Bankers' New Clothes*

"Important."
 —Christopher Matthews, *Time*

"Excellent."
 —Matthew Yglesias, *Slate*

"Anat Admati and Martin Hellwig convincingly make the case for much stronger and simpler borrowing limitations for banks."
 —Roger E. Alcaly, *New York Review of Books*

"Admati and Hellwig have done something extraordinary. They took [banking] frustration and all its complex details and gave it a simple narrative, one that both explains what banks have been getting away with and what we might ask that Congress do about it."
 —Brendan Greeley, *Bloomberg Businessweek*

"A clearly written, sensible analysis of problems and cures for the U.S. banking system."
 —Dale Singer, *St. Louis Post-Dispatch*

"Anat Admati and Martin Hellwig are academics with a gift for taking the mind-numbing minutiae of banking and presenting it in a way that the average reader can understand. One by one, the self-serving protests of the banking industry against tougher regulations are lined up and struck down in *The Bankers' New Clothes*. . . . The authors map out the regulatory flaws that make it easy for debt-junkie bankers to get rich when times are good, and leave them hanging around protesting when times are worse thanks to their own recklessness."
 —Susan Antilla, *Bloomberg News*

"The book pounds quite the drumbeat here: Force banks to borrow less (they should make up the difference through issuing more equity stock) and so inject sanity into the system."
 —Katharine Whittemore, *Boston Globe*

"Admati and Hellwig explain, in layman's terms, some of the silly arguments bankers make for keeping to the status quo and preventing any new regulation of the banks from ever being enacted. . . . Admati and Hellwig have made a gift to you. You don't have to go wrestle with banks' financial statements or their annual reports or their 10Q's. You don't

need to pull out your old accounting textbooks or call your college economics teacher to have her explain to you again why debt leverage increases risk. Admati and Hellwig have done all the hard work for you. But, you have to read their book."
—John R. Talbott, *Huffington Post*

"Buy this book; read this book; give this book to your friends; discuss this book; act on this book."
—Carol Hunt, *Irish Sunday Independent*

"*The Bankers' New Clothes* is a lucid exposition of the intellectual falsehoods deployed by banks to justify the ways in which they went about growing their business beyond any reasonable assessment of risk in the run-up of the crisis of 2008 and which they continue to peddle today. Admati and Hellwig cut through the debates about whether it was too little or too much regulation that was to blame, whether central banks could and should have acted faster, and the rights and wrongs of securitisation or separating commercial and investment banking, and go to the heart of the matter."
—Will Hutton, *New Statesman*

"[Admati and Hellwig's] case that the banking industry still needs a shake-up is persuasive. And you have to admire their nerve in tackling the lobby head-on because, like the emperor in the Hans Christian Andersen fairytale, it wears a smokescreen of competence and confidence. Attacking the illusion takes courage."
—David Wilson, *South China Morning Post*

"In simple and accessible terms, the authors show convincingly that banks are as fragile and destructive as they are, not because they must be, but because they want to be—and they get away with it."
—*Shanghai Daily*

THE
BANKERS' NEW CLOTHES

What's Wrong with Banking and What to Do about It

New and Expanded Edition

ANAT ADMATI and **MARTIN HELLWIG**

PRINCETON UNIVERSITY PRESS

Princeton and Oxford

For our families

CONTENTS

The global banking system was so fragile in 2007–2009 that it was unable to withstand the impact of the decline in U.S. housing prices. The breakdowns of financial institutions and the declines in asset prices were stopped only when central banks and governments provided massive bailouts and supports. We wrote this book to explain why the system had become so fragile and how it had broken down, and to advocate for better rules. The fragility was the result of distorted incentives and poorly designed rules. Reforms after the crisis did not remove the major flaws. The "reformed" rules were still poorly designed and did little to reduce the fragility of the system. They still enabled bankers to profit at the expense of others. We realized that, without broader understanding and engagement, the politics of banking prevented effective reform. To broaden the set of participants, we sought to cut through the confusing jargon and explain the issues so they are accessible to all. Our title, *The Bankers' New Clothes*, indicates that many of the claims made in this discussion are deeply flawed.

Since the book came out in early 2013 we have kept advocating for better rules, but the politics of banking continued to prevent progress. Once public attention was diverted to other subjects, banking regulation even moved backward rather than forward. The absence of a major crisis between 2013 and 2022 made bankers and politicians complacent. They liked to boast that banks are "strong," that the financial system is safe, and that new rules for dealing with failing banks have eliminated the "too-big-to-fail" problem. However, the seeming stability of financial systems between 2013 and 2022 was due to the favorable overall economic environment after 2013 and to the massive supports that governments and central banks provided to the economy and to asset prices during the COVID pandemic. Moreover, on several occasions the authorities went out of their way to avoid applying the new rules for dealing with failing banks, even for smaller banks. We still have too-big-to-fail institutions. Many of them have become even bigger.

Events in 2023 exposed the promises of "no more bailouts" made by bankers, politicians, and regulators since 2010 as vacuous. The U.S. government provided guarantees for tens of billions in uninsured deposits of the failed Silicon Valley and Signature Banks, and it engaged taxpayers in a loss-sharing agreement with JPMorgan Chase in the sale of the failing First Republic Bank. Many banks may be insolvent, but are kept alive by the Federal Reserve's new lending programs. Taxpayer-backed guarantees are also involved in the government-engineered takeover of one of two giant banks in Switzerland, Credit Suisse, by the other one, UBS. These events all show that much remains wrong with banking. They took place just as we were finalizing new material for the new edition of the book that we started writing in September 2022. In this edition we discuss events through May 2023 and place them in the context of developments since 2013.

This edition of the book expands our discussion in a few important ways. First, since the 2007–2009 financial crisis, central banks such as the Federal Reserve, the Bank of England, and the European Central Bank have taken an ever larger and more prominent role in the economy. By now, whenever a problem arises they are expected to step in to support financial markets, banks, and others, including governments. Central banks are powerful and prominent. We mentioned them many times in the first edition of this book, but we did not explain how they work and how they interact with private-sector institutions. In this edition we remove much of the mystery around central banks. The interactions of central banks with private-sector institutions, including the role of some central banks as regulators and supervisors, are important for understanding how central banks have enabled and even exacerbated the fragility of the banking system in recent years and how they continue to do so now.

Second, we explain why bailouts by governments and central banks continue and why new rules for dealing with the failing banks are not workable. Despite earlier promises that these rules would end disruptive failures and bailouts, the Swiss authorities ultimately did not entrust Credit Suisse to their own new procedure, which suggests that they shared our assessment. However, the system, and some institutions, may become "too big to save."

Repeated scandals and breaches of the law in banking raise the question of whether people in banking are above the law. This edition provides a more extensive discussion of issues concerning the rule of law for corporations and their executives, in banking and beyond. When we finished writing the first edition of this book in 2012, the "scandal of the day" involved the so-called LIBOR fraud, coordinated falsifications of reports from banks to the British Bankers Association, which used the reports to construct an interest rate index called LIBOR. This index determined payments in millions of contracts around the world. Prosecution of LIBOR falsifications and many other cases of wrongdoing by financial institutions and people working for them has been very weak. To the best of our knowledge, except in Iceland, none of the top executives of the institutions involved ever faced criminal prosecution. Civil liability, such as clawbacks of bonuses and payments for damages, was hardly ever imposed.

In this edition we discuss why violations of rules could have become a normal way of doing business in banks. Bankers routinely infringe internal rules intended to limit risks without reprimands from their superiors. They also break laws against fraud, price fixing, and money laundering with scant interference from authorities. Regulators and supervisors, auditors and rating agencies are often blind, perhaps willfully blind, to rule breaking. Law enforcement authorities may impose seemingly large fines on banks, but these fines may still be small compared to the gains from the incriminated practices. Moreover, the fines are often parts of settlements that allow banks to claim that they did nothing wrong and that reveal little relevant information to the public. Many in the media and in academia are fascinated by the glamor of bank bosses and extoll the "efficiency" of banking while overlooking the enormous harms it has caused and is still causing.

In this new edition, we maintain the original text, which remains relevant just as it is, and which covers the issues and events through 2012. The new chapters reflect experiences since 2013, including our own extensive engagements with many people in the private sector, the policy world, and academia, as well as our service on advisory bodies of regulatory institutions. These activities have improved our understanding of how political institutions and authorities interact with the industry, the media, and academics. They have also forced us to pay more attention to the details of rules set by legislators and regulators and the nuances associated with enforcement, and to relate these details to our own analysis.

The decade since the book first came out leaves us even more alarmed by the state of our democracies in dealing with powerful corporations and their leaders. The power of financial institutions to influence, in public or behind closed doors, how laws and regulations are written and enforced contributes to the disaffection of many with our political, economic, and legal systems. Fooling others and perhaps oneself, both in trading and in political discussion, is pervasive in banking and far beyond. The challenge is to give truth more power.

May 2023

PREFACE

I N THE FALL OF 2008, it seemed obvious that radical reform would be needed. For more than a year, banks and financial markets had been in a state of crisis. Then, in September, the entire financial system was about to collapse. One institution after another was failing or about to fail. Governments and central banks stopped the panic by massive interventions, but even so, the economy went into a decline of a magnitude unseen since the Great Depression.

We hoped for a serious investigation and discussion of what had gone wrong and what would have to be done to avoid a recurrence of such a crisis. We hoped that the lessons of the crisis would be learned. But we were disappointed. There was no serious analysis of how the financial system might be made safer.

Many claimed that they "knew" what had caused the crisis and what needed—or did not need—to be done, and they did not look any further. Bankers and their supporters argued that not much was wrong with the banking system. Serious reform, they routinely said, would interfere with what banks do and harm the economy. If we wanted banks to lend and to support growth, they wanted us to believe, we had to accept this system pretty much the way it was.

This made no sense to us. Much of the discussion seemed to ignore what had happened. Many arguments seemed downright false. As academics who have spent our lives studying the financial system—Anat as a finance and economics professor at Stanford and Martin as an economics professor and director of a research institute in Bonn—we were shocked to see press reports and policy recommendations with misleading uses of words, flawed understanding of basic principles, fallacious and misleading arguments, and inadequate uses of mathematical models. Banking experts, including many academics, seemed to believe that banks are so different from all other businesses that the basic principles of economics and finance do not apply to them.

We were not surprised that bankers lobbied in their own interest and said whatever might serve their needs; often their paychecks and bonuses were at stake, and the status quo worked for them. But we were dismayed—and increasingly alarmed—to see that flawed narratives and invalid arguments were not challenged but instead seemed to be winning the debate on both sides of the Atlantic. Reform efforts seemed to be stalling. Proposals were headed in the wrong direction. Simple opportunities to improve the system were being overlooked.

We wrote about the issues, arguing for reform and exposing the invalid arguments that were being given against reform. However, important parts of the policy discussion go on behind closed doors. Even when regulators ask for public comment on a proposed regulation, most contributions come from the industry and its supporters, and additional lobbying goes on behind the scenes.

In trying to have discussions with those involved in the debate, we discovered that many of them had no interest in engaging on the issues—not because of what they knew or did not know but because of what they *wanted* to know. Politicians, regulators, and others often prefer to avoid challenging the banking industry. People like convenient narratives, particularly if those narratives disguise their own responsibility for failed policies. Academics get caught up in theories based on the belief that what we see must be efficient. In such a situation, invalid arguments can win the policy debate.

We also discovered that many people, including many who are involved in the policy discussion, do not have a sufficiently full understanding of the underlying concepts to form their own opinions about the issues or to evaluate what others are saying. The jargon of bankers and banking experts is deliberately impenetrable. This impenetrability helps them confuse policy-makers and the public, and it muddles the debate.

We are concerned about this situation because the financial system is dangerous and distorted. We have written this book to explain the issues to the broader public. We want more people to be better informed so they can form their own opinions. We want to expand the set of participants and elevate the level of the debate.

When policymakers ignore risks, all of us may suffer in the end. A stark example was provided in Japan, where corrupted regulators and politicians colluded for years with the Tokyo Electric Power Company and ignored known safety concerns. When an earthquake and a tsunami occurred in 2011, this neglect led to a nuclear disaster that was entirely preventable.

Weak regulations and ineffective enforcement were similarly instrumental in the buildup of risks in the financial system that turned the U.S. housing decline into a financial tsunami. Yet, despite the wreckage, serious attempts to reform banking regulation have foundered, scuttled by lobbying and misdirection.

Banking is not difficult to understand. Most of the issues are quite straightforward. Simply learning the precise meanings of some of the terms that are used, such as the word *capital,* can help uncover some of the nonsense. You do not need any background in economics, finance, or quantitative fields to read and understand this book.

In this book we discuss many statements and views. At times we use generic terms, attributing statements to "bankers," "regulators," or "politicians." Having talked and collaborated with many people connected to banking and public policy, we know that not every banker, regulator, or politician subscribes to the same views. Many in these groups and elsewhere advocate and work to bring about beneficial reform. In each of the groups, however, the views we discuss are so prevalent, and have had such an impact on policy discussions, that we feel justified in generalizing to make our points.

Do not believe those who tell you that things are better now than they had been prior to the financial crisis of 2007–2009 and that we have a safer system that is getting even better as reforms are put in place. Today's banking system, even with proposed reforms, is as dangerous and fragile as the system that brought us the recent crisis.

But this situation can change. With the right focus and a proper diagnosis of the problems, highly beneficial steps can be taken immediately.

Having a better financial system requires effective regulation and enforcement. Most essentially, it requires the political will to put the appropriate measures in place and implement them. Our hope in writing this book is that if more people understand the issues, politicians and regulators will be more accountable to the public. Flawed and dangerous narratives—"the bankers' new clothes"—must not win.

October 2012

ACKNOWLEDGMENTS

I N WRITING THIS BOOK about borrowing and its dark side, we have ourselves borrowed a lot and experienced the bright side of borrowing. We have borrowed a lot of other people's time, attention, and thoughts, and we have experienced the pleasures of interacting with them. Some interactions occurred long ago, in discussing pure research, some more recently, in discussing policy and regulatory reform since 2007.

Writing a book on banks and banking regulation that would be accessible to a nonprofessional reader has been a great challenge. We are very grateful to many friends and colleagues who encouraged us to take on the challenge and kept us going with support and advice along the way.

We are particularly grateful to the following people, who read earlier drafts of at least portions of the book and made numerous useful comments: Philippe Aghion, Neil Barofsky, Jon Bendor, Sanjai Bhagat, Jules van Binsbergen, Christina Büchmann, Rebel Cole, Peter Conti-Brown, Pedro DaCosta, Jesse Eisinger, Christoph Engel, Morris Goldstein, Charles Goodhart, Andrew Green, Susan Hachgenei, Dorothee Hellwig, Hans-Jürgen Hellwig, Klaus-Peter Hellwig, Marc Jarsulic, Bob Jenkins, Simon Johnson, Birger Koblitz, Arthur Korteweg, Tamar Kreps, James Kwak, Alexander Morell, Stefan Nagel, John Parsons, Dieter Piel, Joe Rizzi, Steve Ross, Ingrid Schöll, Graham Steele, Monika Stimpson, Tim Sullivan, John Talbott, Matthias Thiemann, Rob Urstein, Jonathan Weil, and Art Wilmarth. The reviewers of the book for Princeton University Press (PUP) also made very helpful comments. Special thanks to Paul Pfleiderer, who was involved in many brainstorming sessions and made numerous useful suggestions about different drafts.

We also thank members of the financial stability group convened by Anat Admati and Simon Johnson at the Peterson Institute for International Economics in Washington, D.C. Generous funding by the Institute for New Economic Thinking supports this group, including a meeting in June 2012 to discuss this book.

While engaging in the policy debate in the past few years, we have had many helpful discussions with colleagues and with individuals involved in the policy debate and others, which have influenced our thinking and shaped the book. We thank Viral Acharya, Philippe Aghion, Sheila Bair, Mary Barth, Nadine Baudot-Trajtenberg, Jane Baxter, Lawrence Baxter, Urs Birchler, Niklaus Blattner, Jürg Blum, Arnoud Boot, Claudio Borio, Michael Boskin, John Boyd, Dick Brealey, Claudia Buch, Charles Calomiris, John Cochrane, Peter DeMarzo, Thomas Gehrig, Hans Gersbach, Hendrik Hakenes, Andy Haldane, Ian Harrison, Richard Herring, Tom Hoenig, Rob Johnson, Ed Kane, Dennis Kelleher, Mervyn King, David Kreps, Sebastian Mallaby, Maureen McNichols, Hamid Mehran, Allan Meltzer, David Miles, Chuck Morris, Manfred J. M. Neumann, George Parker, Francisco Perez-Gonzalez, Thierry Philipponnat, John Plender, Barbara Rehm, Isabel Schnabel, David Skeel, Chester Spatt, Ilya Strebulaev, Martin Summer, Elu von Thadden, Adair Turner, Jim Van Horne, Larry Wall, Beatrice Weder di Mauro, Juli Weiss, Mark Whitehouse, Martin Wolf, Daniel Zimmer, and Jeff Zwiebel. Some of them may disagree with our views, but all of them have contributed to the book with their insights.

In the book we are critical of politicians and regulators, but many do not fit our characterizations. Our thinking has been influenced, in particular, by serving on policy committees. We are grateful for the opportunity provided by these committees to apply academic thinking to practical questions and to discuss the issues with politicians and administrators, central bankers and regulators, corporate executives, and other academics.

An important predecessor of this book was "Fallacies, Irrelevant Facts, and Myths in the Discussion of Capital Regulation: Why Bank Equity Is *Not* Expensive," a paper that we wrote jointly with Peter DeMarzo and Paul

Pfleiderer from Stanford in the summer of 2010. This paper was addressed to professionals involved in the policy debate about banking regulation. Our subsequent experience in this debate suggested that we should try to make the ideas in the paper available to a wider audience. This book is the result. While writing the book, we also did more research with Peter DeMarzo and Paul Pfleiderer, which led to a sequel article, "Debt Overhang and Capital Regulation," on which the book also draws.

Writing a book when one author is located in California and the other in Germany requires not only time but also support for travel and communication. We are grateful to the Stanford Graduate School of Business and the Max Planck Institute for Research on Collective Goods in Bonn for providing this support. We are also grateful for support from the German Federal Ministry of Education and Research through the Max Planck Research Award 2012.

Research assistants Siddhartha Basu, Matthew Haney, Josh Loud, Michael Ohlrogge, Lucas Puente, Estefania Molina Ungar, Zach Wang, and Yizhou Xiao were very helpful with the endnotes and references. We are also grateful to our assistants, Mandy Ferrero and Monika Stimpson, for their invaluable logistical, administrative, and other support.

Seth Ditchik and Peter Dougherty from PUP gave us many useful suggestions that improved the book. We thank them and everyone else at PUP and at Princeton Editorial Associates for their encouragement, patience, and help with the numerous edits.

Finally, and most importantly, our families—especially our spouses, David Kreps and Dorothee Hellwig—have endured many months of stress and absences while we have focused intensely on writing and communicating about this book. We are immensely grateful for their understanding and support.

ACKNOWLEDGMENTS FOR THE 2024 EDITION

THE IDEA OF WRITING new material for an expanded edition of *The Bankers' New Clothes* a decade after its first publication came up in summer 2022 and we embarked on it in September 2022. We discussed the idea with some of those on whose advice and help we had relied in preparing the first edition and who have been acknowledged already. We are again grateful to them, particularly to Paul Pfleiderer and Graham Steele. We also thank other friends and colleagues who encouraged us to undertake this writing and were supportive and helpful as we struggled to decide how to design the extension to the previous material. Erik Ben Artzi, Sarah Bloom Raskin, Gregg Gelzinis, Thomas Gehrig, Hans Gersbach, Marc Jarsulic, Gudrun Johnsen, Robert Muth, Richard Portes, Farzad Saidi, Gerhard Schick, Heiner Schulz, Wolfgang Schürer, Amit Seru, Justin Simpson, and Lisa Simpson provided advice and comments on early drafts. Research assistants Grace Austin, Aristotle Marangu, and Timur Sobolev provided important help, particularly with the references.

Joe Jackson at Princeton University Press was a great partner in this project and offered invaluable support and advice. We thank him and the teams at PUP and at Green Pelican Editorial Services for their support and patience with this new edition. We are especially indebted to our spouses, Dorothee Hellwig and David Kreps, who again put up with our months of work and virtual collaboration across the Atlantic.

ONE

The Emperors of Banking Have No Clothes

I just think that this constant refrain "bankers, bankers, bankers" is just un-
productive and unfair. People should just stop doing that.

Jamie Dimon, chief executive officer of JPMorgan Chase, Davos, Switzerland,
January 27, 2011

The world has paid with tens of millions of unemployed, who were in no
way to blame and who paid for everything. It caused a lot of anger. . . . We
saw that for the last 10 years, major institutions in which we thought we
could trust had done things which had nothing to do with simple common
sense.

Nicolas Sarkozy, President of the French Republic, Davos, Switzerland,
January 27, 2011

F OR THE FIRST YEAR after the financial crisis of 2007–2009, bankers were
lying low, mindful of the anger that had been caused by the crisis and by
the use of taxpayers' money to bail out banks.[1] French President Nicolas
Sarkozy's response to JPMorgan chief executive officer (CEO) Jamie Dimon
in Davos in 2011 resonated widely with the media and the public.[2]

At that time, most bank lobbying went on behind the scenes. Since then,
however, the banking lobby has become outspoken again.[3] As in the years
before the crisis, bankers have been lobbying relentlessly and speaking up in
public against tighter banking regulation.[4] Leading bankers present themselves as experts who know and care about what is good for the economy.
They are regularly consulted by leading government officials, regulators, and
politicians.[5] Every utterance of a major bank's CEO is extensively reported in
the press. But whereas there is major coverage of such statements, there is
actually little scrutiny of the arguments behind them.

In Hans Christian Andersen's famous tale "The Emperor's New Clothes,"
two self-declared tailors offer to provide the emperor with beautiful and very
special clothes. They claim that the clothes will be invisible to people who are

stupid or unfit for their jobs. The emperor orders a full set of these special clothes. When he sends his ministers to monitor the "tailors," the ministers do not see anything, but, for fear of being considered stupid or incompetent, none of them admits this. Instead, they extol the splendors of the invisible clothes and the nonexistent fabrics of which they are made.

The emperor himself finds his new attire invisible, yet, not wanting to appear stupid or unfit to be emperor, he praises the nonexistent clothes. When he tours his capital "wearing" them, the onlookers also admire his attire, even though they do not see anything. Only when a little child shouts "The emperor has no clothes!" does everyone realize and admit that the emperor is in fact naked.

A major reason for the success of bank lobbying is that banking has a certain mystique. There is a pervasive myth that banks and banking are special and different from all other companies and industries in the economy. Anyone who questions the mystique and the claims that are made is at risk of being declared incompetent to participate in the discussion.[6]

Many of the claims made by leading bankers and banking experts actually have as much substance as the emperor's new clothes in Andersen's story. But most people do not challenge these claims, and the claims have an impact on policy. The specialists' façade of competence and confidence is too intimidating. Even people who know better fail to speak up. The emperor may be naked, but he continues his parade without being challenged about his attire.[7]

Our purpose in writing this book is to demystify banking and explain the issues to widen the circle of participants in the debate. We want to encourage more people to form and to trust their opinions, to ask questions, to express doubts, and to challenge the flawed arguments that pervade the policy debate. If we are to have a healthier financial system, more people must understand the issues and influence policy.

Many have a sense that something is wrong with banking and have questions. Why did banks get into so much trouble in the crisis? Why were banks and other financial institutions bailed out? Were the bailouts necessary? Will these institutions be bailed out again if they run into trouble? Will new regulations help or hurt? Are they too tough or not tough enough?

Leading bankers have simple answers to these questions. They may admit that mistakes were made,[8] but they portray the crisis primarily as a fluke, an accident that is highly unlikely to recur in our lifetimes.[9] It would be costly and wasteful, they claim, to tighten regulation to forestall an event that might happen once in a hundred years. Tighter regulation, we are warned, would interfere with what banks do to support the economy, and this would have serious "unintended consequences."[10]

The English classical scholar Francis Cornford wrote in 1908, "There is only one argument for doing something; the rest are arguments for doing nothing. The argument for doing something is that it is the right thing to do. Then, of course, comes the difficulty of making sure that it is right."[11] He goes on to explain how "bugbears," sources of dread or false alarms, are used to raise doubts or scare. If Cornford was writing today, he would surely talk about the bugbear of "unintended consequences."

Meanwhile, politicians seem to be taken in by the lobbying. For all the outrage they expressed about the crisis, they have done little to actually address the issues involved. For example, one might infer from President Sarkozy's lashing out at bankers that France is a champion of bank regulation. But this inference would be wrong. In the bodies that try to coordinate regulatory efforts across countries, France has consistently opposed any tightening of regulation.[12] In the United States, regulations are often watered down in response to bank lobbying. For example, in passing the Dodd-Frank Act in 2010, Congress weakened the so-called Volcker Rule, which prohibits commercial banks from trading securities on their own account. Lobbying also affects the so-called rule-making process by which the regulatory bodies implement the law.[13]

Much of the research on banking, the financial crisis, and regulatory reform takes for granted that banks and the financial system must be as vulnerable to risks as they are, so that the failure of one bank can pull down the entire financial system. Some academic research suggests that this fragility might actually be a necessary by-product of the benefits banks provide to the economy.[14] However, this work is based on assumptions under which fragility is indeed unavoidable, without assessing the relevance of the assumptions in the real world.[15]

Expanding the policy discussion beyond the circle of bankers and banking specialists is very important, because more action is urgently needed and yet has not been taken.[16] The banking system is still much too fragile and dangerous. This system works for many bankers, but it exposes most of us to unnecessary and costly risks, and it distorts the economy in significant ways.

Can something be done at a reasonable cost to reduce the likelihood of banks' failing and causing a costly crisis? In one word: Yes. Will the reforms that have been decided upon achieve this aim? No. Can we have regulations that greatly increase the health and safety of the system while still allowing banks to do everything the economy needs them to do? Yes. Would we, as a society, have to sacrifice anything substantial to have a better banking system? No.

One clear direction for reform is to insist that banks and other financial institutions rely *much less* on borrowing to fund their investments. The reforms that have been agreed upon since 2008 are woefully insufficient in this respect, and they maintain previous approaches that have not worked well. The benefits of a more ambitious reform would be significant, whereas, contrary to the claims of leading bankers and others, the relevant costs to society would be quite small, if they existed at all.

We are not saying that stricter limits to bank borrowing are the only measures to be considered. However, these measures are important and beneficial no matter what else might be done. Reducing the excessive risks to the economy from the banking system, particularly the large distortions that result from having institutions that are "too big to fail," may well require additional measures. The key is to try to provide better incentives for market participants, and for those who design and implement regulations, so that bankers' actions will be less in conflict with the public interest.

A Sampling of the Bankers' New Clothes

A few examples will illustrate what we mean by *the bankers' new clothes*. Excessive borrowing by banks was identified as a major factor in the crisis of 2007–2008. Bankers themselves sometimes admit this.[17] Nevertheless, the banking industry fights aggressively against tighter restrictions on bank borrowing. The constant refrain is that too much tightening of such restrictions would harm economic growth.

For example, in 2009, when negotiations about a new international agreement on banking regulation were getting under way, Josef Ackermann, then the CEO of Deutsche Bank, asserted in an interview that tighter restrictions on bank borrowing "would restrict [banks'] ability to provide loans to the rest of the economy. This reduces growth and has negative effects for all."[18]

This is a typical bugbear, suggesting that we must make a choice between economic growth and financial stability and that we cannot have both. After all, who would be in favor of a regulation that "reduces growth and has negative effects for all"?

Mr. Ackermann acknowledged that tighter restrictions on banks' borrowing "might increase bank safety," but he insisted that this would come at the expense of growth. He said nothing, however, about how continued financial instability and turmoil would affect growth.

The sharpest economic downturn since the Great Depression of the early 1930s occurred in the last quarter of 2008, and it was a direct result of the worldwide financial crisis that affected numerous banks and other financial institutions. The unprecedented decline in output in 2009 and the resulting loss of output have been valued in the trillions of dollars.[19] The crisis has caused significant suffering for many.[20] In light of these effects, warnings that greater financial stability would come at the expense of growth sound hollow. Warnings that bank lending would suffer also sound hollow. In 2008 and 2009, banks that were vulnerable because they had too much debt cut back sharply on their lending. The severe credit crunch was caused by banks' having too much debt hanging over them.

Why would restrictions on bank borrowing have any effect on bank lending at all?

One argument was given in 2010 by the British Bankers' Association, which claimed that new regulations would require U.K. banks to "hold an extra £600 billion of capital that might otherwise have been deployed as loans to businesses or households."[21] To anyone who does not know what the regulation is about, this argument may look plausible. In fact, it is nonsensical and false.

The nonsense is due to the misuse of the word *capital*. In the language of banking regulation, this word refers to the money the bank has received from its shareholders or owners. This is to be distinguished from the money it has borrowed. Banks use both borrowed and unborrowed money to make their loans and other investments. Unborrowed money is the money that a bank has obtained from its owners if it is a private bank or from its shareholders if it is a corporation, along with any profits it has retained. Elsewhere in the economy, this type of funding is referred to as equity. In banking, it is called capital.

Capital regulation requires that a sufficient fraction of a bank's investments or assets be funded with unborrowed money.[22] This is similar to the requirement that a home buyer make a minimum down payment when buying a house. Having a minimal ratio of unborrowed funds relative to total assets is a way to limit the share of assets that is funded by borrowing. Because unborrowed funds are obtained without any promise to make specific payments at particular times, having more equity enhances the bank's ability to absorb losses on its assets.

From the statement of the British Bankers' Association, however, we would not guess that capital requirements are about how much a bank borrows. The statement makes it appear as if capital were a cash reserve—a pile of cash that banks hold that cannot be used to make loans.

In fact, capital regulation does *not* tell banks what to do with their funds or what they should hold. It tells banks only what portion of the funds they use must be unborrowed. Saying that new regulations would *require* U.K. banks to "hold an extra £600 billion of capital" is nonsensical. The implication that loans to businesses or households are automatically reduced by that £600 billion is false. Capital is not a rainy-day fund.

The confusion about the term *bank capital* is pervasive. Numerous media reports say that banks must "set aside" capital to satisfy new regulations. References to capital reserves suggest that the regulation forces banks to hold cash that sits idly in the bank's tills without being put to work in the economy.[23] A bank lobbyist is quoted as saying, "A dollar in capital is one less dollar working in the economy."[24]

This confusion is insidious because it biases the debate, suggesting costs and trade-offs that do not actually exist. The trade-offs exist for reserve requirements, which call for banks to hold some fraction of their deposits in cash or in deposits with the central bank. However, capital requirements are distinct from reserve requirements and do not give rise to the same trade-offs. Confusing the two makes it easier to argue that capital requirements prevent banks from lending when this is not actually true.

At least for banks that are organized as corporations, bank capital requirements have no automatic effect on bank lending. If capital requirements are increased, there is nothing in the regulation that would prevent these corporations from issuing additional shares and raising new funds to make any loans and investments that they might find profitable.

Banks that do not have access to the stock markets, as well as those that do, can increase their equity by retaining and reinvesting their profits. What the banks would *choose* to do with the funds and why they would make these choices are different matters that are obviously important. But there is no sense in which capital regulation *forces* banks to shrink or prevents them from making loans. Viable banks can increase their reliance on unborrowed funds without any reduction in lending.

In arguing against increased capital requirements, advocates for banks often say that capital, that is, equity, is expensive and that, if they must have more equity, their costs will increase.[25] This mantra is so self-evident to banking specialists that they usually see no need to justify it. But why is it that banks hate equity so much and view it as expensive? In what exact sense is it expensive, and what does this mean for society and for policy?

We can test this argument by comparing banks to other corporations. Corporations in most industries are free to borrow as much as they want if they can find someone to make them loans. Yet there is no other sector in which corporations borrow anywhere near as much as banks do. For the vast majority of nonfinancial corporations in the United States, borrowing represents less than 50 percent of assets. Some highly successful companies do not borrow at all.[26] By contrast, for banks, debt often accounts for more than 90 percent of assets. For some large European banks, the fraction is even higher, above 97 percent; it also was that high for some major U.S. investment banks before 2007, as well as for the mortgage giants, the Federal National Mortgage Association (Fannie Mae) and the Federal Home Loan Mortgage Corporation (Freddie Mac), which were bailed out.[27] The new regulations that the banking industry complains about would still allow debt to fund 97 percent of bank assets.[28]

If capital is expensive, as bankers suggest, and borrowing is cheap, why doesn't this also apply to other corporations? Why don't nonbanks borrow more and economize on the supposedly expensive equity? Are these other corporations doing something wrong? For example, why doesn't Apple, which has not borrowed at all, borrow some money by issuing some debt and use the proceeds to pay its shareholders? Wouldn't this be beneficial, replacing the company's expensive equity with cheap debt? Or is there something fundamentally different about the funding costs of banks?

The business of banking is different, but bank stocks are held by the same investors, or by investors who value stocks in the same way, as those who invest in other companies. They do not look different from other stocks; all stocks allow their owners to receive dividends and sell the shares for cash at the prevailing price in the stock market. Why would bank stocks be any different from those of other corporations?

One difference that is important for bank funding costs became evident in 2008: if an important bank gets into trouble and comes close to defaulting on its debt, there is a good chance that the government or the central bank will support it to prevent default. A few corporations outside the financial sector have also benefited from government bailouts, for example, the auto industry,[29] but those instances have been rare exceptions. In the financial sector, bailouts of large institutions, or of many institutions if they get into trouble at the same time, have become the rule.

If a company can count on being bailed out by the government when it cannot pay its debts and its creditors do not worry much about its defaulting, creditors will be happy to lend to the company. The company will therefore find that borrowing is cheap and, by comparison, other ways to fund investments, such as equity, are expensive. The interest that the company has to pay on its debt will not reflect its true default risk because that is partly borne by the taxpayer. From the perspective of the banks, therefore, borrowing is cheap. But this is true only because the costs of bank borrowing are partly borne by taxpayers.

When bank lobbyists claim that having more equity would raise their costs, they never mention the costs to taxpayers of making their borrowing cheap. At times they even deny the presence of the subsidies to their debt.[30] Yet there is significant evidence that bank borrowing benefits from the prospect of taxpayer bailouts. For example, credit rating agencies sometimes assign higher ratings to bank debt than they would if the banks had no prospect of being bailed out.[31] These higher ratings directly lower the interest rates at which banks can borrow.[32] The value of this benefit is greater the more a bank borrows.

These are just a few examples of what we refer to as the bankers' new clothes, flawed and misleading claims that are made in discussions about banking regulation. Many of the claims resonate with basic feelings, yet they have no more substance than the emperor's fictitious clothes in Andersen's story.

This book will provide you with a framework for thinking about the issues so you can gain a better understanding of them and see flawed arguments for what they are. It does not require any expertise in or prior knowledge of economics, finance, or banking. You might think that this is not your field. However, if the discussion of banking and banking regulation is left only to those who are directly concerned, the financial system will continue to be at risk from unsafe banking, and all of us may suffer the consequences. Only pressure from the public can bring forth the necessary political will. Without public pressure and political will, we can expect little change.

Many of the bankers' new clothes that we expose in this book are related to how much banks borrow. In order to understand the issues, we first explore the impact of borrowing by individuals and companies on risk and on investments more generally. This will enable us to see where banks are similar to other companies and where they are different.

Borrowing is not the only topic of the book. Many more flawed claims are made in the debate on banking regulation. Most of these bankers' new clothes are also bugbears, warnings of unintended consequences meant to scare policymakers out of doing something without focusing properly on the issues or proposing how the actual problems should be solved.

For example, leading bankers often call for so-called level playing fields in regulation.[33] They warn that their ability to hold their own in global competition might suffer if regulation were any stricter for them than for banks in other countries. This argument is also used by other industries, and it can succeed in weakening regulation, but it is invalid.[34] A country's public policy should not be concerned about the success of its banks or other firms as such, because success that is achieved by taxpayer subsidies or by exposing the public to excessive risks—for example, the risks of pollution or of a financial crisis—is not beneficial to the economy and to society.

On the issue of how much banks should borrow, as well as how much risk they should take, there is a fundamental conflict between what is good for bankers privately and what is good for the broader economy. By having policies that encourage bank borrowing and risk taking, we paradoxically make it attractive for banks to choose levels of debt and risk that are harmful without serving any useful purpose.

Whatever else we do, imposing significant restrictions on banks' borrowing is a simple and highly cost-effective way to reduce risks to the economy without imposing any significant cost on society. Curbing excessive and harmful risk taking by bankers may require additional laws and regulations.

Why Bank Safety Matters

Why should we care so much about the safety of banks and about how much banks borrow? The more anyone borrows, the greater the likelihood that the debts cannot be paid. When this happens, most borrowers go into bankruptcy, the lenders' claims are frozen until a court has determined what they can be paid, and then, usually, the lenders are paid much less than what they are owed.[35]

When a borrower is a bank, the damage resulting from its defaulting on its debts can be great, affecting many beyond those directly involved with the bank. This is especially true when the bank is a systemically important financial institution like JPMorgan Chase or Deutsche Bank, with massive operations all over the globe.[36] Excessive borrowing by such banks exposes all of us to risks, costs, and inefficiencies that are entirely unnecessary.

In the run-up to the financial crisis, the debts of many large banks financed 97 percent or more of their assets. Lehman Brothers in the United States, Hypo Real Estate in Germany, Dexia in Belgium and France, and UBS in Switzerland had many hundreds of billions of dollars, euros, or Swiss francs in debt.[37] Lehman Brothers filed for bankruptcy in September 2008. The other three avoided bankruptcy only because they were bailed out by their governments.[38]

The Lehman Brothers bankruptcy caused severe disruption and damage to the global financial system.[39] Stock prices imploded, investors withdrew from money market funds, money market funds refused to renew their loans to banks, and banks stopped lending to each other. Banks furiously tried to sell assets, which further depressed prices. Within two weeks, many banks faced the prospect of default.[40]

To prevent a complete meltdown of the system, governments and central banks all over the world provided financial institutions with funding and with guarantees for the institutions' debts.[41] These interventions stopped the decline, but the downturn in economic activity was still the sharpest since the Great Depression.[42] Anton Valukas, the lawyer appointed by the bankruptcy court to investigate Lehman Brothers, put it succinctly: "Everybody got hurt. The entire economy has suffered from the fall of Lehman Brothers . . . the whole world."[43]

In the fall of 2008, many financial institutions besides Lehman Brothers were also vulnerable. Ben Bernanke, chairman of the Federal Reserve, told the Financial Crisis Inquiry Commission (FCIC) that "out of maybe . . . 13 of the most important financial institutions in the United States, 12 were at risk of failure within a period of a week or two."[44] Some or all of the major banks in Belgium, France, Germany, Iceland, Ireland, the Netherlands, Switzerland, and the United Kingdom failed or were at significant risk of failing had their governments not bailed them out.[45]

Accounts of the crisis often focus on the various breakdowns of bank funding between August 2007 and October 2008.[46] Much bank funding consisted of very short-term debt. Banks were therefore vulnerable to the risk that this debt would not be renewed. The deeper reason for the breakdowns, however, was that banks were highly indebted. When banks suffered losses, investors, including other financial institutions, lost confidence and cut off funding, fearing that the banks might become unable to repay their debts.[47] The Lehman Brothers bankruptcy itself heightened investors' concerns by showing that even a large financial institution might not be bailed out, and therefore that default of such an institution was a real possibility.[48]

The problem posed by some banks being regarded as too big to fail is greater today than it was in 2008. Since then, the largest U.S. banks have become much larger. On March 31, 2012, the debt of JPMorgan Chase was valued at $2.13 trillion and that of Bank of America at $1.95 trillion, more than three times the debt of Lehman Brothers. The debts of the five largest banks in the United States totaled around $8 trillion. These figures would have been even larger under the accounting rules used in Europe.[49]

In Europe, the largest banks are of similar size. Because European economies are smaller than that of the United States, the problem is even more serious there. Relative to the overall economy, banks are significantly larger in Europe than in the United States, especially in some of the smaller countries.[50] In Ireland and Iceland before the crisis, the banking systems had become so large that, when the banks failed, these countries' economies collapsed.[51]

The traumatic Lehman experience has scared most governments into believing that large global banks must not be allowed to fail. Should any of these large banks get into serious difficulties, however, we may discover that they are not only too big to fail but also too big to save. There will be no good options.

The consequences of letting a large bank fail are probably more severe today than in the case of Lehman Brothers in 2008, but saving them might cripple their countries. The experiences of Ireland and Spain provide a taste of what can happen if large banking systems have to be saved by their governments. In both countries, the governments were unable to deal with their banking problems on their own, so they had to ask for support from the International Monetary Fund and from the European Union.[52]

This situation makes it all the more important to prevent scenarios in which governments must choose between letting a major institution fail or committing to an expensive bailout. One approach is to try to create mechanisms that would allow large banks to fail without disrupting the economy or requiring public support. Although useful efforts have been made in this direction, this remains a challenge for global banks. Even the best resolution mechanism is likely to be disruptive and costly.[53]

Whatever else might be done, significantly reducing the reliance of large banks on borrowing is the most straightforward and cost-effective approach to crisis prevention. Current and proposed regulations go in the right direction, but they are far from sufficient and have serious flaws.[54] This situation reflects the success of bank lobbying and the prevalence of flawed arguments, the bankers' new clothes, in the debate. To make progress, the issues must be clarified.

The present situation is perverse. It is as if we were to subsidize the chemical industry to intentionally pollute rivers and lakes. Such subsidies would encourage additional pollution. If the industry were asked to limit the pollution, it would complain that its costs would increase. Would such complaints make us tolerate the pollution? Subsidizing banks to borrow excessively and take on so much risk that the entire banking system is threatened is just like subsidizing and encouraging companies to pollute when they have clean alternatives.

Most investments involve risks. If investments are funded by borrowing, the risks are borne not just by the borrowers but also by the lenders, and possibly by others. The borrowing itself magnifies risk, and it creates fundamental conflicts of interest that can also lead to inefficiencies. These conflicts of interest and inefficiencies explain much of what is wrong with banking and suggest what to do about it.

To understand the issues—and to see through the bankers' new clothes—it is important to understand the relation between borrowing and risk. This is the subject to which we turn now. In the next two chapters we discuss the relation between borrowing and risk without a focus on banking. Then we turn to banking, risk in banking, and the implications of excessive risk for the financial system. This background will frame our discussion of banking regulation and the bankers' new clothes in later chapters. The discussion will also throw light on the politics of banking. Providing a better understanding of the issues and the political challenge has been our motivation in writing this book.

PART ONE

Borrowing, Banking, and Risk

TWO

How Borrowing Magnifies Risk

Loans and debts make worry and frets.
Proverb

B ANKS MAKE LOANS to individuals, businesses, and governments. Banks borrow from individuals and from firms, including other banks. Understanding banks requires an understanding of borrowing. In this chapter and the next, we discuss how borrowing works and how borrowing affects risk. Our discussion applies to any private borrowing, not just to borrowing by banks.[1]

Individuals borrow to buy such things as a car or a house so they can own and enjoy these things earlier than they could if they had to pay for them on their own.[2] Individuals and businesses also borrow to make investments. For example, individuals may use borrowed money to pay for their education, and businesses may invest in new factories or in new product developments. Borrowers hope to pay their debts from money they will earn later, for example, as their investments pay off.

Borrowing creates leverage: by borrowing, individuals and businesses can make investments that are larger than they can afford on their own right away. This leverage creates opportunities for the borrower, but it also magnifies the borrower's risks. The borrower makes promises to pay lenders specific amounts at given times in the future and gets to keep everything that is left after these promised debt payments. On the upside, if the investments turn out well, the leverage magnifies the borrower's profit. On the downside, however, if the investments do not return enough, the leverage magnifies the losses. The more one borrows, the greater this danger.

17

For individuals and small businesses, borrowing might be the only way to invest more than what they can afford on their own. For corporations, however, and particularly for large corporations, borrowing is not the only way to pay for investment and growth. Corporations can also raise funds from investors by issuing equity shares. When corporations make investment decisions, they must choose a mix of debt and equity to fund the investments.

A Mortgage Example

Kate wants to buy a house for $300,000. She does not have enough money to pay cash for the house, but she can take a mortgage of up to $270,000. She must contribute at least $30,000, 10 percent of the price of the house, as a down payment.

A useful way to visualize Kate's purchase of the house is through a balance sheet diagram, shown in Figure 2.1. The box on the left-hand side represents Kate's investment, namely the house, which costs $300,000. The positions on the right-hand side represent the different sources of money for the investment, the $270,000 mortgage and the $30,000 down payment. The difference between the value of the house and the value of what Kate owes is called her equity position in the house. Initially, Kate's equity position is just the value of her down payment.

The mortgage contract for Kate's house specifies the payments that she must make for interest and in repayment of the loan itself. To simplify the discussion, we assume for now that, in the period under discussion, Kate is living in the house and paying only interest, without any repayments on the $270,000 she borrowed.

After a year, Kate wants to move elsewhere, so she sells the house. To settle the mortgage, she must repay the $270,000. Whatever is left over after selling the house, if anything, Kate can keep.

If the value of the house has stayed the same, Kate can sell it for $300,000. After settling the mortgage debt of $270,000, she has $30,000 left, which is just the amount of her down payment. She had to pay interest on the mortgage and also has foregone the money she could have earned if she had invested her own $30,000 elsewhere, but if she liked living in the house, she may still

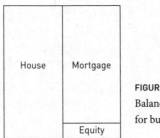

FIGURE 2.1
Balance sheet diagram
for buying a house.

be happy with the investment. The interest she paid can be thought of as replacing the rent she would have had to pay if she had not owned the house.

Kate will be happier, of course, if the house has gone up in value during the year. Suppose the house has increased in value by 5 percent, to $315,000. After paying the mortgage debt of $270,000, Kate will be left with $45,000, which is $15,000 more than her down payment of $30,000. By borrowing, Kate was able to buy a house that she could not have afforded on her own, and in addition she has earned a great return on her investment. Borrowing is wonderful if the borrowed money is invested in something that increases in value.

What if Kate's house has gone down in value? Suppose the value has dropped by 5 percent, to $285,000. After paying back $270,000, Kate will have only $15,000 left of her $30,000 down payment. Relative to her down payment, she will have lost $15,000, or 50 percent of the money she invested in the house.

We can already see in this simple example how borrowing creates a leverage effect that magnifies risks and returns. A small change of 5 percent in the value of Kate's house has dramatic effects on her wealth, generating gains or losses of 50 percent of her investment. Just as a lever multiplies the force one exerts to move a boulder, debt allows borrowers to multiply the assets they can finance with their own money but also magnifies the gains and losses they earn for each dollar of their own money.

On the upside, if the value of Kate's house has increased, Kate will keep every dollar of the $15,000 increase in the value of the house. On the downside, however, a small percentage decrease can be devastating to Kate's investment, because the debt amount is fixed, so her down payment must absorb the full dollar losses, at least until it is wiped out. In the case of a 5 percent decline, she will lose half of her down payment.

The different possibilities are described in Figure 2.2 using balance sheet diagrams. On the left is Kate's position when she bought the house, introduced in Figure 2.1. Her down payment was her initial equity. The other two diagrams show her position a year later, the first assuming that the value of the house has increased and the other that it has declined. Kate's debt is the same in both cases. The value of the equity changes by the full amount of the change in the value of the house. Because the value of the equity is smaller than the value of the house, the change in Kate's equity is larger in percentage terms than the change in the value of the house.

Kate's situation is even worse if the house has declined in value even more. Suppose, for example, that the value has dropped by 15 percent. Now Kate sells the house for $255,000, which is less than the $270,000 that she owes. Kate's entire down payment of $30,000 is lost, and she is "underwater," owing more on the mortgage than the house is worth.

The outcome for Kate when the house is worth less than the amount she owes depends on whether the lender can demand that she pay the difference out of her other assets or even her future salary.[3] In many European countries and in some of the states of the United States, mortgage lenders can ask for

| Original position | Position if house value goes up | Position if house value goes down |

FIGURE 2.2 Balance sheet diagrams for buying a house and selling it a year later.

payments from at least some of the borrower's other assets, such as bank accounts, cars, paintings, or jewelry.[4] Under such rules, Kate could be forced to pay the full $270,000 rather than just the $255,000 she obtains from selling the house. If she does not have enough other assets, she may have to declare personal bankruptcy.

In some states of the United States, mortgages have a so-called non-recourse clause that gives a homeowner the option to abandon a house without making any further payments.[5] In such a case, the bank would receive the abandoned house instead of being paid in full.[6]

How would things be different if Kate's down payment had been $60,000 instead of $30,000? In this case, Kate would have needed to borrow only $240,000 to buy the house. Obviously, Kate's interest payments on the loan during the year she lived in the house would have been lower, but she would have had $60,000 instead of $30,000 tied up in the house.

If Kate started off with greater initial equity, the leverage effect would be less intense than if her initial equity was lower. If the value of the house rises by 5 percent and the house is sold for $315,000, and if Kate owes $240,000, she will end up with $75,000, a gain of 25 percent on her initial investment of $60,000. If the value of the house goes down by 5 percent and the house sells for $285,000, she will end up with $45,000 after paying $240,000. In this case, she loses 25 percent of her $60,000 investment in the house.

In dollar amounts, the gain and the loss on the entire house are the same as before, but they are both smaller as a percentage of Kate's initial equity if she borrowed less. The more Kate borrows, the more dramatic is the effect of leverage, that is, the magnification of the percentage gains and losses on her investment. If Kate bought the house without borrowing anything, she owns it outright, so her percentage gains or losses are the same as the percentage increases or decreases in the value of the house. In that case, a decline of 5 percent in the value of the house would be a 5 percent loss to Kate of her investment; there would be no leverage and no magnification of the percentage gained or lost.

Table 2.1 summarizes the example, showing how the different scenarios play out for Kate. The top panel shows the case we started with, in which Kate made a $30,000 down payment and borrowed $270,000. The bottom panel

TABLE 2.1   Debt and Equity When Buying a $300,000 House in Two Down
             Payment Scenarios (with a nonrecourse mortgage loan)

Buying with a $30,000 down payment (initial equity)

Year-end house price (dollars)	Percentage change in house price	Mortgage debt (dollars)	Final equity (dollars)	Return on equity (percent)
345,000	15	270,000	75,000	150
315,000	5	270,000	45,000	50
300,000	0	270,000	30,000	0
285,000	−5	270,000	15,000	−50
255,000	−15	270,000	0	−100

Buying with a $60,000 down payment (initial equity)

Year-end house price (dollars)	Percentage change in house price	Mortgage debt (dollars)	Final equity (dollars)	Return on equity (percent)
345,000	15	240,000	105,000	75
315,000	5	240,000	75,000	25
300,000	0	240,000	60,000	0
285,000	−5	240,000	45,000	−25
255,000	−15	240,000	15,000	−75

shows the case in which the down payment was $60,000 and the mortgage was $240,000.[7]

To show the leverage effect most dramatically, we include a scenario in which the value of the house increases by 15 percent, to $345,000. In the case in which Kate took the larger mortgage and invested only $30,000, she ends up with $75,000 after paying the debt; her return per dollar invested in the house is 150 percent, which is wonderful indeed! With the smaller mortgage and the larger down payment of $60,000, Kate's return per dollar invested is "only" 75 percent. Leverage is great on the upside.[8] On the downside, represented in the bottom panel, if the house declines in value Kate does better if she borrowed less; in percentage terms, her losses are smaller.[9]

If everyone assumes that house prices can only increase, the scenarios in which there are losses are not considered relevant. But sometimes, as we have seen, house prices do decline even though lenders and homeowners may consider this impossible.

The example illustrates the important role of the down payment, Kate's initial equity position in the house. When Kate bought the house, her equity represented the part of the value of the house that was not paid for with borrowed money. At any later time, Kate's equity is the difference between the value of the house and the amount needed to repay her debt. Equity acts as a buffer that can absorb losses on the house. The greater Kate's equity, the more likely she is to remain above water and have some equity remaining even if the house loses value.

In summary, borrowing creates leverage and makes the equity investment of a borrower riskier. The higher the borrower's reliance on debt, the greater the likelihood that the equity will be wiped out. With a nonrecourse clause, the borrower's loss is limited to 100 percent of the initial equity position. Beyond that, any additional loss hits the creditor rather than the borrower.

In our simplified example, Kate's house is sold after one year, and during the year she lived in it, she made only interest payments, so the amount needed to settle the mortgage is the same as the mortgage. In a more realistic situation, Kate may own the house for a while. As time goes on, she makes payments on her mortgage, possibly refinancing it at some point. While she owns the house, she also maintains it, and maybe improves or remodels it.

Over time, the value of the house, Kate's mortgage debt, and her equity all change. In the balance sheet diagram, all these changes would be represented by changes in the sizes of the different boxes or categories on the balance sheet. At any one time, the larger Kate's equity relative to her debt, the less likely it is that a subsequent decline in the value of the house will wipe out the equity.

In our example so far, we have taken the cost of $300,000 for the house and the down payment, $30,000 or $60,000, as fixed. If Kate wanted to buy a $300,000 house and had only $30,000 for a down payment or she did not want to invest more than this on a house, she would have to live with the risk that comes with borrowing 90 percent of the value of the house. Kate could have reduced her risk by buying a cheaper house. If she had bought a $150,000 house with a $30,000 down payment, for example, her initial equity would have been 20 percent of the value of the house, the same percentage it was when she invested $60,000 in a $300,000 house.

The gains and losses in percentage terms would have been the same if Kate had bought a $150,000 house and invested $30,000 as they are in the bottom panel of Table 2.1, which describes her making a $60,000 down payment for the $300,000 house. In particular, whereas Kate's equity of $30,000 is wiped out if she has bought a $300,000 house whose value declined by 15 percent, a 15 percent decline will not wipe her out if she has bought a $150,000 house with a $30,000 down payment. In deciding which house to buy if she only had $30,000 to invest, Kate has to weigh the benefits of living in a larger house against the much higher interest she would have to pay on the larger loan and the increased risk of losing more of her investment or all of it.

Business Borrowing

Much of the preceding discussion applies to business borrowing as well as personal borrowing. If Kate runs her own business as a so-called sole proprietor with no partners, borrowing enables her to acquire more machines or more space than she could with her own funds. She may also borrow to pay her employees ahead of any sales that she makes.

The balance sheet diagram can be used as easily for Kate's business as for her house. The box on the left-hand side of the diagram in Figure 2.3 represents the value of all the assets of the business, the upper box on the right-hand side the value of Kate's debts or liabilities, the lower box on the right-hand side the value of her equity in the business.

As in the example of Kate's borrowing to buy a house, the balance sheet for her business changes over time. The changes are not only due to changes in asset values but also might be due to changes in the asset holdings themselves. When goods are produced, Kate's inventories go up, and when she sells goods, her inventories go down and her cash reserves go up. When Kate pays her employees, her cash reserves go down. This situation is more complicated than the mere change in house values in the previous example, but the basic logic is the same.

FIGURE 2.3
Balance sheet diagram
for a business.

As in the house example, the difference between Kate's assets and her debts is her equity position, sometimes called her net worth. In both cases, Kate does not know beforehand how her assets, in the house example the value of the house, will evolve. The value of the house and the evolution of the business are both uncertain. Changes in the value of the assets in both cases affect Kate's equity. If Kate makes a profit because her revenue from sales exceeds her costs, the value of her assets will increase, and so will the value of her equity. If she is unlucky and her revenues fail to cover her costs, her equity will go down. But Kate's debt is still the same unless she borrows more or repays some of it.

As in the example of the house, borrowing creates leverage and magnifies risks. Any increase or decrease in the value of the assets translates into an equal increase or decrease in the value of Kate's equity. On a percentage basis, the change in the value of her equity will be a multiple of the change per dollar in the value of her assets. This leverage effect will be more dramatic the more Kate has borrowed and the less equity she has.

As the sole proprietor of her business, Kate is not protected by a nonrecourse clause. If her business experiences a loss, she cannot just abandon it without paying the debt. Unless she can pay all the debts of the business, Kate may be forced into personal bankruptcy. Kate can shield her personal wealth from her business risks if she runs her business as a company with limited liability.[10] The charter of such a company determines the maximum amount for which she can be held responsible or liable. Beyond this, as in the case of a mortgage with a nonrecourse clause, Kate can walk away from the debt of the company.

There is a downside to limited liability. If Kate can walk away from some of her debts, she may find it more difficult to borrow.[11] Customers might also worry whether they have sufficient recourse to be paid if something goes wrong in their dealings with Kate. If Kate is liable and cannot walk away, she is exposed to more risk, but it also gives others the confidence that she has incentives to perform well.

Corporations

The corporation is the most important form of limited-liability company. A corporation is an institution with a set of rules that determine how it works, such as rights and responsibilities of the board of directors and the shareholders. In many contexts, the law treats this institution as if it were an individual with its own identity. As such, it can contract with others, borrow from investors, hire employees, and sell its products. Lawyers refer to this entity as a legal person. In practice, the decisions and actions of corporations result from the actions of the people in charge, such as their managers or members of the board of directors.

If Kate incorporates her business, she will initially hold the equity shares of the business and also manage it. However, there is no reason that she should stick to this arrangement. Kate may want to sell part of her equity to somebody else or to give shares to family members, friends, or key employees. Or she may want to keep the shares but appoint somebody else to run the business. Within the legal framework of a corporation, she can do both. There is no necessary link between the ownership of the equity and the management of the corporation.

Like individuals, corporations can borrow. In the same way, when corporations borrow they receive money in exchange for a legal promise to pay back specific amounts of money at specific times in the future. This promise is kept only if the corporation can pay; if it cannot do so or cannot negotiate other terms, the corporation may have to declare bankruptcy. Shareholders, the owners of the equity, cannot be forced to make additional payments. Their liability is limited to the amounts they invested. The corporation's debt must be paid entirely from the assets of the corporation to the extent that this is possible.

FIGURE 2.4
Balance sheet diagram for a corporation.

The financial position of a corporation can again be represented in a balance sheet diagram. The balance sheet represented in Figure 2.4 is the same as that in Figure 2.3, with one exception: instead of owner equity, the difference between the assets and the liabilities is now called shareholder equity.[12]

The shareholder equity of a corporation represents the difference between the value of the corporation's assets and the corporation's commitments to its creditors. As before, the evolution of equity over time reflects gains and losses on the corporation's investments, with a leverage effect from borrowing. The more equity a corporation has relative to its assets, the larger the losses it could sustain that would still not wipe out the equity. When corporations have little equity, they are like the homeowner whose mortgage is a high percentage of the value of the house. The smaller the amount of equity, the greater the chance that it will be wiped out due to decreases in the value of the assets.

Corporations Can Raise Funds without Borrowing

An individual's investments may be limited by personal wealth and the amount that the individual can borrow. A corporation, however, can raise additional money for investments by selling shares. Corporations can expand quickly without borrowing.

Shareholders hold fractions of the corporation's equity depending on the number of shares they bought. When the corporation earns a profit and distributes some or all of it as dividends, shareholders are entitled to receive their proper share of these dividends. Depending on the dividends they expect to be paid, investors are willing to pay money for the shares.

Corporations can therefore raise funds by issuing shares and selling them to investors. The individual shareholders can also sell shares to others.[13] This is particularly easy if the shares are traded on an active stock exchange. The ownership structure of corporations is very flexible, and this flexibility has contributed to the success of the corporation as an institution.

When a corporation issues new shares, each of the previously existing shares represents a smaller fraction of the corporation's total equity. For example, if the corporation originally has four million shares and then issues one million new shares, after the issuance it will have five million shares outstanding. The four million old shares then account for 80 percent of the corporation's equity, the new shares for 20 percent.

The reduction in the original shareholders' fraction of the equity is sometimes referred to using the word *dilution,* suggesting that somehow the original shareholders are in a worse position. However, whereas their fraction of the corporation's total equity decreases, the resources of the corporation increase. The money that new shareholders pay for their shares becomes available to the corporation for further investments. The total assets of the corporation increase, and the left-hand side of the corporation's balance sheet grows by the amount of money that the corporation receives for the shares.

What is the impact of the issuance of new shares on original shareholders? The answer depends on whether they are better off with a larger fraction of a smaller corporation or with a smaller fraction of a larger corporation. If the corporation can put the new money to good use so that the corporation earns larger profits and is better able to grow, the original shareholders will be better off with the new share issue than without it.[14] Having a smaller fraction of a larger and faster-growing corporation can be more valuable and more attractive than having a larger fraction of a smaller corporation.[15]

The value of the original shareholders' equity may decline, however, if the new funds are used for purposes that do not benefit them, for example, if the firm grows while acquiring other assets at a price that is excessive. Another possibility is that the new funds will benefit the firm's creditors, leaving relatively little of these funds, or the returns generated from investing them, for its shareholders.[16]

Because corporations can issue shares as well as borrow, the extent of their borrowing depends not only on how much they want to invest but also on the *mix of debt and equity* they want to use to fund the investment. In this respect, corporations are quite unlike individuals.

Internal Growth Is a Source of Equity

Private businesses as well as corporations can invest and grow without borrowing by retaining and reinvesting their profits. Money paid out to owners and shareholders is no longer available to the business or the corporation. Investments made with retained earnings do not require any additional borrowing and are therefore attributed to equity. No new equity is required.

Shareholders expect to get something in return for their investments in the corporation. If a corporation retains its earnings and makes bad investments or wastes the money, shareholders are dissatisfied, and this is reflected in low share prices. Managers and shareholders sometimes disagree about how profits should be used, with shareholders demanding that managers pay more of them out.[17]

In some situations, however, shareholders may prefer that profits be retained and reinvested. This is the case if the corporation has tremendous growth opportunities that shareholders would like the corporation to exploit. If the investments are successful, this success will be reflected in higher share prices and larger dividends later. Many corporations do not make any payouts to shareholders for extended periods of time, and their shareholders are happy. Apple, for example, did not pay any dividends between December 1995 and August 2012. Shareholders in corporations that are not paying a dividend but whose shares are traded on an exchange can create a so-called homemade dividend by selling some shares.[18]

Payouts to owners or shareholders can be accomplished in two different ways. When a corporation pays dividends, all shareholders are paid in proportion to their share ownership. Alternatively, the corporation can repurchase or buy back some of the shares. In such a case, some of the shareholders are bought out and paid in cash, while others see the fraction of their ownership increase because there are fewer shares; with fewer shares outstanding, the price per share will be higher than it would have been if the firm had paid a dividend, so these shareholders will benefit as well. In both cases the payouts reduce the total equity of a corporation and its capacity to absorb losses.

Banks Borrow a Lot

Corporations vary greatly in how much they borrow. Some corporations, such as Apple or Bed Bath and Beyond, hardly borrow at all. Most other corporations have some debt, but often not very much. Corporations in Europe generally borrow more than U.S. corporations and rely more on banks to provide loans, but even in Europe there are virtually no healthy large corporations that have less than 30 percent equity. When banks make loans, they insist that borrowers have sufficient equity to absorb losses.[19] Meanwhile, banks themselves tend to rely extensively on debt and typically have less than 10 percent in equity, often 5 percent or even less, relative to their total assets.

This has not always been the case. In the first half of the nineteenth century, banks operated as partnerships with unlimited liability. Bank owners had to pay their depositors or other creditors from the banks' assets or from their other assets. Until the middle of the nineteenth century, equity levels around 40–50 percent of banks' total investments were typical.[20] Bankers were careful not to take too much risk because they could not walk away from the debts when the investments did not work out.

In the United States and many European countries, companies with limited liability, particularly corporations, became prominent in the last third of the nineteenth century. In some countries this form of organization spread less quickly to banking than to other industries. For example, in Britain many banks were initially reluctant to take advantage of new laws enabling them to operate under limited liability. As a banking expert from that period explained, "A depositor would be much more likely to trust his money with a bank" if the shareholders had unlimited liability.[21] Similarly, although limited liability was widely used in other industries, throughout the United States a combination of laws and private contracts kept most banks from adopting limited liability until the 1930s.[22]

Banks with unlimited liability can destroy their shareholders when they run into trouble, and this was seen to discourage wealthy individuals from becoming bank shareholders. Banks could not become too large when operated as partnerships. After the collapse in 1878 of the City of Glasgow Bank, in which depositors did not lose anything but 80 percent of the shareholders were personally bankrupted, the trend toward limiting bank owners' liability accelerated. Still, well into the twentieth century, banks' shareholders frequently had extended liability that required them to cover losses beyond the amount of their original investment.[23]

Extended liability was ineffective in preventing bank runs and losses to depositors during the Great Depression because of many personal bankruptcies.[24] Following that experience, the United States established explicit deposit insurance by creating the Federal Deposit Insurance Corporation (FDIC). Banks that are FDIC members pay a premium, and their deposits are then guaranteed by the FDIC up to a maximum amount, currently $250,000. Similar programs have been developed in many other countries.[25]

The most remarkable trend in the way banks have funded themselves since the middle of the nineteenth century has been their consistently decreased reliance on equity relative to borrowing. Early in the twentieth century, it was still typical for banks to have equity equal to 25 percent of their total assets, but banks' equity levels declined to single digits, around 6–8 percent of their total assets in the United States, by the early 1990s.[26] Similar trends were observed in other countries.[27] Indebtedness further increased for many banks in the run-up to the financial crisis of 2007–2008.[28]

When individuals or corporate managers decide to borrow, they mainly see the bright side of borrowing—the ability to make larger investments and to enjoy greater returns if the investments turn out well. However, the leverage from borrowing works on the downside, not just the upside. The larger the share of the assets funded by borrowing, the more likely it is that the borrower, the lenders, and possibly others will experience the dark side of borrowing. In the next chapter we take a closer look at that dark side, when the borrower runs into financial distress and might fail to make the promised payments. Although we focus on banks only in the chapter after that, the next chapter is a critical part of the book, because the dark side of borrowing explains much of what is wrong with banking.

THREE

The Dark Side of Borrowing

Good old John Sedley was a ruined man. His name had been proclaimed as a
defaulter on the Stock Exchange. . . . The house and furniture of Russell
Square were seized and sold up, and he and his family were thrust away, . . .
to hide their heads where they might.

William Makepeace Thackeray (1811–1863), Vanity Fair

D EBT IS A PROMISE. After debt is put in place, borrowers and creditors
must deal with it. Sometimes the burden imposed by the promise is too
difficult or impossible for the borrower to bear. This is true for the debts
of individuals and businesses, and sometimes also for government debt. The
burden of the debt can cause problems for both borrowers and lenders, and
sometimes also for third parties.

Consider Kate as an individual or as a business borrower. If Kate defaults
on her debts, the legal consequences can be disruptive to her life and to her
business. Kate might try to arrange for an additional credit line, which means
she will take on additional debt to pay loans she has taken previously. For
Kate to be able to borrow again, however, lenders must believe that her difficulties are only temporary and that at some point she will repay the new loan
as well as the original loans.

As a borrower, if Kate runs into any trouble, she may want her creditors to
believe that she has only a *temporary liquidity problem;* she does not have the
cash to pay today but will be able to pay later. She may not want her *solvency*
—that is, her ability to eventually pay her debts—to be in doubt. If the creditors believe her, they may be willing to let her "roll over" her debt. Borrowers
with supposedly temporary problems, however, sometimes end up in default
and bankruptcy.

Does it matter whether Kate has just a liquidity problem or a solvency
problem? If Kate has little hope of recovering and paying her debts but her

creditors let her keep borrowing and doing what she wants with the money, Kate may become reckless. Gambling for resurrection, taking bets in the spirit of "heads, I win; tails, my creditors lose" may be tempting if there is no other way to avoid bankruptcy.

The impact of debt is felt before a borrower actually defaults. Borrowers may make different decisions because of their "overhanging" debt than they would have made had they not been indebted. Distressed borrowers may become excessively cautious or excessively reckless. Both of these behaviors can be quite costly to borrowers, creditors, and third parties.

Issues related to the dark side of debt are important in explaining why most corporations limit their borrowing. Banks, however, experience the burden of debt differently from other borrowers. They see mainly the bright side. This results in banks' borrowing significantly more than other corporations. The dark side of borrowing is not so dark for them because some of the costs are borne by others. By borrowing heavily, however, banks cast a deep shadow on the economy.

Living with Debt

Let us revisit Kate and the mortgage of $270,000. In the last chapter we assumed that she takes this mortgage to buy a $300,000 house. Kate lives in the house for a year and pays only interest. Then she sells the house and settles the mortgage. In a more realistic arrangement, Kate's monthly payments would involve not just the interest but also some repayment of the mortgage. Over time, Kate's remaining debt and the interest on this debt would gradually shrink, and the repayment portion of her monthly payment would rise.

Once Kate takes the loan, she must make the payments specified in the mortgage contract. If Kate has a good job, perhaps the payments seem easily affordable. But what if she loses her job or someone in her family becomes sick and needs expensive treatment? Then the mortgage payment will be a serious burden, and Kate may not have enough money to pay her living expenses as well as the mortgage.

Kate's bank might agree to postpone the payments for a while. Or Kate might be able to take out additional loans. But that would not really solve her problem, because she would then have to pay even more interest, on the new loans as well as the old one. Using new loans to make payments on outstanding debts can be the beginning of a vicious spiral or a debt trap in which obligations become larger and larger. The same might happen if Kate had taken a second mortgage on her house in order to pay for a trip to the Mediterranean; by taking the second mortgage, she would have increased her debts and reduced her equity in the house.

Kate's risks are even greater if the interest on her mortgage can be adjusted to reflect changes in market rates of interest. Adjustable-rate mortgages (ARMs) were used often in the 1980s when banks were worried that the interest rates at which they were borrowing might themselves change. ARMs were also used frequently in the run-up to the recent crisis, when borrowers were offered so-called teaser rates, very low rates of interest for the first two years, with a rule that, after those two years, the rates would be adjusted upward. In Kate's case, if such adjustments are made and the interest on her mortgage goes up, her monthly payment will increase and the burden of debt will become heavier, possibly by a large amount.

In the late 1980s, the risk of changes in interest rates hit many people in the United Kingdom. Because there was no rental market, many had bought apartments while borrowing heavily. Most mortgages had adjustable interest rates. When interest rates increased sharply in 1989, many borrowers could no longer make the payments on their mortgages. This led to many defaults and foreclosures in 1990–1991.[1] The same happened with many adjustable-rate loans and mortgages in the United States when interest rates increased in the late 1980s and again in 2005–2007.[2]

Living with the risk of being unable to pay her debts is unpleasant for Kate. To avoid it, Kate may maintain some cash reserve. She might also have borrowed less in the first place. Of course, borrowing less might not have been an option if her job required her to live in a particular area. If the area was expensive and Kate could not find a comparable job in a cheaper area, she might have had to live with the debt and bear the risk that borrowing entails.

Similar issues arise for businesses and corporations. Because business income is often more uncertain than income from employment, the risks of borrowing might actually be larger for businesses than for individuals. We often see companies that have been successful for a while losing their customers at a later point. As in the case of individuals, the risks of borrowing may temporarily be smoothed over by additional borrowing, but more borrowing can induce a vicious spiral.

For businesses, the costs of defensive strategies as safeguards against risks may be larger than for individuals. When people borrow for personal consumption, consuming less is often a realistic alternative. The investment needs of a business, however, are partly defined by the nature of the business and often cannot be reduced without harming the business. A car manufacturer must have an assembly line. A physician needs a certain set of machines to set up his or her practice and must maintain staff. Having half an assembly line or having a smaller set of machines or no receptionist would not work. Additional investments might also be necessary for a business to keep up with the competition. Being indebted may prevent a borrower from investing. The game of Monopoly can give us a taste of this dilemma. If players are in danger of running out of money, they may have to avoid buying expensive properties even if buying these properties might be very profitable.

As discussed in Chapter 2, corporations can raise funds by issuing equity and not just by borrowing. This gives corporations more flexibility than individuals or unincorporated businesses to avoid the burdens of debt. If a corporation does not issue sufficient equity or if its equity has been depleted by substantial losses, it may also find that outstanding debt is a burden that can endanger its future.

Default and Bankruptcy

No matter how hard they may try, borrowers may end up being unable to keep the debt obligations they have incurred. What happens then depends on the law and on what their creditors and the bankruptcy court decide to do.

When a borrower defaults on a payment, the lender usually waits and sees whether the payment is just late. The lender might impose a penalty for late payment. Going to court to try to collect debts or seizing a property that serves as collateral is time consuming and costly. The lender may eventually take legal actions to enforce the collection or trigger bankruptcy proceedings. If the borrower persists in default, the lender is likely to take legal action. When several lenders are involved, they may be less patient, because each of them might fear that the others might step in and take possession of the borrower's property, which would harm the more patient lenders.

It makes a difference, of course, whether the debt is $50,000 or $50 million and how large it is relative to the total assets and debts of the borrower and the lender. A debt of $50,000 is typically the borrower's problem, whereas a $50 million debt is likely to become the lender's problem.[3] If the borrower is in default on a $50 million debt, the lender may tread carefully so as to avoid destroying the borrower's business, into which the $50 million had been invested. If the lender treads too carefully, however, he or she may find it difficult to be paid back.

When lenders do go to court, the consequences depend on the law, which differs across countries and periods. In ancient Rome, the property of a defaulting borrower was taken, and the borrower and his family could be sold into slavery.[4] Shakespeare's merchant of Venice had a claim to a pound of the borrower's flesh. In the Middle Ages, defaulting borrowers could be placed in debtors' prison until their families paid the debt.[5] Putting defaulting debtors into prison was common in many countries until well into the nineteenth century. In the United States, the federal government and most states abolished this practice in the 1830s, but in some states, even today, borrowers can still be arrested when they default on their debts.[6]

Default and bankruptcy are disruptive. Under today's laws, they are less disruptive than in ancient Rome or in the Middle Ages, but most people still strongly prefer to avoid bankruptcy if possible.[7] For a business, the disruptions caused by default can be fatal. If a creditor seizes a truck or a machine, the business's activities may come to a halt. When the business has several creditors, the danger is greater because the creditors may have competing claims. Each one may want to seize an asset before the other creditors. In this situation, declaring bankruptcy may be a way to prevent creditors from fighting each other under the law of the jungle and letting the business go down the drain.[8]

Disruptions from default and bankruptcy affect not just the borrowers and the lenders who are involved. They may also affect the borrowers' employees, their suppliers, and their customers.[9] Local authorities may lose income from taxes, and local stores may suffer from a downturn in the demand for the products they sell. Housing prices may decline if people move away. If employees are laid off and cannot make their mortgage payments, foreclosures that lead to houses' being abandoned or neglected may also reduce property values in the town.[10]

Before creditors take action, most countries allow borrowers to declare bankruptcy. In that case, a bankruptcy court or trustee becomes involved. Traditionally, the purpose of bankruptcy was to prevent individual creditors from taking actions that would end up harming not just the borrower but also the other creditors. In recent decades, many countries have tried to change their bankruptcy procedures so as to avoid inefficiencies and the negative effects of default and bankruptcy on people other than the borrowers and their lenders.[11]

Whereas in the past the focus was on liquidating assets and paying creditors according to the priority of their claims, now the focus is mostly on maintaining the business as a going concern. Bankruptcy is used to renegotiate contracts with employees, suppliers, and the creditors themselves and perhaps also to shed unprofitable parts of the business and give the company a fresh start. The parties involved may be willing to accept reductions of their claims because the alternative of a forced liquidation would be even less attractive.

For some industries, such as airlines, the bankruptcy process works quite smoothly. An airline typically continues its operation or is acquired by another airline, and the process allows renegotiation of labor and other contracts in light of the new circumstances.[12]

For other industries, the process works less well. Negotiations may involve too many parties. Each party may engage in brinkmanship in order to receive a good part of the spoils. Given the problems that brought the firm into bankruptcy, there is a great deal of uncertainty about the firm's prospects or the value of its assets. The discussions and negotiations can drag on for a long time, particularly when they involve many different creditors and different priorities and interests. During this time the firm may be unable to compete properly in the market and attract or retain customers.[13] For example, car buyers might avoid buying cars from a manufacturer in bankruptcy or about to go into bankruptcy, fearing that, if the firm is liquidated, buying spare parts or being able to resell the cars might become difficult.[14] This type of reaction in itself can be a reason that eventually the firm will not be able to continue in business and must be liquidated.

Although they are disruptive, bankruptcies and liquidations should be seen as normal occurrences in a market economy. All are free to run businesses the way they like under the law. Their business strategies may fail, but if they are successful, they can provide a basis for innovations, growth, and new employment. No one knows in advance which entrepreneurs, firms, and strategies will be successful and which ones will fail. This will be determined in the market. Along with the successful firms, therefore, there will always be unsuccessful firms as well. Bankruptcy and liquidation are ways to deal with these firms, repairing some and eliminating others, so as to prevent more resources from being wasted on them.

"Only a Liquidity Problem"

Borrowers who cannot pay their debts often want creditors and others to think that they have only a temporary problem and will be able to pay their debts later. This will help borrowers to avoid default and bankruptcy and might allow them to continue to borrow or find ways to fund additional investments.

A temporary inability to pay is sometimes called a liquidity problem. To understand what a liquidity problem is and how it relates to default and bankruptcy, suppose that Kate promised to pay Paul $1,000 in cash at 11:00 P.M. on a particular day, but she forgot to take cash out of the bank. After hours the ATM will dispense only $300. Because Kate does not have the cash to pay her debt, she might not actually pay as promised. Unless she finds a way to come up with the money on time or to convince Paul to wait or accept an alternative payment, Kate will default. However, if Kate actually has more than $10,000 in her bank account and the $1,000 promise is her only debt, she does have the ability to pay this debt later.

Kate's problem in this example might be called a pure liquidity problem. This kind of problem can usually be remedied. If Kate can convince Paul that there is enough money in her bank account, he may accept a check from her instead of cash. Or Kate may find someone else who will lend her the cash.

As long as there is no doubt that Kate has the resources to pay, the pure liquidity problem can be solved.

Default and bankruptcy rarely occur due to pure liquidity problems. If it is reasonably easy to verify that a borrower has enough valuable assets to be able to make payments on a new loan, a temporary liquidity problem does not typically lead to default or bankruptcy. Because default and bankruptcy are unpleasant and costly both to the borrower and to creditors, they will try to find some other arrangement.

In practice, however, it is not always clear what a borrower's assets are worth. Suppose, for example, that Kate owns land on a remote island in the Mediterranean. If her creditors do not know the property, they may be unwilling to extend further loans to her. If Kate does not have cash, she may have to sell this land to generate cash and pay her outstanding debts. How well or how fast this can be done depends on how the market for land on the island works. For some such assets, it may take a while to find a buyer. If Kate needs to cash out quickly, she may therefore have to accept a very low price. By doing so, she solves her liquidity problem but takes a loss, which is also damaging.

Liquidity problems are endemic to banking. Much of the debt of banks is short-term debt, due within months or even days. Some borrowing even takes the form of overnight debt. Many of banks' assets, however, are loans and other investments that extend over longer periods. Most of these assets are not traded in markets where they can be converted into cash at short notice without significant losses.

It therefore matters greatly whether banks are able to renew their borrowing from their creditors or to find new investors from whom to borrow when previous debts become due. If banks cannot obtain new funding to replace earlier borrowing, they may have to sell assets at a loss. Selling assets at greatly reduced prices may cause banks to become unable to repay their debts at all, in the future as well as in the present.

To help banks overcome liquidity problems, central banks such as the Federal Reserve allow banks to borrow while posting assets with the central bank as collateral. This safety net has been introduced on the assumption that, if the assets are sound and the banks actually have only a liquidity problem, the central bank has little to lose. Meanwhile, the banks and the financial system may be spared inefficient asset sales and a possible crisis.

Some believe that the financial crisis of 2007–2009 was primarily caused by the liquidity problems of financial institutions that did not have access to the safety net. The liquidity problems came about when lenders to banks and other financial institutions withdrew their funding and, at the same time, the markets for mortgage-backed securities broke down.[15] The focus on liquidity problems, however, avoids the critical question of why lenders withdrew their funding to begin with.

The breakdown of funding for banks and other institutions during 2007–2009 did not come out of the blue. Rather, it reflected investors' legitimate concerns that these institutions were no longer sound and that they might actually be unable to pay their debts ever. The concern, in other words, was whether these banks might be *insolvent*.[16]

Insolvency

Suppose Kate owes $1 million that must be paid by tomorrow morning, but all her assets, including her house, her bank account, and even the likely value of her future wages, are worth no more than $400,000. In this case Kate's assets are insufficient to pay her debt in full. Default is inevitable.

Here is a new twist. What if Kate's debt of $1 million is due only in a month and her assets are worth at most $400,000 today? Because payment of the debt is not due yet, Kate is not yet in default. But there is clearly no realistic prospect that she will be able to pay this debt. She is underwater, broke, or *insolvent*.

The notion of insolvency refers to whether, in principle, a borrower is *able* to pay a debt. This notion is simple to state but quite difficult to make operational. What if by some miracle Kate suddenly finds out that an uncle she never knew has died and left her $10 million? In that case, Kate might still be able to pay her debt.

In practice, it is not easy to determine whether a borrower is actually insolvent. To do so requires making a forecast of future returns on the borrower's assets and profits from the borrower's business. These forecasts depend on the participants' information. The borrowers, or the firm's managers and owners, may have the best information, but they also have strong incentives to hide any adverse information.

Insolvency is suspected when the value of a borrower's assets is assessed to be not much higher, or even lower, than its liabilities. For a corporation, a possible insolvency test is whether it can raise new equity from private investors. An inability to raise equity at any price is a clear sign that the corporation is weak and might be insolvent.[17]

Hidden Insolvency and Distress

Even if borrowers are not actually insolvent, they can be in financial distress. In such situations there is a significant risk that the borrowers will become insolvent. Distressed borrowers exhibit behaviors that may be quite different from those they would engage in if they were not indebted or if their burden of debt was lighter. Specifically, they may be excessively cautious or excessively reckless.

A borrower may become cautious in order to try to avoid going into default. This caution can be inefficient if investments are important for the business or the corporation to remain competitive or as successful as it can be.

Even if the distressed borrower wants to take advantage of a good investment opportunity, the debt contract with the creditor from which the business or corporation has already borrowed might not allow the investment to be made. To protect themselves, creditors may have written conditions in their debt contracts that constrain future investments that would potentially put them at risk or require that their borrowers consult with them before making investments. If a borrower has learned of a promising investment that it would be desirable to make if the debt were not in place, the constraints of the debt contract might prevent the borrower from undertaking the investment. This reduces the borrower's flexibility to continue investing in the business as the need and opportunities arise. In such cases the borrowing that was undertaken earlier harms the borrower's ability to make productive investments.

Sometimes a highly indebted or insolvent borrower may choose to avoid investments because of the effect of the overhanging debt commitments. For an example, let us return to Kate, who borrowed $270,000 to buy a $300,000 house. Kate's mortgage has a nonrecourse clause, so when she leaves a year later, she need not pay the debt in full if the house is worth less than her debt of $270,000.

Imagine that after Kate has taken the mortgage, there is a major flood and Kate's house declines in value by 20 percent, or $60,000. It is now worth only $240,000. Kate has no flood insurance to make up this loss. The flood wipes out Kate's equity, and she is underwater—figuratively and perhaps literally.

Now it happens that Kate has a friend who owns a construction company. Taking pity on Kate, the friend offers to restore her house to its original value of $300,000, a fix worth $60,000, at a bargain price of only $50,000. Would Kate wish to invest $50,000 of her own money to bring the value of the house back to $300,000? From Kate's perspective, this is not an attractive investment. Because she owes $270,000 on the mortgage, her equity in the $300,000 house would again be $30,000. But putting in $50,000 to bring her equity from zero to $30,000 implies a loss of $20,000.

If Kate made this investment, she would be giving a gift to her creditor. Without the fix, the creditor will get the abandoned house worth $240,000. If Kate restores the value of the house to $300,000, the creditor will get the full $270,000.[18] Because so much of the benefit from the investment goes to the creditor, Kate does not wish to invest. By contrast, if she owned the house outright, she would welcome the opportunity to increase its value from $240,000 back to $300,000 by spending $50,000.

In the scenario in which Kate is underwater, any investment she makes in the house will benefit her creditor. But even if she has some equity in the house, a high level of indebtedness discourages her from investing, because some of the benefit of the investment might go to her creditor, while she will have to fund the investment in full. For example, imagine that after buying the house for $300,000, Kate decides to pay $50,000 to add an extra bedroom and expand the kitchen. Now the house is worth $350,000, and Kate has a total of $80,000 invested, her $30,000 down payment and the $50,000 improvement.

The additional investment can benefit Kate's creditor as well as Kate. Suppose, for example, that there is a flood after the $50,000 improvement and that this flood reduces the value of the house by 20 percent, from $350,000 to $280,000. The creditor, still owed $270,000, is unaffected by the flood, and Kate absorbs the full $70,000 decline in the value of the house. If Kate had not invested the $50,000, she could leave the creditor with the house after the flood, that is, the creditor would not be paid in full. The $50,000 for the extra bedroom and larger kitchen also helps protect the creditor.

At the other end of the spectrum, distressed borrowers may be tempted to take on risks that might be reckless and wasteful. The most extreme cases involve insolvent borrowers. Recall the example in which Kate owes $1 million in a month but has only $400,000 in assets today. Kate might consider going to Las Vegas with her $400,000 to gamble on the small chance of making a huge profit. If she wins big, she might be able to pay the $1 million debt and have some money left over. If she loses, she may have wasted the $400,000 that otherwise might have become available to her creditors in bankruptcy. Effectively, Kate is gambling with the creditors' money.

Borrowers usually do not want to admit to being insolvent if they might prevent insolvency by delaying default and bankruptcy.[19] However, during the delay, the conflict of interest between insolvent or highly distressed borrowers and their creditors can impose high costs on creditors and others. Borrowers act in their own interest, which may harm creditors. Creditors have limited ability to control or prevent harmful actions by borrowers. It is therefore important to recognize insolvencies early and to deal with insolvent firms in an orderly fashion.

Borrowing Can Be Addictive

We saw that, once debt is in place, borrowers and creditors can become conflicted regarding risks. Borrowers benefit from the full upside of risks being taken, while the downside is shared by creditors if there is a possibility of default. A risky investment can therefore be more appealing to a borrower than it would be if the borrower had to face the full downside risk.

Borrowers affect their creditors' position not only through their investments but by changes they make in the indebtedness itself, whether increases or decreases. Because borrowing increases risk, borrowers' attitudes toward additional borrowing are similar to their attitudes toward risks in invest-ments. Once they are in debt, borrowers may want to increase their debt even more and to resist decreasing their indebtedness.

For example, suppose that after Kate has taken the $270,000 mortgage for the $300,000 house she inherits some money and spends $50,000 to reduce her mortgage from $270,000 to $220,000. If a flood were to strike after that, reducing the value of the house to $240,000, Kate would suffer the full loss of $60,000. If she had not spent the $50,000 for debt repayment, her loss would be limited to her initial equity of $30,000.

From the lender's perspective, Kate's reducing her mortgage from $270,000 to $220,000 is wonderful, because the remaining debt becomes safer. From Kate's perspective, however, the debt repayment has the disadvantage that her part of any subsequent loss may be larger. Unless the creditor is willing to adjust the interest on the remaining debt to reflect its greater safety, Kate is likely to be unwilling to make this early repayment.[20]

Kate does not like reducing her indebtedness. Might she like to increase it? This is quite possible. One way Kate can increase her indebtedness is to take a second mortgage on the house, thus increasing her indebtedness. For ex-ample, suppose Kate's house increases in value to $315,000 soon after she moves in. She might take a $15,000 second mortgage, essentially a further $15,000 loan that is attached to the house. The effect would be that Kate again has $30,000 of equity in a house worth $315,000, and she owes $285,000.

In effect, Kate has used new borrowing against the value of her house to obtain more cash for other things. With the two mortgages, Kate has a higher likelihood of becoming underwater, because this will happen whenever the value of the house is below $285,000. Without the second mortgage, Kate's debt is only $270,000 and she is less likely to be wiped out.[21]

From Kate's perspective, however, the $15,000 she takes out in the second mortgage is shielded from any possible future losses. Should the house decline in value to $270,000, for example, Kate will lose the entire equity of $45,000 that she has in the $315,000 house. By taking the second mortgage, Kate limits her loss in this scenario to the remaining $30,000 in equity she has in the house after the second mortgage.[22]

The effect described in this example shows that borrowing is addictive in the sense that, once debt is in place, borrowers can become biased in favor of more borrowing and they generally resist reducing their indebtedness.

In Chapter 2 we noted that banks rely on borrowing much more than do other firms. Is there anything about banking that makes it necessary for banks to borrow so much? And how are banks and others affected by the dark side of borrowing? Answering these questions requires an understanding of what banks do.

FOUR

Is It Really "A Wonderful Life"?

Nothing is more responsible for the good old days than a bad memory.

Franklin Pierce Adams (1881–1960), American columnist

SOME WHO ARE UPSET about the financial turmoil since 2007 are nostalgic for the good old days, when banking was simple and bankers were serving their local communities. A model for this nostalgia is the banker George Bailey in the 1946 movie *It's a Wonderful Life*.[1] In the small town of Bedford Falls, New York, his Bailey Building and Loan Association enables working people to buy their own homes so that they no longer have to deal with Mr. Potter, the local real estate tycoon, who is thinking only about profits and is demanding extortionate rents from his tenants.

In the movie George Bailey's bank is a savings institution, taking deposits and lending to homeowners and doing nothing else.[2] In particular, George Bailey's bank does not trade stocks or other securities, nor does it provide brokerage services for its customers. In the United States, between 1933 and 1999, under the so-called Glass-Steagall Act, an institution that obtained funding through deposits was actually forbidden from engaging in such activities. Anything to do with stocks or other securities was left for so-called investment banks and brokerage houses.

Since the repeal of the Glass-Steagall Act in 1999, U.S. banks have again been allowed to combine deposit taking and investment banking activities.[3] Some nostalgia for the good old days is based on a sense that before the repeal of Glass-Steagall banking was better and safer. Even in the movie, however, the good old days are not all that good, and the bank is not safe. At one point in the story, a rumor that the Bailey Building and Loan Association might go bankrupt triggers a run of people wanting their money back. The prospect of bankruptcy is again raised when $8,000 is stolen.

In the movie, the run is stopped by George Bailey, who pays people from the money he had saved for his honeymoon, and the gap from the theft is filled with help from family and friends. The movie thus has a happy ending, but one may wonder whether the Bailey Building and Loan Association should really be seen as an ideal. What would have happened if the needed money had not been provided at the last moment?

In reality, indeed, the fate of traditional banking institutions was often not so happy. The Hollywood happy ending of the movie stood in contrast to the experience of commercial banks, as well as savings and loan associations, in the Great Depression. More recently, in the 1980s and early 1990s, many savings institutions in the United States failed. As we are writing this book, local and regional savings banks in Spain are in a crisis. The problems of U.S. and Spanish savings institutions in these crises were caused by risks the institutions incurred from real estate lending.

George Bailey's mode of banking actually had, and continues to have, substantial problems. To be sure, there were relatively few bank failures and no banking crises between 1940 and 1970, but this had more to do with the strong performance of the economy and the remarkable stability of exchange rates and interest rates than with the high quality of banking in these decades. When economic performance sputtered and exchange rates and interest rates became volatile in the 1970s, traditional banking in the style of George Bailey went into a prolonged crisis.

George Bailey's Balance Sheet

As mentioned, George Bailey's bank in the movie takes deposits and makes loans. Under the Glass-Steagall Act, commercial banks and savings banks focused on taking deposits and making loans. The differences between these institutions do not matter for this discussion, so we treat them as one type of institution and focus on deposit taking and lending, their main activities.

Figure 4.1 describes the broad categories on the balance sheet of a typical commercial bank or savings bank in the United States under the Glass-Steagall Act. These categories, as well as several others, would also appear on

Assets	Liabilities
Reserves	Deposits
Short-term loans	Short-term debt
Long-term loans	Long-term debt
Other investments	
	Shareholder equity

FIGURE 4.1
A traditional commercial bank's balance sheet.

the balance sheet of a so-called universal bank, which engages in all financial activities, including securities trading.

On the liabilities side of the balance sheet, we first find deposits. These are mostly the demand deposits and savings deposits that we all use for our daily transactions and savings. Businesses also have such deposits for their transactions. To the banks, deposits represent a form of debt that they owe depositors. Deposits are the most important form of funding for many banks.[4]

In the case of so-called demand deposits, the bank must pay depositors whenever they demand the money. Savings deposits tend to be somewhat less accessible, but most of them are also available on short notice.[5]

In addition to deposits, some banks also obtain funding by borrowing from other financial institutions. In particular, they might borrow in the so-called money market, the market for very short-term debt; lenders in this market are typically other banks that might have a surplus of funds or other financial institutions, such as money market mutual funds, that specialize in short-term lending. Some banks also borrow by issuing long-term bonds that might be bought by insurance companies or pension funds interested in long-term investments with fairly predictable income streams.

On the asset side of the balance sheet in Figure 4.1, we first find cash reserves. These reserves ensure that the bank has cash available when depositors want to make withdrawals. Because only some of the depositors need their money at any given time, banks do not usually keep large reserves. For traditional commercial banks or savings banks such as George Bailey's and for many banks today, the most important category on the asset side of the balance sheet is loans. These banks use most of the funds they receive from depositors, from other lenders, and from equity investors to make mortgage loans, consumer and business loans, loans to other banks, and loans to governments.

How Banks Benefit the Economy

Among the important services banks provide are those associated with deposits and the payment system. For depositors, it is important that banks make funds that were deposited readily available where and when the depositors want them. The checking accounts in which demand deposits are kept allow people to receive and make payments through checks, bank transfers, or the use of debit cards and credit cards. Because banks provide these services, depositors are willing to accept less interest than they might earn elsewhere.[6] The convenience of the payment system is captured in Paul Volcker's 2009 quip that the ATM had been the only useful banking innovation in the previous twenty years.[7]

Demand deposits and the payment system that is based on them make up an important part of the infrastructure of the economy, akin to a system of roads. If the payments system is efficient, transactions are cheap and easy to make and economic exchange works smoothly. If the payments system is bad, transactions are cumbersome and exchange is costly. By enabling transactions without the need for people to meet to exchange cash, banks contribute to the smooth working of the economy.

Another core activity of traditional banks that brings visible benefits to the economy is lending.[8] In the movie *It's a Wonderful Life,* George Bailey is a hero because he uses the funds of the Bailey Building and Loan Association to allow the people of Bedford Falls to have better and cheaper housing. The loans banks make can also fund productive investments by businesses and individuals and help people buy what they want "on credit."

A bank's task in lending, however, is not just to provide funding to anyone for any purpose. Rather the bank must discriminate between loans that should be made and loans that should not. Successful lending requires information and skill, and it involves specific risks. A lender cannot know for sure whether borrowers will repay their loans. Borrowers may fall on hard times and be unable to repay; they may be reckless and wasteful, or even abscond with the money; or they may simply refuse to pay their debts and find ways to thwart the lenders' attempts to collect payments.

Making successful loans and avoiding those that are best avoided requires reliable assessments of each borrower's creditworthiness before granting a loan, setting appropriate terms for the loan depending on the borrower's conditions and the purpose of the loan, and effectively monitoring the loan after it is granted. Reliable creditworthiness assessments require information about the likelihood that the borrower might default. Acquiring all this information and digesting it properly requires time, effort, and skill.

Many banks have developed special capacities for making loans. Their loan officers are specially trained to assess loan applications and to monitor debtors' performance. Some of the information they use is so-called hard information, such as business plans, statements of profits and losses, or consumer credit scores and bank statements. Other information might be soft, such as assessments of management ability. Even such things as local gossip might be relevant in assessing the creditworthiness of a borrower.[9]

It would appear that banks are in a great position if they can charge a high interest rate on the loans they make, such as 6 percent, and pay depositors a low rate, such as 1 percent. Why don't depositors eliminate the middleman and lend directly to those who are borrowing from the bank?[10] The problem for depositors who want to cut the bank out is that they must find out about the creditworthiness of the borrowers themselves. This is difficult and time consuming, and most people do not have the necessary skills. Especially if the amount each depositor has to invest is small, it makes more sense for them to keep their money in the bank and let the bank do the creditworthiness assessments and the lending.[11]

The bank acts as an intermediary, channeling money from thousands of depositors and other investors to its loan clients. This is likely to improve the efficiency of lending. One thorough investigation of a loan client is likely to be more effective, and cheaper, than multiple investigations by many small lenders. There are also advantages in relying on the expertise that the bank's loan officers gain as they handle many loan applicants and borrowers.[12]

When they improve the efficiency of lending, banks benefit the economy. Without their channeling money from depositors to loan clients, more money might be wasted on bad loans. Loan rates might then have to be higher, or loans might not be granted at all because the risks from lending might seem too large.[13]

Borrowing from banks is particularly important for small businesses that do not have proven track records or reputations. Because they are not well known, such businesses cannot easily gain access to other sources of funds. Without access to borrowing from banks or other financial intermediaries, they might be restricted to using the owner's funds and possibly funds from friends and family.[14]

When banks get into trouble and cannot continue their lending, the effects on small businesses tend to be particularly large. Reductions in bank lending to businesses play a major role in the transmission of banking problems to the rest of the economy. This role was particularly damaging in the Great Depression of the early 1930s.[15]

What Can Go Wrong: Panics and Bank Runs

The use of deposits to fund loans has been a standard practice in banking for centuries.[16] Standard references and textbooks on banking refer to what is called "maturity transformation" as a core function that banks perform for the economy.[17] This means that banks hold assets, such as loans, that extend over several years and cannot be easily sold during this time, and they borrow by taking deposits that can be withdrawn at short notice, whenever the depositors want to make payments or to get cash. In other words, there is a fundamental mismatch between the two sides of banks' balance sheets. Maturity transformation is said to be beneficial because it gives depositors flexibility to decide when they want their money; this flexibility is useful to them even if they do not make use of payment services, for example, if they have their money in a savings account.[18]

Although the use of deposits and short-term debt to fund loans has gone on for centuries and is enshrined in banking textbooks, this practice is in fact inherently quite risky. If short-term funding is not renewed or deposits are withdrawn, and if the long-term loans cannot easily be converted into cash, a bank may run into potentially serious liquidity problems.

With demand deposits and with many savings deposits, a bank can be required to pay the depositor *at any time*. This is not a problem if withdrawals and deposits roughly balance each other and the bank has enough cash on hand to make up any difference between money going out and coming in. Ordinary payment processes show a mixture of randomness and predictability that allows the bank to pay its depositors without difficulties by maintaining some cash reserves.

Problems arise, however, if many depositors demand their money at the same time. This could happen if depositors become worried about the bank's solvency and try to get their money out before it is too late. As we know from the fate of the Bailey Building and Loan Association in the movie, this can give rise to a *bank run*.

Bank runs are sometimes discussed as examples of self-fulfilling expectations; that is, events that become reality just because people expect them and act on the basis of these expectations. If investors fear that other investors are about to run and withdraw their money from the bank, it may make sense for them to run themselves and try to withdraw their money. They know that an important part of the bank's funds is tied up in illiquid investments and that the promises the bank has made to depositors cannot be fulfilled if too many people want their money at the same time. The fear of a run can therefore become self-fulfilling. If the bank sells assets at distressed-sale prices in order to satisfy many depositors who are trying to get their money at the same time, the run itself hurts the bank's solvency.[19]

The notion that runs might happen because people expect them to happen is intriguing, but there is little evidence that bank runs actually occur without any reason other than that some individuals believe that other people's running on the bank will cause the bank to collapse. Most runs are triggered by negative information about a bank's solvency.

In the Great Depression, when many banks were in trouble at the same time, depositors seemed to distinguish fairly well between banks that were really in trouble and banks that could come through on their own.[20] At that time, bank solvency problems were so widespread and the panic so great that one state in the United States after another felt compelled to declare a so-called bank holiday to prevent people from withdrawing their money; finally, on March 6, 1933, the federal government imposed such a "holiday" nationwide.[21] The national bank holiday stopped the panic, but the complete breakdown of all payments caused havoc for the economy.

Following the Great Depression, in 1935 the United States created a federally guaranteed deposit insurance system to protect depositors from the consequences of bank failures and to prevent bank runs.[22] When an insured bank fails, the FDIC takes over and winds the bank down without damage to the depositors.[23] By now this process works so well that depositors do not go a day without access to their funds. Because they have nothing to fear and it is a hassle to move accounts from one bank to another, depositors tend to stay with the same bank for long periods of time. Deposit insurance is less well established in other countries, but depositors can still count on some form of protection in most places.[24]

The Breakdown of "3-6-3" Traditional Banking

In the United States, the reforms of the 1930s were followed by four decades of exceptional stability in the banking industry. Bank runs were a thing of the past. Commercial banks and savings banks flourished because funding was stable and risks in lending relatively small. The atmosphere of that period is well expressed in the saying that savings institutions were following a "3-6-3 business model": take in deposits at 3 percent interest, make loans at 6 percent interest, and make it to the golf course by 3:00 p.m. Commercial banks offered rates on deposits that were even lower, but these banks also offered costly payment services.

This 3-6-3 world of banking came to an end in the 1970s. In the wake of the Vietnam War and the oil price shocks of 1974 and 1979, annual inflation rates rose above 10 percent. In parallel with inflation, interest rates in the money market also rose to double-digit levels.[25] Meanwhile, regulations from the 1930s restricted the interest commercial and savings banks could pay on deposits.[26]

Under these conditions, depositors left commercial banks and savings institutions in favor of newly introduced money market mutual funds. These funds paid much higher rates of interest while allowing investors to withdraw their funds quickly, even on demand. The money market funds could afford to pay more interest because they were lending to the government, to nonfinancial corporations, and even to banks in the money market at the high rates prevailing there. Traditional deposit-taking institutions suffered significant withdrawals, not because people had doubts about the quality of the loans they had made but because people could earn better returns elsewhere, from unregulated institutions.[27]

The tide of withdrawals was stopped when deregulation allowed commercial banks and savings banks to pay whatever interest rates they needed to keep their depositors and possibly attract new ones.[28] After this deregulation, the liquidity problems of these institutions disappeared.

Many savings banks, however, had hidden solvency problems. They had made many mortgage loans with fixed rates of interest and very long maturities.[29] As of 1980, a thirty-year mortgage that was made in 1965 with a fixed interest rate of 6 percent per year would still have fifteen years to go. Interest rates in the money markets, however, were well above 10 percent in the early 1980s. Many savings banks lost substantially because they had to pay their depositors the high interest rates that prevailed in the money market while receiving the low rates of the 1960s from their mortgage borrowers.[30]

Gambling for Resurrection

Because of the gap between the interest payments they had to make to depositors and the interest income they received from their mortgage borrowers, about two-thirds of U.S. savings banks were actually insolvent in the early 1980s, with a total shortfall estimated at $100 billion.[31] Most of these insolvencies were hidden because the banks' accounts did not give an adequate picture of the situation. The actual losses were recorded in earnings statements, but the fact that these losses reflected a substantial worsening of prospects for the future was not recorded or recognized.[32]

When deregulation removed many restrictions on their investments, many savings banks used this new freedom to invest in very risky assets, such as highly speculative commercial real estate investments and high-yield securities, also known as "junk bonds." Junk bonds are corporate bonds with a high risk of default that pay relatively high interest to compensate for the risk. The "zombie banks," those banks that would have been considered insolvent if their accounts had fully reflected their economic situation, were the most reckless in pursuing such strategies.[33] They were gambling for resurrection, on the principle that "heads, I become solvent again; tails, the deposit insurer has a problem."

When interest rates rose and the economy turned down again in the late 1980s, many of the speculative investments made by the savings banks in previous years turned sour and the so-called savings and loan crisis finally broke into the open. By the end of the 1990s, when the mess had at last been resolved, 1,043 out of 3,234 savings banks had been closed and the total cost had been about $153 billion, $124 billion to the general taxpayer and $29 billion in industry support for the deposit insurance institutions.[34] It would have been much cheaper to resolve the crisis in the early 1980s, but at that time, industry lobbyists had convinced Congress that U.S. savings banks had "only a liquidity problem," which would be solved by deregulation.[35]

What Else Can Go Wrong: Risks from Lending

The 1980s experience of savings institutions in the United States is an example of the general problem that lending can be very risky. Reading the media coverage of banking and finance, it is easy to conclude that risk in banking comes primarily from speculation gone wrong. When rogue traders impose multi-billion-dollar losses on their employers, this is big news.[36] By contrast, when banks suffer huge losses from systematic mistakes in lending decisions or from the maturity mismatch between their assets and their liabilities, the problem may not really make the news even if the bank's difficulties create huge problems for others.

In 1995, for example, Barings Bank in the United Kingdom was brought down by Nick Leeson, a trader in Singapore who had made a gigantic bet that Japanese stock prices would go up, a bet that created huge losses after the Kobe earthquake. Mr. Leeson became an instant media personality—and remained one until he was sent to jail. Yet the losses on his trades, roughly £1 billion, were only one-tenth of the losses from bad loans that brought down the French bank Crédit Lyonnais shortly afterward. In the case of Crédit

Lyonnais the stakes were much larger, but the risks were the boring risks associated with traditional business and real estate lending, not the thrilling risks associated with an exotic gamble in a faraway country. Nor was there a single face or a single gamble that could be pinpointed in the media.[37]

Although risks and losses from excessive market speculations are bigger media events, traditional lending can be just as risky and can lead to very large losses. Even if banks try to choose worthy borrowers and set loan rates so that, on average, the losses from bad loans are covered by the profits from good loans, risks in lending often do not average out to prevent losses. Some loans may just be too large. Or a recession may affect many businesses at the same time and reduce their ability to pay. A pervasive drop in house prices that induces many mortgage borrowers to default at the same time is also possible.

These problems are particularly serious if in the period before a downturn or a "bust" borrowers were not carefully screened for creditworthiness. Careless lending often occurs in a "boom," when borrowers and bankers are overly optimistic and bankers may be overburdened by numerous loan applications. Careless lending also occurs if bankers do not have the right incentives to engage in due diligence when making loans. In real estate lending, a boom may actually feed on itself, because rising house prices make bankers feel safer in lending and induce them to lend more, allowing home buyers to bid up prices even more until the "bubble" bursts.

These mechanisms were responsible for some of the major banking crises in recent decades. In the late 1980s, there was a worldwide boom in real estate and business lending. When financial conditions tightened subsequently, many economies experienced recessions and real estate prices declined. This caused many countries, including the United States, Finland, Japan, Norway, Sweden, and Switzerland, to have severe banking crises, all due to losses on real estate and business loans from the preceding boom.[38] Boom-and-bust developments in real estate lending again were central to the U.S. subprime mortgage crisis in 2007, the Irish crisis of 2010, and the Spanish crisis of 2012.

In the 1980s in Latin America and again since 2010 in Europe, banks have found that even governments can have problems paying their debts if they cannot print the money they owe. In Latin America in the 1980s, support for debtor countries from the IMF got most of the banks off the hook. In Europe, support from the IMF and from other Eurozone countries since 2010 has also limited the damage. The Belgian-French bank Dexia and Germany's Hypo Real Estate, however, would have been insolvent without direct government support.[39]

Financial Innovation to the Rescue?

As we have seen, the traditional model of deposit banking has important weaknesses. Activities might be disrupted by runs, the renewal of funding might be impossible or too costly, or returns from investments might not be sufficient to pay depositors. Deposit insurance has all but eliminated the problem of runs by depositors, but it has not addressed the other problems. From the 1930s to the early 1970s, these problems did not play much of a role, but since then the economy has become less stable and interest rates have become much more volatile. Banks' risks from changes in refinancing costs and from changes in returns on loans and other investments have increased.[40]

In the early 1980s and again in the late 1980s, traditional depository institutions turned out to be very vulnerable to these risks. In this risky new world, the 3-6-3 model of specialized savings banks that take deposits and make mortgage loans was no longer viable.[41]

In this much riskier world, the needs of savings banks like the Bailey Building and Loan Association drove financial innovations in the 1980s and 1990s. Many tools were developed to transfer risks from savings banks to other investors. In this context a major role was played by what is called securitization, a procedure that allows commercial banks and savings banks to sell their loans and mortgages to other investors. The word *securitization* refers to the fact that a group of loans that are not directly tradable in a market can be bundled together and turned into bonds, that is, securities that are tradable.

When large and well-known corporations borrow, they can issue tradable bonds. By contrast, the mortgage loan made to Kate in our mortgage example was not easily tradable. Investors did not know Kate or the property that she had purchased with the loan. However, if Kate's mortgage had been put into a package with a few thousand other mortgages, investors would not have particularly cared about Kate as an individual. They would have cared only about the average of the borrowers in the package.

For mortgage securitization, an investment bank acquires a large number of mortgages, puts them into a package, and sells claims on this package, so-called mortgage-backed securities.[42] An example would be a debt security that pays investors out of all the mortgages in the package. Another would be a more "junior" debt security that also pays investors from the mortgages in the package, but only as long as the first, more senior security pays its investors in full.

Mortgage securitization became popular in the early 1980s because savings banks were eager to sell mortgages in order to avoid the risks associated with them. Since then, this innovation has completely changed the way home mortgages are funded. A large part of outstanding mortgages in the United States is no longer held by the likes of the Bailey Building and Loan Association but serves as collateral for mortgage-backed securities held by investors worldwide.

Securitization has solved the problem that savings banks using deposits to fund mortgage loans cannot really bear the risks incurred. At the same time, however, securitization has created a new problem. When the banks that originate the mortgage loans know that they will sell the loans for securitization, their incentives to carefully assess the borrowers' creditworthiness may be quite weak. The investment bank that performs the securitization might impose some quality control, but the investment bank's incentives to do so are also weak if it bears little liability and if it wants to earn large fees from securitizing large numbers of mortgages. Given these incentives, it should not have been surprising that the quality of mortgage loans turned out to be lower than under the old system.[43]

As securitization has become more widespread since the mid-1990s, the quality of mortgage loans has indeed declined. Instances of fraud have become much more numerous, and so have late payments and outright defaults.[44] These developments have been closely linked to securitization; quality problems have been much less prevalent in mortgages that were not due to be securitized.[45] The decline in the quality of mortgage loans contributed greatly to the breakdown of U.S. markets for mortgage-backed securities, mortgages, and real estate in 2007 that marked the beginnings of the global financial crisis.[46]

So far, there does not seem to be a way to protect the U.S. banks that issue mortgage loans from the risks associated with the long-term nature of real estate investments without also destroying their incentives to devote enough resources to the creditworthiness of their borrowers.[47] As long as there is relatively little investment in real estate, this problem may not matter much, but it is bound to become significant again when the financial system and the economy recover and real estate investment picks up again.[48]

In 2007–2008, the downturn in housing and mortgage markets of the United States that had begun in 2006 turned into a massive global financial crisis that affected the broader economy worldwide. Why was the financial system so vulnerable, and why was the damage so great? The next chapter answers these questions.

FIVE

Banking Dominos

It was incredible. In exchange for a few million bucks, this insurance company
was taking the very real risk that $20 billion would simply go *poof.*
Michael Lewis, The Big Short, *regarding American International Group (AIG)*

T HE GLOBAL FINANCIAL CRISIS that broke into the open in the summer
of 2007 is often ascribed to excessive mortgage lending and excessive
securitization of low-quality, subprime mortgages in the United States.[1] At
the peak of the crisis, in October 2008, the IMF estimated that the total losses
of financial institutions from subprime-mortgage-related securities amounted
to $500 billion.[2]

When seen by itself, $500 billion seems huge, but in the context of a global
financial system in which the banking sector's assets are on the order of $80
trillion or more, it is actually not all that large. In fact, the $500 billion
loss from subprime-mortgage-related securities is dwarfed by the more than
$5 trillion of losses in the value of shares on U.S. stock markets in the early
2000s, when the so-called technology bubble of the late 1990s burst.[3]

How could this loss in the value of mortgage-related securities have such a
large effect on the global financial system and on the broader economy? Why
was the subprime crisis so much more damaging than the bursting of the
technology bubble a few years earlier? And why has this crisis been so
much more damaging to the world economy than the many banking crises of
the early 1990s, including the Japanese crisis, which also involved very large
losses in real estate lending?[4]

The one-word answer to these questions is "Contagion." In 2007, U.S.
subprime-mortgage-related securities were mainly held by banks and their
affiliates. These banks were very highly indebted, particularly with short-term

debt that had to be renewed in short order. The banks' losses endangered their solvency and disrupted their funding. Their attempts to deal with the situation further depressed financial markets, which then affected other financial institutions.[5]

When dominos are standing near one another, one piece falling can make all the others fall, too. Similarly, the initial losses on subprime-mortgage-related securities triggered a chain reaction that eventually threatened to bring down the entire financial system. This is why the final damage was much greater than the initial loss might have led one to expect.

By contrast, when the technology bubble burst and stock markets declined in the early 2000s, the losses were mainly borne by final investors.[6] Because of those losses, many people will end up with substantially smaller pensions, but at the time there were few defaults and bankruptcies that dragged down other institutions, and there were no furious asset sales that further stressed the system. Even the 2002 bankruptcies of Enron and WorldCom, the largest bankruptcies before the financial crisis, did not create the kind of havoc that was seen in 2007–2009, especially after the Lehman Brothers bankruptcy.

As for the Japanese crisis, because Japanese banks had borrowed mainly in Japan, financial institutions outside of Japan were not much affected. Subprime-mortgage-related securities, by contrast, were held by financial institutions worldwide, and many of these institutions had borrowed extensively for these investments. The interconnectedness of the institutions involved, their high degree of indebtedness, and the contagion mechanisms that spread losses between institutions explain why the mortgage and real estate crisis in the United States had such an enormous global impact.

Contagion

The simplest form of contagion occurs through the effects of a borrower's default on his creditors. The creditors may lose some or all of their investments. Even if the losses end up being small, when the borrower goes into bankruptcy the creditors suffer from having their claims frozen until the bankruptcy procedure has been completed. During this time, it is often not clear how much, if anything, they will be paid back.

If the defaulting borrower is a large bank, the consequences can be dramatic. Before the introduction of deposit insurance, these consequences affected depositors as well as other creditors. During the U.S. "bank holiday" of March 6–13, 1933, depositors could not get at their funds, and payments came to a complete standstill. When the bank holiday ended, more than 5,000 banks out of 17,800 did not reopen, and millions of depositors were left stranded.[7] Thousands of businesses were at a loss about how to pay their workers and their suppliers, let alone how to fund their investments.[8]

Deposit insurance prevents such damage to depositors and to the payment system, but it does not protect the other creditors of banks. They suffer losses when a bank defaults and also possibly earlier, when the bank is in distress and insolvency seems likely. If the creditors are also financial institutions, the original bank's distress or losses may cause these other institutions to also become distressed or insolvent, which can also cause their funding to break down.

In September 2008, the bankruptcy of Lehman Brothers had a deadly impact on the Reserve Primary Fund, a money market mutual fund, which had lent almost $800 million to Lehman Brothers. As a mutual fund, it was funded by shares and thus was not threatened by insolvency. But when the losses on loans made to Lehman Brothers caused Reserve Primary to "break the buck"—that is, when the value of a share in the fund fell below one dollar—investors rapidly withdrew their money. Within days, Reserve Primary lost some $60 billion of its $62 billion in funds, and it was closed shortly afterward.[9]

At the time, investors in other money market funds, even those not directly affected by the Lehman bankruptcy, treated the fates of Lehman Brothers and Reserve Primary as a signal that other investment banks and money market funds might also be at risk. To protect themselves, many investors abruptly withdrew their money. The run on money market funds was stopped only when a few days later the U.S. Treasury offered them a scheme for government-guaranteed deposit insurance.[10]

The run forced money market funds to reduce their investments. Many of these investments were short-term loans that the money market funds had made to banks, sometimes just for a day or a few days. The value of these short-term loans had become highly suspect after the Lehman bankruptcy.[11] Reductions in money market fund lending affected not only U.S. investment banks, which were at the center of the storm, but also European banks, some of which were heavily dependent on borrowing in the money market. As short-term funding from money market funds evaporated, the banks and other institutions that had relied on this funding ran into serious liquidity problems.[12] Because private markets for short-term lending to banks— including interbank lending in which banks lend to one another—had come to a complete standstill, these banks found it difficult to find new lenders.[13]

Further defaults of major institutions in Europe and the United States were averted only because central banks stepped in as lenders of last resort and provided banks with cash.[14] In addition, governments provided guarantees and new equity in order to reassure investors.[15] In Iceland, defaults and bankruptcies of banks could not be avoided even with government support because much of the banks' debt was denominated in dollars or euros, which the central bank of Iceland could not print.

When financial institutions fear for their funding, they feel pressured to sell assets in order to generate cash.[16] If there are no ready buyers, attempts to sell make the prices of the assets go down. Investors in other institutions that hold similar assets may then believe that these institutions' assets are also worth less, and their solvency may be in doubt. This doubt, in turn, threatens these institutions' funding and can force them to also shed assets and thereby put further pressure on asset markets and prices.

Such asset sales contributed significantly to the pressures on asset markets in September 2008 and similarly in the fall of 2011. In both cases, banks that lost short-term funding tried to shed assets. The resulting price declines made investors' confidence in banks decline even more. The downward spirals of the system were stopped only when governments provided guarantees and central banks made it clear that they would provide all the liquidity that banks needed.

Even before the Lehman bankruptcy, from August 2007 to September 2008, a slow version of this form of contagion could be observed in the markets for mortgage-related securities. Highly leveraged banks tried to reduce their borrowing by selling these securities.[17] Securities prices declined, imposing further losses on banks, which depleted their equity, creating pressure for them to sell even more assets.[18]

In 2007–2009, this contagion through panic sales and asset price declines was particularly strong because many banks had very little equity, on the order of 2 percent of their total assets. If equity accounts for only 2 percent of a bank's total assets, a drop of 1 percent in the value of these assets wipes out half of its equity. The situation is akin to Kate's having only 2 percent, or $6,000, equity in her $300,000 house. If the house declines in value by only 1 percent, or $3,000, Kate loses half of her equity.

Similarly, suppose that the bank's assets were initially worth $100 and its equity was worth $2. With a loss of $1, the assets are worth $99 and the equity is worth $1. Now suppose that no new equity is raised and the bank wants to move the ratio of its equity to its assets back to 2 percent of its total assets. It needs to reduce its assets to $50, almost half of their $99 current value, and pay back $49 worth of debt in order for the $1 it has in equity to represent 2 percent of its assets. This shows how intense so-called deleveraging through asset sales becomes when there is so little equity to begin with.

If instead the bank's initial equity was 20 percent rather than 2 percent of its total assets, a 1 percent drop in the value of its assets would wipe out only 5 percent of its equity. Starting with $100 in assets and $20 in equity, a drop of 1 percent in the assets will lower the equity to $19 out of $99 worth of assets. In this case, selling 5 percent of assets would be more than enough to move the ratio of equity to assets back to 20 percent. Specifically, if $4.95 worth of assets is sold, leaving $94.05, the $19 in equity will represent more than 20 percent of the bank's total assets. This shows that a bank's losses will generally induce larger asset sales and potentially larger price pressures and declines in asset prices if only a small portion of its assets is funded by equity. If banks initially have more equity, the deleveraging effect is much less intense and is less likely to be destabilizing.[19]

Contagion through asset price declines can also be very strong if there are few buyers willing to invest in the risky assets. In this case, the price decline can be steep even if the institution that has to sell assets is insignificant and the sales themselves are small.[20] Particularly steep price declines are to be expected if many institutions holding similar positions are in similar straits and if, in addition, potential buyers expect the sales to continue for some time.[21] In this scenario, buyers might hold off and wait for further price declines.

What Was Different about the 2007–2009 Crisis?

In Chapter 4 we noted that between 1940 and 1970 banking was safe and boring. Across the world, there were relatively few defaults of major banks and even fewer crises of entire banking systems.[22] In the 1970s, risk in banking became a major concern again in the United States as well as in other countries.[23] The systematic historical overview of Reinhart and Rogoff (2009) lists nine banking crises in the 1970s and more than fifty banking crises each in the 1980s and 1990s.[24]

Before 2007, banking crises tended to be limited in scope, and most of them did not cross national boundaries. Contagion did not play much of a role. For example, the U.S. savings and loan (S&L) crisis was not felt in Europe. The 1992 crises in Finland and Sweden had few effects outside those countries. The Japanese crisis, which was the greatest crisis of the 1990s and may have matched the subprime crisis of the United States for the sheer magnitude of initial losses, had no serious impact on the United States and Europe. Some crises, such as the Asian banking crises of 1996–1998, did cross national boundaries because the local banks had borrowed from banks in other countries. For the most part, the cross-border effects of these crises were limited to their direct impact on foreign lenders.[25]

By contrast, the downturn of U.S. real estate and mortgage markets that began in 2006 triggered a truly global financial crisis. Developments in real estate markets as such were not all that different from previous boom-and-bust episodes in such markets, but this time contagion in the financial system played a much greater role.

Three effects seem to have been responsible for the vast reach of the 2007–2009 financial crisis. First, the mortgage-related securities that lost much of their value were held by financial institutions all over the world. These financial institutions were linked to each other by the market prices of the mortgage-related assets. When one institution's asset sales depressed prices, other institutions were also affected because their holdings of these assets became less valuable.[26]

Second, because the institutions that held the mortgage-related securities had very little equity to begin with, solvency concerns arose quickly, and domino effects of defaults arising from the borrowing and lending of institutions from and to one another extended over several stages. Whereas in 1997, for example, the European banks that had lent to financial institutions in Asian countries had enough equity to absorb the losses from the Asian banking crises without too many difficulties, in 2007–2009 losses from subprime-mortgage-related securities quickly threatened the solvency of institutions that held the securities.[27]

Third, much of the borrowing by banks was in the form of short-term debt from other financial institutions, particularly from money market funds. This source of bank funding is especially susceptible to contagion and runs because neither the money market funds nor their investors are officially covered by deposit insurance. The crises of the investment banks Bear Stearns and Lehman Brothers in 2008 were precipitated by the refusal of short-term lenders such as money market funds to roll over and renew their loans when they were worried about the banks' solvency. After the Lehman bankruptcy, investors moved out of money market funds, and the funds, in turn, were forced to withdraw from funding banks.[28]

Increased Interconnectedness

Contagion has become more serious since the 1990s because financial institutions have become more interconnected and more fragile than they were in the past. This greater interconnectedness is to some extent a consequence of globalization, with ever more cross-border financial activities, such as German banks' borrowing from U.S. money market funds to buy mortgage-related securities in the United States.[29]

The interconnectedness and fragility of financial institutions have also increased because new types of financial institutions have come into the system. An important example is the role of money market mutual funds, which have grown in size and have increasingly taken a place between investors and banks. As we explained in Chapter 4, money market funds were developed in the 1970s in the United States as a way of circumventing regulations restricting interest rates on deposits at commercial banks and savings banks. Though some of the regulations were lifted, money market funds have remained active and have become an important part of the financial system, catering in particular to the needs of corporations and institutional investors that hold liquid assets in excess of FDIC limits for deposit insurance.

Money market funds offer almost the same services as deposit institutions, but legally their investors hold shares rather than fixed claims. The trillions of dollars that they raise are invested in short-term debt of nonfinancial companies and banks.[30] When money market funds invest in the debt of nonfinancial companies, they are competing with banks that might also lend to these companies. When money market funds make short-term loans to banks, they create an additional layer of financial intermediation between investors who want services like those associated with deposits and banks seeking short-term funding.

Borrowing from money market funds increases the risk of liquidity problems and runs. Without deposit insurance, the situation is similar to that of George Bailey in the movie *It's a Wonderful Life,* which we discussed in Chapter 4. Managers of money market funds that have loaned to banks may become concerned about the solvency of those banks and attempt to withdraw their money. They can do this by not renewing the short-term loans they gave to the bank. At the same time, the money market funds' own investors may become concerned about the money market funds themselves and rush to take their money out. Therefore, runs can occur in two ways—the money market funds can run to withdraw their funds from the banks, and the money market funds' investors can run to withdraw their money from the funds.

A double run of this sort actually happened in the fall of 2008. Money market fund investors suddenly wanted to move their money into safer assets, such as government bonds or even just cash. This forced the money market funds to withdraw their funding from banks. Having the additional layer of intermediation through money market funds was a source of vulnerability for banks.[31]

Another source of increased interconnectedness has been introduced by new techniques for managing risk. An example is the use of mortgage-backed securities to spread the risks from mortgage lending. As we noted in Chapter 4, these securities were invented in order to enable banks to eliminate their exposure to risks from mortgage lending, which had caused the S&L crisis in the 1980s.

With securitization, more transactions and more institutions are involved. In George Bailey's world, money passes from depositors to a bank that makes a mortgage loan to a home buyer like Kate. Before securitization, this was the final transaction. The bank would hold the mortgage and receive Kate's mortgage payments. With securitization, the bank sells Kate's mortgage, along with many other mortgages, to an institution such as an investment bank that bundles them together. The institution then creates securities, promising to pay investors based on what Kate and the other homeowners in the pool of mortgages pay. These debt promises are sold to different investors, although sometimes the investment bank itself might buy some.[32]

The desire to shift risk away from the original mortgage lender thus lengthens the chain of transactions and increases the scope for defaults to trigger domino effects. If the banks or other institutions that buy the mortgage securities borrow from money market funds, the chain of transactions is even longer.[33]

The use of so-called credit default swaps is another example of how attempts to manage risk can create additional complexity and fragility. A credit default swap (CDS) is a kind of insurance contract. The buyer of a CDS pays a periodic premium to the seller. In return, the seller promises to reimburse the buyer if the loan or portfolio of loans on which the CDS is written does not perform as it had promised. By buying a CDS, the bank shifts the default risk on the loans that are protected to the seller of the CDS, just as a buyer of home insurance shifts the risk of fire to the insurance company.

Prior to 2007, many financial institutions that purchased mortgage-related securities also bought CDSs as insurance against the risk that the mortgage borrowers might default and the mortgage-related securities would not pay the full amount that was promised. This practice added the insurer to the set of entities associated with mortgage-related securities.

Later, CDSs were also written on "synthetic" securities that were not themselves loans or packages of loans but were created to track and mimic the payments of actual loans.[34] This move added further complexity and interconnection.

The CDSs were sold by insurance companies, most prominently by American International Group (AIG), to which the epigraph of this chapter refers. AIG sold CDSs providing insurance for about $500 billion to financial institutions. When default rates rose in 2008, the solvency of AIG was put in doubt, and in the turmoil of that September AIG could not renew its funding. Because practically all the major financial institutions in the world were among AIG's clients, an AIG bankruptcy would have carried an enormous risk of further contagion. Millions of ordinary insurance clients would also have been affected.

To avoid this damage, the U.S. government and the Federal Reserve chose to bail AIG out. In doing so, they made sure that the financial institutions that had bought CDSs from AIG were paid what they were owed by AIG in full.[35]

Derivatives

CDSs are an example of contracts known as derivatives. Derivatives allow the trading and rearranging of risks among different people. The word *derivative* indicates that the participants' payments under the contract depend on, or are "derived" from, something else, such as whether a borrower defaults or the price of some asset that is uncertain at the time that the contract is written.

Derivatives allow nonfinancial and financial companies to manage their risks better. For example, a bank might enter a so-called forward contract with a U.S. manufacturer to exchange dollars for euros at a pre-set rate on a future date when the manufacturer expects to receive a payment in euros from a European customer. For the manufacturer, this contract eliminates the risk that, by the time it receives payment, the euro might be worth much less relative to the dollar.

This contract makes sense if the bank cares less about the exchange rate risk than does the manufacturer. If the manufacturer's costs are paid in dollars, it may not even cover its costs if the euro loses a lot of value (relative to the dollar) by the time the manufacturer receives its payments in euros. The solvency of the firm might then be threatened. It might therefore be important for the manufacturer to transfer the risk to someone else so it is not exposed to this risk. By contrast, the bank might not be much concerned about the risk. Constantly active in currency exchanges, the bank might expect to match the forward purchase of euros from the U.S. manufacturer with a forward sale of euros to a European manufacturer that expects payment in dollars. Even if the bank cannot fully match the contract, it might consider the risk insignificant relative to its total investments. If the bank is a large corporation with many shareholders, the risk to any one shareholder is very small.

Forward contracts have been around for a long time, not only for currencies but also for metals, potatoes, pork bellies, and other commodities. Other derivatives have been traded in exchanges since the early 1970s. Starting in the 1980s, and especially in the 1990s, derivatives have expanded dramatically and have come to play a major role in the financial system. New techniques have been developed that allow banks to manage the risks that they take when they write such contracts.[36] Innovations relying on these techniques have been useful because, as mentioned earlier, risks from exchange rate and interest rate movements became much larger in the 1970s and 1980s than they had been earlier.[37]

Have New Risk Management Techniques Made the System Safer?

Derivatives and new techniques for risk management have benefited society by providing better means of sharing risks. Better risk sharing can reduce dangerous exposures to risks and can transfer risks to those who are best able to bear them. This effect can make individual defaults and bankruptcies less likely and improve financial and economic stability.

However, the new markets and new techniques have also expanded the scope for gambling, and they can be used in ways that increase rather than reduce risks in the system.[38] Over the past twenty or thirty years, many scandals in which banks and their clients lost enormous amounts of money have involved derivatives. In Chapter 4 we mentioned the case of Singapore banker Nick Leeson, who brought down the United Kingdom's Barings Bank in 1995 when he bet that Japanese stock prices would go up and instead they went down.

By using derivatives rather than buying stocks, Mr. Leeson was able to build up extremely large positions in a very short time, with little control from the bank's senior management. Since then, at least twenty incidents involving losses of more than $1 billion each have arisen from the speculations of individual traders, carried out using derivatives.[39] In the case of Orange County, California, in 1994, this involved a significant loss of public money.[40]

Speculation and gambling have always played a role in financial markets. In the case of derivatives, however, the gambles that individual traders take have become much larger and much more difficult to control. Moreover, the domino effects of even small institutions' failing can be disastrous. Warren Buffett was right when he referred to derivatives as "weapons of mass destruction."[41]

Derivatives allow the magnification of risks in ways quite similar to the effects of leverage discussed in Chapter 2. However, the risks cannot be seen by looking at a bank's balance sheet. If a bank concludes a forward contract for an exchange of currencies, the initial balance sheet entry is zero.[42] Yet if the contract is for €1 billion, a 10 percent drop in the value of the euro implies a loss of €100 million.

Risks from derivatives are even larger if payments change more than proportionately with changes in the underlying variables on which the contract depends. Such bets involve complicated formulas that can be used to make large gambles and to hide them from others. Techniques for reducing risks from derivatives often involve complex trading strategies. Traders like to keep these strategies secret because they do not want others to imitate them. Often they go out of their way to obscure what they doing. This secrecy protects them not only from imitation by others but also from control by senior management. If senior management itself is involved in the gambling, the secrecy hides the risks from supervisors, customers, and investors.[43]

The secrecy and the complexity of the contracts and strategies used in derivatives trading allow individual traders and individual banks to build up very large risks, sometimes very quickly, without any effective oversight or control. Because derivatives can magnify risks, extensive derivatives trading can threaten not just an individual institution but, through contagion, the entire financial system. For example, large gambles involving complicated formulas and trading strategies were one reason that a small change in interest rates set by the Federal Reserve gave a large shock to the financial system in 1994; the size of the shock came as a surprise because most people were unaware how sensitive the positions of many derivatives investors were to the Federal Reserve's policy.[44]

Another early example of this risk magnification was seen in the so-called LTCM crisis of 1998, named after the hedge fund Long Term Capital Management (LTCM). With $4.7 billion in equity and $125 billion in debt at the end of 1997, LTCM was a relatively small institution. However, when LTCM incurred large losses in 1998, the Federal Reserve was afraid that an LTCM bankruptcy might trigger a chain reaction, pushing other institutions into insolvency as well.

LTCM had huge derivatives positions, and the fear that LTCM's partners in these contracts might suffer greatly from an LTCM bankruptcy was exacerbated by significant legal uncertainty about the treatment of these contracts.[45] Moreover, because investors were afraid of a major financial crisis, attempts to sell LTCM's assets might have caused the prices of these assets to fall dramatically, with potentially disastrous effects on the many other institutions that had been following strategies similar to those of LTCM.

To forestall such contagion effects, the Federal Reserve Bank of New York pressured major banks, creditors of LTCM, into bailing out LTCM by putting in equity, which would enable a slow unwinding without a bankruptcy procedure.[46] LTCM was treated as a systemically important financial institution even though before the crisis it had not looked like one.

In the spring of 2008, similar concerns made the Federal Reserve want to avoid a Bear Stearns bankruptcy, so it arranged the takeover of Bear Stearns by JPMorgan Chase instead. In the process, the Federal Reserve took over a portfolio of close to $30 billion of dubious assets with a $1 billion contribution from JPMorgan Chase and close to $29 billion of its own money.[47] The Federal Reserve acted in this way because it feared that a Bear Stearns bankruptcy would impose great damage on the partners of Bear Stearns in derivatives contracts.[48]

People in the financial industry often claim that they are experts at detecting and managing risks and therefore that their actual risks are much smaller than others might consider them, certainly much smaller than the risks of nonfinancial companies. Quantitative models and so-called stress tests are said to provide precise and reliable assessments of risks and a basis for reducing risks by sophisticated techniques using derivatives.[49]

These claims should not be taken at face value. Although bankers might be experts at analyzing and managing risks, they often come across risks that they have not anticipated.[50] As former U.S. Defense Secretary Donald Rumsfeld famously said: "There are known unknowns; that is to say there are things that we now know we don't know. But there are also unknown unknowns; there are things we do not know we don't know."

For example, people at LTCM, some of the most sophisticated minds in finance, had carefully calculated the risks of different movements that various interest rates might take, but they had not thought of the possibility that market investors might become more apprehensive about risks altogether so that the values of all debt securities except for the safest U.S. government bonds would go down. Similarly, before August 2007 bankers who purchased U.S. mortgage-related securities had managed their risks on the assumption that these securities could always be traded in the market. In August 2007, however, the markets for these securities suddenly froze up.[51]

The high quality of risk management itself can be a problem if people in the industry become excessively confident about their models and about their ability to manage risks. This is analogous to the observation that the sense of safety provided by seat belts seems to cause many people to drive less carefully.[52] Similarly, the sense of control that is provided by the use of quantitative risk models and derivatives markets for risk management seems to make people less careful about limiting their exposures and vulnerabilities. This may explain why speculative gambles using derivatives have become so large and why some of the most spectacular losses have been experienced by people and institutions that have been particularly highly regarded for the quality of their risk management.[53]

The chosen risk management strategies themselves may also provide a false sense of security. Buying credit insurance from AIG, investors in mortgage-related securities felt that they were safe. They failed to see that, if those credit risks were realized, the contract with AIG itself might be problematic at the very time that it would be most needed. To fully understand the situation, these investors would have had to know the full extent of the contracts AIG had signed with others and the extent of its exposure.

Usually, however, investors do not know the positions of other market participants. As mentioned earlier, market participants often go out of their way to keep their positions and strategies secret. Because most trades are made over the counter, out of the sight of other market participants, it is all but impossible for anyone to have a precise picture of other participants' overall exposures and default risks. In particular, it is all but impossible to know whether the transfer of risks that has been promised will actually work or whether and under what conditions the entity on the other side of the contract might default.[54]

Should We Let Banks Fail?

In 1998 the Federal Reserve Bank of New York was much criticized for pressuring private banks into providing a temporary bailout of LTCM. Similar criticism was raised in the spring of 2008 when the Federal Reserve arranged for JPMorgan Chase to acquire Bear Stearns, providing support through guarantees for some of the assets of Bear Stearns. Such interventions by the central bank or any other government body are in conflict with the principle that firms should be allowed, or even required, to fail if they cannot meet their obligations.

In the fall of 2008, this principle was honored in the case of Lehman Brothers, but the outcome confirmed the worst fears that had been expressed in the LTCM and Bear Stearns episodes. Since then, no other important financial institution has been allowed to fail, even though some are very weak and possibly insolvent.[55] Instead, many have been bailed out, from AIG a few days later to the European banks, Bankia and Crédit Immobilier de France in the summer of 2012. The principle that banks, like all other firms, should be forced to bear the consequences of bad decisions seems to have given way to a general fear of contagion from the failure of large banks.

The decision to let Lehman Brothers go into bankruptcy has been the subject of much debate.[56] At the time, the authorities seemed to believe that a Lehman bankruptcy would not cause too much damage to the system because the weakness of the bank had been well known for months and market participants had had plenty of time to prepare. Bankruptcy would also send the message that even a systemically important financial institution was subject to normal market discipline. However, the events that followed the Lehman bankruptcy were much worse than what virtually anyone had expected.

The question in the heading of this section has no easy answer. In a sense, it is not even well posed. As a matter of principle, without considering any particular bank or any concrete situation, the answer must be "Of course we should let them fail!" If market participants are unable to meet their obligations, they should go into bankruptcy or a similar process and be reorganized or wound down. Under this principle, all individuals and all firms will know that they have to fend for themselves without any prospect of a bailout if they get into difficulties.

However, the question of whether banks should be allowed to fail rarely arises as a matter of principle. Rather a particular bank is in trouble and the authorities must decide whether to let it go into bankruptcy or a similar process or to allow it to continue operating, possibly after an injection of public money. In this situation, authorities will be much concerned with the costs that the bank's failure might impose on the rest of the financial system and the economy. If the bank is small and unimportant, this concern will not be serious, but if the bank is large and systemically important, the fear of disastrous contagion effects might cause the authorities to keep the bank going after all. Even in the case of small banks, if many are affected at the same time, the authorities may be reluctant to let them fail. Once banks are in difficulties and there is a threat of substantial damage to the overall economy, it may actually be better to forget about fundamental principles and to do what can be done to avert immediate damage.

The argument just given highlights the general problem of the credibility of threats. In principle, it may be desirable to threaten banks with failure if they get into difficulties. If this threat is credible, it may induce banks to be more prudent. However, the threat may not be credible. If an important bank gets into difficulties, the government may prefer to prevent it from failing rather than bear the consequences of the failure. Similar credibility problems arise in many contexts, for example, that of nuclear deterrence or committing not to pay a ransom for hostages.

To improve on this situation, it is not enough to affirm the principle that banks should be allowed to fail. The enforcement of this principle will be credible only if the costs of bank failures to the rest of the financial system and the overall economy are reduced.

In the United States, the Dodd-Frank Act attempts to lower the costs of dealing with banks in difficulties by giving authority to the FDIC to take over and resolve any systemically important financial institution.[57] The FDIC is empowered to maintain the institution's activities while attempting to resolve its difficulties, sell some of its assets, and replace its top managers. As a government institution, the FDIC can cover any shortfall temporarily by borrowing from the federal government, and it can impose charges on remaining banks to prevent taxpayers' funds from being used.[58] Because the FDIC has experience in successfully resolving depository institutions, one might expect that it could manage to deal with a crisis situation without creating another Lehman-type shock and at a tolerable cost to the public.

However, the challenge of effective resolution of large, complex financial institutions such as JPMorgan Chase, Bank of America, or Citigroup is daunting. Such institutions have thousands of subsidiaries or other related entities, many of them in different countries. Under international banking law, there would be separate resolution procedures for different subsidiaries in all the different countries. Resolution would require coordination among the different resolution and possibly bankruptcy authorities and procedures, which may well be incompatible with the prevailing laws.[59]

Beyond dealing with the legal mechanisms in different countries, the challenge would be to maintain systemically important activities during the resolution process. For example, Lehman Brothers had used its London subsidiary for many investment banking and brokerage activities. When the bank declared bankruptcy, there were separate bankruptcy procedures in the United

States and the United Kingdom. In the United Kingdom, the authorities were shocked to discover that there was hardly any cash at all in the London subsidiary. Although the different units of Lehman Brothers in different countries were legally independent, their cash management had been integrated so that, at the close of the business day in London, all cash would be sent to New York.[60] Without cash in place, most activities of Lehman Brothers London were immediately stopped. To maintain activities in London, it would have been necessary for the authorities in the United States and the United Kingdom to cooperate so as to keep the integrated cash management going. It is hard to imagine this kind of integration with different authorities dealing with different units in different countries.[61] Even in a single country, taking control of a complex institution with numerous subsidiaries without interrupting important activities is quite a challenge.[62]

Initiatives in the United States, the United Kingdom, Germany, and elsewhere have made some progress in creating better resolution mechanisms for large, complex financial institutions, but as yet there is no internationally agreed mechanism that would preserve a failing bank and its subsidiaries as an operating unit to minimize the fallout for the financial system and the economy. Moreover, given the inherent conflict over how losses should be shared and the intricacies of negotiations about international legal reform, reaching such an agreement is unlikely to be achieved anytime soon.[63]

Because of the complications associated with the resolution of the largest and most complex institutions, there are serious doubts that authorities would actually trigger these mechanisms even if a major institution were insolvent.[64] Requirements in the Dodd-Frank Act and elsewhere that financial institutions submit living wills to facilitate resolution do not provide enough assurance that resolving such institutions can be sufficiently effective to avoid harming the system and the economy.[65] Even if resolution is trusted enough to be triggered, the process is likely to be lengthy and disruptive.[66] This problem is not limited to the largest and most complex financial institutions, but can also arise when a large number of small banks are distressed or insolvent.

Jamie Dimon, the CEO of JPMorgan Chase, has repeatedly suggested that his bank and others like it should be allowed to fail if they become insolvent and that the industry should cover the cost of resolving "dumb banks."[67] This bravado must be taken with some skepticism. JPMorgan is greatly exposed to the ups and downs of markets because so many of its assets are not loans but trading assets.[68] The bank also has enormous derivatives positions and short-term debt, all of which make it highly connected to others around the globe. In the bank's own analysis, a $50 billion trading loss could spark a run on the bank's funding and panic sales that would lead to further losses and possibly a financial crisis.[69] Moreover, Mr. Dimon's suggestion that large banks be allowed to fail ignores the potentially great damage that such a failure could impose on society. The collateral damage, including the domino effects and the potential disruption of the broader economy, would likely be significant even if the direct cost of bankruptcy or resolution were borne by investors or by the banking industry.

The state of affairs just described is bad indeed. Banks can impose great harm on society. If a large bank fails, the contagion effects can be disastrous. The costs of not letting it fail can also be very large. If banks are kept going even though they are distressed or insolvent, the rest of the economy may still suffer because distressed banks tend to make poor lending decisions, which may restrict innovations and growth.[70] If banks expect to be bailed out, the situation is that much worse because bankers may be induced to take more risk, which will increase the likelihood that their distress and insolvency will damage the rest of the economy.

Creating viable ways for banks to fail without harming the economy is analogous to preparing emergency procedures for earthquakes or other natural disasters; reducing the harm is important. However, financial crises are very different from earthquakes. The analogy is convenient for many, but it is misleading.[71] Whereas there is little we can do to prevent earthquakes, there is much we can do to reduce the likelihood of financial crises. The coming chapters will show that the fragility of the financial system is neither essential nor useful and that it can be greatly reduced. Even better, creating a safer and healthier system does not require us to sacrifice any of the benefits the banking system can provide.

PART TWO

The Case for More Bank Equity

SIX

What Can Be Done?

An ounce of prevention is worth a pound of cure.
Benjamin Franklin

D O WE HAVE TO RESIGN OURSELVES to having a fragile and dangerous
banking system, one that harms the economy and requires government
support when the risks turn out badly? As we have seen, there is not much
prospect of dealing with failures of large and interconnected banks, particularly those that are active internationally, without imposing large costs on the
economy. The economy is also harmed when many banks are distressed at
the same time and do not make sufficient loans because of their overhanging
debts. It is therefore important to focus on preventing banks and other financial institutions from running into distress or insolvency. For this purpose,
we need better regulation and supervision.

In any industry, regulation is important when the individual actions of
people and companies can cause significant harm to others.[1] If the banks'
own incentives with respect to the risks they take and the extent of their reliance on borrowing were aligned with those of society, banking regulation
would be less important. As it turns out, however, the incentives of banks
with respect to the risks they take and to their borrowing are perversely conflicted with those of society.[2]

In the last few years, many proposals have been made to address the
risks that the banking system imposes on society. Very few, however, have
been implemented. Most proposals have been rejected, diluted, or delayed,
some of them endlessly it appears, because the banks have convinced policy-

makers, regulators, and sometimes the courts that the regulations might be too expensive.[3]

What does *expensive* mean in this context? Who would be incurring the costs of the regulations? From the bankers' perspective, any regulation that constrains their activities or might reduce their profits is expensive. What is expensive for the banks, however, need not be expensive for the economy. The costs to the banks are important, but other costs must be considered as well, particularly the costs to everyone else resulting from financial crises or bank bailouts.[4]

If a producer of chemical dyes is stopped from polluting a river, the costs of producing his dyes might increase. He might then have to charge higher prices, and the prices of dyed products might also rise. Even so, the overall economy might well benefit. If the dye producer's pollution imposes cleanup costs of $20 million each year on downstream cities but the cost to the dye producer of using alternative ways to dispose of his waste is only $2 million per year, there will be an $18 million yearly gain overall if the dye producer is prohibited from polluting the river. The dye producer will no doubt complain that environmental regulation is expensive because it costs him $2 million a year, but this accounting neglects the $20 million benefit the regulation can bring to others.

When bankers complain that banking regulation is expensive, they typically do not take into account the costs of their harming the rest of the financial system and the overall economy with the risks that they take. Public policy, however, must consider all the costs and not simply those to the bankers. The point of public intervention is precisely to induce banks, or dye producers, to take account of costs they impose on others.

For society, such intervention can be very beneficial. Appropriate banking regulation is available that would reduce the potential for harm to the financial system without imposing any costs on banks other than the loss of subsidies from taxpayers. The simple remedy is to ensure that banks have considerably more equity to absorb their own losses. The fact that this is beneficial and not costly for society is all too often obscured by flawed and misleading claims, what we refer to as the bankers' new clothes. Excessive borrowing increases the fragility of the financial system without providing any benefits to society.

A Fragile "Fortress"

Bankers even dispute that their institutions are fragile. They talk of how much better their situation is now relative to how it was prior to the crisis.[5] Jamie Dimon, the CEO of JPMorgan Chase, often says that his bank has a "fortress balance sheet."[6] With $184 billion of equity on the bank's balance sheet, Mr. Dimon suggests that JPMorgan Chase is well equipped to withstand any adverse developments. Even the almost $6 billion of losses from speculation in derivatives that was revealed in June 2012 made only a small dent in this fortress.

The term "fortress balance sheet" that Mr. Dimon loves to use conveys a sense of safety and security, the opposite of vulnerability and fragility. But if one examines the actual risks lurking around the size and type of the bank's investments and debts, the strength of the fortress can be called into question. A closer look suggests that JPMorgan Chase is highly vulnerable and is imposing significant risk on the global financial system.

Some of the risks that make JPMorgan Chase dangerous cannot actually be seen by looking at its balance sheet because the positions that give rise to them are not included there. These are risks from business units that JPMorgan Chase might own in part or that it sponsors, and to which it has provided guarantees to serve as a backstop if they should have funding problems. These units might be full-blown subsidiaries, or they might be mere "letterhead firms," vehicles without any drivers, that are established for legal or tax reasons only. The bank's commitments to these units amount to almost a trillion dollars, but these potential liabilities of the bank are left off the bank's balance sheet. Yet they are quite relevant to the financial health of JPMorgan Chase.[7]

Entities left off a firm's balance sheet were responsible for the bankruptcy of Enron in 2001.[8] In 2007, guarantees for entities that banks had used to keep their holdings of mortgage-related securities off their balance sheets were called, putting these banks under a lot of pressure and greatly weakening them so that some required bailouts right then.[9] In 2008, similar pressures arose because sponsoring banks had to provide support for money market funds that they had kept off their balance sheets.[10] Mr. Dimon's "fortress balance sheet" ignores these off-balance-sheet commitments and the risks they might impose on JPMorgan.

As for the bank's actual balance sheet, Figure 6.1 provides a rough representation of the different parts of the balance sheet of JPMorgan Chase as of December 31, 2011.[11] The diagram on the left corresponds to the bank's public

FIGURE 6.1   JPMorgan Chase balance sheet, December 31, 2011, by U.S. accounting rules (left) and international rules (right).

disclosures under U.S. accounting rules, the so-called generally accepted accounting principles (GAAP).[12] The diagram on the right adjusts these disclosures to the International Financial Reporting Standards (IFRS), which are used in the European Union.[13] The adjustment concerns mainly the treatment of derivatives; it makes a big difference for the balance sheets of those banks that are heavily involved with derivatives, primarily JPMorgan Chase, Bank of America, and Citigroup.

In both representations of the JPMorgan Chase balance sheet, the liabilities side shows deposits of about \$1.13 trillion, long-term debt valued at about \$257 billion, and equity reported at about \$184 billion. The rest of the bank's debt, which consists of nondeposit short-term obligations and commitments related to derivatives contracts, are included as very different amounts in the two versions of the bank's balance sheet, developed using different reporting standards. Under GAAP, the other debts besides deposits and long-term debts are valued at about \$698 billion; under IFRS they are valued at \$2.49 trillion, a much larger figure.

A similar discrepancy appears on the assets side of the balance sheet. In both representations of the JPMorgan Chase balance sheet shown in Figure 6.1, we find cash reserves of about \$145 billion and loans valued at about \$696 billion. However, the trading and other assets are reported as \$1.43 trillion under U.S. accounting rules and \$3.22 trillion under international accounting rules.[14] The total assets are therefore \$2.27 trillion under GAAP and \$4.06 trillion under IFRS.[15]

These differences have dramatic effects on how one sees the loss absorption capacity of the bank's equity. According to the "fortress balance sheet" that JPMorgan Chase shows in its official reports, its equity amounts to about 8 percent of its total assets. However, if JPMorgan Chase used the same accounting rules as its European counterparts, this number would shrink to a mere 4.5 percent.

The difference between the amounts reported under U.S. and European accounting rules has to do with the treatment of derivatives that the bank may have with the same trading partners or counterparties. Under GAAP, derivative positions valued at around \$1.8 trillion are not counted on the JPMorgan Chase fortress balance sheet because the bank can use netting agreements to eliminate them from both its assets and its liabilities, as if they did not matter to the bank's financial position.[16] IFRS rules do not allow most of this netting.

The practice of netting that is allowed under U.S. accounting rules for derivatives masks important risks. For example, in the final phase of the Bear Stearns crisis, the attempts of derivatives counterparties to close their positions or pass them to others played an important role and contributed to the run on the bank. Similar dynamics were observed in the case of Lehman Brothers. These experiences suggest that, if JPMorgan were to become distressed, the bank's enormous derivatives positions could be a major source of instability, for the bank and for the financial system.[17]

Whereas banks emphasize their role in making loans, the balance sheet of JPMorgan Chase shows that lending is only a small fraction of the bank's activities. Loans represent only about $700 billion of the bank's assets, less than a third of its assets under U.S. accounting rules and less than a fifth under international accounting rules. Large global banks have been increasingly focused on trading assets since the 1990s.[18] Making business loans, in particular, has been less attractive to them than trading financial claims, particularly claims that promise high returns and whose risks can be hidden.[19]

JPMorgan's fortress looks even more fragile if we consider the market value of the bank's equity. On December 30, 2011, the date of the bank's financial disclosures, the stock price of JPMorgan Chase was $33.25 per share, which gave its equity a total value in the stock market of about $126 billion. This figure is significantly lower than the $184 billion in shareholder equity that JPMorgan Chase reported on its balance sheet, the so-called *book value* of its equity. If we use the market value figure of $126 billion instead of the book value of $184 billion for the bank's equity, JPMorgan's ability to absorb future losses would seem even weaker and its equity ratios even less than the 8 percent under GAAP and 4.5 percent under IFRS calculated on the basis of book values.[20]

What do we make of the discrepancy between the book value and the market value of JPMorgan's equity? The book value is based on the balance sheet, which is prepared and made public by the bank; it is equal to the difference between the value of the bank's assets and the value of its debts as assessed by the bank under the prevailing accounting rules. In determining the book value of the bank's assets, the bank must place a value on its loans. If some borrowers are behind on their payments, the bank must decide how long to wait to classify the loans as "impaired" and to recognize that it will almost surely incur a loss on the loans. A loss can be substantial if a house goes into foreclosure or if the loan is the borrower's second mortgage and will not be paid at all unless the borrower pays the first mortgage in full. The bank's management may have incentives, of course, to delay such recognition so as to present the bank's assets to investors and regulators as being more valuable than they actually are, which also overstates the value of its equity.

Market investors, however, form their own views about what a bank's assets are worth, and these views are reflected in the bank's stock valuation. The fact that the market value is lower than the book value suggests that investors believe the book value is overly optimistic.[21] This discrepancy between book values and market values is of immediate practical importance if the bank wants to raise new equity by selling shares in the market. The price at which this can be done depends on the value that stock market investors place on new shares, not on what the bank puts in its books as a book "value."

For some banks, the discrepancy between the stock market valuation of their equity and the book value of this equity reported on their balance sheets has been even greater than it is in JPMorgan's case. For example, the stock market values of Citigroup and Bank of America in recent years have often been less than half of their book values.[22]

Bear Stearns was considered a strong bank in 2006, eighteen months before it succumbed.[23] JPMorgan Chase is several times larger and more complex than Bear Stearns or Lehman Brothers were prior to their downfalls. Its equity may be able to absorb occasional losses during normal times. However, in a downturn, when many financial institutions tend to suffer losses at the same time, the contagion mechanisms described in Chapter 5 can easily lead even a relatively strong bank like JPMorgan Chase to become distressed or even insolvent.

Controlling Risks from the Banks' Investments

How can risk in banking and the fragility of the system be controlled and reduced? Approaches can be thought of in reference to the banks' balance sheets. One approach is to try to change the assets or investments of a bank, the left-hand side of the balance sheet. A simple measure is to limit the amount that the bank can lend to any one borrower, thus reducing the impact of a default by any borrower. This might seem uncontroversial, but recent proposals for stronger position limits in the United States have met with resistance from banks.[24]

Limiting banks' exposures to individual counterparties is useful. It reduces the risk—which is particularly prevalent among a small number of very large megabanks—that the failure of one institution will bring down one or more other institutions, a threat that played a role in the Federal Reserve bailout of AIG. But merely limiting large exposures is not enough to limit the risks banks are taking. For example, it does not prevent a bank from making many small loans with a significant chance that many borrowers might default at the same time.

In the past, some regulations actually forced banks to lend in a poorly diversified manner. For example, before the S&L crisis most savings institutions were restricted to mortgage lending in their states. Similarly, in many European countries banks were restricted to lending in their own countries, sometimes by explicit regulations, sometimes by restrictions on moving funds abroad.

Restrictions of banks' activities to their home territories have a long tradition. Ostensibly designed to force banks to invest safely, these rules have often been used to ensure that local borrowers, including the government, would get ample funding at good terms.[25]

The crises of the 1980s and 1990s, however, showed that investing at home is not the same as investing safely. For example, in Texas the S&L crisis of the late 1980s came sooner, beginning already in 1986, and was stronger than in most other states because Texan real estate and mortgage markets were uniquely affected by the oil price slump of 1985. In Sweden the banking crisis of 1992 was stronger than other countries' banking crises in the early 1990s because, in trying to protect the exchange rate, the Swedish central bank pushed interest rates for overnight borrowing to a record 500 percent per year, after which there was a dramatic downturn in real estate markets.[26]

In the United States, such rules were also meant to prevent banks from becoming too large.[27] By now, these rules have mostly been lifted. Over the past two decades, concentration in banking has grown dramatically, much of it through mergers and acquisitions.[28] The trend toward ever larger banks was further reinforced in the financial crisis when some institutions were "saved" from bankruptcy by having them acquired by other, usually larger, institutions.

The largest institutions by now are not just too big to fail in the sense that failure could cause disaster but, as the experience of Iceland and Ireland shows, they may also be too big to save in the sense that rescuing them would overburden taxpayers. Large banks and financial institutions are by far the largest corporations in the world by asset size, and they are also arguably among the most complex.[29] As discussed in Chapter 5, the enormous complexity is one of the reasons that the bankruptcy or resolution process is so costly and disruptive. Simpler institutions would make the use of resolution mechanisms more credible.[30]

One approach to reform is therefore to find a way to break up the banks into smaller, more manageable, and less complex entities. Although large banks boast that big is beautiful and scoff at size restrictions, there is little to suggest that banks that grow beyond about $100 billion in assets create gains in efficiency; in fact, at the largest sizes, institutions might become more inefficient and subject to serious governance and control problems.[31] The incentives for banks to become large through mergers can be partly attributed to cost advantages from implicit subsidies they obtain by becoming too big to fail. But these cost advantages come at the expense of taxpayers.

Combining many types of businesses under one roof does not necessarily increase efficiency. This has been demonstrated by the history of the conglomerates that were formed in the United States during the 1960s. Many of these large conglomerates failed to perform well and were later broken into smaller, more focused corporations.[32] Reducing the size and scope of large banks could make them more efficient as well, but the subsidies associated with size—as well as managerial entrenchment, which is also observed in other industries—have so far prevented this from happening.[33]

Several reform proposals aim to protect depositors and deposit insurance from the risks of investment banking. In the United States the so-called Volcker Rule seeks to ban proprietary trading by deposit-taking institutions. In the same spirit, the Independent Commission on Banking (ICB) in the United Kingdom has proposed to "ring fence" retail banking, deposit taking, and lending in special institutions that would not be allowed to engage in investment banking. In the European Union, a group of experts set up by the European Commission under the chairmanship of Finnish central bank governor Erkki Liikanen has put forward a similar proposal.[34]

These proposals presume that concerns about depositors and the payment system are, or should be, the major reason for government interventions in banking, for guarantees and bailouts as well as banking regulation. For example, the ICB's ring-fencing proposal for the United Kingdom is based on the assumption that retail banks will benefit from government guarantees and that investment banks will not be able to count on such support. Given the prospect of government support for retail banks, the ICB wants to insulate these banks from the risks of activities such as speculating on the banks' own accounts, participation in derivatives markets, or, more generally, investment banking.[35]

This approach has two weaknesses, however. First, protection of depositors and the payment system is not the only concern that might induce governments to bail out banks. Second, commercial banking activities can also be a source of risks that cause banks to fail unless they are bailed out.

On the first point, we note that both Bear Stearns and Lehman Brothers were non-deposit-taking investment banks, AIG was an insurance company, and LTCM, seen as systemically important in 1998, was a hedge fund. None had depositors, and none was involved with the payment system, yet Bear Stearns, AIG, and LTCM were deemed sufficiently important to be kept out of bankruptcy for fear that otherwise they might seriously damage the rest of the financial system. Lehman Brothers did go into bankruptcy, but, with hindsight, this is seen as having been very costly.[36] The experience with these institutions suggests that concerns about government guarantees and bailouts should not be limited to deposit-taking institutions or even to banks.

Systemically important financial institutions need not be taking deposits; they need not even be called banks.[37]

Second, as noted in Chapter 4, traditional commercial banking activities have caused many banking crises in the past. The collapse of commercial banks in the United States in the Great Depression was in large part due to the fact that many loan customers could not pay their debts, especially businesses that were unable to sell their products in the slump.[38] Business and real estate lending played a key role in the banking crises of the late 1980s and early 1990s.[39] The troubles in recent years of Irish and Spanish banks, and indeed those of many U.S. and European banks, can be traced to loans to real estate developers and buyers that turned out badly. In some cases, in fact, the problem has been one of too many to fail rather than too big to fail, because many banks were exposed to the same risks and thus were in danger of failing at the same time.

The German experience of 2009 provides an interesting perspective on this discussion. Retail banking in Germany, deposits and small-business lending, is dominated by banks that are active only locally, in particular savings banks in public ownership. These local banks were hardly affected by the crisis and the economic recession. Therefore, there was not much of a credit crunch for small and medium-sized businesses.

However, the Landesbanken—public banks that are active globally but do not have any retail business, deposits, or loans—were much affected by the crisis; in fact, most of the costs of the crisis to German taxpayers were caused by these banks, which had gone into various adventures because they did not have a profitable retail business. Some of this cost, in fact, was borne by the local savings banks, which are co-owners of the Landesbanken and put their surplus funds in deposits with the Landesbanken. In this experience of a banking system with some separation of retail (deposit) banking and investment banking, retail banking was somewhat protected from the risks of investment banking, but these risks did hit the system—and the taxpayers —nonetheless.[40]

The key objective of banking regulation should be to reduce the fragility of individual banks and of the system so that it can support the economy reliably. Achieving this would likely require a combination of measures.

The structural reform proposals discussed here focus on the banks' assets, the left-hand side of their balance sheets. The fragility of the financial system, however, is critically related to the ways in which financial institutions fund themselves, the right-hand side of their balance sheets. No matter what other steps are taken to reduce the risk to the economy from the financial system, correcting the distortions in the funding mix of banks must be a key part of any reform.

Controlling Liquidity Risks

Banks can run into liquidity problems because the deposits and other short-term debt that they use for funding can suddenly be withdrawn, while many of the investments that they make cannot always be converted into cash easily. A traditional way to deal with this problem is to require banks to invest sufficient amounts in assets that are deemed to be liquid. The simplest such requirement is that banks hold a certain fraction of their deposits in cash or in accounts with the central bank that can be drawn on for cash at any time. This regulation is called a reserve requirement.

Reserve requirements are often viewed as costly because the funds kept in reserves earn little or no interest.[41] Increasing reserve requirements may ultimately lead banks to charge higher fees for their services. In setting reserve requirements, such additional costs to clients must be considered along with any benefits from banks' having cash readily available.

Over the past few years, international bodies have proposed to reduce the incidence of liquidity problems in banking by regulating the liquidity of the banks' assets. For example, Basel III proposes to introduce a so-called liquidity coverage ratio regulation in order to ensure that at all times banks have enough assets that can be converted into cash quickly and without incurring a loss to meet all their payment obligations over the next thirty days.[42] This regulation has less effect on the banks' ability to earn interest than do reserve requirements. By focusing on the banks' ability to fulfill their upcoming obligations, it also gets at the core of the liquidity problem, which simple reserve requirements do not.[43]

The liquidity coverage ratio regulation raises new questions, however. For instance, what kinds of assets should be considered sufficiently liquid?[44]

Practically all assets other than cash and claims on the central bank may suddenly turn from very liquid to very illiquid. Banks would like liquidity regulation to treat many assets as liquid so they can satisfy the requirements easily without reducing the interest they can earn. But if the regulation is very loose, there is a danger that supposedly liquid assets will not actually provide banks with needed cash in a crunch.[45]

In the distant past, liquidity problems were often associated with runs by depositors. For example, as discussed in Chapter 5, in the United States the Great Depression of the early 1930s was accompanied by disastrous bank runs and banking crises. Since the creation of the FDIC, however, there have been hardly any runs by depositors.[46] Money market funds did not have this protection and suffered runs by investors in September 2008; these runs stopped when the government provided money market funds with a form of deposit insurance. At the same time, the remaining major investment banks, Goldman Sachs and Morgan Stanley, turned themselves into standard bank holding companies so as to obtain access to the Federal Reserve as a lender of last resort.[47] In many other countries as well, in September and October 2008, government guarantees and government funds were used to quell the financial turmoil that had followed the Lehman bankruptcy.[48]

Does it follow that we should rely more generally on government guarantees to forestall liquidity problems? According to one view, government safety nets should be expanded to cover the entire system of short-term debts of financial institutions, nonbanks as well as banks.[49] Addressing liquidity problems by means of government guarantees without considering solvency is misguided, however, because solvency problems are much more dangerous than liquidity problems. Indeed, liquidity problems are quite often *caused* by solvency problems, because concerns about solvency induce creditors to pull out. If creditors are confident that a bank is solvent and able to pay them back, they are not likely to withdraw their funding from the bank.

Guarantees can actually be quite harmful if banks are insolvent or nearly insolvent and highly distressed. The guarantees enable distressed banks to roll over their debt, and even to borrow more, without doing anything to reestablish solvency and, because of distorted incentives, not necessarily making the most productive investments. This can be costly to the economy as well as taxpayers.

In Chapter 4 we discussed the experience of the 1980s, when insolvent U.S. savings institutions were treated as if they had only liquidity problems. The institutions were freed from regulations and became reckless, with large costs eventually paid by taxpayers.[50] Another example is provided by the Landesbanken in Germany, public banks that had traditionally been guaranteed by the state. Following a 2001 ruling by the European Commission that these guarantees had to end after 2005, they borrowed more than one hundred billion euros while the guarantees were still in effect and invested much of the money in toxic securities in the United States. Losses from these investments are likely to amount to more than €50 billion.[51]

Controlling Banks' Ability to Absorb Losses

The approaches to reducing risks from banking just discussed were focused on either trying to control the volume or the type of activities in which banks engaged or trying to control the mismatch between the short-term nature of the banks' debts, on the right-hand side of their balance sheets, and the long-term nature and poor salability of their assets, on the left-hand side. A third approach to the challenge of reducing the fragility of banks and the banking system is called capital regulation; it focuses on the banks' ability to absorb losses without becoming insolvent.

Capital regulation focuses on how banks fund their assets rather than on the assets themselves. It deals with the mix of debt and equity on the right-hand side of their balance sheets.[52] As we saw in Chapters 2 and 3, a borrower like Kate, who buys a house or has a business with a given set of assets, is better able to absorb losses when she has more equity. The more equity she has, the less likely she is to become insolvent. Capital regulation is intended to make sure banks do not have too little equity.

Requiring banks to have more equity and less debt addresses banks' solvency most directly. Recall the example discussed in Chapter 2, in which Kate buys a $300,000 house using borrowed money and some of her own money. If Kate's down payment or initial equity is $30,000, a subsequent drop of 10 percent or more in the value of the house will wipe out her entire equity and leave her underwater. By contrast, if Kate invests $60,000 as a down payment, she will lose her entire equity only if the price declines in value by 20 percent or more; otherwise she will continue to have equity in the house. Similarly, when equity represents less than 5 percent of the total value of the assets, as is often the case for banks, a small drop in the value of the assets endangers the bank's solvency.

Capital regulation also reduces fragility in indirect ways. If solvency risk is reduced, the likelihood of liquidity problems and runs is also reduced because depositors and other creditors are less nervous about their money. Moreover, beyond the bank's own ability to absorb losses without becoming distressed, the fraction of assets that a bank may have to sell after losses in order to recover its equity ratio is smaller if it has more equity. Therefore, the contagion caused through asset sales and interconnectedness is weaker when banks have more equity. Increasing banks' ability to absorb losses through equity thus attacks fragility most effectively and in multiple ways.

Capital regulation does not impose restrictions on banks' activities and investments. In fact, the more equity a bank has, the more the choice of assets to hold, and the management of risks associated with these assets, can be left to the bank.

Capital regulation also improves the incentives of bankers with respect to risk taking. If a bank has more equity and less debt, more of the downside of its activities will be borne by the bank and its shareholders rather than by creditors or taxpayers. This increased equity gives bankers better incentives to manage the risks in their investments, and it gives shareholders better incentives to make sure managers do not take too much risk. The decisions made by banks with more equity will therefore take better account of risks. Such banks are less likely to encounter the conflicts of interest from the dark side of borrowing that we discussed in Chapter 3. This is beneficial to everyone who would suffer the consequences if the risks turned out badly, including taxpayers and the broader economy.

The Debate over Capital Regulation

Capital requirements have been the main instruments of banking regulation since the early 1990s.[53] Many of the regulations that were put in place after the Great Depression had been dismantled in the 1970s and 1980s. In a world with large swings in interest rates and exchange rates, as well as more intense competition from nonbank intermediaries and from banks in other countries, many of the older regulations had become counterproductive.

In the late 1980s, regulators from major countries got together to coordinate banking regulation internationally. The idea was to set minimum standards so that, if a country adhered to these standards, the other countries would allow that country's banks to operate in their territories. In 1988 these negotiations led to the so-called Basel Accord ("Basel I"), named after the city of Basel in Switzerland where the regulators met. Under Basel I, banks were required to have "regulatory capital" equal to at least 8 percent of their business lending. Subsequently, "Basel II," concluded in 2004, allowed the requirement to be much more finely calibrated to the risks of the different loans and investments. Banks operating under Basel II, which included banks in Europe and U.S. investment banks, found many creative ways to have very high leverage and to evade the requirements by shifting risks to others or hiding them behind flawed risk models or misleading credit ratings.[54]

When the financial crisis began in 2007, the equity of some of the major financial institutions worldwide was 2 or 3 percent of their total assets. The fact that these margins of safety were so thin played a major role in the crisis.[55] For example, without help from the Singapore Sovereign Wealth Fund and from the Swiss government, the Swiss bank UBS would have become insolvent, destroyed by losses from mortgage-backed securities and related derivatives that had been treated as riskless.[56]

In the aftermath of the crisis, regulators set out to strengthen capital regulation. Although the resulting accord, "Basel III," eliminates some abuses, it fails to address the basic problem that banks can easily game the regulation. Banks' equity can still be as low as 3 percent of their total assets. It is not clear that anything would have been substantially different in the 2007–2009 crisis had Basel III already been in place.

The weakness of Basel III was the result of an intense lobbying campaign mounted by bankers against any major change in regulation. This campaign has continued since. By now even the full implementation of Basel III is in doubt.[57]

Nonsense in the Debate

According to bankers, higher equity requirements for banks will restrict bank lending and reduce economic growth. They argue that, to have safer banks, we must sacrifice growth. In Chapter 1 we quoted Josef Ackermann, then CEO of Deutsche Bank, claiming that higher equity requirements "would restrict [banks'] ability to provide loans to the rest of the economy," and that "this reduces growth and has negative effects for all."[58] The Institute of International Finance, a key bank lobbying organization, forecast that the planned Basel III reform would substantially raise interest rates on bank loans in the United States and Europe and lower real growth rates for a number of years.[59] Other bankers and their lobbying organizations echo the same warnings that higher capital requirements would "greatly diminish growth."[60]

These claims and many others made in the debate about capital regulation are invalid—as insubstantial as the emperor's new clothes in Andersen's tale. As discussed in Chapter 1, capital requirements do not prevent banks from lending. Claims suggesting that they do are nonsensical and fallacious— articles of the bankers' new clothes. In later chapters we show that higher capital requirements do not impose meaningful costs on society. If bankers see them as expensive, the reason is the same as that given by the dye producer, who objects to a prohibition on his dumping waste in a river as being expensive because it would cost him $2 million, whereas it would provide a benefit of $20 million for others, for a net benefit of $18 million.

In the debate on bank capital regulation, there are many flawed and muddled arguments. As discussed in Chapter 1, the pervasive confusion of capital with reserves is particularly insidious. Consider the statements "Capital is the stable money banks sit on" and "Think of it as an expanded rainy day fund."[61] These statements would make sense if they referred to banks' cash reserves, but they are false if applied to bank equity. Capital and reserves are on different sides of the banks' balance sheets. Capital requirements refer to the banks' funding, whereas reserve requirements restrict how banks use their funds.

To understand the confusion, consider again the mortgage example from Chapter 2. If Kate makes a $30,000 down payment on her house, she is using this equity, together with the mortgage loan, to pay for the house. That money is not "set aside" like a cash reserve. The value of the equity will fluctuate as the value of the house changes after the loan is put in place, but at all times the equity is invested in the house. The same is true for corporations. The equity of any corporation—think of Apple or Wal-Mart—just like Kate's investment in her house, is not sitting idle. The same is also true with regard to the equity of banks, or what the banks call their capital.[62] If a bank holds cash as a reserve, this is part of the bank's assets. The bank's depositors and other creditors, as well as the bank's shareholders that own its equity, have claims that will be paid out of the bank's assets.

The confusion between equity and reserves is reflected in the language of public debate. In many news reports as well as official writings, banks are said to "hold" or to "set aside" capital as if it were an asset. The word *capital* itself contributes to the confusion because in other contexts it does refer to assets. For example, when economists say that a firm's production is capital intensive, they mean that the firm has lots of machines that help it save on labor. In the world of banking and banking regulation, however, *capital* refers to equity.[63] This equity is held by the investors who fund the bank, its shareholders. To say that the bank "holds capital" is an inappropriate and confusing use of language. The bank is not holding its equity, the part of its balance sheet that represents unborrowed funds; the bank holds loans and other assets *funded* by equity and debt. Similarly, Apple and Wal-Mart are not said to "hold" their equity.

This is not a silly quibble about words. The language confusion creates mental confusion about what capital does and does not do. This confusion helps bankers, because it creates the false impression that capital is costly and that banks should strive to have as little of it as regulators will allow.

For society, there are in fact significant benefits and essentially no cost from much higher equity requirements. By contrast, reserve requirements have costs, and their benefits in reducing the risks in banking are limited. Unless reserve requirements are so high that banks face virtually no risks, they do not actually address the solvency problem that results from banks' using borrowed money to make risky investments.

Making false statements that create confusion between capital and reserves is not the only nonsense in the debate. In 2010, when one of us was involved in writing a report to the German government that advocated capital requirements of at least 10 percent of total assets, an industry association objected, saying that the proposal would reduce business lending by 40 percent.[64] Subsequent discussion showed that they had taken the banks' equity as fixed and concluded that, if capital requirements were to double, lending must be cut in half.

For example, if banks have equity worth €500 billion and this must be 5 percent of their total assets, banks can have assets worth €10 trillion, because they can borrow €9.5 trillion to "leverage" this equity. If the same €500 billion must be 10 percent of the banks' total assets, according to the reasoning of the industry association, banks would be able to have only €5 trillion in assets because they could borrow only €4.5 trillion using this equity, and presumably their lending would be cut in half.

This argument is misleading, though—another article of the bankers' new clothes. As discussed in Chapter 2, banks can grow and invest without borrowing. Banks whose shares are traded on a stock exchange can raise money by issuing additional shares and selling them to investors. If the additional funds are used to make new loans, the higher equity levels will actually allow the banks to lend more rather than less.

Banks that do not have access to a stock exchange can increase their equity by reinvesting their earnings. These banks have at most a problem of transition. After a while, they will have enough equity to support lending at the same levels as before, and they can continue growing by reinvesting their earnings or selling new shares.

When bankers lobby against higher equity requirements, they also claim that such requirements would increase banks' costs and harm the economy. However, as we show in the next three chapters, these claims are also invalid. Some of their arguments are simply wrong, while others fail to address the relevant issues by confusing the costs and benefits of public policies to banks and bankers and the costs and benefits of the policies to society.

Is Equity Expensive?

> The banker sitting next to me was lamenting the profitable lending opportunities being passed up by capital constrained banks, when I broke in to ask: "Then, why don't they raise more capital?" . . . "They can't," he said. "It's too expensive. Their stock is selling for only 50 percent of book value." "Book values have nothing to do with the cost of equity capital," I replied. "That's just the market's way of saying: We gave those guys a dollar and they managed to turn it into 50 cents."
>
> *Merton Miller, 1990 Nobel Laureate*

T HE CONVERSATION REPORTED by Merton Miller and quoted above focuses on a key question for banking regulation.[1] To bankers it seems obvious that equity is expensive.[2] But what does this statement refer to, and what are the costs of having banks fund their assets and investments with more equity? The banker in the conversation is suggesting that because capital regulation forces banks to have some equity funding of loans, and because "equity is expensive," the banks must pass up lending opportunities that would be attractive if they could just fund them with debt. Why should funding with equity be expensive?

The view that it is more expensive to use equity funding than to fund by borrowing is sometimes justified by the observation that for each dollar they invest in a bank's shares, shareholders "require" a higher return than debt holders require. For debt the required return might be 4 percent per year, and for equity it might be 15 percent per year. This is taken by some to mean that it would cost a bank $40 million of interest expenses per year (4 percent of the total amount) to raise $1 billion by issuing debt and $150 million per year (15 percent of the total amount) to raise $1 billion by issuing equity. According to this view, if regulation forces banks to fund their investments with more equity, their costs will increase and they will have to charge their clients more, for example, by charging higher interest on loans.[3]

At first sight the argument may seem convincing, but actually it is quite flawed, yet another article of the bankers' new clothes. If equity were so expensive, why would nonfinancial companies rely so much on it? Why wouldn't they borrow as much as they possibly could? The statement that "the required return on equity is higher than the cost of debt" applies to all corporations, not just to banks, and there is no regulation constraining how most companies fund their investments. Yet there are virtually no corporations that rely so much on borrowing and use so little equity funding as banks. Are nonbanks doing something wrong by not economizing on equity? Is there something special about banks that makes equity expensive for them while for other corporations equity is somehow cheaper?

Take a corporation like Apple, which is funded almost entirely with equity and was worth around $630 billion in the stock market on October 11, 2012. Suppose that Apple issued $10 billion in debt and used the funds to repurchase some of its stock. If equity costs 15 percent per year and debt costs 4 percent, it appears that Apple could save $1.1 billion per year by doing that. There is no regulation that controls how much Apple borrows. So why doesn't this company borrow more?

The claim that "equity is expensive because shareholders require higher returns than debt holders" involves two basic flaws. First, the required rates of return for debt and equity for a particular corporation are not fixed but rather depend on the risk associated with the investments the corporation makes. Second, the costs of debt and the costs of equity cannot properly be considered separately and in isolation, without referring to the *mix* of debt and equity that is used.

Shareholders require higher returns because equity bears more risk than debt. The risk of $100 invested in a firm's stock, however, depends critically on how much borrowing the firm is doing. Our discussion in Chapter 2 implies that if a corporation uses more equity and borrows less, the return on equity will become less risky (per dollar invested) because it will be affected less intensely by the uncertainty associated with the investments. When shareholders bear less risk per dollar invested, the rate of return they require is lower. Therefore, taking the costs of equity as fixed and independent of the mix of equity and debt involves a fundamental fallacy.

The reported conversation between Merton Miller and the banker does not actually mention rates of return. The banker argues that equity is expensive because the banks' value in the stock market is only 50 percent of its book value (the value reported on the banks' balance sheets). Miller's response indicates that he considers the banker's reference to book values quite flawed. Using book values as a guide for making investment decisions is indeed another article of the bankers' new clothes. Book values usually reflect historical valuations that are no longer relevant. Investment decisions must be made in light of current valuations.

The fallacies discussed in this chapter are less obvious than the fallacy of confusing equity with reserves, but they are no less important.

The Costs of Borrowing

For debt, the notion of cost seems straightforward. If a corporation issues a bond with an interest rate of 4 percent per year, each year it will have to pay the bond holders 4 percent of the amount owed, for example, $40 million on a bond issue of $1 billion.

The interest rate on a loan or a bond depends on many factors. For example, a borrower who lives in a remote village with a single bank might have to accept whatever interest rate the bank charges because there are no alternative ways to obtain funds.[4] By contrast, if there are many competing banks, the best rate that the borrower can get will reflect mainly the costs of making this loan.[5] These include not only the costs of assessing the borrower's creditworthiness and monitoring the loan but also the costs to the lender of obtaining the funds or of not using them for alternative investments.

For example, in making a mortgage loan a relevant comparison would be to making a loan to the government. If government bonds pay, say, 3 percent per year, the interest on the mortgage must be high enough that the bank will not prefer to invest the same funds in the government bond instead. Compared to a U.S. government bond, the mortgage is likely to be less safe for the lender.

Lending dollars to the U.S. government is essentially riskless because the U.S. government can always pay such debts. If necessary, the Federal Reserve can print dollars to pay the debt.[6] By contrast, when lending money to a mortgage borrower there is a risk of default and a risk that if the borrower defaults on the loan, the house might be worth a lot less than the debt. In making the loan, the lender must consider how likely it is that the promised amount will not be repaid in full and how much the lender would get in that case. If a substantial decline in the value of the house seems likely, the lender may refuse to make a large loan at all and ask the borrower to put in much more of her own money as down payment. Alternatively, the lender may charge higher interest to reflect the risk of less than full payment.

Interest rates charged on loans reflect the likelihood that the borrower might default and the amount the lender would likely recover in that case. This principle can be seen in the market for the bonds of European countries. As we are writing this text, for example, Spain must pay over 5 percent on a ten-year bond, while Germany borrows at less than 2 percent over this period.[7] It might be tempting for anyone to try to borrow at the German rate and use the money to lend to Spain, benefiting from the "spread" of more than 3 percent. European banks could do something similar with the loans at 1 percent interest that they can obtain from the European Central Bank.[8]

Borrowing at a low rate to invest in something that promises a higher rate of return is called a "carry trade." If there was no risk involved in the investment, borrowing at 2 percent and receiving 5 percent *for sure* would actually be called an "arbitrage opportunity." An arbitrage opportunity is a kind of money machine. Such money machines usually do not exist in competitive markets.[9]

In general, if one can borrow at a particular rate and use the borrowed money to make risky investments, there *must* be a chance that the return on the investment will be less than the borrowing rate, that is, that the borrower will incur losses. Being able to make more money *for sure,* without putting in any equity to absorb potential losses, is typically too good to be true.

In fact, if Spain has to promise more than 5 percent interest on a ten-year loan while Germany can promise less than 2 percent, the reason is that investors believe Spain might not be able to pay its debt as promised. This means that someone borrowing at 2 percent and investing in Spanish bonds promising 5 percent may have to take a loss. For government bonds, this may seem unusual, but in fact investors who had bought Greek government bonds in previous years suffered significant losses when Greece defaulted on some of its debt in March 2012.[10]

Higher interest rates compensate lenders when they face a risk of default in making loans. The amount of the compensation depends on how likely they consider a default and how large a loss they expect in default. For loans to borrowers that might default, interest rates will also include some extra charges because lenders dislike risk. Unless lenders earn a "risk premium," they prefer investing in safe bonds over making risky loans. The idea of a risk premium is that, on average, and also taking account of the possibility of default, the lender must expect to earn more than the 3 percent the government pays on its loans.

There are many different rates for borrowing in the economy. Mortgage rates are usually lower than rates charged on business or consumer loans, in part because a house serves as collateral that the lender can possess if the loan is not paid. Interest rates on business loans are usually lower than those on consumer or credit card debt. Interest rates charged on credit card debt are particularly high because people who delay payment and use this debt most are those who are short of cash and have a relatively high likelihood of default.[11]

The same considerations apply when corporations borrow. The lenders may be different, but their concerns are similar, namely, whether they will be paid in full and what will happen if they are not. Whereas an individual would borrow from a bank or a mortgage company to buy a house, a corporation like IBM would typically issue bonds that may be purchased by banks, insurance companies, mutual funds, and private investors.

The principle that the interest rate charged on debt depends on the default risk of the debt applies to all borrowing. If debt is perceived as riskless, the rate charged will not be much higher than the rate for riskless government debt. In making a risky loan, however, investors require that the interest rate be higher. An exception to this principle is made only if the debt is insured by a reliable third party such as the government. Bank depositors whose deposits are insured by the FDIC do not care much whether the bank is safe or risky.

We can already see that something is missing in the argument that "4 percent is less than 15 percent and therefore funding by debt is cheaper than funding by equity." If this argument were correct, any corporation would want to forget about equity altogether and fund itself exclusively with debt. But as a corporation takes on more and more debt, it owes more and more to its creditors. If there is any risk associated with the corporation's investments, the likelihood of default will go up, and therefore the interest on the debt must go up. In other words, as the corporation borrows more, the cost of borrowing will eventually rise above 4 percent.

Back to Kate's mortgage. If Kate borrows $270,000 and her house drops in value below what she owes a year later, she may walk away from the mortgage debt if she has a nonrecourse mortgage that allows it. By contrast, if she borrows only $240,000, she will be less likely to default because her debt is lower. From the lender's perspective, therefore, lending to Kate carries much less risk if she has $60,000 of her own money in the house than if she has only $30,000. The higher equity provides the lender with better protection because debt must be paid first, and with less debt and more equity, the debt is more likely to be paid. As a result, if there is a possibility that the house will go down in value—from $300,000 to $250,000, for example—Kate will face a higher interest rate if her initial equity is $30,000 than if it is $60,000.[12]

For corporations, too, the risk of default depends on the mix of debt and equity used for funding, and this affects the cost of borrowing. Quite generally, if a borrower is more highly indebted, there is a greater likelihood of default and typically more will be lost when default occurs. For both of these reasons, a higher interest rate is charged when more is borrowed.

The Cost of Equity

The shareholders of a corporation are like the owners of a business. If the corporation earns a profit, the profit belongs to the corporation and its shareholders. Profits can be paid out as dividends, or the corporation can buy back some of its shares. Another possibility is that the firm will retain the profits and use them for new investments that, it hopes, will provide shareholders with even greater profits in the future. If the corporation's shares are traded on a stock exchange, the shareholders can sell the shares whenever they prefer to invest the money elsewhere—or need the money to take a trip around the world. If the corporation has made profitable new investments, shareholders can create a "homemade dividend" for themselves any time.

When shareholders buy shares of stock, or equity, in a corporation, they are buying the uncertain future dividends they might receive and the ability to sell the shares for a price that will be determined in the market at the time the shares are sold. In this context, what does the "cost" of equity funding refer to? How is the corporation "paying" for equity?

The cost of equity essentially corresponds to the returns that the corporation must provide to shareholders to justify the money it has received from them. Unlike debt holders, the shareholders do not have any contractual commitment from the corporation to pay them. However, they have bought their shares in the expectation of future returns. If these expectations are not met, many shareholders may sell the shares, which may cause the share price to decline. This price decline would likely have negative consequences for the corporation and its management. If managerial compensation is based on the stock price, management might be directly hurt. The board of directors may also be concerned with keeping the value of the shares sufficiently high, which may help the corporation raise more equity funding in the future.[13]

Of course the company's earnings and stock price fluctuate from year to year, and shareholders know this when they buy shares. In some years the corporation flourishes; in others, profits wither away and prospects may be poor. The company may thrive because of a new patent, or it may lose money because sales drop off in a recession.

Although shareholders understand that business might sometimes be poor, they want to have some assurance that better earnings in good times will make up for poor business in bad times; otherwise they will not be willing to pay as much for the shares of the company. The notion of a required return on equity refers to an average or expected return that shareholders would need to anticipate on average in order to be willing to invest in the company's shares at the price that is quoted in the market.[14] Although there is no contractual requirement that the corporation generate a particular return for its shareholders, shareholders will compare the average return that they expect to receive with what they consider an appropriate return given the risks of the investment. If investors expect to receive too low a return, the share price will have to decline.

Required returns on stocks are generally higher than on bonds. The difference compensates investors for accepting the higher risks associated with stock investment. The historical record shows that there is a relation between average returns and risks, so the riskier the investment, the higher the average return. For example, the average return earned on U.S. Treasury bills from 1926 to 2010 was 3.6 percent. The average annual return on a broad portfolio of corporate bonds over the same time period was 6.14 percent. For investment in an index of medium-sized stocks, the average return was a much greater 13.7 percent.[15]

How the Debt-Equity Mix Affects the Required Return on Equity

We are now ready to explain why the statement that equity is expensive because it has a higher required return than debt is false. As just discussed, the cost of borrowing depends on how much debt is taken: the more indebted the borrower, the more likely the risk of default. How does the amount of borrowing affect the cost of equity?

We saw in Chapter 2 that borrowing has a leverage effect that magnifies the risk that the borrower bears on his investment. We consider this effect again, this time by comparing Kate and Paul when both put up $30,000 in equity, but Paul borrows less than Kate. Whereas, Kate borrows $270,000 to buy a $300,000 house; Paul borrows only $120,000 to buy a $150,000 house. Kate has 10 percent equity in her house; Paul has 20 percent. Paul's indebtedness is the same as Kate would have if she had $60,000 invested in the house, a case we discussed in Chapter 2. The difference between Kate and Paul is that they use different amounts of debt to leverage their investment of $30,000 in the equity of their respective houses.

Imagine that both Kate's and Paul's houses increase in value by 5 percent; the value of Kate's house goes up by $15,000, the value of Paul's house by $7,500. This means that Kate will make a 50 percent return on her investment of $30,000, while Paul will make "only" a 25 percent return on his. As discussed in Chapter 2, leverage is wonderful when investments go up in value because it magnifies the gains.

But the downside is magnified as well. Suppose that Kate's and Paul's houses decrease in value by 5 percent. For Kate this will mean a loss of $15,000, or 50 percent of her $30,000 investment. For Paul the loss of $7,500 will not be as painful, because it will amount to only 25 percent of his initial investment. A 12 percent decline in housing prices would wipe Kate out and leave her underwater, but Paul would still have equity in his house.

Leverage works the same way for shareholders of corporations, including banks and their shareholders. The more the equity is leveraged through borrowing, the more shareholders can profit from windfall gains on the firm's investments and the more vulnerable they will be to losses on these investments.

For a concrete example that involves a bank and its shareholders, consider the payment of $8.5 billion in settlement of litigation related to mortgage derivatives that Bank of America announced on June 29, 2011.[16] As long as the bank continues to pay its debt, the shareholders will be the sole bearers of this loss.

When Bank of America announced the $8.5 billion settlement, the total value of its equity in the stock market was approximately $110 billion. This means that the $8.5 billion that Bank of America had to pay represented about 7.5 percent of the market value of its equity at the time. If a shareholder had $100,000 invested in Bank of America at that time, the part of the loss that was borne by his shares was approximately $7,500.

What if, instead of having $110 billion in equity, Bank of America had had only half that amount, $55 billion? In that case the $8.5 billion loss would have been spread over half as much equity, amounting to 15 percent rather than 7.5 percent of the total equity. A shareholder who had invested $100,000 in the stock would have lost $15,000, not $7,500. Just as in the example of the mortgage, the leverage of the corporation magnifies losses as well as gains to shareholders.

We can now see the fundamental flaw in the simple math that takes the required return on equity (ROE) as fixed at some rate, such as 15 percent, regardless of the firm's leverage. When there is more debt in the funding mix and therefore more leverage, the risk to shareholders per dollar invested is greater. Because they bear more risk, they require higher returns as compensation. In other words, the required ROE will be lower when there is more equity and less debt in the mix and, conversely, higher if the funding involves less equity and more debt.

In assessing how changes in the funding mix affect the overall, or total, costs of a corporation for funding its investments, one must take into account the fact that the required ROE, as well as the interest rate on all forms of risky debt, depend on the entire funding mix. As leverage is reduced and there is more equity, the "expensive" equity becomes cheaper, just as more of it is being used. What is the overall effect on funding costs? If we compare two corporations that have the same assets, but one has 50 percent debt and 50 percent equity while the other has 30 percent debt and 70 percent equity in their funding mix, which of them has higher funding costs?[17]

For a long time, the answer to this question was not well understood. A key insight came in 1958, when Franco Modigliani and Merton Miller argued that a change in the funding mix—one that affects *only* the division of risks among those who do the funding but does not otherwise affect the total returns from the investment that must be shared among those who provide the funding—cannot have any effect on funding costs.[18]

The idea is simple. If the investments of the corporation are fixed and the returns from investments are used to pay all the investors who fund the corporation, a basic conservation principle is at work. If there is any risk involved in the investments, *someone* must bear this risk. For example, the $8.5 billion in legal damages that Bank of America had to pay had to be borne by *someone*. In a manner similar to that seen in the physical principle that energy is conserved in a closed system, as long as the risks of the investments are collectively borne by the investors who provide the funding, changing how the risks are divided among them will not by itself change the overall funding costs.

Think about the total returns of the corporation as a pie and the funding mix as a way of cutting the pie into different pieces. Baseball legend Yogi Berra is said to have once asked a waiter to cut his pizza into four slices, saying, "I am not hungry enough for eight today."[19] This is funny because we know that changing the way in which a pizza is cut does not affect its food content. Similarly, the way in which the funding mix divides the risks and returns among debt and equity investors does not by itself affect the value of the firm or its funding costs.

The food content of the pizza would have changed if somehow the way the pie was cut affected its content. If, for example, some of the pizza stuck to the knife and was lost every time the pie was cut, an eight-slice pie might in fact have had less food content than a four-slice pie. (If instead the knife had had a special device for adding cheese in the process of cutting, the pie would have had more substance when it was cut into eight pieces, so Yogi Berra would indeed have needed to be hungrier to eat an eight-slice pie than to eat a four-slice pie.)

Similarly, if the mix of debt and equity funding affects the value and the funding costs of a corporation, the reasons must be related to how the size of the total "pie" available to investors is affected rather than to how the pie is divided among them. In this case, any impact on overall funding costs that the mix of debt and equity has is not due to the fact that a particular security that the corporation issues to investors in exchange for funds is riskier relative to other securities. Rather it is due to the fact that using a different mix might affect such things as the amount of taxes the corporation pays, the subsidies it receives, or the investment decisions it makes.

The Big Question: Are Banks Special?

Bankers and many banking experts often claim that banks are different from other corporations, and therefore the insights discussed earlier about how the costs of funding depend on the mix of debt and equity are irrelevant for banks. The persistent refrain is that M&M (as the result of Modigliani and Miller is often referred to) does not apply to banks. Is this true?

The question "Does M&M apply to banks?" was posed by Merton Miller in the title of the article from which the epigraph to this chapter is taken. In that article he gave the succinct answer "Yes and no," the same answer that anyone would give when asked about the applicability of M&M to *any* industry. "Yes" because the basic considerations underlying the result apply in banking as well as in any other industry; "no" because the underlying assumption, that there are no frictions in the system, is not satisfied in reality, in banking or in other industries. The critical question is not whether there are deviations but whether and how the deviations might be relevant for the individual company and for policy considerations.[20]

In Chapter 4 we saw that some of the main functions of banks are tied to their borrowing. For example, deposits, which are the basis for the payments system, are debts to the bank whereby the bank effectively borrows from depositors. Because banks provide many services and conveniences in exchange for deposits, the interest rates banks pay on deposits are typically very low. But paying low rates to depositors does not necessarily make deposits cheap for the bank. Banks have to incur expenses in providing ATMs and payment services (though of course they may charge fees for some services). If deposits are insured with the FDIC, the bank must also pay an insurance fee, so how cheap or expensive it is for the bank to use deposits for funding also depends on the insurance fee. For all these reasons, bank funding by deposits is different from other types of funding that banks use and the logic of M&M does not apply to changes in deposit funding.[21]

However, banks typically have a lot of debt other than deposits. Some actually borrow much more in the form of non-deposit debt than through deposits. For these other forms of debt and for equity that is traded in stock markets, the relation of funding costs to the funding mix is determined by the same logic that we previously discussed and by the same logic that applies to the funding of all corporations. Those holding uninsured debt issued by a bank assess the risk that they might not be paid and set the terms of the debt accordingly. If there is a risk of default, they charge higher rates or require the bank to give them collateral that they will own if the bank fails to pay them back. The principles of what determines the cost of different funding mixes are the same for banks as for nonbanks, particularly when the bank must choose between adding equity and adding non-deposit debt to the mix.

In the case of equity, in particular, the investors who invest in bank stocks and become shareholders of the bank think about the risk of their investment in bank stocks in the same way they think of the risk of any other stocks or investments they might make. Bank equity investors are often the very same investors as those that invest in other stocks. They are mutual funds investing on behalf of individuals in broad diversified portfolios, or they are other investors that think of the risks and returns of all the various investments they can make. Many of us have some bank stocks as part of our pension fund investments.

The notion that the required ROE is fixed and independent of the funding mix is as fallacious for banks as it is for nonfinancial corporations. It is an article of the bankers' new clothes that must be seen as the fiction that it is.[22] There is in fact substantial empirical evidence that the average returns on the shares of banks that rely on more borrowing are higher than the average returns on shares of banks that rely on less borrowing and have more equity.[23]

The debt-equity mix that corporations use does have an impact on their overall funding costs. For example, if more debt is used relative to equity, any corporation may be able to pay less in taxes to the government, which allows investors to share more returns in total than they would have shared if their corporation had not borrowed at all. The tax saving may give borrowing an advantage for corporations relative to funding their investments with equity.

For banks, there are also other considerations that make funding matter. But these considerations are not related to the fact that equity is riskier and thus has a higher required return than debt. For banks, the assumption that the risk of an investment is borne by the investors who provide funding for the corporations does not hold.

For example, some of the downside risk of the investment is borne by the FDIC, which provides deposit insurance. If the bank loses so much that it does not have enough assets to pay its depositors, the FDIC will pay what the banks' assets do not cover. In the recent crisis, the government offered guarantees for many nondeposit bank debts. This can make borrowing cheaper and more attractive for banks, but such cost savings are paid for by others and therefore should not affect policy.

The Irrelevance of Book Values

In the conversation reported by Merton Miller, the banker who claims that equity is expensive refers to the difference between the book value and the market value of equity, not to the required returns for different mixes of debt and equity funding. Our discussion so far has not considered his objection. We have hardly referred to the share price at all. Where does the price come in?

Our discussion has focused on how the required ROE depends on the risk of the stock. The return that shareholders "require" matters because, as we discussed, if shareholders expect a lower return, they will reduce their demand for the stock, which will force the stock price to decline. The stock price must be low enough so that, with their expectations of the average return, shareholders will be willing to hold the stock.

The banker in the conversation complains that banks' stock prices are only 50 percent of their book values. In his view, it seems, issuing shares is "expensive" because the shares will have to sell for 50 percent of their value as reported on the banks' balance sheets. Bankers do not want to fund new loans by issuing new shares under these conditions, says the banker; they would, however, be happy to fund them by borrowing more.

Miller's answer is very clear: book values, whether they are smaller or larger than market values, have nothing to do with the cost of equity. Or, as we would say, the banker's claim is an article of the bankers' new clothes. Making lending decisions according to whether the market price of a bank's shares is lower or higher than the value of the stock in the bank's books is bad business strategy.[24]

We noted in Chapter 6 that, as of December 30, 2011, JPMorgan Chase reported that the book value of its equity was equal to $184 billion. This translates to a per-share book value of $48.55, significantly higher than the $33.25 at which the bank's shares were selling in the stock market at the same time. For weaker banks, the situation resembled the banker's statement that "their stock is selling for only 50 percent of book value."

If the book value of $48.55 per share for JPMorgan Chase was the right value for a share of JPMorgan, issuing a new share at anywhere near the stock price at the time, $33.25, might seem to be a bad deal for the bank. However, was the stock really worth $48.55 per share? As we discussed, the market price of a share reflects shareholders' assessments of the future returns that the shares will bring, which depend on the returns that the bank will earn from its assets, the interest the bank has to pay on its debt, and the bank's decisions whether to make dividend payments or to reinvest these returns. If JPMorgan Chase shareholders believed that the bank's prospects warranted a price of $33.25 per share, perhaps that was the right value after all.

If a bank has made many loans that are "nonperforming" and seem unlikely to be paid in full but are not recognized as problematic and are instead reported at historical values, the book value of the stock may be too optimistic as an estimate of what the stock is worth. If the bank were to acknowledge the problems, it would take a loss and assign a lower value to these loans. As we saw in Chapter 2, such a loss would directly reduce the value of the bank's equity on its balance sheet. The book value per share would then also be lower.

Quite often, the market value of a bank's stock is lower than the book value because bank managers are reluctant to acknowledge losses. This may be due to wishful thinking, with the managers hoping that the borrowers' problems will not be so serious after all. Or managers may want to delay disclosing losses so they can first reap a bonus for the current year's reported profits. Higher balance sheet valuations also help satisfy capital requirements. Bankers have clear incentives to delay recognizing losses if they can do so, and the accounting rules are sufficiently flexible to leave much room for such delays.

The bankers' refusal to admit and recognize losses, however, does not make the losses disappear.[25] If a bank forgoes profitable opportunities just because it lost on its previous investments and is unwilling to be upfront about the losses, it may well be harming its shareholders. If the losses are in fact real, issuing new shares at the price that is paid in the market seems "expensive" to the banker who must acknowledge that he has managed to turn a dollar into fifty cents but not to the shareholders who will have to bear the losses anyway. The shareholders truly lose if the banker's fear of losing face by making that acknowledgement makes him forego some profitable opportunities.[26]

When bankers make investment and funding decisions and when they lobby against higher capital requirements, on whose behalf are they acting? Not surprisingly, as we discuss in the next chapter, first and foremost bankers act on their own behalf.

EIGHT

Paid to Gamble

It is difficult to get a man to understand something, when his salary depends upon his not understanding it!

Upton Sinclair, I, Candidate for Governor: And How I Got Licked *(1935)*

WHEN ARGUING AGAINST higher capital requirements, bankers and others routinely claim that having more capital would "lower returns on equity" (ROE).[1] These lower returns, they claim, would harm their shareholders and could "make investment into the banking sector unattractive relative to other business sectors."[2]

Arguments against higher capital requirements that are based on such reasoning are fundamentally flawed. Such arguments ignore the basic connection between borrowing and risk, discussed in Chapter 2, and the basic connection between risk and required returns, discussed in Chapter 7. The arguments also say little to the policy issue because they neglect the need to protect the economy from the risks implied by banks' being funded with very little equity.

The focus on ROE is deeply imbedded in the culture of banking. For example, a leading textbook, written by a prominent academic and former central banker, states that bank capital "has both benefits and costs. Bank capital is costly because, the higher it is, the lower will be the return on equity for a given return on assets."[3]

As a general statement about *actual* ROE, this is simply false: more equity does *not* always cause ROE to be lower. In Chapter 2 we saw that borrowing magnifies risk on the downside as well as the upside. Therefore, if a bank's assets decline in value, its ROE will actually turn out to be higher, less negative, if there is more equity.

It is true that the *average* ROE may decline if the bank uses more equity. However, as we saw in Chapter 7, when more equity funding is used, the *required* ROE is lower because shareholders bear less risk for each dollar invested. Therefore, shareholders need not be harmed when more equity is used. The lower average return may compensate them sufficiently for the risk they are exposed to. In this case, the textbook's assertion that increasing bank capital is harmful to shareholders is also false.

ROE by itself is a flawed measure of performance. *Actual* ROE reflects economic developments such as the level of housing prices, as well as luck— for instance, how speculative trading in derivatives turned out. The *average* ROE may be high because a bank is taking inordinate risks, which can be rewarded with higher average returns in financial markets. Just taking risks by itself, however, does not help shareholders, because there are many ways for shareholders to take risks on their own and receive appropriate returns other than investing in banks.

Investors care whether the average return they receive on any of the assets they hold is appropriate *relative to the risk they bear.* As discussed in the last chapter, average returns on safe investments are lower than average returns on risky investments. Investors agree to buy safe assets such as bonds even though, on average, they receive lower returns. And the risk associated with any investment depends critically on whether and how much the investment is leveraged through borrowing.

Why are bankers so focused on ROE? The quote from Sinclair in the chapter epigraph provides an important clue. Bankers may target high ROE because it is treated as a performance measure that affects their compensation. If compensation depends on ROE, bankers have direct incentives to take risks. Bank managers also have incentives to increase bank borrowing in order to increase the average ROE as well as the bank's risk.

As long as the gambles are successful, shareholders gain on the upside. Losses, however, also harm creditors and taxpayers. Nevertheless, even shareholders can be harmed if managers go after high ROE with insufficient concern for risk.[4] If bank managers find ways to hide risks for a while, investors and regulators may not even be aware of them. By the time the risks materialize, the managers may have already reaped the bonuses for today's profit.

Governance problems related to risk controls in banks are particularly challenging, because risks are difficult to judge and can be easy to hide. Risk management and risk controls do not seem to be high priorities for banks. The incentives of top managers may be distorted as well, or they might be unable to control those they manage. Even boards may have distorted incentives and have trouble controlling the overall risks taken by the banks.

On the Downside, ROE Is Higher with More Equity

To understand the mechanics of ROE, consider again the mortgage example of Chapter 2, in which Kate buys a $300,000 house with either a $270,000 mortgage or a $240,000 mortgage. We saw in Chapter 2 that if Kate borrows less, the impact of any subsequent change in the value of the house on her equity position will be less pronounced.

In Chapter 2 we simplified the discussion by ignoring the interest payments Kate makes during the year, as well as the rent she saves by living in her own house. This allowed us to see most easily how borrowing creates leverage and magnifies risk.

The same effect can be seen when the interest is taken into account, as is appropriate in comparing different rates of return.[5] Table 8.1 presents the same calculations as Table 2.1 under the alternative assumption that Kate pays 4 percent interest on her mortgage. Simplifying again to make the discussion easier, we assume that all the interest will be paid at the end of the year when she sells the house and settles the mortgage. (We also neglect Kate's savings on rent, which does not affect our conclusions.)

If Kate borrows $270,000, the 4 percent in interest payment amounts to $10,800 and she owes $280,800 on her mortgage at the end of the year. If she borrows $240,000 at 4 percent, her interest cost is $9,600 and she owes $249,600.[6]

Kate's ROE is calculated as what she makes per dollar of her initial investment. For example, if she invested $30,000 and the house sells for $345,000 (as in the top panel), she ends up with $64,200 after paying the mortgage, which represents a return of $34,200 on her investment of $30,000, or 114 percent.

As the table shows, whether Kate's actual ROE is higher or lower with more borrowing depends on whether the house increases in value by more or less

TABLE 8.1   Borrowing at 4 Percent to Buy a $300,000 House in Two Down
Payment Scenarios (assuming a nonrecourse clause)

Borrowing with a $30,000 down payment (initial equity)				
Year-end house price (dollars)	Percent change in house price	Mortgage debt (dollars)	Final equity (dollars)	Return on equity (percent)
345,000	15	280,800	64,200	114
315,000	5	280,800	34,200	14
300,000	0	280,800	19,200	−36
285,000	−5	280,800	4,200	−86
255,000	−15	280,800	0	−100

Borrowing with a $60,000 down payment (initial equity)				
Year-end house price (dollars)	Percent change in house price	Mortgage debt (dollars)	Final equity (dollars)	Return on equity (percent)
345,000	15	249,600	95,400	59
315,000	5	249,600	65,400	9
300,000	0	249,600	50,400	−16
285,000	−5	249,600	35,400	−41
255,000	−15	249,600	5,400	−91

than the interest she must pay, or 4 percent.[7] If the house increases in value by more than 4 percent, such as by 5 percent or 15 percent, Kate's ROE is higher if she borrows more (as in the top panel) than if she borrows less and has more equity (as in the bottom panel). Leverage magnifies her high returns in these good scenarios, and the more leverage, the greater the magnification.

If the house increases in value by less than 4 percent, however, Kate's ROE will be higher if she borrows less and has more equity. In particular, if the value of the house stays the same or even goes down, as in three cases shown in the table, Kate's ROE will be negative and her loss will be greater if she borrows more (as in the top panel) than if she borrows less and has more equity (as in the bottom panel). Her ROE will therefore be greater (less negative) with less borrowing in these bad scenarios. Leverage magnifies her losses and lowers her already negative ROE even further.

The same considerations apply when corporations borrow. When a corporation uses more equity, its actual ROE will be lower only in scenarios in which the assets earn more than the interest rate on the debt. Otherwise, the actual ROE will be higher when more equity is used. The statement that ROE always declines with more equity is therefore false, an article of the bankers' new clothes.

Can the unpleasant possibility that assets earn a lower return than the borrowing rate be neglected? An optimistic banker might think so; in many scenarios the spread between the rate of return earned on assets and the rate paid to borrow is seen as positive, and large returns can be earned without ever worrying about possible losses. If losses were impossible, there would be no need for any equity to absorb losses.

Being able to use borrowed money to invest in assets that always pay more than the costs of borrowing is too good to be true, at least for ordinary people and nonfinancial businesses and corporations. If normal borrowers invest borrowed funds in risky assets whose value is uncertain when the investment is made, there must be *some* likelihood that the return on the assets will turn out to be below the borrowing rate. If the assets always return more than the borrowing rate, the borrower cannot ever lose. He will therefore have the proverbial money machine, allowing him to make money for sure without risking any money of his own.[8]

It may seem that banks are not normal borrowers and sometimes have access to such a money machine. For example, for the few years since the financial crisis, U.S. banks have been able to borrow at close to zero interest from the Federal Reserve. If banks can borrow at such a rate for ten years and invest the money in U.S. government bonds that are perfectly safe and pay 2 percent interest for ten years, they can be said to have a money machine.[9]

However, there is a snag even here: if the low interest is available just for a short-term loan and not for a ten-year loan, banks face the risk that at some point during the ten years their borrowing cost might go up, perhaps even higher than the 2 percent they are making on the ten-year bonds they hold, at which point the banks will lose money on their investment.[10] Thus, even banks cannot ignore the risk that the rate of return on their assets may actually be lower than the interest rate at which they can borrow.

The More Equity, the Lower the Required ROE

On average, of course, banks hope to—and usually do—earn returns that are well in excess of their borrowing rates. In such a case, a change in a bank's funding mix so as to have more equity and less debt will lower the average ROE of the bank.[11]

However, a decline in average ROE does *not* mean that shareholders would be harmed. Whereas shareholders receive, on average, less compensation for bearing risk, they also bear less risk. As discussed in Chapter 7, the risk per dollar invested in a bank's equity is lower if there is more equity. Therefore, the *required ROE*, which we introduced in Chapter 7 as a benchmark return that shareholders expect to receive on average, is also lower when banks have more equity. If the decrease in average ROE and the decrease in required ROE are the same, the compensation shareholders receive is still sufficient for the risk they bear. Shareholders are harmed only if the average ROE actually decreases by more than the required ROE.

Target ROE and Shareholder Value

Bankers often set high figures for target ROE that they promise their shareholders they will try to achieve. They also tell politicians, regulators, and the public that shareholders "require" them to strive to hit these targets. In the years before the financial crisis, Josef Ackermann, the CEO of Deutsche Bank from 2002 to 2012, repeatedly announced that an ROE of 25 percent before taxes was the benchmark for a competent investment bank and that Deutsche Bank was aiming to meet this benchmark, at least on average, over a number of years.[12] On a more modest scale, Bob Diamond, CEO of Barclays from 1996 to 2012, announced in April 2011 that he was targeting a 13 percent ROE by 2013.[13]

These statements presume that ROE is a meaningful measure of performance and that it makes sense to set benchmarks and targets for ROE. However, if no account is taken of how much debt has been taken to create leverage and, more generally, of the risk of the equity per dollar invested, ROE is not a meaningful measure of performance, nor does it measure shareholder value. If no account is taken of the market environment, such as market rates of interest, comparison of ROE with a given benchmark is also not meaningful. Implying otherwise is another article of the bankers' new clothes.

Mr. Ackermann's 25 percent would have meant something different at a time when the interest rate on long-term bonds was 6 percent than it does at a time when this interest rate is at 2 or 3 percent. Similarly, the compensation that investors require to be willing to take on risks can change over time, and this will affect the required ROE for all corporations.

As discussed earlier, if a corporation uses more equity to fund its investments or if its assets are less risky, the risk per dollar invested in the equity will be lower, which means that the required ROE will be lower. Shareholders who find the average ROE too low for their taste and would like to dramatically increase the average return on their investments can do so on their own—for example, by borrowing to create leverage. When banks do the borrowing instead of their individual shareholders, they add risk to the financial system and may harm the economy.

Shareholders might actually be harmed by actions that managers take to try to achieve a target ROE. Managers have many ways to take risks with investors' money, for example, by trading in derivatives markets. This can expose shareholders to risks that they might prefer not to take and for which they may not be sufficiently compensated. Moreover, because derivatives trade over the counter and not on organized exchanges with fully transparent transactions and prices, shareholders might not even be aware of the risks that are taken.[14]

The target of 25 percent that Mr. Ackermann had set for Deutsche Bank was much higher than the average actual ROEs that the bank achieved during his tenure. The average of Deutsche Bank's pretax ROEs from 2003 to 2012 was just 11.7 percent. The ROE was above 20 percent in just three years, 2005–2007, when the bank was earning large profits from producing and selling mortgage-related securities. In all other years since 2003, Deutsche Bank's ROE has been below 16 percent; in 2008, the worst year of the crisis, it actually was negative 16.5 percent; in that year, the bank suffered a large loss.[15]

When a bank sets a target that is so much out of line with experience, it cannot reach that target merely by becoming better at what the bank has done before.[16] Reaching the target may be possible only if the bank takes additional large risks.

On the face of it, the target ROE of 13 percent that Mr. Diamond set for Barclays in April 2011 may seem more realistic. However, even this target seems daunting when market interest rates are low and banks are facing many challenges.[17]

In announcing his ROE target of 13 percent, Mr. Diamond said that the bank was ready to increase its "risk appetite" in order to achieve the target. He did not discuss whether the increase in returns that he would achieve by taking the additional risks would be sufficient to compensate his shareholders for the added risks they would have to bear.

If bankers such as Barclays' Bob Diamond or his successors are able to find investments with sufficiently better return prospects to compensate them for their risk, shareholders will want them to take advantage of the opportunities anyway, regardless of what target they have for ROE. If the return prospects are not good enough to compensate for the higher risks, the shareholders will be harmed if the bank tries to reach the ROE target by just increasing its risk appetite.

In other words, if the risky investments a bank like Barclays plans to make because of the bank's increased risk appetite are already available, why hasn't the bank made them already to benefit its shareholders? Why does a bank need to increase its risk appetite to make good investments? Conversely, if the bank takes risks just to achieve a target ROE, how is it creating value for its shareholders? Investors who are keen to take more risks can find plenty of opportunities on their own to make risky investments and raise their average returns in the financial markets. Like any company in the economy, a bank should do something for its shareholders that shareholders cannot do by themselves without allowing bankers to invest on their behalf.[18]

Performance Pay

The focus on ROE may actually have more to do with the way bankers are paid than with the wishes of shareholders. Bankers in positions of responsibility are paid on the basis of the profits their banks make. Through stock-related compensation, they are also given incentives to care about how the stock price develops. The idea is that high earnings reflect good management performance, and a high stock price reflects a good assessment of this performance by investors.

However, the profits a bank makes depend on the extent of its borrowing and the risk it takes as well as on the performance of its management.[19] High profits can also be achieved if the bank's managers invest in a weekend of gambling in Las Vegas and they happen to be lucky and come back with a large gain. Such a lucky outcome is of course quite unlikely, but if compensation is arranged so that the banker gets to keep 5 percent of profits and faces no penalty for losing, he may still find gambling in Las Vegas an attractive option. The downside risk is borne by others.

In reality, of course, bankers do not gamble in Las Vegas (although Deutsche Bank has recently invested $5 billion in the Cosmopolitan casino there[20]). Gambling in derivatives may have more favorable odds than gambling in casinos. The principle, however, is the same: if compensation allows bankers to benefit from large gains while not suffering much from losses, taking risks may be attractive.

When risks are taken, shareholders may benefit or lose depending on whether their share on the upside provides enough compensation for the downside risk that they have to bear. If the performance pay of bank managers and traders is sufficiently geared toward gains and less toward losses, their incentives to take risks may be such that shareholders will dislike their gambles if they know about them.[21] In addition, of course, downside risks that cause distress or default harm creditors and possibly taxpayers.

Risks to taxpayers are particularly large if bank managers of different banks follow similar strategies, so that many banks may experience losses at the same time.[22] Such herding behavior can be attractive because it provides a way to deflect blame when things go wrong. Excuses like "We all made this mistake" or "We cannot be immune to a crisis of the overall system" are meant to reduce personal responsibility. Herding can also be made attractive by the prospect that when many banks experience losses, the government might feel compelled to provide support.

The large ROEs that banks achieved before the financial crisis provided the basis for large bonuses and high compensation levels for bankers even as banks took on significant risk and increased their reliance on borrowing. When banks suffered large losses during the crisis and since, however, bankers' compensation did not decrease proportionally to reflect the decline in ROEs.[23]

Showing Profits, Hiding Risks

So far our discussion has focused on returns over one specific period, such as a year. In reality, however, investments affect risks and returns over longer periods. After a year, it is often not yet clear what returns an investment will provide. Yet compensation is determined annually on the basis of the bankers' performance over the past year. For CEOs, banks' earnings and ROE over the past year provide the basis for determining an important part of the compensation. For bank employees, such as traders or salespeople, the contribution they made to earnings typically provides the basis for their bonuses.[24]

To determine earnings over a particular period, some values must be assigned to the investments that were made over the period. These value assignments are often coarse or even speculative. For investments that can be traded in organized markets, such as stock exchanges, one can rely on market prices. For investments for which such markets do not exist, values are given on the basis of accounting conventions or mathematical models that assign so-called fair value to trading positions.

In the latter situation, bankers at all levels have strong incentives to follow strategies that will show high profits upfront although the risks may not appear until later. Profits are front-loaded to boost short-term performance, whereas risks and losses that may appear later are not properly taken into account. One method for doing this might be to hide risks in subsidiaries or other entities off the balance sheet using methods similar to those used by Enron before it went into bankruptcy.[25]

Sometimes such an extra effort to hide risks is not even needed. Investors may believe, for example, that securities stamped totally safe and given AAA ratings by credit rating agencies carry essentially no risk. The notion that risk must be the reason that the interest on a AAA-rated security is slightly higher than the interest on U.S. Treasury securities is ignored.

In the years before the recent crisis, bankers used large amounts of borrowed money to buy such securities. Because the returns on these securities were slightly higher than the costs of funding, the banks' books showed large profits. The return differentials were small, but, with tens of billions of dollars invested, even an extra return of 0.1 percent provided a nice profit—and a nice bonus to the investment bankers involved. The risk of the mortgages underlying the securities was not taken into account.[26]

When many of the securities were discovered to be toxic in 2007, traders, investment bankers, and top executives had already cashed in their earlier bonuses. The losses were left to the banks' shareholders and creditors—and to taxpayers. If managers themselves still held shares, they participated in these losses, but, given the large amounts of compensation they had previously received, they still came out with huge gains.[27]

Risk Control and the Bonus-and-ROE Culture

The problem of risk control goes beyond the individual traders and can concern entire affiliates or divisions of a bank. Swiss Bank UBS's "Report to UBS Shareholders on Write Downs" (2008) explains in great detail how the bank's subsidiary, UBS Investment Bank, had taken huge risks in securitizing and selling, or even holding, mortgage-related securities.[28] The report also explains that UBS senior management had never received a full account of the business model UBS Investment Bank was pursuing or a comprehensive systematic analysis of the risks involved. Until June 2007, UBS Investment Bank could obtain additional funding from the parent bank at an interest rate that did not properly reflect the risks.

From reading this report, one gets the impression that UBS Investment Bank went out of its way to make sure that UBS senior management would not look too closely at what the investment bank was actually doing. However, one also gets the impression that UBS senior management did not make a very serious effort to find out—until it was too late. Similar observations were made in the case of Enron prior to its bankruptcy and in other accounts of the decade before the recent financial crisis. Taking risks and cutting corners may be tolerated as long as a unit generates profits. This is a general problem of focusing on short-term corporate profits as a measure of successful management.[29]

The ROE culture extends beyond the individual bank. Analysts and journalists commenting on the quarterly or annual reports of a bank will usually highlight the bank's earnings and mention the bank's ROE but say little about risks. Risks are difficult to observe, measure, and communicate in an accessible way. By contrast, earnings and ROE figures provide precise numbers to discuss, and they can be compared with numbers from other years or other banks.

The UBS report also suggests that competitive pressures push banks to engage in the same activities as others, and to take some of the same risks, in order to "keep up with the Goldmans."[30] Citigroup CEO Chuck Prince put it this way in July 2007: "As long as the music is playing, you've got to get up and dance."[31] Outside assessments based on comparisons of earnings and ROE targets contributed to these pressures.

What about the banks' boards of directors? The boards typically focus fully on *their banks.* This means that their concern is primarily with shareholders, especially those who have substantial shareholdings in the banks. Like others inside and outside of the banks, boards of directors often focus on short-term profitability and return measures. Board members may find it difficult to ask whether the past quarter's record earnings might be due to the banks' having taken on a lot of risk and been lucky rather than to the CEOs' being capable. It takes courage to challenge what everyone else regards as a record of success. In addition, board members often lack expertise in banking, and they are likely to be unwilling or unable to challenge reports by management.[32]

Directors and some large shareholders may be conflicted with other shareholders, with creditors, and with the public, particularly when it comes to the safety of the bank. One example concerns payouts such as dividends and share buybacks. As mentioned in Chapters 2 and 3, when cash is paid to shareholders or owners, it is no longer available to pay creditors. This corresponds to the case in Chapter 3 in which Kate takes out a second mortgage and uses the money for consumption. She lowers her equity and raises the likelihood that she may end up underwater. If bank creditors allow these payouts because they are protected by guarantees, the payouts put taxpayers at risk. If bank boards of directors do not concern themselves with the impact of the banks' decisions on creditors, taxpayers, or the economy, they will proceed with such decisions even if they are harmful to others.[33]

In order to address the risks that individuals within the banks take, some banks have recently put in place delays of bonus payments and "clawbacks" that allow the banks to demand that their managers pay back some of their bonuses in case of losses. In practice, however, clawbacks have only rarely been used so far, and it is unlikely that the threat of clawbacks will have a major effect on risk taking unless compensation structures change.[34] Because excessive risk taking can harm the economy, some politicians and regulators have proposed the regulation of compensation in banks.[35]

Even if compensation systems are improved, however, the treatment of short-term profits as a key measure of performance will continue to induce decisionmakers in banks to gamble with investors' money. One reason for this is ambition. For example, in the early 1990s Mathis Cabiallavetta, a member of the executive board of Union Bank of Switzerland, was proud to have a derivatives trader in London earning substantial profits. On the strength of these profits, Mr. Cabiallavetta was promoted to CEO of the bank. Then, in 1997, the profits from derivatives turned into much larger losses and he arranged to have his bank taken over by Swiss Bank Corporation to form the new UBS.[36]

Banks do not seem to put significant resources into risk management. Those involved in managing and controlling risk are not rewarded as highly as those who take risks. Risk managers are often not provided with enough timely information, and they have little authority to interfere.[37] Shareholders seem helpless to promote better risk management, even when they try.[38]

The 2001 bankruptcy of Enron, among the largest and most complex bankruptcies in U.S. history, revealed significant governance problems, as well as problems related to accounting and auditing practices.[39] In response to these problems, the Sarbanes-Oxley Act, passed in 2002, sets new standards for the boards, management, and accountants of public companies in the United States. However, the issues that motivated this legal reform remain problematic. Auditors might be in a position to alert boards and investors to questionable practices and hidden risks, but they might have their own conflicts of interest. As a result, investors and regulators may not receive sufficient information to judge the risks taken by large financial institutions.[40]

Nobody can borrow unless someone agrees to lend to them at acceptable terms. Why can banks, despite being so highly indebted, find willing lenders and continue to borrow at terms that are sufficiently attractive for them? As we will see in the next chapter, guarantees and subsidies play a critical role in answering this question.

NINE

Sweet Subsidies

I don't know how you measure that subsidy. . . . That's why they say it's invaluable.

Mark Zandi, chief economist of Moody's Analytics, part of the credit rating agency Moody's, April 2009

YOGI BERRA'S SUGGESTION that the content of a pizza might depend on how it is cut is absurd. Yet when banks borrow excessively and econo-mize on equity, the total "pie" available to their investors grows.[1] When banks borrow, they benefit from subsidies that they would not enjoy if they relied more on equity. The more banks borrow, the larger are the subsi-dies, as if the pizza chef added more cheese when the pizza was cut into more slices.

The main source of subsidies for banks is the support the government pro-vides to protect banks, their depositors, and sometimes their other creditors and their shareholders. Banks and their creditors benefit from explicit and implicit government guarantees. Depositors are protected by deposit insur-ance, which is guaranteed by the taxpayers. Other creditors, and even the bank's shareholders, benefit if the government provides additional equity to prevent the bank from going bankrupt—for example, in a crisis.

Because depositors and other creditors count on this support, they are willing to lend to banks on more favorable terms than the terms they would require otherwise. In particular, the interest rates banks must pay on their debt are lower than they would have been without government support. This gives banks strong incentives to prefer borrowing over other types of funding they might obtain for their investments. In effect, taxpayers subsidize the use of borrowing by banks. Paradoxically, these subsidies encourage banks to be more fragile. They reinforce the distortions from the bias that heavy borrowers have toward even more borrowing, the effect of debt overhang discussed in Chapter 3.

Excessive borrowing by banks can expose the public to great risks. A bank exposing the public to risks is similar to an oil tanker going close to the coast or a chemical company exposing the environment to the risk that toxic fluids might contaminate the soil and groundwater or an adjacent river.[2] Like oil tankers or chemical companies that take too much risk, banks that are too fragile endanger and potentially harm the public. Cleaning up coastlines and rivers and bailing out banks are all costly to taxpayers. The risks and costs to the public in all these cases are very real. For society, containing the risks of oil tankers, chemical factories, and banks is therefore important, even if there is a cost involved. In the case of banks, in fact, requiring more equity produces large benefits at virtually no cost to society.

Explicit and implicit government guarantees have perverse effects on the extent of borrowing and risk taking of banks. The preferential tax treatment of debt also encourages borrowing. With the additional borrowing, the incentive to take excessive risks, discussed in Chapter 8, becomes stronger.

Government guarantees and subsidies thus reinforce the effects of bankers' compensation and the focus on ROE, as well as the effects of debt overhang, all of which encourage borrowing and risk. The prospect of becoming systemically important or too big to fail provides banks with incentives to grow and become more complex. The implicit guarantees reduce the funding costs of the too-big-to-fail institutions and give these banks an advantage over other banks and over other companies in the economy. If banks respond to these incentives by growing and becoming more complex, this in turn increases the damage to society should these institutions become distressed or insolvent. It is as if the government subsidized ever larger tankers going ever closer to the coast.

Isn't It Wonderful to Have Such an Aunt?

To see how guarantees work, let us again consider the example of Kate who takes out a mortgage to buy a $300,000 house that she sells a year later.[3] In the case discussed in Chapter 8, we assumed that Kate borrows $270,000 at 4 percent interest and puts down $30,000 in down payment or initial equity.

If Kate settles her mortgage and pays all the interest after a year, she owes $280,800, including $10,800 in interest, to settle the mortgage a year later. If Kate has a nonrecourse mortgage, as we have been assuming, she does not pay her debt in full when the house subsequently declines in value to below the amount of the mortgage debt, $280,800.[4] We can assume that the 4 percent interest rate that Kate is charged includes some compensation for the risk to the bank of not being paid in full.

Now let us change the example slightly by assuming that Kate's Aunt Claire offers to guarantee Kate's mortgage. If the house subsequently sells for less than Kate owes on her mortgage, Aunt Claire will make up the difference. The local banker knows that Aunt Claire is wealthy. With the mortgage guaranteed by Aunt Claire, the bank faces virtually no risk and therefore allows Kate to borrow at the riskless interest rate of 3 percent.

In borrowing $270,000 at 3 percent instead of at 4 percent, Kate pays only $8,100 in interest instead of the $10,800 she must pay without the guarantee. She saves 1 percent in interest on the loan of $270,000, which amounts to $2,700 for the year. This leaves Kate with more money after paying the mortgage debt. For example, if the house subsequently increases in value by 5 percent to $315,000, we saw in Chapter 8 that Kate will be left with $34,200, a 14 percent return on her equity investment, if she borrows at 4 percent. If she borrows at 3 percent and owes only $278,100, she will instead have $36,900 left, a 23 percent return on her equity investment, after selling the house for $315,000 and paying her mortgage debt.

The saving of $2,700 in interest will also soften the blow should Kate lose some of her investment, assuming that she is still "above water" and able to pay her mortgage. For example, if the house sells for $300,000, Kate will be left with $19,200 if she borrows at 4 percent, a loss of 36 percent of her investment, but she will have $21,900 if she borrows at 3 percent, losing only 27 percent of her investment. Similarly, she will lose less if the house declines in value by 5 percent to $285,000. In the worst-case scenario, if the house ends up below $278,100 in value, Kate will lose everything whether she borrows at 3 percent or 4 percent; Aunt Claire's guarantee does not benefit Kate in this case.

The situation is summarized in Table 9.1. The top panel reviews the case discussed in Chapter 8, in which Kate pays 4 percent interest, while the bot-

TABLE 9.1   How Kate Benefits from Guarantees When Borrowing

Kate's position with no guarantees (borrowing at 4 percent)

Year-end house price (dollars)	Percent change in house price	Mortgage debt (dollars)	Final equity (dollars)	Return on equity (percent)
345,000	15	280,800	64,200	114
315,000	5	280,800	34,200	14
300,000	0	280,800	19,200	−36
285,000	−5	280,800	4,200	−86
255,000	−15	280,800	0	−100

Kate's position with guarantees (borrowing at 3 percent)

Year-end house price (dollars)	Percent change in house price	Mortgage debt (dollars)	Final equity (dollars)	Return on equity (percent)
345,000	15	278,100	66,900	123
315,000	5	278,100	36,900	23
300,000	0	278,100	21,900	−27
285,000	−5	278,100	6,900	−77
255,000	−15	278,100	0	−100

tom panel shows the case in which Kate borrows at 3 percent with the guarantee from her aunt. Kate benefits from the guarantee even when she is able to pay her debt, and this is reflected in her ROE.

We saw in Chapters 2 and 8 that borrowing magnifies risks for the borrower both on the upside and on the downside. With the guarantee from her aunt, the upside for Kate is even better and the downside is either better or no worse. Kate is obviously quite happy with the guarantee, and the bank is getting paid for sure. Aunt Claire, however, must put up money in the one case in the table in which Kate cannot pay. If the house sells for only $255,000, Aunt Claire will have to add the missing amount of $23,100 so the bank is paid $278,100 in full.

If she can, would Kate like to reduce her down payment and borrow more? Suppose Aunt Claire is in fact willing to guarantee Kate's mortgage even if

Kate borrows $290,000. The bank would allow Kate to take a larger mortgage because it knows that it will get paid in full no matter what happens to the value of the house. The interest rate it would charge Kate would again be 3 percent even for a larger mortgage.

How does the situation in which Kate invests only $10,000 instead of $30,000 in the house compare to that in which she invests $30,000? If Kate borrows $290,000 for a year at 3 percent, her interest payment is $8,700, so she owes $298,700. In this case, Kate will become underwater and will be unable to pay her mortgage debt from selling the house if the house subsequently sells for less than $298,700. For example, if the house sells for $285,000, Kate will default on her mortgage debt if she borrows $290,000. In this scenario, Aunt Claire will have to pay $13,700 to make sure the bank is paid the full $298,700 that is owed. By contrast, if Kate borrows only $270,000 and puts $30,000 in as a down payment, she will absorb the entire loss without needing the guarantees.

Table 9.2 summarizes the positions of both Kate and her aunt if Kate invests $30,000 in equity and borrows $270,000, as shown in the top panel, which is the same as the bottom panel of Table 9.1, and if Kate invests $10,000 and borrows $290,000, both loans at 3 percent interest.

Obviously, if Kate borrows more, Aunt Claire will bear much more of the downside risk. For example, if the house subsequently declines to $255,000 in value, Aunt Claire will have to put in $23,100 if Kate borrows $270,000 and owes $278,100. In the bottom panel of Table 9.2, which represents the situation in which Kate borrows $290,000 and owes $298,700, Claire will have to cover a whopping $43,700 to live by her guarantee. Although Kate will lose all her investment in both cases, the loss will be only $10,000 if she borrows $290,000, whereas it will be $30,000 if she borrows $270,000.

The guarantees are a gift from Aunt Claire to Kate. The more Kate borrows, the larger is the value of the gift. If Kate borrows more, as represented in the bottom panel of Table 9.2, Aunt Claire will sometimes have to pay more than she will if Kate borrows less. (In the cases in which Kate can pay the mortgage by selling the house, her aunt will pay nothing in both cases.)

If Aunt Claire asks Kate to put more of Kate's own money into her down payment, Kate might claim, "Equity is expensive!" Indeed, once she has the

TABLE 9.2   How Guarantees Make Borrowing More Attractive to Kate

$30,000 down payment (initial equity)				
Year-end house price (dollars)	Percent change in house price	Mortgage debt (dollars)	Kate's final equity (dollars)	Aunt Claire's position (dollars)
345,000	15	278,100	66,900	0
315,000	5	278,100	36,900	0
300,000	0	278,100	21,900	0
285,000	−5	278,100	6,900	0
255,000	−15	278,100	0	−23,100

$10,000 down payment (initial equity)				
Year-end house price (dollars)	Percent change in house price	Mortgage debt (dollars)	Kate's final equity (dollars)	Aunt Claire's position (dollars)
345,000	15	298,700	46,300	0
315,000	5	298,700	16,300	0
300,000	0	298,700	1,300	0
285,000	−5	298,700	0	−13,700
255,000	−15	298,700	0	−43,700

guarantees, it will become expensive for Kate to invest more money in the house, because by investing more she puts more of her money at risk of being lost, when instead she can leave more of the downside risk for Aunt Claire, letting her aunt absorb more losses. (We are ignoring, of course, family considerations or hard feelings that might result from Kate's taking advantage of her aunt's generosity.)

Whether Kate actually ends up doing better or worse investing $30,000 in the house depends on what she does with the $20,000 that she does not invest in the house if she puts only $10,000 into the down payment and borrows $290,000. Kate might take an expensive trip with the money, and very much enjoy the experience.[5] If instead she invests the $20,000 elsewhere, the question is whether the alternative investment will end up earning more or less than what Kate can earn by investing the money in the house and saving on interest payments. If Kate can invest the money at 3 percent without risk, she will make the same in those scenarios in which she remains above water, but in the scenarios in which she is underwater and must make use of Aunt Claire's guarantees, she will do better if her money is invested elsewhere, because she will not have to bear the losses. Therefore, Kate wants to put as little equity as possible into the house; without equity in the house, she will enjoy the upside and will lose less on the downside.[6]

In summary, Kate benefits from her aunt's guarantees by being able to pay less on her loan when she borrows. This allows her to save on interest expenses. Kate can increase her gains further by borrowing more and putting less equity into the house. The more Kate borrows, the greater will be the value that Kate will derive from Aunt Claire's gift. Putting her own money into the house seems expensive to Kate because it exposes her to downside risk that she can otherwise leave for Aunt Claire.[7]

Debt guarantees of the type Aunt Claire gives to Kate make borrowing very attractive. The bright side of borrowing—the magnification of the upside—looks even brighter to the borrower, while the dark side, the magnification of losses, affects the person making the guarantees, in Kate's case Aunt Claire. With lower interest on borrowing, it is easier for investments to surpass the low borrowing rate, thereby providing larger magnified returns. The worst of the downside is shared by the guarantor.

Taking this logic a step further, suppose that Aunt Claire agrees to guarantee a mortgage of any size and the bank knows that Aunt Claire is trustworthy and able to pay. Then Kate would actually prefer, and be allowed, to have no equity at all in the house. She would have zero initial equity and borrow the entire $300,000 at 3 percent interest, promising to pay $309,000.[8] If the house ends up increasing enough in value to pay the mortgage, Kate will be able to enjoy the full upside. Otherwise, she will lose nothing.[9]

The scenario in which Kate puts in zero initial equity is wonderful for her. With no investment in the house, she is not at all exposed to the risk that the subsequent value of the house might not be enough to pay the mortgage debt; she can never lose, but she will gain if the house appreciates by more than is needed to pay the mortgage debt. The house will become a kind of money machine for Kate; allowing her to enjoy the full upside while facing no downside. The downside will be fully borne by Aunt Claire.

Banks Have Uncle Sam

The relation between Kate and Aunt Claire in the example is similar to the relation between banks that are too important to fail and taxpayers. Just as Aunt Claire steps in when Kate cannot pay her mortgage debt, governments often support banks when they cannot pay their debts. And banks, like Kate, want to economize on equity and use debt as much as possible. Borrowing is made attractive to them through subsidized guarantees. The banks' creditors are more confident that they will be paid in full than they would have been without the guarantees; because of this, creditors are willing to lend to the banks for lower interest, and creditors care relatively little about the banks' own equity or the risks banks take.

The safety net for banks takes different forms. Some guarantees are given explicitly, and some are implicit, implied by expectations that, in a crunch, the government will most likely step in and help. In the turmoil that occurred after the Lehman Brothers bankruptcy, many of the institutions that received government support had not previously been covered by any explicit guarantees.

Explicit guarantees are limited, and banks must make payments intended to cover their costs, which is similar to paying insurance premiums. For example, in the United States deposit insurance from the FDIC is available for deposits up to $250,000.[10] The FDIC charges banks a deposit insurance premium, and it is supposed to be self-financing. However, for close to a decade, until 2006, the FDIC did not charge any deposit insurance premium at all because its fund was well-capitalized given the lack of defaults in previous years.

As a result of its calibration of funding to average default rates, the FDIC is short of funds when default rates are unexpectedly high. If it runs out of funds, the FDIC can increase its insurance premium. Increasing the premium in a crisis, however, may itself exacerbate the crisis because the charges represent a tax on surviving banks to make up for the losses of failing banks. If many banks are in trouble and the industry is not able to cover the losses, taxpayer support may be needed to make up the shortfall.[11]

Under this arrangement, the contributions of any individual bank to the FDIC do not properly reflect the risk that the bank imposes on the deposit insurance system. Once a bank fails, of course, it no longer makes contributions, and any shortfall of funds or other expenses are covered by the FDIC, that is, by the other banks or taxpayers.

Implicit guarantees are potentially unlimited, and banks do not pay for them. In the fall of 2008, banks received large amounts of support from their governments in various forms. In the United States, the government put up $900 billion, $700 billion for TARP and $200 billion for Fannie Mae and Freddie Mac, the giant mortgage corporations that had dominated housing finance for decades. In other countries, governments committed comparable amounts—for example, £550 billion in the United Kingdom, €480 billion in Germany, and €360 billion in France.[12] These operations ended up protecting most debt holders, even those with "hybrid" debt that was meant to share in absorbing losses and that banks had been allowed to use to satisfy some of their capital requirements.

Additional support was provided by central banks acquiring assets from many private banks, either directly or as collateral for loans. In the United States, the Federal Reserve increased the money supply by more than $1.3 trillion, from just below $900 billion to over $2.2 trillion. In the process, it acquired assets of lower quality, taking on debts of private companies and individuals that included questionable mortgage-backed securities and related derivatives. Such interventions also affect taxpayers, because any losses on the acquired assets reduce the Fed's profits and therefore the payments it makes to the Treasury. Altogether, the bailout operations of 2008 put about $2.2 trillion of U.S. taxpayer money at risk, $900 billion through the Treasury and $1.3 trillion through the Federal Reserve.[13]

Another form of subsidy to banks comes through cheap borrowing from central banks. Since 2008, central banks in the United States, the United Kingdom, and Europe have allowed private banks to borrow at interest rates of 1 percent or less. If this money is invested in safe securities that pay more than 1 percent in interest, the central banks are effectively providing a money machine to the private banks.[14]

In the United States, this kind of support was also provided in 1990, when, in response to information that large commercial banks were in trouble, the Federal Reserve lowered the short-term rate it charged banks that wanted to borrow money.[15] U.S. commercial banks used this cheap borrowing to invest in long-term bonds, earning large profits from 1990 to 1994, rebuilding their equity.

In Europe, since December 2011 the European Central Bank (ECB) has provided more than €1 trillion in cheap loans to banks within the so-called long-term refinancing operations (LTRO), three-year loans at very low rates. Borrowing from the ECB at 1 percent in order to lend to Italy or Spain at 4 or 5 percent may look like an attractive way to rebuild the bank's balance sheet by means of a carry trade. (As discussed in Chapter 8, this practice may involve significant risk.)[16]

In all these examples of central banks' lending at below-market rates or of governments' providing guarantees of banks' debts, the institutions that have access to these loans and guarantees are provided subsidies that other companies in the economy cannot obtain. At the peak of the financial crisis in 2008, money market funds were provided guarantees, and Goldman Sachs and Morgan Stanley, the two remaining pure investment banks in the United States, changed their legal status so as to have access to various supports. They have made use of the supports and have maintained this status.[17]

Since the crisis, many have demanded that there should never be bailouts again. The Dodd-Frank Act in the United States forbids government bailouts and certain forms of support by the Federal Reserve, such as those used in the bailout of AIG.[18] In signing the Act into law, President Obama said, "The American people will never again be asked to foot the bill for Wall Street's mistakes. There will be no more taxpayer-funded bailouts. Period."[19] The Act tries to deliver on that promise by giving authority to the FDIC to take over and resolve any systemically important financial institution and by mandating that no taxpayer money be used. It requires that the costs of the FDIC's taking over and unwinding a financial institution be covered by the institution's creditors or by contributions from other financial institutions. This requirement corresponds to the principle that the FDIC should be self-financing.

However, the FDIC is guaranteed by taxpayers. If the entire banking industry is in trouble and if imposing additional charges on remaining banks would deepen a crisis, taxpayers would have to step in and support the FDIC, as in the case of the S&L institutions in the late 1980s and early 1990s. As the entire industry was failing, taxpayers paid $124 billion to support the deposit insurance system.[20] In the face of a looming crisis, most governments and central banks will likely again step in to help the banks and limit the damage. If the law forbids a bailout, lawmakers can quickly change the law again, particularly in a crisis situation. As a result, hardly anyone considers the no-bailout commitments credible. Support is most likely to be given to the largest and most "systemic" banks because winding them down would be highly disruptive and costly. As discussed in the last section of Chapter 5, there are as yet no workable procedures for winding down internationally active banks with branches and subsidiaries in different countries and no agreements on how to share losses among the different countries involved.

If governments are afraid to let systemically important banks fail, these banks enjoy essentially unlimited implicit guarantees that are similar to the blanket guarantees Kate receives from her aunt. It is very difficult for governments to convincingly commit to removing these guarantees. In a crisis it will be even more difficult to maintain this commitment and provide no support to institutions that are deemed critical to economic survival. Once a crisis is present, it may even be undesirable to do so, because letting banks fail in a crisis can be very damaging. Perversely, the prospect of government support in a crisis makes creditors willing to lend to banks at low rates of interest and provides banks with a reason to view equity as expensive.

Tax Subsidies to Borrowing

In addition to the incentives to economize on equity because of guarantees, borrowing by all corporations is encouraged by the tax systems of most countries. To see how this works, let us go back to Kate's purchase of her house without Aunt Claire's guarantees. Suppose Kate could pay for the house without borrowing but she considered borrowing anyway. Would it make a difference? In the United States, the answer is generally "Yes," because the interest paid on mortgages is tax deductible. In determining her taxable income, Kate could deduct the mortgage interest payments as an expense.[21] Borrowing could therefore reduce Kate's taxes, essentially making Uncle Sam contribute to the purchase of her house.[22]

Corporations can similarly save on taxes by borrowing. In most countries, corporate taxes are paid on a corporation's "income," defined in such a way that interest paid on the corporation's debt is considered a tax-deductible expense.[23] The more debt and the less equity a corporation uses in its funding, the less it pays in taxes. The part of the pie available to investors grows with more borrowing because a smaller part of the earnings goes to the government in taxes. This encourages corporations to borrow more than they might otherwise choose to do.[24]

Some countries (for example, Australia, Germany between 1977 and 2000, and, since 2004, Belgium) have tried to neutralize the tax penalty for equity funding. Many commissions in the United States have also recommended changes to the tax code to eliminate or reduce the tax incentives for corporations to borrow.[25]

Whereas tax legislation is usually driven by considerations and politics different from those that drive banking regulation, it is important to recognize that a corporate tax code that subsidizes debt and penalizes equity works directly against financial stability. By giving corporations tax incentives to use debt, the tax code encourages the excessive borrowing of financial institutions that harms the financial system by increasing its fragility.

Life without Guarantees

The tax subsidy of debt applies to all corporations. Yet most nonfinancial corporations refrain from borrowing extensively, and some corporations, like Apple, use virtually no debt.[26] How can we explain this? The primary reason has to do with the burden of debt discussed in Chapter 3, which can make high levels of indebtedness costly and undesirable to nonbank corporations.

Borrowing obviously increases the likelihood of distress and bankruptcy. Bankruptcy is costly in the sense that it depletes a corporation's remaining assets further than they have already been depleted prior to bankruptcy. For example, lawyers and bankruptcy courts charge fees that must be paid out of the corporation's remaining assets or by its creditors. These costs are entirely due to the use of debt, and the likelihood of incurring them would be lower if the corporation had more equity and less debt. If bankruptcy can be avoided, losses from investments will be a concern for shareholders, but there will be no expenses for bankruptcy lawyers and courts.

In terms of Yogi Berra's pizza, the bankruptcy costs reduce the amount of the total "pie" that is available to investors. Anticipating that a corporation's assets will be depleted in bankruptcy, creditors charge a higher rate of interest than they would absent the bankruptcy costs. This makes using debt more "expensive" for the corporation and acts to discourage too much borrowing.

As discussed in Chapter 3, the costs of bankruptcy go beyond those for lawyers and court fees. For example, the bankruptcy process may freeze a firm's activities. Even before bankruptcy, as distress sets in, the firm's flexibility and its ability to compete in its markets may be impaired. High levels of indebtedness also exacerbate conflicts of interest between owners or managers and creditors. Owners or managers might choose risky investments that can harm creditors, or they might pass up good investments, just as a homeowner who is underwater is less likely to invest in home improvements.

When creditors agree to lend to the corporation, they try to protect themselves in advance by charging higher interest rates or by attaching conditions, generally called "covenants," to the loans they make. Banks do the same when they lend to individuals and businesses. These conditions restrict the borrower's flexibility and can make borrowing less attractive.

For example, creditors may forbid a borrowing corporation from taking additional debts or from making dividend payments to shareholders in certain situations in which such actions would harm the creditors. Creditors may also require that major investment decisions be approved by them. This requirement can prevent the borrower from quickly taking advantage of investment opportunities as they arise.

Without guarantees, the costs and inefficiencies associated with distress and default are reflected in the interest rates and conditions attached to debt contracts, raising overall funding costs. This helps explain why, despite the tax advantage of debt, most nonfinancial companies avoid becoming highly indebted even if they can borrow more.

With debt guarantees, however, the burdens of debt become lighter. Creditors believe that their debts will most likely be paid in full. Therefore they do not charge as much, and do not impose as many conditions, as they would if the bank made the same investments without guarantees.

For banks, therefore, the costs of added debt are much lower with guarantees, even if they are already highly indebted. They view equity as expensive; borrowing is always attractive. As discussed in the previous chapter, the focus on ROE in banking reinforces the effect by compensating bank managers in ways that encourage risk taking and borrowing.

Perverse Incentives

When large banks are treated as too big to fail, this status has strong and perverse effects on the banks' behavior. The prospect of benefiting from too-big-to-fail status can give banks strong incentives to grow, merge, borrow, and take risks in ways that take the most advantage of the potential or actual guarantees. Banks may also want to draw advantages from taking risks that are similar in that they are all likely to turn out well or to turn out poorly at the same time. If things go wrong, the entire industry may be affected, which will generate strong pressures for government support. These effects of government guarantees on banks' behavior are counterproductive in that they further increase the likelihood that the economy might suffer harm from the fallout of risks taken in the financial sector.

Some of the perverse incentives banks are given can be seen by going back to Kate and her Aunt Claire. If Aunt Claire guarantees Kate's mortgage to buy only the $300,000 house, Claire will not lose more than $309,000, Kate's debt if she puts in no equity; most likely, the house will not become worthless, so the cost to Aunt Claire will be lower. Uncle Sam's exposure to the risks of large, systemically important banks, or to those of the entire banking system, is not so limited, particularly when the banks and the banking sector can keep growing and taking risks.

The banks' situation is as if Aunt Claire gave Kate a guarantee for *any* debt, not just for a particular $300,000 mortgage. With blanket guarantees, Kate can buy a bigger house. She can also set up a corporation and make risky investments with borrowed money. If she maintains very little equity, she cannot lose much; yet, as she continues borrowing and investing, her profits can become very large.

How wonderful indeed this would be for Kate. As long as Aunt Claire's guarantees remain good, Kate can borrow cheaply and can try to maintain her equity at near zero. If her investments are profitable, Kate can pay herself a dividend and continue to borrow. And with little equity, risk does not scare Kate. She actually finds risk attractive, because it holds the prospect of large gains on the upside, with hardly any consequences on the downside. At most she might worry that, if her gambles do not succeed and Aunt Claire has to pay for them, her aunt might not be willing to provide more guarantees in the future.

In this fantasy, there are no limits to how much Kate can benefit by growing her business and taking more risk or to the amount Aunt Claire might have to put up. The more Kate borrows, the more she stands to gain on the upside while being protected on the downside. Similarly, there are no limits to the amounts that taxpayers may have to put up if they do not constrain what the banks can do, how large they can grow individually or as an industry, and how much they can borrow. In the most recent crisis, governments provided banks with blanket guarantees to avoid a potential meltdown of the financial system. In a similar crisis in the future, the cost of such guarantees could be higher.

If Kate racked up enough losses, Aunt Claire might have run out of funds. Similarly, banks can overburden taxpayers with their losses. This is essentially what happened in Iceland and Ireland in 2008. Banks in those countries grew and invested so much that their losses were larger than the countries could bear.[27] Spain may be facing a similar experience.

Being considered too big to fail is extremely valuable for a bank, because it lowers its borrowing costs. Just as Kate was able to borrow at a lower rate because of Aunt Claire's guarantees, banks that benefit from implicit guarantees are given higher credit ratings, and thus pay less interest when they borrow. This reduces the banks' overall funding costs and increases the amount of the total pie available to their investors.

There is significant evidence that subsidies associated with being too big to fail can make these banks seem more profitable, when in fact they are not generating more value but simply benefiting from more subsidized funding.[28] Banks do not seem to become more efficient when they grow beyond about $100 billion in assets, yet growing can allow them to enjoy the subsidized funding that comes with the implicit guarantees.[29] With subsidized funding through guarantees, growth is easy, and building empires can be quite profitable.[30]

Mergers in banking have also been shown to be partly motivated by a desire to attain too-big-to-fail status, which generally lowers costs and makes for easier borrowing terms. A bank is willing to pay more to acquire other banks if the merger will result in a bank that is considered too big to fail.[31]

A recent study estimated that at the peak of the financial crisis, the guarantees to the U.S. financial sector were worth close to $160 billion.[32] The value of the subsidies associated with guarantees was estimated to be about $2.3 trillion worldwide in 2009.[33] The banks would have had to pay someone in the private market very large amounts to provide the guarantees the government provided. The magnitude of the implicit subsidies has generally grown since the crisis because the largest banks have grown in size.[34] Of course the value of the guarantees changes with economic conditions and is at its highest when the economy is weak and banks are more distressed.

Even when they do not cause banks to merge, guarantees can have strong and damaging effects on the behavior of banks. In the United States, mortgage giants Fannie Mae and Freddie Mac have always been considered to be protected by the government. They have not benefited from any explicit guarantees, but investors have thought they were too big to fail, and indeed they were bailed out in September 2008. Their too-big-to-fail status allowed the mortgage giants to grow at the tremendous rate of 16 percent per year from 1980 until the crisis, while their involvement in residential mortgages and mortgage guarantees rose from $85 billion to $5.2 trillion and their share of the mortgage market rose from 7.1 percent to 41.3 percent.[35]

This growth was facilitated by their being able to borrow at very low rates even though their equity was between 2.5 and 5 percent of their total assets; if their mortgage guarantees had been put on their balance sheets, their equity would have been even less, between 1 and 2 percent of their total assets. Borrowing cheaply with hardly any equity was possible only because of implicit guarantees. For the year 2000, the Congressional Budget Office estimated that the value of these guarantees amounted to $13.6 billion. Of this amount, at least one-third was estimated to be a simple wealth transfer from taxpayers to the shareholders and managers of these companies, and no more than two-thirds were estimated to have improved the terms under which home buyers could borrow. By some accounts, the value of the implicit government guarantees accounted for almost the entire market value of these companies.[36]

In an industry in which there is intense competition, particularly for growth, guarantees tend to encourage recklessness.[37] If the banks' creditors expect their investments to be safe because of the guarantees, they do not pay much attention to the risks the banks take. This enables the banks to grow fast by expanding their borrowing without seeing their borrowing rates increase. Fannie Mae and Freddie Mac are examples of this problem. Other examples, from the 1980s, were U.S. S&Ls, which attracted large amounts of funding by offering high rates of interest on federally insured deposits. In each case, the explicit or implicit government guarantees provided a basis for extraordinary growth, which ended up being very costly for taxpayers.[38]

Excessive Borrowing: Expensive for Aunt Claire, Uncle Sam, and the Rest of Us

The guarantees that allow banks to borrow cheaply and take excessive risk are a burden on taxpayers. As the subsidies become more valuable to banks, they also become more costly to society. In our example involving Kate and Aunt Claire, any equity that Kate puts into her house reduces the payments Aunt Claire may subsequently have to make to honor the guarantee she gave to cover Kate's debt. Equity is expensive *for Kate,* but any cost to her of more equity is fully balanced by lower expenses for Aunt Claire. For Kate and Aunt Claire together, Kate's using more equity and less debt is not expensive; the two of them together always pay the mortgage in full. Any benefit Kate sees in different arrangements comes at the expense of Aunt Claire. Meanwhile, Kate benefits from the upside, but the best-case scenario for Claire is that she does not have to pay.

The combined cost to Kate and Claire will in fact be lower if Kate becomes motivated to make sounder decisions when she has more equity and thus more "skin in the game." If Aunt Claire provides Kate with blanket guarantees and Kate cannot be made liable for her debt, there will be nothing to prevent Kate from using borrowed funds to gamble in Las Vegas. Such wasteful investments would be less likely if Kate had more of an equity stake that might be lost by gambling.

Similarly, when considering the costs and benefits of banks' using different mixes of debt and equity, from the perspective of society, the costs to taxpayers of providing guarantees and subsidies must be considered. Also relevant is the damage to the economy when banks are in distress, even more so when they go into default and bankruptcy; this damage includes the cost of valuable loans' not being made. A funding mix that relies on a lot of borrowing and little equity and that appears cheap to a bank can in fact be very expensive to society. Conversely, although banks consider equity funding more expensive than borrowing, additional equity funding of banks can actually be significantly *cheaper* for society once we factor in the costs and risks to society of banks' becoming fragile through borrowing.

The magnitudes of the costs banks impose on society can be large. The recent financial crisis has led to significant loss of output, likely in the trillions of dollars. The losses of the U.S. government from its various rescue operations since 2008 have been between $200 and $500 billion.[39] Beyond the costs of the bailouts, the collateral damage to the economy has been enormous.[40] If this money had not been lost but rather invested at 4 percent per year, a typical rate for fairly safe long-term investments, it would provide $8–20 billion of additional revenue per year. In a federal budget that includes $129.8 billion for education and $94.5 billion for transportation in 2012, $8–20 billion a year could make a noticeable difference in education or transportation.

As noted in Chapter 2, in the nineteenth century and the early twentieth, equity levels in banks were often 25 percent or higher (even as high as 40 percent or 50 percent in the first half of the nineteenth century). The reduction of bank equity to the present low levels over the past century paralleled the expansion of the government safety net of banks, with equity levels decreasing as the safety net expanded.[41]

If banks were to rely less on subsidized borrowing and use more equity, any increase in their cost of funding would be fully matched by taxpayers' savings on the cost of providing subsidies to the banks. Society would benefit by having healthier and safer banks that are less likely to become distressed and impose additional costs, and the distorted incentives to take advantage of the guarantees would be reduced. Would having more equity interfere with any of the services that banks provide? As the next chapter shows, the answer is a clear "No." In fact, safer banks that use more equity can serve the economy much better.

TEN

Must Banks Borrow So Much?

The Phoenicians invented money—but why so little of it?

Johann Nepomuk Nestroy (1801–1862), Austrian playwright

A S WE SAW IN CHAPTER 4, banks benefit the economy by taking deposits and making loans. Of these two activities, deposit taking is unique to banks. Loans can also be made by any other institution that has the capacity to assess the loan applicants' creditworthiness and to monitor their performance. The concentration of banks on lending is due to the ready availability of funds from deposits.[1]

As we also saw in Chapter 4, banks provide depositors with important services, such as making payments and standing ready to provide cash at any moment. Because deposits are a form of debt, borrowing is an essential part of banking. Does this mean that banks would provide fewer benefits to the economy if they relied less on borrowing and used more equity? The answer is "No."

Banks have always been fragile and prone to trouble. The very word *bankruptcy*, common to many languages, alludes to banks.[2] The history of banking has been full of crashes and crises. The period between 1940 and 1970, when there was hardly a banking crisis and few bank failures, was a remarkable exception.[3] The incidence of crashes and crises since 1970 is not much different from past experience of financial instability, for example, in the nineteenth century.[4]

Banking experts often start from the observation that, with their reliance on deposits, banks have always been susceptible to runs, and they conclude that fragility in banking is inevitable. By this account, banking crises are similar to natural disasters such as earthquakes or hurricanes, which cannot be prevented. When a natural disaster strikes, governments usually provide emergency support. If banking crises are like natural disasters and cannot be prevented, one might conclude that all governments can do is provide emergency support when a crisis hits.[5]

Is this analogy of banking crises with natural disasters appropriate? Are banking crises as unpreventable as earthquakes? No. If deposits and other forms of bank debt can provide benefits, does it follow that banks must rely on as much borrowing as they currently do or as much as proposed regulations would allow? Again, the answer is "No."

When banking experts discuss the benefits that banks provide to the economy, they typically ignore the role of equity in bank funding. But, as we have argued, banks can increase their equity funding without reducing their debt. For example, banks can retain their earnings or issue new shares. Would doing so reduce the benefits they provide through their deposits and other debts?

This question is rarely asked, but the answer is striking. If banks added more equity while leaving their deposits and other borrowing unchanged, the benefits that depositors and other creditors would obtain would actually be *larger*. As we saw in Chapters 2 and 3, with more equity there is less risk that a bank might become insolvent when its investments do not work out as hoped. If the risk of distress and insolvency is lower, deposits and other loans to the bank are safer. The greater safety of the bank benefits depositors, other creditors, and the deposit insurance system. One clear benefit of more equity is that the bank is more trustworthy and a costly run on the bank is less likely.

The fact that banks have always been fragile does not prove that this is unavoidable, essential, or efficient. In fact, the fragility that we observe in banking is largely a result of conflicts of interest between bankers and their creditors (or taxpayers). Without regulation, these conflicts of interest are usually not resolved in an efficient manner. Moreover, the impact of banks' decisions on the stability of the financial system and on the overall economy is not given enough attention.

Deposits, Payments, and the Fragility of Banks

On a five-pound note in England, one can find the inscription "I promise to pay the bearer on demand the sum of five pounds." In an earlier era, this represented an obligation of the Bank of England to redeem the note for an equivalent amount in gold.[6] When the Bank of England was founded in 1694, it was actually one of many institutions issuing such notes. At that time many banks, as well as other institutions, were taking deposits of gold, particularly gold coins, and issuing notes against these deposits, essentially promises to pay back the deposits to the holders of these notes.[7] People used the bank-notes for payments the way we now use cash. These early bankers realized that they did not have to hold all the deposits in reserves, so they engaged in lending, providing loan customers with gold or with additional newly cre-ated banknotes.[8]

Over time issuing banknotes has become a privilege of central banks, but deposits still provide an important part of the funding of private banks, and they are still closely tied to the payment system.[9] People treat their deposits as akin to money, something that can be readily used for payments, by means of checks or bank transfers or through credit and debit cards.[10] In the words of one author, from "a money view perspective," banking is part of "the sophisticated mechanism that operates to channel cash flows wherever they are emerging to meet cash commitments wherever they are the most pressing."[11]

The role of banks in the payment system, in the past when they issued banknotes, as well as later with demand deposits in checking accounts, has made them vulnerable to the risk of runs. In the eighteenth century, there were even runs on the Bank of England when wars and government finances made the bank appear unsafe. In the United States, the experience of runs and panics under the National Banking System was one reason for the cre-ation in 1913 of the Federal Reserve, which was given a monopoly on issuing notes.[12]

Vulnerability to runs may appear to be a necessary consequence of the promise banks make to depositors that they can get at their money whenever they wish. This promise makes deposits useful for payments, but, as explained in Chapter 4, it also exposes banks to the risk that all depositors might want their money at the same time. This risk has been a feature of banking for cen-turies and therefore is often taken for granted, something that cannot be avoided if we want to have an efficient payments system.[13]

However, the links between the payment system, deposits, money, and the fragility of banks are not as simple and mechanical as this reasoning suggests. First, important parts of today's payment system have no risk of default. Banknotes are issued by central banks and in most countries do not actually promise anything.[14] The inscription on English banknotes is no more than a historical relic.[15] A demand deposit that a private bank has with the central bank is a debt of the central bank, but this debt obliges the central bank only to deliver the equivalent amount in banknotes. Because the central bank itself can print the notes, this is a debt without default risk.[16]

Second, the fragility of private banks—that is, the likelihood that they will get into trouble—depends on the extent to which the arrangements for payments in the economy rely on banknotes and deposits with the central bank. The more people rely on cash and the more private banks rely on reserves of central bank money, the more the payment system is immune to the danger of a run. Because the interest paid on cash and deposits with the central bank is low if any is paid at all, investors and private banks are always tempted to reduce their reliance on cash and central bank deposits as means of payments.[17] This is a matter of choice rather than necessity.

Taking deposits and promising to repay them whenever the depositors want does not automatically make private banks prone to trouble. If deposits were treated as safekeeping arrangements, as in the case of a storage facility, and if the banks did not invest the funds, the banks would not be vulnerable at all because, even if there was a run, the banks could return what they owe.[18] The banks become vulnerable only if they use funds from depositors to make investments that cannot readily be converted into cash. The more they do so, the more vulnerable the banks become.

Some of the lending and other investments made by banks are both profitable for the banks and desirable for the economy. This observation by itself, however, provides little help in assessing how much banks should invest and how much they should hold in reserves. It also says nothing about how much equity banks should use in funding themselves. The downside risks from the loans and investments must be dealt with and borne by *someone*. How risks are dealt with depends on the banks' investment choices and on the amount of loss-absorbing equity they have.

When banks rely mostly on borrowed funds and then make risky investments, they become vulnerable to insolvency risk as well as the risk of illiquidity problems and runs. As discussed in Chapters 4 and 5, the two types of risk are related but distinct. Most runs are actually caused by concerns about banks' possible insolvency.[19] Deposit insurance or guarantees can greatly reduce or eliminate the risk of a run, but they do nothing to reduce the risk that banks might become insolvent. In fact, the costs of insolvency can be magnified if guarantees and so-called liquidity support enable banks to retain their funding and continue operating even though they are actually insolvent.

If banks take deposits that customers can use to make payments, this fact does not by itself determine how likely banks are to run into trouble. The risk of a run or an insolvency depends on how the banks use their funds, how risky their investments are, and how much equity there is to absorb potential losses. The more equity a bank has, the lower the risk of distress and insolvency and the less vulnerable the bank is to the risk of runs and, more generally, to the risk of having to default on its debt promises.

The banks' choices as to the amount of their reserves or their use of equity have little to do with the fact that deposits are available for payments or, more generally, with the benefits banks provide through deposits or other borrowing. If anything, the benefits from the easy availability of deposits will be *greater* if a bank has more reserves or more equity because its depositors and other creditors will be less concerned about the bank's ability to pay them.[20]

For example, if a bank issues additional shares or if it retains its profits rather than paying them out to shareholders, it can increase its equity without reducing any of its deposits or other borrowing. With the additional funds the bank can make worthy loans that can provide additional benefits to the economy. If it finds no loans it considers worthy to make, the bank can invest the money it raises in other assets, such as stocks and bonds, receiving appropriate returns. The returns on the additional investments will allow the bank to pay its debts more reliably, and this will reduce the likelihood of insolvency.[21]

Additional equity, therefore, makes the bank safer and bolsters investors' confidence in the bank. If the deposits are not insured, depositors and other creditors are the beneficiaries. If instead there is deposit insurance or some sort of guarantee for the deposits, the institutions providing the insurance and guarantees may benefit most. Uninsured creditors also benefit because everyone knows that the bank is safer if it has more equity. If everyone knows that the bank is safer—and everyone knows that everyone else knows the same —everyone will become less worried that anyone might start a costly run.

In earlier times, when banks issued notes, information that a bank had a lot of equity would make its notes more acceptable as means of payment. Checks on uninsured accounts with a bank would also be more acceptable if the bank was known to have more equity. Recall the assessment of a nineteenth-century banking expert, referred to in Chapter 2, that depositors have more trust when banks' owners have full liability, as they did at that time. With more liability of owners, banks will be better able to pay back their depositors and other creditors. Similarly, when a modern corporation has more equity, it is better able to pay back its depositors and other creditors. The very benefits that banks provide because deposits or other short-term debts are readily available and acceptable as means of payment are thus *enhanced* when banks have more equity.

The Insatiable "Need" for Liquidity

Money is wonderful: we can use it to pay for anything we want. For some payments, however, using cash is cumbersome. Moreover, cash does not pay any interest. A bank deposit may be even better than money: it can be used to pay for almost anything, sometimes more conveniently than using cash, and it may even pay interest. A share in a money market mutual fund may be better yet: it can also be used for payments, and it pays even more interest.

We want to have it all. We want our investments to be as easy to use as cash, safe and readily available when we want to pay for something. At the same time, we want the investments to provide us a better return than cash so we can have more money later. We may know deep down that it may not be possible to have it all, but we may gladly listen to a fund manager, a banker, or a spin doctor who offers an investment that is just as easy to use as cash but pays a much better return.

Banks cater to people's desire for assets that seem like cash but pay a higher return than cash.[22] According to one banking expert, "Banks produce debt" the way automobile manufacturers produce cars.[23] Not just any debt, of course, but deposits and other kinds of very short-term debt that are considered to be like money. The economy is seen as having an unbounded need for such "liquid assets."[24] Banks, money market funds, and other institutions performing banking services are said to be there to satisfy this "need." Innovations that allow banks and other institutions to produce more of this liquid debt should therefore, goes the narrative, be considered useful and beneficial.[25]

However, the notion that the economy has an unbounded "need" for liquid assets is another example of the bankers' new clothes. It is impossible to discuss coherently the *need* for anything without considering its cost. When a young adult tells a parent that she *needs* a fancy car, she actually means that she *wants* the car and expects the parent to pay for it—and perhaps also the insurance and maintenance. If she has to pay for everything herself, her so-called need might be quite different. Similarly, it makes no sense to talk about the need for liquidity without talking about its cost.

Money, in the form of cash or reserves with the central banks, is of course perfectly liquid. Cash can be used in practically any transaction. Even so, under realistic market conditions, the actual need for cash is bounded. Beyond a certain point, people prefer to put their funds into assets that provide them with a return, such as interest-bearing deposits, stocks, or bonds.

These interest-bearing assets are less liquid and/or less safe than cash, and they are less frequently used to make payments. Even the deposits and other money-like assets that banks and other financial institutions create are not quite the same as actual money. Whereas money—that is, cash—is nobody's debt, the kind of money-like debts that are represented by deposits and other kinds of very short-term borrowing *do* represent promises made by the issuing institutions. Whereas there is no risk of default associated with cash, in the case of deposits and other forms of debt there is a risk that a bank may not be able to honor its promises, for example, if it makes poor investments with the money and incurs large losses.[26]

The reality is that anything that is just as safe and as convenient as cash cannot pay a higher return than does cash—that is, zero.[27] If banks offer alternative investments with higher returns, these investments must have *some* disadvantage relative to cash. Perhaps the investments are risky. Or they may become illiquid, that is, difficult to sell quickly and convert to cash without a discount. To obtain higher returns than with cash, investors must give up *something*.

However, it is always tempting to cut corners, to neglect risks, and to hope for higher returns without giving up any of the advantages of cash. The bankers who want our funds want us to believe that their debts are money-like even when they are not, and we want to believe them.[28] The suggestion that the economy has an unbounded need for liquid assets reflects these wishes but is not based on sound reasoning.

If differences in risks, liquidity, and the interest promised are taken into account, the need for the most perfect form of liquid asset, namely cash, is in fact fairly small. And the need for less perfect forms of liquidity depends on people's willingness to ignore the hidden risks of these assets.[29] Of course people may believe that the government will step in to make sure all claims are paid. If this happens, the attractiveness of the asset to the individual investor may turn out to be very costly for society, because financial institutions receive funding at subsidized interest rates that do not reflect the true costs and because the fragility of the financial system is increased.

In Chapter 4 we noted that banks traditionally used the funds they obtained from deposits to make loans and that they used to hold the loans until they were repaid, typically a number of years. The deposits were due on demand and were therefore perceived as very liquid by depositors, but the loans that backed these deposits were very illiquid; it was virtually impossible to sell them for a reasonable price.[30]

Banking experts refer to this use of liquid debts such as demand deposits to fund illiquid loans and other investments using the term *liquidity transformation*.[31] By contrast to the statement that banks just "produce money-like debt," the term liquidity transformation draws our attention to the relation between the illiquid assets in which banks invest and the liquid debt that they create.

The risks of the investments a bank makes can actually limit its ability to produce money-like debt. If there is a significant risk that the bank might default on its debts, the debts may be less liquid, because their liquidity depends on how much people can be sure about their value. This is similar to the way that a gift card from a large department store is almost as useful as cash because one can use it to buy whatever is in the store, but this can only be done as long as the store is in business. Likewise, an airline ticket is useful for flying only if the airline does not go into bankruptcy (unless other arrangements are made, such as for another airline to honor the ticket).

Similarly, a demand deposit, which is very liquid in principle, may become perfectly illiquid if the bank at which it is held goes into bankruptcy and is not part of a deposit insurance system. Banknotes or bank bonds may suddenly stop being easily tradable if people are worried that the bank may be unsafe and that someone else with these notes or bonds might be taking advantage of them by selling the notes or bonds on the basis of bad news that they have just obtained.[32] If people are afraid that sellers of such assets are trying to take advantage of them, they will buy only if prices are very low— lower even than the information available about the bank might suggest.

The short-term debt that a bank produces may therefore not be very money-like if the bank does not have much equity. Without sufficient equity providing a buffer against losses, there is a risk of distress, insolvency, and possibly default. With debt that can be withdrawn or must be renewed, there may also be a high risk of a run. All these risks imply that debt may suddenly become illiquid—even if, initially, it might not look that way.

Poor lending decisions can also destroy the money-like quality of a bank's deposits and other short-term debt. Such decisions increase the risk that the bank might become insolvent. As a result, its debts might be neither liquid nor safe.

An example of the destruction of the liquidity of money-like debt by risks from lending was provided by mortgage-related securities in 2007. As we explained in Chapter 5, many of these securities had been created in the preceding years. Securitization allowed mortgage banks to sell their loans. Investment banks and others would buy many mortgages, bundle them together, and then issue various tradable securities that would pay investors from the money paid by the mortgage debtors.

For a while before 2007, these securities—or at least those that had the first claim on the mortgage debtors' payments and that received the highest credit rating, AAA—were treated as both extremely safe and very liquid, easy to convert to cash. However, in the vast expansion of mortgage lending and securitization during 2004–2006, the standards for assessing the credit-worthiness of mortgage borrowers and the quality of mortgages had declined dramatically.[33] When investors realized the extent of the credit risk in the summer of 2007, the markets for these mortgage-related securities suddenly froze. Instead of being very liquid, the securities became completely illiquid, and their prices plummeted.[34] At the same time, lenders became unwilling to accept these securities as collateral.

On several occasions since 2007, central banks have stepped in and supported private banks by accepting mortgage-related securities as collateral for bank borrowing or even purchasing mortgage-related securities outright. For someone who believes that liquidity is everything, this was just the right thing to do, and maybe it was a way of preventing a disastrous collapse of the banking system.[35]

However, such interventions can be costly. If the securities purchased end up being bad risks, the central bank will have incurred a loss. To be sure, the cost of printing the money needed to buy securities or to lend against collateral is negligible. However, if this money had been used to acquire safe assets instead, the central bank would be earning higher returns. These returns would supplement the public budget and perhaps provide additional funding for highways or schools. If mortgage-related securities purchased by the central bank are affected by debtors' defaults, there will be that much less money for highways or schools.[36]

There is also a danger that when the central bank prints money the purchasing power of money will go down, so that people in the economy will find that any money they have is worth less.[37] Indeed, in this case inflation will erode not only the value of the money that people hold but also the value of bank deposits and any other assets that are denominated in units of money. Printing money is costless for the central bank but can impose a large "inflation tax" on the public.

The power of central banks to print money has often been abused. Most importantly, governments have used the printing press to provide themselves with funding that they could not obtain from their taxpayers, sometimes with disastrous consequences.[38] To prevent such abuses, many countries have established institutional safeguards and legal rules that limit the scope for printing money as a source of funding.[39]

Some of the rules that limit central banks' activities concern their interventions in support of private banks. In particular, liquidity supports from central banks are not meant, and should not be used, to keep insolvent banks afloat. Without such a restriction, there would be a danger of excessive lending by private banks. Lending decisions of poor quality imply that resources are put into investments that will not pay off. If private banks use deposits to fund bad loans, the liquidity transformation and the lending must be considered excessive and inefficient. When things go wrong and the bad credit risks appear, there will be a temptation for central banks to print money to provide what will be referred to as "liquidity support"—but will in fact be disguised bailouts. As indicated earlier, such bailouts impose costs on the public even though the costs may be covered up because, in the short run at least, printing money seems costless. (Later, of course, those who engaged in printing the money may well be out of office or the link to them will not be made.)

Cutting Corners through Innovations

Another one of the fancy terms in banking textbooks that we mentioned briefly in Chapter 4 is *maturity transformation*. The term sounds impressive, just as the word *cauliflower* sounded to Mark Twain until he realized that "cauliflower is nothing but cabbage with a college education."[40] Maturity transformation simply means that banks use short-term debts like deposits to finance long-term investments like loans. According to banking textbooks, this is one of banks' core functions.

Maturity transformation is closely related to liquidity transformation, but it is not the same. For example, a bank might fund a set of mortgage loans that have ten years to go by issuing a ten-year bond, that is, debt that is paid over ten years. In this case, the length of time until the loans expire—their maturity—is the same as the length of time until the bond expires, so there is no maturity transformation. However, the bond may be traded in the bond market, in which case it can be easily converted into cash, unlike the individual mortgage loans, so there is some liquidity transformation.[41]

Funding ten-year mortgage loans by means of short-term debt, however, would be a form of maturity transformation. In Chapter 4 we discussed this type of transformation as characteristic of traditional commercial banks or savings banks such as the fictional Bailey Building and Loan Association. Such banks were funded by deposits that could be withdrawn at short notice, and the banks used the deposits to make long-lasting home mortgages.

When banks engage in liquidity transformation and in maturity transformation, they face not only a risk of liquidity problems and runs but also a risk of insolvency, which is much more serious. For example, if interest rates on the home mortgages are fixed, and at some point in the lifetime of those mortgages the interest rate on deposits becomes much higher, the bank can become insolvent. As we discussed, this happened to many U.S. savings institutions in the early 1980s.

Securitization of mortgages was a response to this experience. Selling home mortgages off to others looked like a good way to eliminate the risks that maturity transformation created. However, the risks were not eliminated; they were merely moved elsewhere.

To see how the risks persisted, consider a typical funding chain, as discussed in Chapter 5. The chain would begin with a private individual or a nonfinancial company investing in a money market mutual fund. The money market mutual fund, in turn, provided an overnight loan to a bank or to a so-called structured investment vehicle, a subsidiary created by a bank, usually to avoid regulation.

Next the bank or the bank's subsidiary used the money it got from the money market fund to buy mortgage-related securities that had been created by subsidiaries of investment banks out of large packages of mortgages that they had acquired from the original mortgage banks. The mortgage banks, in turn, had these mortgages to sell because they lent money to homeowners.

In this chain of transactions, the investment that we started with, that of the private individual or the nonfinancial company in the money market fund, was "transformed" into an investment in the properties that homeowners bought. The investment went from a money-like short-term debt commitment that the money market mutual fund made to the investor to houses that would likely last a few decades. The mortgage-related securities ended up being held by banks, and again these investments were funded by short-term debt.[42]

If one believes that the role of banking is to "produce liquid debt," one will marvel at the wonders of financial engineering that have made it possible to transform trillions of dollars of the money-like debts of banks and financial institutions into housing and real estate investments.[43] If instead one is concerned about having a safe and healthy financial system, one may wonder about the risks that might arise from so much maturity transformation. As in the case of the Bailey Building and Loan Association in the movie *It's a Wonderful Life*, one type of risk is a run that disrupts the funding of the banks holding the mortgage-related securities. A more serious risk is the possibility that the bank will become insolvent, which is precisely what happened to a number of banks in 2007 and 2008.

Unlike the insolvencies in the early 1980s, those in 2007 and 2008 were not directly caused by interest rates' changing. Many mortgages had adjustable interest rates, which went up along with market rates in 2005–2007. However, these rate adjustments led to many defaults on mortgages because borrowers could not pay the higher interest.[44]

The interest rate increases in the United States in 2005–2007 were much smaller than those in the late 1970s and late 1980s, but, coupled with the questionable creditworthiness of borrowers, the increases were enough to usher in the turnaround in U.S. real estate prices and trigger many delinquencies on mortgages. When the risks in mortgage-related securities became apparent in the summer of 2007, the prices of these securities declined significantly. Given that the institutions holding them had very little equity, many became distressed, some insolvent.[45]

In Chapter 5 we discussed the contagion risks associated with long and complicated chains of transactions. These chains allowed participants to fool themselves about the risks to which they were exposed. There was a substantial amount of maturity transformation in the system, but none of the participants seemed to have seen the risks from where they stood. Quite possibly, given the incentives of many of the participants, they preferred to ignore the risks.

By splitting the overall operation into many different and connected steps, market participants were able to hide the risks and tell themselves, their supervisors, and their customers that everything was safe and liquid because each step by itself seemed safe. Creditors were enthusiastic about the ability to invest in money-like debt that paid slightly more interest than government debt, and lots of questionable mortgages were made to feed the rush to securitization and the "production" of liquid debt.

Why All This Complexity?

The complicated chain of transactions just discussed is an example of the increase in the interconnectedness of the financial system in recent decades. As we noted in Chapter 5, this interconnectedness was key to the contagion that caused the 2007–2009 financial crisis to be as damaging as it was.

The increase in interconnectedness was not due just to a desire for greater efficiency. At least some elements of the chain of transactions were due to participants' trying to get around the prevailing regulations. For example, the continued prominence in the U.S. financial system of money market mutual funds, which played a major role in the post-Lehman panic, is due to their being able to offer the same services as banks without being subject to the same regulations. They can generate higher returns for investors because they are not part of the deposit insurance system and therefore do not have to pay insurance fees. In September 2008, however, the U.S. government chose to provide them with guarantees anyway rather than allowing the run of investors on money market mutual funds and the run of money market mutual funds on banks to continue to destabilize the financial system.[46]

In Chapter 5 we mentioned that the bailout of AIG was motivated by the fear of contagion from an AIG default on its commitments to credit insurance. Banks had bought this insurance in order to reduce estimates of their risks and, by implication, their required equity. Without the AIG bailout, the credit insurance might have been worthless, and the banks would have been hit by the credit risks that they thought they had insured.

Putting mortgage-related securities into structured investment vehicles (SIVs), entities that could be kept off the banks' balance sheets, was also motivated by the desire to get around regulation. Regulators treated the SIVs as if they were separate from the sponsoring banks. Therefore, the banks were not required to have any equity funding of the investments. However, the SIVs could obtain outside funding only because the sponsoring banks provided guarantees for them.[47] Banks bore the risks of the SIVs without backing this commitment by equity and thus without the ability to absorb losses.[48]

There was (and still is) an element of make-believe in all of this. As bankers and investors pursued higher returns, actual or imagined, they downplayed the risks. Banks claimed to hedge risks in ways that fooled supervisors and possibly the bankers themselves but ended up being ineffective. No one bothered to keep track of where in the system the risks were going. Some of the gains in returns seemed extremely small relative to the risks involved. For example, the extra interest earned on relatively "safe" mortgage-related securities might be as low as 0.1 percent, which was hardly enough compensation for the actual risks involved.[49]

Why were people so willing to fool not only the regulators and their bosses but possibly also themselves? The answer is that they had incentives to do so.[50] As discussed in Chapter 8, bankers are paid bonuses on the basis of their assessed contributions to profits, with little accounting for risks. Investing $1 billion in a security whose return promises to be 0.1 percent above the borrowing cost may seem very attractive and a reason for paying a high bonus because, if nothing goes wrong, the investment will show a profit of $1 million per year. If, a year later, the security's value declines by 10 percent, the bank loses $100 million, but that need not affect the bonus that the banker had received for making the investment.

Bankers generally act in response to the incentives they are given, even if their actions do not generate sustainable benefits for anyone but themselves. Borrowing a bit more in order to make a risky investment that pays barely more than the borrowing rate may be attractive to a banker if he does not have to take the additional risk into account. Because of the risk, however, this borrowing and the investment made with the borrowed funds may well be undesirable for the bank's shareholders, its other creditors, and society.

As discussed in Chapter 3, heavy borrowers are affected by debt overhang, which makes them resist reducing their indebtedness if doing so would make their remaining debt safer at their expense. In fact, heavy borrowers have incentives to increase their borrowing even if it is inefficient.

In our mortgage example, we saw that Kate might be reluctant to invest $50,000 in renovating her house even if the renovation increases the value of the house by more than it costs; the reason is that the investment will increase the value of her equity by less than $50,000 if there is a possibility that she might end up underwater. In this case the investment will benefit Kate's creditors rather than Kate. Kate might also be tempted to take a second mortgage, increasing the likelihood that she will default. Similarly, managers and shareholders may have reasons to resist taking actions to make banks safer, and they may even try to take additional risk at the expense of their creditors—and of society.[51]

Why do creditors agree to lend to banks under such circumstances? One answer is that at least some of them are insured and have nothing to worry about. This is the case of depositors whose claims are covered by deposit insurance. Insured creditors have no reason to monitor what a bank does and how much risk it takes. Since the introduction of deposit insurance, deposits have actually been a rather stable source of funding for banks.

Another reason creditors lend under such circumstances is that they believe they can protect themselves by providing only short-term loans. Providing short-term loans enables creditors to react quickly to bad news about a bank by withdrawing their funding. By providing only short-term loans, creditors also protect themselves against the bank's issuing new debt that might have priority over their claims.[52]

Bank borrowing involves a kind of rat race in which every creditor tries to make sure that he will be repaid before the others.[53] One way to do this is to lend for very brief periods only—for example, overnight. The maturity transformation that banks engage in, which involves using deposits and short-term debt to fund longer-term investments, is at least partly a result of this rat race. People lend to banks through deposits and other types of money-like debt not only because this is convenient but also because they want to make sure they have priority over all other creditors. Repeated overnight lending that must be renewed every day gives creditors a sense of being in control.

Creditors have an enhanced sense of control and protection if a bank puts up collateral—that is, if the bank assigns assets to a debt that creditors can take over if the debt is not paid. In the past decade, borrowing with the use of collateral has increasingly taken the form of so-called repo agreements, where *repo* stands for *repurchase.*

Legally, a repo agreement is not a loan contract with a borrower and a lender but rather an agreement in which the borrower sells the collateral to the lender, that is, to the party that provides the money, and at the same time agrees to repurchase the collateral at a specified price in the future, often the next day. The legal treatment of this arrangement as a sale and repurchase rather than a loan effectively allows the creditor to sidestep bankruptcy proceedings that might freeze the borrower's assets. Should the borrower go into bankruptcy and fail to repurchase the asset as promised, the lender just keeps the collateral, which legally is his own.[54]

Like the shortening of debt maturities, the use of repo agreements is a device by which new creditors can jump ahead of previous creditors and make sure they are paid even in the event of a bankruptcy.[55] The assets that are used as collateral become unavailable to pay a bank's other debts. Many derivatives contracts are similarly protected by collateral and therefore benefit from this type of exemption as well. Even if the bank is distressed or insolvent, it can continue to borrow in this fashion and keep posting collateral, reducing the assets available to the deposit insurer and other creditors if the bank fails.

Some have argued that short-term debt is useful and efficient for banks because it provides discipline to bank managers; managers are said to act in the interest of investors for fear of a run.[56] However, it is abundantly clear that in the run-up to the financial crisis of 2007–2009, short-term debt did not discipline bankers. As long as they had collateral for repo and other kinds of short-term borrowing, bankers could borrow and invest as they wished, and lenders did nothing to discipline them. The breakdowns of Bear Stearns and Lehman Brothers were precipitated when creditors had doubts about the quality of the collateral as well as the viability of these banks.[57] In the context of the policy debate, the notion that short-term debt disciplines managers is yet another article of the bankers' new clothes.

When short-term creditors at last withdrew funding and markets froze in the several crisis episodes in 2007 and 2008, much of the overexpansion of the system had already occurred, and it was too late to change much. By then the strategies bankers had chosen had led to concerns with banks' solvency and with the quality of the supposedly safe and liquid mortgage-related securities that they created and held.

The effects of debt overhang and the rat race of borrowing are further strengthened by government guarantees and the subsidies given to bank borrowing that were discussed in Chapter 9. Guarantees and subsidies lower the costs and the burden of borrowing to banks and remove incentives for creditors to monitor the banks. As a result, banks experience the burden of borrowing differently from other firms. In particular, they do not experience the reluctance of creditors to lend to highly indebted borrowers and the costs and constraints that usually accompany such borrowing, which induce other corporations to avoid becoming so highly indebted. Bankers respond to the opportunity to borrow by borrowing as much as they possibly can. In so doing, they impose costs and risks on taxpayers and the public.

Excessive "Debt Production": Far from Efficient

Why do banks borrow as much as they do and rely so much on short-term borrowing? The reason is *not* that banks must economize on equity in order to be banks. Although some of the business of banking, such as deposits, involves short-term borrowing, there is nothing to prevent banks from increasing their reliance on equity. Doing so would not reduce the benefits they provide to the economy. To the contrary, as we noted, banks with more equity are even better placed to make loans and to create money-like assets, and they have better incentives to make loans to creditworthy businesses and individuals.

Equity is not scarce for viable businesses and corporations. This is as true for banks as for other businesses. Banks can raise their equity levels internally, as most corporations do before they seek any new funding from debt or equity, by retaining their profits. Banks also have access to the same investor community that provides equity funding for other companies. In the case of banks whose shares are traded on an exchange, these investors include mutual funds, pension funds, and individual investors.

Banking experts and others often imply that banks are special because they make long-term investments using short-term funding. This refers to the textbook notion of maturity transformation discussed earlier, in which short-term deposits are used to fund long-term loans. However, making long-term investments is common elsewhere, and this does not by itself make banks special. For example, many pharmaceutical companies invest in projects for developing new medicines that take decades to become marketable. These investments are obviously very risky. For this very reason, companies that make long-term investments tend to fund those investments with a lot of equity. They want to avoid the dark side of borrowing.

By contrast, banks are less concerned with the dark side of all their borrowing. They do not want to use more equity and become safer. They prefer to live on the edge, with borrowing that magnifies the upside of their investments, leaving the downside risk to others, later. This behavior has little to do with the benefits banks can bring to the economy; rather it has to do with the way bankers are paid, with the guarantees and subsidies that their borrowing confers, and with their ability to borrow repeatedly using collateral. It satisfies the banks' addiction to borrowing but is far from efficient.

The past four chapters exposed all the arguments made against much higher equity requirements as false or flawed. Society would, in fact, benefit greatly, and the financial system would be able to serve the economy even better, if banks and other financial institutions were much less fragile than the current and proposed regulations allow. Is it possible to transition from the unhealthy and dangerous system we have to a safer and healthier one? Can we maintain a thriving and more stable banking system that supports the economy consistently? The answer to both questions is "Yes." The next chapter explains how.

PART THREE

Moving Forward

ELEVEN

If Not Now, When?

Time . . . has a trick of getting rotten before it is ripe.
Francis M. Cornford (1874–1943), English classical
scholar, Microcosmographia Academica, 1908

W E HAVE ARGUED that if banks have much more equity, the financial system will be safer, healthier, and less distorted. From society's perspective, the benefits are large and the costs are hard to find; there are virtually no trade-offs. Yet the claim is often made that this reform would be costly to realize in practice. Banks are said to be unable to raise equity by issuing new shares, implying that higher equity requirements would reduce bank lending. Reduced lending, it is claimed, would hurt the economy, which has yet to recover fully from the sharp downturn in 2008.[1]

Because of such concerns, Basel III, the new international agreement on requirements for bank equity, has a long transition period, until 2019.[2] The slow transition was intended to avoid abrupt shocks from the new regulations. However, this meant that the insufficiency of bank equity was not dealt with right away. The resulting solvency concerns contributed greatly to financial turbulence in 2011.

It is actually best for the financial system and for the economy if problems in banking are addressed speedily and forcefully. If bank equity is low, it is important to rebuild that equity quickly. It is also important to recognize hidden insolvencies and to close zombie banks. If handled properly, the quick strengthening of banks is possible and beneficial, and the unintended consequences are much less costly than the unintended consequences of delay. This is true even if the economy is hurting.

The long transition period is not the only flaw of Basel III. Other flaws are the very low level of equity that is still permitted and the complexity of the regulation. Regulations that attempt to fine-tune equity requirements using quantitative risk models and stress tests can be easily manipulated. Flawed regulation has caused excessive fragility in the past; it has diverted banks away from making loans to small- and medium-sized enterprises and toward investing in tradable assets. Basel III maintains this flawed approach with hardly any change.

"Now Is Not the Time"

After the financial crisis of 2007–2009, the equity level of banks has not been much increased. Basel III, the international agreement designed to increase bank equity, has a transition period that will last until 2019. In 2011, the European government debt crisis raised serious concerns about the solvency of European banks. These concerns caused U.S. money market funds and other investors to stop lending to many European banks.[3] The loans were partly replaced by loans from central banks, but this did not reduce the solvency problems.[4] Because European banks were operating with little equity, they were correctly seen as being very vulnerable.

As we are writing this in October 2012, the European government debt crisis is still unresolved. The focus has moved from Greece and Greek government debt to Spain, Spanish banks, and the Spanish government.[5] The numbers involved and the risks for French and German banks are probably larger, but there seem to be fewer concerns about their solvency than there were in 2011 about the effects of a Greek default.

A major difference between 2012 and 2011 is that in the meantime European banks have been forced to increase their equity. This resulted from a decision made at the October 2011 summit of the leaders of the European Union.[6] The immediate aftermath of this decision seemed to confirm the view that equity requirements must be imposed judiciously, not when banks are in trouble and the economy is doing poorly.[7] However, the higher equity levels that banks had as a result of the requirements have contributed to the greater robustness of European banks in 2012.[8]

From the banks' perspective, the time is never ripe to increase equity requirements or to impose any other regulation. As for the regulators, when the industry is doing poorly, they worry that an increase in equity requirements might cause a credit crunch and harm the economy. When the industry is doing well, no one sees a need to do anything.[9] The discussion is governed by the "Principle of Unripe Time," as the English classicist Francis Cornford called it, the principle "that people should not do at the present moment what they think right at that moment, because the moment at which they think it right has not yet arrived."[10]

The Principle of Unripe Time is a bugbear. In banking, being scared by this bugbear can be very costly.[11] For example, in Japan in the 1990s, the authorities failed to force their banks to recognize losses from bad loans that they had made. There was a fear that doing so might show that the banks were insolvent and that this would disrupt the financial system. The banks continued to lend to bad borrowers while reducing their lending to new firms. As a result, economic growth was lacking. The denial of solvency problems and deferral of resolution in banking was a major reason the Japanese crisis lasted for more than a decade, with huge economic and social costs.[12]

In Chapter 3 we discussed the distorted and potentially dangerous behaviors of borrowers in distress and particularly those in hidden insolvency. The Japanese experience shows that these concerns are relevant to banks. Weak banks do not serve the economy. In lending they may continue to roll over loans to their existing distressed or insolvent clients and even provide them with additional funds in order to avoid having to acknowledge losses; this behavior hurts the economy by maintaining unsuccessful old firms and restricting funding for potential new firms. Distressed or insolvent banks also tend to take excessive risks to gamble for survival or for resurrection. Allowing weak or insolvent banks to continue operating—and especially supporting them with loans or loan guarantees—is costly and inefficient.[13]

When large banks and even an entire banking system are in trouble, politicians and supervisors fear that strict enforcement could cause a credit crunch and a recession.[14] They believe that the time is not ripe to resolve the problems. Instead they allow insolvent or highly distressed banks to continue operating, and, if necessary, they provide bailouts.[15] Research on banking crises, however, has shown that failing to deal with banking problems early and forcefully often results in more serious crises and in more severe credit crunches and recessions later.[16] Kicking the can down the road can be very expensive.

Sometimes the concern is not just about the distress or hidden insolvency of individual banks. Individual banks may run into problems because there are too many banks in the market. When there is too much capacity, competition can be very intense, and banks may find it difficult to earn the interest margins or the fees that they need in order to cover their costs. Although such a situation may please the banks' customers, at least for a while, it may endanger the financial system because banks may take undue risks in order to have a chance of surviving.[17] If excess capacity in banking is the underlying source of the problems, government or central bank support for the banks can perpetuate the problems by preventing the needed adjustments.[18]

The crisis of 2007–2009 and subsequent developments in Europe have weakened many banks. Although some of the banks' losses have been recognized and some banks have disappeared, there are many indications and a strong suspicion that many losses may still be hidden and that there still may be too much capacity in banking. Investors are therefore not willing to pay much for banks' shares, and banks' stock prices are relatively low. As discussed in Chapters 6 and 7, the fact that the stock market values of bank equity are significantly below the banks' reported book values is evidence of investors' being skeptical that losses have been fully acknowledged.[19]

In the United States, banks are making fewer new mortgages and not recognizing losses on existing loans.[20] This is similar to what happened in Japan in the 1990s. Yet authorities in Europe and the United States have been reluctant to address the continued weakness of many banks. The lessons from the past have not been learned.

Strengthen Banks Immediately!

The easiest way to increase the health and stability of the financial system is to ban banks from making cash payouts to shareholders and to require banks to retain their earnings until they have significantly more equity. This measure would bring immediate benefits and have no harmful side effects on the economy; it would strengthen banks most quickly and directly and would entail no "unintended consequences."

What will happen if banks do not pay their shareholders and retain their earnings for a while? If there are worthy loans to be made, the banks can make these loans using their retained earnings rather than by additional borrowing. Successful companies use retained earnings as a key source of funds for new investments. In fact, retained earnings are the most popular source of funding for corporations.[21] If banks find no worthy loans to make, they can use retained earnings to pay some of their debts or to invest in marketable securities that will earn appropriate returns. In all these cases, the banks' equity levels will increase without harming the banks' ability to make loans.

How will shareholders feel if banks retain their earnings and refrain from making payouts to the shareholders? Shareholders of companies that have little or no debt are happy if the money is invested productively, because the added value of the investments will be reflected in the value of their shares. Whatever the company does with its earnings, even if it invests in Treasury bills and awaits an opportunity to invest quickly in the future without needing to raise funds, shareholders are entitled to all of the profits, now and in the future, and the value of their shares will adjust to reflect the investments.[22] If the shares are traded on an exchange, shareholders who need cash can create homemade dividends by selling some of their shares.[23]

What about banks, which use debt to fund more than 90 percent of their assets? As we discussed in Chapter 3, once debt is in place, borrowers' attitudes toward risk in investment and additional borrowing are affected by the overhanging debt. Highly indebted borrowers tend to be biased toward taking more risk in investment and toward more borrowing. The presence of debt makes risk more palatable to a borrower because he benefits from the upside but shares the downside with his creditors, and possibly with others that provide insurance for creditors. This is a fundamental conflict of interest that is due to borrowing and is particularly strong when borrowing is heavy.

Because banks are heavily indebted, their actions affect not only their shareholders but also their depositors and other creditors, the deposit insurance fund, and the public. Payouts to shareholders are a way for banks to maintain or increase their indebtedness—an analog to the case, discussed in Chapter 3, of a borrower's (Kate in our example) taking a second mortgage to finance consumption or other investments.

Prohibiting payouts does lower the value of a bank's shares if the bank's solvency is questionable, and the ban on payouts makes the bank safer. In this case, some of the costs of a payout to shareholders are borne by creditors and possibly by the deposit insurance fund or the public, because the bank is more likely to fail if it makes the payouts. Conversely, if the debt is made safer, the benefits of a ban on payouts will accrue to creditors and possibly to the deposit insurance fund or the public. Moreover, society as a whole will benefit from a ban because, if the bank is safer, it will be in a better position to make good loans and provide other services.

When bankers make payouts to their shareholders rather than retaining the funds for investments or to pay debt, they effectively resist reducing their indebtedness and instead choose to maintain or increase it. Paying share-holders may keep shareholders happy for a while, but it harms society. As discussed in Chapter 8, managers might also take too much risk for which their shareholders are not sufficiently compensated. From the policy per-spective, there is no reason to allow banks to endanger the public by making payouts to shareholders. If a bank is sufficiently healthy that its debt is per-fectly safe even after making payouts to its shareholders, similar to that of companies with little or no debt, and there is no conflict of interest with cred-itors. As long as the debt is paid for sure, shareholders bear the upside and the downside of all investments.

If a bank is healthy enough so that shareholders bear the downside as well as the upside of all investments, they may not actually lose much when pay-outs are delayed. For the most part, when payouts to shareholders are made, the value of the equity declines by exactly the amount of the payouts; share-holders' total wealth is therefore independent of whether payouts are made. Therefore, as long as shareholders bear all the risks—and aside from the tax subsidies associated with debt (which we discussed in Chapter 9)—share-holders' wealth is not affected if payouts are prohibited.[24]

In 2007 and 2008, U.S. regulators allowed banks to make large dividend payments. They allowed this even after the subprime crisis broke into the open in August 2007.[25] The payouts weakened banks significantly. The amounts that the largest banks had paid to their shareholders were equal to about half of the funds that the government provided them subsequently through TARP. Had the banks not made those payouts, there would have been less need for government support in the fall of 2008.[26]

Since 2011 the Federal Reserve and authorities elsewhere have allowed most banks to make cash payments to shareholders even though banks are still weak and some of them have still not reached the level of equity required under Basel III. Profitable banks could reach Basel III equity levels much more quickly if they retained their earnings. It makes no sense to delay the implementation of Basel III on the grounds that banks need time to adjust and at the same time to allow payouts that make the adjustment slower. Allowing the payouts before the new equity levels have been reached benefits the banks and harms the public.[27]

Healthy banks do not need to wait for equity to be built internally by re-taining profits. Such banks can immediately become safer by raising new equity from investors, and regulators can require them to do so. New shares can be sold to existing shareholders (in a so-called rights offering) or offered to new shareholders.[28] Funds raised in this way can be used to make loans or other investments or to pay back debts.

Bank managers, and possibly shareholders, would resist a requirement that they issue new shares for the same reasons that they resist a ban on payouts—debt overhang and the potential loss of taxpayer subsidies. As noted earlier, however, none of these concerns relates to any cost to society.[29] It is legitimate to ask that more of the downside risk be borne by the banks' managers and shareholders than by creditors and taxpayers.

Requiring banks to reach a particular ratio of equity to assets may have harmful side effects if banks respond to this requirement by making fewer loans rather than increasing their equity levels through retained earnings or by issuing new shares.[30] A reduction in lending, however, can be prevented if, instead of a target ratio, the regulation specifies an amount of equity that must be reached.[31]

If a bank is unable to raise new equity because it has no profits to retain or cannot sell shares, there is reason to suspect that the bank is highly distressed or even insolvent.[32] In such a case, supervisors should step in, examine the loans and other assets one by one, and assess their values and the likelihood of future losses. Doing so is costly, but it is essential in order to avoid having dysfunctional zombie banks. Closing insolvent banks early is an important task for supervisors.[33]

When an entire banking system is affected, intervention is all the more important; once the assets have been assessed and investors are confident that the bad assets have been cleaned out, the remaining "good banks" can be sold on the market again, as happened in Sweden in the 1990s. As part of the cleanup, it may also be important to reduce the size of the banking sector.[34] If losses have been caused by too many banks' being engaged in reckless competition, then, as we discussed earlier, the underlying problems will not disappear unless the size of the banking sector is reduced.[35]

Beyond Basel: Increase Equity Requirements Substantially!

In addition to the unnecessarily long transition period, Basel III has two other major flaws. First, its equity requirements are far too low. Second, for the most part the required equity is related not to a bank's total assets but to what is called "risk-weighted assets," which are just a fraction of total assets. Basel III requires that banks have equity equal to at least 7 percent of their risk-weighted assets by January 1, 2019.[36]

It can make a great difference whether the 7 percent equity requirements relate to the total assets of a bank or to its risk-weighted assets. For example, the roughly €55 billion in equity that Deutsche Bank had on its reported balance sheet at the end of 2011 represented more than 14 percent of the bank's risk-weighted assets of €381 billion but only 2.5 percent of the bank's total assets of €2.2 trillion.[37] More generally, when a European bank proudly proclaims that it has 10 percent "core capital," we can safely bet that its equity is less than 5 percent of its total assets—quite likely only 2 or 3 percent.[38]

The idea behind risk weighting is that if the assets banks hold are less risky, less equity may be "needed" for a bank to be able to absorb potential losses. The simplest way to think about the notion of putting "risk weights" on different assets is to imagine that each of the assets of the bank has a separate equity requirement that depends on the risk of that asset. For example, because cash is not risky, banks are not required to back their holdings of cash with equity. A bank that has $1.8 trillion in loans and $200 billion in cash is required to have the same amount of equity as a bank that has just $1.8 trillion in loans.

The minimum required equity is also the same if a bank in the United States has $1.8 trillion in loans and $200 billion in U.S. government securities instead of cash. And in Europe, a bank that has €1.8 trillion in loans and €200 billion in Spanish or Greek government debt is not required to have more equity than a bank that has €1.8 trillion in loans and €200 billion in cash. The regulations presume that such government debt is as riskless as cash, but in Europe this presumption was proven wrong when Greece defaulted on its debt in March 2012.[39]

Whatever the merits of stating equity requirements relative to risk-weighted assets may be in theory, in practice many banks have used this feature of the "Basel approach" to reduce their equity to a very small fraction of their total assets. When equity is 2.5 percent of a bank's total assets, a 2.5 percent decline in the value of assets is enough to wipe out the equity and make the bank insolvent. Since 2007 several large banks have had this experience and become insolvent (Lehman Brothers, Washington Mutual) or would have become insolvent if they had not been bailed out with taxpayer money (UBS, Hypo Real Estate, Dexia). In some cases, the losses that wiped out the equity came from assets that had been considered as riskless as cash by regulators and therefore had not required any backing by equity at all.[40]

The United States never fully implemented Basel II, which had introduced the complex risk-weights system, for commercial banks, largely because Sheila Bair, chair of the FDIC at the time, believed that the Basel II approach to risk weights was problematic. This lack of implementation helped FDIC-insured banks to be stronger than European banks or U.S. investment banks regulated by the Securities and Exchange Commission, which allowed the use of risk weights.[41] In a major innovation, Basel III proposes to introduce regulation based on a so-called leverage ratio. This regulation will set a minimum level for equity relative to total assets. Basel III fixed this minimum level at 3 percent.[42]

If this number looks outrageously low, it is because the number *is* outrageously low. When the agreement was announced in September 2010, Martin Wolf's column in the *Financial Times* was appropriately titled "Basel:

The Mouse That Did Not Roar."[43] He sarcastically noted that the claim that the requirement triples the previous requirements "sounds tough, but only if one fails to realize that tripling almost nothing does not give one very much."

Banks' having 3 percent equity is akin to Kate's having $9,000 in equity and a mortgage of $291,000 funding a $300,000 house. As we have seen, if Kate borrows so much, a very small subsequent drop in the value of the house can put her mortgage underwater, with more owed than the house is worth. For banks, this type of situation means distress or insolvency.

If bank equity is as low as the regulation allows, we must be prepared to see recurrent bank failures and banking crises, with large costs to taxpayers and significant and lasting damage to the economy. At these low levels of equity, banks—and bank regulators—are gambling on their combined ability to properly assess risk weights and on the banks' ability to avoid losses that would bring distress or insolvency. The actual experience since 2007, however, shows that neither ability can be trusted. The required bank equity should be *much* higher than the 3 percent of total assets proposed in Basel III.

History provides some guidance. As discussed in Chapter 2, for much of the nineteenth century, when banks were partnerships whose owners were fully liable for their debts, it was common for banks to have equity on the order of 40 percent or even 50 percent of their total assets. Around 1900, 20–30 percent equity for banks was common in many countries. These equity levels were not mandated by any regulation. Rather, they emerged naturally in the markets in which the banks' owners and managers, depositors, and other investors interacted.

The decline that occurred subsequently in the twentieth century was closely related to governments' needs for finance in World War I and to the development and repeated extensions of the various safety nets by which governments support the banking industry, from explicit guarantees provided by deposit insurance to the bank bailouts and implicit guarantees for too-big-to-fail banks.[44] As discussed in Chapter 9, the ever-increasing safety nets that support banking have made it attractive and possible for banking institutions to "economize" on equity and increase their borrowing. Governance and control problems, discussed in Chapter 8, have also contributed to a decline in bank equity levels.

The notion that banks cannot be made much safer at their own expense is flawed. Banks and their creditors should be in a position in which public support and bailouts most likely will not be needed. Requiring that banks' equity be at least on the order of 20–30 percent of their total assets would make the financial system substantially safer and healthier. At such levels of equity, most banks would usually be able to cope on their own and require no more than occasional liquidity support.[45]

Because the use of deposits and other forms of short-term debt can give rise to inefficient runs, deposit insurance in the style of that offered by the FDIC benefits society. Central banks' occasionally providing liquidity support to sound banks can also be beneficial. However, the banks' safety net distorts the incentives of bankers and their creditors, inducing them to take or to tolerate excessive risks from borrowing and risky investments.

Requiring significantly more equity is the most straightforward way of counteracting these distortions; it simply asks banks to reduce the risk of becoming distressed and thereby harming others. Banks whose shares are traded on stock exchanges can do so by raising equity at market prices, determined in the same markets where other companies in the economy raise their funding. Regarding banks' economizing on equity at the expense of others, the Nobel laureate Merton Miller, whose attempt to discuss capital requirements with bankers was featured in Chapter 7, said, "I can't help smiling at complaints from bankers about their capital requirements, knowing that they have always imposed even stronger requirements on people in debt to them."[46]

Much higher equity requirements should be imposed on all institutions that offer banking services to the public, in particular services in connection with payments.[47] In addition, significant equity requirements should be imposed on other institutions that are systemically important in the sense that their distress, insolvency, or default could significantly destabilize and harm the system.[48]

Determining who should be subject to capital regulation requires regulators and supervisors to keep track of where risks build up in the system. As discussed in Chapter 6, hedge funds can become systemically important, and the crisis has shown that insurance companies should be watched as well.[49] Equity requirements for different types of institutions might differ. In some cases—for example, that of investment banks that can take uncontrollably large risks in securities trading and derivatives or that of institutions serving as central counterparties in derivatives trading—it might be appropriate to have particularly high equity requirements because the systemic risks that these institutions' activities create can be very large and because derivatives markets can be used to take and hide substantial risk.[50]

There is no legitimate reason for the proposed Basel III requirements to be so outrageously low. These requirements reflect the political impact that the banks have had on the policy debate and the flawed and misleading claims that are made in discussions about banking regulation—the bankers' new clothes.

Without proper evaluation of the social cost and benefits, the approach taken by regulators has been based on the misplaced notion that there are significant trade-offs for society associated with much higher equity levels for banks. The approach has been to require that banks have the minimum amount of equity to "get by," and no more. As we have shown in this book, however, the view that there are significant trade-offs is flawed. At current levels of bank borrowing, the purported trade-offs do not exist.

The research that has been offered in support of the proposed regulation understates the benefits and makes up fictional "costs" for substantially increasing equity requirements. For example, practically all of the studies that have been provided in support of Basel III assume that there is a cost to society when banks issue new equity, but these studies do not provide a satisfactory explanation of this assumption. In particular, the studies fail to take full account of the key distinction between the private costs of equity to banks and the costs to society.[51]

When analyzed more properly from society's perspective, the long-term benefits of much higher equity requirements are large, and the costs are hard to find.[52] There is therefore no reason whatsoever to economize on banks' equity to the extent that proposed regulations do. If the adjustment to higher equity levels is handled properly, the transition need not take long and need not have harmful side effects on bank lending.

Among the advantages to the stability of the financial system of banks' operating with much more equity is the fact that losses to banks' assets deplete equity much less intensely and thus do not require as much of an adjustment as when banks have less equity. A loss of 1 percent in the value of a bank's assets wipes out fully one-third of the bank's equity if it has only 3 percent of its assets in equity but reduces its equity by only 4 percent if the bank's equity represents 25 percent of its assets. If the bank wants to sell assets to restore the relation between equity and total assets or for other reasons following a loss, it must sell 32 percent of its assets if the initial equity was 3 percent of its assets but only 3 percent of its assets if the initial equity was 25 percent. The contagion effects of deleveraging through distressed sales after losses are much smaller if the initial equity is much higher.

Another important benefit to the system of requiring much greater bank equity would be that financial institutions would have more confidence in each other. Financial institutions routinely borrow from and lend to each other in order to smooth fluctuations in their funding that might be due to customers' transfers, withdrawals, and deposits. If banks had greater confidence in each other, this smoothing would be less vulnerable to disruptions and would work more efficiently.

Many have argued that the Basel III requirements are too low.[53] Even among advocates of higher equity requirements, however, few advocate levels as high as we do.[54] Most seem to take the equity levels of recent decades as a reference point. For several reasons, however, this is problematic. First, the equity levels of recent decades were artificially low because banks and their creditors had become used to the government safety net. Second, the increases in the intensity of competition in financial markets that we have seen since the 1970s have decreased the banks' ability to withstand shocks. Third, the high degree of interconnectedness in the system that has come with financial innovation and with globalization has magnified the potential fallout from the failure of a systemically important financial institution for the global economy. Moreover, institutions tend to be exposed to the same shocks and therefore run into trouble at the same time. All these concerns lead to the conclusion that the levels of equity banks have had in recent decades do not provide appropriate guidance as to what bank equity should be.[55]

Since 2010, when we became more outspoken about the need for an ambitious reform of capital regulation, we have engaged in many discussions on the subject, yet we have never received a coherent answer to the question of why banks should *not* have equity levels between 20 and 30 percent of their total assets.[56] (A caveat on providing specific ratios is that their meaning will depend on accounting conventions.)

Some would say that banks cannot raise so much equity. Such concerns are misplaced. First, as we emphasized, any bank that is profitable should be able to increase its equity by retaining its earnings. For 2012, for example, JPMorgan Chase has been planning to pay around $19 billion to its share-holders. If it retains this money instead, its equity will increase by this amount, roughly 10 percent of its book value, and a higher percentage of its market value.[57] If viable banks avoid making payouts to shareholders and raise new equity, the 20–30 percent range for equity relative to total assets should be achievable fairly quickly.

Second, when it comes to raising equity from investors, there is no dis-tinction between bank stocks and other stocks. All stocks are held by the same investors, who value them using the same criteria. New shares can be sold to investors at prices that are appropriate given investors' assessments of risks and returns. Diversified investors such as pension funds and mutual funds buy a broad mix of stocks, and there is nothing special or different about banks' stocks relative to other stocks.

Third, if banks have no profits that they can retain or if they cannot raise new equity, they may already be insolvent or they may not have viable busi-ness models. Such banks should be forced to leave the market, like other companies that do not have viable business models. It may be, in fact, that the current size of the entire banking sector is too large, and some downsiz-ing may be called for. If this is actually the case, using public support to main-tain existing institutions is highly inefficient.

Nobody knows what the proper size of an industry is. Finding this out is one use of a market system in which profitable firms thrive and nonviable firms are forced out. In banking, this market mechanism has been distorted by guarantees and bailouts, by excessively cheap borrowing, and by the artifi-cial prevention of bank failures. Higher equity requirements that impose greater liability on bank shareholders and that lower the value of the subsi-dies may lead the industry to shrink to a more appropriate size. Requiring more equity would reduce the distortions and allow markets to operate more successfully, benefiting the broader economy.

Beyond Basel: Abandon the Illusion of Fine-Tuning

As we stated earlier, Basel III specifies equity requirements for banks relative to their risk-weighted assets rather than their total assets. The leverage ratio approach, which specifies equity requirements relative to total assets, is considered a backstop to limit the excessive reduction of equity requirements by risk weights. There has been resistance even to the very lax leverage ratio requirement, however. Some of this resistance comes from institutions in the industry that would be directly affected even at a 3 percent equity level; some comes from regulators and others who like the sophistication of risk weighting.[58]

The risk-weighting approach gives the impression of being scientific; the risk of each of a bank's assets is measured "scientifically," and equity requirements are determined on the basis of these measurements. It may seem obvious that a rule based on science is better than a crude rule.[59]

Such reasoning has dominated the work of regulators from many countries who have been meeting in the Basel Committee for Banking Supervision.[60] The first international agreement, concluded in 1988, had only crude categories for distinguishing between assets according to their risks. Since then, regulators have been searching for the holy grail of the "right" risk weights. Basel II, concluded in 2004, was considered to be doing it properly, but the financial crisis showed that Basel II was flawed.[61] Basel III attempts to correct some of the flaws in Basel II, but it has not changed the overall approach.[62]

The risk-weighting approach is extremely complex and has many unintended consequences that harm the financial system. It allows banks to reduce their equity requirements by concentrating on investments that the regulation treats as safe. Banks might also use derivatives to shift the risks of their investments to others, and this can increase interconnectedness. An example would be a bank's purchase of credit default swaps in order to insure against the credit risk of debt securities held by the bank. As we saw in Chapter 5, such credit insurance served to justify treating mortgage-related securities as perfectly safe; it was also a source of systemic risk and played an important role in the government's decision to bail out AIG.

Banks have developed various techniques for "risk-weight optimization" that allow them to choose investments that are in fact riskier than the supervisors believe and have return prospects reflecting these risks so that, on average, returns are higher than the returns on investments that are in fact safer.[63]

In theory, risk weights are meant to adapt equity requirements to the risks of the banks' investments; in practice, the weights are determined by a mixture of politics, tradition, genuine and make-believe science, and the banks' self-interest. In this mixture, some important but real risks are completely overlooked.[64] For example, as mentioned earlier, a bank in the euro area need not use any equity when investing in euro-denominated Greek or German government debt if the investment is funded in euros. Within the euro area, such debts have been treated as riskless even after the Greek default of March 2012.[65]

Since the mid-1990s, banks have been allowed to use their own models to assess the risks of their investments.[66] Regulators allowed this because they realized that banks generally have better and more up-to-date information about these risks, as well as better techniques for evaluating them. Despite the obvious problems that the crisis exposed in the risk-weight approach, the pervasive view among regulators and many others—including politicians, banking experts, and much of the financial press—is that it is good to use "scientific" techniques to fine-tune risk measurements.

However, in the process of determining how best to measure risk, the purpose of regulation was lost. Regulators overlooked the fact that the banks' interests in measuring and managing risks are not the same as the public interest in having a safe financial system; the possibility that banks might use their control over risk models to manipulate risk measurement in their own interest was neglected. Regulators and others also neglected the implications of risk weighting for the banks' investment strategies.[67] Even when there are no manipulative intentions, there are reasons to believe that the risk-weighting approach might be fundamentally flawed.[68]

Basel II contributed greatly to the fragility of the global financial system in 2007–2009. Bank leverage was so high because, in the run-up to the crisis, many banks had used the right to compute equity requirements on the basis of their own risk models to economize on equity, treating risks as nonexistent if it served their interests.[69] Banks' investments had been concentrated in assets for which such manipulation of risk assessments was easy as opposed to assets for which such manipulation was difficult. This explains why so many funds went into mortgage-related securities as opposed to small-business lending.[70] The funds that went into mortgage-related securities ultimately served to finance the construction of many residential buildings that are now standing empty and rotting, an awful waste that was encouraged by the regulation.

In Chapter 5 we noted that the increased interconnectedness in the financial system was one reason that something as relatively small as the U.S. subprime crisis could upset the whole world. This interconnectedness was partly due to the Basel approach to computing equity requirements on the basis of risk weights. An example of this, which we have repeatedly mentioned, was the excessive use of credit default swaps to justify ignoring credit risk and having no concerns for the credit insurer's ability to pay.

Another example was the creation of multiple layers layers of securitization that was discussed in Chapter 5.[71] At each stage in this process, some poorly rated securities would be put into a package, new securities would be issued with claims depending on the returns of the securities in the package, and some of the new securities would be given the best possible credit rating, AAA, so that banks would be able to hold the securities with hardly any backing by equity.

All this was done because banks wanted investments that would not require them to have much equity and that would allow them to raise ROE with little concern for possible losses. By creating an artificial demand for AAA-rated securities, the regulation made it attractive to create such securities. Effectively, therefore, the regulation contributed to the complete breakdown of market discipline in mortgage lending and securitization and, later, to the complete breakdown of many markets. The buyers had no realistic way to find out what the credit risks were, and the sellers had no incentive to do so. The outbreak of the crisis in the summer of 2007 occurred when the riskiness of these securities was suddenly recognized and the supposedly extremely safe AAA ratings, which equated the risk of these securities to that of U.S. government debt, were replaced by much lower ratings.

The attempt to fine-tune equity regulation is based on an illusion. Besides the problems of corruption by politics and manipulation by the banks, the risks themselves are changing all the time, and even the banks lack the information necessary to measure them properly.[72] For example, the risks of counterparties' defaulting may change as the counterparties' positions change, as happened when AIG sold many more credit derivatives over time. The ability to convert assets into cash may suddenly change when investors realize that they know too little about these assets, as happened in the case of mortgage-related securities in 2007. Asset price risks may also change because other investors incur losses and have to engage in fire sales. Such developments could not be predicted in time on the basis of the information that the banks had. Given these limitations, it is dangerous to rely exclusively on the fine-tuning of risk measurements, no matter how "scientific" the quantitative risk models of banks are made out to be.[73]

Empirical research on the financial crisis has actually shown that a high ratio of equity relative to risk-weighted assets did not mean that a bank was safe. By contrast, a high ratio of equity relative to total assets, without risk weights, meant that the bank was in a better position to deal with the crisis.[74]

Despite the experiences of the financial crisis, trust in the fine-tuning of risk measurements on the basis of the banks' quantitative models has not disappeared. Except for the proposed introduction of the leverage ratio, Basel III provides little substantial change. Regulators and supervisors are also relying on models in the periodic stress tests they use to determine whether banks have "enough equity." Such tests have been carried out in the United States in 2009, 2011, and 2012 and in Europe in 2010 and 2011.[75]

Like the stress tests used in engineering or medicine, stress tests in banking are intended to check whether banks have enough equity to withstand some shocks, such as an economic recession leading to defaults of borrowers or a stock market decline. This approach, however, is no more scientific or trustworthy than the one used to fine-tune equity requirements.

Predictions of what would happen under the specified stress scenarios are based on models developed by banks and regulators. Stress tests, like risk measurements, are therefore subject to the limitation that something like the dynamics of contagion discussed in Chapter 5 is not captured in the models, and in fact there would not be enough data to do so. In addition, of course, the predictions are colored by the politics of how the stress tests are done and by the self-interest of banks, and possibly regulators, in constructing their models.

Given these limitations, it is hardly surprising that in 2010 as well as 2011, some European banks that had passed the stress tests with flying colors went into distress and had to be bailed out shortly afterward.[76]

"Anything but Equity"

In another misguided effort at fine-tuning that allows banks to cut corners, at times capital regulation treats some debts as if they were equity. For example, a bank might issue debt that gives investors the right to receive a fixed interest payment every year except for years in which the bank does not earn a profit. From the shareholders' perspective, such a claim is a kind of debt, because those who hold the security have priority over shareholders' receipt of dividends. Some regulations, however, say that this type of security is like equity because the bank is not required to make payments if it incurs a loss.

Under Basel II, many such hybrid securities (as they are called) were counted toward equity requirements even though they were not in fact equity. The notion was that investors in these securities would participate in losses just as shareholders do. In the bailouts of 2007–2009, however, government support saved the holders of these hybrid securities, along with depositors and other creditors, from losses.[77] Governments seem to have been afraid that if these hybrid securities were actually made to share in banks' losses, there might be another "Lehman event."[78]

The clear lesson is that only equity can be relied on to absorb losses in a crisis. The drafters of Basel III tried to apply that lesson, but, especially in Europe, bankers have been lobbying strongly to get other securities approved as equity-like.[79] Their approach can be called *anything but equity*. The search for anything but equity to absorb losses has recently focused on so-called contingent convertible bonds, often referred to as co cos, long-term bonds that can be converted to equity when some trigger event occurs.[80] The idea is that some creditors would be forced to become shareholders if the bank's equity were depleted by losses.

There are numerous complications with this approach and serious reasons to doubt that it would be effective or reliable. Should a bank come near one of the triggers meant to begin the conversion of some debt into equity, there might be turmoil, because the conversion would benefit some investors and harm others, and many participants, including the bank's managers, might take actions to influence whether the trigger was hit. Such actions might cause panic in the markets for these securities or for the bank's shares and impose significant losses on some investors.[81]

Co cos may be better at protecting the safety of the bank than simple debt. However, they are clearly less reliable than equity. There is no valid reason for non-equity alternatives to be considered instead of equity when using equity would be simpler and more effective in achieving the goals of a stable and healthy financial system.[82]

The effort to include anything but equity in capital requirements is entirely based on flawed claims.[83] It seems to reflect the flawed focus on ROE that we discussed in Chapter 8. As long as the equity-like security is not actually equity, it has the same effects as debt in calculating ROE. Bob Diamond, then CEO of Barclays, stated in April 2011, "Barclays is counting on being able to fund part of its capital requirements with new contingent convertible instruments, or co cos, which will not dilute ROE numbers."[84]

The attraction to non-equity securities may also reflect a concern for maintaining the tax subsidies associated with borrowing if such securities can be classified as debt for tax purposes.[85] However, this observation only suggests that a tax code that gives banks a penalty for equity and encourages debt or anything but equity is perverse and should be changed. Compromising financial stability to give banks a tax break makes no sense.

How to Make Equity Regulation Work

It is important to determine what laws and regulations should mandate, but what happens if they are violated? In principle, if a bank has too little equity, the supervisor must intervene and force the bank to increase its equity while threatening to take disciplinary action against the bank, including revoking its license and closing it down.

The threat of closing a bank may not be credible if the bank is large and highly interconnected with other banks. The supervisor may also be afraid that, if a bank is shown to have lost a lot, people may raise questions about its past supervision. Rather than close the bank, the supervisor may therefore prefer to overlook the bank's losses, allowing it to maintain delinquent loans on its books without acknowledging losses. As we've already discussed, this can be very dangerous and costly.

We must get away from the simple dichotomy of having enough versus not enough equity and more carefully consider what supervisors should do when a bank's equity is reduced. On this point, Basel III goes in the right direction. The 7 percent requirement that we mentioned has two components, an equity requirement of 4.5 percent and a so-called capital conservation buffer of 2.5 percent of risk-weighted assets. The idea is that if equity lies between 4.5 percent and 7 percent, a bank will be forced to retain its profits and avoid paying dividends so as to rebuild its equity internally, but it will not need to raise new equity right away.

This idea can be applied to equity requirements at the much higher and safer levels that we propose. For example, a requirement of equity in the amount of 20–30 percent of banks' total assets, as we suggested earlier, could be managed in such a way that banks would be expected to have at least 30 percent equity in good times. If banks incurred losses that reduced their equity below 30 percent but not below 20 percent, they would be instructed not to make payouts to shareholders but to rebuild their equity, at least by retaining earnings. Some payments, such as those to managers, might be made with new shares.[86] If banks' equity went below 20 percent, however, it would be appropriate to require them to rebuild their equity immediately, if necessary by issuing new shares.[87]

More generally, it makes sense to have a graduated system of equity requirements involving different responses of supervisors and banks depending on how little equity the banks actually have. In the United States, the Federal Deposit Insurance Corporation Improvement Act of 1991 provides for a graduated system of responses involving various "prompt corrective actions" depending on how serious a problem is. Extending this approach would allow us to get away from a regime in which infringements of regulatory requirements immediately raise the question of whether a bank should be closed.

The practical implications of specifying any ratios of equity relative to assets depend critically on the rules that determine which assets and liabilities are listed on a bank's balance sheet and how their values are determined. The principle here should be that any investment or commitment that exposes the bank to risk must be included. Investors and regulators must be able to evaluate the risks. For example, banks should not be allowed to keep entities off their balance sheets to which they are promising liquidity support or other guarantees. And derivative positions that might cause fragility should be included rather than netted and ignored.[88]

Equity ratios based on book values do not always indicate solvency concerns in a timely manner. Such ratios would not always have pointed to problems through the fall of 2008 because, as discussed in Chapter 6 and earlier in this chapter, they are not adjusted to losses in a timely manner and banks may be able to manipulate them.[89] Regulators should consider other information, such as stock prices and other market indicators, in trying to maintain the safety and soundness of the financial system. Any concerns about the buildup of risks should lead to prudent steps, such as a ban on payouts to shareholders, to prevent the depletion of equity. Maintaining sufficient equity using such tools can be a powerful way to make sure that we can rely on the financial system to support the economy.

Supervisors must keep in mind that their basic job is to protect the public. Concerns about the details of regulatory requirements, accounting rules, and other measurements must not divert attention away from this objective. If risk is said to disappear because it has been hedged, who has actually taken on this risk? Spreading risk or passing it on is beneficial only if the institutions that bear the risk are able to do so without problems. Otherwise the very shifting of risk that regulation encourages can harm the financial system and the economy.

Regulators should also be more concerned with risks of rare events. Dangers should not simply be neglected if they are expected to occur with a probability of less than 1 percent. If such events occur, the damage to the financial system and the economy can be great, and this possibility should be taken into account even if the probability is thought to be small.

It is useful to compare equity and other regulations meant to keep the banking system safe to speed limits and other rules for trucks carrying explosives or other chemicals on a highway through a settled area. Speed may be easier to measure than the equity levels of banks, but the key objectives of protecting the public are quite similar.

Trucking companies may argue that they have excellent drivers, and therefore the speed limit need be no lower than seventy miles per hour. They may also argue that their drivers can take care of themselves, and therefore no public regulation of rest breaks is needed. Lower speed limits or mandated rest breaks for drivers, they might also say, would make the transportation of goods by trucks more expensive and reduce economic growth. The response might be a debate on whether the trucking companies' risk models are taking adequate account of sudden side winds or of ice on the road, but after the first disaster authorities would likely conclude that protecting people might be more important than fine-tuning the regulations.

The same considerations that apply to trucks, airplanes, or nuclear reactors should apply to banks. Public safety must be the focus. A remarkable difference, however, between much higher equity requirements and safety measures in many other contexts is that high equity requirements are such an incredible bargain to society: the significant benefits of much more equity are actually free!

If truck drivers had to drive more slowly or stop for thirty minutes every two hours and could not drive at night, they would drive fewer miles each day, and this might increase the cost of transportation. By contrast, increasing equity requirements from 3 percent to 25 percent of banks' total assets would involve only a reshuffling of financial claims in the economy to create a better and safer financial system. There would be no cost to society whatsoever.[90]

Why has banking regulation failed so miserably, and why, despite the crisis, hasn't it been fixed? The answer has much to do with the politics of banking, where invalid claims are often successful with conflicted regulators and politicians. We take up the political issues in the final two chapters of the book.

TWELVE

The Politics of Banking

"The king is naked!"—but under such splendid robes.
Stanislaw Jerzy Lec (1909–1966), Polish aphorist, Unkempt Thoughts

W
E OPENED CHAPTER 1 by quoting French President Nicolas Sarkozy angrily chastising U.S. bankers who had lost their "common sense." From that quote one might assume that French banks are so tightly supervised that French bankers do not have a chance to lose their common sense.

In fact, French banks have been a major focus of concern in the European crisis. Throughout, they have had very little equity and a lot of short-term funding, in particular from U.S. money market funds. In 2011 the money market funds were worried about the sovereign debt crisis in Europe and withdrew their money. Without liquidity support from the European Central Bank (ECB), French and European banks would have been in serious trouble.[1]

Funding from the ECB could provide liquidity support, but this was not enough for the Belgian-French bank Dexia.[2] This bank had already been bailed out with a taxpayer investment of €6.4 billion in 2008. By the end of 2010, Dexia's equity amounted to €11 billion, less than 2 percent of its assets. Over the first nine months of 2011 this equity was further depleted, and nothing was left to absorb additional losses on Greek debt in October 2011. The bank had to be bailed out again; in the process, the Belgian and French parts were split up, and each was nationalized.[3]

Less than two months before Dexia was nationalized, the executive director of the International Monetary Fund, Christine Lagarde, had warned that European banks were very weak and needed more equity.[4] Christian Noyer, the governor of the Bank of France, who is also responsible for financial supervision, commented: "Perhaps she was very badly informed by her staff."

Similarly, the French finance minister saw no reason "to question or worry about the French banking system." Earlier Mr. Noyer had warned against "excessive capital cushions" and insisted that the French banks' holdings of Greek debt were not a reason for particular concern.[5]

In international negotiations about the reform of banking regulation over the past few years, France has consistently opposed any tightening of regulation. In Chapter 11 we referred to the characterization of Basel III as "The Mouse That Did Not Roar" in the title of Martin Wolf's column in the *Financial Times*. The watering down of regulatory reform was largely due to the efforts of France, Germany, and Japan.[6]

Many politicians exhibit a remarkable discrepancy between speech and action. In public speech they are often critical of banks, but they do little to curb the risks that banks impose on taxpayers. Yet the French and German politicians who resist tighter regulation should know from their own experiences that bank bailouts are very expensive.[7]

Politicians, regulators, supervisors, and others often align themselves with bankers because they want to promote their countries' banks' interests in international competition. In international negotiations they fight for their countries' banks even if the rules they fight for might endanger financial stability.[8] Complaints that new regulation might disadvantage their countries' banks in global competition have greater weight with them than concerns about the risks to which these banks are exposing the taxpayers.

Protectionist arguments appeal to nationalist instincts, but they are flawed. Promoting the global competitiveness of banks regardless of what it costs does not serve national interests. When banks succeed in global competition by imposing risks and costs on the rest of the economy and on taxpayers, this is actually harmful to society.

Another reason banks succeed in lobbying is that politicians and others see them as sources of funds rather than as sources of risks. Regulating banks can interfere with their provision of funds for favorite causes, including the government. The bankers' new clothes can provide a cover for ignoring risks when doing so is convenient.

Bankers take advantage of this situation. Politicians in government might be thinking about "their" banks, but the bankers, in turn, are thinking about "their" governments. Given their expertise and their control over money, bankers are in a strong position to influence public discussion as well as the decisions of politicians and regulators, affecting public policy in their interest. The phenomenon of "regulatory capture," by which politicians and regulators are taken in by those they regulate, appears in most regulated industries, but it is particularly striking in banking and finance.[9]

Because different countries have different institutions and traditions, the politics of banking and banking regulation differs from country to country.[10] However, beneath the differences there are some important common undercurrents.

"Global Competition Needs Level Playing Fields"

Representatives of banks and other industries often complain that government regulation unfairly harms their ability to compete with firms in other countries—and they make the argument expressed in the heading of this section. For example, Jamie Dimon, CEO of JPMorgan Chase, called Basel III "anti-American."[11] According to him, Basel III is biased in favor of European institutions and might lead to Asian banks' taking some of the U.S. market share. Similarly, French banks complained that the new rules do not take account of the special situation of their bank and insurance conglomerates, and German public banks thought the new rules were biased against them.[12]

Public officials often sing the same songs. When criticized for watering down Basel III in response to French and German lobbying, Michel Barnier, the European commissioner for Internal Markets and Services, who is in charge of financial regulation, complained that the United States was slow to adopt Basel III, had not even fully adopted the previous Basel II agreement, and had gone back on a G20 agreement to limit incentives for bankers' risk taking.[13] The U.S. Treasury responded by emphasizing that the regulation of derivatives trading is more advanced and more stringent in the United States than in Europe.[14]

In this blame game, everyone is calling for level playing fields, and everyone is blaming others for giving special privileges to their own banks. Bankers and their lobbyists say that for the sake of fairness, all banks must be subject to the same rules. In fact, they complain about unfairness in order to fight rules that they dislike, trying to gain advantages for themselves. As a result of their success, international coordination of banking regulation has tended to reduce regulation to the lowest common denominator.[15]

In sports, competitors often complain about rules and about umpires' being biased in favor of others. The home media join in, knowing that their audience is rooting for the home team. The global economy, however, is not a sporting event. In the Olympic Games, the competitions in different events are separate, and a country may hope that its athletes will do well or even win medals in all competitions. In the global economy, however, different industries are interrelated, and it is not possible for a country to win the competition in all industries at the same time.

The economy is a system of production, exchange, and consumption. Businesses employ people and buy other inputs to produce goods and services that they can sell to other businesses and to individuals.[16] They use the revenues from their sales to pay their employees and the suppliers of other inputs; any surplus is available to the owners of the business. Employees and owners of firms can use the income they earn for consumption, for purchases, or for productive investments in assets.

In this system, businesses and individuals specialize in certain activities and do not try to provide everything for themselves. They buy things they do not provide for themselves from someone else. The division of labor, whereby different people do different things and trade, is beneficial because, by specializing in activities they are good at, people and firms contribute to making the economy more productive.

Specializing and doing something well necessarily means not being as good at other things, and nobody is the worse for it. For example, doctors specialize in medical practice, and they are happy to get their strawberries from a farmer or from a supermarket that might have acquired them from farmers in California or Israel.

This logic also applies in international trade. Politicians sometimes talk about countries' being in competition with each other. This is a flawed argument, an article of the bankers' new clothes. If financial institutions in the United Kingdom or Switzerland have leading positions in global financial markets, their successes are directly related to the inability of their countries' firms to compete in other activities. Just as doctors use the fees they earn for medical treatments to pay for strawberries, so do the United Kingdom and Switzerland use their revenues from selling financial services worldwide to buy computers in the United States or wine in France. In fact, these purchases are made not by the United Kingdom or Switzerland but by people and firms in these countries, who may be paid for working in the financial industry.

Banks in a country are not just competing with banks in other countries. They are also competing with other industries in their own country. Most importantly, they are competing for people, particularly those with scarce talents, whom firms in other industries would also like to hire. If the financial industry can offer high salaries and interesting careers, it is more likely to draw highly qualified people—at the expense of industries that cannot make competitive offers. If the other industries cannot afford to pay high enough salaries, they do less well in competing for people. Consequently, they may not do as well in selling their products or services, either locally or globally.

Switzerland and Iceland illustrate how the success of banks comes at the expense of other industries. A hundred years ago, tourism in Switzerland benefited from cheap labor in the remote mountain regions. Nowadays this cheap labor is no longer available because people can easily move to the cities and get high-paying jobs in the financial industry. The success of the financial industry (and some others) has come at the expense of the tourism industry. Similarly, the rise of the financial sector in Iceland during the decade before 2008 drew people into banking out of other activities such as agriculture, fishing, and tourism.[17]

For a country as a whole—or, more precisely, for the people in the country —the important question is not whether the country's banks or car producers are successful in the global economy. The important question is whether resources, most importantly people, find their most productive uses.

For example, modern banks employ mathematicians and physicists to run their mathematical risk models. The physicists who work for banks are not available for work in other industries—for example, for developing nanotechnology or electricity-powered cars that would reduce our dependence on oil. Do we know that these physicists are better employed in running risk models for banks than in developing nanotechnology? And might some of those smart people in investment banking be more productive in developing new software?

Nobody can answer such questions directly. An indirect way to find out is to see which firms win in competing for people. If markets work well, the firms that make best use of them will best be able to attract talented people. Success in selling their products and success in attracting people go together; good revenues from sales enable firms to pay good wages. Unless the market system is distorted, a firm's success in its markets is a sign that the firm's use of the talent and other resources it acquires is good for the overall economy.[18]

Markets can be distorted, however. When firms do not bear the full costs of their activities and rely on others to pay some of the costs, too many resources may go into the activities whose costs the firms are not fully taking into account. In this case, the market outcome may not be efficient. An example is a company that pollutes a river and does not pay for the damage that the pollution imposes on people and firms downstream. The company may be a world leader in its markets, but if its products are cheap because the costs of its pollution are borne by others, such success is not beneficial to society.

This conclusion also holds if the activity imposes risks on others. Examples would be chemical products that are cheap because of insufficient safety measures to prevent explosions, transportation that is cheap because a truck company saves on maintenance, and, in the same way, financial activities that involve a risk of a financial crisis. There is not much difference between banks engaging in risks that may blow up the financial system and trucks with explosive loads that may blow up a residential area.

In Iceland everyone paid dearly for the global successes of Icelandic banks prior to 2008. The financial crisis led to a sharp recession, a rise in unemployment, and a fall in wages. Inflation and the devaluation of the krona relative to other currencies eroded the purchasing power of people's savings. The costs of bailing out depositors stifled the government.[19] Ireland had a similar experience. As part of the Eurozone, however, Ireland could not devalue its currency, and the Irish government had to apply for assistance from European institutions.[20]

When markets are distorted, a government can try to correct the distortions by taxing activities that are harmful to others or subsidizing beneficial activities that the market does not reward sufficiently. Taxes and subsidies, however, can create their own distortions. Unless subsidies are needed to reward a firm for providing benefits to society for which they are not compensated by markets—for example, through research whose insights can also be used by others—subsidized firms are likely to have a disproportionate advantage in competing with firms from other countries or with firms from other industries that do not receive subsidies.

Subsidized firms are likely to attract too many resources and to be more successful than is good for society. This conclusion holds whether taxpayer money is spent to subsidize farming, steelmaking, or bank bailouts. It also holds if the subsidies support firms' successes in global markets.[21]

Implicit guarantees to large banks are especially problematic and perverse because they encourage excessive borrowing that increases the risk of costly financial instability. These are similar to corn subsidies in the United States that lower the cost of high-fructose corn syrup and thus indirectly increase the incidence of obesity-related diseases.[22] With banks there is the added concern that the subsidies have no natural bound. Too-big-to-fail policies encourage banks to become very large and complex and to make very large bets.

Whenever individuals or firms do not bear the full costs of their actions, it is important to correct the resulting distortions. Even if regulations reduce the ability of the affected institutions to compete in global markets, society may be better off. If banks are less successful in global markets, the available talent and other resources will be attracted by other industries. This may be better than exposing the economy and taxpayers to excessive risks.[23]

If the funding costs of banks increase because some of the subsidies to their borrowing are withdrawn and the banks increase the costs they charge on their loans, the effects are still likely to be beneficial. The subsidized rates may be inappropriately low. Large amounts of cheap lending to homeowners may seem good for a time, but they are inappropriate if the risks are too large. Societies worldwide would have been better off if banks had not lent so much to small firms in the late 1980s and to homeowners in the years before 2007.

The firms themselves, of course, suffer when they lose subsidies and can no longer impose some of their costs on others. In their lobbying, they do not mention this. Instead they appeal to economic nationalism and warn of a loss of competitiveness in the global economy—as if they were their country's entries into the global Olympics. Their argument is another article of the bankers' new clothes.

In the 1970s and 1980s, similar complaints were brought against environmental regulation designed to curb emissions from steel, textile, or chemical plants.[24] Since then, perhaps partly as a result of environmental regulations, many traditional steel and textile producers have disappeared.[25] The regions where these industries had been located suffered from the change, but the overall economy has prospered. Would anyone—with the possible exception of the people in the industry who had benefited from subsidies—wish to return to an economy with polluted rivers, darkened skies, and taxpayers subsidizing coal mines and steel mills that cannot pay for themselves?

Politicians and regulators, however, often fall for the rhetoric about global competition and the need for level playing fields, and they fight to make sure that international standards do not hurt their nation's banks. Others, even some who should know better, join in, not mentioning the cost to the public of helping the banks become successful.[26]

When the CEOs of major banks complain that a regulation would prevent them from winning in global competition, it takes courage and firmness on the part of a politician to assert that national interests are better served by subjecting bankers to certain constraints than by allowing banks to achieve success by taking risks that may harm the rest of the economy. The bankers' complaints are very audible, but the risks are invisible and seem abstract—until they actually materialize. When the risks materialize, the causes are so tangled together that it is difficult to assign responsibility. The bankers, politicians, and regulators involved are rarely held accountable or suffer significant consequences.[27]

It is not a coincidence that the United Kingdom, Sweden, and Switzerland have been most forceful in promoting stricter banking regulation in the international negotiations since the crisis. The financial sectors in these countries are especially large, and they have been hard hit by financial crises.[28] In other countries, politicians and the public seem to be less aware of how costly the successes of their countries' banks can be.

"Banks Are Where the Money Is"

There is a deeper reason for the reluctance of politicians to impose strict regulations to reduce the risk of banks. Banks deal with money.[29] Money is an object of desire and a source of power. Almost anyone has views on how banks should use their money.

When politicians want banks to fund something they like, reducing risks in banking becomes less important to them. Those running the government may even believe that the primary job of banks is to fund the government. Regulations that reduce banks' desire to take risks will therefore seem counterproductive. A regulation that requires the banks to fund the government will seem much more convenient. So will a regulation that requires or encourages the banks to fund anything else that politicians consider desirable, such as homeownership.

The history of banking regulation is full of rules directing banks to fund activities to which the political system wants to give preference, most importantly the government itself. A typical example is a requirement that banks hold large reserves with the central bank. If the interest rate on these reserves is zero, the requirement forces banks to give a large interest-free loan to the central bank and, indirectly, to the government.

This kind of regulation played an important role in some European countries before 1990. Ostensibly, the regulations were intended to make banks safer by avoiding risky private loans. In fact, they made for easier funding of government deficits. Because lending to private borrowers was restricted, the interest that banks charged on loans to businesses and individuals was quite high. This reduced investment and growth.[30]

Most of these regulations in Europe were dismantled when the European Union required its members to open their markets for banking services. As banks were subjected to competition with banks from other countries, such regulations became unsustainable and might have endangered financial stability if they had been maintained.

As mentioned in the previous chapter, banking regulation still favors banks' lending to the government. It allows banks to ignore the risk of government default even when it exists. In the government debt crisis, pressures on banks to fund their own governments have again increased so that, for example, Greek banks were hardest hit by the Greek default in March 2012.[31]

If U.S. banks lend to the U.S. government, treating such lending as riskless might be justified on the grounds that the government can effectively print the money that it owes.[32] In the Eurozone, the situation is different. When the government of Greece or Germany borrows and promises to make payments in euros, the situation is similar to that if the government of Mexico or New York City borrows and promises to pay in U.S. dollars. Just as the governments of Mexico and New York City cannot print dollars, so the governments of Germany and Greece cannot print euros.[33]

In the euro area, the creation of money is the responsibility of the ECB, which is independent of the different member states and is in fact forbidden by law from lending to governments. When governments owe euros, there is no assurance that they can pay their debts.[34]

Nevertheless, European banking regulation treats the euro-denominated debt of Eurozone governments as perfectly safe.[35] Banks can fund these loans entirely with borrowed money. The Belgian-French bank Dexia that was mentioned earlier had in fact used this rule to acquire a lot of government debt with very little equity.[36] When it became clear that Greece would default on its debt, Dexia was brought down and many other banks in Europe were sorely strained. Even so, no change in the regulation is in sight.

When regulations are designed to give preference to government debt, banks are more willing to lend to the government. This is convenient for governments, so they are reluctant to change the regulation. If at some point the taxpayers have to pay for a bailout, voters will not be able to identify who was responsible. Nor will they understand the connection if the bailout cripples the government's finances and everyone is affected by austerity policies. In many cases, the responsible politicians actually leave office before the risks from their policies materialize.

Banks and governments have always had a symbiotic relationship. Since the beginnings of modern banking in medieval Italy, lending to governments has been a key activity of banks. It is easy to make large loans to governments, and they can be very profitable—until the governments default on them. Historically, governments failing to pay their debts have been the most important causes of banking crises.[37]

Other regulations have also been motivated by the idea that banks are sources of money. For example, as discussed in Chapter 6, before the deregulation of the 1980s, savings institutions in many states of the United States were required to restrict their mortgage lending to properties located inside their states. The argument was that lending close to home is particularly safe, but in fact such rules prevented the savings banks from diversifying their investments and left them vulnerable to the specific risks of the states in which they were located. Politically, such rules were motivated by a desire to provide home buyers in the states with cheap credit rather than a desire to make the savings institutions safe.

For politicians such rules have the advantage that the costs of directing banks to specific investments do not appear in the government budget—until the banks get into trouble. At that point, again, voters are unlikely to make the connection between the banks' troubles and the regulations or the political interventions.[38]

The view of banks as sources of funds for politically desired purposes pervades the treatment of banks, particularly state-owned banks, in Europe. In Germany, public banks have long played a major role. Until 2005 these banks were guaranteed by the government and could borrow very cheaply. Even so, the Landesbanken, public banks at the regional level, were not profitable.[39] Since their creation in the 1970s, hardly a decade has passed without a multibillion scandal associated with one or several of these banks. Their lack of profitability has reflected both a lack of competence and an involvement in the flawed industrial policies of the regional governments.

In the financial crisis, the Landesbanken were among the hardest-hit institutions, requiring many billions of euros of taxpayer money. Despite this, the political authorities in charge have been unwilling to wind them down.[40] To a politician, the power to move a few million euros by a mere phone call, without having to go through parliamentary procedures, is worth every euro of taxpayer money. This is why excess capacities have been a permanent source of instability in the German financial system.[41]

France is another example of where banks are regarded as public institutions.[42] After the election of 1981, French banks were nationalized and their CEOs were appointed by the government. Subsequently the banks were privatized again, but their CEOs still come from the same group of "Enarques," former students of the elite École Nationale d'Administration (ENA).[43] The CEOs have made their careers in government, usually the Ministry of Finance, and at some point switched into banking.

A typical example can be seen in the career of Pierre Mariani, who spent about thirteen years in various ministries, culminating in the position of director of the cabinet of the budget minister, Nicolas Sarkozy, in 1993–1995. Mr. Mariani then moved into the financial sector, where he worked with BNP Paribas before being appointed CEO of Dexia after the first government bailout of the bank in 2009, under President Nicolas Sarkozy.[44]

The resistance of France and Germany to tighter banking regulation is partly explained by the role of the Landesbanken in Germany and by the networking of the French *Enarques*. The Landesbanken cannot raise equity in the stock market, and their public owners prefer not to put in additional money if they can help it. Giving up control, however, is out of the question. Similarly, the *Enarques'* network of politicians, bankers, and bureaucrats in France does not want to subject the banks to the control of market investors.[45]

Regulatory Capture

Although they can put in place any laws and regulations that they see fit, politicians are not in the driver's seat in their relation with banks. Bankers know more about banking than politicians. Moreover, politicians want the bankers' cooperation to make the investments the politicians favor—or campaign contributions.[46] When bankers warn that capital requirements will hurt bank lending and reduce economic growth, they are rarely challenged by politicians, not only because politicians do not see through the banks' claims but also because they do not want to upset their symbiosis with bankers.[47] Bankers and politicians have a two-way dependence. In this situation, politicians can forget their responsibilities, and the political system fails to protect the economy from banking risk. Even after the financial crisis, as one politician admitted, the banks "own the place."[48]

The three decades leading to the financial crisis of 2007–2009 were marked by enormous growth in the financial sectors of the United States and Europe. Banks and financial firms convinced politicians and regulators that tight regulations are not needed because markets work well enough. Bankers gained prestige and wealth, and their political influence increased. An anti-regulation ideology helped as well.[49]

Prior to the financial crisis, regulators failed to set proper rules and supervisors failed to enforce the rules in place so as to prevent the reckless behavior of bankers.[50] In the United States, for example, Alan Greenspan (chairman of the Federal Reserve), Arthur Levitt (chairman of the Securities and Exchange Commission [SEC]), and Robert Rubin (Treasury secretary) prevented an initiative in 1998–2000 that would have imposed more transparency on derivatives markets. Such transparency was sorely missing in the run-up to the financial crisis.[51] A 2004 ruling of the SEC allowed U.S. investment banks to determine their regulatory capital on the basis of their own risk assessments, and this enabled Lehman Brothers and other investment banks to become highly indebted and vulnerable.[52] The United Kingdom also instituted so-called light-touch regulation in order to expand its role as a major financial center.[53]

An important factor underlying the financial crisis of 2007–2009 has been the failure of regulators and supervisors in the United States and in Europe to set and enforce proper rules to prevent the reckless behavior of bankers.[54] Supervisors in the United States and Europe allowed banks to circumvent capital requirements by creating various entities that did not appear on the banks' balance sheets. Investors were willing to lend to these entities because the sponsoring banks were providing guarantees. The supervisors did not object to banks' keeping these exposures off their balance sheets, nor did they try to limit the banks' obligations from the guarantees. The obligations ended up greatly weakening the sponsoring banks and bankrupting some of them when the crisis broke in the summer of 2007.[55]

What causes regulatory capture? First, regulating and supervising an industry requires some expertise. This expertise is best found among people in the industry. Regulators and supervisors therefore tend to have significant numbers of recruits from the industry. If these people are competent, they may eventually be hired back by the industry. In such a revolving-door situation, a regulator may start out with some sympathy for the bank that he or she has just left.[56] Also, regulators may not want to be tough on banks from which they hope to receive job offers in the future.

In the United States, bankers serve on the boards of the regional Federal Reserve banks, which are in charge of supervising banks and even in setting the regulations. For example, Jamie Dimon, CEO of JPMorgan Chase, has been on the board of the Federal Reserve Bank of New York since 2007 and will serve through 2012, even as the New York Fed is directly involved in formulating and enforcing capital regulations and other policies impacting JPMorgan Chase and other banks.[57] This situation can create significant conflicts of interest.[58]

Second, regulators exhibit what is known in sports as the home-team bias of referees, the subconscious sympathy of referees for the team that is cheered by the home crowd.[59] If the crowd of onlookers, such as segments of the press, politicians, and industry specialists, favor certain people and institutions, supervisors may become biased and favor them as well. The home-team bias is particularly strong if the affected firms claim that a regulation unfairly damages their ability to compete with away teams, firms in other countries.

In this context, it is important to realize that special interests tend to be much more vocal than the general public. As regulation matters greatly to them, so they invest heavily in lobbying. To any individual without a special interest, the regulation may seem too unimportant to warrant much of an investment of attention or energy. Even if, in the aggregate proper enforcement of the regulation would be called for, because so many people are affected, special interests that fight the regulation may have much more influence.[60]

Third, firms in the industry influence politicians and administrators by lobbying and by providing money, particularly for election campaigns. Firms in regulated industries want to make sure that appointees to regulatory positions will not be too challenging. Top bankers and politicians interact in many informal ways as well. For example, Jamie Dimon cultivates his relations with high-level government officials and has stated that JPMorgan Chase gets "a good return on the company's 'seventh line of business'— government relations."[61] If a regulatory agency is zealous in trying to control the industry, the legislature can cut the agency's budget to restrain the zeal.[62]

In other industries, the effects of regulatory capture might be weakened by resistance from the firms' clients and competitors, the public, and politicians.[63] For example, safety standards that would allow a risk of plane crashes would not be tolerated for long.[64] The harm is evident, and it is easy to trace damage back to negligence and recklessness.

In banking, however, the damage from ineffective regulation and supervision is harder to detect. Moreover, for the reasons we discussed earlier, politicians may find it quite appropriate or convenient for regulators and supervisors to be lax toward banks. The public is dispersed and disorganized, and other individuals and firms have little to gain individually from pushing banking reform.[65] Everyone has dealings with banks, and many find it beneficial or necessary to maintain their good relationships with the banks. In this environment, confusing and flawed arguments—the bankers' new clothes— are more likely to affect policy.

This situation can change only with significant pressure from the public. Nonprofit citizens' and public-interest groups try to provide a counterweight to lobbying by industry groups, but their resources can hardly compete with those of the financial industry, and they often find it difficult to gain access to politicians and regulators.[66]

An interesting comparison can be made with the Japanese authorities that were in charge of supervising the Tokyo Electric Power Company (TEPCO) before the earthquake and tsunami on March 11, 2011. According to the parliamentary committee investigating the nuclear disaster at the Fukushima Daiichi Nuclear Power Plant after those events, the disaster could have been avoided if the supervisor had been more diligent in imposing safety rules and the company had been more forthcoming in complying.

In what the report on the nuclear disaster calls a "culture of complacency," the behavior of TEPCO and its supervisors was shaped by collusive ties among the nuclear industry, regulators, and politicians. Regulators allowed TEPCO to operate reactors that were known to have significant problems, and TEPCO was able to hide some problems that were even more serious. Regulations were nonexistent or inconsistent or were not enforced. The individuals involved seemed more concerned with their own interests than with the safety of the plants. The so-called nuclear power village represented revolving doors and a web of connections among government officials, regulators, and TEPCO.[67] The reports about the regulatory and political environment that emerged in the context of TEPCO show a striking similarity to the situation of the financial industry. In both cases, regulatory and political capture went unchecked, and still does, because the risks were hidden—until disaster struck.

Much is wrong with banking, and much can be done about it. If politicians and regulators fail to protect the public, they must face pressure to change course. The next chapter pulls together the key themes from our discussion in this book and exposes more of the convenient and flawed narratives that help justify the lack of action. The challenge is to make those who handle other people's money—including bankers, politicians, and regulators—bear more of the consequences of their decisions.

THIRTEEN

Other People's Money

I am disappointed because many of these behaviours happened on my watch. It is my responsibility to make sure that it cannot happen again. . . . We did not have appropriate controls in place. Frankly, we misjudged the risk associated. . . . We know that a small minority have let us down. We also know that we need to rebuild bonds of trust with the society we serve.

Bob Diamond, Barclays CEO, July 2, 2012

THE ABOVE QUOTE is taken from a letter to the employees of Barclays, the giant U.K. bank.[1] The letter concerns Barclays' involvement in a scheme whereby traders of several large banks allegedly conspired to manipulate reporting for LIBOR, a key index for interest rates, whose value affects trillions of contracts around the globe.[2] A few days earlier, Barclays had agreed to pay more than $450 million to U.S. and U.K. authorities to settle allegations that Barclays had manipulated LIBOR. The chairman of the board of Barclays had just resigned, and Mr. Diamond was forced out as CEO the next day.[3]

In his letter Mr. Diamond is remarkably vague about the "behaviours" he is referring to. He talks about insufficiently controlled "risk" but does not mention any violation of the law. Nor does he let on that manipulating reports for personal gain might raise concerns about criminal behavior such as fraud. Mr. Diamond attributes the manipulation to a small group of people whom the bank had not sufficiently controlled. Yet the manipulation had gone on for years, and even outsiders had had suspicions about it.[4] Why did the bank fail to control the people in question? If senior management knew that they might misbehave, why did it put them in positions in which misbehavior might matter? If management did not know, why not?[5]

According to many accounts, greed has come to dominate the culture of major banking institutions over the past two or three decades.[6] With ever larger speculative positions, the banks' traders have taken ever larger risks. If

208

their bets succeed, the traders can earn large bonuses, and many of them have become extraordinarily rich. This behavior sets an example for others to emulate; they strive either to become as rich or to prove that they are just as daring as their role models.[7] Large rewards and a sense that "everyone is doing it" have eroded behavior codes focusing on clients' trust.[8]

Convenient Narratives

Mr. Diamond asserts that the LIBOR scandal had nothing to do with the culture of the bank. Despite recognizing that "our culture, and that of the industry overall, needs to evolve," he insists that "a small minority have let us down."

A major theme of this book has been that people often use convenient narratives, stories they tell to explain what happened or what is going on, hoping that others will not ask too many vexing questions. In the case of bankers and banking experts, most of these narratives are examples of the flawed claims we refer to as the bankers' new clothes. Mr. Diamond's letter fits this pattern perfectly. By insisting that the LIBOR scandal was due to the misbehavior of a few individuals, Mr. Diamond tries to deflect any demands for wider investigation or reform.

Downplaying problems has also been a standard response to the financial crisis of 2007–2009.[9] For example, many politicians and regulators downplay the costs of the crisis. The U.S. Treasury and the Federal Reserve proudly announce that they made a profit on the assets they acquired to relieve banks, but they leave out important parts of the intervention, such as the support using taxpayers' money that was given to Fannie Mae and Freddie Mac.[10] Most importantly, in limiting attention to the costs of the intervention, politicians and regulators, like bankers, frequently ignore the enormous costs of the crisis to the broader economy—the loss of output in the recession, job losses, and hardships associated with foreclosures.[11] By minimizing the costs of the crisis, this narrative aims at silencing calls for more reform.

A related narrative often advanced by bankers, regulators, and economists is that the financial crisis of 2007–2009 was primarily a "liquidity crisis."[12] According to this interpretation, investors lost confidence, first in mortgage-related securities and then in banks. The runs that followed caused extensive damage, with strong contagion effects on other banks and markets.

If it had not been for these runs, so the narrative goes, losses would have been much smaller. The runs are compared to depositors' bank runs before the introduction of deposit insurance, except that the recent runs were driven by companies rather than individuals, and the focus was on short-term lending to banks and investments in money market funds.[13]

In the liquidity narrative, the financial system is sometimes compared to the plumbing of a house, invisible but essential.[14] The metaphor is intriguing, but it is not clear what it is meant to tell us, and unclear metaphors are bad guides for policy. Seeing the words *plumbing* and *liquidity* next to each other, one might suspect that the message concerns the need to make sure that fresh water—or money—is available where and when we need it. (Or does the metaphor refer to the part of the plumbing that is used to flush waste down the drain?) The analog of a liquidity problem in the financial system would then presumably be a lack of water coming from the tap, and the central bank's pumping money into the system would be like getting an additional water supply to fill the pipes.

But why is no water coming from the tap? Is it because of leakage through rusty pipes or because of a drought that has forced the water company to limit the water supply? If the pipes are rusty and have holes, more water will hardly help; if there is a drought, even the government might not be able to provide more water.

Plumbing must also be seen in the context of the structure it serves. A highly indebted bank is like an unstable, shoddily constructed building. When such a building is exposed to a strong storm or an earthquake, the walls may not be able to withstand the pressure, and their shaking may damage the plumbing. This will cause a "liquidity problem" at the water tap, but we should be most worried about the instability of the walls. Just as the lack of water flow is really due to the building's being badly built, so the lack of liquidity is often due to a bank's being highly indebted.

In the liquidity narrative, the main problem for policy is to prevent runs and liquidity problems from occurring and provide liquidity when they occur. If this is actually the key issue, one might conclude that policy should focus on extending the government safety net, that is, on providing government guarantees to strengthen investors' confidence and liquidity support by the central bank to help banks in need.[15] This focus on the safety net is inappropriate, however, if liquidity problems and runs are just symptoms of deeper difficulties of banks.

The liquidity narrative benefits from people's fascination with runs and panics, which contributes to the success of movies such as *It's a Wonderful Life* and *Mary Poppins*. Scholars, analysts, journalists, and the public are intrigued by how a small spark of mistrust, even one that is based on a misunderstanding, can kindle a panic that destroys a bank. The fascination with runs and panics makes the liquidity narrative attractive, but that does not mean that this narrative is true.

Throughout this book we have emphasized the critical importance of solvency for banks and other financial institutions. If these institutions are highly indebted, it does not take much of a shock for solvency concerns to arise. Such concerns can lead creditors to withdraw their money as soon as they can, causing liquidity problems for the banks. As we discussed in Chapters 3–5, runs and other liquidity problems rarely appear out of the blue but usually start when a bank's solvency is in doubt. Even during crises, investors tend to distinguish between institutions according to their strength.[16] A run can sometimes even be the mechanism for discovering a hidden insolvency and triggering corrective action.[17]

In explaining the crisis of 2007–2009, solvency concerns must be taken very seriously. Banks faced substantial losses from mortgage lending due to homeowners' defaulting on their debts. These losses would have caused serious problems even if there had been no liquidity problems. Many banks were so highly indebted that they did not have enough equity to absorb the losses. Even those that did not become insolvent found that their equity was much impaired, and this forced them to reduce their activities or sell assets.[18] The subsequent credit crunch for the real economy was a result of banks' financial distress caused by excessive borrowing.

Describing the financial crisis as a liquidity crisis without much concern for the underlying solvency issues is convenient for many, but it is inappropriate for this crisis, just as it is for most—virtually all—recent financial crises.[19] This narrative diverts attention away from much more important underlying questions, such as why low-quality mortgage lending had expanded so much, why so many banks were so vulnerable to losses, and why regulators and supervisors had looked on passively as the risks were building up.[20]

The liquidity narrative diverts attention away from the question of responsibility for the vulnerability of the banks and of the system. It therefore masks the numerous failures of governance and of regulation, in the financial sector and among supervisors, which contributed greatly to the buildup of risks in the run-up to the crisis. Bankers took many risks and hid them. Regulations were poorly designed and counterproductive. Supervisors allowed banks to get away with practices that bent or broke the rules and that proved to be very harmful in 2007 and 2008.[21]

The crisis was not caused by pure liquidity problems. It was driven by serious and legitimate solvency concerns about a number of banks and other institutions.[22] The liquidity narrative distracts audiences from trying to understand why the solvency problems arose.

Many politicians, regulators, bankers, and others want us to believe that banks and the financial system are in much better shape now than they were before the crisis, that dangerous activities have been much reduced, and that many new rules have made the system safer.[23] But some improvements for which regulators take credit cannot really be attributed to them. For example, banks can appear profitable by taking advantage of cheap interest rates to borrow. At the same time they can delay the refinancing of mortgages so their borrowers cannot benefit from the low rates. These actions make banks look better, but they do not reflect any real improvement in the system.

The new reforms that are being put into place are far from satisfactory. Banks may be more robust today than they were in 2008, but this statement does not say much about where they really are and where they should be. As discussed in Chapter 11, bankers and bank regulators prefer to deny the banks' weaknesses rather than deal with them properly. This attitude has meant that concerns about hidden insolvencies have still not been addressed, and the financial system remains vulnerable to problems inherited from the past. As of this writing, in October 2012, this system does not appear to be better equipped than it was in 2000–2006 to limit the buildup of risks or than it was in 2007–2009 to bear losses.[24]

Why Invalid Arguments Can Win

Like other articles of the bankers' new clothes, convenient narratives are often successful even when they are invalid. They are too rarely challenged, and they impact policy. As we saw in Chapter 12, politicians and regulators often have their own reasons for siding with banks in the debate about regulation or for protecting their own past conduct. Politicians are concerned about campaign contributions from banks and bankers. They may also be concerned about banks' lending to the government, to home buyers, or to businesses. Taking their cues, and sometimes explicit directions, from politicians —or maintaining options for future careers in banking—regulators and supervisors also shy away from conflicts.

Lobbying is often successful because it faces few challenges. The benefits for special interest groups of bending laws and regulations or getting them changed are large and focused. They find it worthwhile, therefore, to spend money and effort for this purpose. By contrast, the harmful effects on the public, which may be much greater in total, tend to be spread over so many people that each individual person hardly notices the damage.[25]

In such a situation, it is quite possible for the lobby to succeed even though, on balance, the harm from its proposals may outweigh the good; the special interests that benefit are just so much louder than the general public, even though the harm to the latter may be very great. Individuals who know the issues may have little to gain from challenging the lobby and limited ability to actually have an impact.

As discussed in Chapter 12, nonprofit citizens' and public interest groups try to provide a counterweight to special-interest lobbying, but these groups can hardly compete with corporations and industry lobbyists for organization and resources. Citizens' groups or others often find it difficult to gain access to politicians and regulators if what they say is inconvenient for the politicians or regulators, and as a result, special interest groups are often more successful in affecting policy.[26]

In the area of financial regulation, despite the public anger over the financial crisis and the bailouts, bankers and their lobbies continue to wield the greatest influence. As discussed in several chapters of this book, bankers have succeeded in watering down regulatory reforms both in the process of legislation and at the implementation stage. Lobbying with politicians and regulators away from the public eye has been particularly effective. When conversations do occur in public, convenient narratives divert attention away from the critical questions.

Unfortunately, making valid arguments is not necessary to affect policy. In the United States a striking example was provided by the battle, around 1994, over the treatment of executive stock options in corporate earnings statements. The Financial Accounting Standards Board (FASB), the body of experts that is charged with developing accounting rules for corporations in the United States, had proposed that options be treated as expenses at the time the options were granted.

Special interest groups warned of the dire consequences that would follow if this proposal to change the accounting rules were implemented. They claimed that the change would make it more difficult for U.S. firms to raise funds, that it would stifle innovation and make U.S. firms less competitive globally. Under the influence of their lobbying, the U.S. Senate passed a resolution opposing the proposal, and the FASB desisted. Ten years later, after the Enron bankruptcy and other accounting scandals, the rule was at last implemented, and none of the earlier warnings was confirmed.[27]

In this case it took accounting and governance scandals to enable the enactment of a simple change in accounting rules whose advocates had previously been silenced by invalid arguments. So far we have not learned a similar lesson from the financial crisis of 2007–2009; invalid claims have continued to dominate the debate.[28]

Financial Stability Has No Constituency
but Is Everyone's Business

The bankers' new clothes have contributed to an anti-regulation atmosphere in which politicians, regulators, and supervisors shy away from interfering with banking industry practices and in which the banking industry feels entitled to evade the government and the supervisors.[29] This atmosphere provided the context for much of the deregulation of the 1980s and 1990s, as well as for the reluctance of politicians or regulators to introduce new regulation or even to enforce the existing rules strictly.[30]

In the LIBOR case discussed earlier, regulators had information that should have led them to suspect that the law had been violated, but they failed to take action in time.[31] For the past decade or more, few individuals and corporations in the financial industry have been prosecuted for possible violation of the law.[32] Individuals working in the financial sector face minimal punitive consequences of wrongdoing, even of fraud.[33] Most cases are settled out of court with penalties that are tiny relative to the bonuses and profits the offending individuals have earned by engaging in illegal or unethical practices.[34] The penalties are often paid by the banks, which effectively means by shareholders and, in the case of default, even creditors; the individuals responsible pay little or nothing, and banks become weaker.

Such out-of-court settlements may be convenient for the authorities because prosecution is costly and, given the complexity of the issues, the verdicts are often uncertain. Pressing charges might also reflect badly on supervisors who failed to intervene in time. Indeed banks often defend their actions by arguing that regulators were present, allowed them to take the actions, and did not interfere as the actions continued. As a result, there is too little accountability for wrongdoing.[35]

This lack of accountability is harmful. Effective banking regulation and enforcement are needed to protect the public interest. Leaving people and firms free to act as they like, subject only to the so-called discipline of the market, is best in many areas of economic activity but not in banking. If banks are left free to act as they like, they will endanger and distort the economy, and the public interest will suffer. The public has already been greatly harmed, and the dangers have not abated.

In 1914 Louis Brandeis, who later went on to serve on the U.S. Supreme Court, emphasized the fact that bankers use "other people's money."[36] The risks that bankers take affect not just themselves but also those other people whose money they use, and many others besides. In making and controlling the laws and regulations, politicians, regulators, and supervisors make decisions that affect many other people, including not only the banks' investors but also the public as a whole. The "other people," however, do not have a say in the bankers' decisions, and often also in decisions by policymakers.

Banks and other financial institutions must be regulated because their distress and insolvency can have a significant negative impact on the rest of the financial system and on the economy. When banks borrow too much and take too much risk, they harm the public. If the government tries to limit the damage by bailing banks out, taxpayers bear the direct costs.

The problem is not risk taking per se. Risk taking is part of most investments, and without it we would experience very little innovation and growth. Funding innovative entrepreneurs, for example, requires that venture capitalists or other investors make highly risky investments. The investors do their best to evaluate the odds, but they know that many start-up businesses will fail and that spectacular performers like Apple or Google are extremely rare.[37] Established companies must also take risks to innovate or even to remain in business: pharmaceutical companies take risks in developing new medicines, car manufacturers in further increasing fuel efficiency.

Risk is unproblematic for society when those who make the decisions also bear the consequences and when they do not harm others who have little control over the decisions. Bankers, however, do not bear the full consequences of their decisions, and they can harm others who have little control over them. Banks borrow from a large and dispersed set of depositors who simply want their deposits to be safe and their payments to be made smoothly but do not have sufficient information or ability to assess or influence the decisions and the risks that are taken. Moreover, banks' risk taking affects not only depositors and other creditors but also the broader public through the different forms of contagion discussed in Chapter 5.

Because the bankers' decisions significantly affect others, the principle that everything should be left to the unregulated free market is not appropriate in the context of banking. The bankers' decisions can endanger too many "other people." Effective regulation and enforcement are therefore essential.

The public has a much greater interest in the banks' safety than do the banks themselves. Individual banks may be very sophisticated in managing their risks, but their assessments do not consider the interests of other people and institutions, such as the costs of contagion from their problems. Exacerbating this problem, the costs and benefits faced by individual people working for banks are different again from those faced by the banks' investors and the broader public. Bankers often benefit from banks' potential profits but face no personal costs from the banks' possible bankruptcy, let alone from harming the rest of the economy with the risks they have taken.

The key objective of banking regulation must be to guard the safety and soundness of the financial system in the public interest.[38] Other concerns should not interfere. Promoting the competitive success of banks in global markets is not in the public interest if this success is due to banks' taking excessive risks at the expense of the taxpayers. Many countries have paid dearly for the successes of their banks.

Encouraging the banks to fund the government is also not in the public interest if such funding endangers the banks. Such funding may be convenient for politicians who want to hide the costs of their policies, but if a government defaults on its debt and this is accompanied by a banking crisis, the consequences can be disastrous for many people.[39]

The need for effective regulation is acute. The large scale of bankers' gambles and the high degree of interconnectedness in the financial system make that system very fragile. If some large and highly connected bank or other financial institution fails, it can destabilize the entire financial system and inflict enormous damage on all of us.

Politicians, regulators, supervisors, and even central bankers are also in control of other people's money. They are charged with protecting the public interest, but they sometimes become captured or respond to other incentives and forget their duty. By allowing flawed arguments to impact policy and by failing to design and enforce effective laws and regulation in the public interest, they also abuse their control of other people's money. Only public pressure can solve this governance problem.

Sensible, Cost-Effective Regulation

In the aftermath of the bailouts of 2008–2009, there has been much debate about what is wrong with the banking system. Often the discussion focuses on the largest banks, called "too big to fail."[40] Other financial institutions have the distinction of being too interconnected, too important, or perhaps too political to fail. They are referred to as "systemically important."

One of the worst effects of having institutions that are "too important (too big, too systemic, or too political) to fail"—that is, institutions whose failure the government wants to avoid—is the creation of distorted and dangerous incentives for such institutions or for others that want to attain this status. In addressing this problem, one possibility is to focus on how such institutions might be made smaller, less interconnected, important, or political, so that there would be no problem in letting them fail.[41]

Our approach instead takes its cue from the quote from Benjamin Franklin with which we opened Chapter 6: "An ounce of prevention is worth a pound of cure." Rather than focusing only on how to prepare for the possibility of failure or how to rearrange the activities of these institutions so failure becomes palatable, can we do something, at a reasonable cost, to prevent financial institutions from getting to the point of failing in the first place? This question can be asked about small and large institutions alike and for all types of institutions whose failure might be harmful to the system. However, it is obviously more urgent for the institutions whose failure would be most harmful to the economy.

Financial failure involves a failure to pay debts, that is, legal promises to pay. Banks and other institutions harm the economy most when they become distressed or insolvent—that is, when they get into a situation in which they cannot pay their debts or when investors fear that they might not be able to pay their debts. This is most likely if the banks take on too much debt to begin with and if the people in charge, in the banks or among the regulators, do not take proper precautions to prevent financial distress.

Importantly, the damage that failures or insolvencies of financial institutions create is not limited to the impact on depositors, those who provide deposit insurance, and existing and new loan customers. For example, Lehman Brothers did not engage in commercial banking activities, and yet the damage from its bankruptcy was enormous.[42] This observation suggests that banking regulation should focus on protecting the financial system from risks arising in investment banking at least as much as it aims to protect depositors and make sure banks provide consistent and appropriate loans.[43]

The interconnectedness of financial markets and financial institutions that we discussed in Chapter 5 implies that contagion effects arise in activities other than commercial banking. In 1998, authorities thought of the hedge fund LTCM as systemically important and intervened to prevent it from failing in the normal way. Bear Stearns and Lehman Brothers were both pure investment banks; the takeover of Bear Stearns by JPMorgan Chase was subsidized by the Federal Reserve, and Lehman Brothers' bankruptcy caused havoc. Also, in September 2008 the U.S. government bailed out the insurance company AIG rather than allowing it to go into bankruptcy.[44]

Even if the largest banks become smaller, the interconnectedness of the financial system and the danger of contagion will still be likely to create excessive fragility unless more is done to control this fragility.[45] Financial institutions might still get into trouble and, if and when they do, the implications of failure for the rest of the financial system might be so frightening that they still might not be allowed to fail.[46]

This reasoning explains our focus on improving the safety and soundness of banks. If failures become less likely, the financial system will become more robust and stable, and it will be able to serve the economy more consistently. Regulation must focus first and foremost on making banks more resilient against shocks, particularly because there is a cost-effective way to do so. Whatever else is done, it is critical to find ways to reduce the likelihood that banks will become distressed or insolvent.

In this book we have argued that achieving this objective most directly, with little if any cost to society, would involve requiring banks to have *much* more equity and rely less on borrowing. If banks have considerably more equity funding, they will be less likely to become insolvent or fail, and governments will be less likely to get into a position in which they must choose between bank bailouts and contagious bank failures.

Regulation of equity funding is required because, if banks are left to choose their levels of equity on their own, they have incentives to choose too little. As we explained in Chapter 9, deposit insurance and other guarantees, as well as the tax system, bias banks' preferences for borrowing. The fact that banks are already highly indebted also creates biases in favor of continuing to borrow and resisting more equity. As we have explained throughout the book, borrowing can be addictive, especially if the borrower benefits from guarantees. Quite simply, banks are as indebted and fragile as they are only because they *want* to be and not because of any benefit this brings to society. Nothing that banks do requires that they borrow as much as they do or as much as they lobby to be allowed to do.

Good regulation should directly address the key problems that must be solved, and it should do so in the most cost-effective way possible.[47] If a key diagnosis is that banks and other institutions are too fragile, making sure that they have much more equity is the simplest and most cost-effective way to address this problem, and it will correct or reduce many distortions created by government guarantees and subsidies. The benefits of this approach are particularly strong for banks and other institutions whose distress and insolvency would impact the overall system.

Capital regulation is already in place, and improving it does not require much in the way of new laws. Regulators often have plenty of authority to act. By requiring only that banks fund their assets with more equity, capital regulation is less intrusive than any other types of regulation that may intervene in the actual business activity of the banks. As discussed in Chapter 11, prior capital regulations failed because they were insufficient, flawed, and poorly enforced. We can and must do significantly better than current proposals call for.

There are many advantages to a situation in which banks and other financial institutions would be required to have substantially more equity. First, more equity would reduce the likelihood that banks will fall into financial distress or insolvency. As we discussed in Chapter 6, this situation would increase the stability of the system and addresses contagion concerns, but it would have additional benefits. Less indebted banks are in a better position to make good loans. By contrast, highly indebted banks are more prone to taking excessive risks in lending, and they may stop lending if they get into financial trouble.

Another benefit of higher equity requirements is that they would naturally reduce the sizes and the distortive effects of guarantees and subsidies. With fewer subsidies, large banks might break up without being forced to do so by law or regulation, under pressure from investors concerned about their inefficient size or complexity. High equity requirements would make it more likely that banks would become smaller naturally.

Higher equity requirements would therefore alleviate the problem of banks' being too big, too interconnected, or too political to fail. Not only would banks be less likely to fail; they would bear more of their own losses should they incur losses, and they would be less able to take advantage of the subsidized cheap borrowing that their status as too big to fail has conferred on them.

Best of all, these many critical benefits of significantly higher equity requirements could be obtained at virtually no cost to society. Taxpayers would save on subsidies, and the public would benefit from a more stable and healthier financial system. There are therefore no trade-offs associated with this approach. Society would obtain large benefits for free.

Bankers fight higher equity requirements, but the only way that having more equity might actually be costly to them is by preventing them from benefiting at the expense of taxpayers and creditors. Throughout this book we have exposed a large collection of what we call the bankers' new clothes, invalid reasons bankers have given as to why moving to a system with much more bank equity, even at the level of 20 percent or 30 percent of banks' total assets, is undesirable or impossible.[48] These flawed arguments and bank lobbying have prevented highly beneficial reform.

For example, in discussing the cost of more equity, bankers frequently refer to the return that investors require, lamenting that they cannot deliver those required returns if they have more equity. This reasoning goes against the basic principles operating in the financial markets in which banks operate. One of these principles is that investors require compensation for risk. For example, investors are currently willing to receive almost no returns at all when investing in safe government bonds. Any discussion of returns that does not recognize this principle is fundamentally flawed. In targeting high returns, bankers may take risks for which their shareholders are not adequately compensated and that definitely harm their creditors or the public.

The concern most often heard about higher equity requirements is that they would reduce lending. This concern is misplaced. Making loans, like other investments in the economy, should be guided by the quality of the potential loans and by the appropriate economic cost of funding them. Having banks funded with more equity would not interfere with this process; rather, it would make credit markets work better.

Bankers choose loans and other investments in light of their own incentives. As we saw in Chapter 6, for many of the major banks, making loans is currently only a small part of their business. Reductions in lending have less to do with equity requirements, instead reflecting the incentives banks have to use their funds otherwise.

The current structure of the regulations may actually introduce biases against making loans. For example, when bankers focus on investments that regulators view as less risky than they actually are, making business loans may seem less attractive than other investments. The investments that bankers find attractive may endanger the system, as happened in the run-up to the financial crisis of 2007–2009 when banks "innovated" to create AAA-rated securities that turned out to be quite risky. Requiring banks to have more loss-absorbing equity, with requirements that cannot be manipulated by conveniently designed risk models or through the flexibility of accounting rules, is likely to remove the biases and therefore encourage responsible lending that can benefit the economy.

As we have also seen, the fact that banks have so much debt also distorts their incentives, in lending and investing as well as in further borrowing. The incentive distortions are exacerbated by guarantees and debt subsidies. As bankers respond to these incentives, they endanger the financial system and the public. This situation must be corrected.

Adair Turner, chair of the Financial Services Authority of the United Kingdom, in urging radical reform and a reassessment of the role of the financial system in the economy, said in 2010, "There is no evidence that the growth in the scale and complexity of the financial system in the rich developed world over the last twenty to thirty years has driven increased growth or stability, and it is possible for financial activity to extract rents from the real economy rather than to deliver economic value." He continued: "We need to challenge radically some of the assumptions of the last thirty years and we need to be willing to consider radical policy responses."[49]

In Chapter 11 we made specific proposals that would be highly beneficial to the financial system, and we urged that they be taken up immediately. These proposals require nothing but the will of governments and regulators to take the essential steps. First among our recommendations is to determine which banks are insolvent and to unwind them even if the immediate costs seem daunting. Experiences in Japan and elsewhere have shown that keeping insolvent or "zombie" banks in business is harmful and costly.

Second, we strongly recommend strengthening banks by banning payouts to shareholders, such as dividends or share repurchases, until the banks have reached much higher equity levels than they currently maintain. Banks whose shares are traded on an exchange can be strengthened further by requiring them to raise more equity. As we explained in Chapter 11, these steps would entail only benefits and no costs to society, and they would not interfere with banks' ability to make loans during the transition. Indeed, if banks refrained from making payouts to their shareholders and raised more equity, they would have additional funds for loans.[50]

The standard objection to this proposal, that a ban on payouts or a request to raise new equity would make the banks' stock prices decline, fails to recognize that any such decline would be due only to the fact that, with more equity, bank shareholders who benefit from the upside of decisions taken on their behalf would also have to bear more of the downside risks. This would merely correct a situation in which they can rely on others to bear some of the downside risks.

The official approach to the regulation of bank equity, enshrined in the different Basel agreements on so-called capital regulation, is unsatisfactory. Even the recent Basel III, which is said to be much stricter than its predecessor, permits banks to have very little equity, as little as 3 percent of their total assets. Moreover, the complex attempts in this regulation to fine-tune equity requirements—for example, by relying on risk measurements and weights—are deeply flawed and create many distortions, among them a bias against traditional business lending.

Ultimately, all risks must be borne by someone. Some risks are unavoidable, and some are the result of decisions taken by individuals, companies, and governments. The financial system can help the economy grow and prosper by spreading risks more efficiently and by facilitating the funding of productive investments. However, this requires that the responsibility and liabilities be clearly assigned and enforced. So far, this condition is not satisfied, and therefore the financial system has become too dangerous and distorted. Correcting the distortion would not prevent any productive activity in the economy from being undertaken, and it would not interfere with the beneficial spreading of risk and funding of investments that the financial system engages in.

In Chapter 8 we noted that bankers are often given direct incentives, through their compensation, to borrow too much and to take too many risks. In that context, a legitimate concern is that, if higher equity requirements prevent bankers from magnifying the risks of their investments through the leverage associated with borrowing, they might become more reckless in order to achieve these targeted high returns.

This concern suggests that it is important to improve governance and risk control in banks. If banks have more equity, shareholders may have better incentives to control risk taking. However, because shareholders benefit from the upside of risk taking while the public shares some of the downside risk, and because effective shareholder governance can also be difficult, additional oversight—or even regulation of banks' governance and controls—may be desirable.[51]

The Bugbear of Shadow Banking

The bankers' new clothes that we have discussed so far include convenient narratives that downplay problems and also bugbears, warnings of unintended consequences meant to scare politicians and regulators out of tightening regulation. Among the claims we discussed are "Higher equity requirements would harm lending and growth," "Equity is expensive," and "Our competitive position in global markets will be harmed." As we have seen, with regard to at least equity requirements, and often to other proposed policy reforms, these claims are all invalid.

Another bugbear involves the warning that tighter regulation might cause financial activities to move from regulated banking to the so-called shadow banking sector, where there is less regulation and possibly no regulation.[52] A typical example is money market mutual funds, discussed in several earlier chapters.[53]

The argument that we should not have regulation because banks or other financial institutions might evade regulation is somewhat perverse. It turns the failure to enforce regulation into an argument against having regulation at all.

To see the fallacy, imagine a suggestion that we should not outlaw robbery because, with the police patrolling well-lit streets, would-be robbers would move to back alleys where they would be even more difficult to control. With regard to robbery and other crimes of violence, we do not accept such arguments; instead we ask the police to patrol the back alleys as well as the well-lit streets. Movies such as *High Noon* remind us how lawlessness tyrannizes society. Effective law enforcement may require courage and energy, but it improves people's lives. Similarly, we do not give up on collecting taxes just because many try to take advantage of tax loopholes. Like law enforcement and collecting taxes, regulating banks and other financial institutions is essential for society, and enforcing regulation effectively is a challenge we must take on.

In fact, the bugbear warning that risky financial activities will move to unregulated parts of the system is wrong in terms of why shadow banking has been a problem. The reason has not been excessive regulation, the inability of regulators and supervisors to enforce the regulation as needed, or a lack of tools at their disposal. Rather the source of the problem has been that regulators and supervisors have been *unwilling* to apply the tools they have had and to enforce regulations effectively.

Regulators and supervisors, at least in Europe and the United States, have always had the authority to regulate and supervise deposit-taking institutions to maintain the safety of the financial system. Yet they have allowed such institutions to sponsor and to guarantee the debts of many entities in the shadow banking system, providing substantial commitments and "liquidity supports." These actions contributed greatly to the buildup of risks prior to the financial crisis of 2007–2009. The Financial Crisis Inquiry Commission concluded that "widespread failures in financial regulation and supervision proved devastating to the stability of the nation's financial markets. The sentries were not at their posts."[54]

In fact, some of the most dangerous shadow banking institutions that had a harmful impact on the financial system in 2007 and 2008, entities that held and issued mortgage-related securities, were affiliated with the regulated banks.[55] These affiliations meant that regulated banks were taking substantial risks, which should have set off alarms for regulators and supervisors. Supervisors should have treated some of the banks' risks as unacceptable, and they could have intervened. Instead, regulators and supervisors stood by.[56]

The bugbear that we should not regulate because we cannot enforce the regulation is another article of the bankers' new clothes. Rather than throwing up our hands, we should take up the challenge of effective regulation and enforcement. The stakes are high.

Bankers and Society: How to Deal with the Conflict

The bugbear of shadow banking turns the failure of previous regulation and enforcement into an argument against beneficial regulation. Because regulation is essential, the focus must be on making enforcement easier and more effective. Some laws and regulations, however, are counterproductive and make enforcement more challenging, because they actually give banks more incentives to borrow excessively. For example, as discussed in Chapter 9, the tax codes in many countries allow corporations to deduct interest payments on debt as an expense. This treatment creates a tax penalty for funding with equity and encourages more borrowing.

Penalizing the use of equity while encouraging more debt funding is especially perverse as applied to banks, because their excessive borrowing harms the financial system by increasing its fragility. Paradoxically, the tax codes subsidize borrowing, but then capital regulation tries to reduce it. It is as if we provided tax incentives that encouraged reckless driving or pollution while at the same time enacting laws forbidding these behaviors. Giving banks tax incentives to borrow is bad public policy. The tax code should not interfere with financial stability; if anything, it should try to reduce the distorted incentives.

Other laws also make it easier for banks to borrow too much. For example, many short-term debt contracts that are used in the financial system are exempt from normal bankruptcy procedures. These exemptions can play a role in enabling the type of "borrowing rat race" that we discussed in Chapter 10, which makes the banking system more fragile;[57] they should be reexamined.

Regulation would be easier to enforce if it were supported by policies allowing investors and supervisors to better monitor and control bankers' risk taking. Making derivatives markets more transparent, for example by forcing many of them to public exchanges, would make it harder for bankers to hide the risks they are taking. Effective corporate governance is also important. If bank managers cannot be controlled by their boards and shareholders, their behavior can be particularly dangerous. Laws and regulations that promote responsible corporate governance can help reduce the conflict between those who make decisions within financial institutions and others in the economy who might be harmed but have no control.

The Essential Element: Political Will

Once the problems in the financial system are identified properly, much can be done to create a better system that supports the economy without subjecting all of us to excessive risks. This will require appropriate laws and regulations, as well as effective enforcement.

Despite the enormous damage of the financial crisis of 2007–2009, the effort to reform the financial system has been stymied. The main reason has been political. Those who prefer the status quo have dominated the debate, while those who argue for effective reform have not been as successful.[58]

Politicians often prefer to neglect or forget the risks that the financial system imposes on the public. They may falsely believe that these risks are unavoidable. Or they allow other considerations, such as campaign contributions or the desire for banks to make certain investments, to interfere. The flawed and invalid claims we have called the bankers' new clothes contribute to the problem by creating confusion and providing rationalizations to those who oppose reform and regulation.

When politicians prefer to neglect the risks from banking, regulators and supervisors may also wish to avoid challenging banks. They may find it easier or more convenient, or they may feel pressured politically—for example, because Congress might threaten to reduce their budgets.[59] In the present revolving-door system, individual career concerns could also play a role. With so many factors contributing to the inability or unwillingness of regulators and supervisors to impose greater accountability and enforce regulation of the financial industry, the public interest in having a safe and stable financial system is forgotten.[60]

When people have a chance to see the reality of enforcement from up close, they sometimes react strongly. In the summer of 2012, following a trial in which the SEC brought crisis-related fraud charges against a midlevel banker, the jury felt strongly enough to take the unusual step of attaching a note to their verdict. In the note jurors urged the SEC to "continue to investigate the financial industry and modify existing regulations as necessary." The jury foreman said that "the industry seemed completely out of control with no oversight," adding that "Wall Street actions hurt all of us and we badly need a watchdog who will rein them in."[61]

We can have a financial system that works much better for the economy than the current system—without sacrificing anything. But achieving this requires that politicians and regulators focus on the public interest and carry out the necessary steps. The critical ingredient—still missing—is political will.

PART FOUR

Undermining Democracy and the Rule of Law

FOURTEEN

Too Fragile Still

Without reform of the financial system, . . . , another crisis is certain, . . .
*Mervyn King, Former Governor of the Bank of England, The End of Alchemy
(2016)*[1]

ON THURSDAY, March 9, 2023, there was a depositor run on Silicon Valley Bank (SVB), at that time the sixteenth largest bank in the United States with total assets of more than $200 billion. On Friday, March 10, the Federal Deposit Insurance Corporation (FDIC) closed the bank, citing "inadequate liquidity and insolvency."[2] SVB was the largest bank in the United States to fail since Washington Mutual in September 2008. Initially, the FDIC announced that insured depositors would be able to access again on Monday, March 13. After protests from investors with deposits above the deposit insurance limit of $250,000, Treasury Secretary Yellen announced on Sunday, March 12, that uninsured deposits would also be protected. At the same time, the Federal Reserve opened new lending programs for banks in order to prevent runs on other banks.

A few days later, on March 15, there was also a run on Credit Suisse (CS), one of two megabanks in Switzerland.[3] CS had problems of its own. In 2022, the bank had reported a loss of 7.3 billion Swiss francs (almost $8 billion), including 4 billion just in the third quarter. Following the announcement of these third-quarter losses, the bank lost many depositors and other investors. A new equity issue of almost 4 billion Swiss francs in December 2022 did not restore confidence. On March 9, 2023, the bank announced that, because of a request from U.S. authorities, it would delay the publication of its 2022 Annual Report. The publication of the report on March 14 was followed by the final run on March 15–17.[4] An announcement that the central bank of

Switzerland would support CS with up to 50 billion Swiss francs in loans did not end the run. Four days later, on Sunday, March 19, the Swiss government, central bank, and supervisory authority, together with the managements of CS and UBS, the two globally systemic banks in Switzerland, announced that UBS would acquire CS for 3 billion Swiss francs' worth of UBS shares. The merger would be accompanied by substantial loans from the Swiss central bank with government backing of up to 100 billion Swiss francs and by government guarantee against losses on CS assets.[5] The Swiss authorities preferred this bailout to an application of the new procedure they had installed for dealing with failing banks.

The cases of SVB and CS are different in that the problems of the two banks came from different sources. SVB suffered because the long-term securities it held had decreased in value as market rates of interest rose in 2022. CS had substantial losses in many business lines, particularly in investment banking.

In the same week as SVB, two other banks in the United States, Silvergate and Signature Banks, also suffered massive withdrawals of deposits and were closed, Silvergate through voluntary liquidation, Signature by intervention of the authorities; these banks had suffered losses from their involvement with crypto currencies and the bankrupt crypto exchange FTX. Like SVB and CS, these banks had funded their investments with little equity and much borrowing.

These events reminded people that banks are still fragile and potentially dangerous. Bank share prices worldwide plummeted. Moreover, in the United States many depositors moved their deposits from regional banks to larger banks and to money market funds hoping that they would be safer there.[6] For First Republic Bank, another regional bank in California, support through $30 billion in deposits from eleven large banks was not enough to stop the bleeding, and on May 1, 2023 the authorities intervened and sold it to JPMorgan Chase.[7]

On May 3, Jay Powell, the Chair of the Federal Reserve, suggested that "the resolution and sale of First Republic Bank" was "an important step towards drawing a line under [the] period of stress" that started with SVB's failure, but investors and markets did not seem to believe him. Bank stock prices did not recover after Mr. Powell's statement.[8] Empirical research suggests that the problems to which SVB and First Republic succumbed were in fact widespread among U.S. banks in spring 2023.[9]

The theme of this chapter is the persistence of fragility in banking since the 2007–2009 crisis.[10] For a long time, this fragility was hidden because outward circumstances were favorable. In 2022, however, conditions changed. Dangers arose and created turmoil. Most importantly, central banks raised interest rates to fight inflation. From March 2022 to March 2023, the discount rate, at which the Federal Reserve itself lends to banks overnight, rose from 0.25 percent annually to 5 percent annually. By historical standards, 5 percent is not spectacularly high, but coming from a rate close to zero, which had prevailed for two years, the increase was dramatic.

When interest rates rise, the market values of existing securities tend to decline, because investors compare the returns on these securities to the returns they can get on newly issued assets. As newly issued securities such as new government bonds offer more attractive rates of return, outstanding securities become relatively less attractive, and their market prices decline. SVB became insolvent through losses from such price declines. As we discussed in Chapters 4 and 5, increases in market rates of interest have regularly caused financial turmoil.

Society remains very much at risk from the fragility of banks and the overall financial system. In this chapter, we first provide a brief overview of developments since 2013. We then explain why many banks are still too fragile, too complex, and too opaque. In the process, we explain in more detail the cases of Credit Suisse and SVB, including the failures of regulators and supervisors. Finally, we discuss why regulatory reforms that should have reduced the fragility of financial institutions have been insufficient and why false and misleading arguments about the effects of banking regulation, what we call *the Bankers' New Clothes*, still have a powerful impact.

Backlash on Regulatory Reform

The years since this book first came out in 2013 have not been propitious for effective regulatory reforms. At that time, the participants in rule-making, in the Basel Committee on Banking Supervision, the United States, and the European Union, had a sense that the job was finished.[11] The Basel III agreement had been concluded, reform legislation had been passed or was about to be passed, and the rest of the reform was seen as a task for regulators and supervisors. In the United States, regulators took their time with the implementation of the Dodd-Frank Act.[12] In the European Union, attention had moved from the implementation of Basel III to the reform of procedures for dealing with failing banks and to the so-called banking union that consolidated the supervision of large banks in a new organization attached to the European Central Bank (ECB). This legislation was completed in 2014.[13]

Political changes in the United States, the United Kingdom, and the European Commission also worked against further reform of banking regulation. In the United States, key appointments by President Trump to positions relevant to banking involved veterans of the industry who favored light-touch rules if any at all.[14] In the United Kingdom, the Tory government followed the City's, i.e., the financial sector's, wishes in 2013 and appointed Mark Carney, then governor of the Bank of Canada and a thirteen-year veteran of Goldman Sachs, to succeed Mervyn King as governor of the Bank of England. Proponents of stricter financial regulation left or were removed from positions relevant to banking regulation and supervision.[15] In 2015, the U.K. Treasury again followed the wishes of the City and forced out the head of the Financial Conduct Authority because he had been too active in pursuing misconduct.[16] More recently, there have been several initiatives to reduce U.K. financial regulation quite drastically, ostensibly to take advantage of Brexit to make the London City "more competitive" in global competition.

In the European Union, the rules of financial regulation depend on the European Commission, which has a monopoly on proposing new legislation.[17] In 2014, the new European Commission was headed by Jean-Claude Juncker, the former prime minister of Luxembourg, a financial center, and the new Commission member in charge of Financial Stability, Financial Services, and Capital Markets Union was Jonathan Hill, the representative of the United Kingdom. Mr. Juncker was mainly interested in getting banks to provide funding for his Investment Plan for Europe. Mr. Hill was mainly interested in promoting "capital markets union" to benefit the City, which in practice meant relaxing restrictions on asset-backed securities, ignoring the shortcomings of these securities that had contributed so much to the 2007–2009 crisis. Since the United Kingdom has left the European Union, this particular interest has receded, but the politics of banking still work the way we described in Chapter 12, with member state governments wanting to promote the interests of "their" industry players in global competition even if these interests endanger financial stability.[18]

When our book first came out, high officials of the European Commission complained that we had unfairly presented the Commission as having resisted stricter regulation of banks. A few years later, in 2016, one of the same officials was proud to proclaim that stricter equity requirements would come at the expense of lending and growth, one of the bugbears that we had debunked in Chapter 1. From 2013 to 2016, fear of being seen as siding with bankers had turned into pride at parading the Bankers' New Clothes.

In the United States in 2014, lobbyists allied with members of Congress pushed for a bill that would repeal a part of the Dodd-Frank Act requiring risky trading to be separated from deposit banking. To eliminate the possibility of a veto or a full discussion of the issues in the usual process, the bill was appended to a must-pass spending legislation that was essential to keep the government open. President Obama signed the bill in December 2014. By following this procedure, the lobby avoided a public debate and a separate vote on the merits of the bill it was pushing. According to media reports, Citigroup lobbyists were particularly involved in crafting the language of the legislation, and JPMorgan Chase CEO Jamie Dimon made personal phone calls to individual lawmakers, urging them to vote as the banks wished.[19]

Subsequently, early on in the Trump administration, an executive order mandated that "regulations should be efficient, effective, and appropriately tailored."[20] The Treasury Department followed up with 101 recommendations on how "tailoring" should be done to fit the banks' business models. The word "tailoring" was in fact a code word for deregulation. Not one of the proposed recommendations increased the stringency of regulation anywhere.[21] With the Economic Growth, Regulatory Reform, and Consumer Protection Act of 2018, Congress made "tailoring" mandatory even though the meaning of the term itself was unclear. The new law also mandated that stricter regulation for systemically important institutions should only be applied to institutions with total assets above $250 billion; previously the limit had been $50 billion. Silicon Valley and Signature Banks had total assets between these two limits, so their managers were among the beneficiaries of the change. Gregory Becker, the CEO of SVB, had actively campaigned for the legal change.[22]

Even before Congress passed this law, in 2018 the Federal Reserve introduced its own "tailoring." It effectively reduced regulatory requirements for both large and small banks. In particular, it reduced equity requirements for the large, systemically important institutions that had stood at the center of the 2007–2009 financial crisis.[23] Because the Federal Reserve is independent and the details of regulation, including the setting and operationalizing equity requirements, are not written into the law, it might have resisted President Trump's call for tailoring, the more so since the objective of "efficiency" has no basis in the law. The administration and the Federal Reserve were in fact pushing aside the objective of financial stability, which Title 1 of the Dodd-Frank Act specifically assigns to the Federal Reserve.[24]

The eagerness of the Federal Reserve to reduce equity requirements in the Trump era followed an unwillingness to increase these requirements in the early 2010s. Given its mandate and given its independence, in the early 2010s, the Federal Reserve might have responded to a bipartisan appeal from U.S. senators Brown, Democrat from Ohio, and Vitter, Republican from Louisiana, to raise equity requirements to 15 percent of total assets for the largest institutions, and to 8 percent of total assets for medium-size institutions.[25] Because the Federal Reserve failed to act, senators Brown and Vitter introduced their proposal in Congress in April 2013. Shortly before that, in March 2013, Federal Reserve Chair Bernanke had publicly admitted that the "too-big-to-fail" problem had not yet been solved.[26] A unanimous resolution by the U.S. Senate to end too-big-to-fail subsidies had no noticeable effect on the Federal Reserve's policy stance. Yet, the Dodd Frank Act had mandated the Federal Reserve to eliminate the too-big-to-fail problem.[27]

The changes in policy stance since 2013 were greatly helped by the fact that, until 2022, the fragility of the financial system was largely hidden. There were leftover problems from the crisis of 2007–2009 and from the European crises of 2010–2013, but these problems were smoldering rather than erupting dramatically.[28] Whatever new problems arose were largely contained. The Greek crisis of 2015 stands out, but, massive though it was for Greece, it did not spill over to other countries.[29] Moreover, this crisis had less to do with problems of the banks than with the political conflict between the newly elected Greek government and the European institutions.[30]

On the face of it, the COVID pandemic left the financial sector largely unscathed, but this outcome was mainly due to public support to asset markets and to nonfinancial businesses.[31] For a while, in March 2020, the pandemic seemed to cause a panic, but dramatic interventions by governments and central banks quieted markets down quickly. The pandemic itself and the lockdowns mainly affected companies outside the financial sector. Financial institutions actually benefited because they played a big role in handling government subsidies to individuals and to nonfinancial businesses.[32] They also benefited because the supports prevented defaults of individuals and non-financial businesses on their borrowings from banks, and because they enabled more profitable investment banking business. Without all the supports, there might well have been a financial crisis. As yet, it is not clear to what extent damage suffered by nonfinancial businesses will end up hurting their loans performance.[33]

The seeming stability of the financial system has created a sense of complacency. For example, at a workshop of the Stakeholder Group of the European Banking Authority in January 2022 that one of us attended, industry participants, as well as some academics and supervisors, vaunted the strength of the banks' equity and the fact that the banks had coped so well with the COVID pandemic. None of them mentioned the fact that during the pandemic banks had benefited substantially from government support to their debtors and from central bank asset purchases that stopped asset prices from falling. Nor did anyone mention upcoming risks, such as risks from increases in interest rates and real estate price declines. Yet, such changes were already on the horizon, and shortly after some of them have materialized.

Such complacency is dangerous. The financial system is still much too fragile, as recent events illustrate. Banks are still too highly indebted, and many of them are too large, too complex, and too opaque. The absence of a global financial crisis since 2013 does not mean that today's financial system is robust and safe. The seeming stability of the financial system in the years before 2023 reflects the benefits banks obtained from the favorable macro-economic environment in 2013–2019 and from the support that governments and central banks provided during the COVID crisis. Since early 2022, the environment has become much more challenging.

In Europe, the public support provided in 2007–2009 and since then has allowed too many banks to survive. They have procrastinated acknowledging losses in the various crises, so their accounts overstate their strength and their solvency is in doubt.[34] There is still significant excess capacity in banking, which makes for intense competition.[35] Consequently, bank profitability in Europe has been low throughout the decade. Since 2015, the European Central Bank has contributed to this development because its policies served to compress the margins between the rates of return that banks could earn on loans and securities and the interest rates they had to pay to their depositors and other lenders.[36] This low profitability has hampered the ability of European banks to rebuild equity from current profits.

In the United States, since around 2013, the authorities have been somewhat stricter in forcing banks to acknowledge losses on nonperforming loans and to raise new equity if they wanted to stay in business.[37] In this past decade, U.S. banks have been fairly profitable, but they have also made large payouts, in dividend payments and stock repurchases, to benefit their shareholders. They were therefore ill prepared for the turbulence associated with the beginnings of the COVID pandemic and needed the authorities' forbearance with respect to equity requirements in 2020.

Remarkably, while granting such forbearance and easing the rules in 2020, the Federal Reserve did not impose more than temporary restrictions on payouts to shareholders.[38] For the Federal Reserve, Trump's "efficiency" mandate seemed to call for maximum payouts to shareholders. In early 2021, Federal Reserve researchers declared that the COVID experience proves that regulatory reforms worked well, but like the European regulators they neglected to note the critical role of the government supports that greatly benefited banks indirectly, and they did not seem concerned about looming risks such as from interest rate increases.[39] The latter risks became evident a year later and even more so in March 2023.

Central Bank Supports in the COVID Crisis

In February and March 2020, a growing awareness of dangers from the COVID pandemic and fear of a recession caused many investors to liquidate their holdings of assets. In particular, investors in money market funds and other mutual funds asked to redeem their investments.[40] To comply with these requests, the funds had to liquidate assets, creating a strong downward pressure on asset prices. Further pressures on asset prices came from heavily indebted hedge funds that had to sell assets quickly for cash in order to reduce their borrowing as their lenders became more restrictive.[41] The selling pressures were particularly strong for U.S. Treasuries, debt securities of the U.S. government, which are normally among the safest securities available. Many funds had held these securities as reserves, to be liquidated if a need for cash were to arise. In March 2020, there were many sellers of these securities—and hardly any buyers—so prices started to decline sharply.

In this situation, the Federal Reserve intervened massively and purchased large amounts of U.S. Treasuries and many other financial assets to support financial markets.[42] The Federal Reserve also recreated facilities it had first established in 2008, which provided loans to institutions and purchased financial assets.[43] By these interventions, it enabled funds to comply with their investors' redemption requests. It also stopped the abrupt decline in asset prices and the investors' panicky reactions to these price declines. The intervention achieved its goals, but it also created a heightened expectation among investors that, if something goes seriously wrong, the central bank will always step in as a "market maker of last resort."[44]

The term market maker of last resort, however, is a misnomer in this context. Ordinarily, *market maker* refers to intermediaries who are ready to buy an asset at a *buying price* with an expectation of reselling it shortly at a *selling price* that they hope will be higher. In a decentralized system of exchange in which most participants do not know or meet each other, a market maker relieves sellers and buyers of the need to search for each other. Usually, market makers do not hold on to assets for long unless an unpleasant surprise prevents a quick resale.[45]

By contrast, in 2020 and later, the Federal Reserve, as well as other central banks that followed its lead, accumulated large amounts of all kinds of assets.[46] Central banks are now holding large portfolios not only of government debt but also of corporate debt, loans to small and medium businesses, mortgage-related securities, and covered bonds.[47] Their interventions have provided long-term support for asset prices and not merely prevented momentary panics. Effectively, the central banks acted as long-term investors, *asset buyers of last resort*, rather than market makers of last resort.[48] This development is dangerous. The long-term support of asset prices may prevent downward price adjustments when return prospects become less favorable, thus maintaining inflated asset valuations in the economy.

The events of March 2020 echoed the events of September 2008, when the Lehman Brothers bankruptcy and the ensuing losses of the Reserve Primary Fund caused a run by investors on money market funds, which in turn forced money market funds to withdraw from lending activities and caused a freeze of money markets and a worldwide scramble for cash. In 2008, the run on money market funds ended when the U.S. Treasury provided these funds with access to a type of deposit insurance.

After this experience, it was clear that the susceptibility of money market funds to runs was problematic not only for investors in these funds but also for institutions such as banks that had come to rely on borrowing from money market funds. This fragility was also dangerous for the financial system as a whole. It became clear as well that regulatory reform was needed. Yet, both in the United States and in the European Union, initial reform proposals were watered down substantially, and the post-crisis rules that were eventually passed, after much procrastination, did not provide any protection in the 2020 crisis.[49] New reform initiatives have now been introduced, but as of this writing (May 2023), they have not been finalized and it is not clear they will do any better next time the funds incur runs.[50]

The acuteness of the 2020 crisis was due in part to the enhanced vulnerability of U.S. bank holding companies after the Trump-era deregulation. The weakening of liquidity requirements had allowed banks to hold fewer so-called high quality liquid assets, which meant that they were more dependent on being able to generate cash by selling less liquid assets.[51] Selling such assets is difficult and costly when asset markets are in turmoil and asset prices depressed. Moreover, banks that had set up, or "sponsored," their own money market funds would be exposed to losses when supporting these funds in a panic. The ability of banks to bear these losses was already low before but had been much further reduced by the Federal Reserve's relaxation of equity requirements in the years 2017–2019.[52]

High Indebtedness and Fragility

Bankers like to proclaim that they have much more "capital" than regulators ask for and much more than before the crisis. Their statements usually refer to accounting values of equity relative to the so-called risk-weighted assets.[53] In Chapter 11, we criticized the use of risk weights in determining equity requirements as resting on a combination of tradition, pseudo-science, and politics, which is unsuitable and deficient for capturing the actual risks banks are taking.

Relative to the banks' total assets, the equity levels of large banks are still much too low. For large European banks, one study found that Basel III had only moved equity levels from a range of 2–4 percent to a range of 4–7 percent of total assets, which is roughly where they were in 1998 and which was already much lower than in the decades before that.[54] At these low equity levels, it still does not take much to put such banks into distress and to cause investors to lose confidence, as happened to Silicon Valley Bank, whose reported equity amounted to less than 8 percent of total assets.

In Chapter 11, we proposed graduated equity requirements of 20–30 percent of total assets, with the proviso that, below 20 percent, the bank must issue new shares, and between 20 percent and 30 percent, the bank must try to rebuild equity by abstaining from payouts to shareholders through dividend payments or share repurchases. The harmful effects of heavy indebtedness would thereby be much reduced.[55] Had SVB entered the period of higher interest rates with 20 percent equity, it probably would not have become insolvent.[56]

There is *no justification* from society's perspective for tolerating equity levels anywhere as low as those that current regulations allow and banks maintain. Since writing this book more than a decade ago, we have still not heard any satisfactory argument to explain why the equity levels we proposed are somehow too high. These levels were common in banking a century ago, before government subsidies began to play such a large role, and they are considered normal outside banking.

Some regulators seem to believe that large banks are relatively safe.[57] Deposit outflows from regional banks to large banks in the wake of the SVB closure suggest that depositors share this view. However, risks from their investments can threaten the solvency even of very large banks if these banks rely mainly on borrowing and have very little equity to absorb losses. The size of the globally systemic bank Credit Suisse did not protect it from becoming distressed and subject to a run when the flaws in its investments caused large losses.

As another example of fragility from high indebtedness and risky investments, consider Deutsche Bank. Just before the financial crisis of 2007–2009, that bank's equity amounted to less than 2 percent of its total assets. In the crisis and its immediate aftermath, the bank had to manipulate its accounts in order to meet the equity requirements. For this manipulation, it was subsequently fined by U.S. authorities.[58] After the crisis, the bank reduced the scale of its activities but, according to Basel III standards, the ratio of equity to total assets did not rise above 4 percent.[59] In the years 2014–2019, the bank reported losses adding up to more than $14 billion. Repeated issues of new equity were just large enough to avoid falling short of regulatory requirements but not enough to restore investor confidence. Investors came to interpret new equity issues as harbingers of bad news, such as announcements of additional fines by U.S. authorities.[60]

In 2016, Deutsche Bank was highly distressed. New equity that it had raised had been immediately wiped out again by a loss of almost €6.8 billion. Business was not going well, and the bank was facing significant legal risks.[61] In September 2016, U.S. authorities announced a new fine of $14 billion for fraud in selling mortgage-related securities. The fine was subsequently reduced to $7 billion, but for a while the announced number loomed large and triggered public discussion of whether the bank was or might become insolvent and whether the German government would or should support the bank if its existence was threatened.[62] Two months earlier, in June 2016, the

International Monetary Fund had reported that, because of its size, complexity, and interconnectedness, Deutsche Bank was the most important net contributor to global systemic risk. According to the IMF, many important financial institutions across the world would be deeply affected if Deutsche Bank were to get into serious difficulties.[63]

At the time, the value of equity shown in Deutsche Bank's published accounts amounted to roughly €60 billion, but the market value of the bank's shares was less than €14 billion.[64] The low market value was a sign that investors considered the accounts to be too optimistic about the bank's prospects.[65] Many wondered whether Deutsche Bank was still solvent. The bank further reduced the scale of its operations and survived this crisis, but it continued to have problems until in 2021 its renewed focus on its traditional German business seemed to be paying off.[66]

The fact that the market value of Deutsche Bank's equity was positive throughout does not prove that it was actually solvent. Because their liability is limited, shareholders cannot lose more than what they have invested. If the bank cannot pay its debt, shareholders can just walk away. Because they know that shareholders will not have to pay anything if events turn out badly, the share price will *never* be negative, and it can only be zero if equity is entirely wiped out. Even if the bank is in severe distress or insolvent, as long as it does not default and there is a chance that it might turn around and survive after all, investors are willing to pay a positive price for the bank's shares because, with some probability, they will get some positive returns.[67] In the case of a systemic institution like Deutsche Bank that investors expect to be bailed out with public money, the prices of shares in the market also reflect the benefits from prospective taxpayer subsidies in a bailout.[68]

Opaqueness

For outsiders, and perhaps also for the banks' managers and their regulators and supervisors, correctly assessing the solvency of a bank is often very difficult, if not impossible. As we discussed in Chapters 3 and 11, solvency itself is a tricky concept because the actual ability to pay debt when it is due often depends on the valuation of assets that live beyond the time the debt is due. Moreover, existing rules leave a fair amount of leeway for creative accounting.

The banks' accounts might therefore not reflect all losses that have already occurred or that might be forthcoming.[69] For example, if the borrowers to whom the bank had lent fail to make payments on time, the bank's managers may be unwilling to report the loan as "nonperforming," arguing that the payment is merely delayed and will soon be made after all. Managers may also underestimate the prospective losses from prosecutions by authorities and other legal disputes. The 2010s witnessed many examples of both.[70] Investors have no way of assessing how great these risks actually are.

The accounting for derivatives, securities whose value depends on other asset prices or on the occurrence of uncertain events, is particularly opaque. If derivatives are traded in open markets, one can value them at their market prices, but these prices, as well as the risks involved, can change often and quickly. If derivatives are not traded in open markets, their valuations are based on mathematical models involving a set of assumptions that can be quite arbitrary; sometimes the valuation is effectively a guess.[71] The numbers involved are sometimes large: In June 2016, Deutsche Bank reported €615 billion in derivatives on the asset side of the balance sheet and €598 billion on the liabilities side.[72] If the risks were perfectly matched so that the values of a claim and a liability always go up or down by the same amount, one might not worry about these positions. In fact, they are not perfectly matched, and there have been cases where illusions or self-deception about the matching of risks were at the root of large losses.[73] At this order of magnitude, it does not take much of a modeling error to wipe out the bank's equity with a book value of roughly €60 billion.[74]

Reported measures of "safety" can be deceiving. In the run-up to September 2008, for a full year after the first signs of the global financial crisis, most large banks showed equity just above the levels required by regulation. In its last balance sheet before bankruptcy, Lehman Brothers showed equity equal to about 3 percent of total assets. Months before the bankruptcy, many suspected, and one critic commented publicly, that Lehman Brothers had not properly accounted for its losses on home mortgages and mortgage-related securities and was in fact insolvent.[75] It later became clear that the bank had used many accounting tricks to hide the extent of its problems.[76] Similarly, many institutions that showed equity equal to or slightly above regulatory requirements until mid-September 2008 then got into trouble and required massive supports and bailouts. This assessment includes several institutions whose solvency was in doubt.[77]

Given the opaqueness of balance sheets and the leeway given to banks in valuing their assets, even sophisticated investors have trouble assessing a bank's financial health.[78] Uncertainty about the health of a bank contributes to the risk of a run. In the case of Lehman Brothers, some argue that such a run destroyed what was fundamentally a solvent investment bank. However, mounting losses and the brinkmanship of its management led many to question Lehman Brothers' solvency. This skepticism caused lenders to withdraw funding, so the bank could no longer function and had to file for bankruptcy.[79]

For Credit Suisse (CS), the developments leading up to the final crisis in March 2023 followed a similar pattern. In 2021, CS lost close to $5 billion in the collapse of investment fund Archegos, which we discuss later in this chapter.[80] As mentioned, the bank reported a loss of 7.3 billion Swiss francs in 2022, including a loss of more than 4 billion Swiss francs in the third quarter. Its newly installed top management thus started its reign by taking a large write-down.[81] At about the same time this new management announced that CS was going to reduce its financial distress by raising 4 billion Swiss francs' worth of new equity in November and December.[82] This equity increase was too small to neutralize the previously reported losses. The announcements did not give investors much confidence that the new management was up to solving the bank's problems.

Throughout 2022, the market value of the equity of Credit Suisse was only a fraction of its book value.[83] Also throughout 2022, the bank lost customers, depositors as well as clients for its wealth management services. In early October, after the announcements of the third-quarter results and of the new equity issue, the drain of customers became a run.[84] From November through early March, the drain of customers slowed again, but then, in March 2023, the run returned in full force. The reasons are a matter of speculation, but the March 14 publication of the 2022 Annual Report seems to have played an important role.[85]

This 2022 report of CS reads as if the authors had wanted to confirm our warnings about the opaqueness of banks' financial accounts. It contains two sets of accounts with different numbers for equity, 45 billion Swiss francs and 22 billion Swiss francs. The different sets of accounts also gave different numbers for 2022 losses, the 7.3 billion Swiss francs mentioned above and another figure of 24.4 billion Swiss francs.

Which numbers should investors believe? The two sets of accounts were set up under different rules and with different purposes. Some differences in numbers are therefore normal. However, the size of the differences in this case is highly unusual. They arise from differences in values assessed for the different subsidiaries and units of CS.[86] In one set of accounts these values are much lower than the previous year, whereas in the other they are not lower.

The more optimistic set of accounts is accompanied by a comment from management that they had not seen any need to reduce assessed values for different units. However, the auditors' certification of the accounts contains a warning that management had failed to design a good method for assessing risks of errors in valuations. Management itself conceded that "internal control over financial reporting was not effective."[87] These statements from the auditors and management undermine the credibility of the more optimistic valuations.[88]

The 2022 report of CS also gives the impression that the bank was suffering an existential crisis and management was unaware of it or chose to ignore it. As mentioned, the bank suffered large losses of depositors and clients for wealth management services. Revenues shrank dramatically, but costs hardly declined. The report announced planned cost savings, but these were hardly enough to bring costs in line with the adverse developments.[89]

When the final run began, the Swiss authorities tried to suggest that CS was only suffering a liquidity problem, but its own actions belied that message. The liquidity support provided by the central bank was too small to reassure investors, so it did not stop the run. The authorities then used strong political pressure to arrange the shotgun takeover of CS by UBS, the other "globally systemic" bank in Switzerland. To get UBS to agree, they promised significant support from the central bank and guarantees from the public purse, relying on emergency powers of the government to impose the out-come without participation of the legislature or the shareholders of the two banks. The need for taxpayer involvement suggests that ultimately all partici-pants saw a serious possibility that CS might actually be insolvent, despite the positive equity numbers in the 2022 annual report.

The actions of the Swiss authorities, government, central bank, and super-visor show that nobody should believe the incantations of policymakers, reg-ulators, and bankers that, after the reforms they have introduced, large global banks can fail without substantial damage to the rest of the economy. In an early draft of this chapter, in January 2023, we wrote: "We therefore expect that, if the crisis of Credit Suisse were to deepen, the authorities, most impor-tantly the Swiss National Bank, would step in to provide support." The actual events in March 2023 have confirmed this expectation; the Swiss central bank and government were heavily involved, not only with loans and guarantees but also with new legislation and regulation that eliminated shareholder par-ticipation in the decision and that legitimized the wipeout of some subordi-nated debt.[90] We expect that any other systemically important bank would also receive support from its government and central bank if such support was needed to avoid default. Chapters 15 and 16 provide more detailed dis-cussions of bailouts and their persistence.

For many investors, the expectation that central banks and governments will prevent a bank from defaulting is an important reason they are willing to do business with that bank at all. Without explicit or implicit guarantees, institutions that are so highly indebted and so large, complex, and opaque would hardly be trustworthy enough to other market participants. Outside of banking, no healthy corporation is anywhere near the indebtedness levels that banks routinely maintain, or anywhere near the size and complexity of the largest banks.

In the so-called shadow banking system, most of the institutions that are not funded by deposits and that do not enjoy the explicit guarantees given to banks maintain much higher levels of equity as they respond to market forces that affect their funding costs, including pressures from the banks that lend to them.[91] By contrast, in the regulated banking sector, explicit guarantees and expectations of central bank or government support remain important ingredients of the banks' business models and allow the banks to operate with much lower levels of equity funding.[92]

Incompetence and Recklessness

In a conversation in 2010, Martin Hellwig asked an investment banker with whom he was serving on a committee about quality differences between investment bankers. The question was motivated by the consideration that the vast expansion of investment banking in the preceding decades had also brought a vast expansion in the number of investment bankers, and that some of this expansion might have come at the expense of quality. The answer was blunt: "Yes, some people did not understand what was going on. We used to call them 'stuffies' because you could always stuff them with securities that you wanted to get rid of." This answer aligns with Michael Lewis's reference in *The Big Short* to the "folly of subprime mortgage investors, some large number of whom seemed to live in Düsseldorf," a German city with two banks whose folly cost taxpayers dearly.[93] The folly of the "stuffies" enabled the mortgage lending and securitization growth in the years leading up to the 2007–2009 crisis, which involved misrepresentations and even fraud in selling mortgage-related securities, as well as flawed notions about real estate markets and prices and flawed incentives, as discussed in Chapter 5.[94]

Discussions of banks and bank regulation often presume that the participants are competent and only rarely commit major errors and that, if an error does occur, it is quickly corrected. This presumption is unrealistic. Moreover, with the small amounts of equity funding that prevail, the consequences of incompetence can easily destroy the affected banks.

One cannot always distinguish incompetence and recklessness. In Chapters 8 and 9, we discussed recklessness as a cause of excessive risk taking and subsequent bank failures.[95] Recklessness may result not just from flawed incentives but also from flawed perceptions, particularly of risks. Flawed perceptions of risks are probably partly due to a lack of understanding and partly due to willful blindness. In either case, the ensuing behavior can be very dangerous.

The two banks that collapsed in March 2023, SVB and CS, illustrate the impact of incompetence paired with recklessness. In 2021, CS reported a loss of $5.5 billion (4.7 billion Swiss francs) from its involvement with Archegos Capital Management. Archegos was a hedge fund that bought shares or placed enormous bets with derivatives on the value of a few stocks using significant borrowing from several banks.[96] Its investments were concentrated in a small number of stocks, particularly ViacomCBS and Discovery. In March 2021, the share prices of these two companies dropped dramatically.[97] The banks that had lent to Archegos asked for additional collateral for their loans, in cash or securities. When Archegos could not provide that, the banks rushed to sell the shares that they held as collateral. Archegos defaulted and went bankrupt. CS had not been alone in blundering over Archegos, but some of the other banks were able to recover most of their money. CS reacted last and was harmed the most.

Archegos showed poor judgment in concentrating its funds in just a handful of stocks and doing so with much borrowed money. CS showed even worse judgment in lending to Archegos for such risky investments without a proper understanding and control of the risks. An outside investigation that CS initiated showed that people at CS had overlooked many warning signals and exerted forbearance on many occasions when Archegos violated barriers that been set in place to control the bank's risks. The investigation concluded that the disaster was due to a "lack of competence" and the "weakness of a risk culture" with a prioritization of current profits, $16 million in 2020 and an expectation of $40 million for 2021, over sound risk management. Employees concerned about their bonuses were said to be reluctant to have serious discussions with Archegos when yet another red line was crossed.[98]

Around the same time, CS also incurred large losses through its involvement in Australia-based Greensill Capital Group, which also became insolvent in 2021. Greensill specialized in lending to nonfinancial firms in order to help them overcome delays in payments for the goods they sold along a supply chain.[99] Greensill also succumbed to the effects of overconcentration of its activities, in this case, on the India-based GFG Alliance Group of the Gupta family, which eventually owed several billion dollars to Greensill.

CS was involved as an organizer of investment funds that bought packages of claims from Greensill and sold shares in these packages to outside investors, with assurances that these were low-risk investments because a large part of the claims would be insured. In fact, CS left it to Greensill to put the packages together and to arrange the insurance, without control. Greensill failed when the insurers withdrew because they were suspicious of the lack of diversification. CS became liable for misrepresentations in selling the asset-backed securities of its funds. As in the Archegos case, the bank had made elementary mistakes in failing to oversee and control Greensill. The final report of the Swiss bank supervisor on this case, which was released on February 28, 2023, hardly two weeks before the run on CS took up speed again, is scathing.[100]

Recklessness and the 2023 U.S. Banking Crisis

The failure of SVB also reflects incompetence and recklessness. Its causes are much simpler than you would guess from initial media reports emphasizing that SVB had specialized in lending to high-tech startup companies and venture capital firms in Silicon Valley. George Bailey, from the movie *It's a Wonderful Life* that we discussed in Chapter 4, would have known all about SVB's problems. So would the managers of U.S. savings institutions in the early 1980s, whose depositors withdrew funds in favor of money market funds offering higher returns while the banks only earned low interest rates on previously made long-term mortgage loans.

SVB used almost exclusively uninsured short-term deposits to fund long-term investments. Such a mismatch creates a risk of a bank run, the subject of the movie *It's a Wonderful Life*. Ordinarily, it is unlikely that all depositors want their money back at the same time, but if there are reasons for them to do so, they will. One reason would be information that the bank might be insolvent. The introduction of deposit insurance has greatly reduced the risk of a run because insured depositors no longer worry about losses from an insolvency of the bank. However, SVB had an unusually high share of deposits above the $250,000 limit up to which the FDIC provides insurance. At the end of 2022, out of $173 billion in deposits, more than $150 billion were not covered by the FDIC.[101]

Between the end of 2019 and the first quarter of 2022, deposits at SVB had more than tripled, from $51 billion to $198 billion. Deposits grew in this period because the low interest rate environment created by the Federal Reserve's reactions to the COVID pandemic changed investors' assessments of the trade-off between the flexibility provided by a deposit and the higher returns provided by money market assets and longer-term investments.

Because of the uncertainty created by the pandemic, loan demand in this period was relatively low, at SVB and at other U.S. banks, and thus most of the additional funds they received through deposits did not go into new lending but rather into securities such as Treasury bonds and mortgage-backed securities.[102] By March 31, 2022, SVB held $127 billion in securities, more than four times the $29 billion it had held at the end of 2019. Interest on these securities was on the order of 1.6 percent per year. With deposit rates close to zero, this constellation looked wonderful.

In the spring of 2022, however, the Federal Reserve began to raise interest rates in order to fight inflation. Therefore, interest rates in money markets rose steeply. For example, between March 7, 2022 and March 6, 2023, the federal funds rate, the interest rate at which banks lend to each other overnight, rose from 0.08 percent to 4.57 percent. For SVB, this change had two negative effects. First, as in the experience of the S&Ls in 1980, deposits began to flow out because the depositors could earn higher returns elsewhere. This is why SVB deposits at the end of 2022 were already $25 billion below the peak of March 2022. Second, the market values of securities held by SVB declined significantly. As we explained earlier, increases in interest rates generally lower the market prices of existing assets and securities because the returns they offer are relatively lower than those on newly issued debt.

By September 2022, and perhaps earlier, losses from the price declines of securities made SVB insolvent, in the sense that the market value of its assets was less than its liabilities.[103] The insolvency was not evident in the bank's accounts because the bank made use of a rule that certain assets need not be "marked to market" as the phrase goes, i.e., valued at their market prices, because they are classified as "held to maturity."[104] As of September 30, 2022, SVB held $93 billion of securities in this category, but the market value of these securities was only $77 billion, i.e., there was a hidden loss of $16 billion. If this loss had appeared in the bank's balance sheet, SVB's equity would have been wiped out.[105] However, SVB leaders refused to acknowledge the obvious distress the bank was in and continued to make enthusiastic projections based on invalid assumptions.[106]

Outflows of SVB deposits continued in early 2023. The bank used cash, money obtained through other borrowing, and non-renewals of maturing securities to pay the depositors who withdrew their money. Eventually, however, the bank's management was compelled to sell securities at a loss. When the bank announced on March 8 that it had sold $21 billion of securities at a loss of $1.8 billion and that it wanted to raise $2.25 billion in new equity, the announcement made investors aware that the bank was in deep distress or insolvent. The announcement of an ultimately unsuccessful equity offering caused the stock price to decline dramatically, and the combination of bad news led depositors to run as fast as they could, attempting to withdraw a staggering $42 billion on March 9.[107] The authorities closed the bank the next morning.[108]

SVB was special in having had such extraordinary deposit growth in 2020 and 2021, in catering to a very small, socially connected clientele, and in having more than 90 percent uninsured deposits. These facts explain the extent and speed of the run, but *the ultimate cause of the bank's failure was the underlying solvency problem.*

The developments that we have described and the problems they caused were not unique to SVB. The story of First Republic Bank, mentioned above, is similar to that of SVB.[109] More generally, between early 2020 and March 2022, many banks in the United States saw substantial deposit growth because money market investments were unattractive. Much of deposit growth went into fixed-income securities because loan demand was not growing as much if at all. When interest rates increased again in 2022, these securities declined substantially in value.

As of April 2023, according to one study, the total unrealized losses on securities in U.S. banks amounted to some $2 trillion.[110] If half of all uninsured deposits were withdrawn, about 190 banks would have to realize losses so large that they might be unable to repay even the insured deposits. If asset prices fell because many banks had to sell securities simultaneously, the number of banks affected and the size of the losses would be even larger. Such concerns explain why investors and markets did not come to rest after the reassuring speech of Federal Reserve Chair Jay Powell on May 3 that we quoted above.

The risks created when banks use deposits to invest in fixed-interest long-term assets are well known. Many U.S. bank managers, particularly at SVB, showed incompetence and recklessness in taking these risks without suitable protection. The question is why no one had stopped the banks from taking such large risks. Apparently, asset manager BlackRock warned SVB management about their risks in January 2022, but they chose to ignore the warning.[111]

Were the bank, its depositors, and its supervisors blind or reckless, or were they willfully blind? The bank's managers may have been fully rational. As long as their ride lasted, they reaped high rewards for the profit growth associated with a growing balance sheet and the margin, however small, between the returns on securities and the costs of deposits.

The behavior of depositors is harder to understand, unless they expected to be bailed out or trusted regulators to make sure the bank was safe. The average uninsured deposit in SVB was more than $4 million, with one deposit exceeding $3 billion.[112] Putting that kind of money into a bank deposit would seem to require some investigation of the bank's business model and the bank's financial health. Given that the business model and the associated risks were obvious from even a superficial perusal of the bank's quarterly reports, why did the depositors not take account of the fact that, with interest rates near zero, the bank was taking a very lopsided bet and that, if interest rates did go up, the bank would be in serious trouble?

Failures of Regulation and Supervision

As for the regulators and supervisors, they might have raised questions about the bank's exorbitant growth in 2019–2022 and about the risks associated with this growth. They also should have raised questions about the bank's solvency and even closed the bank as early as September 2022. The fact that the bank did not have to adjust its disclosures to reflect losses on securities classified as "held to maturity" did not mean that losses in market values of these securities were irrelevant, and regulators certainly had the information and should have been aware of these obvious risks. The supervisors should have intervened by September 30, 2022 at the latest. They failed to do so until the massive run of March 9, 2023.

Some supervisors had issued alerts to the bank, but they failed to act to force the bank to do more to protect itself and its depositors. They do not seem to have seen the existential threat from risks the bank was bearing and the urgency of corrective action.[113] The Federal Reserve's report on SVB's failure refers to management recklessness and to the supervisors' slowness in addressing this recklessness, but hardly gets to the heart of the issues.[114] In fact, SVB received high ratings from its supervisors in most categories, including capital adequacy, and most of the issues the supervisors raised were procedural. A preliminary review by the Government Accountability Office (GAO) notes that the Federal Reserve failed to engage in prompt corrective action.[115] The laxness of the supervisors mirrored the "light touch" approach to regulation and supervision of the Federal Reserve.[116]

The Federal Reserve's report fails to discuss the bank's solvency problem and the supervisors' blindness toward this problem.[117] It treats the interest rate risks of SVB's investments and the liquidity risks of SVB's funding as though they had nothing to do with each other. Yet, changes in asset values and changes in refinancing conditions were two sides of the same coin. The decline in value of the bank's securities, which caused its insolvency, was caused by the same increases in interest rates that made depositors leave the bank after March 2022. The Federal Reserve's report fails to discuss the problem that the supervisors' focus on regulatory capital ratios based on accounting valuations and risk weights blinded them to the impact of market value losses that were not reflected in the accounts.

Importantly, supervisors should have recognized the declines in the market values of SVB's assets as highly relevant to its viability and should have acted on this information. The Federal Reserve's policy reaction to the SVB failure, expanding its lending programs to banks, neutralizes the effects of deposit withdrawals temporarily, *but it does nothing to alleviate the underlying solvency problems of banks.* If a bank pays off depositors by borrowing from the Fed at 5 percent while earning less than 2 percent on government bonds bought or mortgages made in 2021, it is a path to failure.[118]

The issue of hidden solvency problems is well known from the Savings and Loans (S&L) crisis of the 1980s in the United States that we discussed in Chapter 4.[119] Regulators and supervisors seem to have forgotten the lessons of that crisis about dangers from failing to recognize losses promptly. Then as now, accounting rules for assets classified as "held to maturity" concealed losses and allowed many insolvent institutions to persist without intervention of the supervisors. In the 1980s, the "zombie" S&Ls went on to "gamble for resurrection," using funds from depositors to take risks that blew up when interest rates rose again in 1989. The depositors were attracted by the high interest rates that the S&Ls offered and by the promise of protection from government-backed deposit insurance. The ultimate cost to taxpayers was much higher than it would have been if the insolvencies had been addressed in 1981.

If the banks' solvency issues are not addressed, a new round of gambling for resurrection is to be expected. In fact, some such gambling has already begun in 2022. When interest rates started increasing, those banks that were most strongly affected tended to increase their risk exposures even more, by buying even longer-term securities or by reducing hedges against these risks.[120] By contrast, banks that were less strongly affected tried to reduce their risk exposures.

As we discussed in Chapters 3 and 10, the liquidity narrative—"it is just a liquidity problem"—is convenient but dangerous. It is especially convenient if the illiquidity involves a run. In this case, the banker will claim that he is merely a victim of bad luck. The supervisor will claim that it would have been impossible to foresee the run. And the economist will glory in demonstrating that runs can occur out of the blue, just because suddenly every depositor believes that every other depositor is about to run and therefore rushes to be first in line to withdraw money.[121]

In the real world, runs hardly ever occur without a concrete reason. As we discussed in Chapter 4, runs occur when bad news causes depositors and other investors to take a closer look at the bank and they do not like what they see.[122] This is precisely what happened at SVB and other U.S. banks, as well as CS.

In the U.S. banking crisis of 2023, the liquidity narrative abuses the fact that flawed accounting rules hide the insolvencies. If a bank claims that it intends to hold debt securities until they are repaid, the accounting rules require no recognition of value losses that are caused by interest rate increases in the interim. These rules are based on the flawed argument that losses in market value matter only if the securities are to be sold. If they are to be held until they are repaid, supposedly the only issue is whether the borrower is creditworthy. If the borrower is creditworthy, for example, if the borrower is the U.S. government and the debt is denominated in dollars, it is clear that the debt will eventually be paid in full, together with the specified interest.

However, the bank may be unable to hold the debt securities until they are repaid. At any time, depositors may want their money back, and then the bank must pay up. If the bank's cash reserves do not suffice, the bank may have to sell assets even if, originally, it intended to hold them until they expired. Alternatively, if the bank replaces departing depositors with new deposits or other funding at currently prevailing rates of interest, it may have to pay much higher interest than before, higher even than the return on its securities.

This problem is relevant even when there is no run. In the case of SVB, significant deposit withdrawals occurred throughout the twelve months preceding the run. SVB had a large cash reserve and it did obtain funds through additional borrowing from the Federal Home Loan Bank (at relatively harsh terms), but eventually SVB had to sell securities, and the fiction of holding securities until they expired became untenable. The withdrawals before March 2023 appear to have been motivated by the same kinds of considerations as the deposit inflows in 2020 and 2021, namely, comparisons of deposits with other short-term investment opportunities. A bank that relies on funding from such investors must always be up to the danger that they might want to leave. For such a bank, the notion that large parts of the bank's assets could be held forever at the bank's discretion is deeply flawed. So is the accounting rule that is based on this notion.

Reforming Accounting Rules and Equity Requirements

Accounting rules should be changed so that banks must apply fair-value accounting to all assets regardless of how long they intend to hold them. Fair-value accounting relies on market value for assets where markets exist, such as government bonds.[123] It also relies on continuous assessments of asset quality, such as the creditworthiness of borrowers.[124] In the context of changes in interest rates, market value accounting for securities would greatly reduce the scope for hiding insolvencies. It would also force supervisors—or give supervisors the chance—to identify solvency problems quickly and take prompt corrective action. The desirability of prompt corrective action was embodied in reforms after the S&L crisis.[125] Unfortunately, these reforms did not encompass the accounting rules, despite the experience that the hidden and unrecognized insolvencies from the early 1980s had contributed very much to the costs of the S&L crisis.

The suggested reform of accounting rules would prevent banks from pretending that the risks they take are minimal. For a bank that takes deposits and invests in long-term loans or securities, the risk from changes in interest rate is substantial. In the case of SVB, the market value losses on supposedly safe securities came to over 15 percent of the original investments. Bankers do not like to talk about risks of this magnitude—and perhaps supervisors do not like to challenge the bankers about these risks. However, hiding the losses through flawed accounting does not eliminate them, and the pretense that there is no risk from such losses is dangerous.

Since the first edition of this book appeared, we have often been asked why we propose equity requirements of 20–30 percent of total assets, a multiple of the 3 percent leverage ratio demanded under Basel III. Without repeating the arguments from Chapter 11, we note that the market value losses of SVB on its securities were much higher than the 3 percent presumed in Basel III. If SVB had followed our proposal, it would not have become insolvent. Shareholders would have absorbed all losses without money from the FDIC. Probably the bank would have grown less in 2020 and 2021, but that might have been an advantage. After all, SVB did not even use all of its growth to make loans and instead bought securities for which no banking expertise was required.

With equity required to be at least 20 percent of total assets, the supervisors would have had to recognize the bank's problems early on. They would have had an opportunity to step in and force the bank's management to take corrective measures at a time when there was no risk of insolvency yet and probably also no risk of a run. The same is true of CS, where the supervisors also preferred to kick the can down the road, hoping for better days, until it was too late, and the final run closed off any solution that would not have required taxpayer money.

In Chapter 11, we remarked that the risk-based approach to equity requirements rests on "politics, tradition, genuine and make-believe science, and the banks' self-interest." The treatment of risks from potential increases in interest rates follows regulatory tradition despite the negative experience of the 1980s, and it persists today.[126] This continued reliance of regulators on metrics that ignore important risks is misguided.

Regulatory Reform and Politics

Many insiders share our assessment that regulatory reform after the great financial crisis has been unsatisfactory. When on one occasion one of us posed the question: "If all the reforms of banking regulation that have been introduced since 2008 had already been in place in 2000, would the global financial crisis have been avoided?," a former central bank governor answered with a resounding "No!"[127] In the United States, Thomas Hoenig, vice chair of the FDIC between 2012 and 2018, said publicly in 2014 that the resilience of individual banks and industry "is still sorely lacking," and in 2018 that "too big to fail remains with us."[128] In private, many others have told us the same.

Announcements of regulatory reforms should not be interpreted to mean that the reforms being announced will be effective. Quite often, these announcements merely reflect the pride the officials involved take in having reached an agreement. Most reforms of banking regulation since 2008 were not based on any thorough analysis of what had gone wrong before the crisis.[129] And they were not accompanied by any thorough analysis of how and why the new rules would work.[130]

In a discussion with high-level regulators about the ongoing agenda of the Basel Committee on Banking Supervision, one of us raised the question of why the regulators were discussing regulatory measures without any account of how and why these measures were expected to work. The answer was: "You must understand: This is about politics!" An analysis of leaked voting records and public speeches shows that the participants in the Basel Committee's negotiations were mostly interested in promoting the interests of their own national champions, confirming our discussion in Chapter 12.[131]

The politics of regulatory reform sometimes depend on the regulators and sometimes on legislators and governments. For money market fund regulation, in the United States, reform was watered down by the Securities and Exchange Commission (SEC), the designated regulator. In the EU, the watering down came from the member state governments, particularly France.[132]

Politics enters many aspects of banking regulation and supervision, including assessments of risk. For example, in most jurisdictions, banking regulation still treats government bonds denominated in the country's own currency as entirely riskless despite the huge losses that those who held Greek government debt incurred in 2012.[133] A 2015 report of the European Systemic Risk Board initiated a discussion on the treatment of risk from government debt but, so far, this discussion has not led to any rule changes.[134] The Basel Committee on Banking Supervision and the European Commission have not gone beyond recommendations for transparency about holdings of government debt and for diversification, i.e., risk reduction by spreading the holdings over the debt of several governments.[135] Anything more effective meets strong opposition from governments that benefit from easy funding conditions if their debt is treated as riskless.[136]

Meanwhile, in the middle of the 2010s, the leadership of the Basel Committee on Bank Regulation and Supervision seems to have been concerned that the risks were still large and that regulatory reform had not gone far enough.[137] Among other things, it concluded that reliance on the banks' own risk models for determining the required equity left a lot of room for manipulation.[138] Several studies undermined the trustworthiness of the risk models. In response to questions about the treatment of risks attached to certain assets and contracts, banks had given extremely heterogeneous answers, which suggested that these risk assessments were based on guesswork or, worse, manipulations, rather than any "science."[139] In 2017, therefore, the

Basel Committee introduced an amendment to the Basel Accord that limited the scope for reducing equity requirements by use of such models.[140]

The banking lobby referred to this new agreement as "Basel IV" and campaigned vehemently against it.[141] So did the governments of France and Germany and the European Commission. The European Commission's proposal for implementing this new agreement in the European Union falls short of the agreed standards "in order to take account of European specificities."[142] The shortfall is in conflict with the understanding that the Basel Accord sets *minimal* regulatory standards that are a precondition for allowing the banks of one jurisdiction to operate in other jurisdictions without being subject to supervision there as well. Negotiations about the legislation are due to be completed before the end of 2023. In the United States, the industry's Bank Policy Institute and the Financial Services Forum are also trying to get the regulators to dilute the implementation of the new Basel rules. As of this writing (May 2023), the final details of the implementation are still unclear.

In its attempt to limit abuses of the risk weights approach to determining equity requirements, the Basel Committee is on the right track, though much too timidly. As we have noted before, the way they are actually used in bank regulation, the risk weights have little to do with genuine science and a lot to do with politics, tradition, make-believe science, and the banks' interests.[143] The failure to take proper account of the risks that hit SVB, namely, risks from changes in interest rates when using short-term liabilities to fund long-term investments, is one example where tradition—and the banks' self-interests—outweigh any common sense.

Some, particularly academics, prefer the risk-weighted approach because it seems more sophisticated. A simple leverage ratio approach is despised as being too crude.[144] Surely, so the argument goes, a bank must be required to have more equity funding if it takes higher risks. When this argument is presented by a banker, the speaker usually means something quite different: if a bank *claims* to be taking less risk, it should be allowed to get away with *less* required equity funding. In practice, the promotion of the risk-weighted approach aims at lowering required equity, not at raising it. The basis for requiring less equity is the claim that a bank has little risk, without any objective risk measurement.

The lowering of equity requirements is dangerous. Some of the risk weights are close to zero, so that the implied equity requirements are also close to zero. For example, in the run-up to the crisis of 2007–2009, many banks had used risk weighting to have equity backing on the order of 1 percent of the assets in their trading books, including mortgage-related securities.[145] Such low risk weights and such low equity requirements allow banks to magnify their gambling a lot. For some bankers, the scope for such gambling with very little equity and a lot of borrowing seems to be the real purpose of a risk-weighted approach to determining equity requirements with their own risk models.

Such gambling with assets requiring little equity backing enables bankers to take huge risks and should be prohibited. Therefore, equity requirements should be based on a leverage ratio approach. It might make sense, however, to combine a simple leverage ratio approach with an asymmetric risk-weighted approach that requires banks to use *more* equity funding for large risks but does not allow them to get away with less equity funding for purportedly small risks. The basic leverage ratio ought to be much higher than the 3 percent of Basel III and even the higher ratios in the United States, up to the range of 20–30 percent as recommended in Chapter 11. When leverage ratio requirements are increased, it is important to ensure that in the transition, the banks cannot simply get to the higher ratio by selling assets, particularly safe assets.[146]

The Parade of Bankers' New Clothes Continues

Bankers and their lobbyists are in on all discussions of banking regulation, either officially or behind the scenes.[147] In part, this situation reflects the symbiosis of bankers and politicians that we discussed in Chapter 12. In part, it also reflects a sense that bankers are the experts.[148] Bankers, however, are interested parties.[149]

Bankers often complain that regulation is expensive and threaten that it will harm the economy and prevent them from making loans. They have objected strongly to regulators' attempts to limit the abuses of the banks' risk models. They have also fought even temporary bans on dividend payouts and stock repurchases meant to improve banks' resilience during the COVID crisis and more recently when facing risks from interest rate increases and a possible recession.[150]

Quite often, the only "cost" of the regulation is that the bankers must give up something that benefits them personally but imposes a cost on others. As we discussed in Chapters 8 and 9, costs to the bankers and banks are not the same as costs to society. If the regulation constrains the banks' ability to shift their costs and downside risks to others, all it does is remove their privilege to benefit themselves while harming society. The bankers' claims about "costs," as discussed in earlier chapters, is similar to chemical companies complaining about increased costs when they are prohibited from dumping toxic chemicals into rivers next to their plants.[151]

President Trump's executive order to the effect that regulations should be efficient, effective, and appropriately tailored, and Secretary Mnuchin's 101 recommendations on appropriate tailoring, must be seen in this context. As mentioned earlier, the efficiency mandate has no basis in the law.[152] Its implementation in the Treasury's recommendations focuses on the costs to banks, with scant regard for costs to the rest of society. And the notion of "tailoring" makes the regulation subservient to the banks' business strategies no matter how risky these strategies may be and how large the potential damage to the overall economy. The European Commission's attention to European "specificities" is not much different.

As for the bankers' warnings, the late Paul Volcker, revered former chair of the Federal Reserve, told a U.S. senator in 2010 that bankers' threats that credit and growth will suffer because of regulation are "all bullshit."[153] The experience of the 2010s has confirmed his assessment, as the implementation of higher equity requirements imposed by Basel III was followed by increased lending and growth.[154]

In Hans Christian Andersen's tale *The Emperor's New Clothes*, people are aware that the emperor is naked but are nevertheless acting as if he wore fine clothes, for fear of being considered stupid or incompetent. When a child shouts: "The emperor has no clothes," even the emperor realizes that he is naked and is ashamed, but he decides that he must go through with the parade. Those making flawed claims in banking remain proud of parading the

Bankers' New Clothes. They have even added some new items to the wardrobe. We comment on these developments in a document entitled "The Parade of Bankers' New Clothes Continues" which presents a list of dozens of claims and explains briefly why they are flawed.[155]

An interesting addition to the wardrobe was provided in 2013 by John Stumpf, the CEO of Wells Fargo Bank at the time. In an article in the *Financial Times*, he was quoted as saying: "Because we have this substantial self-funding with retail deposits, we don't have a lot of debt."[156] Even though deposits are clearly debt that the bank owes depositors, bankers like to think of depositors as customers rather than creditors. Deposits provide a basis for services, in particular for payments, and depositors like to avoid the hassle of switching from one bank to another. For the banks, customers' deposits are therefore a convenient form of funding, but even so, as discussed in Chapter 4, they are a form of debt. A bank that is only funded by deposits can still become insolvent if its assets lose much of their value and it becomes unable to pay depositors what it owes them. The only significant difference between deposits and other debt of Wells Fargo and other banks is that, up to a limit, the deposits are explicitly insured while other forms of debt do not have that type of an explicit guarantee, although they may still benefit from government bailouts.

The bankers' mantra is that "equity is expensive" and therefore equity requirements are harmful. In Chapters 7–9, we explained that the claim that equity is expensive is often based on fallacious claims and that, in fact, it reflects the bankers' self-interest in getting high bonuses and preserving subsidies. Nevertheless, the mantra can still be found in banking textbooks, including one written by a prominent academic and former Federal Reserve governor.[157] For society, in fact, there is virtually no relevant cost if banks are required to have much more equity, with properly designed rules as we outlined in Chapter 11. *It is heavily indebted banks that are expensive for society, not only because their defaults may cause damage to the financial system or impose costs on taxpayers, but also because their heavy indebtedness and distress tend to distort their lending and investment decisions.*

Bankers seem to think that, with a given level of equity at a given instant, a stricter equity requirement would prevent them from borrowing more and making more investments. This view presumes that bank lenders do not worry about not being paid, i.e., that the government will provide bailouts if the bank fails. If lenders do not expect to be bailed out, they will worry about the possibility of bank failure and determine the conditions under which they lend to be compensated for the risks to which they are exposed. Bankers must therefore consider that the terms at which lenders are willing to lend to them depend on whether the lenders expect the bank to be cautious or reckless in future decisions.

If lenders are exposed to risks from the bank's failing and if they expect the bankers to be reckless in future decisions, for example by expanding their borrowing ever more, they may refuse to lend altogether, or they may ask for very high interest.[158] In general, the presence of existing debt creates incentives for more borrowing and more risk taking. These incentives create a sort of "addiction" to borrowing, as explained in Chapter 3 on the dark side of borrowing.[159]

Corporate debt contracts typically have conditions intended to protect creditors and to give them confidence about the borrower's future behavior. Government-imposed restrictions on bank borrowing provide a substitute for such restrictions. In the case of banks, such a substitute is needed because creditors are highly dispersed and cannot easily organize to impose and enforce such restrictions. With deposit insurance, some creditors may not even care. The statement discussed earlier of Wells Fargo CEO Stumpf, who seemingly "forgot" that deposits are the banks' debt, may reflect the fact that banks funded primarily with deposits may not *feel* the normal burden of such heavy indebtedness, particularly if regulation and supervision are lax. Ultimately, the restrictions that the government imposes are needed to protect taxpayers and the public from the harm caused by the excessive and addictive borrowing and risk taking of banks.[160]

In this context, the reaction of academic economists specializing in banking to the 2007–2009 financial crisis is also of interest. Whereas most observers thought that this crisis was caused by excessive borrowing of banks, particularly short-term borrowing, many of the economists specializing in banking treated the crisis as a "shock" to a system that mostly works well. They claimed that regulation limiting such borrowing would deprive society of important benefits from liquidity provision, managerial discipline, and cheap lending to nonfinancial firms, which is a more sophisticated way to say that "equity is expensive."[161]

However, much of the research on which these claims are based makes highly unrealistic assumptions and does not pass basic smell tests for capturing real-world phenomena. Academic authors rave about the market outcomes their models predict while ignoring key elements of reality, particularly systemic risks and the monitoring and commitment problems discussed in the last paragraph, as well as the bankers' incentives to take excessive risks and to deceive.[162] These omissions raise serious doubts about the relevance of this research.

Because academic research is inaccessible to most people, it provides lobbyists and policymakers with material whose conclusions they can use when it serves their own interests. If they like the conclusions, they do not care whether the analysis on which they are based has anything to do with reality.[163] The experience of the last decade shows that robust equity is a source of strength that supports lending and economic growth.[164]

A Perverse Tax Subsidy

Among the reasons bankers are so intensely resistant to using more equity funding is that the corporate tax code subsidizes borrowing and penalizes equity funding for corporations. Thus, using more debt and less equity reduces the amount of taxes the banks need to pay. As discussed in Chapter 9 and again in Chapter 13, the deductibility of payments of interest on debt from taxable income has no justification and is bad policy.

The tax deductibility of interest on debt, for corporations as well as home buyers, encourages borrowing and can create or reinforce the distortions that arise from the dark side of borrowing that we discussed in Chapter 3.[165] For banks, the tax advantage of debt contributes significantly to the addictiveness of borrowing that is already intense at the high levels of indebtedness banks maintain.[166] Encouraging debt in this way is paradoxical if at the same time regulators need to reduce the fragility of the financial system and therefore the likelihood of distress, insolvency, and default. This tax policy exacerbates the conflict of interest between what is good for the banks and what is good for society. Therefore, regulations to keep the system safer and healthier are more difficult to enforce.

The extent of corporate borrowing, partly motivated by the desire to take advantage of the tax subsidies to debt, meant that many corporations were much more vulnerable when the pandemic hit in spring 2020 than they would have been had they relied on more equity and less debt. The massive supports of financial markets helped corporations in these markets avoid the consequences of their borrowing, showing that "too big to fail" is not only a problem in banking.[167]

Ideally, taxes and subsidies should be used to achieve desired policy objectives with a minimum of distortions. Often, policymakers continue to support counterproductive policies even when better approaches are available. Encouraging and enabling homeownership or higher education, for example, is better accomplished through measures directly targeted at these objectives rather than by subsidizing private debt and creating excessive burdens and distortions.

Ways to change the corporate tax code so it treats debt and equity more symmetrically have been implemented in various jurisdictions.[168] The issue is not how much tax in total banks or others should pay but how the amount of taxes is determined. A change in the tax code that would encourage, rather than discourage and penalize, the use of equity to fund corporations, particularly banks, would be a step in the right direction and might reduce the extent of excessive borrowing with its negative consequences by reducing the conflict of interest between bank managers and shareholders on one hand and the public interest on the other.

Politically, eliminating the tax subsidy of debt, which can be done in such a way as to maintain the same total amount of corporate and other taxes, would be difficult. Not only banks, but other businesses as well, are likely to oppose it. Yet, just for banks, one might achieve the desired objective of reducing the bias toward borrowing if one imposed a levy on them that corresponds to their tax savings from debt finance. Such an arrangement may be the only way to make globally systemic banks bear at least a part of the cost they impose on the rest of the financial system and of society.[169]

In arguing for higher equity requirements for banks, we sometimes meet the objection that equity requirements are not so important anymore because the reforms of the past decade have eliminated the problem that some banks are so big, so connected, so important that one cannot let them fail without causing great damage to the rest of the economy. In Chapter 5, we expressed doubts about the scope for effective too-big-to-fail reforms. By now, a decade later, we have seen many new rules and procedures for how to deal with failing banks. We have also seen that most of the time the new rules and procedures are not applied because governments and central banks prefer bailouts. Bailouts persist, and not only of the largest banks. SVB and its peers are only the most recent examples. The next two chapters explain how and why.

FIFTEEN

Bailouts and Central Banks

It was not quite a Lehman moment. But it got close.

London Banker, September 2022[1]

I N PREVIOUS CHAPTERS we discussed the many forms of supports and subsidies from governments that benefit banks and their creditors. These subsidies will be reduced if banks increase their reliance on equity funding as we suggest they should be required to do. In the last chapter, we saw that central banks also provide important supports. The supports and subsidies are key to understanding why the bankers who receive these benefits resist higher equity requirements so aggressively.

Debt is a promise. If debtors default on their promises, their creditors suffer. If the debtor is actually able to pay, creditors can take recourse to the legal system to enforce their claim. If the debtor does not have sufficient resources, the damage to the creditors is unavoidable unless a third party steps in and provides help, either in the form of a direct payment to lenders or in the form of a subsidy to the debtor that enables creditors to be paid more than they would have obtained otherwise.

Most debtors and creditors do not get such help. By contrast, banks and their creditors have come to expect support from central banks or governments as a matter of course. We refer to such support from central banks and governments, which we discussed in Chapters 4 and 9, as *bailouts*. Central banks and governments provide bailouts because they are afraid of the consequences of bank defaults. They may fear the economic, social, and political consequences of the damage done to lenders. For example, a bank may have millions of depositors, many of whom may not be well off. Defaults on these deposits may hit and impoverish a significant part of the population, forcing them to reduce their consumption and causing a depression for the industries that normally supply them.

Central banks and governments may also fear the systemic implications of bank failures and even the prospect of bank failures. Creditors without hopes of being bailed out have incentives to protect themselves, for example by withdrawing their deposits or not renewing loans to the bank if they become nervous about the risk of a default. If the bank's creditors themselves also rely on funding from others, there may be a domino effect on the ultimate sources of funding. Chapter 5 shows how such systemic effects played out with money market funds after the Lehman Brothers bankruptcy. The AIG bailout, also discussed in Chapter 5, benefited many U.S. and foreign banks that had purchased credit insurance from AIG.[2] Similarly, the interventions by European institutions and the International Monetary Fund prevented a default of the Greek government in 2010, thus protecting banks, particularly French and German banks.

Bailouts can take many forms. One form is by guaranteeing deposits when a bank is in trouble. Deposit insurance was introduced in the United States in the 1930s in reaction to the runs during the Great Depression. Deposit insurance typically covers deposits up to some statutory limit. Since 2008, this limit has been set at $250,000 in the United States. However, in the cases of Silicon Valley Bank (SVB) and Signature Bank, which were closed in March 2023, U.S. Treasury Secretary Yellen announced that *all* deposits would be paid, including the more than $150 billion deposits above the $250,000 limit. According to declarations from May 2023, the FDIC expects costs of $15.8 billion from covering the uninsured as well as the insured deposits of SVB and Signature Bank and costs of $13 billion from sharing losses of First Republic Bank with JPMorgan Chase.[3] Losses will be covered by the FDIC's Deposit Insurance Fund, which as of December 31 had a balance of $128 billion. The Deposit Insurance Fund is financed by a levy on the industry, a fee that each bank is obliged to pay.[4]

President Biden and Treasury Secretary Yellen emphasized that the support for uninsured depositors of SVB and Signature would not come from taxpayers but from the fees that banks will have to pay to the FDIC. Like taxes, however, these fees are forcibly extracted from banks by the FDIC using the power of the state. The banks that must pay the fees are likely to resent the bailout of uninsured depositors of SVB and Signature Bank just as much as taxpayers would.

In the case of Credit Suisse (CS), the Swiss government provided UBS, the large bank that took over CS, with a guarantee, a promise to compensate for certain losses from the acquisition.[5] Any payments to UBS under this guarantee would come out of the government budget and ultimately from taxpayers. In the crisis of 2007–2009, many government supports also took the form of guarantees. However, some governments also provided direct funding of banks in difficulties, in some cases by acquiring equity, newly issued or outstanding, more often however by acquiring subordinated debt claims that counted as equity for regulatory purposes.[6]

Central banks are usually not allowed to provide direct subsidies to financial institutions or others in difficulties. Even so, they can also provide support. One way they do so is to offer the institutions loans. The institutions are usually required to put up collateral, specific assets that the lender can possess if the borrower fails to make promised payments.[7] On March 12, 2023, the Federal Reserve announced that it will freely provide one-year loans to banks using debt securities held by the banks as collateral. It also announced that it would value these securities *at par*, i.e., at the nominal values of the claims on the debtors rather than their market values. At the same time, the Department of the Treasury created a $25 billion fund to absorb losses that the Federal Reserve might incur on these loans.

On March 15, 2023, when the final run on CS had begun, the Swiss National Bank offered to lend the bank up to 50 billion Swiss francs (nearly $55 billion) to help pay depositors who wanted to leave. In the context of the takeover by UBS, the Swiss National Bank provided the newly merged bank with massive loans, with a government guarantee for up to 100 billion Swiss francs. In Chapter 11 we also referred to the European Central Bank's Long-Term Refinancing Operation of 2011, which quieted down what seemed to be a repetition of the turbulence of September 2008.

Whereas loans involve central banks in direct business relations with the banks to which they lend, central banks can also provide support without engaging in business relations with the institutions they support, merely by buying assets such as government bonds or mortgage-related securities. The assets—and the risks attached to them—are thereby removed from the books of the institutions that held them previously. The purchases also tend to raise the assets' prices, or at least to prevent them from falling, which benefits all institutions that hold such assets. As we discussed in Chapter 14, such interventions played a major role in the incipient financial crisis at the beginning of the COVID pandemic in March 2020.

Bailouts are highly problematic even if there may be good reasons for going through with them. When they occur, they generate a sense of unfairness particularly among those who might be forced to pay for them directly or indirectly. Resentment is likely to be particularly strong among those who did not benefit from bailouts, such as investors in a bank that was not bailed out or homeowners whose mortgages were foreclosed in the crisis of 2007–2009.[8] The support provided to other banks in the turmoil following the Lehman Brothers bankruptcy must have galled the creditors of Lehman Brothers, and some of them still have a sense that they were treated unfairly compared to creditors of Bear Stearns a few months earlier.

As we discussed in Chapter 9, bailouts and expectations of bailouts create distortions. A depositor who expects to be bailed out need not worry about the quality of the bank. In the 1980s, many brought deposits to savings and loans institutions in the United States offering "high interest rates, federally insured." The consequence was a vast increase in savings deposits and a spree by institutions that were "gambling for resurrection."

A government guarantee of deposits may look like a wonderful way to avert runs on depository institutions, but years later the taxpayers may have to pay dearly for all the losses incurred by protected institutions' taking risks with funds from "federally insured" deposits. Bailouts in the forms of loans or loan guarantees to a distressed borrower that enable that borrower to continue borrowing may prevent default, but they allow or even encourage that borrower to pile on more debt and kick the can down the road, sometimes increasing the ultimate overall costs to those providing the funding and the guarantees and to the rest of society.

The massive bailouts and supports that propped up the financial system after 2008 were extremely unpopular. When President Obama signed the Dodd-Frank Act in July 2010, he declared: "No more bailouts. Period." and received a two-minute applause.[9] Policymakers and bankers often claim that reforms have made it possible for any bank, including the largest, most complex, and global "systemic" institutions, to "fail" through a process akin to bankruptcy without causing harm to the system and without needing government bailouts. We are asked to believe that financial institutions are no longer too big to fail or too important to fail.

The events of March 2023 in the United States and in Switzerland have refuted these claims. Despite promises and claims to the contrary by bankers, policymakers, and others, bailouts persist even if policymakers do all they can to avoid using the dreaded word.[10] In fact, the ever-broader safety net for the financial system suggests that the system may be becoming "too big to save."

In the past, there was a principle that the government should be in charge of bailouts dealing with solvency problems, and central banks should only deal with liquidity problems.[11] This principle was based on the idea that bailouts in insolvencies involved outright subsidies and that such subsidies should be decided by governments that draw legitimacy from winning elections. By contrast, interventions in cases of liquidity problems were seen as a more technical matter, which could be left to central banks because they did not involve outright subsidies and might actually earn money for the central bank.

In the crisis of 2007–2009 and the subsequent European crises, in the COVID pandemic and the developments of 2022 and 2023, central banks played a critical role. By now, there seems to be a general presumption that, whenever any problem arises in the financial sector, central banks will step in to help. However, it is not always clear that they adhere to the principle of not bailing out insolvent banks.

So far in this book, we mentioned central banks many times, but we did not explain how these banks work, why they are important, and why they are able to provide bailouts and other support to the financial sector.[12] What central banks and central bankers do and say is often front-page news, yet there is little public understanding of their power and impact on the economy. For a better understanding of the role of central banks in the context of bailouts, we will explain in some more detail in this chapter how central banks operate. We will not say much about monetary policy, the main task of central banks, but limit our discussion to the interaction between central banks and private-sector institutions, and to the relevance of central banks for the stability of the financial system—or its fragility.

In the remainder of this chapter, we explain the way central banks work and their role as so-called *lenders of last resort*. We also discuss the dark side of central bank bailouts.

Central Banks and the Money They Create

The most important function of a central bank involves the creation of money, particularly banknotes such as dollar bills. Money facilitates exchange so that, for example, one can earn wages from one person or business and buy goods from another person or business.[13] Banknotes allow making payments without requiring the intervention of a third party such as a credit card company or a bank.[14] Central banks are in charge of issuing banknotes. They are public institutions created and enabled by parliaments and governments. Special laws give central banks specific responsibilities and privileges, including monopolies for issuing banknotes.

As we mentioned in Chapter 10, in a distant past, banknotes were legal claims to receive payments in gold.[15] Today's banknotes, however, are just printed pieces of paper with a certain shape and design, imprinted with copies of official signatures and seals. They do not confer any legal claims and have no intrinsic value. Yet, they are generally accepted in payment for real goods and services. People are willing to provide goods and services in return for banknotes because they believe they will in turn be able to use the notes for payments themselves. The law considers a payment in banknotes as a final settlement of a financial obligation.[16]

In practice, we do not much use banknotes (cash) for payments today, especially when the amounts involved are large. We pay by checks, credit cards, debit cards, or bank transfers, including through mobile applications.[17] These payments rely on the accounts that we have with commercial institutions for which the term "banks" is normally used.[18]

The fact that cash is not used much does not mean that it is unimportant.[19] Indirectly, cashless payment mechanisms also rely on banknotes. Kate's deposit with "her" bank is a legal claim for banknotes that the bank must pay her if she demands them.[20] If Kate's bank transfers $100 from her account to the account of her aunt Claire, Kate's claim on her bank is reduced by $100 while Aunt Claire's claim on her bank is increased by $100. This transaction is equivalent to Kate giving Aunt Claire $100 in cash.[21]

In this transfer of $100 from Kate to Aunt Claire, if Kate and Aunt Claire have accounts with different banks, the two banks will likely use the central bank to handle the transaction. If both banks have accounts with the central bank, Kate's bank may ask the central bank to transfer the money from its account to the account of Aunt Claire's bank, which will then put the amount in Aunt Claire's deposit account.[22]

In addition to issuing banknotes, the central bank serves as "the banks' bank." The different commercial banks have deposit accounts with the central bank. Like Kate's and Aunt Claire's deposits with their banks, the banks' deposits with the central bank are also legal claims to receive the amount of the deposits in banknotes. These deposits are often called "reserves." Depending on the law, the central bank may choose to pay interest on reserves or to impose a charge on them (negative interest).[23]

Because the central bank is committed to converting the banks' reserves into banknotes on request from the banks, the sum of the banks' reserves with the central bank and the outstanding banknote issue are often lumped together under the name of "central bank money." In August 2022, the amount of central bank money outstanding in the United States was roughly equal to $5.6 trillion. This amount consisted of roughly $2.3 trillion in "currency," or cash banknotes held by banks ($0.1 trillion) and nonbanks ($2.2 trillion), and roughly $3.3 trillion in banks' reserves, that is deposit accounts with the Federal Reserve.[24] In the euro area, at this time, there were €1.6 trillion in outstanding notes and €4.6 trillion in reserves.[25]

Banks and their reserves play an important role in connecting the central bank to the overall economy. During the financial crisis of 2007–2009, Federal Reserve chair Bernanke sometimes referred to the possibility that the central bank might deliver money into the economy by having banknotes dropped from helicopters, but he meant it as a joke.[26] In fact, central banks create money by buying assets or making loans. If a central bank buys an asset from a bank or makes a loan to a bank, it puts the amount it is paying into the account of that bank, increasing the bank's reserves. Since the amount in that account is a component of central bank money, the total amount of central bank money is thereby increased. If the central bank buys an asset from someone other than a bank, or if it makes a loan to a nonbank, it asks the bank of the beneficiary to put the payment into the beneficiary's account and compensates that bank by increasing its reserves by the same amount.

Banks also hold some central bank money in the form of cash, for example, in ATMs. They need this cash to accommodate customers who want to make withdrawals. Banknotes are thus created when commercial banks exchange reserves, that is, deposits at the central bank, for cash delivered to the banks by the central bank. This cash enters the wider economy when customers make cash withdrawals from their banks.

Banks need to hold reserves of central bank money in order to meet the demands of their own depositors when they want to obtain cash or to make payments to people and businesses that have accounts at other banks. Sometimes, such demands by depositors may be motivated by a lack of trust in the bank or if they are concerned that the bank may default, which creates a desire to get out and move to another bank.

Since banks use some of the funds provided by depositors to make loans and other investments, their reserves are usually too small to satisfy depositors' demands to take their money out if a large number make these demands at the same time. On such occasions, a bank might borrow from other financial institutions, as was common before the crisis of 2007–2009, or it might borrow from the central bank. In the United States, banks can take out short-term loans from the Federal Reserve's "discount window" if they provide sufficient collateral and promise to pay interest, assessed at the "discount rate."[27] The discount rate set by the Federal Reserve also affects the interest rates at which banks lend to each other, the so-called federal funds rate.[28]

On May 31, 2023, the discount rate for so-called primary credit was 5.25 percent per year.[29] During the pandemic, from March 2020 to March 2022, it had been 0.25 percent per year, a historical low. Between March 2022 and this writing (May 2023), the Federal Reserve has raised the discount rate in several steps, most recently on May 3, 2023. These developments reflected the Federal Reserve's fear of a financial crisis and/or recession during the pandemic and concerns about inflation since early 2022.

Central Banks' Balance Sheets

As we did for private-sector banks in Chapters 4 and 6, we rely on a balance sheet diagram to explain how central banks operate and how they fit into the overall economy.[30] Figure 15.1 shows the major categories of a typical central bank balance sheet.

Assets	Liabilities
Gold and foreign currencies Loans, including to banks Securities, including government bonds	Foreign currency liabilities Banknotes Deposits of banks (Reserves) Deposits of the government Other debt liabilities
	Equity

FIGURE 15.1   A traditional central bank's balance sheet.

On the asset side, the categories in a typical central bank's balance sheet are similar to those found on other banks' balance sheets and that we discussed in Chapters 4 and 6. There are two important differences, however: First, there is no entry for cash on this side of the central bank's balance sheet, because the central bank itself issues cash.[31] Second, many central banks hold substantial reserves of gold and foreign currencies.[32] A central bank needs the foreign currency reserves if it wants to stabilize the value of its own currency relative to another currency by intervening in the exchange markets in which these currencies are traded. For example, a central bank that wants to prevent a devaluation of its currency relative to the dollar needs a dollar reserve that it can use to buy back its own currency.[33] For central banks that do not intervene in these markets, these reserves are merely historical relics.

On the liabilities side, we first see foreign currency liabilities. These are usually owed to other central banks or to the International Monetary Fund (IMF). For example, in 2008, central banks outside the United States, such as the European Central Bank (ECB), the Bank of England, and the Bank of Japan, borrowed dollars from the Federal Reserve in order to provide support to domestic banks that were owing dollars and were unable to find lenders in the dollar markets.

Also on the liabilities side, we see the banknotes issued by the central bank and the deposits that commercial banks place in the central banks, the two components of central bank money. There are also deposits that the government itself places in its central bank, since a government typically relies on its central bank for its transactions. The government's deposits are not considered part of central bank money.

Finally, the equity (or "capital") of the central bank is, by definition, the difference between the reported values of assets and liabilities. As with private-sector institutions, the owners of the central bank's equity (corresponding to shareholders in the case of corporations) have a right to receive any profit distributions the central bank might make. Central banks make profits because the returns on their assets usually exceed their costs, including the interest they may pay on their liabilities.[34]

In the past, many central banks were owned by private investors, but today most central banks belong to their governments.[35] For example, the Bank of England started out in 1694 as an investor-owned institution and was nationalized in 1946. In the United States, the Federal Reserve System as a whole is not owned by anyone, but the twelve regional Federal Reserve banks are organized as corporations whose equity is owned by commercial banks of the region.[36] The ECB is owned by the national central banks of the member states of the euro area; most of those are owned by their governments. In all central banks, including those that have private shareholders, the policies and the actions they choose are largely a matter of public policy.

The notion that banknotes are an actual liability of the central bank is an anachronism. Nowadays, banknotes do not impose any legal liability on the central bank.[37] The situation was different when central banks were first created.[38] At that time, the banknotes they issued obliged them to pay specified amounts in gold if the holders of the banknotes demanded such payments. There was a real risk that the central bank might not have the amount of gold needed to meet all the demand. To forestall this risk, the central bank had to ensure that it had sufficient gold reserves to satisfy the claims of the holders of banknotes. Today there is no more obligation to redeem banknotes in gold or anything else.[39]

At present, issuing banknotes can be thought of as similar to the production and sale of books. A book publisher produces books at some cost and sells them for a price. Once a book is sold, except possibly for a limited period in which the book is returnable, the publisher has no further obligation to the buyer, and the difference between the price at which the book was sold and the cost of producing it counts as profit for the publisher. Similarly, a central bank produces banknotes, imprinted pieces of paper with a certain shape and design, and then sells these pieces of paper (or claims to them) in return for a financial asset such as a government bond.

The logic of banknotes not carrying a default risk also applies to the reserves that other banks hold at the central bank. These reserves do involve legal claims, but these are claims to receive banknotes, which the central bank can produce at a negligible cost. If there is no interest on these deposits, then, like the issuance of banknotes, the issuance of deposits imposes no real burden on the central bank.[40]

If the central bank's balance sheet was drawn up under the same accounting principles as the balance sheet of a publisher, the difference between the value of an acquired asset and the cost of producing the currency or the reserves used to buy it would be counted as a profit.[41] Retaining the profit would then increase the amount of equity in its balance sheet just as it would for a book publisher.

Central banks, however, do not use the same accounting conventions as normal businesses. In their reporting, central banks treat the banknotes they issue as if they were liabilities even though the banknotes impose no legal obligations. This convention enables central banks to avoid showing profits when they expand their balance sheets by issuing more banknotes and similarly avoid showing losses when they contract banknote issuance. The profits from the issuance of banknotes only appear over time as the assets purchased by the central bank provide returns. If they showed these profits openly in their accounts, central banks would be under much pressure to distribute them to the government and others who might have a claim to returns on their equity.

Since the beginning of 2023, we have seen much discussion about central banks' losses. As interest rates rose in 2022, the securities that central banks hold in their portfolios decreased in market value.[42] These losses reduce and may even eliminate the payouts that central banks make to their governments. In consequence, central banks may lose popularity in the political arena.[43] However, they need not fear for their economic viability. Unlike Silicon Valley Bank, they cannot be forced into default by such market value losses on securities.

In Chapter 14, we mentioned that John Stumpf, then CEO of Wells Fargo Bank, suggested falsely that customers' deposits in his banks are not the bank's debt.[44] In the same interview, Mr. Stumpf also said: "We've got $100 billion with the Fed right now. We lend them money. They don't lend us money." The contrast between Mr. Stumpf's view that Wells Fargo's deposits with the Federal Reserve are a loan from Wells Fargo to the Federal Reserve and thus debt of the Federal Reserve and his view of customers' deposits at Wells Fargo as not being debt of Wells Fargo is absurd. Although both customers' deposits in private-sector banks and these banks' reserves with the central bank give deposit holders the right to receive a certain amount of banknotes, *the central bank can always fulfill this claim without effort, whereas the commercial bank must make an effort to avoid default.*

The losses that central banks showed for 2022 will likely revive debates about the policies that the Federal Reserve, the European Central Bank and others have pursued in the past decade. In public discussion during this period, one could sometimes hear the warning that the central bank should not buy so many risky assets because, if the risks were to materialize, the central bank would make a big loss.[45] Since the purchases would be paid for with newly created money, these warnings were based on the notion that central bank money is actually a kind of debt of the central bank. Yet, any money forger knows that if he creates false €100 bills and sells them in return for the common stock of some corporation, he will make a profit; subsequent declines in stock prices reduce the profit but do not eliminate it. In this respect, the economic position of the central bank is not unlike that of the money forger, except that its money creation is legal and it does not have to fear the police.

In the past, when banknotes were promises to pay the bearers in gold, the position of central banks and of commercial banks were more similar than they are today. The central banks of those times had to manage their issuance of banknotes and their gold reserves to avoid default. The transition to a pure fiat money regime removed these constraints for the central banks, but it did not remove the constraints on private-sector banks.

A central bank's *foreign-currency* liabilities, however, are still genuine liabilities that the central bank must manage carefully. If the ECB borrows dollars from the Federal Reserve, for example, as it did in 2008 and in 2011, it must pay back dollars. Because the ECB itself cannot produce these dollars, it must make sure that it has sufficient dollar reserves by the time the repayment comes due. Debt in a currency that it does not produce must be taken seriously as a liability of the central bank.

Central Banks as "Lenders of Last Resort"

Following the failures of SVB and Signature Bank, on March 12, 2023, the Federal Reserve announced an expansion of its lending to banks, through the discount window with loans of up to ninety days and through a new "Bank Term Funding Program" that will make up to one-year loans available to eligible banks. Under this program, the Federal Reserve would accept the debt securities that banks post as collateral *at par*, in other words, at the face values of the debt even though their current market value might be lower.[46]

Immediately after this announcement, in the turmoil following the failures of SVB and Signature Bank, banks' borrowing from the Federal Reserve under the new terms for collateral valuation rose dramatically.[47] In the first week after the SVB failure, banks borrowed $152 billion from the discount window, much more than the $10 billion borrowed the week before.[48] Banks also borrowed $52.7 billion under the new Bank Term Funding Program within the first ten days of its existence.[49]

To understand how this type of support from the Federal Reserve to commercial banks works, think about the balance sheet of a commercial bank as shown in Chapters 4 and 6. This balance sheet lists customers' deposits among the liabilities and reserves of central bank money among the assets. If depositors withdraw their money, both the deposit liabilities and the reserves of central bank money decline by the amount of the withdrawal. A one-year loan from the central bank allows the commercial bank to replenish its reserves. However, this loan also creates an additional liability, to repay the debt to the central bank with interest after one year. In the balance sheet of the central bank, the loan raises the commercial bank's reserves, reported on the liabilities side of the central bank balance sheet, and the central bank's claim for repayment of the loan appears as an additional asset on the asset side of the central bank's balance sheet in the same way that a loan that a commercial bank makes is one of its assets.

The operation has no effect on any of the other assets and liabilities or on the equity of the commercial bank. Nor does it have any effect on the other assets of the central bank or on its reported equity. It does, however, increase the amount of central bank money outstanding. By replenishing the commercial bank's holdings of central bank money, the central bank enables the commercial bank to satisfy more depositors, perhaps even all of them if the loan from the central bank is large enough or repeated often enough. Thus, the liquidity problem of the commercial bank that is caused by the many withdrawals is solved. With enough loans from the central banks, runs by depositors do not destroy a commercial bank. The central bank, meanwhile, cannot have any liquidity problem in its own currency because it can itself produce banknotes to pay whatever it owes. Under current law, the owners of banknotes have no claims on the central bank.

Importantly, because the equity of the commercial bank is unaffected, *such lending by the central bank does not address any solvency problems of the commercial bank*. As we explain below, the Federal Reserve's support to commercial banks in the crisis of 2023 may actually exacerbate these banks' solvency problems. Solvency problems for private-sector banks call for *equity injections*, by private parties or by the government. If no one is willing to provide additional equity, this fact in itself may be evidence that the bank's solvency problems are fatal.

In principle, any liquidity problems of commercial banks might also be solved through borrowing from private parties. In some situations, however, borrowing from private parties may not be available, as we described in Chapter 5 for the weeks that followed the Lehman Brothers bankruptcy. In such situations, central banks can still be available to provide commercial banks with liquidity. This is why they are sometimes called *lenders of last resort*.

The idea that central banks should act as lenders of last resort and support financial institutions in a time of crisis is very old. In the first analysis of central banking, in 1873, the English journalist and expert Walter Bagehot famously suggested that, in a crisis, the central bank should "lend freely to solvent banks against good collateral and at penalty rates" of interest.[50] A central bank that followed this prescription would defuse the crisis. With money provided by the central bank, the other banks would be able to meet withdrawals of deposits and to avoid fire sales of assets. The central bank itself would actually earn a profit by charging the banks high rates of interest. Moreover, by forestalling the crisis, or at least reducing its impact, the intervention would protect the values of the central bank's own assets.

Bagehot's recommendation reflected the experiences and activities of the Bank of England in the 18th and 19th centuries. At that time, the Bank of England was already powerful enough to be an effective support of the financial sector in a crisis.[51] Private attempts for dealing with crises were often not working because the stronger financial institutions would not be interested in helping weaker institutions with whom they were competing. While being aware of the dangers of contagion across institutions, they tended to see crises as occasions to make competitors disappear through bankruptcy.[52]

The United States did not have a central bank until 1913. For a long time, fears that a central bank would have too much power and that it would take business away from the other banks had created effective resistance to such an institution.[53] Following a panic in 1907, however, as mentioned in Chapter 10, the Federal Reserve System was founded in 1913 with the hope that, in accord with the Bagehot view, this new central bank would forestall the panics and runs that had been typical of the National Banking System, in which banknotes had been issued by competing private banks and there was no central bank.[54]

During the Great Depression of the 1930s, however, the Federal Reserve as well as most other central banks did very little to support financial institutions and prevent banking crises and panics.[55] There were several severe crises, and many banks failed, exacerbating the economic downturn.[56] Central bank policies, including failures to do something about the banking crises, were a major reason why the depression of the 1930s became the "Great Depression."[57]

The passivity of central banks in the 1930s stands in marked contrast to the activism of central banks in the global financial crisis of 2007–2009 and since then. The difference is explained by the fact that, in the 1930s, central banks were constrained by international currency considerations, but in 2007–2009 they were not so constrained. At the time of the Great Depression, central banks were subject to the gold standard. To maintain their ability to fulfill this obligation, they focused on protecting their gold reserves rather than supporting the banks, let alone counteract the economic depression.[58]

Since 1973, central banks have no longer been constrained by international currency considerations.[59] In the ensuing decades, there have been many instances of central bank supports of financial institutions, most extensively in the global financial crisis of 2007–2009.[60] In that crisis and since then, Bagehot's recommendation has often served to justify central bank interventions. Not much attention has been paid, however, to the fact that many of these interventions benefited banks whose solvency was dubious, that the quality of the collateral was questionable, and that the interest rates banks had to pay were low.

The Dark Side of Bailouts and Deposit Guarantees

When SVB was closed, there were suggestions that the Federal Reserve could have and should have provided this bank with funding to prevent its failing, thus fulfilling its role as a lender of last resort. A business blog of the *New York Times* and an opinion piece in the *Wall Street Journal* suggested that SVB was just illiquid and had no solvency problems.[61]

Such suggestions are both misleading and dangerous. The lender-of-last-resort function of a central bank presumes that the institutions to which it lends are solvent. The view that SVB was solvent seems to rest on the fact that the bank's accounts showed a positive value of equity. As we explained in Chapter 14, by September 2022, the equity shown in the bank's accounts was positive *only* because the accounting rule used allowed the bank to hide certain losses. If these losses had been laid open, the accounts would have shown negative equity.

The accounting rule used rests on the idea that changes in the market values of debt securities are irrelevant if the bank wants to hold these securities until the debt is repaid and if there is no doubt that the debt will in fact be repaid, as is the case with U.S. Treasury bonds. As we explained in Chapter 14, this idea is flawed. Even if the bank declares that it wants to hold the debt securities until they are paid, it may be unable to do so if its depositors want to withdraw their funds. In this case, the bank may have to sell the securities to pay depositors, so the value that the bank can get in the market is highly relevant for its solvency. If the bank holds on to the securities and manages to get new funding, but the interest rates on this funding are higher, the solvency problem does not disappear but is merely kicked down the road.

Suppose, for example, that the Federal Reserve had provided SVB with support by lending to it at current rates of interest. Then the bank would have to pay more interest on the loan from the Federal Reserve than it would earn on the securities, more than 5 percent versus 1.6 percent. With more than $100 billion in securities, this would lead to a loss of more than $3 billion in a year. If this constellation of interest rates were to persist, the bank would probably end up failing despite the support from the Federal Reserve.

Believers in the accounting rule used by SVB and proponents of Federal Reserve support for SVB betray a poor knowledge of history. As we discussed in Chapter 4, in the early 1980s, about two-thirds of U.S. savings institutions were de facto insolvent. However, the same accounting rule used by SVB allowed them to hide that insolvency.[62] They were holding mortgages from the 1960s with fixed interest rates of, say, 6 percent and twenty or thirty more years to go. Interest rates in money markets at that time were on the order of

15 percent. Initially the interest rates these institutions paid their depositors were kept down by regulation, but then depositors took their money away and invested it elsewhere. The deregulation allowed the savings institutions to pay those high rates themselves, which solved their immediate liquidity problem. However, the solvency problem attached to having to pay 15 percent while earning 6 percent did not disappear. In subsequent years, the S&Ls attracted substantial funding by advertising high rates on federally insured deposits, but much of that funding went into reckless investments, making the subsequent cleanup all the more onerous and expensive.[63]

The S&L experience is also relevant for thinking about the Federal Reserve's Bank Term Funding Program and about proposals by many to extend the FDIC's deposit insurance to all deposits regardless of size and eliminating the $250,000 limit.[64] The Federal Reserve lending under the Bank Term Funding Program is intended to protect banks from the effects of deposit withdrawals in a situation where many banks have hidden losses of the kind that SVB experienced and depositors have lost trust. The research on which we reported in Chapter 14 suggests that these hidden losses may be substantial relative to the banks' equity levels. This research also suggests that, if only half of all uninsured deposits were withdrawn and the banks had to sell assets to meet the withdrawals, the realized losses would bankrupt hundreds of banks right away.[65]

One must wonder how many hidden insolvencies there are among the banks to which the Federal Reserve is lending. One must also wonder how the difference between the interest charged by the Federal Reserve and the interest earned on the securities held will affect the banks' future health. The Federal Reserve's promise to value the collateral at par does not mean that it charges less interest. This promise only means that the amounts banks can borrow will not be reduced because market values of securities are below their nominal values.[66]

Some might argue that the Federal Reserve should adapt the interest it charges to the interest banks earn on the collateral. Such a policy would outrageously subsidize banks to cover up the consequences of the risks they have taken. It would also mean giving up the effort to fight inflation and returning to the low interest rates that prevailed during the pandemic. Such a policy shift would be highly problematic.[67]

The runs on SVB, Signature and First Republic Bank have also triggered a discussion about the limits on deposit insurance.[68] In these three cases, uninsured deposits ended up being bailed out after all, and there are many proposals to abolish limits on deposit insurance. Such proposals must be treated with caution, however, if we want to avoid a repeat of the S&L debacle. As we discussed in Chapter 9, allowing financial institutions to attract deposits with a promise of government guarantees provides these institutions with implicit subsidies at the expense of taxpayers. In the case of the S&Ls, such guarantees provided the basis for the expansion and the recklessness of the 1980s. By 1990, there was a consensus that the influence of government guarantees for deposits on the behavior of depositors and savings institutions in the mid- and late 1980s had been harmful and costly. Proponents of extending guarantees for deposits seem to have forgotten that experience.

The main argument for deposit insurance concerns the protection of day-to-day transactions. In the course of these transactions, people do not want to think constantly about whether their bank is trustworthy. Deposit insurance for amounts corresponding to daily transactions eliminates this friction. For private households, in this context, the statutory limits of $250,000 in the United States and €100,000 in the European Union should be more than sufficient, except perhaps for real estate transactions. For businesses or public entities that must meet payrolls, these numbers may not be sufficient, i.e., for these entities, transactions needs may exceed current deposit insurance limits.[69] However, in the case of SVB, the largest depositor was Circle Corporation, a crypto business with a deposit of $3.3 billion. With such an amount, the deposit has little to do with transactions and is merely a convenient way to hold wealth. However, corporate wealth management should not benefit from a government-backed deposit insurance that is funded by a levy on the banking industry and, if the industry is too weak to pay, a backstop from taxpayers.

Bailouts, whether from governments or from central banks, prevent or at least delay bank failures. If the failures are only due to liquidity problems, that might make sense. However, the bankers—and some commentators in the media and in academia—will always claim that a bank has "only a liquidity problem," as in the cited comments on the SVB failure. They will be applauded by anyone who finds bank failures and bank closures painful. However, the consequence of not letting banks fail and not closing them can also be painful. In addition to the distorted incentives of banks in distress or even hidden insolvency, there may also be a cost to the industry as a whole.

Technological innovations such as in data processing, information, and communication technologies may expand the capacity of individual institutions to handle customers' needs. Unless some institutions leave, there may then be excess capacity in the banking industry, too many banks and shadow banks, and intense competition between them. Borrowers likely believe that loan rates can never be too low, but if the intensity of competition drives banks to charge low interest rates to borrowers with exorbitant risks, merely to survive, and if these risks must ultimately be borne by taxpayers, competition is too intense and loan rates may be too low. In such a situation, some exit of banks from the market is called for.

In Chapter 14, we noted that in the 2010s many banks in Europe have been unprofitable. In the crisis of 2007–2009 and since then, most European banks were bailed out by their governments, and only a handful of banks disappeared.[70] From the early 1990s to the crisis, European banking had increasingly been marked by excess capacities and intense competition. This fact was one reason why continental European banks had ventured into investment banking activities and investment banking products in the United States and the United Kingdom. Bailouts meant that excess capacities were not much reduced in the crisis, and the problem has persisted. Low profitability is the major reason these banks find it hard to acknowledge the non-performing loans they hold, let alone rebuild equity from current profits.[71]

Problems caused by excess capacity in the market, as well as solvency problems, would be most directly addressed *if banks were forced to raise more equity.* If a stricter equity requirement were imposed in value terms, prorating the desired ratio to the assets that banks hold, banks could not fulfill the requirement by selling assets, "deleveraging" as the jargon calls it, but would have to acquire additional equity funding. Some banks might be unable to do so, but that would be an indication that investors have doubts about their solvency as they did when SVB tried to raise equity in early March 2023. *These banks are failing a basic market "stress test" and should be candidates for closure*. The exit of such banks from the market would improve the prospects of those that remain, increase their profitability, and make them more resilient. Such a development is painful for the affected banks, but the alternatives are likely to be painful for all of us.

Bailouts through Asset Purchases

The reference to a "Lehman moment" in the epigraph to this chapter comes from a September 28, 2022 news report about a massive program by the Bank of England to purchase long-term U.K. government bonds ("gilts") in order to stop sharp declines in their prices. The turmoil in U.K. markets had been triggered by announcements from the Bank of England and the U.K. government. On September 22, the Bank of England announced an increase in its base rate of interest; on September 23, the U.K. government announced a "mini budget" plan involving tax cuts and cancellations of planned tax increases, which generated expectations of rising government deficits and further increases in interest rates.[72] These announcements led to a plunge in the price of government bonds, which became a "death spiral" as pension funds that had borrowed to fund their investments were forced to sell assets, including government bonds, exacerbating the price declines. The Bank of England's purchases served to protect these pension plans from insolvency, which otherwise might have come within days.[73]

The Bank of England's intervention on this occasion followed the same pattern as the Federal Reserve's interventions during the COVID pandemic and amid the crisis of 2007–2009. As we discussed in Chapter 14, during the COVID pandemic, a large part of the Federal Reserve's interventions consisted in buying assets such as government bonds and mortgage-related securities in the open market to support the prices of these assets. The interventions benefited money market funds and mutual funds that were trying to sell assets to meet redemptions. Without the Federal Reserve's interventions, the fire sales of these institutions might well have triggered a "death spiral" in asset prices. The interventions also benefited other financial institutions, including banks, by maintaining the values of their investments. Institutions that had borrowed to buy such assets were saved from the difficulties of meeting lenders' demands to provide more collateral as market values of collateral declined. Similarly, in 2008 and 2009, the Federal Reserve and other central banks bought massive amounts of government bonds and corporate bonds, mortgage-related securities, and covered bonds in order to provide banks with cash and to support the prices of these securities.

As discussed in Chapter 14, a central bank purchasing assets in a crisis is sometimes referred to as a *market maker of last resort*. A better term would be *asset buyer of last resort*. In contrast to market makers who try to resell the assets they bought as soon as possible, central banks have been holding on to their asset purchases for years.

As with other forms of bailouts, such interventions in support of asset prices and asset-holding institutions may be called for in a crisis, but they also have a dark side. Prospects of central bank protection against downturns in asset prices reduce the downside risks for investors and weaken their incentives for taking care in choosing which assets to buy. The support also weakens the incentives of managers in charge of the institutions that issue or have issued these securities. These effects are similar to those seen for mortgage lending and securitization that we discussed in Chapters 4 and 5. Central banks that routinely act as "asset buyers of the last resort" may end up in the position of the "stupid German bankers in Düsseldorf" that are mentioned in the book *The Big Short*, willing buyers of toxic securities created by Wall Street investment bankers.[74]

Policymakers repeatedly promise they are doing everything possible to avoid bailouts in the future. Yet bailouts persist. In principle, bailouts are unpopular, but recognizing and imposing losses is sometimes even more unpopular. And despite many vaunted reforms, the rules and procedures for dealing with failing banks are still unwieldy. There is no way a megabank can fail without causing major harm. Why do governments keep bailing out banks? Can we afford to have megabanks that impose unconscionable risks on society? The next chapter takes up these questions.

SIXTEEN

Bailouts Forever

[A] globally active systemically important bank cannot simply be wound up according to the "too-big-to-fail" plan.

Karin Keller-Sutter, Head of the Swiss Finance Department, March 25, 2023[1]

THE DODD-FRANK ACT in the United States promised the end of bailouts and "too-big-to-fail" institutions. The European Union's 2014 legislation for dealing with banks likely to fail was claimed to provide "a framework" to "deal with banks that experience financial difficulties without either using taxpayer money or endangering financial stability."[2] In November 2014, Mark Carney, at the time the governor of the Bank of England and chair of the Financial Stability Board (FSB), a body of financial regulators from around the world, announced triumphantly that an agreement about new rules for the thirty largest and most complex, "globally systemic" financial institutions would prevent bailouts in the future.[3] Many people in politics and the media believed these claims.[4]

In a similar vein, as of this writing (May 2023), Finma, the Swiss bank supervisor, announces on its website: "Financial market participants can become so large at a national and even international level that their disorderly failure could undermine financial stability and force a government bailout. Following the global financial crisis of 2007 and 2008, the "too big to fail" problem was therefore addressed both in Switzerland and abroad."[5] Notice the factual claim: "the problem was addressed."

The confidence expressed in these statements stands in marked contrast to the actual events in March 2023. When faced with a run on Credit Suisse, one of those thirty "globally systemic" institutions, the Swiss authorities, including Finma, did not actually use the new procedures that had been developed to deal with banks that are in trouble. Instead they engineered a bailout. The bailout announced on March 19, 2023 took the form of a take-over by larger rival UBS, with liquidity support from the Swiss National Bank guaranteed by the government for up to 100 billion Swiss francs and with a government guarantee of up to 9 billion Swiss francs against certain losses.[6]

So much for the promise that bailouts are a thing of the past! In the epigraph to this chapter, we quoted the Swiss finance minister who was responsible for this plan. The interview continued: "Legally this would be possible. In practice, however, the economic damage would be considerable."[7] The Swiss finance minister and the head of the supervisory authority also explained that the new procedures could not be used because CS had lost all trust with investors.[8]

One may wonder why the regulators designed rules for dealing with failing banks without considering the possibility that such a bank would lose the investors' trust. If a bank is highly distressed, it is natural for investors to doubt whether it is solvent and for trust to disappear. Any rules for dealing with failing banks should be designed to work even in that plausible scenario. If the regulators did not imagine such a scenario, the question is why they were so naïve.

Financial markets have long shown skepticism about the effectiveness of new rules and procedures intended to end bailouts. Empirical research has shown that globally systemic institutions are still able to fund their investments at lower costs than other institutions taking similar risks. This funding advantage reflects investors' expectations that these institutions are still *too important to fail* and will receive government support should they run into problems or in a crisis.[9] We share the skepticism about the end of too-big-to-fail. Long before the Credit Suisse weekend, we wrote that government support and bailouts were still to be expected if an important institution were to fail. Therefore, we were not surprised that the Swiss authorities proceeded as they did.

In the remainder of this chapter, we discuss the rule changes that were introduced since 2010 and their shortcomings. The major problem is that no matter what they may say in public, most politicians prefer bailouts to anything else. They hate to impose losses on anyone, particularly on people whose votes (or financial support for campaigns) they want to have in the next election. They also shy away from the difficulties and intricacies of dealing with actual bank operations. Finally, they continue to fear the collateral damage caused by failing banks.

Ending Too-Big-to-Fail—A Pipe Dream

The optimism expressed by Governor Carney in late 2014 rested on two innovations, but these innovations will not fulfill the hopes attached to them. The first innovation is called Single-Point-of-Entry (SPE) resolution, the second is called Total Loss Absorbing Capacity (TLAC). The term "resolution" is short for "bank resolution," used for procedures by which authorities intervene to "resolve" the problems of failing banks without subjecting the banks to a bankruptcy procedure. In a SPE resolution, one authority takes control at exactly one point, usually the headquarters of the overall group. Most large banking institutions are organized as bank holding companies whose subsidiaries carry out the actual business operations. In an SPE resolution, the authorities enter the bank holding company but *not* the subsidiaries.

In theory, SPE resolution has two advantages: First, the authorities do not have to interfere with the actual operations. Operations take place in the subsidiaries, which the authorities do not enter. Second, for banks with subsidiaries in multiple jurisdictions, SPE resolution eliminates the problem of what happens when the subsidiaries in different jurisdictions are entered by different authorities, namely one for each jurisdiction in which the bank has a legally independent subsidiary. Because of these advantages, the Financial Stability Board has repeatedly urged for the authorities of different countries to agree on SPE resolution.[10]

Both supposed advantages are illusory, however. First, the idea that a resolution authority need not concern itself with the subsidiaries and their operations presumes that all relevant information is easily available at the level of the bank holding company. In particular, it presumes that there is no need to interfere with ongoing operations or even to wind some operations down.[11] Second, the idea that different countries and jurisdictions will allow the resolution authority in charge of the bank holding company to decide on the fate of subsidiaries in their territories is unrealistic. U.S. authorities have made clear that they will not submit to interventions of foreign banks' home country authorities using SPE procedures that might impose losses on the clients of these banks' subsidiaries in the United States. Instead, they have required large foreign banks to organize their U.S. operations under bank holding companies in the United States, and they intend to apply "SPE" resolution to these holding companies and their subsidiaries. True SPE resolution of the overall organization, in the home country and in the United States, is thereby impossible. U.S. authorities thus avoid submitting to the organization's home country authorities.

The other innovation, Total Loss Absorbing Capacity (TLAC), is not an innovation at all but a marketing trick. The idea is that banks should maintain a minimum amount of funding that can absorb losses in bank resolution. Equity has this ability automatically. In addition to equity, however, the holders of some debt securities might have no claim to be bailed out.[12] Together with equity, these securities would provide TLAC. Whereas equity would absorb losses at any time, "loss-absorbing debt" would absorb losses in a resolution or bankruptcy procedure.[13] The slogan was "Equity before bankruptcy, TLAC in bankruptcy!"[14]

The presentation of debt that can absorb losses as something special is a rhetorical sleight of hand. Outside of banking, there is a general presumption that lenders must absorb losses if the borrower defaults and goes into bankruptcy. Because of the disruptions associated with standard bankruptcy procedures, alternative and more flexible resolution procedures have been created for banks. However, this change is not a reason for deviating from the general principle that uninsured creditors must share in losses according to the seniority of their claims if the bank fails. The exemption of insured deposits and several other liabilities from sharing a bank's losses is a privilege.[15] The TLAC discussion suggests that politicians and bankers see this privilege as the rule, and debt that must share losses in resolution or bankruptcy as the exception.

The mantra "Equity before bankruptcy, TLAC in bankruptcy" suggests falsely that equity and "loss-absorbing debt" serve different needs and that one is not a substitute for the other. In fact, equity and loss-absorbing debt are different ways to fund the banks' activities, and funding by equity *instead* of loss-absorbing debt will *avoid* the need to go into bank resolution in the first place, so loss absorption by debt becomes much less relevant. Equity absorbs losses automatically and prevents a corporation from becoming distressed or failing. Debt absorbs losses only when the trigger for a bankruptcy or resolution procedure is pushed.

To be sure, once a resolution is triggered, loss absorption by debt may reduce the need for taxpayer money. In some circumstances, loss absorption by debt may even eliminate the need for taxpayer money altogether. Whenever TLAC debt absorbs all losses, however, the need for triggering a bankruptcy or resolution procedure would not even have arisen had the same funding taken the form of equity. This greater equity funding would prevent the bank from failing in the first place.

The trigger for a bankruptcy or resolution procedure is only pushed if governments and regulators are confident that they will not cause harm to themselves and their friends or to the financial system. If the authorities have reasons to avoid triggering a bankruptcy or resolution procedure, it makes no difference that some debt securities are available for absorbing losses in such a procedure. In the case of CS, the authorities preferred to have the bank taken over by UBS with much public support even though, in addition to equity and the contingent-convertible debt that was devalued, the bank also had about 50 billion Swiss francs' worth of TLAC debt, so loss absorption by TLAC liabilities should have been easy.

As we discussed in Chapter 11, before the financial crisis of 2007–2009, banks had issued a variety of debt securities that, under the then-prevailing rules, counted toward capital requirements as "Tier 2 Capital," available for immediate loss absorption in bank resolution.[16] In the crisis of 2007–2009, however, these securities did not contribute to the absorption of losses because governments preferred to bail out the banks and all their creditors for fear of the possible contagion effects of triggering a bankruptcy or resolution procedure.[17] We expect the same choices to be made again if there is another systemic bank failure or crisis.[18]

For the banks, as well as the politicians and regulators, the focus on TLAC has the advantage of diverting attention away from equity. Bankers focus narrowly on their own bottom line and ignore the substantial benefits of equity requirements for society.[19] Politicians and regulators shy away from conflict with the bankers. By discussing TLAC and loss-absorbing debt, they

promise the end of too-big-to-fail and unpopular bailouts and present themselves to voters as champions of financial stability while avoiding the conflict
with bankers that would accompany increases in equity requirements.[20]

The Politics of Bail-Ins and Bailouts

There is indeed no reason to believe that the authorities' willingness to pull
the trigger for a resolution or bankruptcy procedure and to impose losses on
debt holders is any greater today than it was in 2008. In the European Union,
legal reforms since 2008 have created a legal basis for putting banks through
a resolution procedure rather than a bankruptcy procedure and for "bailing
in" a bank's creditors so that they must bear those losses that are not absorbed
by shareholders. Since the introduction of the new rules, in the euro area
excluding Greece, six medium to large banks have required public interventions.[21] Three of these banks avoided resolution procedures through government support.[22] Another two went into liquidation because the European
Commission disallowed the support that the government wanted to provide.[23] Only one bank went through a resolution procedure without any consideration of government support.[24]

Imposition of losses on debt holders occurred in four of the six cases, in
Spain and Italy, where shareholders and holders of subordinated debt that
had counted toward capital requirements were wiped out. The Italian government would have preferred to avoid such loss absorption by investors and
proposed to recapitalize the banks. However, the European Commission,
which has oversight over any public subsidies to commercial enterprises, so-
called state aid, intervened and forced the Italian authorities to impose a
bail-in.[25]

Politicians do not always mean what they say when they assert that taxpayer money should never again be used to bail out banks. Policymakers,
including politicians and regulators, often want to engage in bailouts for reasons of their own, which have nothing to do with the prevention of damage
to the financial system and the overall economy. For example, if they have
control over a bank, they may want to recapitalize it before any resolution
procedure begins, thus preserving the bank as a source of funding over which
they have control without having to ask their legislatures.[26] They also may

want to protect investors in the bank either because these investors are close to them or because they are otherwise important, economically or politically.[27]

In the cases of SVB and Signature Bank in the United States, the extension of deposit protection to uninsured depositors may have been motivated by a desire to protect Silicon Valley tech firms, a desire to avoid contagion effects with runs on other banks, or simply a desire to avoid a public outcry. In cases involving the German Landesbanken, the regional governments that owned these banks went out of their way to avoid a resolution procedure because they were afraid that such a procedure would impose losses on the local savings banks that had deposited surplus funds with these institutions.[28] The warning "This might be a Lehman moment" always provides a convenient pretext.

In debates about bailouts, the term "systemic risk" is often used as a bugbear. The word *systemic* is a weasel word, one that suggests something specific when in fact it has no well-defined meaning at all. It works wonders, however, to call an event, an institution, or the creditors of an institution "systemic" if you want to orchestrate a bailout. Thus, some called SVB systemic for the tech companies it served, and the tech companies systemic for innovation. The failure of SVB and Signature Bank were called systemic because they triggered contagion as the depositors of other banks became concerned about their bank's solvency.[29]

In Italy, before the 2017 closure of Banca Popolare di Vicenza and Veneto Banca, both banks were said to be systemic for the economy of the region around Venice where they were located.[30] In March 2013, the Cypriot banks and their depositors were called systemic because of potential contagion effects in other southern European countries. Ultimately every business may be important for its customers, employees, and others and might thus be called systemic. But a market economy cannot work well if every business or even just every bank can expect bailouts. In the above examples, the dire warnings of systemic damage from the closures of the Venetian banks and the bail-in of large deposits in the Cypriot banks did not materialize. Investors who lost money were affected, but that did not have many additional repercussions.[31]

Because the word "systemic" appears in legal documents, such as the Dodd-Frank Act, the authorities must form views about its meanings. In practice, these views may change from decision to decision. In 2008, Bear Stearns was considered systemic but Lehman Brothers was allowed to fail. Washington Mutual was sold and its shareholders were wiped out, but Citigroup, including its shareholders, were repeatedly bailed out.

Since the 2018 change in the law, Silicon Valley Bank was not "systemic" enough to warrant stricter regulation than any small bank. In June 2021, the Federal Reserve itself explained its approval of SVB's $900 million acquisition of Boston Private Bank and Trust by the comment: "The organization would not be a critical services provider or so interconnected with other firms or markets that it would pose significant risk to the financial system in the event of financial distress."[32] Yet when SVB was closed on March 10, 2023, a *systemic exception* was made to guarantee all its depositors, including those with millions or even billions in deposits. At this time, the Federal Reserve also used a systemic exception to offer changes in its main discount window policy and a new lending program.[33]

In the EU, the cleanup of the banking sector after the global financial crisis was significantly delayed and is still not complete. Insolvencies were hidden by maintaining unrealistic asset values in bank balance sheets, for example maintaining loan valuations long after it had become clear that these loans would not be paid in full. Supervisors found it convenient to tolerate such practices, and so did governments, effectively kicking the cans down the road. Procrastination became a major policy tool. In Chapter 4, we discussed this kind of procrastination in the context of the savings and loans crisis in the United States in the 1980s. The recently observed tardiness of supervisors in intervening in Silicon Valley Bank and Credit Suisse followed the same pattern.

The supervisors, like the bankers, always hope for better times. Laying the problems open would raise nasty questions about risk taking by the bankers and about negligence by the authorities. It would also necessitate disagreeable actions, such as forcing banks to raise additional equity, or imposing losses on investors, or even closing the banks. By contrast, keeping the banks open without doing anything, with funding provided by the central bank, might seem much more convenient.[34] Governments would thereby avoid the nasty choice between imposing losses on investors and imposing losses on taxpayers. In 2011/12 the weakness of their banks even provided governments in Europe with an indirect access to money from the central bank, as the weakest banks used money they obtained from the central bank to lend to their own governments.[35]

For example, the Spanish authorities took a very long time to recognize the losses of their banks from the bursting of the real estate bubble that their lending had created in the 2000s. They only changed track in the spring of 2012, when the failure of Bankia showed that something needed to be done.[36] In Italy and Germany, the authorities procrastinated about the valuations of nonperforming loans, particularly loans to nonfinancial businesses and homeowners in Italy and loans to shipping companies in Germany.[37]

Procrastination was eventually reduced in 2014 when the EU created the so-called banking union and the European Central Bank (ECB) began to take charge of supervision.[38] Demands from the ECB to revalue nonperforming loans required banks to cover the shortfalls by raising additional equity. Many banks managed to do so in the open market. Some did not, which led to the discussions about government support that we mentioned above.[39]

When procrastination cannot be continued, the authorities must choose between imposing losses on investors and putting in taxpayer money. In the cases of the Italian banks, the Italian government feared the political fallout from imposing losses on investors, particularly small retail investors. However, as mentioned, the European Commission vetoed its proposals to maintain all banks and bail out all investors.[40] As a result, investors who had purchased shares or subordinate debt securities lost their investments.[41] The harshness of the Commission in these cases was probably due to the fact that the competition policy unit at the Commission stands apart from others and has a certain autonomy as well as a rather uncompromising stance. However, the fact that these were middling banks without systemic importance also played a role. In systemic crises, in 2020 as well as 2008, the Commission has been keen to provide rule exemptions and forbearance.

The imposition of losses on investors created massive outrage in Italy. This outrage contributed significantly to the government's loss in the 2018 general election. As the securities that were "bailed in" had previously counted toward meeting equity requirements, one might believe that investors who had bought and held these securities were aware of the risk. In fact, the banks had sold these securities to their retail customers as perfectly safe investments. The authorities had not interfered with this mis-selling, perhaps because they were pleased that these sales enabled *their* banks to continue to meet regulatory requirements. Some of the subsequent outrage was directed at the authorities' connivance with the banks, as well as their submission to the European Commission, seen here as a foreign power. The media and the electorate would have preferred a full bailout of all investors.

This episode contains a lesson about TLAC. Who should buy the bail-in-able debt that banks must issue? Hedge funds, insurance companies, or other banks? All these institutions are themselves borrowers, so there is a serious risk of contagion. Mutual funds or pension funds? If they hold bail-in-able debt of banks, the contagion risk would probably be small, but investors in these funds may end up being hard hit, like those retail investors in Italy. One may presume that the managers of these funds would appreciate the risks, unlike the Italian retail investors who were misled. However, the shareholders may not know about the risks, and the fund managers may disregard them because they like the higher yields such risky bank debts offer. Once a bank fails, however, the funds' shareholders will be hit by losses that create outrage. If the authorities fear that, as in Italy, there might be a strong political backlash, they will end up bailing out the bail-in-able debt as well as all other debt.[42]

The imposition of losses on the holders of contingent-convertible debt of CS does not refute these considerations. The holders of the contingent-convertible debt of CS were investment funds all over the world. The holders of shares in these funds do not vote in Switzerland. Nor were they represented in the negotiations about the takeover to CS by UBS. The shareholders of Credit Suisse were represented by the bank's management, which could have vetoed the transaction and in fact did veto it in early rounds of the negotiation when it considered the bids of UBS to be too low.

Moreover, it seems that there were many shareholders in Switzerland, so the government had to be concerned about their votes. These considerations explain the paradox that the shareholders ended up getting UBS shares worth 3 billion Swiss francs, while the holders of contingent-convertible debt got nothing, which reversed the hierarchy of claims in a resolution or bankruptcy procedure. The outcome raised doubts about contingent-convertible debt of other banks and contributed to the persistence of turmoil after the CS weekend, but that turmoil abroad seems to have been of no concern to the participants.

The Need for Time and Resources

When a nonfinancial corporation goes into bankruptcy, a judge or a receiver may try to restructure the corporation's commitments by renegotiating its debts with a view to maintaining profitable operations. The creditors may go along because the maintenance of profitable operations may end up benefiting them even when their claims on the corporation are reduced. If necessary, assets are liquidated. Doing so slowly may avoid destroying value by selling at excessively low, "fire sale" prices. All this requires time and resources, human as well as financial. With banks, resources may also be needed to maintain operations that are important for the overall financial system, at least for a while, in order to avoid damage from abrupt change.[43]

Given the many expressions of concern about the need to prevent a failing bank from disrupting the rest of the financial system, one might expect that reforms since 2008 have designed bank resolution for this purpose. The resolution authorities should be able to sort out which activities of the bank are systemically important and how these activities should be wound down so that the shock of an abrupt disappearance is avoided. In fact, the rules for bank resolution give the authorities hardly any time and resources at all. Impracticality is another reason why the authorities are likely to avoid resolution if they can.

In the aftermath of the U.S. savings and loans crisis of the 1980s, FDIC took some ten years to liquidate the assets of the defunct institutions. In the absence of a functioning market for nonperforming loans, it seemed best to be patient and see how much the debtors would eventually be able and willing to pay. By the end of the 1990s, the losses from the savings and loans crisis were seen to be much smaller than had been expected in the early 1990s.[44] By contrast, in the Swedish banking crisis of 1992, the actual losses were larger than necessary because the government had wanted to get out quickly and liquidated problem loans at discount prices.[45]

Whereas dealing with the savings and loans crisis required the FDIC to spend enormous amounts of labor time, now authorities often try to save on resources by selling a failing bank's assets and some of its liabilities to another bank. For example, in 2008, the FDIC sold Washington Mutual's assets to JPMorgan Chase on the same day it seized the bank; JPMorgan Chase also assumed Washington Mutual's deposit liabilities and secured debts.[46] The takeover of Credit Suisse by UBS is another example. The Swiss authorities are probably pleased that they do not have to sort out and clean up the assets and operations of CS but instead have UBS to carry out this task. There are reasons to believe that under this arrangement, the cleanup will be more professional and systemic damage may be better contained, but one must also wonder about the strain on the resources of UBS.

In the cases of Lehman Brothers and of many European banks in 2008 and later, there were no willing buyers.[47] In such cases, the authorities may have to choose between an immediate shutdown of operations and an intervention that tries to contain the damage by having the government itself take over the operations. The first alternative avoids a bailout with taxpayer money but involves a risk of repeating the experience of the Lehman Brothers bankruptcy. The second alternative may reduce the latter risk, but it also puts taxpayer money at risk and it requires active involvement in managing the failing bank and its assets. Governments that dislike active involvement may only provide funding, but then there may be a conflict with the bank's managers, whose interests usually do not accord with those of the government. To avoid such a conflict, the government must take some control.[48]

One way to handle a bank failure is for authorities to take over the bank, sort out which assets are good assets and which assets are bad assets, create a new bank with the good assets, and sell this new bank to investors while keeping the bad assets and liquidating them without time pressure. This procedure was followed by Sweden in the early 1990s and by other European governments in various crises since 2007.[49] In each case, the initial sorting as well as the subsequent liquidation of bad assets required significant human and financial resources.

If a bank is systemically important, as Lehman Brothers was in 2008, it is desirable to manage resolution in such a way that damage to the rest of the financial system and the overall economy is minimized. For this purpose, it may be necessary to maintain some systemically important operations, at least for a while. In such cases, management and funding needs may be even more challenging. The United States and the United Kingdom have addressed these issues by giving the resolution authorities appropriate powers and funding.[50] By contrast, the European legislation on bank resolution hardly addresses the problem at all. The competence of resolution authorities to administer and fund their operations is narrowly restricted.

This legislation seems to assume that resolution can happen swiftly over a weekend: On some Friday after the close of business, the authorities walk into the bank. They spend Saturday figuring out what the bank's assets are and what they are worth and on Sunday they tell the shareholders and the creditors with loss-absorbing debt what their portions of the losses are; some of the creditors might also be told that the debt they hold is converted into equity. Then, before the opening of business on Monday, the authorities declare that the bank is solvent again and that it presents no risk to anyone entrusting it with their money.

This view is naïve, but it is one reason why the discussion of loss-absorbing debt has never been concerned with the actual process of how resolution works in practice. Even if one does not worry about contagion effects, merely determining what the bank's assets and activities are worth takes time. Therefore, the evaluation of overall losses and the attribution of losses to investors cannot be done just over the weekend.[51]

One also cannot presume that, on the Monday after the intervention, investors will trust the bank in question to be solvent again and will therefore be willing to provide the funding it needs to stand on its own again. In practice therefore, the authorities are likely to be helpless unless they can arrange a fire sale or are willing to violate the rules. U.S. authorities sought to sell SVB over the weekend that followed its closure, but neither the government nor potential buyers were able to evaluate the bank's assets and liabilities in such a short time. SVB was of course much smaller and much less complex than banks like JPMorgan Chase or Bank of America.[52]

The omission cannot have been due to carelessness. The need for time and resources in resolution is well known and has been asserted, for example, in a report of the Financial Stability Board entitled "Key attributes of effective resolution regimes for financial institutions."[53] However, to some participants, it must have seemed better to leave these matters unaddressed even though this meant that bank resolution remained unworkable.[54] When asked by one of us about this failure to deal with important details, an official participating in the negotiations about the European legislation answered: "This is a problem for the ECB [the European Central Bank] to handle." Yet, the ECB is not allowed to lend to insolvent banks, and it has publicly declared that it will not do so.[55]

Megabanks—Still Too Large and Complex

The preceding discussion has pointed to the lack of political will to impose effective resolution without bailouts on even medium-sized banks that are not "systemic." For large and complex, "globally systemic" institutions, the problems are much deeper. Even if the requisite human and financial resources were available, there is virtually no viable way for any type of bankruptcy or resolution of such an institution to take place without causing much collateral damage. If today a bank of the size and complexity of Lehman Brothers were to encounter serious liquidity problems or become insolvent and there was no willing buyer, as for Credit Suisse, the choices for authorities would again be stark, namely a bailout or a disaster. The fear of another "Lehman moment" is often merely a pretext, but for certain institutions it may be fully justified because these institutions are as dangerous as Lehman Brothers was or more so.[56]

Risks from these institutions are not just a matter of bank size. The problem is also that these banks are so complex that, no matter how the process of resolution is organized, the intervention of the authorities in the event of default will destroy some of the functions they perform, with potentially disastrous consequences for the rest of the financial system.[57] So far, we do not have a feasible and smooth "orderly resolution" process for one of the systemic big banks that would avoid such disruptions. Moreover, there are reasons why it may be impossible to have such a process at all.

One way to see the problem is to consider the resolution plans that large, systemically important institutions are now required to submit to the regulatory authorities, often referred to as *living wills*.[58] These documents are meant to facilitate "orderly resolution" by providing the authorities with guidance on the structure of the subsidiaries and activities of the institutions and about potential resolution strategies. The authorities can raise objections if the plans suggest that the institution is too complex and would be too difficult to resolve, and they can require banks to revise them. U.S. authorities have repeatedly done so.[59] The submitted plans are said to have thousands of pages, sometimes more than 10,000.[60] Even disregarding the question whether the assumptions built into the analysis are still relevant a year or two later, a document of this size hardly seems a practical guide for any intervention that requires quick decisions over a few days such as the weekend. A realistic road map for such a scenario would have to be much more concise.[61]

Central clearinghouses for derivatives may be even more difficult to deal with. As part of the new rules in the wake of the financial crisis, some derivatives trading must now be done through these institutions, which interact separately with the different sides of derivatives transactions.[62] Because they are involved in numerous, possibly millions of different contracts, and because they have almost no equity to absorb losses should any participant default, these clearinghouses can be quite fragile. In 2017, a bankruptcy expert in the United States pointed out the gaps in current rules about whether and how clearinghouses might be able to "fail" and concluded that, "absent reform, there is a serious risk that the instability of a major clearinghouse would cause systemic harm or necessitate a bailout."[63] The situation has not changed since, and clearinghouses remain dangerous as a source of systemic risk.[64] If a clearinghouse fails and the contracts are torn up, the result would most likely be chaos.

A key issue that remains unresolved concerns the treatment of institutions that are systemically important in several countries or jurisdictions. As discussed in Chapter 5, when Lehman Brothers went bankrupt, the parent bank in New York was in the hands of U.S. authorities and the subsidiary in London was in the hands of U.K. authorities. The separate interventions of the different authorities disrupted the relationship between the parent bank in New York and the subsidiary in London. The subsidiary had been in charge of the derivatives business and was unable to continue separately, even temporarily.[65] The abrupt disappearance of Lehman Brothers as a market maker in derivatives markets caused many of these markets to freeze, creating problems for many who had counted on them for their own risk management. The experience might have been repeated with the London derivatives business of CS if CS had gone into a resolution procedure rather than being taken over by UBS.

According to a 2021 evaluation of the effects of too-big-to-fail reforms by the Financial Stability Board, "the average globally systemically important bank still has over a *thousand* subsidiaries in over 40 jurisdictions."[66] Even small, non-systemic institutions tend to set up shop in multiple jurisdictions, creating problems for the authorities when they become insolvent. The November 2022 bankruptcy filing of FTX, a cryptocurrency exchange with "only" $9 billion in liabilities, headquartered in the Bahamas with 134 subsidiaries and customers and investors around the globe, provides a recent illustration of the problems that arise when authorities in multiple jurisdictions with different laws, powers, and interests handle insolvent corporations with assets and stakeholders across many jurisdictions.[67] To be sure, FTX was not regulated, but even so, for such a small operation, the complexity is already astounding.

To avoid disruptions, the Financial Stability Board has repeatedly urged authorities of different jurisdictions to coordinate their strategies and their interventions in failing financial institutions. As mentioned above, they propose a Single-Point-of-Entry approach such that only one country's authorities would be in charge of the entire operation of disposing of the failing bank.[68]

For banks operating in multiple jurisdictions, this proposal is a political pipedream. The IMF declared in 2016 that "there remains considerable additional work to be done to establish an effective regime for cross-border resolution" and has not updated this conclusion since. It is unrealistic to expect governments to give up their own control and allow foreign authorities to manage a process that may impose losses on their citizens. As mentioned above, U.S. regulators have been very clear about this and have turned down the living wills of foreign banks that proposed leaving everything to their home countries' authorities.[69] Regulators in other countries have been less outspoken, but in private many of them have told us that they would not leave control over essentials to the authorities of another country. For example, in the case of Nordea, the Scandinavian megabank headquartered in Helsinki, the Norwegian authorities are unlikely to trust the Finnish or Swedish authorities to provide for continued lending to private households and non-financial companies in Norway.

There is also the question of how to allocate losses across the different units and across the investors funding them. Whoever oversees a resolution that extends across several jurisdictions would have a great deal of power to influence the distribution of losses. Some claim that the inevitable conflicting views about how losses should be distributed are partially or completely resolved by using "internal TLAC," financial contracts between parent banks or bank holding companies and their subsidiaries, requiring that the parent company absorb the losses of subsidiaries. These arrangements would limit the scope for attributing losses to a subsidiary.[70] However, if losses are large, this arrangement may not be sufficient. It would also not help the subsidiary raise new funding or ensure the renewal of existing short-term funding for its ongoing operations.[71]

The Federal Reserve's approach focuses on the top of each organization, the so-called bank holding company that controls the different subsidiaries. The idea is that, by taking control at the top, one can solve problems throughout the organization without disturbing the different subsidiaries and their operations. A problem like Lehman Brothers London's suddenly disappearing would not arise because the subsidiaries would not be part of the process. If a subsidiary were to be insolvent, it would become solvent again if the parent, or the authority in charge of the parent, converted its TLAC debt into equity. A public authority that has taken control of the parent can do this without doing anything more to the subsidiary, at least if the parent holds enough TLAC debt of the subsidiary.

This is again the idea of the "weekend resolution," which is based on wishful thinking. The Federal Reserve or the FDIC may like the idea that a bank's problems can be solved over a weekend, without requiring many resources, personnel, or funding, from the authorities. But how would the authorities assess the solvency of the subsidiaries if they do not have their own information about their assets and their operations? Why would outside creditors, of the holding company or of the subsidiaries, believe that their debtors' problems have been resolved?

For CS, a weekend resolution might even have worked. Total loss-absorbing capacity amounted to more than 100 billion Swiss francs, surely enough to absorb the bank's losses, hidden as well as open. But that would not have dealt with the problem that major activities of the bank had become unprofitable and that management gave no evidence of being up to the challenge.

Restructuring requires involvement and resources. The notion that a combination of TLAC and single-point-of-entry approach will allow the authorities to resolve banks without using many resources is also an illusion.[72] The bottom line is that, if a bank like Lehmann Brothers were to get into difficulties again, dealing with the situation without bailouts will be highly disruptive and damaging. The problem of cross-border coordination between the different authorities has not been solved and is probably not solvable at all. Those claiming otherwise are willfully blind to the issues and conflicts that stand in the way of a solution.[73]

Too Big to Save?

Since 2008, some megabanks have grown even larger.[74] At the end of 2021, JPMorgan Chase reported total assets of around $3.75 trillion, more than twice the $1.5 trillion reported at the end of 2007 and much more than the $2.25 trillion at the end of 2011 as discussed in Chapter 6. In 2021, the total reported assets of this bank amounted to 16 percent of U.S. Gross Domestic Product (GDP), compared with "only" 11 percent in 2007. As we discussed, the bank also has enormous risk exposures "off balance sheet." If it reported under different accounting standards, its total size in terms of both assets and liabilities would be even larger.[75]

In the financial crisis and then again in the 2023 crisis, the importance of JPMorgan Chase to the global financial system and the overall economy has become even greater than it had been before.[76] The acquisitions of Bear Stearns in March 2008 and Washington Mutual in September 2008 contributed significantly to the bank's growth. The acquisition of Bear Stearns was orchestrated by the Federal Reserve, which also provided JPMorgan Chase with guarantees against potential losses on Bear Stearns assets.[77] The acquisition of Washington Mutual was arranged by the FDIC with a price that many observers considered cheap. Jamie Dimon, the CEO of JPMorgan Chase, likes to present these transactions as acts of heroism with which he helped the government, but many, including himself, viewed the acquisitions as valuable for JPMorgan Chase at the time. If Bear Stearns had filed for bankruptcy, JPMorgan Chase most likely would have incurred significant losses.[78]

In 2023, the takeover of First Republic Bank followed the same pattern as the previous acquisitions. Moreover, following the failures of SVB and Signature Bank, tens of billions in deposits were moved from small and medium banks to the largest banks, including JPMorgan Chase, Bank of America, and Citi.[79]

Some of the growth of megabanks is due to public policy. Takeovers of failing banks by others often provide simple solutions to what would otherwise be a headache to the authorities, for example the 2008 takeovers of Bear Stearns and Washington Mutual by JPMorgan Chase. The 2008 takeover of Merrill Lynch by Bank of America is another example. So is the recent acquisition of Credit Suisse by UBS. Sometimes the authorities also allow mergers of banks that are not quite so big in order to create new competitors to the megabanks.[80]

Unfortunately, though, the effect of such a merger of mid-size banks on competition is usually not large—but the effect on the too-big-to-fail problem is. So far, in the United States as well as Europe, the law and practice of merger control are limited to the competition implications of such mergers, without also considering the implications for the too-big-to-fail problem.[81]

Since the financial crisis, a number of megabanks, such as the French bank BNP Paribas, the U.K. bank HSBC, and U.S.-based Citigroup also experienced significant growth. For example, reported total assets of BNP Paribas grew from €1.7 trillion at the end of 2007 to €2.6 trillion at the end of 2021. A few institutions, such as Deutsche Bank and UBS, have shrunk somewhat but they still have total assets well above one trillion dollars, euros, or Swiss francs. There are thirty institutions classified as "Global Systemically Important Banks" by the Financial Stability Board.[82]

In our discussion so far, we have presumed that governments are strong enough to bail out failing banks and their creditors. For megabanks, however, or for an entire national banking system, this presumption may be unwarranted. These banks are too big to fail, but they may also be too big to save. In earlier parts of the book, we discussed Iceland, where the dollar debts of the banks were so high that a bailout by the government was impossible, even if they had tried. We also mentioned that the two megabanks in Switzerland might be too large and too heavily indebted in foreign currencies for the Swiss Confederacy to take on the task of bailing them out. The take-over of one of these megabanks by the other, CS by UBS, reinforces these concerns because now the mega-risks are all in one bank.[83]

In 2012, the government of Spain found that cleaning up the Spanish banking crisis and recapitalizing the Spanish banks was too much to deal with on its own. It therefore asked for support from the European Stability Mechanism (ESM).[84] Similarly, in 2010, the Irish government needed support from the European Financial Stabilisation Facility (EFSF), the precursor of the ESM, in dealing with its banking crisis.[85] Such examples show that if the banking sector, and in particular the largest banks, are too large, even the government may not be able to provide effective bailouts.

In these two cases, one problem for the governments was that they did not have power over their currency. The creation of their means of payment, the euro, was and is controlled by the European Central Bank. This observation does not make the concerns raised by these examples irrelevant for others, however. First, governments always have this problem if banks are indebted in foreign currencies. For example, for the past few decades, European banks have borrowed extensively in U.S. dollars to finance their U.S. operations. Some did so through U.S. subsidiaries, which had direct access to the Federal Reserve. Others did so without having subsidiaries in the United States. In the great financial crisis, and again in the crises of 2011, the European authorities, which cannot create dollars, benefited from support by the Federal Reserve, which lent dollars to the central banks of other countries.[86]

Second, even if the government has power over the currency in which the banks' debt is denominated, the funds needed for effective support may be so large that ordinary budgetary considerations, and thus citizens' welfare, are affected. For example, in the Swedish banking crisis in 1992, the government had to accompany its support of the banks by cutting back on a lot of other spending, and the country entered the most severe depression since the 1930s. In the Japanese crisis of the 1990s, fears that the problems might be too big to handle seem to have been one reason why the government shied away from stepping in and cleaning up the Japanese banking system. As we discussed in Chapters 3 and 5, the persistence of zombie banks for an entire decade was a major reason for Japan's lack of economic growth in the 1990s.

Could such dynamics be a problem for the United States, the country with the largest economy and a currency that serves as a global means of payment? In considering this question, it is useful to note that in early 2023, total bank deposits in the United States were about $18 trillion, of which nearly $10 trillion were explicitly insured by the FDIC. On March 31, 2023, the deposits of JPMorgan Chase were $2.38 trillion, about 69 percent of the bank's $3.44 trillion total liabilities under U.S. accounting rules.[87] According to JPMorgan Chase's 2022 Annual Report, about 60 percent of its deposits, roughly $1.4 trillion, are uninsured, which means that about $1.1 trillion were guaranteed by the FDIC and other authorities, even if there is no rule change.[88]

However, as in the failures in early 2023, there will be strong pressures for providing protection also to uninsured deposits and possibly other short-term debt should any bank run into serious difficulties.[89] In the financial crisis in October 2008, the limit of deposit insurance was officially raised from $100,000 to $250,000, but in fact, the FDIC provided unlimited guarantees on all non-interest-paying deposits between October 2008 and the end of 2012.[90]

In the cases of SVB and Signature Bank, the FDIC also extended its guarantees to cover all deposits. In a panic, we therefore expect uninsured deposits to receive public support again. As mentioned above, some observers even propose such an extension of deposit insurance as a matter of principle. For JPMorgan Chase, the amount guaranteed would go up to the full amount, $2.38 billion as of March 31, 2023.[91] For the U.S. banking system as a whole, the guarantees would go up to the full amount of deposit holdings in all banks.[92] If deposits swell as money comes in from elsewhere because people become concerned about the safety of their savings, or if the guarantees are also extended to other assets such as money market fund shares, as they were in 2008 and 2020, the amounts would be even larger.

All these numbers are *much* larger than any funds available to the FDIC.[93] They are also larger than anything that might realistically be raised by imposing a levy on the other banks, particularly if the other banks are also distressed. Ultimately, therefore, taxpayers are at risk for an amount so enormous that it would be political dynamite. Should the banking system—or even just one or two megabanks—run into serious trouble, the U.S. government would have to choose whether to follow the Swedish or the Japanese approach. Citizens will be affected by whatever the government does.

Following the Swedish approach might require the government to take over banks' obligations to investors in amounts that would require such actions as issuing large amounts of additional public debt, possibly with help from the Federal Reserve's purchasing this debt with newly created money. Such a policy would involve serious political conflicts.

To avoid such conflicts, the government and the Federal Reserve might therefore follow the Japanese approach and kick the can down the road, using loans from the Federal Reserve to prevent weak banks from defaulting while obscuring insolvencies by maintaining book values of assets at past levels without acknowledging losses.[94] The repeated bailouts of Citigroup during the financial crisis illustrate this scenario, as do the failures to address banks' solvency problems in 2023.[95] Such a policy would avoid political conflict about using taxpayer money to support banks, but the Japanese experience of the 1990s suggests that its effects on the overall economy would be similar to the effects of a layer of mildew on plants.

In 2009, Mervyn King, then governor of the Bank of England, said that, "if some banks are too big to fail, then . . . they are too big."[96] We must ask whether the benefits of having large, globally systemic institutions are worth the costs of exposing society to the risks of their failing or the costs of being unable to avoid bailouts when these institutions get into trouble. The largest financial institutions have been described as "too big to supervise," "too big to succeed," and "too big to manage."[97]

We have never received a convincing answer to the question of what exactly the benefits of such institutions to society are, especially those operating in many jurisdictions. The only answer that remotely addressed the question claimed that an airline like Lufthansa, which has transactions all over the world, must surely benefit from being able to handle all these transactions with the same banking partner everywhere. Somehow, this explanation did not convince us that Deutsche Bank must have investment banks in London and New York.

In 1919, the U.S. Congress passed the Edge Act, which allowed U.S. banks to set up subsidiaries that would pursue banking activities abroad without being subject to the usual bank regulation in the United States. Such subsidiaries, so-called Edge Act corporations, were supposed to help nonfinancial firms in the United States that wanted to compete in international markets. In fact, these subsidiaries did not much serve this purpose. Instead, the Edge Act has become a self-serving tool of large U.S. banks to escape U.S. regulation, always in the name of "global competitiveness." Edge Act corporations have been the major basis for the global activities of U.S. banks, and they have been at the core of crises and scandals, such as the London component of the Lehman Brothers crisis and the "London Whale" scandal of JPMorgan Chase.[98]

An author who interviewed people from across the financial sector in London summarized his conclusions as follows in 2015: "Seven years after the collapse of Lehman Brothers, it is often said that nothing was learned from the crash. This is too optimistic. The big banks have surely drawn a lesson from the crash and its aftermath: that in the end there is very little they will not get away with."[99] This assessment is particularly worrisome when the recklessness turns into lawlessness and banks and bankers get away with breaking laws. The next chapter considers the extent to which banks and bankers behave as if they were already above the law and the challenges this poses for democracy and the rule of law.

SEVENTEEN

Above the Law?

[Power struggles in the economy] are not fought by people who are
infinitely progress-minded, but by people who have developed sophisticated
and brutal techniques of fighting for power.

Walter Eucken, German economist (1891–1950)[1]

The 2015 feature movie *The Big Short*, based on Michael Lewis's book with
the same title, ends with the lament that none of the executives of the
many corporations whose conduct brought about the crisis of 2007–2009
went to jail despite the havoc that their behavior had caused. Whereas some
of the misbehavior was lawful because the rules were inappropriate, there
was also a lot of illegal behavior, particularly pervasive fraud in mortgage
lending and securitization marketing. Millions of people lost their homes
and jobs, yet many of those who worked in the financial sector, including
mortgage lenders, banking institutions, credit rating agencies, and auditors,
fared well—particularly executives. In most countries, no high-level individuals faced any charges, let alone went to prison, for any of the frauds.[2]
Assessments of civil damages have also been rare.

Recklessness and lawlessness in the financial system persist. In the run-up
to the crisis of 2007–2009, as in the years since then, there have been numerous instances of scandalous behavior. Banks have deceived and defrauded
consumers and investors, falsified reports to institutions publishing indices
for interest rates and exchange rates, manipulating bets on these indices, and
engaged in money laundering, tax evasion, and tax fraud, to name just some
of the violations.[3] The authorities, however, have often failed to hold those
responsible for the violations accountable and to tighten the rules where
appropriate. In settlements with authorities, corporations paid large fines, in
most cases without any admission of wrongdoing and without any of the

detail becoming public. Banks could just move on without much if any changes in their culture and conduct.

In this chapter, we give many examples of rule breaking and lawlessness in banks and by banks. We also show that the enforcement of rules is very weak. The underlying attitudes, rationales, and narratives, including "profits trump rules," or "efficiency must be a guiding principle," and "regulation threatens free market and could lead to tyranny," are dangerous for our societies and our polities.

When corporations cause harm or break rules, creating proper consequences poses significant difficulties. Corporations are abstract entities, created by the law. U.S. law permits the prosecution of corporations for any criminal conduct done by anyone "on behalf" of the corporation.[4] As abstract entities, corporations cannot go to jail. Criminal convictions may result in fines and, possibly, the imposition of compliance procedures and the appointment of a monitor to ensure that the corporation abides by the ruling.

In most cases, the authorities actually avoid the costs and the uncertainties of a court trial by reaching a settlement with the corporation that requires the payment of a fine but does not require the admission of wrongdoing.[5] If the fines are small in relation to the size and profits of the institution, there is little if any deterrent effect; fines are merely a "cost of doing business," never mind the unlawfulness. However, authorities often shy away from large fines because they might damage the financial health of the corporation and harm its ability to do business, with collateral effects on their employees and their customers.[6]

In March 2013, U.S. Attorney General Eric Holder highlighted the problem by telling the Senate Judiciary Committee that he is "concerned that the size of some of these [financial] institutions becomes so large that it does become difficult to prosecute them." As he explained the matter, prosecution might have "a negative impact on the national economy, perhaps world economy," implying "that some of these institutions have become too large," thus preventing the Department of Justice from dealing with them properly.[7]

Prosecution of individual executives for wrongdoing requires proving these executives committed specific actions with criminal intent.[8] Such proof may be difficult to obtain, since typically there is no one person knowingly orchestrating the overall scheme of misbehavior.[9] People at the top may be careful to ensure that they do not have "too much information" about what is going on below. To indict an individual at the top might require the collaboration of many people along a chain of command, and the distance between the wrongdoing and the person at the top may enable deniability. Recklessness may be excused as a way of taking standard business risks. The victims of wrongdoings may be widely dispersed and hard to identify individually. Even when wrongdoings or crimes persist for a long time, meeting ordinary standards of proof for executives' responsibility is difficult if not impossible.[10] The case of the blood-testing company Theranos, where people at the top were clearly responsible for the company's wrongdoing, was an exception.[11]

This state of affairs is dangerous. Since the financial crisis of 2007–2009, trust in our institutions has seriously eroded.[12] Large parts of the population have come to believe that the enforcement of laws and other rules for large corporations and their executives is seriously lacking, and that our economic, political, and legal systems are rigged against ordinary people. The resulting sense of unfairness undermines the legitimacy of our economic and political systems.[13] This sentiment has contributed to the radicalization of politics and to the success of politicians who appeal to people's anger. Unless we can create a system with better incentives and better accountability, the anger and discontent will increase further and may end up overthrowing our political order altogether.

The Cum-Ex Tax Fraud

A blatant kind of fraud occurred in the "cum-ex" scandal in Europe.[14] This fraud began in the late 1990s, gained momentum in the late 2000s, and slowed down after 2012, when the authorities started to crack down on it. The parties involved claimed that it was legal because there was no law that explicitly forbade it, but several courts have made clear that the conduct was inherently illegal because it was clearly based on fraud, and fraud is illegal. As of this writing, however, some versions of cum-ex fraud are said to be still going on.[15]

Those engaging in the fraud used false certifications to obtain "reimbursements" of taxes that had never been paid. In many European countries, corporations withhold capital income taxes when they pay dividends to shareholders. Certain institutional investors, however, such as banks and other corporations, and some foundations, are exempt from paying income taxes on dividends. The corporations paying the dividends do not know which investors are tax exempt, so they withhold the taxes for all as they make the payments and leave it to the investors to ask for reimbursements if they are eligible. The investors' banks certify the tax payments when they process the dividend payments so the appropriate clients can ask the tax authorities for the reimbursements.

The cum-ex fraud involved complicated schemes that generated two or more reimbursement certificates when the tax had only been paid once.[16] In the words of Correctiv, a journalists' cooperation that played an important role in uncovering the extent of the fraud: "It is a bit like parents claiming a child benefit for two or more children when there is only one child in the family."

When done on a large scale, the profits from this scheme can be extraordinary. The costs to taxpayers are estimated to be more than €10 billion in Germany and more than another €40 billion in the rest of Europe.[17] Most of the gains seem to have gone to the banks that arranged the transactions and to the lawyers that invented the schemes.[18] The banks charged the investors large fees. In Germany, all large private-sector banks were involved, as were at least four Landesbanken (public-sector banks owned by regional governments) and Lehman Brothers' German subsidiary. In other countries, names such as Bank of New York Mellon and Merrill Lynch in the United States, Barclays in the United Kingdom, ABN Amro in the Netherlands, Santander in Spain, Bank Safra Sarasin in Switzerland, or Bank Macquarie in Australia appear on the lists of institutions investigated by the authorities. Some pension funds registered in the United States have also been involved.[19]

The large-scale cum-ex frauds, which persisted over many years, were enabled by incompetent or captured government bureaucrats, by tax lawyers and tax law academics, and by politicians who did not want to interfere with the banks. The government bureaucrats put loopholes into the tax laws, in one case with a text instigated by a mole paid by the Bankers' Association.[20] The German financial supervisor BaFin chose to overlook the matter. Two whistleblowers' alerts, one of them made as early as 2007, were not acted on but were passed on to the banks in question without any investigation.[21] BaFin only concerned itself with cum-ex when the government's reclaiming money from the German subsidiary of the Canadian Maple Bank caused that bank to become insolvent.[22] The myth that cum-ex was legal because the law did not explicitly forbid it dominated the discussion. This myth was propagated enthusiastically by leading tax lawyers, including the global head of tax law for one of the world's most prominent law firms. It was also supported by paid experts' briefs from several tax law professors.[23]

The tenaciousness with which the scandal was eventually pursued owed a lot to the competence and courage of Anne Brorhilker, a public prosecutor in Cologne, who was unwilling to accept that a particular fraud was lawful because the general prohibition against fraud in the law did not make special mention of it. The prosecutor's office had been alerted by the tax authorities after one investor whose application for a "tax reimbursement" had been rejected hired a lawyer, and the lawyer notified the authorities of the scheme.

Ms. Brorhilker's previous assignments had included cases of organized crime in the construction industry and tax fraud to support Al Qaeda, and she quickly saw parallels between cum-ex and those earlier cases. However, she had an uphill fight because, even in her own institution, there were many who would have preferred that she go for settlements by which the accused and the banks would pay fines without admitting wrongdoing.[24] It took the intervention of the regional minister of justice to free her from interference by her colleagues.

A somewhat different prosecution took place in Switzerland. A German client of Swiss Bank Safra Sarasin had lost a large part of a €50 million investment when the German tax authorities refused the tax "reimbursements" that he claimed. (A large part of the investment itself had been used for special fees that the bank charged.) When he sued Bank Safra Sarasin for damages in Germany, his lawyer obtained help from two whistleblowers, one of them the bank's outgoing head of legal affairs and compliance. Among the documents he received was a legal assessment of his own case that the bank's lawyers had prepared. According to this assessment, the bank stood little chance of winning the case because it had failed to provide the investor with enough information about the nature and risks of the investment. The bank had not followed the lawyer's advice and instead had hired another lawyer. It had also declared all matters concerning cum-ex to be a bank secret and had asked the public prosecutor in Zürich to initiate criminal proceedings against the German lawyer and the whistleblowers, for "economic espionage" and violation of bank secrets. The public prosecutor in Zürich was eager to pursue the case while neglecting to deal with an accusation for fraud against the bank that had come from the German client's lawyer. Sometimes, Swiss authorities seem more interested in protecting Swiss banks than in prosecuting fraud.[25]

As of this writing (May 2023), five individuals have been given prison sentences for cum-ex tax fraud. Well over a thousand criminal cases are still being pursued. Some authorities are trying to force perpetrators to return the spoils of their fraud. Remarkably, however, in 2016 the regional government of Hamburg, which at the time was headed by Olaf Scholz, who later became Federal Chancellor, decided to forgo repayments of fraudulently obtained tax reimbursements from Hamburg-based Warburg Bank![26]

In the population at large, such decisions, and the entire cum-ex affair, reinforce the view that politicians and bankers illicitly connive at the expense of ordinary people. Politicians and those charged with law enforcement who tolerate substantial law infringements undermine the legitimacy of governments and their institutions. The sense that democratically elected governments and regulatory bodies are powerless in dealing with financial institutions, or even worse, are complicit in their excesses and transgressions, has contributed much to the anger that has increasingly come to dominate the political discourse in our societies.

LIBOR Manipulations at Deutsche Bank

In the introduction to Chapter 13, we reported that Barclays Bank in London had just agreed to pay $450 million to U.S. and U.K. authorities to settle allegations that it had been involved in manipulating LIBOR, the London Inter-Bank Offered Rate, a key index for interest rates whose value affects trillions of contracts worldwide.[27] We also mentioned that the LIBOR scandal had forced Bob Diamond, the CEO of Barclays, whom we quoted in Chapter 13, as well as the chairman of the board, to step down even as they claimed that they had been "let down" by "a small minority" of people in the banks, of whose misbehavior they had not been aware.

The index LIBOR was meant to provide a measure of the interest rates at which banks in London lent to each other. The value of this index was determined as an average of interest rates that the different banks reported to the British Bankers' Association. The index was important because many contracts referred to it and it determined the amounts owed under these contracts. For example, in the late 1970s, international banks would lend to Latin American countries at an interest rate equal to LIBOR plus x percent, so in any year the interest owed by the debtor depended on actual London interest rates in that year. LIBOR also served as a reference in many derivatives contracts.[28]

For traders who had taken bets on whether interest rates were going to rise or fall, the outcomes of their bets would depend on whether LIBOR would rise or fall. Misreporting LIBOR would therefore affect the outcomes of such bets. If the person submitting the report on behalf of a bank knew the positions of the bank's traders, a manipulation of the report could be used to increase both the traders' and the bank's profits at the expense of whoever was on the other side of the traders' contracts.[29]

Barclays was not the only institution involved in these manipulations. The list of banks that ended up paying fines for their involvement in LIBOR and similar manipulations reads like a Who's Who of global banking.[30] Deutsche Bank, for example, paid nearly $3 billion to U.S. and U.K. authorities and €725 million to the European Commission, all related to LIBOR manipulations.[31]

The leadership of Deutsche Bank, however, did not suffer the same consequences as the leadership of Barclays. In 2012, Anshu Jain, who had been the head of investment banking at Deutsche Bank, became one of two co-CEOs, succeeding Josef Ackermann, who stepped down after ten years. As the bank's involvement in LIBOR manipulations became known, Mr. Jain always asserted, like Mr. Diamond, the CEO of Barclays, that he had known nothing about the manipulations. Whereas such assertions did not help Mr. Diamond, they helped Mr. Jain to stay on even though the manipulations had occurred on his watch.

Mr. Jain only left as co-CEO in 2015. At the 2015 general meeting, share-holders had expressed their dissatisfaction with the large fines Deutsche Bank had to pay. Around the same time, Deutsche Bank had also received a highly critical letter from Frauke Menke, the department head in charge of large banks at Germany's supervisory agency BaFin.[32] In this letter, Ms. Menke asserted that, even if Mr. Jain did not know about the LIBOR manipulations, of which Ms. Menke expressed serious doubt, he was responsible for not having looked into the matter when the first rumors arose in 2007–2008 and for having maintained a structure of organization and control that enabled the traders' wrongdoings.

Ms. Menke's letter was based on the results of an investigation by the auditing company Ernst & Young. This report had shown, among other things, that in 2007, Mr. Jain had the seating arrangements in the London trading rooms of the bank changed in such a way that the people in charge of submitting reports about interest rates to the British Bankers' Association would be closer to the traders in interest rate derivatives. The new seating arrangements allowed for easier communication between the two groups. The letter also notes that, shortly after this change, the profits earned by Christian Bittar, the best trader of Deutsche Bank, increased dramatically. In 2008, they amounted to €500 million, obtained through bets on the index EURIBOR, the Euro Inter-Bank Offered Rate, whose outcomes were distorted by manipulations in EURIBOR reporting.[33]

In the turbulence that followed the Lehman bankruptcy, these EURIBOR submissions, as well as LIBOR submissions, were significantly biased downward because the banks wanted to present the impression that, despite the crisis, they were still able to borrow and lend at low interest rates. A trader who knew about this bias could profit by betting on relatively low EURIBOR values. Anyone in charge of transmitting reports to the British Bankers' Association who knew the trader's bets could benefit the bank by submitting reports that would make the bets succeed.

For his performance in 2008, Mr. Bittar received a bonus of €80 million, with strong support from Mr. Jain. Subsequently, when the authorities established that he had been involved in LIBOR manipulations in 2006 and 2007, he had to leave the bank, and the bank withheld some €40 million in unpaid bonuses. In 2018, a London court sentenced him to more than five years in prison.

Rule Infringements and Power Struggles

In her 2015 letter, Ms. Menke, the bank supervisor, had criticized the fact that Deutsche Bank's overall organization and culture had failed to deter misdeeds such as LIBOR manipulations. One aspect of this criticism concerns the incentives given to investment bankers. Withholdings of bonuses that had already been committed, as in the case of Mr. Bittar, must be seen as an exception. As long as Mr. Jain was at the helm, investment bankers were paid large bonuses, and the bank's accounting made sure that subsequent charges, such as payments of fines for investment bankers' misdeeds, would not be attributed to the investment bankers and would not cause subsequent decreases to investment bankers' bonuses.[34]

According to the analyst Dieter Hein of Fairesearch, Deutsche Bank paid investment bankers' bonuses amounting to €37 billion between 2007 and 2018. In the same period, it raised €37 billion in equity.[35] This new money from shareholders had mainly served to pay the investment bankers' bonuses. The bank's total profits over the period were a little more than €5 billion.[36]

In an earlier report, in 2012, Fairesearch had recommended that Deutsche Bank should close down its investment banking business and concentrate on private banking and portfolio management for wealthy investors. For the years 1998–2011, this report showed that the rate of return earned by the bank in investment banking amounted to 11.1 percent, the rate of return earned in private banking amounted to 21.5 percent.[37] These numbers differ from the numbers issued by the bank itself. According to Mr. Hein and Fairesearch, the difference was due to the fact that the bank had understated the equity attributed to investment banking and overstated the equity attributed to other activities. In private conversations, we have heard similar assessments, together with indications that internal whistleblowers pointing to the misattributions were not well received.

An even stronger plea for giving up on investment banking altogether had already been presented in 2011 by Markus Granziol, a former head of investment banking at the Swiss bank UBS, another globally systemic bank.[38] Granziol argued that wealth management was more profitable, and that having wealth managers and investment bankers side by side created ongoing conflicts of interest. One example he gave was Goldman Sachs taking bets that real estate prices would decline and take mortgage-related securities down with them, even as the bank was also advising investors to buy mortgage-related securities.[39] To be trustworthy as a wealth manager, Granziol argued, UBS should get rid of its investment banking. This was exactly the strategy followed by Axel Weber, the former president of the German central bank, who in 2012 became president of the board of UBS. Under his guidance, UBS greatly reduced its investment banking and became a world leader in wealth management services.

Ironically, Mr. Weber had previously been Josef Ackermann's favorite for his own succession as CEO at Deutsche Bank. The chair of the Supervisory Board of Deutsche Bank, however, claimed that Weber was not a banker and thwarted the plan. He wanted to promote Anshu Jain and got his wish.[40] In this context, Deutsche Bank also appointed an outsider as the new chair of the Supervisory Board, Paul Achleitner, who was firmly committed to the idea that investment banking must be the core activity of the institution.[41] He strongly supported Mr. Jain until 2015, when further support became inadvisable, perhaps because shareholders rebelled, perhaps also because Ms. Menke, the supervisor, had made her views clear.[42] After the leadership change, downsizing and cleanups began, but change was very slow.

In April 2016, nine months after the replacement of Mr. Jain, an Achleitner-led nomination committee recommended that the appointment of the head of the bank's integrity committee should not be renewed, as this person was too intent on investigating scandals and too little concerned with the future of the institution.[43] The removal of this person occurred shortly before the announcement of a large new fine from the United States caused the deep financial distress discussed in Chapter 14. Change only accelerated when Christian Sewing, who had no affiliation to investment banking, was appointed CEO in 2018.[44]

These power struggles are reminiscent of events at certain Italian courts in the Renaissance era. No poison or daggers were involved, but in an intense rivalry, different individuals fought for power in the institution, and the personalization of the struggle shaped the strategic discussion. To some extent the participants acted like members of different families or even different tribes, and tribal loyalties biased the discussion about strategic choices, sometimes overruling principles. The notion that bonuses ought to reflect performance, including damage from past misbehavior, was thrown overboard, as was the notion that internal rules had to be respected.

In the case of Deutsche Bank, the power struggle between investment bankers and traditional bankers goes back to the late 1990s. In 1999, Deutsche Bank bought Bankers Trust, originally a commercial bank that had moved aggressively into derivatives in the 1980s. Their aggressiveness showed in many instances of mis-selling and other forms of unlawful behavior. The record of Bankers Trust in the years 1990–1994 reads like a prelude to investment banking in the years after 2005, bringing the bank a fair amount of litigation, a substantial loss of reputation, and a culture of aggressiveness.[45]

For Deutsche Bank, the acquisition was an attempt to widen the bank's business beyond the home market. Deutsche Bank did not try to take control over the investment bankers at Bankers Trust but let them do their thing, with easy funding from the parent, Deutsche Bank. Sometimes it seemed as if Bankers Trusts' investment bankers had taken over Deutsche Bank rather than the other way round. They were in the driver's seat throughout the Ackermann years and then also during the Achleitner-Jain years, even as other institutions had begun to wonder whether investment banking was such a great business.

Power struggles also played a key role in Citigroup in the United States, one the largest globally systemic institutions in the world. Citigroup had been formed in 1998 when the former commercial bank Citicorp, with CEO John Reed, merged with the financial conglomerate Travelers, with CEO Sandy Weill. Travelers included insurance, mutual funds, and investment banking. The investment banking part of Travelers was led by Salomon Brothers, the institution that Michael Lewis writes about in *Liar's Poker*. Mr. Reed left in 2000 after a power struggle with Mr. Weill. Subsequently, he blamed "the dominance of Salomon Brothers sort of culture," which in his view had contributed to the disaster that Citigroup experienced in the 2007–2009 financial crisis. Citigroup survived this disaster only because massive support from the government hid its solvency problems. Mr. Reed's own time in leading Citicorp, however, included much the same behavior and also required bailouts.[46]

The Weakness of Internal Enforcement

Mr. Bittar, the trader at Deutsche Bank who earned the bank €500 million in 2008, violated the bank's rules limiting the size of the bets that traders could take. This rule violation seems to have had no consequences for Mr. Bittar at the time. Someone who earned that much money for the bank seems to have stood above the rules. Such an attitude suggests that the bank's management considered it more important for people to earn money than to abide by the rules, raising the question why rules are there in the first place.

The experience of some banks where bets turned out badly suggests that such an attitude is dangerous. In Chapter 5, we discussed the case of Mr. Leeson, whose unrestricted bets bankrupted the U.K.'s Barings Bank in 1995. We also mentioned that, from the mid-1990s to 2012, there have been at least twenty cases in which individuals' uncontrolled betting with derivatives imposed losses of more than $1 billion on the banks that employed these individuals.[47] More recently, Credit Suisse (CS) lost $5.5 billion from its dealing with the Archegos investment firm, which CS employees had pursued without imposing proper controls on Archegos, strongly resisting any calls to confront Archegos about violations of agreements on risk limits and even disobeying some of these calls.[48] A rule limiting the bets a trader can take makes sense because, no matter how "good" the trader may be, there is always an element of luck determining the outcomes of the bets. The bank must ensure that potential losses from bad luck remain limited.

In January 2013, JPMorgan Chase reported that, in 2012, derivatives traders in London had caused losses of $6.2 billion, after bringing in $400 million in profits in 2011.[49] A single trader, Bruno Iksil, nicknamed "the London Whale," had caused losses of about $2 billion; the number grew to more than $6 billion because Mr. Iksil's superiors chose to maintain his bets rather than liquidate them when the losses first appeared. The bank released a 129-page report about the episode and announced that, despite high overall profits in 2012, the pay of its CEO, Jamie Dimon, would be cut in half, from $23 million in 2011 to $11.5 million in 2012.[50] Several managers and traders, including Mr. Iksil, were dismissed.

Two months later, in March 2013, the Senate Committee of Investigation posted a report of some 1,300 pages, "JPMorgan Chase Whale Trades: A Case History of Derivatives Risks and Abuses."[51] The report found that the trading operation "piled on risk, ignored limits on risk taking, hid losses, dodged oversight, and misinformed the public." Moreover, limits on all the five risk measures used by the bank were breached. Between January 1 and April 30, 2012, there were a total of 330 breaches.[52]

Despite the loss caused by the London Whale, the bank's overall profit for 2012 was $21 billion, but the incident raised the question how a small group of traders could have had so much discretion over trades. The senate report suggests that internal risk controls were broken with no consequences and immediate superiors were complicit in prolonging the breaches. Later in 2013, JPMorgan Chase had to pay more than $1 billion in fines in connection with the episode.[53]

Mr. Bittar got away with taking excessive bets because he made a large profit for the bank. His superiors at Deutsche Bank chose not to enforce their own rules. Mr. Bittar's luck only turned when the authorities found that he had profited from the illegal manipulations of LIBOR reporting, which ultimately sent him to prison. For those involved in the derivatives trading for JPMorgan Chase in London that ended up causing the loss and the legal troubles, luck ran out earlier as they incurred large losses.[54]

For rules to be effective, they must be enforced. Enforcers, however, are often inactive, because of fear, complicity, or sheer laziness. With such motivation, enforcers may prefer to be willfully blind to a rule transgression.[55] In the case of Mr. Bittar, the lack of enforcement was likely due to fear and complicity—fear of losing this trader to another bank, and complicity in benefiting from the high profits for the bank and corresponding high bonuses for the bankers. The CS report on the Archegos disaster also mentions the weakness of enforcement in a culture focused on current profits.[56]

In the book *Liar's Poker*, author Michael Lewis tells the story of his own education and socialization as a bond trader at Salomon Brothers in the late 1980s. The blurbs on the book's cover emphasize how funny the book is. Though the book is funny indeed, the story it tells is quite disturbing. It presents the training of a bond trader as a course in aggressiveness and immorality. It presents lying as a normal form of discourse, both in relations between bankers and in relations with clients. In a key sentence, the author writes: "I had made the mistake of trusting a Salomon Brothers trader." Selling a bunch of AT&T bonds for $60,000 more than the bankers knew them to be worth was considered an act of heroism, never mind what the transaction might imply for the buyer. The principle *caveat emptor—buyer beware!*—was treated as an excuse for dishonest salesmanship.

In another book, *Traders, Guns & Money*, the former banker and derivatives trader Satyajit Das describes derivatives as "weapons of mass deception" and writes: "There are salespeople—they lie to clients. Traders lie to sales and to risk managers. Risk managers? They lie to the people who run the place—correction, think they run the place. The people who run the place lie to shareholders and regulators."[57]

In one interview, a risk and compliance officer described the low status of risk and compliance officers, who are treated as "business blockers." The person described the hierarchical nature of the banks, the challenge of getting information from traders, dealing with all their jargon, selfishness, and callous attitudes, and the fear of rocking the boat too hard. The person also emphasized the great job bank lobbyists have been doing to weaken the rules.[58]

The critical letter that Ms. Menke from BaFin sent to Deutsche Bank in 2015 emphasized the responsibility of the bank's leadership for the impact of organization, structure, and culture on the behavior of the bank's traders and the ability of the leadership to control illicit behavior. The education that Michael Lewis writes about seems to have had little to do with rules, except perhaps as things to be ignored and violated. Rule compliance would hardly go together with the aggressiveness that was taught. To the extent that disrespecting rules was part of the culture of investment bankers, the banks had a fundamental governance problem. If they insisted on respect for rules, they risked losing the traders. If they did not insist on such respect, they ran a risk of large losses—from flawed speculations of overconfident traders or from fines imposed by the authorities for transgressions of rules.[59]

The Weakness of Enforcement by Public Authorities

The March 2013 Senate report about the JPMorgan Chase London Whale episode mentioned earlier describes how JPMorgan Chase repeatedly misled its main regulator or neglected to provide information requested by the regulator. In addition, this report strongly criticized the regulator for failing to question the bank's valuation models and to investigate the many breaches of risk controls at the bank.[60] In January 2015, the Inspector General of the Federal Reserve issued a report arguing that the Federal Reserve Bank of New York, which also has a responsibility to supervise JPMorgan Chase, failed to examine the bank's investment unit ahead of the 2012 debacle even though a team of experts had recommended a "full scope examination" in August 2009.[61]

The same forces that allow bank employees to get away with breaking internal rules also allow banks to get away with breaking rules set by lawmakers and regulators. Ensuring that a bank complies with such rules requires enforcement. Outside enforcement is even harder than enforcement inside the organization because outside enforcers have much less information about what is going on. At the same time, fear, complicity, and laziness can be just as powerful in inducing willful blindness in outside enforcers as in inside enforcers.

In Chapters 12 and 14, we explained the phenomenon of politicians, regulators, and supervisors being complicit with "their" banks. Such complicity is as important today as it was when we first wrote the book more than ten years ago.[62] One cause of complicity is mistaken nationalism, based on a view that the banks' success in international markets promotes national welfare. Another cause of complicity is the view of banks as sources of funding for beloved projects or campaign contributions. Politicians love low interest rates for homeowners, an important group of voters, and are therefore responsive to warnings that stricter regulation might force them to raise mortgage rates.[63]

Finally, politicians, regulators, and supervisors may simply be "captured." They accept bankers' claims uncritically because of concerns about the bankers' dominating public discourse, because of their socialization, and because of career concerns. Career concerns are particularly important in jurisdictions in which people may move back and forth between banking and regulation.[64]

Quite often, supervisors and regulators refer to legal concerns as a pretext for their inactivity. These concerns are often convenient excuses.[65] For example, the German supervisor BaFin justified inactivity in the cum-ex affair on the grounds that tax fraud was not their responsibility and that they were not allowed to divulge information to tax authorities. However, the laws on data protection did not forbid their passing whistleblowers' warnings to the public prosecutors rather than to the whistleblowers' employers.

In fact, the legal powers of regulators are usually great, giving them many options to intervene if a bank engages in activities and practices that are incompatible with professional banking, including excessive risk taking. However, supervisors and regulators tend to shy away from using these powers.[66] Perhaps the very scope of their power makes them cautious because, if they use their power fully, they must expect blame from those they hurt.[67] As for the rest of society, regulators and supervisors may also be afraid that, if something is wrong and they intervene, they will be blamed for not having intervened earlier. In the case of Silicon Valley Bank, an intervention would have been called for at least by September 2022, but at that time already, it would have been appropriate to ask why the intervention did not take place even earlier. Supervisors should have ensured that SVB control its risk properly long before the bank collapsed in March 2023.[68]

Since the 2007–2009 crisis, one must add the fear of financial turbulence to the list of fears. In the years since that crisis, governments, regulators, and supervisors have often been soft on banks because they feared the consequences of toughness for the banks and the overall economy, for the funding of public debt and for themselves. For example, the authorities' toleration of procrastination in acknowledging losses on nonperforming loans that we discussed in Chapter 14 was very much due to fears that acknowledging such losses might reveal hidden insolvencies and needs for bank closures or recapitalizations that the authorities might not be able to handle. In the case of Credit Suisse, in September 2022, supervisors even seem to have lowered the equity requirements for the bank in order to avoid an intervention.[69]

Inaction by regulators and supervisors may also be motivated by other fears. For example, they may fear that bankers will call them incompetent. This fear played a big role in the years 1993–1995, when bankers fought for—and obtained— the right to use their own risk models in determining equity requirements for "market risks," that is, risks attached to changes in interest rates, exchange rates, and other market prices. The initial proposal of the regulators was ridiculed as being behind the times because the proposed requirements were ill-attuned to the actual risks.

Regulators and supervisors may also fear that the government or the courts will overrule them. For example, even before the financial crisis of 2007– 2009, the financial stability department of the Swiss national bank worried that the big Swiss banks were abusing the right to use their own risk models to determine their equity requirements.[70] However, they knew that an equity requirement without risk weighting would not go over well with the big banks, the government, or the media that at the time adored the big banks as champions for Switzerland in worldwide competition.[71]

The regulators and supervisors, as well as the public prosecutors, also worry about the proper use of their own resources.[72] Focusing their attention on any particular bank may require significant resources, which comes at the expense of looking at other cases. Such concerns may make the authorities willing to agree to a settlement, rather than go through with their investigations and possibly subsequent legal proceedings. Some regulators may also have reason to fear that intense activity on their side may induce the government to reduce their funding in subsequent years.

The 2015 intervention of BaFin against Deutsche Bank, supposedly the clearest case of a national champion in Germany, does not refute our considerations. Around 2005, politicians and media may have been excited at Deutsche Bank's promising to become a global leader in banking,[73] but by 2015 there was a sense that Deutsche Bank was no longer wholly a national institution. The role of Anshu Jain as co-CEO and the impression that the bank was being exploited by investment bankers in London and New York had created significant hostility towards the bank.

By contrast, in the case of payment company Wirecard in the late 2010s, BaFin was more concerned about defending Wirecard from foreign short sellers and media than about defending investors and taxpayers. BaFin, as well as the German finance ministry, to which BaFin is subordinated, seem to have regarded Wirecard as the one financial firm in Germany that was promoting cutting-edge technology for electronic payments.[74] In fact, their business was initially in "high-risk payments," such as payments related to pornographic movies or gambling on the internet. Later on it was a sham, which allowed participants to embezzle some €1.9 billion. The embezzlement involved the use of borrowed money to buy "firms" with no serious business whose owners were close to Wirecard managers. These fictitious firms paid dividends that were used as evidence of "profits," and allowed Wirecard to continue borrowing and purchasing fictitious firms.[75]

When a *Financial Times* journalist demonstrated that the published accounts of Wirecard contained evidence of irregularities, BaFin saw only an attack by foreigners on a German "champion." Instead of going after the fraud, the regulator scandalously imposed a prohibition on short sales of shares to protect Wirecard and even asked the public prosecutor to go after the *Financial Times* and the journalist who had uncovered the fraud.[76] Eventually, the president of Bafin had to resign—because Bafin employees were found to have speculated in Wirecard shares.

The agency's behavior in the years before the crisis of 2007–2009 was also marked by inaction. Its supervisors raised no objections to German banks' use of Special Purpose Vehicles to hold mortgage-related securities off-balance-sheet without any equity funding, as we dicussed in Chapter 11. They also did not object to the 2007 shotgun takeover of Austrian bank Hypo Group Alpe Adria by Bayrische Landesbank. In their view, this takeover was covered by the bank's freedom to do business as it liked. Yet, the risks were already obvious, and procedures for due diligence had been blatantly violated. The takeover ended up costing taxpayers some €5 billion when Hypo Group Alpe Adria became insolvent in 2009.[77] BaFin's inaction toward nonperforming loans of several banks to shipping companies fits fully into the pattern described here, particularly in the cases of HSH Nordbank and NordLB, two of the Landesbanken, whose losses on shipping loans amounted to several billion euros.

Fragmented Authorities

Given the involvement of Wirecard in "high-risk" transactions, you might expect that the company was regularly examined for potential participation in money laundering. In fact it was not. The financial supervisor BaFin claimed that Wirecard was not a bank and not even a financial holding company but a provider of payment services, and therefore BaFin was not in charge.[78] The government of Bavaria, the state where Wirecard headquarters was located, was in charge of controlling money laundering by nonfinancial businesses, but did nothing. Neither institution informed the other until, at a very late date, the government of Bavaria declared that Wirecard was a financial holding company after all. For almost two decades, therefore, this provider of payment services was not investigated for money laundering.

This episode illustrates a more general problem: Responsibilities for financial regulation and supervision are often split between multiple authorities. This fragmentation is a cause of inactivity. The different authorities have different rules and objectives and different routines, and they do not always share all the information they have with each other. This fragmentation and the potential information gaps it creates may enable banks to pile up risks— or frauds—without any one authority realizing the extent of the problem.

In the United States, for example, there are often multiple federal regulators as well as state regulators involved with each institution. The main regulator assigned to any banking institution is supposed to supervise it to ensure that it acts prudently. However, if they fail and instead tolerate excessive risk taking and insufficient equity, they may have incentives to withhold information about the bank's weakness from the FDIC, which is concerned with protecting the deposit insurance fund and taxpayers but may not be in control until such time as the bank is declared weak enough and potentially failing.[79]

Conflicted "Gatekeepers": Auditors and Rating Agencies

The behavior of regulators and supervisors is often driven by a fear of losing when banks contest their decisions. They shy away from confrontations with bankers because they fear that, in a conflict, they might be forced by the government or by a court to rescind their decisions and "lose face." Remarkably, regulators and supervisors are timid even in cases where both the letter of the law and the facts are clear. The letter of the law may be unimportant since it is up to the interpretation of the legal authorities, particularly the courts. Moreover, the authorities may fear that they cannot match the armies of professionals, lawyers, auditors, and consultants that a bank can mobilize to appear in court.

Some of these professionals are called "gatekeepers" because they provide information and certification about corporations to outside investors and thereby affect the terms on which the corporations can offer securities in the market. Important examples are auditors and rating agencies.

Auditors certify the financial disclosures that corporations with publicly traded shares, and some others, make at regular intervals. These disclosures should provide a correct picture of the corporation's financial development and status using a common set of accounting standards. Beyond checking that the corporation complies with the relevant accounting rules, auditors are also supposed to certify that the disclosures do not provide misleading information.

Auditors should also provide information about risks that the corporation and its investors may be exposed to, including risks concerning solvency, liquidity, and potential legal fines. The auditors' certifications should rest on the investigations that they have carried out, examining physical assets, such as real estate, and financial assets, as well as the documentation of financial claims, contracts, and bills to which the accounts refer. The auditors' reports also rest on conversations the auditors have had with managers and other people inside the business.

Auditors are in principle independent of the executives of the corporation to which they provide auditing services. The executives cannot tell them what they should put into their reports. However, the auditors are paid by the firms they audit, and they know that, if they want to get the auditing assignment again in the future, their report should be friendly rather than confrontational. Therefore, auditors' reports and certifications will often reflect the interests of those who hired them. The effect is reinforced if the auditing company also has a consulting business and is interested in serving the firm as a consultant, as well as auditing it.[80]

As we discussed in Chapter 8, such conflicts of interest played an important role in the scandals of the early 2000s, particularly the scandal around the bankruptcy of Enron. In the United States, the Sarbanes-Oxley Act of 2002 set new standards for accountants and auditors of public corporations and established a new regulator for auditors. Other countries followed with similar reforms. The Sarbanes-Oxley Act particularly tried to strengthen the independence of external auditors, pushing them to consider the interests of the corporation as a whole and of its shareholders, rather than the interests of the executives who hired them.

However, these laws could not eliminate the underlying conflicts of interest. In numerous cases corporations go into bankruptcy or need bailouts shortly after auditors give them a clean bill of health. Recent collapses of firms such as Carillion in the United Kingdom in 2018, Wirecard in Germany in 2020, or Greensill in Australia in 2021 all seem to have involved major flaws in external auditing.[81] In the Wirecard scandal, Ernst&Young, one of the leading international accounting firms, accepted the firm's accounts without ever engaging in a serious investigation of those sham "third-party acquisitions," which did not generate profits that would have corresponded to the money that was paid for them.[82]

In the cum-ex fraud scandal, one bank simply deleted an alert about legal risks from the published version of their auditor's report, apparently without any reaction from the auditor or the supervisor.[83] The financial statements of the three failed U.S. banks in 2023, SVB, Signature, and First Republic Bank, were all approved by their auditors. These auditors came from the same auditing firm, KPMG. Although, as discussed in Chapter 14, the weaknesses of the banks were in plain sight for months, the auditors did not raise any concerns, for example, about the sustainability of the funding as deposits were flowing out, the risks attached to funding by uninsured deposits, or the feasibility of holding a very large amount of securities until they would expire. As in other cases, auditors likely did not challenge managers because they wanted to maintain the lucrative engagements with the banks.[84]

Rating agencies can be similarly conflicted. Their task is to assess the risks associated with debt securities. Until the 1970s, it was common for them to be paid by investors. Since then, it has become common for them to be paid by the issuers of the debt securities. The switch seems to have been induced by the difficulties that rating agencies had when cheap photocopying made it easy for some investors to free-ride on the ratings purchases of others. With the transition to issuer payments, however, rating agencies came to have the same conflict of interest as auditors: They knew that, if they wanted to keep the firm as a client, they had better give its debt good ratings.

In the run-up to the crisis of 2007–2009, this conflict of interest was magnified by the rating agencies providing consulting services on how to package mortgages and mortgage-related securities to get good ratings. Surely, the ratings branch of the agency would not go counter to the recommendations of the consulting branch, especially since the consulting part of the business was often more lucrative than the rating part. The problems this caused became apparent in the summer of 2007 when multiple mortgage-related securities were downgraded by several steps at once and it became clear that a AAA rating, the best rating of all, for a mortgage-related security did not mean what AAA ratings had traditionally been taken to mean.

Auditors and rating agencies benefit from rules that require mutual funds or pension funds to use their certifications and ratings. Regulators and supervisors also rely on their work. As we have discussed many times throughout the book, several investigations have shown that inaccurate and misleading credit ratings played a key role in causing the financial crisis. The post-crisis Dodd-Frank Act signed in 2010 requires federal agencies to find "appropriate" substitutes for the credit ratings provided by rating agencies in financial regulations. It also calls for enhancing the accountability and transparency of credit rating agencies, and mandates the creation of a new Office of Credit Ratings to oversee them. However, the hoped-for changes have not materialized as the powers of the new regulator are limited, and regulators still rely on rating agencies.[85]

Lawyers

The Sarbanes-Oxley Act of 2002 in the United States set standards not only for corporate executives, accountants, and auditors but also for lawyers appearing before the Securities and Exchange Commission (SEC) in representation of issuers. Lawyers are hired to provide advice to executives, looking over the executives' shoulders as they design their strategies and telling them what they can legally do and what not. If the executives engage in behaviors the lawyers have advised, or at least allowed, as legal, the executives will feel safe and, if the matter comes before the SEC or goes to court, they will argue that any accusation of criminal intent is false because they listened to their lawyers.

Neither the law nor the SEC have provided much substance to the standard required of lawyers. The only standard that the SEC has developed concerns the so-called up-the-ladder reporting, a requirement that, if lawyers observe unlawful behavior of an employee of a corporation, they report the matter to the employee's superior. Even this rule, however, has not been systematically enforced, nor has the SEC put in place any broader set of rules. There have been court judgments against reckless "can do" advice, but no clear definition of what professional standards require.[86] The issue is difficult because, on the one hand, the lawyer is obliged to act in the best interests of the client and, on the other hand, the lawyer is also professionally pledged to fidelity to the law as a kind of public service.[87]

To understand the issues, it is useful to go back to the cum-ex fraud cases. The lawyers who developed and promoted the cum-ex schemes and who profited from them certainly pursued a "can do" approach. In so doing, however, they proceeded recklessly because they overlooked the fact that reimbursement claims for two or more tax payments when only one tax payment had been made was fraudulent. No best-service-for-clients requirement can justify advising such fraud, let alone turning it into a business model, for the banks as well as the lawyers.

In a daring investigation in 2014, the anticorruption organization Global Witness secretly recorded prominent lawyers in the United States expressing willingness to help a person posing as a lawyer representing a foreign leader interested in setting up corporate structures in order to be able to spend funds that were quite obviously illicit in the United States. One of the attorneys is recorded saying, "They don't send the lawyers to jail, because we run the country."[88]

Corporate Settlements

Any attempt by authorities to bring banks or bankers to court requires substantial resources, patience with a lengthy legal process, and a willingness to take a chance at losing in court, as often happened in cases where authorities tried.[89] Because of a lack of resources and the fear of losing cases in court, U.S. authorities typically find it too costly and risky to use the courts against corporations and executives.[90] As mentioned above, the German prosecutor in the cum-ex cases also was under pressure to abandon the prosecutions and settle for money. The cheapest and easiest path often taken by government authorities is to delegate the investigation to the corporation itself, extract a high settlement amount, and declare success even if the outcomes deliver little in the way of justice, accountability, or deterrence.

When corporate settlements are announced, representatives of the corporations usually say they are glad to put the allegations of wrongdoings behind them, but they typically neither admit nor deny the wrongdoings.[91] The representatives of public authorities may proudly announce that they have extracted large fines to hold the corporations accountable. In fact, it is impossible to assess whether a settlement is appropriate relative to the total harm that a corporation had caused and whether the perpetrators have been made properly accountable. The settlements are decided behind closed doors, not in a courtroom where the public can see the evidence in the case and the legal consequences. The "statements of fact" that accompany settlements usually reveal very little about the facts of the case even when the settlements are enormous. Everything else is subject to nondisclosure rules with serious penalties in case the rule is broken. Even the corporation's shareholders do not get the information they would need to impose discipline on managers in order to ensure compliance in the future.

As an example of these issues, consider one large settlement involving JPMorgan Chase. On November 19, 2013, the U.S. Department of Justice, in collaboration with a group of state attorneys general, announced "a record

\$13 billion global settlement with JPMorgan Chase for misleading investors about securities containing toxic mortgages."[92] This settlement was the largest civil settlement with a single entity in the United States until it was eclipsed by a \$16.65 billion settlement with Bank of America in August 2014.[93] In the announcement of the JPMorgan settlement, Attorney General Holder said: "Without a doubt, the conduct uncovered in this investigation helped sow the seeds of the mortgage meltdown," and he declared that "no firm, no matter how profitable, is above the law."

This settlement covered several different cases and involved not only the Department of Justice, but also several states, and one government agency. The \$13 billion consisted of \$2 billion in civil penalties, \$7 billion in retrieval of ill-gotten gains, and \$4 billion that the bank promised to spend assisting homeowners over four years. The \$7 billion retrieval of ill-gotten gains was considered a tax-deductible expense, so the effective cost to the bank was much less than \$7 billion.

When the \$13 billion settlement was announced, some in the financial media viewed it as too harsh, and in January 2014, CEO Jamie Dimon stated that the settlement was "unfair."[94] The "statement of facts" associated with the settlement does not provide a basis for assessing this claim. This statement describes in broad terms how JPMorgan Chase, as well as Bear Stearns and Washington Mutual, the institutions it bought in 2008, marketed mortgage securities that its employees knew were of poor quality while misrepresenting the quality to investors or providing inaccurate information when asked. Few details were given about the extent of the problems.

In February 2014, the nonprofit organization Better Markets filed a lawsuit in the District of Columbia challenging the \$13 billion settlement on grounds that the agreement was not subject to independent judicial review. Better Markets argued that "the Department of Justice served as investigator, prosecutor, judge, jury, sentence and collector" without anybody being able to review its decision and without sufficient information about the underlying conduct to assess whether the settlement was appropriate.[95] This lawsuit was dismissed in March 2015 because the Department of Justice argued, and the judge accepted, that Better Markets does not have "standing" in the case that would enable it to challenge the settlement.[96] The Department of Justice argued that it represents "the people," and, apparently, the law takes it for granted that the Department acts in the people's interest and that there is no need for transparency in the matter.

Mr. Dimon's claim that the settlement was unfair raises the question why he accepted it. One answer might be that the settlement enabled him to continue claiming that most cases of lawless behavior had involved employees of Bear Stearns and Washington Mutual, the two banks JPMorgan Chase acquired in 2008 rather than employees of JPMorgan Chase itself. Media reports at the time suggested that negotiations about the settlement had been languishing for months, with JPMorgan Chase not making any substantial offers, and only picked up in September 2013 when the bank was threatened with a civil suit by a federal prosecutor in California.[97]

Subsequent media reports indicated that this civil suit was based on evidence provided by a whistleblower from inside JPMorgan Chase, who was prepared to testify about low-quality mortgage-related securities having been sold to unwitting investors with false presentations by managers of the bank. This suit would have publicized the fact that such misbehavior had occurred not only at Bear Stearns and Washington Mutual, but also at JPMorgan Chase itself, under Mr. Dimon's watch.[98] Whereas all the civil claims related to the case were settled in November 2013, the Department of Justice kept open the possibility of bringing criminal charges. However, no action was taken and the witness never got to testify.

The Department of Justice does not need judicial approval for its settlements, but some other settlements need approval from a judge, for example those between a bank and an agency such as the SEC. In these cases, the approval is a rubber stamp because the judge does not have much information about the settlement.

In one case that made headlines, Jed Rakoff, a senior judge in the Southern District of New York, refused to sign a $285 million settlement between the SEC and Citigroup in 2011, saying that he could not determine whether the settlement was "fair, reasonable, adequate and in the public interest."[99] Asking the court to employ its power to approve the SEC's interpretation of the law without knowing the facts would be inappropriate, he argued. The fine, in fact, could have been too large and yet the corporation may have chosen to settle rather than go to court. Whereas many applauded Judge Rakoff's courage, an appeals court later forced him to approve the settlement. When following the appeals court's decision, Judge Rakoff commented: "That court has now fixed the menu, leaving this court with nothing but sour grapes."[100]

Most jurisdictions outside the United States did not even impose substantial fines after the 2007–2009 crisis.[101] Some authorities even tried to intervene to reduce fines from the United States, viewing them as a threat to global financial stability.[102] Mark Carney, whose activities we discussed in Chapter 14, the governor of the Bank of England and chair of the Financial Stability Board for a major part of the 2010s, even asserted that the $320 billion in fines that had been levied could have supported $5 trillion in new lending.[103]

Whistleblowers

We saw that auditors, rating agencies, and lawyers often have weak incentives to deal with wrongdoings in corporations even though the very purpose of these actors is to help investors, regulators, and the public gain information on what is going on inside corporations, including dangers from reckless or unlawful behavior. As they are hired by executives or directors and paid by the corporation, their business interests may be in conflict with the public interest to which they should in principle be committed.

Alerts from victims and witnesses, as well as investigative media that can magnify their message and do their own research as well, can therefore be critical for dealing with corporate lawlessness, deterring it and providing victims with compensation for harm.[104]

If victims or whistleblowers get media attention, there may be pressure on enforcers to take action, but publicity is only likely if the offense or the offender are important enough to make the story newsworthy. States like Delaware make it easy for many small businesses to organize as corporations, and the rules and regulations help these businesses hide what they want to hide. Certain other jurisdictions also enable secrecy, corruption and worse.[105] If nobody follows up, justice may not be served. If cases are settled out of court, even the federal judge who must approve a settlement may not get enough information to determine if it is in the public interest.

Victims may be the only ones who can file a civil complaint.[106] However, doing so and prevailing in the legal process is time consuming and costly.[107] Offenders may have sufficient resources and power to frustrate such attempts, even if lawsuits are brought on behalf of the government.[108] Ordinary citizens meanwhile may not be able to afford any legal expenses.[109] In connection with a panel of an American Bar Association meeting in 2014, Anat Admati was told that homeowners could not get any legal representation to sue banks on mortgage-related cases. A banking lawyer confirmed that, because many large banks have ongoing relationships and often long-term retention contracts with most of the relevant law firms, victims may indeed have trouble lining up representation to pursue claims against a bank.

If powerful people cause harm, break laws, or benefit when others do it on their behalf, they will try to prevent the truth from emerging.[110] They might intimidate, threaten, or take legal action against victims and whistleblowers.

Whistleblowers, people who observe and communicate wrongdoings within organizations, are often ignored, fired, and may themselves become victims. One example is the securities lawyer who worked at JPMorgan Chase between 2006 and early 2008. She informed higher-ups in the corporation of mortgage securities fraud at the bank, but failed to get attention from her bosses and the executives she approached. She was fired in February 2008. Her testimony is cited in the Statement of Facts of the $13 billion settlement of JPMorgan Chase discussed above. In subsequent interviews, she said that she could not get another job as a lawyer in the United States, so she returned to her native Canada. Potential employers in the United States were deterred by the revelation that she might have to serve as a witness against JPMorgan Chase.[111]

This whistleblower, like many employees in banks and elsewhere, signed a nondisclosure agreement (NDA) that forbade her from revealing anything about her work at JPMorgan Chase. When she approached prosecutors, they agreed to maintain her anonymity. After the draft complaint was shared with the bank's lawyers in early September, those who had been clearly alerted to the frauds could no longer claim that they had not been aware of it. By contacting the Department of Justice to renew settlement negotiation just before the complaint would become public, Mr. Dimon made sure that this evidence would remain secret. The "statement of fact" attached to the settlement referred to an employee who alerted her superiors and executives to the problem but kept all the names hidden and did not provide much detail about the frauds.

There are many other stories of whistleblowers who were treated harshly. For example, a former Citigroup employee alerted top executives in Citigroup, including former U.S. Secretary of the Treasury Robert Rubin, in early November 2007, about pervasive fraud in selling mortgage securities. He was ignored and then fired. Parts of his testimony to the Financial Crisis Inquiry Commission were sealed.[112] Above we also mentioned two whistleblowers on the cum-ex tax fraud whose complaints the supervisor just passed on to the incriminated banks. One of them got fired immediately.[113]

In yet another case, a risk manager alerted his superiors at Deutsche Bank in 2011 that the valuation methods they had been using at least since 2009 for some complex derivatives were flawed. The flaw led to an over-valuation of the bank's net derivatives position by about $10 billion in 2010. This over-valuation induced an exaggeration of the bank's equity by the same amount, a substantial fraction of the reported equity.[114] The risk manager was fired in November 2011 and could not find another job in the banking industry. The information obtained from him and two other whistleblowers enabled the SEC to pursue the case. In late 2015, it settled the case for a $55 million fine.[115] Subsequent market developments, which contributed to the bank's poor performance in later quarters, provided indirect evidence that the valuations had been significantly inflated.

Protecting whistleblowers who expose wrongdoing in the financial sector and elsewhere, including in government bodies, and encouraging them to come forward is critically important. In many jurisdictions, however, the law offers little protection.[116] The Dodd-Frank Act in the United States established a whistleblower program in a few regulatory agencies that rewards whistleblowers with a cut of the fines if their tips turned out to be helpful, and offers some protection against retaliation.[117] Such programs are a step in the right direction, but whistleblowers still face great uncertainty, harsh treatment, and difficult dilemmas.

Enablers and Spin

The movie *The Big Short*, which we cited in the introduction to this chapter, was nominated for the 2016 Academy Awards but lost out to the movie *Spotlight*, which deals with the decades-long sexual abuse scandal in the Catholic Church. For many years, the Church had kept this scandal well hidden. When settling claims of sexual abuse by priests through payments to victims, victims had to commit to keep quiet about what they had suffered. The pervasiveness of the abuse only came to light through an in-depth investigation by journalists from the *Boston Globe*. This investigation is the subject of the movie, and it illustrates how powerful people can cause harm repeatedly and conceal it.[118]

In one scene in *Spotlight*, a lawyer who had represented victims of sexual abuse says to a journalist: "If it takes a village to raise a child, it takes a village to abuse a child."[119] This statement points to the tacit collusion of many people over many years. The victims themselves often remained silent, out of shame or because they were silenced by nondisclosure agreements. Before the investigation by the *Boston Globe* journalists, media coverage of abuse allegations had been minimal and sporadic, treating incidents as isolated events. The role of higher-ups in the hierarchy and the Church as an organization played in covering up and perpetuating the abuse had not been addressed.

For scandalous and abusive behavior to persist, there are usually many enablers, people who look away as well as people who provide outright support. The perpetrators may try to present the behavior as "normal," not scandalous at all, or they may try to cover the behavior up, with settlements and an imposition of secrecy. For such strategies to be successful, the media must be willing to support the perpetrators' narratives. It must either overlook the scandals or present them as regrettable exceptions, the abuses or aberrations of people who have abused the trust of their superiors as well as their victims. The "spin doctors" of public discourse, the people who create the narratives that drive public discussion, must also fall in line.[120]

In the context of banking and finance, public discourse is made difficult by the fact that many important issues are technical and complicated. Making these issues understandable to readers who are not specialists may require more space and more effort than are available in general-audience media, whether print or electronic.[121] In such media, simple messages win. Prominence of a bank executive or a government official may be more important than the substance of what they say. Moreover, a populist or nationalist twist improves the speaker's chances of success.

In 2011, Jamie Dimon, JPMorgan Chase CEO, complained that some rules proposed by the Basel Committee for Banking Supervision were "anti-American."[122] This statement got attention. Because he is a successful banker and the public face of JPMorgan Chase, Jamie Dimon's utterances are newsworthy in the United States and the financial media, and the nationalist twist was very effective. Substantive considerations were too complicated to prevail against the simple nationalist message conveyed by a prominent banker.[123]

Another example involves Swiss media commenting on the development of the Swiss champion banks UBS and Credit Suisse (CS) in the 2010s. As mentioned earlier in this chapter, during this period, UBS reduced its involvement in investment banking in favor of growth in its wealth management activities. The major high-quality newspaper *Neue Zürcher Zeitung* was very critical of this change, complaining that UBS was leaving far too many profitable opportunities in investment banking to foreign competitors such as Deutsche Bank. The criticism coincided with applause for CS, which had not changed its strategy in the 2010s. By now, it is clear that UBS fared better than either CS or Deutsche Bank—because of the strategy it had chosen. Indeed, UBS has fared so well that it could acquire the failing CS in March 2023. However, at the time, the idea that UBS, newly led by a German, might cede territory to Deutsche Bank made for a good story.

In Chapter 16, we reported that, in Italy, the imposition of loss sharing on the holders of subordinated debt in insolvent banks in 2017 did not go over well with the public and that the media fueled the outrage. Populist and nationalistic sentiment beat the simple notion that someone who willingly buys subordinated debt receives higher interest as a reward for bearing greater risk and must therefore accept losses when the risks materialize.

With specialized media such as the *Wall Street Journal* or the *Financial Times*, there is a different problem. The readers of such media are probably sophisticated enough to understand the issues, but many of them are part of the industry and are to some extent biased. The papers themselves depend on subscriptions and advertising from the financial industry, and their journalists are keen to get and maintain access to people and institutions in the industry. Promoting the bankers' messages can improve such access and may advance journalists' careers. Journalists who ask inconvenient questions of people in positions of power may in fact be subject to pressure behind the scenes or even be denied opportunities and access. Content that is objectionable to powerful people and institutions may be changed by editors or later removed.[124]

In one extreme case, in 2015, the editor of the British newspaper *The Telegraph* resigned because the paper failed to cover unfavorable news about the bank HSBC, a major advertiser. Explaining his resignation, Editor Peter Osborne wrote that "the coverage of HSBC in Britain's *Telegraph* is a fraud on its readers. If major newspapers allow corporations to influence their content for fear of losing advertising revenue, democracy itself is in peril."[125] Coverage may also be affected by the media company's own business relations with banks.[126]

Narratives are developed and promoted by many people and many institutions. Some of those who develop and promote the bankers' narratives are outright lobbyists. An example is the International Institute of Finance, which works on behalf of globally active banks and whose criticism of Basel III we mentioned in Chapter 6. Their forecast that Basel III would raise interest rates on bank loans in the United States and Europe and would lower real growth rates for a number of years was strongly refuted by subsequent events.[127] In contrast to outright lobbyists, nonprofit think tanks are not directly linked to industry organizations or industry members. However, they depend on donors whom they may not wish to antagonize, and who in some cases they directly collaborate with.[128] The boards of directors of many important think tanks are dominated by corporate executives, including from major financial institutions.

On one occasion, when we co-organized a conference on financial regulation in collaboration with one of the think tanks in Washington, DC, after the program was nearly finalized we were instructed that each panel must include a participant from the banking industry. Not wishing to compromise the quality of the discussion, we arranged to move the conference elsewhere and included industry participants where they fit into the program.[129]

The Oscar-winning 2010 movie *Inside Job* suggests that *academic economists* are also creators of misleading narratives about the economy and particularly about banking.[130] These narratives often involve the notion of "efficiency." Obviously, if a policy produces an outcome that makes *everyone better off in every respect*, then that policy may be deemed to be unambiguously better for society as a whole—it improves "efficiency."

The trouble is that it is very rarely the case that policies make *everyone better off in every respect*, which makes this condition essentially irrelevant for any real-world analysis. Economists therefore like to replace it with the notion that a policy should be preferred if *hypothetically* it could make everyone better off in every respect provided there was a suitable redistribution of income and wealth. For example, opening the country for international trade leads to outcomes that are "more efficient" in this weakened sense, even though some people may lose substantially, as happened to the people in the north of Italy who lost their jobs when China was given unrestricted access to world markets in the early 2000s.

The notion of efficiency was introduced as a criterion for assessing how "good" economic outcomes are. In the past fifty years, economists have begun to use this notion to "explain" much of what we see in the economy. Certain results in economic theory show that, under some conditions, economic outcomes in what is referred to as "free, competitive markets" are efficient. Many have concluded from this observation that whatever we see in markets must be efficient; we live in the best possible world.[131] Thus, if there are market outcomes that we do not immediately understand, our task is to find an explanation of them as being an efficient way to deal with whatever "frictions" will serve the explanation.

By this logic, for example, the heavy short-term borrowing of banks that we observe in the real world must serve some useful purpose. The economist who wants to understand it must come up with a story to "explain" what this purpose is. We discussed some such "theories" in Chapters 10 and 14, and in a more detailed "omitted chapter" from this book.[132] Many studies suffer the shortcoming that the empirical validity of the theories is often not tested, either individually or in competition between different theories, all of which are consistent with what we observe but some are more plausible than others.

If you take the view that what we see must be efficient, you are ill prepared to deal with something like the 2007–2009 financial crisis. This observation explains why, in that crisis, academic economists who are experts in banking and finance stood apart from most other observers. Most other observers thought that the financial crisis was a result of distorted incentives, particularly for short-term borrowing by banks, but many academics maintained that such borrowing is beneficial and that regulation to limit such borrowing would deprive society of important benefits.[133] None of the proponents of such theories bothered to show that the conditions they postulated were satisfied in the years before the crisis. The models that support the theories are often intricate and intellectually cute, but many of them do not pass basic smell tests for realism.[134]

Such theorizing is not limited to banking. In the area of competition policy, one sometimes sees the argument that a monopolist is not really a monopolist because it is subject to *potential* competition.[135] Because the monopolist must fear that any attempt to use monopoly power will induce others to enter the field and take the market away from him, he behaves as if he had no market power at all. Under certain highly special assumptions, one finds that, in theory, there can be circumstances in which this analysis is valid, but these assumptions bear little relation to the real world. Using a theory that is unmoored from reality as a guide to public policy toward monopolies is clearly inappropriate.[136]

Those who consider the current situation in banking to be close to efficient in creating benefits for the economy are avoiding the key question of whether the purported benefits of the system outweigh its costs. The costs include the consequences of the bad investment decisions of heavily indebted banks, of the pervasive fraud in the system, and of the financial crises that keep requiring taxpayer bailouts.[137]

Few read the details of academic research, and if they did, they might find it difficult to spot the weaknesses and flaws in many of them. The bankers only care that the policy recommendations agree with them. Academics, meanwhile, may not care whether the bankers and politicians read and understand the arguments. It is often enough for them to feel welcome and to have the policy recommendations of their research praised by important people in banking and politics. A risk manager for a major globally systemic bank, who had been a doctoral student in finance and can read the academic literature, quipped to Anat Admati with respect to academics: "With such friends, who needs lobbyists?"

"Efficiency," "Free Markets," Fairness, and the Rule of Law

The epigraph to this chapter is taken from a remarkable essay in which the German economist Walter Eucken commented on the hero worship that a previous generation of economists in Germany had devoted to the creators of cartels, arrangements to eliminate price competition, in the late 19th and early 20th centuries. In opposition to this hero worship, Eucken observed that daily life in the economy consists of power struggles and that people succeed in these struggles because they are experts at fighting for power. After the sentence in the epigraph, his text continues: "Some may be tempted to belittle the brutality because each of the groups involved will be interested to present its own struggle as promoting the common good. For this very reason, the duty of scholars is to be extremely skeptical. However, such skepticism is often lacking."[138]

Arrangements for eliminating price competition have a long history. In the Middle Ages, and in many countries, artisans had to belong to guilds, and the guilds prescribed the prices that members could charge, and sometimes also the quality of products they could offer. England was the exception in that English courts had an early tradition of prohibiting *price fixing*, as it was called. Even so, in the 1770s, Adam Smith, the founding father of modern economics, wrote: "People of the same trade seldom meet together, even for merriment and diversion, but the conversation ends in a conspiracy against the public, or in some contrivance to raise prices."[139] The United States prohibited "agreements in restraint of trade," including price fixing, in the Sherman Act of 1890.

Around the same time, the highest German court ruled that cartel agreements fixing the price that members could charge were not only legal, but also legally binding, so members of the cartel could sue violators for damages. Legal scholars saw such agreements as falling under the "freedom of contracting," and contemporary economists were enthusiastic about the power obtained by German businesses. Unlike medieval English judges, they averted their eyes from the fact that this power served to exploit consumers through excessively high prices.[140] In Germany, and under German influence also in the European Economic Community, the predecessor of the European Union, cartels only became illegal in the 1950s. Adam Smith's assessment, however, is still relevant: Hardly a year passes without the discovery of some cartel by which major producers have eliminated competition among each other and charged the buyers of their products excessively high prices. Disregard of the law occurs not only in banking.

Many lawyers and economists believe that laws against restraints of competition, such as the Sherman Act in the United States, aim—or perhaps should aim—at improving efficiency. They know that market outcomes with cartels are inefficient, so presumably the law must be about that.[141] As they focus on efficiency, they overlook the fact that the law does not refer to efficiency and that, historically, prohibitions of price fixing were motivated by considerations of *fairness*. Profits obtained by suspending competition between producers were deemed unfair. The law is rooted in concerns about excessive power and about unfairness involved in the use of such power. Its prohibition of price fixing is not based on any comparison of the gains to cartel members with the losses of the buyers, but on the much simpler assessment that gains to cartel members are illegitimate.

Fairness is also a key concern in the violations of laws and other rules that we discussed in this chapter. Fraud is illegal because telling a falsehood in order to get someone to pay some money is deeply unfair. It is not much different than *theft*. Getting a reimbursement for a tax payment that one has never made is a fraud, effectively stealing from taxpayers. Selling mortgage-related securities to investors without telling the truth about the quality of the assets underlying the security is a kind of fraud, especially if one is at the same time betting that these securities will lose value. So is a misreporting of interest rates for LIBOR and similar indices that allows the bank's own traders to bet on the false reports. The extent to which major banks engaged in these fraudulent activities is deeply disquieting. So is the degree to which the perpetrators and their superiors seem to have regarded fraudulent activities as normal. The weakness of rule enforcement likely has reinforced these attitudes.

In Chapter 14, we reported that, in 2016, U.S. President Trump issued an executive order asking that bank regulators pursue the objective of efficiency, an objective that does not appear in the law. As an objective for regulators, efficiency is not even well defined, but the bankers may claim that all their actions improve efficiency, and therefore the regulators should stop putting constraints on them. Such claims are akin to the second part of Eucken's text: Bankers and other industry leaders claim that they are promoting the common good and that any power they might gain or profits they might earn are coincidental.[142] The skepticism about such claims that Eucken requests from scholars is often missing.

Some people clamor for *free markets*, but they do not explain what exactly makes a market *free*. In a completely free market, where any economic transaction can occur as long as two parties agree to it, would you be free to hire someone to steal goods you might desire and deliver them to you? Would you be free to engage in any sort of deception to sell your goods and services and be allowed to plead *caveat emptor* whenever challenged? In the Middle Ages, trade fairs and markets in trading cities were protected by armed guards. We are fortunate that the rule of law and the power of the state protect people properly, in markets and elsewhere.

Functioning markets require proper rules and forces strong enough to enforce these rules. In financial markets, the need for rules is particularly great because trade in these markets is not organized so that all parties see what they get but rather involves promises of future payments or returns, and enforcement requires policing long after the actual trade. For someone with a history of bankruptcies, breaking promises may seem like normal financial activity, but if all issuers of debt and other securities were to behave that way, banks, financial markets, and the overall economy would be in deep trouble.

Rules and regulations promote the functioning of markets because they provide a basis for participants' trusting each other. Many will rail against the constraints imposed by the rules and the requirement for compliance with the rules. However, without rules, the markets would not get off the ground in the first place. As Tariq Fancy, former chief investment officer for Sustainable Investments at asset manager BlackRock, put it recently, "No rules, no market."[143] If the law constrains some people, it is often to prevent them from taking away the *rights* and freedoms of others.

Like the games of basketball or football, the rules that govern markets need enforcers akin to referees. The enforcers must not be partial. In a basketball or football game, we take it for granted that the referees are not aligned with one of the teams and that they enforce objectively by the rules as best they can. By contrast, the accounts we have given of enforcers in banking suggest that perhaps the enforcers are too much beholden to some of the privileged and powerful players and therefore shy away from full enforcement of the rules.

Those who speak of free markets often also embellish the concept by adding the loaded term *capitalism*. They champion *free-market capitalism*, presenting it as the obvious choice over the dreaded alternative of *big-government socialism*, or even totalitarian dictatorship. The need for effective rules and rule enforcement is overlooked. Yet the very existence of corporations depends on such rules, and so do the contracts and markets on which all economic activities depend. The resentment that some may feel at being constrained by the rules is often an indication that the rules—and their enforcement—are serving the very purpose for which they were introduced, namely to provide protection to some by restraining others.[144]

Enthusiasm about free-market capitalism sometimes involves visceral hostility toward government, harkening back to Ronald Reagan's famous proclamation that "Government is not the solution to our problems; government *is* the problem."[145] To be sure, there are many problems that cannot be solved by government, and there are many instances where flawed government activities are a problem, but without laws and without law enforcement by government, markets would not work and we would all be *much* worse off. The blindness to the need for government and the radicalism with which supporters of free-market capitalism have denied many of the constructive roles that governments can and must play have muddled the political discourse and contributed to unfocused anger. This delusionary thinking about government is one of the reasons for the "crisis of democratic capitalism" that Martin Wolf of the *Financial Times* has decried.[146]

The poor design and lack of enforcement of rules that we have witnessed raise the specter of a class society, in which some people have privileges that allow them to put forward flawed and deceptive claims, create confusion, and defraud others with impunity, while others are powerless to defend themselves against these depredations.[147] In an earlier era, conflicts between aristocrats and ordinary people would be decided in favor of the aristocrats no matter what; judges who were themselves aristocrats took it for granted that people of their own class must prevail. Some of the developments that we have sketched suggest that we may be returning to such a system.[148] This situation poses a fundamental threat to our democracies, which are built on a rule of law in which all people are treated as equal before the law.

The distorted and flawed narratives that we discussed divert attention from these deeper issues. In a 1985 book entitled *Amusing Ourselves to Death*, the media expert Neil Postman expressed deep concern that "our public discourse has become dangerously nonsense."[149] He was concerned with the effects of television and the power of pictures on public discourse, but he would probably have seen the development of social media in the same light, namely as distorting discourse in the direction of entertainment and away from serious discussion about matters of substance.[150] He feared that communication in our society might be so much dominated by concerns for entertainment that all serious discourse would disappear: Concerns for the competence of political leaders would be displaced by concerns for their good looks, arguments would be displaced by quips and sound bites, and concerns for truth and for facts would be displaced by narratives supported by "alternative facts" that might be much more entertaining even if they are based on falsehoods.[151]

Democracy and the rule of law rest on the assumption that citizens of a country have equal access to participation in politics and inhabitants are equal before the law. These basic conditions of equality are endangered if people associated with banks and other corporations enjoy privileges in political and legal processes. They are also endangered if power dominates public communication and determines the narratives influencing legislation and jurisdiction even though these narratives have no more substance than the Emperor's new clothes in Andersen's tale.[152] To avoid these dangers, we must see to it that public discourse gives more *power to truth*.

NOTES

ONE *The Emperors of Banking Have No Clothes*

1. Our timing of the crisis takes its cue from the turbulences of summer 2007 and the requests for support from the financial industry that continued through early 2009. See the descriptions of the Financial Crisis Inquiry Commission (FCIC 2011). Before summer 2007, mortgage and real estate markets in the United States had already been in decline for a year. After 2009, some would say that the crisis continued right into the more recent European crisis that broke out in 2010. However, the European crisis is in many ways distinct from the events of 2007–2009. Reinhart and Rogoff (2009) give a detailed history of financial crises for about eight centuries. Laeven and Valencia (2012) analyze systemic banking crises during 1970–2011.

2. Mr. Dimon's statement is from an earlier session on the same day. These quotes were reported by Reuters ("DAVOS—Sarkozy to JPMorgan Chief: Banks 'Defied Common Sense,'" January 27, 2011).

3. Around the time of the Davos exchange between Dimon and Sarkozy, in January 2011, Bob Diamond, then CEO of Barclays, said similarly that the time for remorse was over. See "Bob Diamond: No Apologies. No Restraint. No Shame," *The Independent*, January 12, 2011. A more recent interview with Jamie Dimon by Jessica Pressler was published under the title "122 Minutes with Jamie Dimon: The JPMorgan Chase CEO Is Really, Really, Really Sorry. Except When He's Not" in *New York Magazine*, August 12, 2012. In this interview Mr. Dimon is quoted as saying, "I'm an outspoken defender of the *truth.*"

4. According to the Center for Responsive Politics, the financial industry spent $477,607,675 on lobbying in 2011. This is an increase of 13.7 percent relative to 2007. (Total inflation during this period was about 7.8 percent.) We discuss lobbying and the politics of banking more generally in Chapter 12.

5. See, for example, Victoria McGrane and Jon Hilsenrath, "Fed Writes Sweeping Rules from Behind Closed Doors," *Wall Street Journal*, February 21, 2012. Sheila Bair, chair of the Federal Deposit Insurance Corporation (FDIC) from 2006 to 2011, describes in detail how bank lobbying and political and regulatory capture affect the determination and

implementation of laws and regulations in the United States and in international regulatory bodies such as the Basel Committee on Banking Supervision (Bair 2012).

6. For example, Richard X. Bove, a bank analyst who is frequently interviewed on television, found fault with a Bloomberg editorial (see Neil Hume, "Bove vs. Bloomberg," *Financial Times* Alphaville, September 26, 2011). Patrick Jenkins and Brooke Masters, in "Higher Capital Ratio Talk Cuts Banks' Appeal" (*Financial Times,* March 27, 2011), quote a "leading London investment manager" who referred to people in the Bank of England pushing for financial reform by saying "There is a Taliban faction of fundamentalists and purists within the Bank." When describing lobbying by banks, Barofsky (2012, 148) writes, "A key tactic is to argue that issues related to high finance are so hopelessly complex that it is nearly impossible for mere mortals to understand the unintended consequences of the legislation. The advocates . . . so the argument goes, just don't have the requisite experience to understand."

7. We are not the only ones who refer to Andersen's tale in the context of banking and financial regulation. The first chapter of Hayes (2012), which discusses Alan Greenspan, Robert Rubin, and Larry Summers, the leading policymakers of the 1990s, is titled "The Naked Emperors."

8. For example, at a conference held in New York in November 2009, Lloyd Blankfein, Goldman Sachs CEO, admitted that they "participated in things that were clearly wrong and . . . have reasons to regret and apologize for." (Blankfein's statement was reported by the *New York Times* in its editorial note "Goldman's Non-Apology," November 21, 2009.) Similarly, in his testimony before the FCIC in January 2010, Brian Moynihan, Bank of America CEO and president, recognized that "over the course of the crisis, we, as an industry, caused a lot of damage. Never has it been clearer how poor business judgments we have made have affected Main Street" (FCIC 2011, 389).

9. Alan Greenspan, past chair of the Federal Reserve, compares trying to protect citizens against risks from the financial system to building a buffer that "may encompass expensive building materials whose earthquake flexibility is needed for only a minute or two every century, or an extensive stock of vaccines for a feared epidemic that may never occur" (see "Regulators Must Risk More to Push Growth," *Financial Times,* July 27, 2011). This prompted a letter from twenty academics (Admati et al., "Greenspan's Reasoning on Excessive Equity Is Misleading," *Financial Times,* August 2, 2011). The logic of not worrying about a "once-in-a-century event" is also behind models used by banks and regulators that use the so-called value at risk measures, which are aimed at calibrating bank capital at three times the amount needed to have a 99 percent probability of withstanding losses. Losses that might happen with a probability of less than 1 percent are ignored, even though they might be extremely large and costly for society as well as for the banks. Uncertainty about the probabilities and doubts about the models and the data that are used to estimate probabilities are also ignored. See Tett (2009), Das (2010), Smith (2010), Taleb (2010), and our discussion in Chapter 11.

10. In a typical example (reported to Martin Hellwig in private communication), a lawyer working for the financial industry warns that rules restricting a bank's exposure to any one counterparty "could hurt the cost of capital, hurt liquidity, and force institutions to take different risk management approaches that may not be as effective. . . . There are a whole

bunch of unintended consequences that haven't been completely thought through" ("Banks Fight Fed's Push to Make Them Less Entwined," Reuters, June 25, 2012). Discussing the Volcker Rule, a JPMorgan Chase official is quoted as saying, "We think [the proposed specifics] could have huge negative unintended consequences for American competitiveness and economic growth" (Edward Wyatt, "Bank Lobbyists Sought Loopholes on Risky Trading," *New York Times,* May 12, 2012). Bankers from Japan and other countries also joined U.S. banks in lobbying (see Michael Crittenden, "BOJ's Nishimura: Volcker Rule May Hurt Liquidity in Sovereign Debt," Dow Jones Newswires, March 5, 2012). We give more examples in later chapters, starting in Chapter 6.

11. Francis M. Cornford (1874–1943) was a renowned classical scholar at the University of Cambridge. His short treatise "Microcosmographia Academica: A Guide for the Young Academic Politician," published in 1908, is the source of a number of catchphrases such as "Give the present system a fair trial" and "The time is not ripe," which we discuss in Chapter 11. Written as a satire on academic politics, it contains insights that apply to the politics of any organization. It is available online at http://larvatus.livejournal.com/222591.html, accessed September 28, 2012. On the background of Cornford's piece, including the text of the piece itself, see Johnson (1994).

12. A piece titled "Sarkozy's Bark Worse than Bite on Banks" (Reuters, February 18, 2011) describes France as softer than the United Kingdom or Switzerland. Another, headed "Behind French Bank Drama, a Relaxed Regulator?" (Reuters, September 15, 2011), states that the bank lobby is stronger in France than elsewhere. Yet another, Tom Braithwaite's "FDIC Chief Says Watchdogs 'Succumbing' to Bank Lobby" (*Financial Times,* July 21, 2010), states that Germany, France, and Japan argued for more relaxed requirements in the Basel III discussions (see note 22 and Chapter 12). Bair (2012) provides more detail. We return to the political issues in Chapters 11–13.

13. Acharya et al. (2010, Chapter 7) discuss the adoption of a "modified Volcker Rule" in the Dodd-Frank Act. On the lobbying efforts that led to this situation, see Yalman Onaran, "Volcker Said to Be Disappointed with Final Version of His Rule," Bloomberg, June 30, 2010. On lobbying during the process of implementation see, for example, Ben Protess, "Behind the Scenes, a Lawmaker Pushes to Curb the Volcker Rule," *New York Times,* September 21, 2012. As explained by Senators Carl Levin and Jeff Merkley, "Financial lobbyists are too successful at watering down regulation of the industry" ("Senators Slam JPMorgan over London Losses and Demand Tighter Regulation," *The Guardian,* May 11, 2012).

14. For example, Gorton (2010) suggests that banks benefit the economy by "producing" opaque short-term debt that is highly liquid so that its holders can easily convert it into cash. French et. al. (2010, Chapter 5), written by fifteen prominent academics, states that short-term debt has a disciplining role that makes banks more efficient. See Admati et al. (2011) and Chapter 10 for additional references and discussion.

15. The issues are discussed in sections 5, 7, and 8 of Admati et al. (2011), in the concluding remarks of Admati et al. (2012a), and in Chapters 10 and 11 of this book.

16. In a similar vein, Bair (2012) calls on Main Street to push politicians and regulators to impose more effective control of Wall Street. Although there has been much discussion

of reforms, little has actually been implemented. In the United States, many of the numerous regulations introduced by the Dodd-Frank Act have still not been implemented. For an extensive discussion of the act, see Acharya et al. (2010) and Skeel (2010). As of this writing, the full set of systemically important financial institutions has not been confirmed, and some of the key provisions are going through a lengthy process of discussion and commentary. Despite urging by many, the Securities and Exchange Commission failed to move on reforming the money market funds industry. See, for example, Christopher Condon, "Money Fund Tests Geithner, Bernanke, as Shapiro Fails," Bloomberg, August 24, 2012.

17. For example, in his January 13, 2010, testimony before the FCIC, Bank of America CEO Brian Moynihan identified excessive leverage as one of the causes of the crisis. In his own words, "Leverage was a crucial factor" (see p. 6 of his written testimony, available at http://fcic-static.law.stanford.edu/cdn_media/fcic-testimony/2010-0113-Moynihan.pdf, accessed September 22, 2012). In the same testimony he further said that "capital is important, and the leverage of investment banks was untenable" (p. 11). Similarly, Jamie Dimon, JPMorgan CEO, recognized in the same hearing that one of "the key underlying causes of the crisis [was] excessive leverage that pervaded the system" (see p. 8 of his written testimony, available at http://fcic-static.law.stanford.edu/cdn_media/fcic-testimony/2010-0113-Dimon.pdf, accessed September 22, 2012). Finally, John Mack, then CEO of Morgan Stanley, pointed out that "many firms were too highly leveraged, took on too much risk and did not have sufficient resources to manage those risks effectively in a rapidly changing environment" (see p. 1 of his written testimony, available at http://fcic-static.law.stanford.edu/cdn_media/fcic-testimony/2010-0113-Mack.pdf, accessed September 22, 2012).

18. See "Josef Ackermann im Gespräch: 'Ohne Gewinn ist alles nichts'" (Talking to Josef Ackermann: 'Without profits everything is naught'), interview, *Süddeutsche Zeitung*, November 20, 2009, http://www.sueddeutsche.de/geld/josef-ackermann-im-gespraech-ohne-gewinn-ist-alles-nichts-1.144881, accessed September 22, 2012. Along the same lines, see Citigroup CEO Vikram Pandit's op-ed "We Must Rethink Basel, or Growth Will Suffer," *Financial Times*, November 10, 2010. The argument was also made in studies by the Institute of International Finance (IIF) (2010), a key lobbying institution of internationally active banks, which assumes that capital markets are unable to price equity properly, so stricter equity requirements have a substantial impact on banks' funding costs. We discuss this fallacy in Chapter 7. In BCBS (2010a) the fallacy is maintained for the sake of the argument, but the conclusions are quite different from those of the IIF. Empirical studies find that a lack of bank equity may have a negative impact on bank lending in the short run but that this effect disappears over the course of two or three years and that in the long run higher equity requirements do not have a negative effect on bank lending and growth. (For the short-run effects, see, for example, Aiyar et al. 2012 and the studies cited by Hanson et al. 2011, 12–15; for the long-run effects, see Hanson et al. 2011, 18–19, Buch and Prieto 2012, and Junge and Kugler 2012.) As discussed by Admati et al. (2012a) and in Chapters 9 and 11 of this book, the short-run effects can be explained by the effect of the overhanging debt that banks already have and by the use of risk weights, and they can be avoided if increased

capital requirements are introduced in a suitable manner, for example, by making sure banks do not make payouts to shareholders and raise more equity. Finally, one may also question Ackermann's assertion that a reduction in bank lending "reduces growth and has negative effects for all." Not all bank lending is desirable. If banks had lent less and with greater care in the years before 2007, the economies of the United States and of many European countries would be much healthier today. See Jordà et al. (2011) and Schularick and Taylor (2012) on the consequences of excessive credit expansions and Turner (2010, 2012) on the need to distinguish between different types of lending.

19. For data on the worldwide economic downturn of 2008–2009, see IMF (2009, 2010a). IMF (2009, Chapter 4) gives projections on the long-term impact on the real economy. In 2009 there was a *contraction* of 0.6 percent in global output, as opposed to an average growth of 4 percent in the preceding years; in advanced economies, the output contraction amounted to a much larger 3.2 percent, as opposed to an average growth of more than 1 percent in the preceding years. Past experience indicates that significant parts of the output loss will be permanent, so over the years they may well add up to "astronomical figures" (Haldane 2010). For the United States, the Congressional Budget Office estimate of the loss in gross domestic product (GDP) from the recession by 2016 will be $5.7 trillion relative to potential. The Federal Reserve estimates that during 2007–2010, median household wealth declined 38.8 percent in real terms. Better Markets (2012) estimates that the total cost of the crisis will eventually come to more than $12.8 trillion. (See http://bettermarkets.com/reform-news/cost-crisis-caused-wall-street-no-less-128-trillion-dollars, accessed September 22, 2012.) In the United Kingdom, Haldane (2010) expects the long-run total output loss to be at least £1.8 trillion; in the world economy, he expects a total output loss of at least $60 trillion. See also Huertas (2010, 1) and Laeven and Valencia (2012). Sinn (2010, Chapter 1) points out that without government intervention, output losses would have been even greater. Jordà et al. (2011) and Schularick and Taylor (2012) show that historically, recessions that have been associated with credit booms gone bust and with subsequent financial crises have been much larger and costlier than other types of recessions. On the slow recovery from the financial crisis in the United States, see Carmen Reinhart and Kenneth Rogoff, "Sorry, U.S. Recoveries Really Aren't Different," *Bloomberg*, October 15, 2012, and Martin Wolf, "A Slow Convalescence under Obama," *Financial Times*, October 24, 2012.

20. For example, according to the Federal Reserve Bank of St. Louis, from February 2008 to September 2009, total nonfarm employment declined by 8.138 million. Subsequent gains have totaled only 3.36 million. See Better Markets (2012).

21. This warning was raised before the G20 in June 2010, using as a basis a preliminary report prepared by PricewaterhouseCoopers, as per the banking industry's request ("Tighter Banking Rules Will Drain £1tn from Financial System, Study Shows," *The Guardian*, July 10, 2010).

22. We discuss bank capital regulation in some detail in Chapter 11. National regulation is based on international agreements that are worked out by the Basel Committee on Banking Supervision, a body of bank regulators from major countries that meets regularly

in the Swiss city. The agreement that the IIF (2010) and the British Bankers' Association objected to, also known as Basel III, is contained in BCBS (2010c, 2010e). This agreement strengthens and adds to the earlier Basel II agreement, contained in BCBS (2004).

23. Among numerous examples are the following: "U.S. pressure to toughen up how banks set aside capital suggests reform on capital adequacy could be drawn out for years," in "U.S. Turns Up Heat on Basel Bank Reform," Reuters, September 3, 2009; "New capital regulations would also require banks to set aside capital for one year for any instruments, even if they have maturities under a year," in "Regulate and Be Damned; Basel III Was Designed to Prevent Another Financial Crisis, but the Unintended Consequences Could Lock Up Global Trade," *Wall Street Journal,* February 7, 2011; and "The new Basel rules would demand that banks maintain more dollars on reserve for the same amount of business, or more capital for no new economic work," in Wayne A. Abernathy, "Shrinking Banks Will Drag Down the Economy," *American Banker,* August 27, 2012. Even Alan Greenspan, former chairman of the Federal Reserve, suggested that capital regulation would "require the building up of a buffer of idle resources that are not otherwise engaged in the production of goods and services," in "Regulators Must Risk More to Push Growth," *Financial Times,* July 27, 2011. As mentioned in note 9, this prompted a letter from twenty academics (Admati et al., "Greenspan's Reasoning on Excessive Equity Is Misleading," *Financial Times,* August 2, 2011).

24. Steve Bartlett, head of Financial Services Roundtable, as quoted by Floyd Norris in "A Baby Step toward Rules on Bank Risk," *New York Times,* September 16, 2010.

25. See, for example, IIF (2010) and the initial quote in Chapter 7 from Miller (1995). We provide additional references and discuss these statements in some detail and in Chapters 7–9.

26. For example, as of 2012, Apple, Bed Bath and Beyond, Citrix, and other companies have virtually no debt. Equity markets, as well as public debt markets, are more developed in the United States than in Europe. See, for example, La Porta et al. (1997, 1998, 1999). Although much debt is often used in so-called leveraged buyouts (LBOs), typically the debt is paid off relatively quickly. Companies taken private in an LBO often return to public equity markets within a relatively short period of time. See Berk and DeMarzo (2011). In other countries, borrowing by nonfinancial companies is often more important because stock markets are less well developed. For companies whose shares are traded on stock exchanges, indebtedness is not substantially different than in the United States; see, for example, Rajan and Zingales (1995, 1998) and Jostarndt and Wagner (2006). For non-traded companies, indebtedness is higher; however, the banks that lend to these companies impose limits on their borrowing.

27. For example, according to its annual reports, Deutsche Bank had only about 2.5 percent equity relative to its total assets at the end of 2011. For Fannie Mae and Freddie Mac, Acharya et al. (2011a, 25 ff) give numbers between 2.5 percent and 5 percent, noting that these numbers understate the problem because reported debt does not include obligations from guarantees. McLean and Nocera (2010), FCIC (2011), and Morgenson and Rosner (2011) describe the buildup of indebtedness and risk at Fannie Mae and Freddie Mac and their takeover by the government.

28. The 3 percent lower limit for equity as a fraction of total assets is given by the so-called leverage ratio regulation. Most Basel rules name higher ratios, but these refer to equity relative to what is called risk-weighted assets. Risk-weighted assets are lower, indeed often much lower, than total assets. The idea is that assets that are deemed safer may be backed by less equity, so they are not taken at face value but only at a fraction of face value; the fraction corresponds to the "risk weight" of the asset. Basel III requires common equity to be at least 7 percent of risk-weighted assets. By investing in assets that have low risk weights, banks can comply with this rule and still have equity at less than 3 percent of their total assets. A detailed discussion appears in Chapter 11.

29. See FCIC (2011, 375) and Bair (2012, 175–177, 358–359). It should be noted that General Motors Acceptance Corporation (now Ally Financial) and Chrysler Financials were large financial institutions and that GMAC in particular was involved in mortgage lending.

30. Jamie Dimon's 2010 Annual Letter to Shareholders (http://files.shareholder.com/downloads/ONE/2103717927x0x458384/6832cb35-0cdb-47fe-8ae4-1183aeceb7fa/2010_JPMC_AR_letter_.pdf, accessed October 5, 2012). In the same document Dimon also affirms that "banks did not benefit from any kind of implicit guarantee."

31. For example, in a statement explaining downgrades of Bank of America's debt rating, Moody's Investors Service made it clear that such "downgrades result[ed] from a decrease in the probability that the U.S. government would support the bank, if needed" (Moody's Investors Service, "Moody's Downgrades Bank of America Corp. to Baa1/P-2; Bank of America N.A. to A2, P-1 Affirmed," Ratings News, September 21, 2011). Similarly, when explaining Citigroup's ratings, Moody's Global Credit Division explained that "Moody's continues to see the probability of support for highly interconnected, systemically important institutions in the United States to be very high, although that probability is lower than it was during the financial crisis" (Moody's Investors Service, "Moody's Downgrades Citigroup Inc. to P-2; Citibank Prime-1 Affirmed; All Long-Term Senior Ratings Confirmed," Ratings News, September 21, 2011).

32. In the 1990s, the effect of government guarantees on borrowing costs was at the center of complaints against the Landesbanken, public banks in Germany that enjoyed such guarantees. For these banks, rating agencies actually published separate credit ratings with and without the guarantees. Typical ratings would be AAA, the best possible, with the government guarantees, and CCC, many grades lower—in fact "junk bond" status—without the guarantees. Because this effect gave the Landesbanken a substantial advantage in borrowing, the European Commission ruled that the (explicit) guarantees represented a form of state aid that distorted competition and was therefore incompatible with what is now the Treaty on the Functioning of the European Union (Art. 107). Germany initially contested the Commission's ruling but eventually gave in. Avoiding a lengthy trial before the European Court of Justice, in 2001 the Commission and the German government agreed that, from 2005 on, no further guarantees would be given. See European Commission, "Germany Agrees on the Implementation of the Understanding with the Commission on State Guarantees for Landesbanken and Savings Banks," press release, February 28, 2002, http://europa.eu/rapid/pressReleasesAction.do?reference=IP/02/343&format=HTML&aged=1&language=EN&guiLanguage=en, accessed September 28, 2012. In the United States,

a similar effect could be observed with Freddie Mac and Fannie Mae, two of the so-called government-sponsored enterprises. For years these banks enjoyed high credit ratings, between A and AAA, even though they were very risky and had little equity. The rating agencies were confident that, if necessary, the U.S. government would bail them out, and this is exactly what happened in 2008; see Acharya et al. (2011a) and Chapter 17 of FCIC (2011). The importance of implicit guarantees for the funding costs of banks, particularly those that are considered too big to fail, is discussed in Chapter 9.

33. For example, see "RBC Chief Nixon Concerned over Uneven Regulatory Playing Field," Dow Jones News Service, September 20, 2011; "Regulation: Wariness over EU's Level Playing Field," *Financial Times*, May 9, 2011; and "JPMorgan's Dimon: 'We Want a Global Level Playing Field,'" Dow Jones Business News, March 30, 2011.

34. See, for example, "Geithner: International Banking Deal to Establish 'Level Playing Field,'" Dow Jones Business News, September 22, 2010. We take up this issue more fully and provide more references in Chapter 12.

35. Some exceptions to the bankruptcy laws are in fact used extensively by the financial industry, such as the exclusion from the so-called stay that has been granted to repurchase agreements (repos), swaps, and derivatives. Their exclusions may be contributing to the fragility of the financial system by encouraging the excessive use of short-term funding and derivatives by banks and other financial institutions. See Skeel and Jackson (2012). We discuss this issue in Chapter 10.

36. The term *systemically important financial institutions* has come to be commonly used. For example, the Dodd-Frank Act includes provisions for the special treatment of such institutions. We discuss the notion of systemic risk starting in Chapter 5.

37. In 2008, when Lehman Brothers announced its bankruptcy, it had $639 billion in total assets and $613 billion in debt. Of course these numbers are based on accounting conventions. In more than three years of bankruptcy proceedings, there was much less for creditors to receive, and most creditors received much less than they were owed. See Valukas (2010). Hypo Real Estate had €400 billion in total assets and €394 billion in debt on December 31, 2007, and had €395 billion in total assets and €391 billion in debt on September 30, 2008; see the company's financial reports at http://www.hyporealestate .com/eng/6375.php, accessed September 22, 2012. According to its annual reports, Dexia had €605 billion in total assets and €588 billion in debt (see also Thomas 2012), and UBS had 2.27 trillion Swiss francs in total assets and 2.23 trillion in debt at the end of 2007.

38. The German government initially supported Hypo Real Estate with €124 billion in guarantees for its debt. In addition, it provided Hypo Real Estate with €7.4 billion in new equity, in the process buying out the old shareholders. In the fall of 2010, in return for government bonds, €173 billion in assets was transferred to FMS Wertmanagement, a so-called bad bank installed in order to eliminate toxic assets from the bank's balance sheets; with this transfer, the bank itself no longer needed the guarantees (see Expertenrat 2011, 94). In 2010 and 2011, this bad bank had to make provisions for losses of €3.9 billion and €11.4 billion, respectively; see press releases of May 13, 2011, and April 27, 2012, in Pressearchiv, http://www.fmsa.de/de/presse/index.html, accessed September 22, 2012. In the case of Dexia, the bank received bailouts for €6 billion from the governments of

Belgium, France, and Luxembourg in 2008. In 2011 Dexia received an additional €4 billion bailout and a €90 billion guarantee from the same parties. Similarly, in 2008 UBS received a $60 billion credit line from the Swiss National Bank. At the time UBS also received a capital injection of 6 billion Swiss francs ($5.2 billion) from the Swiss government. Bair (2012, 118) suggests that, at the time, Citigroup, Merrill Lynch, and AIG were also "truly sick" and insolvent. We discuss bailouts and the safety net of banks in more detail starting in Chapter 9.

39. On the causes and effects of the Lehman Brothers collapse, see the opinion of Judge Lewis A. Kaplan on the matter (U.S. Bankruptcy Court, S.D. New York 2011) as well as the report of the examiner Anton Valukas (2010).

40. For a detailed description, see Chapter 20 of FCIC (2011).

41. According to data from the European Policy Studies Task Force (2010), "During the crisis, 20 bank debt guarantee and 15 bank recapitalization schemes and 44 cases of individual bank aid cases were dealt with by the European Commission under the state aid rules. At the height of the crisis, the effectively committed aid amounted to some 13% of the GDP of the EU." Recent numbers are even more dramatic. The European Commission reports that "between October 2008 and October 2011, the . . . Commission approved €4.5 trillion (equivalent to 37% of EU GDP) of state aid measures to financial institutions. This averted massive banking failure and economic disruption, but has burdened taxpayers with deteriorating public finances and failed to settle the question of how to deal with large cross-border banks in trouble" (European Commission, "New Crisis Management Measures to Avoid Future Bank Bail-Outs," press release, June 6, 2012, http://europa.eu/rapid/pressReleasesAction.do?reference=IP/12/570&format=HTML&aged=0&language=EN&guiLanguage=en, accessed September 28, 2012). On the supports and bailouts in the United States, see FCIC (2011, Chapters 19–20) and Barofsky (2012). We provide more details in Chapter 9.

42. According to the United Nations, in 2009 global output contracted by 2 percent and global unemployment rose from 178 million persons in 2007 to 205 million in 2009. Furthermore, in that same year 52 countries experienced declines in per capita income (UNDESA 2011). The World Bank Group reported a decline in average GDP growth from 6 percent in 2005–2007 to 1 percent in 2009 (Independent Evaluation Group 2012). See also IMF (2009, 2010a). Haldane (2010, 102–103) estimated that the total loss of output worldwide as a result of the financial crisis would eventually amount to between $60 trillion and $200 trillion and that the loss of output in the United Kingdom would be between £1.8 and £7.4 trillion. As for the effects in the United States, according to data from the Bureau of Economic Analysis, the U.S. output (GDP) fell 3.1 percent in 2009. The FCIC (2011, 390) reports that within twenty-one months, American households lost $17 trillion and that reported unemployment hit 10.1 percent at its peak in October 2009. As mentioned in note 19, Better Markets (2012) estimates that the overall cost of the crisis to the United States economy will eventually be more than $12.8 trillion.

43. CBS, interview with Mr. Valukas, *60 Minutes*, April 22, 2012.

44. Statement provided by Ben Bernanke in a private interview before the FCIC, as transcribed in the Commission's final report (FCIC 2011, 354).

45. For details of the banks that were involved, see Expertenrat (2011), especially 44–50. The lists provided there do not include Iceland and Ireland, where all major banks were affected. See also Onaran (2011).

46. For example, in its 2010 *Global Financial Stability Report* the International Monetary Fund focuses on the breakdown of short-term funding and systemic liquidity risks as drivers of the crisis. According to the report, "The inability of multiple financial institutions to roll over or obtain new short-term funding was one of the defining characteristics of the crisis. Systemic liquidity risks were under-recognized by both the private and public sectors and required unprecedented intervention by governments and central banks during the crisis" (IMF 2010b, 57). Along the same lines, see also Hesse et al. (2008), Brunnermeier (2009), Gorton (2010), and Copeland et al. (2012), among others.

47. For accounts of the causes and the dynamics of the crisis, see, for example, Hellwig (2009), Sorkin (2009), Sinn (2010), FCIC (2011), and Bair (2012). According to his testimony to the FCIC (2011, e.g., 241 and 353), Ben Bernanke shares the assessment that the solvency of major financial institutions was a critical factor in causing the breakdown in funding. See also King (2010) and note 17.

48. Meltzer (2012, 34) states that the Federal Reserve followed a "too big to fail" policy, preventing the failure of banks, and increasingly nonbanks, since the 1970s; the Lehman bankruptcy was shocking because there had been an expectation that that bank, too, would not be allowed to fail. Bair (2012, 107) states that the bankruptcy "defied market expectations. Bear Stearns had been bailed out and most market players assumed that the government would step in with Lehman as well given that it was a much bigger institution."

49. The relative size of the largest U.S. banks keeps growing. A measure of overall economic activity is provided by the country's GDP, which indicates the value of annual production. Based on official data (balance sheets from the Federal Deposit Insurance Corporation, or FDIC, and GDP from the Bureau of Economic Analysis), the assets of the six largest U.S. banks as a percentage of GDP was 60.1 percent as of the first quarter of 2012. The same banks had combined assets of 48.4 percent of GDP in 2005, up from only 17.1 percent of GDP in 1995. These numbers would be larger if assets were valued using accounting conventions used in Europe. We discuss the balance sheet of JPMorgan Chase in Chapter 6.

50. According to the World Bank, in 2008 the total bank liabilities were 93.9 percent of GDP in the United States; the ratio for the United Kingdom was 550 percent, for Germany 135 percent, for France 273 percent, and for Switzerland 629 percent. The liabilities of UBS alone were 372 percent of Switzerland's GDP.

51. Bank assets relative to GDP per year amounted to 800 percent in Ireland and 1,500 percent in Iceland. When Icelandic banks collapsed, the national deposit insurance system was unable to fulfill its obligations to depositors and had to be supported by the Icelandic government. This support was limited to deposits in Iceland, however. Those with deposits in the Netherlands and the United Kingdom, where Icelandic banks had been active through branches, were paid by those countries' own governments. Agreements by which Iceland would have compensated the Netherlands and the United Kingdom for this money, €3.8 billion plus interest, around two-thirds of the annual government budget, were twice

voted down in popular votes. The conflict is pending in the European Free Trade Association Court. After the collapse of its banking sector in October 2008, Iceland faced a currency crisis, as well as a severe economic recession. Its government fell, and the country negotiated a multibillion-dollar loan from the IMF and had to seek further financial support from a number of countries (see "Iceland's Rescue Package Flounders," *Financial Times*, November 12, 2008). Iceland's banking collapse was the worst relative to the size of an economy ("Cracks in the Crust," *The Economist*, December 11, 2008). See also OECD (2009) and Lewis (2011).

52. The EU summit of November 2010—that is, the meeting of the heads of state or government of the different members of the EU—provided Ireland with loans of €85 billion, of which €17.5 billion came from the Irish Treasury and National Pension Reserve Fund and €67.5 billion from the IMF, the newly created euro-area support institutions the European Financial Stability Facility and the European Financial Stability Mechanism, and several non-euro-area members of the European Union. Of these loans, €35 billion has been used to support Irish banks; see RTE News [Ireland], "Government Statement on EU/IMF Rescue Deal," November 28, 2010, http://www.rte.ie/news/2010/1128/govtstatement .html, accessed September 22, 2012. The EU summit of June 2012 decided to provide €100 billion from the newly created European Stabilization Mechanism to support Spanish banks once an effective mechanism for European supervision of banks has been developed; see http://consilium.europa.eu/uedocs/cms_data/docs/pressdata/en/ec/131359.pdf, accessed September 22, 2012.

53. Some countries have tried to create a process for the resolution of large financial institutions that would make it possible for financial institutions to fail without damaging the economy. Most notably, the Dodd-Frank Act in the United States gave the FDIC expanded authority for the resolution of problems with "systemically important" financial institutions. The United Kingdom has developed a process similar to that of the United States, and Germany created a somewhat different mechanism. However, for global institutions with operations in many different countries with inconsistent legal systems, determining how losses are to be shared is a major problem. We discuss this at the end of Chapter 5.

54. We discuss the flaws in proposed capital regulations in Chapter 11. The tax code also encourages borrowing by allowing corporations to deduct interest paid on debt as an expense. Exemptions from normal bankruptcy provisions granted for derivatives and repurchase agreements used extensively in the financial industry also encourage fragility. See our discussion of these issues in Chapters 9 and 10.

TWO *How Borrowing Magnifies Risk*

1. Government borrowing follows a somewhat different logic. Whereas the resources that private borrowers can use to pay for expenditures and to repay debts are determined by their incomes and their assets, the resources that governments can use depend on their ability to raise revenues through taxes. Borrowing is a way to relieve current taxpayers, for instance, from the burden of a war or to mislead the public about the costs of current government policies. Reinhart and Rogoff (2009) provide a comprehensive account of

government borrowing and bank–government relations over eight centuries. They show that excessive government borrowing has repeatedly led to defaults; given the involvement of banks in financing governments, these defaults were often accompanied by bank failures and banking crises. In some countries in Europe, the causation was recently reversed as banking problems in Iceland, Ireland, and Spain and government support for the banking systems of those countries crippled the finances of those countries' governments. As the Spanish and other Southern European governments have come under pressure, they have, in turn, leaned on their banks to lend to them.

2. As explained by Hyman (2012), buying on credit has exploded in the twentieth century in the United States, with the General Motors Acceptance Corporation among the pioneers in allowing people to buy first and pay later.

3. We discuss the situation of default in Chapter 3 on the "dark side of borrowing." The costs and considerations from the lender's perspective are discussed in Chapters 7 and 9.

4. For example, many borrowers in Ireland went into personal bankruptcy because of their mortgage debt (see Lewis 2011). More recently, Spanish borrowers have been faced with losses and legally owe some of their debts even if evicted (see "Spanish Homeowners Rally Together to Fight Evictions by Banks," *The Telegraph*, May 2, 2012).

5. For example, mortgages are nonrecourse in Florida, Arizona, and Texas. In California, only the first "purchase money" mortgage is nonrecourse (Ghent and Kudlyak 2009). In the case of second mortgages, which are "junior" to first mortgages and receive payments only after the first mortgages have been paid, borrowers are not entitled to this protection. California Senate Bill 458, introduced in July 2011, would extend nonrecourse protection beyond first mortgages (see "Real Estate: New Short Sale Law," *The Examiner*, July 15, 2011).

6. The creditor might have trouble selling the house, and additional value could be lost in the foreclosure process, as well as due to lack of maintenance. The process can be quite inefficient. Campbell et al. (2011) show that the "foreclosure discount" is 27 percent. See also Michael Wilson, "Foreclosures Empty Homes, and Criminals Fill Them Up," *New York Times*, October 14, 2011.

7. This example is simplified, without affecting the points we make, by ignoring the interest rate on the loan and the benefits from living in the house. In Chapter 8 we discuss return on equity relative to the total cost of borrowing, including the interest.

8. More generally, the magnification of the upside applies when the investments increase in value by more than the interest rate charged for borrowing. In the case of the house purchase, the interest payment can be thought of as a rent Kate pays to live in the house. We will return to the effect of borrowing on the return on equity in Chapter 8, where we also take into account the interest on borrowing, ignored in this chapter for simplicity.

9. Note that Kate's equity, which will be the equivalent of "capital" in the banking context, is always invested in the house; it is tied up there but is not idle and is not a cash reserve. Chapter 6 discusses again the pervasive confusion about the term *bank capital*, already mentioned in Chapter 1.

10. There are many forms of limited-liability companies, with legal details varying across countries and even across companies. For joint-stock companies, that is, corpora-

tions whose shares are publicly traded, many features of governance and control, such as public reporting obligations, are specified by law or regulation; this provides investors with the means to acquire the information they need for their purchasing decisions. In companies whose shares are not publicly traded there is much less need for investor protection, so there is great flexibility to determine the company's governance in the corporate charter. See Allen et al. (2009, 86–92, 183).

11. For information on the impact of walking away from debts on credit ratings, see Les Christie, "How Foreclosure Impacts Your Credit Score," *CNN Money,* April 22, 2010, and Michelle Singletary, "What's Worse for Credit Score—Foreclosure, Short Sale or Deed in Lieu?," *Washington Post,* August 30, 2011.

12. Public corporations, whose equity is traded on the stock exchange, must disclose their balance sheets or statements of their financial position periodically, such as every three or six months, to give information to investors. Equity is defined as the difference between the so-called book, or accounting, value of the bank's assets and its liabilities or debts. Accountants have rules about updating balance sheets over time. As discussed in Chapter 6, accounting conventions vary across countries. For more detailed information on accounting principles, see Horngren et al. (2012).

13. Sometimes there are restrictions on the ability to sell shares. For example, shares that are awarded to executives as part of their pay may be subject to a so-called vesting period during which they cannot sell the shares. Or the shares may be issued as registered shares rather than bearer shares, and the registration of a new shareholder may be subject to certain restrictions. For example, in Switzerland, from the 1970s to the early 1990s, many corporate charters gave top management the right to refuse the registration of a potential buyer of registered shares; see Hellwig (2000).

14. The benefits of the new investments may well be incorporated into the price at which the new shares are issued. If investors buying the new shares know that the funds will increase the value of the firm's assets, they will agree to pay more for the shares than the earlier price, and fewer shares will have to be issued.

15. Having more shares may also have an effect on the control of the corporation by creating a more dispersed ownership structure with more shareholders, each holding a smaller fraction of the total. However, in the case of large corporations with many millions of shares, shareholders do not individually have much impact on corporate decisions. It is a fallacy that just because the equity of a company is divided into more pieces, existing shareholders are automatically worse off when new shares are issued. See Berk and DeMarzo (2011, 469).

16. As we see in later chapters, this is particularly likely if the firm has already borrowed a lot and its ability to repay its debt is in doubt. In this case, existing shareholders might avoid making an investment that would be profitable for the corporation as a whole and might also be biased against new equity issues. The reason is that the new investments partly benefit creditors, whereas shareholders effectively fund them fully on their own. In that sense, borrowing can become addictive. This is part of an important effect called "debt overhang," which will be introduced in Chapter 3 and will come up in many later discussions in this book. We discuss new stock issuance again in Chapters 7 and 11.

17. For much of the twentieth century, in continental Europe corporations were very stingy with dividends, retaining earnings even if the projects in which they invested were not all that promising. For a description of dividend policies in Europe, see La Porta et al. (2000a, 2000b). For a contrasting view of the origins of these tendencies, see Bancel (2009). In the United States, in the early 1980s oil companies, which had rich earnings from existing oil wells, came under attack for wasting those earnings on new exploration, which was not very successful, rather than paying them out to shareholders. For example, during 1982–1984 the industry was receiving on average only 60–90 cents for every dollar invested in exploration and production, and the total market value of these returns to oil companies was even lower than if the corporations had obtained them by drilling holes in the ground. In a survey of thirty large oil companies, twenty-three of them were urged to cut 25–35 percent from their exploration and production spending. See Jensen (1986). For data and other information on the rates of exploration projects during the 1970s and 1980s, see Reiss (1990).

18. On dividend policies, see Berk and DeMarzo (2011, Chapter 17). Some managers and investors disfavor dividend payments because they can subject shareholders to unfavorable tax treatment. We discuss dividends and the potential conflicts of interest regarding payouts in Chapters 3 and 11.

19. There is evidence in the literature on lending standards suggesting that credit standards vary cyclically with banking market conditions and that lending standards have an impact on loan portfolio performance (Rajan 1994; Weinberg 1995; Dell'Ariccia et al. 2008; O'Keffee 2009). We discuss the costs of borrowing in Chapter 7. How much equity creditors require from borrowers depends on other terms of the transaction, such as collateral. For example, mortgage loans may have lower equity requirements than other types of loans because the house can serve as collateral.

20. See Holtfrerich (1981), Berger et al. (1995), Alessandri and Haldane (2009), Buch and Prieto (2012), and Haldane (2012a). For 1910, Riesser (1912, 447–448) reports that German banks had equity exceeding one-third of their debt, that is, equity exceeding one-fourth of their total assets.

21. Haldane (2011b, 3). By contrast, in Germany banks were among the first institutions to exploit the opportunities provided by the 1870 law on incorporation. See, for example, Tilly (1989).

22. One of the prominent supporters of such laws, Senator Sherman of Ohio, remarked that contingent liability would "prevent the stockholders and directors of a bank from engaging in hazardous operations" (Esty, 1998, 190). On the history of banks' limited liability and issues associated with it, see Tilly (1989), Grossman (2001), Alessandri and Haldane (2009), Acheson et al. (2010), Grossman and Imai (2011), and Haldane (2011b).

23. See Macey and Miller (1992) and Grossman (2007).

24. See Grossman (2001, 2007).

25. The amount covered by the FDIC was increased from $100,000 to $250,000 in October 2008, first until the end of 2010 and later until the end of 2013. In the European Union, Directive 94/19/EC of the European Parliament and Council of May 30, 1994, on deposit-guarantee schemes, initially required all member states to have a deposit guaran-

tee scheme to cover at least 90 percent of deposited amounts, up to at least €20,000 per depositor. As a response to the 2007–2008 crisis and to restore confidence in the system, on March 11, 2009, the European Parliament and Council adopted Directive 2009/14/EC, which increased the minimum insured amounts to €50,000 initially and to €100,000 by December 2010. In Australia, on October 12, 2008, the government announced temporary arrangements to enable the guarantee of 100 percent of deposits made to Australian deposit-taking institutions. This amount was reduced to a maximum of $1 million per customer per institution. Finally, on September 11, 2011, it was announced that the guarantee would be reduced to $250,000 as of February 1, 2012 (see "Questions & Answers about the Guarantee on Deposits," http://www.guaranteescheme.gov.au/qa/deposits.html#3, accessed October 5, 2012). We discuss deposit insurance further in Chapters 4 and 9.

26. For example, in "Banks Need More Capital, Not More Rules" (*Wall Street Journal*, May 16, 2012), Allan Meltzer states that "during America's booms following the Civil War and World War I, commercial banks served as both commercial and investment banks. For safety they held much more capital per dollar of assets. In the 1920s, capital ratios for large New York banks ranged from 15% to 20% of assets." For more recent ratios of equity capital to assets, see FDIC, "Basel and the Evolution of Capital Regulation: Moving Forward, Looking Back," An Update on Emerging Issues in Banking, January 14, 2003, http://www.fdic.gov/bank/analytical/fyi/2003/011403fyi.html, accessed September 25, 2012.

27. See Berger et al. (1995) on the United States, Allessandri and Haldane (2009) on the United Kingdom, Holtfrerich (1981) and Buch and Prieto (2012) on Germany, and Junge and Kugler (2012) on Switzerland.

28. See, for example, Acharya et al. (2011b, 2013). As discussed in multiple later chapters (e.g., Chapters 5, 6, and 10), some of the ways in which banks borrow are through operations off the balance sheet or through derivatives and are therefore harder to see.

THREE *The Dark Side of Borrowing*

1. The repossession rate during 1991 was 2.5 times the twenty-year long-run average; see Satchell (2011). For additional information on the U.K. housing market and, more specifically, the 1989–1991 mortgage crisis, see Muellbauer and Murphy (1997), Aron and Muellbauer (2010), and Oxford Economics (2012).

2. For data on the use of ARMs in the United States in the late 1980s, see Schwartz and Torous (1991). In certain parts of the U.S. mortgage market, ARMs again became prevalent in the years before 2007. These mortgages often had artificially low initial teaser rates. Subsequent sharp increases in interest rates led many borrowers into distress and sometimes into default (see, for example, IMF 2007). The FCIC (2011, Chapter 7) and Bair (2012, Chapter 7) describe how losses from such mortgages forced WaMu (formerly Washington Mutual) to write off $1.1 billion for the fourth quarter of 2007 and another $1.1 billion in the first quarter of 2008. Gorton (2010) extols the benefits of ARMs as instruments allowing a lender to force a renegotiation of a mortgage after two years, but he neglects to describe the consequences of borrowers' being unable to pay.

3. A debt of $50 billion is even more the creditor's problem. This is why sovereign debt crises are so dangerous. See Reinhart and Rogoff (2009) for an extensive treatment. In the most recent sovereign default and debt restructuring, in March 2012, private creditors of Greece accepted an exchange of old debt securities for new debt securities that involved a write-down in nominal values of debt exceeding €100 billion (see, e.g., Spiegelonline International, "Greece Pulls Off Historic Debt Restructuring Deal," http://www.spiegel.de/international/europe/historic-opportunity-greece-pulls-off-debt-restructuring-deal-a-820343.html, accessed September 29, 2012).

4. The institution that allowed for this practice was the *manus iniectio*, which literally means "laying the hand on." As explained by Peter Struck, "In the oldest Roman legal procedure [*manus iniectio* is] a kind of execution levied on the person of one who had been condemned to pay a certain sum. If this was not done within thirty days of the condemnation, the plaintiff could seize the debtor and bring him before the praetor, who handed him over to the creditor with the word *addico* (I hand over), unless he paid there and then, or a *vindex* came forward to pay for him or to show there was no ground for complaint. The creditor kept the debtor in chains at his house for sixty days; if his claims had not been satisfied during this period, he might kill him or sell him as a slave in foreign parts" (see *Online Latin Dictionary*, http://www.classics.upenn.edu/myth/php/tools/dictionary.php?method=did&regexp=719&setcard=1&media=1&link=0, accessed August 16, 2012). For more information, see Ford (1926) and Silva (1973, 68).

5. See Ford (1926), Freedman (1928), and "Timeline: A Brief History of Bankruptcy," *New York Times*, November 16, 2005.

6. On the history and abolition of debt prisons in the United States, see Ford (1926) and Jill Lepore, "I.O.U.: How We Used to Treat Debtors," *New Yorker*, April 13, 2009. It is worth bearing in mind that, even though debtors' prisons are illegal in the United States, "it's becoming increasingly common for people to serve jail time as a result of their debt" (Susie An, "Unpaid Bills Land Some Debtors behind Bars," *Morning Edition*, NPR, December 12, 2011). Along the same lines, see Jessica Silver-Greenberg, "Welcome to Debtors' Prison, 2011 Edition," *Wall Street Journal*, March 16, 2011. According to this report, "More than a third of all U.S. states allow borrowers who can't or won't pay to be jailed. Judges have signed off on more than 5,000 such warrants since the start of 2010 (and until March 2011) in nine counties with a total population of 13.6 million people."

7. In Thackeray's novel *Vanity Fair*, from which the epigraph to this chapter is taken, the bankrupt member of the London Stock Exchange is not sent to debtors' prison, but nonetheless his life, and that of his family, is devastated. The word "ruined," so central in Thackeray's account, meant utter social destruction. The Free Online Dictionary explains this word as the past participle of "1. to destroy completely, demolish; 2. to harm irreparably; 3. to reduce to poverty or bankruptcy; 4. to deprive of chastity." See http://www.thefreedictionary.com/ruined, accessed October 23, 2012.

8. The German word *Konkurs*, used for bankruptcy proceedings until 1999, was derived from the fact that all creditors are called together to list their claims and provide the basis for an orderly settlement (Latin *concurrere*, French *concourir* mean "to run to the same place, appear together").

9. Unless their past bills have been paid, the suppliers will also be among the lenders. Beyond that, they are also harmed by the loss of future business.

10. There is evidence suggesting that home prices in neighborhoods with foreclosures are lower than those in neighborhoods without foreclosures (Harding et al. 2009; Campbell et al. 2011; Whitaker and Fitzpatrick, 2012) and that lower prices may be the result of a contagion effect (Harding et al. 2009). Barofsky (2012) argues that TARP (the Troubled Asset Relief Program) was not used effectively to solve the problem. Bair (2012, Chapters 6, 11, and 13) discusses the government's failure to promote efficient restructuring of mortgages and foreclosures. In light of these failures, San Bernardino County officials have announced a plan to seize and restructure troubled mortgages using eminent domain laws. More than a dozen local governments, including those in Suffolk County, New York; Berkeley, Ontario; Fontana, California; and Chicago are considering the proposal (see Alejandro Lazo, "San Bernardino Eminent Domain Plan Draws Wall Street Criticism," *Los Angeles Times*, August 16, 2012, and Joe Nocera, "Housing's Last Chance," *New York Times*, July 9, 2012).

11. In the United States, this development goes back to nineteenth-century legal rulings in favor of employees. To date, the 1978 reform of the insolvency procedure under Chapter 11 of the U.S. Bankruptcy Code provides the most business-friendly regime. In the United Kingdom the Insolvency Act of 1986 developed the concept of administration as a mechanism for guaranteeing the survival of a company as a going concern, with the benefit of a moratorium with respect to certain debts. In Germany, the 1999 replacement of the previous bankruptcy and settlement procedures by a single insolvency procedure was also aimed at improving prospects for continuing a company as a going concern. Apart from some seemingly minor exceptions, the arrangements involved are similar to U.S. procedures under Chapter 11. For the exceptions and their impact, see note 19.

12. In the airline industry, major assets are airplanes and slots, that is, rights to take off or land at specified airports. These assets are easy to transfer from one airline to another, with little uncertainty about their value. According to LoPucki (2005), the smoothness of the procedure can depend on whether there is prepackaging. With prepackaging, the debtor corporation develops the insolvency plan ahead of time and has creditors vote on it. If creditors holding 90–95 percent of the debt agree, there is not even a need to file. If more than 50 percent of creditors holding more than two-thirds but less than the required 90 or 95 percent of the debt agree, the debtor corporation files for bankruptcy and the court can approve the plan in thirty days, imposing it even on those creditors who have disagreed with the plan. Prepackaging gives creditors little say and leaves the incumbent management in charge.

13. See Berk and DeMarzo (2011, 511–517). Enron paid $793 million in fees to lawyers, administrators, and other advisers; Lehman Brothers has already paid $1.6 billion in legal and administrative expenses, and the number is still growing. See Linda Sandler and Lindsay Fortado, "Lehman Fees Could Reach $1.4 Billion, Besting Enron," Bloomberg, October 23, 2008, and Maureen Farrell, "Lehman Bankruptcy Bill: $1.6 Billion," *CNN Money*, CNN, March 6, 2012. Davydenko et al. (2012) estimate that the average cost of default is as high as 21.7 percent of the value of the assets. We discuss the Lehman bank-

ruptcy again at the end of Chapter 5 and the impact of bankruptcy costs on the choice of funding mix by banks and other corporations in Chapter 9.

14. As experienced by Martin Hellwig—who at the time was serving on a committee dealing with applications of nonfinancial companies for government loans or loan guarantees in the crisis—this concern was raised in connection with the application of the General Motors subsidiary Opel for temporary state aid in Germany in 2009 and 2010.

15. See Hellwig (2009), Gorton (2010), Gorton and Metrick (2010), Mehrling (2010), and FCIC (2011, Chapters 19–20). The FCIC (2011, 429) states that the Commission was unpersuaded by the claims that banks had only liquidity problems and not solvency problems. Whereas bank managers claimed that their problems were due to unjustified liquidity runs, the FCIC concludes that "these firm managers knew or should have known that they were risking the solvency and therefore the survival of their firms." This assessment is shared by Hennessey, Holtz-Eakin, and Thomas in their dissenting statement; see FCIC (2011, 429 f). We discuss the focus on liquidity problems as diverting attention from the much more important solvency concerns in Chapters 4, 10, and 13.

16. Ben Bernanke, chairman of the Federal Reserve, told the FCIC that Lehman Brothers did not have sufficient collateral to enable it to obtain additional funding (FCIC 2011, 354). Essentially this means that Lehman Brothers was insolvent when it went into bankruptcy. Timothy F. Geithner, U.S. secretary of the Treasury, said in a testimony before the House Financial Services Committee that "Lehman caused Lehman's insolvency" (http://www.treasury.gov/press-center/press-releases/Pages/tg645.aspx, accessed September 29, 2012). Bair (2012) implies that the problems that led to the crisis were due to excessive borrowing and to the distress and insolvency of banks and other institutions when borrowers started defaulting on mortgages. See also notes 19–21 in Chapter 13.

17. Note that the shareholders or managers of a distressed corporation would resist raising new equity because it would protect the creditors from default at the expense of shareholders. This is because, with more equity, the debt will bear less of the downside risk. The dilution in the value of a share reflects an effective transfer of wealth from shareholders to creditors. We discuss this issue further in Chapter 11.

18. The observation that distressed borrowers may underinvest because of the overhanging debt was made by Myers (1977). When banks suffer from debt overhang, they make fewer loans, as happened in late 2008 (see Ivashina and Scharfstein 2010). There is evidence that homeowners who are underwater do not invest in their houses, and this further reduces the value of the houses and creates inefficiencies (see Melzer 2012). Ideally, of course, a creditor would share in the cost of repairing a house, but such negotiations are often difficult, particularly if the loan was sold in securitization, as discussed in the next two chapters. For corporations, Korteweg (2010) estimates the cost of financial distress at 15–30 percent of the market value of the assets of highly leveraged (distressed) firms.

19. A typical finding in bankruptcy proceedings is that the borrower delayed bankruptcy as long as possible, sometimes even resorting to fraud. This was the state of affairs in the United States before the 1978 reform of the Bankruptcy Code. The 1978 reform

strengthened the prospects that managers of large corporations could retain control. Under the new Chapter 11 of the code, they have had much stronger incentives to file for bankruptcy voluntarily, especially because competition between bankruptcy courts gave them an opportunity to shop around and see which court offered the best prospects of their not losing control. This is particularly important when management wants to present a prepackaged insolvency plan, asking the court to approve a plan that has not received the 90–95 percent rate of approval by creditors that would make a bankruptcy filing unnecessary; see LoPucki (2005). LoPucki notes that corporations getting prepackaged insolvency plans approved in Delaware, the state with the bankruptcy court that attracts most cases, are most likely to refile, that is, to declare bankruptcy again after a few years. In most other countries, the position of management in bankruptcy is much weaker, and corporate managers as well as other borrowers try to delay bankruptcy or insolvency proceedings if they can. For example, Germany's replacement of bankruptcy and settlement procedures with a single insolvency code in the 1990s did not lead to a spate of voluntary filings as occurred in the United States. Three seemingly minor differences can explain this. First, German corporations cannot engage in forum shopping but must file with the court in whose district their headquarters are located. Second, unlike U.S. courts that may or may not appoint a trustee, a German court always appoints an insolvency administrator, and, even if corporate management remains in charge, this administrator must agree to any disposal of company assets; even before the formal opening of the procedure, a temporary insolvency administrator is entitled to full access to the company's books. And third, the rules for creditors' assent to an insolvency plan are fairly strict. See, for example, "Introduction to German Insolvency Law," http://www.justiz.nrw.de/WebPortal_en/projects/ieei/documents/public_papers/german_insolvency.pdf, accessed September 29, 2012.

20. If there is only one creditor, Kate might negotiate a package involving not only the debt prepayment but also a rate decrease reflecting the fact that the prepayment will lower her default risk. When there are many creditors, such negotiations are difficult and costly.

21. Typically, the creditors of the first mortgage would be more senior and thus paid first. In such a case they would receive the entire house, while the second-mortgage creditors would get nothing because they are only paid when the first-mortgage creditors have been paid in full. However, the first-mortgage creditors might lose if the foreclosure process and the neglect of the house would lead to an even lower value for the house. If the house were to drop in value to only $280,000, Kate would default, because she owes $295,000.

22. In this scenario, assuming that the second mortgage is more junior, Kate will pay her first mortgage in full and default on her second mortgage. Still, the first-mortgage creditor will lose in foreclosure if the value of the house declines further in the process due to neglect and other problems.

FOUR   Is It Really "A Wonderful Life"?

1. In the movie, the figure of George Bailey is played by the actor James Stewart. The title of Kotlikoff's book *Jimmy Stewart Is Dead* (2010) refers to the nostalgia. Kotlikoff

makes clear that George Bailey's type of banking was fragile and unsafe, but he shares the nostalgia for the banker who is wedded to his local community (see Kotlikoff 2010, 1–3).

2. There is a slight anachronism here. Savings and loan associations, previously "building societies" or "building and loan associations," were first organized early in the nineteenth century as mutual institutions in which people held shares rather than deposits. Their original objective had been to pool resources so as to allow the participants to acquire their own homes. Subsequently the link between saving and borrowing disappeared, so institutions received savings even from people who would not borrow to acquire their own homes. Even then, however, most of these institutions did not take deposits until the advent of federal deposit insurance in the 1930s. In the Great Depression, many savings and loan associations failed, but, contrary to the story told in the movie, this was due to delinquencies and defaults on loans rather than runs. Because they did not take deposits that were due on demand, savings and loan institutions did not suffer the kind of runs commercial banks suffered. They did, however, suffer withdrawals as members drew down their savings in order to maintain their consumption. For details, see Barth and Regalia (1988).

3. On Glass-Steagall and its demise, see, for example, Fink (2008), Acharya et al. (2010, 187–191), and Johnson and Kwak (2010, Chapter 3). In Europe, so-called universal banks, which engage in all activities, have been common all along.

4. For the Bailey Building and Loan Association, like most savings banks, the liabilities side of the balance sheet included primarily savings deposits. For commercial banks, the liabilities side includes demand deposits as well as savings deposits.

5. The distinction between checking accounts and savings accounts was eroded when in 1974 some savings banks in New England began to offer NOW accounts, savings accounts that allowed depositors to use "negotiable orders of withdrawal" to pay their bills. Before that, savings accounts could not be used directly for transactions.

6. Under the Glass-Steagall Act, until the early 1980s depository institutions were actually forbidden from paying interest on deposits that could be used for checking. This regulation allowed commercial banks to earn substantial net returns by investing a large part of the funds they received in deposits. They used these returns to cover the costs of services. See, for example, Klein (1974). Today substantial parts of the costs are covered by fees.

7. See, for example, "Paul Volcker: Think More Boldly," *Wall Street Journal*, December 14, 2009.

8. The economic historian Alexander Gerschenkron went so far as to claim that bank lending to industry had made the difference between German and English economic development in the late nineteenth century, because German banks were willing to provide loans for large-scale, long-term industrial investments (see Gerschenkron 1962). Similar views have been expressed about post–World War II Japanese economic development (see Mayer 1988). For a review of the analytical and empirical bases of these assessments, see Hellwig (1991). For the case of pre–World War I Germany, more recent accounts are given by Tilly (1989) and Fohlin (2007).

9. Rajan et al. (2010) document that increased use of securitization to sell mortgages to other investors in the years leading up to the financial crisis of 2007–2009 was associated with a decline in the use of soft information in mortgage lending.

10. On a limited scale, some of this is actually happening, for example, through Web sites offering "peer-to-peer" lending (see Ron Lieber, "The Gamble of Lending Peer to Peer," *New York Times*, February 4, 2011).

11. The presumption here is that the bank is more trustworthy than a nonfinancial borrower. If the bank is more trustworthy, its trustworthiness might be due to its being relatively less risky because it makes many different loans whose individual risks, by and large, cancel each other out; the bank might also have an established reputation, which a start-up does not. Both arguments must be taken with a grain of salt, however: if the many loans that the bank makes have risks that depend on a common underlying factor—for example, the business cycle or housing prices—the bank may be strongly affected. Moreover, the bank's reputation may be irrelevant if new developments induce the bank's management to take large risks. See Diamond (1984), Keeley (1990), Hellwig (1998), and Allison (2011).

12. See Diamond (1984) and Hellwig (1991, 1998). As discussed by Hellwig (1991) and Rajan (1992), problems can arise if the concentration of funds with the banks gives them monopoly power, which might allow them to impose extortionary conditions on their borrowers. Weinstein and Yafeh (1998) suggest that this was indeed the case in Japan for a long time. Boyd and De Nicolò (2005) show that such monopoly power of banks can be bad for financial stability because it can induce their borrowers to become reckless.

13. However, it is not always clear that banks put in the effort required for proper screening and monitoring of loan customers. They might try to economize on effort by using standardized screening procedures that are too coarse to provide valid assessments of borrowers or by making fewer and larger loans so they do not have to monitor as many borrowers. Such economizing on effort is not bad per se; after all, it does save real resources. However, it can be bad if, in making these loan decisions, the bank fails to consider the damage to third parties, such as the bank's creditors, that will arise if low-quality lending—the reduced diversification that results from taking fewer and larger risks—raises the bank's own default risk. Banks might also encourage excessive borrowing by individuals who cannot really afford the expenditures for which they borrow. Some banks have used questionable collection techniques whereby distressed individual borrowers are at a disadvantage in legal challenges. See, for example, Joe Nocera, "Why People Hate Banks," *New York Times*, April 4, 2012, and Jessica Silver-Greenberg, "Problems Riddle Moves to Collect Credit Card Debt," *New York Times*, August 12, 2012. The Consumer Financial Protection Bureau established under the Dodd-Frank Act is meant to help provide better information to consumers of financial products.

14. In contrast, large corporations with proven track records can go directly to the financial markets, raising money by issuing bonds that are bought by individuals or institutions such as insurance companies or pension funds. See Hoshi et al. (1990, 1991), Diamond (1991), and Rajan (1992).

15. Bernanke (1983, 1995). See also Bernanke and Lown (1991) and the work of Bernanke et al. (1996) on the credit crunch of the early 1990s, as well as Reinhart and Rogoff (2009).

16. Whereas both deposits and loans were known in antiquity, the combination of payment services, deposit taking, and lending dates back to the late Middle Ages. In travelling from fair to fair all over Europe, merchants did not want to carry gold or foreign

coins. Instead they carried paper, bills of exchange, or letters of credit, which they used to pay their suppliers or to obtain cash in distant places. These documents allowed the recipients to draw on another merchant for the amount owed. Typically the recipient would resell the claim to someone else, who would present it to a merchant or bank elsewhere, and so on, until at last it was presented to the issuer with whom the first merchant had initially made a deposit. These early bankers realized that they did not have to keep all deposits in reserve and that some of the money could be used for loans and other investments. See Lopez (1976, 78–79, 103 ff) or Kindleberger (1984, 35 ff). This earlier development repeated itself in the experience of the Amsterdam Bank, founded in 1609, and the Hamburg Bank, founded in 1619. Both banks were founded as public banks of deposit in order to enable merchants to make payments to each other without using the coins of uncertain metal content that were then circulating. When these banks subsequently learned that they did not need to have all the gold in store at all times, they took up lending as well, beginning with overdraft loans to their depositors. In the middle of the seventeenth century, people in England began to deposit gold with goldsmiths, and the goldsmiths discovered that they could use some of the gold for lending. Since then, the triad of offering payment services, taking deposits, and lending has been rediscovered several times and has come to be regarded as the essence of banking. On the Amsterdam Bank, see Kindleberger (1984, 47 ff), and on the Hamburg Bank, see Lütge (1966, 390 ff). On English goldsmiths, see Kindleberger (1984, 50 ff), Rothbard (2008), and Selgin (2010).

17. See, for example, Wikipedia (http://en.wikipedia.org/wiki/Financial_intermediary, accessed September 30, 2012). The textbook treatment by Mishkin (2007, 223) describes banking as "asset substitution" and says that "banks make profits by selling liabilities with one set of characteristics (a particular combination of liquidity, risk, size and return) and using the proceeds to buy assets with a different set of characteristics." Besides maturity transformation, the literature on banking stresses banks' liquidity transformation, using deposits that can be withdrawn at any time to make loans that are not easily tradable. (The term *liquidity* refers to the ease with which an asset can be turned into cash. We return to this subject in more detail in Chapter 10.) The asset transformation approach to banking, which was originally formulated by Gurley and Shaw (1960), has been criticized by Hellwig (1991, 1994, 1998) for failing to relate the banks' activities to the markets in which the banks, their depositors, and their borrowers operate.

18. Before central banks were given a monopoly on the issue of banknotes, banks also gave bearer notes to depositors. Depositors might present these bearer notes to the banks at any time, but they might also use them directly for payments without going back to the banks. See Friedman and Schwartz (1963) and Gorton (1988, 2010) on the national banking era in the United States. Mehrling (2010) emphasizes liquidity creation in describing the so-called money view of banking. We discuss these ideas more fully in Chapter 10.

19. See Merton (1957). Bryant (1980) and Diamond and Dybvig (1983) provide formal models of bank runs arising from self-fulfilling prophecies. In the movie *Mary Poppins,* a run is triggered by a boy crying, "I want my money back," referring to his pocket money, which others interpret as evidence that the bank has payment problems.

20. Calomiris and Mason (1997) and Schnabel (2004). Calomiris and Gorton (1991) give a more general account of the role of information in triggering runs.

21. For an authoritative account of the 1933 crisis, see Friedman and Schwartz (1963, 324 ff).

22. In addition to the FDIC, charged with providing insurance for deposits at commercial banks, the United States created the Federal Savings and Loan Insurance Corporation (FSLIC) to insure deposits at savings and loan (S&L) institutions. As a result of the S&L crisis of the 1980s, however, in 1989 the FSLIC was dismantled and its tasks given to the FDIC. The FDIC is supposed to be self-financed through fees it charges member banks. So was the FSLIC, but in the S&L crisis the funds it could obtain in fees did not suffice to compensate for the failing institutions' losses. The FDIC can borrow from the U.S. Treasury up to $100 billion (Federal Deposit Insurance Act, Section 14, available at http://www.fdic.gov/regulations/laws/rules/1000-1600.html, accessed September 30, 2012). We discuss this issue again in Chapter 9.

23. The amount insured by the FDIC is limited. The limit was $100,000 from 1980 to 2008 and was raised to $250,000 in 2008. For a history of the evolution of insurance coverage, see "A Brief History of Deposit Insurance in the United States," Table A-2, available at http://www.fdic.gov/bank/historical/brief/brhist.pdf, accessed September 30, 2012.

24. See, for example, Demirgüç-Kunt et al. (2008). We return to the topic of deposit insurance and guarantees in Chapter 9.

25. Short-term interest rates in the United States reached 10 percent in 1974 and 15 percent in 1981, then fell to more normal levels and rose again to 8 percent in 1990. Historical data on commercial paper and federal funds rates are available at the Federal Reserve's Web site, http://www.federalreserve.gov/releases/h15/data.htm, accessed on September 30, 2012.

26. This so-called Regulation Q was imposed by the Federal Reserve using powers conveyed by the Glass-Steagall Act.

27. The first money market fund was the Reserve Fund, created in 1971. The industry took off when the leading brokerage firm Merrill Lynch began offering a "cash management account" in a money market fund. For customers this provided a way to get around Regulation Q; for Merrill Lynch it provided a way to get around the prohibition of combining deposit taking and brokerage. See also Chapter 5, note 28, and Chapter 10, note 46.

28. The Depository Institutions Deregulation and Monetary Control Act of 1980 was the key piece of federal legislation that ended the regulation of the banking industry. This act deregulated banks while giving the Federal Reserve more authority over nonmember banks. Particularly, it required nonmember banks to abide by Federal Reserve decisions but allowed for greater leeway in bank mergers. It also allowed savings institutions to offer demand deposits, eliminated interest rate ceilings for all deposits other than demand deposits, and permitted individual banks to set their own interest rates for loans. In addition, the Act raised deposit insurance to $100,000 per account. Further deregulation—in particular, of savings institutions—came through the Garn–St. Germain Depository Institutions Act of 1982, which authorized savings institutions to make commercial loans and gave the federal agencies the ability to approve bank acquisitions.

29. After the introduction of deposit insurance in the 1930s, mortgage maturities had been significantly lengthened. See Benston et al. (1991, 309).

30. See Kane (1985), Benston et al. (1991), Dewatripont and Tirole (1994), and Hellwig (1994).

31. See Kane (1985, Table 4.6).

32. In the banks' accounts, a 6 percent fixed-rate thirty-year mortgage from 1965 would have been carried at face value without consideration of the fact that, with market rates of interest at 15 percent, return prospects on this mortgage were less than the return prospects on a new investment of half the face value. The discrepancy between the 6 percent rate on the mortgage and the rate of more than 10 percent on deposits entered the accounts only when actual payments indicated an actual loss. In addition, there also were delays in acknowledging losses. See White (1991).

33. See Benston et al. (1991), Hendershott and Shilling (1991), White (1991), and Dewatripont and Tirole (1994). As explained by Akerlof and Romer (1993), there was also outright looting, with "loans" to private companies used, for instance, to transfer resources from a savings institution to private investors related to the institution's manager.

34. See Curry and Shibut (2000).

35. In following this advice, Congress disregarded warnings that deregulation might worsen the problems. See, for example, Kareken (1983). Kane (1985) was even more outspoken. But even as late as 1987, congressional pressure prevented supervisors from dealing with apparent solvency problems and from restraining reckless investments. In the best-known episode, five senators, the so-called Keating Five, who had received financial contributions from the Lincoln Savings and Loan Association, interfered in 1987 by putting a stop to a federal investigation of the institution. When the institution failed in 1989, it cost taxpayers some $3 billion. The Keating Five were Senators Alan Cranston, Dennis DeConcini, John Glenn, John McCain, and Donald W. Riegle Jr.

36. In this respect, modern banking history began with the 1974 crash of Germany's Herstatt Bank, brought down when Danny Dattel, a rogue trader, lost close to 500 million Deutsche Marks in currency speculation. The crash of Herstatt marked the end of the period of stability in banking that had begun in the 1930s. Herstatt was a small bank, but its bankruptcy raised doubts about the international payments system. At the time that the authorities closed Herstatt, the bank was in the middle of a currency exchange with U.S. banks. The exchange was intended to be an exchange of cash against cash, without any element of credit, but due to the time difference between the United States and Germany, the different parts of the transactions did not occur simultaneously. The bank was closed after the U.S. banks had paid Herstatt but before Herstatt had paid the U.S. banks, leaving the latter as unwitting creditors to a bankrupt bank.

37. Crédit Lyonnais did receive some attention, because there were rumors of government involvement in some of that institution's lending and other investment decisions. Moreover, for a while it seemed as if investigations might harm the prospects of Jean-Claude Trichet, the senior Finance Ministry official involved, to become the head first of the French and then of the European Central Bank.

38. In the United States, the downturn affected not just the S&Ls, as sketched earlier, but also many commercial banks; see, for example, Bernanke and Lown (1991) and Boyd and Gertler (1994). For other countries, see the annual reports of the Bank for International Settlements as well as Staub (1998), Berglöf and Sjögren (1998), and Englund (1999).

39. Dexia was nationalized in October 2011. Hypo Real Estate had already been nationalized in 2009, and in 2010 most of its toxic assets had been put into a "bad bank," a separate institution that was managed by a government agency. In return for the toxic assets, Hypo Real Estate had received government bonds, so the bank was not affected by the additional losses on these assets, and these losses are borne by the government. In March 2012, the bad bank suffered more than €6 billion in losses on Greek sovereign debt. If Hypo Real Estate had still held this debt and if it had not received government support already, these losses would have pushed it over the brink. On Dexia, see Michael Birnbaum, "France, Belgium Agree to Nationalize Troubled Dexia Bank," *Washington Post,* October 6, 2011, and Thomas (2012). On Hypo Real Estate, see "Hypo Real Estate Is Nationalized with Squeeze Out," Reuters, October 13, 2009; Oliver Suess, "Hypo Real Will Move $256 Billion of Assets to Bad Bank, Gets More Capital," Bloomberg, September 22, 2010; and Expertenrat (2011).

40. Goodhart (1996) argues that the increase in financial risk should be seen as a return to normality. In comparison to the nineteenth century, the quiet period from, say, 1935 to 1975 must be seen as the exception, not the more turbulent period that we have experienced since then.

41. Commercial banks in the United States also came under pressure, but because business loans tend to have shorter lifetimes than mortgage loans, their losses and risks were somewhat smaller. Commercial banks responded to the pressure by diversifying into other activities, in particular derivatives, discussed in Chapter 5. They also began to campaign for a repeal of the Glass-Steagall Act on the grounds that universal banking would allow for a better diversification of risks across different activities. The experience of Switzerland in the early 1990s would seem to confirm this claim. In that country, regional banks with a specialization in real estate and business lending suffered a severe crisis; the large universal banks had similar problems, but they could balance their losses in traditional banking activities with profits from dealing in new kinds of financial contracts and securities such as derivatives, which are discussed in the next chapter. In other countries, such as Sweden, however, universal banking did not save the banks from the consequences of the boom-and-bust cycle in real estate.

42. The investment banker Lewis Ranieri at Salomon Brothers was among those who introduced securitization (see Lewis 1990). Technically, securitization involves the investment bank's creating a so-called special-purpose vehicle, an independent legal entity that acquires the package of mortgages and issues different types of debt. The debt holders are paid from the payments on the mortgages in the package. For more on securitization, see Das (2010, 292–300) and FCIC (2011, Chapter 3).

43. In the 1980s and 1990s, mortgage securitization was largely in the domain of Fannie Mae and the Freddie Mac, the so-called government-sponsored enterprises of the United

States. These institutions guaranteed the debt service on the mortgage-backed securities. They also imposed minimum quality standards for mortgages that they would securitize, so-called prime mortgages. When private investment banks entered the mortgage securitization business in the early 2000s, they did not give any guarantees, and they focused on "subprime" rather than prime mortgages, that is, mortgages that did not meet the minimum quality standards that had been set by Fannie Mae and Freddie Mac. For a systematic discussion of mortgage securitization and of flaws in mortgage securitization, see Hellwig (2009) and Bair (2012, Chapter 5). Gorton (2010) denies the incentive effect without, however, considering the evidence presented by UBS in its report to shareholders (UBS 2008), or by Shiller (2008), Demyanyk and Van Hemert (2009), and Ben-David (2011). Ben-David's work (2011), which had been available in 2007, shows that mortgage performance was significantly worse for mortgages that were passed on for securitization than for mortgages held by the originating mortgage bank. Keys et al. (2010) also show that securitization is associated with a higher likelihood of default.

44. See Demyanyk and Van Hemert (2009).

45. See Agarwal et al. (2011) and Ben-David (2011).

46. See Hellwig (2009) and FCIC (2011, Chapters 5–7).

47. From a theoretical point of view, the question is how to reconcile the desire of investors to have easy access to their funds if they need them with the long-term nature of investments in housing. Hellwig (1994) shows that the problem can be solved if housing investments are funded by long-term borrowing, for example, by banks' issuing so-called covered bonds, with portfolios of mortgage loans serving as collateral. Covered bonds differ from mortgage-backed securities in that the issuing bank is liable for the debt. In the United States, covered bonds would not eliminate but would merely transform the solvency risks associated with maturity transformation. Because borrowers in the United States have the right to repay their mortgages prematurely, a bank that issues a covered bond at a time when interest rates are high must fear that interest rates will go down and borrowers will refinance and repay their mortgages. See also note 48.

48. It is interesting to compare mortgage-backed securities to covered bonds, which were discussed in note 47 and which are common in Europe. In the case of mortgage-backed securities, neither the originating mortgage bank nor the securitizing investment bank has liability for the debt that is issued. By contrast, the issuer of a covered bond remains liable even if the mortgage borrowers do not pay. By issuing a covered bond, the bank eliminates the risk that the mortgage loan may have to be refinanced at a higher interest rate but it retains the credit risk. Covered bonds may therefore provide better incentives to engage in creditworthiness assessments than do mortgage-backed securities. The preference for mortgage-backed securities in the United States seems to have resulted from the prepayment option that a borrower has under U.S. law. The prepayment option is most likely to be used if the initial interest rate on a mortgage was high and in the meantime interest rates have gone down. For a bank funding mortgage lending by issuing covered bonds, there is therefore a risk that if the market rates of interest decline, borrowers might prepay and the investments the banks could make will not earn enough to pay the interest on the covered bond. By contrast, the distinction of multiple tranches of mortgage-

backed securities provides some flexibility for handling prepayment risk. In most countries other than the United States, Japan, and Denmark, borrowers incur prepayment penalties for fixed-rate mortgages that are meant to compensate lenders for lost income when interest rates decline. Germany has the most severe penalties, which are waived only if a homeowner moves. See, for example, London Economics et al. (2009).

FIVE *Banking Dominos*

1. The chapter epigraph, from Lewis (2010, 72), refers to the enormous risk that insurance company AIG had taken by selling so-called credit default swaps (CDSs), insurance contracts that pay in the event of default, for a total value of close to $500 billion. AIG greatly underestimated the possibility that many defaults might occur at the same time. We discuss this issue later in this chapter and in Chapter 11.

2. For the distinction between subprime and other mortgages, see note 43 in Chapter 4. We use the term *mortgage-related securities* for a broad class of securities containing not only mortgage-backed securities (MBS) but also securities resulting from the securitization of MBS. MBS themselves might serve as collateral for collateralized debt obligations (CDOs) (see, for example, Das 2010, Chapter 9). The idea and the procedure are the same as those for the creation of a mortgage-backed security out of a package of mortgages except that the collateral consists of MBS or more general asset-backed securities (ABS) rather than mortgages. The resulting MBS CDOs or, more generally, ABS CDOs—collateralized debt obligations with MBS or ABS as collateral—might even be securitized further to create ABS CDOs^2, CDOs whose collateral consists of ABS CDOs. For the loss estimates, see IMF (2008b). The estimated total losses of financial institutions from the financial crisis in this report are higher than just the losses on subprime-mortgage-related securities ($1.4 trillion), but this larger estimate already includes significant follow-on losses.

3. Data on the values of shares traded on stock markets in the early 2000s and the year-to-year changes in these values can be obtained from the World Federation of Exchanges at http://www.world-exchanges.org/statistics/time-series/market-capitalization, accessed October 7, 2012. Losses in U.S. stock markets in the early 2000s involved declines in the values of financial securities held by investors; such losses are often referred to as paper losses. The losses in real resources were much lower. Similarly, for mortgage-related securities, losses from borrowers actually defaulting on their debts have so far been much lower than the $500 billion estimated by the IMF in 2008. The relation between so-called paper losses and losses from borrowers actually in default is extensively discussed by the IMF (2008a, Chapter 2, esp. 65–66, and 2008b, Chapter 3). The full extent of actual mortgage-related losses is not yet known because many of the mortgages are still on banks' books, foreclosures have been delayed by problems with documentation, and some of the losses, such as those on second liens, have not yet been recognized.

4. On the Japanese crisis, see Hoshi and Kashyap (2010).

5. IMF (2008b), Hellwig (2009, 2010a), FCIC (2011, Chapters 12–15), and Acharya et al. (2013). The reasons for this vulnerability of the system are discussed in Chapters 10 and 11.

6. Banks were not major investors in the dot-com companies. If banks had held just 10 percent of outstanding shares of listed companies, their losses would have been greater than the subprime losses.

7. According to Friedman and Schwartz (1963, 422 ff), deposits in the United States fell by one-sixth from December 31, 1932, to March 15, 1933, with 70 percent of the decline in banks that did not reopen. Of the five thousand banks that did not reopen, about three thousand were reopened later and two thousand were closed for good.

8. The German banking crisis of 1931, with a "bank holiday" on July 14 and 15 and restricted operations through August, had similar consequences. The deepening of the depression from the collapse of bank lending formed the background to the political developments of 1932–1933 that led to Hitler's accession to power (see Eichengreen 1992).

9. See BIS (2009, 26). According to the FCIC (2011, 357), within a week of Lehman's bankruptcy, $349 billion was withdrawn from prime money market funds.

10. See FCIC (2011, 359).

11. See FCIC (2011, 358).

12. In line with our previous assertion that runs do not come out of the blue, the withdrawals were concentrated in institutions that were known to be in trouble, such as U.S. investment banks, or that subsequent developments would show to be in trouble because they had excessive leverage, such as Dexia in France or Hypo Real Estate in Germany. However, less risky institutions such as Aareal Bank in Germany were also hit (see Expertenrat 2011).

13. As banks came to be perceived as very risky, interest rates for unsecured lending rose dramatically. One example is the behavior of the London interbank offered rate (LIBOR), an index for the rates that London banks charge each other in unsecured borrowing and lending. Before August 2007, the difference between LIBOR and an interest rate for lending that was considered riskless was around 10 basis points (0.01 percent). On September 14, 2007, the day that the Bank of England announced emergency funding for Northern Rock, one of the largest mortgage lenders in the United Kingdom, the difference reached 85 basis points. The difference reached an all-time high (until then) of 108 basis points on December 6, 2007; another high of 83 basis points on March 17, 2008, after the collapse of Bear Stearns, and finally a record 365 basis points on October 10, 2008, after the turmoil caused by the Lehman bankruptcy. See Sengupta and Tam (2008), Acharya et al. (2010, 335–340), and FCIC (2011, 252). (Recent revelations about misreporting of rates for the LIBOR index suggest that the actual rates in interbank borrowing and lending may have been even higher in October 2008. We discuss these revelations in Chapter 13.) Each time interbank markets were in turmoil, central banks stepped in to provide banks with the liquidity they could no longer achieve in markets. For example, on August 9, 2007, after the large French bank BNP Paribas had temporarily halted redemptions from three of its funds because it could not reliably value the assets backed by U.S. subprime mortgage debt held in those funds, the European Central Bank responded with the largest short-term liquidity injection in its nine-year history until then—€94.8 billion ($130 billion at the time) worth of overnight sale and repurchase (so-called repo) agreements (which will be discussed in Chapter 10)—and the Federal Reserve Bank of New York used

one-day repo agreements to inject $24 billion into the U.S. banking system. See Cecchetti (2009).

14. For example, the Bank of England provided U.K. banks with an aggregate total of £500 billion in loans and guarantees. See U.K. Treasury, "Statement by the Chancellor on Financial Stability," from October 8, 2008, available at http://webarchive.nationalarchives .gov.uk/+/http://www.hm-treasury.gov.uk/statement_chx_081008.htm, accessed October 8, 2012. The CNNMoney channel provides a full list of bailout programs and costs in United States, which is available at http://money.cnn.com/news/storysupplement/economy/ bailouttracker/index.html, accessed October 1, 2012. See also Phil Kuntz and Bob Ivry, "Fed Once-Secret Loan Crisis Data Compiled by Bloomberg Released to Public," Bloomberg, December 22, 2011. Sinn (2010, Chapter 9) gives an overview of bank rescue programs in different countries. We discuss the bailouts and various supports given to banks in Chapter 9.

15. For a detailed account, see BIS (2008, Chapter 2, and 2009, also Chapter 2).

16. According to FCIC (2011, 282), Bear Stearns engaged in some asset sales, but this was "too little too late." To reduce its leverage, in May 2008 UBS also sold assets with a nominal value of $22 billion to hedge fund Black Rock, taking a loss of $7 billion (see http://www.ubs.com/global/de/about_ubs/investor_relations/releases/news-display- investor-releases.html/de/2008/05/21/2008_05_21a.html, accessed October 1, 2012).

17. Recognition of the extent of the crisis in July and August 2007 was triggered by two hedge funds' becoming insolvent from losses on mortgage-related securities and related derivatives and by rating agencies' deciding that credit risks on many securities were substantially higher than they had said before. The equity of some banks came under immediate pressure from the losses these banks had to take. Other banks had held these securities "off balance sheet" through so-called conduits, affiliates without equity for which the parent banks had given guarantees. In August 2007, market funding for the conduits broke down and the parents had to step in and take the securities into their balance sheets, at which point the reported ratio of equity to assets on their balance sheets went down. For details, see Hellwig (2009) and the references given there, as well as Acharya et al. (2013).

18. Pressure to raise the ratio of equity to assets came not only from supervisors but also from institutions from which banks borrowed in the money markets. See IMF (2008a, 2008b), BIS (2008, 2009), and Hellwig (2009).

19. Of course the banks do not always need to sell assets in order to reduce their indebtedness. They might also raise more equity and either buy back some of their existing debt or use the proceeds to invest in additional assets. In 2007, in the early stages of the financial crisis, when the seriousness of the crisis had not yet been fully recognized, some banks actually issued new equity to compensate for losses. In 2008 the new equity issues came to a standstill. See, for example, IMF (2008b, 23–24). Admati et al. (2012a) discuss the different ways in which firms might reduce their leverage and show that, although banks are sometimes indifferent, under certain conditions they may have a strict preference for asset sales for the purpose of buying back junior debt. Banks choose this method if it allows them to worsen the position of senior creditors. In Chapter 11 we discuss how this form of "deleveraging" worked in Europe in the fall of 2011.

20. As we discuss later in the chapter, the fear of a systemic chain reaction associated with asset liquidations and price declines was also an important reason that in 1998 the Federal Reserve did not want the insolvent hedge fund Long Term Capital Management (LTCM) to be put into bankruptcy. A historical example of how liquidation sales in bankruptcy triggered contagion in a crisis is analyzed by Schnabel and Shin (2004).

21. This role of expectations in the developments of 2007–2008 is noted by BIS (2008).

22. See Reinhart and Rogoff (2009, Table A.3.1). Their Table A.4.1 gives a brief historical account of each crisis. The only two banking crises between 1940 and 1970 occurred in India following that country's independence in 1947 and in Brazil in connection with a downturn of the Brazilian economy in 1963.

23. As mentioned in the previous chapter, this was largely due to a change in the environment in which banks operate. In addition to movements in interest rates, which we discussed in Chapter 4, after 1973, when the system of fixed exchange rates for currencies was dismantled, exchange rate risk became important. In 1974, Herstatt in Germany and Franklin National in the United States were the first victims of this risk (see Grossman 2010, 267).

24. See Tables A.3.1 and A.4.1 in Reinhart and Rogoff (2009). For the early 2000s, Reinhart and Rogoff (2009) list seven crises; before 2007, there actually was a sense that the system might have become more stable.

25. The Japanese banking crisis did put an end to the 1980s expansion of Japanese banks in the United States, especially California. However, any effects of this retrenchment—for example, on California real estate prices, which had started to decline even before the Japanese crisis—are hard to identify given that, even before 1992, the Japanese–U.S. agreement regarding voluntary export restraints in Japan had diminished the Japanese trade surplus and hence the funds that Japanese investors could invest in the United States; moreover, in California real estate finance was already affected by the S&L crisis and the distress of major commercial banks.

26. Many banks treated these securities as available for sale, which meant that they had to be valued at going market prices. (Doing so allowed banks to arbitrage between different ways of computing regulatory equity requirements.) To stop the downward spiral, in October 2008 regulators allowed banks to transfer these securities to the so-called bank book, treating them as loans that they would hold until they expired. After that, banks no longer needed to adjust their asset valuations to changes in market prices. The role of fair-value or mark-to-market accounting has been a subject of dispute. The IMF (2008a, Chapter 3, and 2008b, also Chapter 3) discusses how this accounting rule can exacerbate a crisis and actually harm a bank that reacts by selling assets that the market values too pessimistically. Laux and Leuz (2009) and Barth and Landsman (2010) suggest that in 2008 the problem was due not so much to the use of fair-value accounting as to the reactions of banks, investors, and regulators to the results of applying these rules. Haldane (2011c) calls for a different accounting regime for banks. We further discuss the issues around the book and market value of banks in Chapter 6 and 7.

27. The problems of Germany's Industriekreditbank and Sächsische Landesbank and the U.K.'s Northern Rock appeared as early as August 2007 (see Hellwig 2009). Over the

twelve months that followed, the downward spiral in asset markets destroyed the solvency of many other highly indebted banks.

28. Briefly in this chapter, and more fully in Chapter 10, we discuss how money market funds developed and how they came to play such a key role in the interconnectedness of the system (see Fink 2008 and Goodfriend 2011).

29. Lewis (2010, 67) reports that each time someone asked who was stupid enough to buy U.S. mortgage-related securities, the answer would be "Düsseldorf." That city in Germany was the seat of both West LB and Industriekreditbank, major buyers of mortgage-related securities that subsequently needed billions of euros in bailout money. (Under orders from the European Commission, West LB actually was split up and largely closed down in the summer of 2012; see "State Aid: Commission Approves Splitup of West LB," http://europa.eu/rapid/pressReleasesAction.do?reference=IP/11/1576&format=HTML&ag ed=1&language=EN&guiLanguage=en, accessed October 1, 2012.) For other examples, see Hellwig (2009) and Kaserer (2010).

30. Money market funds were introduced in Chapter 4, especially note 27. Reform efforts have failed recently (see Nathaniel Popper, "Changes to Money Market Funds Stall," *New York Times*, August 22, 2012). We discuss money market funds again in Chapters 10, 11, and 13.

31. See FCIC (2011, 356–360).

32. Decisions to hold these securities on the bank's own account were partly influenced by governance problems inside the bank and partly by flawed regulation and supervision (see UBS 2008, Hellwig 2009, Merkley and Levin 2011, Better Markets 2012, and Acharya et al. 2013). We discuss these governance problems in Chapter 8 and distortions from regulation and supervision in Chapters 11 and 13.

33. In addition to all these parties, rating agencies were paid for consulting and providing credit ratings, and law firms were paid for writing the various contracts. The large number of parties involved may explain the remarkable finding in Acharya et al. (2013) that banks investing in mortgage-related securities earned 10–30 basis points (0.1–0.3 percent) above the cost of borrowing in the money market when mortgage rates for subprime borrowers were actually 600 basis points higher.

34. See Tett (2009), Das (2010), Lewis (2010), McLean and Nocera (2010), FCIC (2011, Chapters 9–10), Dunbar (2011), and Morgenson and Rosner (2011). The word *swaps* was used so they would qualify for exemptions from regulation that were given to so-called swap agreements. According to Dunbar (2011, 16), "Calling them swaps would ensure that CDS would remain off the regulatory radar for a decade." Also, although they are insurance contracts, CDSs were not overseen by regulators of the insurance industry, which often require that there be an insurable interest (so that one cannot buy insurance on another person's house or life). Lewis (2010, 88) describes how little AIG understood about the enormous risk of the mortgages in the pools they insured, stating, "In retrospect, their ignorance seems incredible—but then an entire financial system was premised on their not knowing, and paying them for this talent." He and others also describe the ignorance of credit rating agencies that neglected correlations between defaults and gave AAA ratings to numerous mortgage securities that later turned out to be anything but as safe as the rating indicated.

35. The bailout is described by the FCIC (2011, Chapter 19). It was triggered by AIG's needing to post cash collateral with the banks to which it sold CDS contracts because of the downgrades of the mortgage securities. The use of taxpayers' money for the bailout has been controversial, particularly because banks were paid in full even as the government invested $85 billion and added many billions of dollars in guarantees and lines of credit while acquiring a significant stake in AIG. See Barofsky (2012) for a discussion of the AIG bailout.

36. These techniques are based on the pathbreaking work of Black and Scholes (1973) and Merton (1973), which was recognized in the 1997 Nobel Memorial Prize.

37. Among the most popular derivatives have been interest rate and currency swaps. For a description of derivatives trading and markets, see Partnoy (2009, 2010), Hull (2007), Das (2010), and Dunbar (2011).

38. Das (2010, 333) gives a definitive answer to the question we ask in the heading of this section, stating that "risk transfer proved to be the shell game of credit markets. A *short con,* quick and easy to pull off. Financial innovation did not decrease risk but increased risk significantly in complex ways."

39. Prominent examples include Sumitomo Corporation in 1996, Société Générale and Morgan Stanley in 2008, and JPMorgan Chase in 2012. For a record of large trading losses in history, see http://en.wikipedia.org/wiki/List_of_trading_losses, accessed October 1, 2012.

40. Significant amounts of public money were again put at risk in the 2000s, before the financial crisis, when public treasurers eager to improve their finances were willing victims of the banks' sales forces. In many cases, the buyers were misled about the risks of the products they bought. In a case involving so-called spread ladder swaps, bets on the future of the difference between the interest rates on long and short maturities, in 2011 the highest German court ordered Deutsche Bank to pay damages of €540,000 to a small firm that had bought these swaps. The court ruled that Deutsche Bank should have provided the customer with better information; in particular, it should have made clear that because of fees, the market value of the position the customer acquired was negative. See "Deutsche Bank to Pay Damages Over Swaps: Court," Reuters, March 22, 2011. The case received wide attention because sales of this kind of product to hundreds of small firms and municipalities were said to be valued at around €1 billion. Partnoy (2009), Lewis (2010, 2011), Dunbar (2011), and Cohan (2012) also discuss fraud.

41. See Warren Buffett, "What Worries Me," *Fortune,* March 3, 2003, available at http://www.tilsonfunds.com/BuffettWorries.pdf, accessed October 6, 2012. The risks and hidden leverage associated with derivatives are described by Partnoy (2009, 2010) and Das (2010).

42. This follows because, if the price that was set is considered the appropriate competitive forward price, the two sides of the forward transaction, buying euros and selling dollars, cancel themselves out. The accounting rules for derivatives use the market value of the derivatives to record the transaction, and at its initiation, this is zero. As the exchange rate changes, one side of the transaction would be indebted to the other, depending on the direction in which the exchange rate moves. This would lead one side to record the value of the position as an asset and the other side to record it as a liability or debt. See Hull

(2007). We further discuss the treatment of derivatives in accounting statements in Chapter 6.

43. See Partnoy (2009, 2010), UBS (2008), and Das (2010). Das (2010, 54) describes the hierarchy of the trading floor to a trainee in this way: "There are salespeople—they lie to clients. Traders lie to sales[people] and to risk managers. Risk managers? They lie to the people who run the place—correction, think they run the place. The people who run the place lie to shareholders and regulators." When asked about the clients, he says that they "lie mainly to themselves" and concludes (53): "To enter the world of derivatives trading is to enter the realm of beautiful lies." (Those are "the lies we would like to believe.") We discuss incentives and governance problems in Chapter 8.

44. See, for example, Partnoy (2009). Among the victims of large losses at the time were Procter and Gamble, Orange County, Credit Suisse First Boston, and Salomon Brothers.

45. See The President's Working Group on Financial Markets (1999), in particular 17–23 and 26–28. Legal uncertainty was exacerbated by the fact that the LTCM Fund was a partnership organized in the Cayman Islands. Acharya et al. (2010, 213 ff) note that ten years after the LTCM crisis the problem of contagion from the failure of an internationally active, systemically important financial institution had not been reduced.

46. For details, see Lowenstein (2001) and Das (2010).

47. FCIC (2011, 290) and Cohan (2012).

48. These partners were expected to grab the collateral that Bear Stearns had pledged; while trying to sell the collateral, they would exert great downward pressure on asset prices. Even before the end, people trying to get out of derivatives contracts with Bear Stearns played a significant role in the run on Bear Stearns (FCIC 2011, 286–291). This issue is discussed in the next chapter.

49. See, for example, Wuffli (1995) and the contributions of Freeland and Gummerlock in Hellwig and Staub (1996). At the time, Wuffli was the chief financial officer and Gummerlock the chief risk officer of Swiss Bank Corporation, which later merged into UBS; Freeland was the deputy secretary general of the Basel Committee for Banking Supervision. The limitations of quantitative models and stress tests are discussed in Chapter 11.

50. Taleb (2001, 2010) refers to such risks as "black swan" risks. Black swans are events that have been deemed impossible and that have significant consequences when they occur anyway. Taleb gives several examples in which neglect of black swan risk led to disaster. Das (2010, Chapter 5) discusses the pitfalls of "risk management by the numbers," including the story of LTCM. Gillian Tett, in "Clouds Sighted off CDO Asset Pool" (*Financial Times,* April 18, 2005), noted that "if a nasty accident did ever occur with CDOs, it could ricochet through the financial system in unexpected ways," and that "while banks insist that these risks can be accurately measured by their models . . . projecting default probabilities remains an art, not science." Frydman and Goldberg (2011) argue that ever-imperfect knowledge and interpretation of information by market participants is important for understanding wide price swings and the poor performance of economic models that ignore this issue.

51. See Lewis (2010). Hellwig (2009) gives an account of developments in 2007 and 2008 and argues that, on the basis of the information that was available beforehand, the

unfolding of events could not have been predicted with any degree of precision. The data that were available did not permit the drawing of any reliable conclusions about the behavior of what is an extremely complex social system. The general proposition that, as a matter of principle, the most important developments are unforeseeable is argued by Taleb (2001, 2010). Another example in which complex strategies and trust in a model had systemic fallout is provided by the stock market crash of October 1987, which involved the use of portfolio insurance. In that case, companies that offered to insure the portfolios of pension funds and other investors relied on program trading that required markets to respond quickly to submitted buy and sell orders. When such orders overwhelmed the trading systems on the exchanges, portfolio insurers could not deliver on their promises. The stock market declined by 19 percent in one day because investors were unsure of the source of the large sell orders. See Anice C. Wallace, "The Brady Report: Looking for Flaws; Study Cites Portfolio Insurers' Role as a Key to the Market Meltdown," *New York Times*, January 11, 1988.

52. This is known as the "Peltzman effect" after the seminal research of Peltzman (1975), who showed that the effects of improvements in car safety are to a large extent neutralized by changes in drivers' behavior. Das (2011, Chapter 8) provides an insider's perspective on the failures of models to truly capture risk and of the false confidence that they inspired in market participants and regulators. We return to this issue in Chapter 11.

53. Lewis (1990, 2011), Partnoy (2009, 2010), Lowenstein (2001), and Das (2010) describe the culture. See FCIC (2011, xxix–xxv and 298–301) about the growth of derivatives markets.

54. On this point, see Hellwig (1995, 2009, 2010a).

55. See Onaran (2011) and Expertenrat (2011).

56. This decision is discussed extensively by the FCIC (2011, Chapter 18 and 433 ff).

57. See Acharya et al. (2010, 220–226), Bair (2012, 194–195), and a speech given by Martin Gruenberg, acting chair of the FDIC, on May 10, 2012, posted at http://www.fdic .gov/news/news/speeches/chairman/spmay1012.html, accessed October 1, 2012.

58. We discuss bailouts and subsidies in Chapter 9.

59. Under the so-called home country principle, any independent legal entity undergoes a resolution procedure in the country where it is incorporated. On the complexity of the largest institutions, see note 62.

60. See Matthew Goldstein, "Lehman Bankruptcy Gets Ugly," *Business Week*, October 2, 2008, and Cumming and Eisenbeis (2010, 12–13).

61. For a discussion of the issue, see ASC (2012).

62. Resolution would require untangling the complex legal structures of megabanks and selling the pieces (see Bair 2012, 331). Some of these are hidden from investors and possibly from regulators. For example, Herring and Carmassi (2010) state that eight large financial institutions have more than 1,000 subsidiaries and Citi has more than 2,500 subsidiaries. However, these numbers are likely understated, and many subsidiaries and entities that are off the balance sheets of banks are not fully disclosed to investors or regulators. For example, in its 2006 financial filings (the so-called Form 10-K), Lehman Brothers listed 168 subsidiaries. Herring and Carmassi (2010, Table 8.1) report that

Lehman Brothers had 433 majority-owned subsidiaries in 2006 (with data from BankScope). Yet in highlighting the challenge of resolution, Harvey A. Miller and Maurice Horowitz, in "A Better Solution Is Needed for Failed Financial Giants" (*New York Times*, October 9, 2012), state that Lehman's bankruptcy involved about 8,000 subsidiaries in more than 40 countries. Cumming and Eisenbeis (2010, 7) state that "interestingly, Lehman Brothers was relatively uncomplicated by comparison with less than half the average total number of subs of other large complex financial institutions (LCFIs)," mentioning that it had "operations in 20 countries compared with the average of 44 for LCFIs in general." (Clearly, they were not aware of some of the subsidiaries mentioned by Miller and Horowitz.) A list of the subsidiaries of Bank of America as of December 31, 2011, as disclosed to the Securities and Exchange Commission (SEC), can be seen at http://www .sec.gov/Archives/edgar/data/70858/000007085812000155/bac-12312011x10kex21.htm, accessed October 8, 2012. On the increasing complexity of large banks and the challenges it poses, see also Boot (2011).

63. Documents from the Financial Stability Board (FSB 2011a, b) list conditions for the viable resolution of systemically important institutions. The Basel Committee on Banking Supervision (BCBS 2011b) provides an overview of what has been done. A comparison of these documents shows how far we are from having a viable system. For the European Union, in June 2012 the European Commission proposed a new directive that would require every member state to install a resolution system on the lines of what is outlined by the Dodd-Frank Act in the United States or the Banking Act of 2009 in the United Kingdom. The European Commission's proposal for a European directive would provide for some coordination of authorities in the EU but not for the kind of joint management that would prevent the disintegration of business procedures. See http:// ec.europa.eu/internal_market/bank/crisis_management/index_en.htm#maincontent Sec2, accessed October 1, 2012, and Daniel Gros and Dirk Schoenmaker, "Cleaning Up the Mess: Bank Resolution in a Systemic Crisis," *Vox*, June 6, 2012. On the lack of an ex ante loss-sharing agreement, see Schoenmaker (2010). On the overall issues, see Hellwig (2012).

64. On the credibility issue, Kane (2012c, 655) draws an analogy between the reactions of the government and those of the public to the crisis and the different stages of grief. Kane's assessment is that "federal authorities are cycling between the stages of denial and superficial political bargaining, while the public is cycling between anger and depression." See also Daniel Indiviglio, "Will the FDIC's New Power End 'Too Big to Fail'?," *Atlantic*, January 20, 2011, and "Still Too Big, Still Can't Fail," *Wall Street Journal*, March 5, 2011. Mayo (2011, loc. 3121-25) states, "When it comes down to it . . . the end result will be the same. The pain of letting one of these institutions go under is almost always too much for politicians and our government to bear."

65. For example, in the United States the Dodd-Frank Act mandates that financial institutions prepare living wills in which each institution describes how it would be unwound if it had to go through bankruptcy. Whereas the logic of giving the FDIC or similar authorities elsewhere expanded resolution authority is based on the recognition that the bankruptcy process does not work well for systemically important banks, the living

wills requirement asks institutions to consider their own resolution under bankruptcy law. The living wills are costly for the institutions to produce and for the regulators to evaluate, and the information must be updated regularly to be relevant. Because systemically important institutions expect to avoid bankruptcy and resolution, their incentives to write useful living wills are quite different from those of individuals who write living wills in part to help their loved ones. Overall, the cost effectiveness of including living wills as part of the regulation is not clear. Obviously, resolution planning requires good information about the institutions to be resolved, but if there is a credibility problem and the institutions do not actually fear failure, they have few incentives to become less complex; instead, they might have incentives to become more complex so that resolution will be even more difficult. The living wills requirement can be useful if these wills allow regulators to use their authority to impose higher capital requirements on complex institutions or force them to simplify their structures so that resolution will become an acceptable option (see Bair 2012, 329–330). However, the politics of banking, discussed in Chapter 12, is likely to make this difficult.

66. Among the reasons resolution would be lengthy and costly is the interconnectedness of the system. Jessica Silver-Greenberg and Nelson D. Schwartz, in " 'Living Wills' for Too-Big-to-Fail Banks Are Released" (*New York Times*, July 12, 2012), quote analysts who point out that "the big banks were so intertwined that if one failed, it would probably take others with it, making it unlikely that enough healthy banks would remain to buy assets from the ailing one."

67. See, for example, Dashiel Bennett, "The One Quote Jamie Dimon Probably Hopes Won't Come Back to Haunt Him," *Atlantic Wire*, June 13, 2012. In his 2010 letter to shareholders (available at http://files.shareholder.com/downloads/ONE/2103717927x0x458384/6832cb35-0cdb-47fe-8ae4-1183aeceb7fa/2010_JPMC_AR_letter_.pdf, accessed October 5, 2012), Mr. Dimon proposed that the industry pay for the resolution of what he called "dumb banks," referring to the resolution process (on page 25) as "Minimally Damaging Bankruptcy for Big Dumb Banks (MDBFBDB)." For a comment on this idea, even from JPMorgan's perspective, see the final part of Anat Admati, "An Open Letter to JPMorgan Board," *Huffington Post*, June 14, 2011.

68. We discuss JPMorgan's "fortress balance sheet" in Chapter 6.

69. See Tom Braithwaite, "JPMorgan Doomsday Scenario Revealed," *Financial Times*, June 12, 2012. The slides of the presentation by a JPMorgan representative are available at http://www.law.harvard.edu/programs/about/pifs/symposia/europe/baer.pdf, accessed October 15, 2012.

70. The distorted incentives and inefficiencies associated with distress and insolvency were discussed in Chapter 3. We discuss the impact of guarantees and bailouts in Chapter 9. We further discuss the importance of timely intervention to forestall these distortions in Chapter 11. The Japanese experience of the 1990s shows that failing to address resolution issues promptly can be detrimental to the quality of lending and to economic growth (see Hoshi and Kashyap 2004 and 2010 and ASC 2012).

71. See, for example, Alan Greenspan, "Regulators Must Risk More to Push Growth," *Financial Times*, discussed in Chapter 1, note 9.

SIX *What Can Be Done?*

1. For an accessible discussion of why markets can fail and regulation may be needed, see Wheelan (2003, Chapters 3 and 4).

2. In the same vein, Meltzer (2012), an economist who is usually known for extolling the virtues of the free market, states that banking regulation is essential in order "to limit banks' size and appetite for risk" and to protect the public (9). He specifically endorses high equity requirements, stating that "bank equity capital deters excessive risk-taking by requiring the bank to pay for its portfolio mistakes and unforeseen changes. . . . If regulators raised capital requirements, bank stockholders would bear the risk of mistakes, which would encourage prudence. Taxpayers would not pay for bankers' errors" (35). (See also Chapter 11, note 54.)

3. See, for example, notes 10 and 13 in Chapter 1 regarding delays in the implementation of the Volcker Rule. Securities and Exchange Commissioner Troy Paredes (2010) said that, although Congress had passed the Dodd-Frank Act, the SEC still had to study whether to implement the law. On legal challenges, see Ben Protess, "U.S. Judge Strikes Down Commodity Speculator Limits," *New York Times,* September 29, 2012.

4. "Reform Group Defends U.S. CFTC's [Commodity Futures Trading Commission's] Position Limits" (Reuters, April 23, 2012) quotes Dennis Kelleher, the president of the nonprofit organization Better Markets, saying, "The CFTC must be guided by the dictates of the public interest, not the burdens of regulation on industry." For details, see Better Markets, "Industry False Claims about Cost-Benefit Analysis," available at http://bettermarkets.com/blogs/industrys-false-claims-about-cost-benefit-analsyis, accessed October 18, 2012. The industry's delay tactics include bringing forward many "studies" that claim to estimate the cost of the regulation to the industry and requesting that regulators respond to these studies. The costs that financial instability imposes on the public are not considered. On these costs, recall the estimate of $12.8 trillion for the cost of the financial crisis in the United States (Better Markets 2012), discussed in Chapter 1, note 19.

5. For example, in a hearing before the House Financial Services Committee on June 16, 2011, arguing against so-called SIFI (systemically important financial institutions)—capital "surcharges," additional capital requirements imposed on a set of the largest banks in the world—Barry Zubrow, chief risk officer at JPMorgan Chase, said that the capital requirements of Basel III (described later in this chapter and taken up in detail in Chapter 11) would "effectively require JPMorgan Chase to hold 45 percent more capital than it took to weather the crisis." Statements about how much better capitalized banks are now and how strict the new requirements are can be found in many bank disclosures and shareholder letters. As discussed in Chapter 11, however, the Basel III requirements are actually not very stringent. We show in Chapters 7–9 that if the banks' costs are increased by having more equity, it is only because taxpayers currently pay some of the banks' costs by bearing some of the risks that should be borne by shareholders and through other subsidies of debt. Zubrow (2011) is an example of the way the industry complains about costs of regulation to them without any concern for the costs of their behavior to the public.

6. The expression is used in every letter to shareholders and comes up frequently in statements and interviews. See, for example, Dawn Kopecki, "JPMorgan's Dimon Says Balance Sheet Built to Handle 'Surprises,'" Bloomberg, May 15, 2012. Mr. Dimon is quoted as saying, "Our fortress balance sheet remains intact" (see, e.g., *BBC News*, BBC, June 13, 2012).

7. According to its 10-K form for 2011, a report that is required by the U.S. Securities and Exchange Commission (SEC) and that summarizes the performance of a public company, JPMorgan Chase had a total of loan-related commitments that amounted to $975 billion (note 29 of the report), of which only $1 billion appears on the balance sheet. In addition, it had guarantees and other commitments with a contractual amount of $316 billion, of which the amount carried onto the balance sheet was only $4 billion.

8. On Enron, see Healy and Palepu (2003) and McLean and Elkind (2004).

9. This was the case with Germany's Industriekreditbank and Sächsische Landesbank and the United Kingdom's Northern Rock (see Hellwig 2009). Thiemann (2012) discusses why supervisors let banks get away with these commitments.

10. See Brady et al. (2012).

11. The numbers are based on the 10-K form for 2011 (see note 7 above) that JPMorgan Chase filed with the SEC, particularly note 3 in the report (p. 189). Under the U.S. GAAP, the net derivative assets on the balance sheet are $92.5 billion. If JPMorgan Chase instead reports under IFRS, according to the International Swaps and Derivatives Association (ISDA) (2012), derivative receivables should be reported on a gross basis, with an asset balance of $1.884 trillion and a corresponding liability balance of $1.792 trillion. Comparable information is provided in the footnote on derivatives but is structured differently.

12. Information on GAAP is given in most accounting textbooks, for example, Horngren et al. (2012).

13. IFRS are prepared by the International Accounting Standards Board (IASB), a private organization. Subject to being approved by an official endorsement process, IFRS are mandatory for all corporations in the European Union that are listed on a public stock exchange. The main difference in the U.S. standards is the way they handle derivatives. See ISDA (2012) and a statement from IASB and FASB on this issue, available at http://www.fasb.org/cs/ContentServer?site=FASB&c=FASBContent_C&pagename=FASB%2FFASBContent_C%2FNewsPage&cid=1176159547684, accessed October 6, 2012. David Reilly, in "Derivatives Tide Rises at Big Banks" (*Wall Street Journal,* November 8, 2011), suggests that investors pay attention to the gross number, not just the net, because "when assets are counted in the trillions of dollars, even a very small problem can quickly become a big one." On controversies regarding how to account for losses on loans, see also Floyd Norris, "Accounting Détente Delayed," *New York Times,* July 19, 2012.

14. These investments reflect the investment banking activities in which JPMorgan Chase, as a universal bank, is also engaging. Traditional investment banking involves financial services for corporations and investors as well as securities trading on a bank's own account, so-called proprietary trading. Investment banking services for corporations traditionally involve advice and marketing in connection with offerings of securities and with mergers and acquisitions. Investment banking services for investors traditionally

involve investment advice and portfolio management services. Trading on their own account arises naturally if the investment bank "underwrites" a public offering, that is, if it buys the entire lot of equity shares or bonds and resells them to the public. The development of derivatives has vastly expanded the scope of these activities.

15. ISDA (2012, 8–9) makes the same calculation using 2009 figures for the largest banks in Europe and the United States. The adjustment for netting in 2009 would have been $1.485 trillion for JPMorgan Chase, $600 billion for Citigroup, and $1.414 trillion for Bank of America. This means that the total assets of JPMorgan Chase in 2009 would have been $3.437 trillion under IFRS (instead of $2.032 under GAAP), those of Citi $2.389 trillion under IFRS (instead of $1.856 under GAAP), and those of Bank of America $3.557 trillion under IFRS (instead of $2.224 trillion under GAAP).

16. This means that if on net JPMorgan Chase has a position where it owes Bank X $1 million worth of derivatives and the same Bank X owes JPMorgan Chase $1.5 million worth of derivatives, the balance sheet with netting would have a debt of only $0.5 million that Bank X owes JPMorgan Chase. This is based on netting agreements drafted by ISDA that supposedly would allow the positions to be netted in the event that one of the counterparties were to default and go into bankruptcy. The legal validity of the agreement has not been tested when the parties are under different legal regimes. If a bank is considered "too big to fail," scenarios in which it defaults through bankruptcy are actually irrelevant.

17. The argument usually given for the U.S. approach is that, according to the netting agreements signed by the trading partners, only the net position matters in bankruptcy. This argument overlooks the possibility that concerns of derivatives counterparties about a possible failure of the bank could be destabilizing *before* bankruptcy or resolution is actually triggered. For example, the counterparties of a distressed bank may try to transfer their exposures to others if they become concerned about the bank's failure. The FCIC (2011, 287–288) describes the behavior of Bear Stearns counterparties. For example, "On Wednesday, March 12, the SEC noted that Bear paid another $1.1 billion for margin calls from 142 nervous derivatives counterparties" (288). And later, "Bear experienced runs by repo lenders, hedge fund customers, and derivatives counterparties" (291). A run on derivatives also played a role preceding the Lehman failure (343). See also Bryan Burrough, "Bringing Down Bear Stearns," *Vanity Fair,* August 1, 2008.

18. Loans are 31 percent of the assets of JPMorgan Chase under GAAP but about 17 percent under IFRS. Interestingly, when IFRS is used, equity, deposits, long-term debt, and other debt as fractions of the bank's total assets are remarkably similar for JPMorgan Chase and for the Swiss bank UBS. However, the absolute size of JPMorgan Chase is about three times that of UBS as measured by assets. For UBS, equity amounts to 6.1 percent of total assets, as calculated under IFRS. Loans represent 28.2 percent of the bank's total investments. For more information, see UBS (2011). ISDA (2012, 8) provides the reported derivatives and total assets of five European banks in 2009. For a discussion of trends in bank activities, see Haldane et al. (2010) and Turner (2010, 2012).

19. As we discuss in Chapters 8–12, there are reasons to believe that the relative displacement of bank lending by other activities is due to distorted incentives of bankers and banks, which are caused by a combination of flawed compensation structures and gover-

nance problems, government guarantees and subsidies, regulations, and distortionary effects of debt overhang.

20. An equity ratio based on market value could be calculated by dividing the market value of the bank's equity (so-called market capitalization) by the sum of its liabilities and the market value of the equity. Berk and DeMarzo (2011, 496) provide equity ratios calculated similarly for different industries. On accounting issues and banking regulation, see Haldane (2011c).

21. Reported balance sheets represent a mix of valuations done at historical values and adjusted under certain conventions, as well as market or "fair" values, which are taken from active markets. For banks, many trading assets are valued by market value. However, assets that do not trade frequently are often "marked to model," which gives banks significant latitude to use mathematical models and historical data to place a value on their assets. See Beattie et al. (1995), Beaver and Engel (1996), and note 26 in Chapter 5. Obviously, unrecognized losses can hide insolvencies. As already discussed in Chapters 3 and 4, bank insolvencies are dangerous and damaging. We return to the distinction between book and market values in Chapter 7 and discuss insolvencies and loss recognition again in Chapter 11. Smith (2010, 190) states, "There are plenty of ways to goose the numbers," discussing some of the same issues we raise here. Mayo (2011), a bank analyst, also mentions significant delays in recognizing losses and estimates (3091–3092) that, as of mid-2011, the banks had not recognized about $300 billion in their financial disclosures. For healthy nonfinancial companies, one should note, market values are often significantly higher than book values. For example, on June 30, 2012, Apple reported a book value of its equity of about $112 billion, while at the same time the market value of its equity was about $547 billion. For Wal-Mart, on July 31, 2012, the book value of its equity was $70 billion, while the market value was about $253 billion.

22. According to Onaran (2011), these two banks may well be insolvent even though the books do not show it. For the largest banks that benefit from implicit guarantees, there may be a positive market value of their shares on the basis of the assumption that the banks will eventually recover, with government and central bank support, as the economy recovers. Requirements to increase equity can provide a test of solvency. If a bank cannot raise equity at any price, this is a clear signal that it might be insolvent. We return to this issue in Chapter 11.

23. For example, see "Fitch Affirms Ratings for the Bear Stearns Companies Inc.; Outlook Stable," Business Wire, August 25, 2006. Lehman Brothers made itself appear stronger than it was by using accounting tricks that masked its true indebtedness. See Michael J. de la Merced and Julia Werdigier, "The Origins of Lehman's 'Repo 105,'" New York Times, March 12, 2010, and Valukas (2010).

24. The Dodd-Frank Act (Section 610) extended existing counterparty and affiliate credit limits to include more types of positions and certain other liabilities. On industry lobbying on this issue, see Lauren Tara LaCapra, "Banks Fight Fed's Push to Make Them Less Entwined," Reuters, June 25, 2012. The proposed rules known as the single-counterparty credit limit proposal would force financial institutions with at least $500 billion of assets to limit their exposure to one another to 10 percent of their capital. According to the

article, the industry "is spooked by these rules" because they would show just how exposed to each other these institutions are. Goldman Sachs is said to estimate that "U.S. banking titans are up to 18 times more exposed to one another under the proposed rule's methodology than banks consider themselves to be now." The piece includes many standard threats that the rules will have "unintended consequences." Our comment letter to the Federal Reserve on this matter, Admati et al. (2012b, 7), suggests that the information contained in banks' comment letters, including the one by The Clearing House, only point to their dangerously large exposures. See also David Clarke, "CEOs of Big U.S. Banks Bend Fed's Ear," Reuters, May 2, 2012, describing meetings of major bank CEOs lobbying on this matter. Mexico tried to help banks' effort as well (see Victoria McGrane, "Mexico Balks at Fed Proposal," *Wall Street Journal,* May 2, 2012).

25. In the United States, from 1927 to 1994 the McFadden Act prohibited banks from having branches in more than one state. For more information on the McFadden Act, see Markham (2002). In Europe, between the 1930s and the 1970s many countries regulated what banks invested in, and banks were often prohibited from moving funds abroad. For Europe, see Baltensperger and Dermine (1987) and Dermine (1990). We discuss the politics around this kind of regulation in Chapter 12.

26. For a thorough discussion of the S&L crisis in Texas, which was particularly strong, see Kane (1989). On Sweden, see Englund (1990, 1999).

27. This was a main purpose of the McFadden Act of 1927 and of many state regulations, such as rules requiring banks to do all their business under the same roof. Concentration in U.S. banking has increased dramatically since these regulations have been lifted, in particular the prohibition on interstate banking. See Johnson and Kwak (2010).

28. Examples are the 1995 merger of Crédit Communal de Belgique and Crédit Local de France to form Dexia and the 2000 merger of Banque Nationale de Paris and Compagnie Financière de Paris et des Pays-Bas (Banque Paribas) to form BNP Paribas. Another example of such a merger is that between the Swiss Bank Corporation and UBS in 1997. Such mergers are often justified by saying that globalization is creating larger markets, and larger markets need larger "players." The risks that these larger institutions create for their home countries are overlooked in such arguments. See Johnson and Kwak (2010), Barth et al. (2012), and Thomas (2012).

29. Of the largest companies in the world, in 2011 the top seventy-nine corporations in the world by asset size were all banks. The largest nonfinancial corporation, Royal Dutch Shell, ranked eightieth, with "only" $340 billion in assets. (See "The World's Biggest Companies," *Forbes,* April 12, 2012.) Of course these rankings are subject to the caveat that accounting rules that differ, as we discussed earlier. Moreover, by market value measures Apple was larger than Royal Dutch Shell at the end of 2011.

30. Hu (2012) addresses the challenge of disclosure and comprehension for the large institutions, referring to them as "too big to depict." Boot (2011) also discusses the complexity of large banks and suggests restructuring them so as to simplify their structure. Bair (2012, 328–331) suggests that the FDIC and the Federal Reserve use their authority to mandate that large institutions restructure if they are unable to show that going through bankruptcy would not be disruptive and harmful to the economy.

31. Davies and Tracey (2012), for example, show that, with a correction to remove the value of the subsidies associated with being too big to fail, the largest banks are no more efficient, and are possibly less so, than smaller banks. Allison (2011), a long-time industry veteran, argues that the business model and recent practices of megabanks are fundamentally flawed. He states (433) that "the presumption that the megabanks have more staying power is little questioned, but it is wrong." (However, he concedes that the banks are unlikely to break up on their own and proposes regulation to achieve this.) We discuss governance issues in Chapter 8, further discuss subsidies and excessive growth in Chapter 9, and consider distorted incentives to borrow excessively using short-term debt in Chapter 10.

32. See, for example, Berk and DeMarzo (2011, 893).

33. Johnson and Kwak (2010) call for breaking up the large banks partly to reduce their political power. Hoenig and Morris (2011) and Allison (2011) make specific proposals as to how this might be done. A recent attempt to limit the size of the largest banks was the 2010 introduction by Senators Sherrod Brown and Ted Kaufman in 2010 of the SAFE (Safe, Accountable, Fair, and Efficient) banking act, which sought to restrict the nondeposit liabilities of any one bank relative to GDP, as well as to the total size of the banking industry. On the failure of this attempt, see Ryan Grim and Shahein Nasiripour, "Senate Votes for Wall Street; Megabanks to Remain Behemoths," *Huffington Post,* June 17, 2010. Senator Sherrod Brown introduced the SAFE banking act of 2012 (and a similar act was introduced by Congressmen Brad Miller and Keith Ellison). These proposals would also constrain banks' leverage. See http://www.brown.senate.gov/newsroom/press/release/brown-introduces-bill-to-end-too-big-to-fail-policies-prevent-mega-banks-from-putting-our-economy-at-risk, accessed October 12, 2012. As our discussion of the JPMorgan Chase balance sheet suggests, accounting conventions can make a difference in the actual implementation of such laws because they can change how liabilities are measured.

34. The Volcker Rule was included in the Dodd-Frank Act in modified form. The rule has become mired in complexity because the exemptions that banks lobbied to include in the law make it very difficult to distinguish allowable trades, such as those defined as related to hedging or market making, from trades that are not allowed under the regulation. As discussed earlier, there have been much recent debate and lobbying over the implementation of the Volcker Rule. For example, see "Volcker Author: Ban Banks' Physical Prop Trades," Reuters, July 31, 2012, the Independent Commission on Banking (ICB 2011) in the United Kingdom, and the October 2012 report of the Liikanen Commission is available at http://ec.europa.eu/internal_market/bank/docs/high-level_expert_group/report_en.pdf, accessed October 15, 2012.

35. For some assessments, see Martin Wolf, "Liikanen Is at Least a Step Forward for EU Banks," *Financial Times,* October 4, 2012; Helia Ebrahimi, "Paul Volcker: Ring-Fencing Banks Is Not Enough," *The Telegraph,* September 23, 2012; and Admati and Hellwig (2011a). Turner (2010, 60) similarly states that "Volcker Rules are in principle desirable, but they are not a sufficient response."

36. Other examples are Dexia and Hypo Real Estate. Neither bank had much by way of deposits, yet these banks were bailed out, Dexia because it was important in lending to local governments in Belgium and France, Hypo Real Estate because it was an important

issuer of covered bonds and the German government feared a loss of confidence in covered bonds. There were also concerns that other banks as lenders might be adversely affected by the failures of these institutions.

37. The Dodd-Frank Act recognizes that nonbanks and other institutions can be systemically important. For example, Section 165 places all institutions with total assets of at least $50 billion in this category and allows the new Financial Stability Oversight Council (FSOC) to place nonbank financial companies under heightened supervision under certain conditions. However, the designation remains controversial. FSOC declared eight institutions "financial utilities" under Title Eight of the Dodd-Frank Act. See Ian Katz, "FSOC Designates Eight Financial Market Utilities," Bloomberg, July 12, 2012. The Basel Committee has developed principles for identifying and regulating globally and nationally systemically important banks (see BCBS 2011b, 2011c, 2012a). The Basel Committee has also identified twenty-seven globally systemically important banks to which the stricter regulation should apply. See Jim Brunsden, "Basel to Disclose Banks Facing Surcharges," Bloomberg, November 3, 2011.

38. At the time, this experience motivated proposals for what is called *full reserve banking* or *narrow banking*. Under such a regime, deposit-taking institutions would be restricted to investing only in highly liquid and safe assets, that is, in cash, deposits with the central bank, and possibly short-term government debt. See, for example, Douglas et al. (1939) or Friedman (1960). Full reserve banking is also part of Kotlikoff's (2010) reform proposals. As we explain in Chapter 10, full reserve banking would provide for effective protection of depositors without any need for a government bailout, but it would not eliminate the problem that non-deposit-taking institutions might also be too important to fail. Kay (2010) also proposes "narrow banking," which drastically restricts the activities of deposit-taking institutions to remove credit risk. Turner (2010, 60) argues, as we do, that such an insulation of deposits and payments from risks of other activities is unlikely to solve the problem of financial instability because the rest of the system can become unstable and dangerous, in developments similar to those we have witnessed, unless it is strictly regulated.

39. Interestingly, in Switzerland, in the early 1990s a crisis rooted in losses from lending was actually mitigated by the fact that the three big banks had large profits from investment banking which balanced their losses from real estate and business lending, and also enabled them to acquire many local and regional banks that would have likely failed otherwise. On the Swiss crisis of the early 1990s, see Staub (1998). Some of the profits from investment banking, however, involved significant risk taking in derivatives, which later caused the downfall of the old UBS; see Schütz (1998).

40. This is not due just to the public nature of the Landesbanken and the local savings banks. The cooperative banks in Germany have a similar structure and had similar experiences. What is true is that, as indicated by very low margins and high risks, Germany has excess capacities in both wholesale banking and investment banking, which is why all banks, public and private, that used to rely on this business have run into problems. See Expertenrat (2011) and Chapter 11.

41. Cash pays no interest at all. In the United States, since October 2008 required reserves in accounts with the Federal Reserve Bank have earned interest at a rate of 0.25

percent per year, which is roughly comparable to the rates that banks pay each other in the money market. Before 2008 in the United States, and still today in many other countries, the interest earned on required reserves was zero. Minimum reserve requirements effectively forced banks to provide interest-free loans to the central bank. Because the profits of the central bank are distributed to the government, the government budget was the main beneficiary. This explains why minimum reserve requirements have traditionally been high in countries that have had difficulties levying taxes. In the United States today, they are at 10 percent of deposits. This compares to 1 percent in the Eurozone (where minimum reserves pay interest at the same rate that the European Central Bank uses when refinancing banks), 20 percent in Brazil, and 30 percent in Lebanon. In southern Europe in the 1970s and 1980s, they stood at around 20 percent and higher. See the essays on Italy, Spain, and Portugal in Dermine (1990). We discuss liquidity in Chapter 10 and the politics of reserve requirements in Chapter 12.

42. In addition to the liquidity coverage ratio, Basel III also proposes to introduce a so-called net stable funding ratio (NSFR), putting limits on the extent to which banks use short-term funding for long-term investments. This regulation is intended to limit liquidity risks and solvency risks from maturity transformation, which we discussed in Chapter 4. Much remains to be worked out, however, and the NSFR regulation will not come into effect before 2019, if at all.

43. It is not clear that a 10 percent reserve requirement really eliminates a bank's liquidity risk. If a depositor withdraws $1,000, that frees just $100 of the required reserves. The remaining $900 must come from the bank's "free reserves," the amount of its overall reserves in excess of required reserves, or the bank must violate the reserve requirement and pay a penalty. For the 1 percent reserve requirement of the Eurozone, doubts must be even greater. The regulation of liquidity coverage ratios aims at very high percentages for foreseeable cash needs.

44. For example, are long-term government bonds that are denominated in the country's currency sufficiently "liquid"? Or does the experience with Greek sovereign debt provide a warning? What about securities such as covered bonds that are backed by specific eligible assets, such as mortgages? Such bonds might be traded in open markets, but these markets can suddenly freeze when there are concerns about default. For U.S. mortgage-backed securities, such a freeze occurred from one day to the next on August 7–8, 2007, when uncertainty about these securities made investors unwilling to trade them. See, for example, FCIC (2011, 471).

45. A disastrous example of this problem occurred during the German crisis in 1931. The major banks held bills of exchange as their major reserve of liquid assets, assuming that if they needed cash they could always present these bills of exchange to the Reichsbank, the German central bank, as collateral for borrowing. This had already been the practice under the Prussian Bank, the predecessor of the Reichsbank, in the middle of the nineteenth century. Because of the assurance that the central bank would always provide them liquidity, German banks were much more involved in long-term industry finance than were their U.K. counterparts (see Tilly 1989). In July 1931, however, when there was a run on the banks, the Reichsbank could not provide the banks with cash. Because there was also a

run on the currency, the Reichsbank had insufficient reserves of foreign currencies and gold, which by law it needed to back the money it created; see Ferguson and Temin (2003, 2004) and Schnabel (2004, 2009). The German banking system collapsed, and this greatly exacerbated the economic depression.

46. In the absence of deposit insurance, there have been critical bank runs quite recently. Examples are the runs on banks in Argentina in 2001 and on Northern Rock in the United Kingdom in 2007. Despite FDIC insurance, in the United States there was a run on Washington Mutual, a bank that collapsed in September 2008. Depositors withdrew $16.7 billion over nine days (Jim Zarolli, "Washington Mutual Collapses," All Things Considered, NPR, September 26, 2008). The bank was closed on September 25, 2008, and was placed under FDIC receivership.

47. See Michael J. de la Merced et al., "As Goldman and Morgan Shift, a Wall Street Era Ends," *New York Times*, September 21, 2008.

48. Deposit insurance was also expanded to cover individual deposits up to $250,000 in any one bank account. Moreover, under a two-year temporary liquidity guarantee program, also called the Transaction Account Guarantee Program, FDIC insurance was available for all non-interest-bearing deposits. This program is set to expire at the end of 2012, but banks are lobbying to extend it. See Jed Horowitz, "Banks Urge Congress to Extend Crisis-Era Deposit Insurance," Reuters, July 30, 2012. Government guarantees are discussed in Chapter 9.

49. See Gorton (2010). Mehrling (2010) instead proposes that the central bank intervene through markets, standing ready to buy assets from banks if no other buyers can be found. We discuss these suggestions in Chapter 10 and return to the narrative that the crisis was due only to liquidity problems in Chapter 13.

50. Savings institutions invested in risky commercial real estate developments and in so-called "junk bonds," corporate bonds that pay high interest and have a high risk of default. On the recklessness of S&Ls, see White (1991, 2004) and Curry and Shibut (2000).

51. Kaserer (2010) estimates the losses at €34–52 billion. Information that has become available since then suggests that the losses will actually be much greater than even the larger of these two numbers. Onaran (2011) argues that many banks in Europe and the United States, including Landesbanken, Citigroup, and Bank of America, have become de facto insolvent. We return to this discussion in Chapter 11.

52. Strictly speaking, this statement is true only for the simplest form of capital regulation, which imposes a lower limit for the share of assets funded by equity. The more complex versions that have been developed by the Basel Committee on Banking Supervision, the body that prepares the international agreements on banking regulation, make the amount of equity that a bank must have depend on the mix of risky and less risky assets that it holds, as well as the total amount. The details of capital regulation, including the dependence of capital requirements on asset risks, are discussed in Chapter 11.

53. Basel II, concluded in 2004, did not come into force until 2008. However, a precursor to Basel II, an amendment extending equity regulation under Basel I to "market risks"—that is, the risks that market prices of assets might change—was already concluded in 1996 and played a major role in determining banks' behavior before the crisis. Goodhart (2011) provides an extensive discussion of the process through 1997, covering Basel I and

the start of Basel II. Tarullo (2008) discusses Basel II. See also Roubini and Mihm (2010, 203–209).

54. Basel II has actually never been implemented in the United States for banks insured by the FDIC. Sheila Bair, chair of the FDIC, objected to the leeway the regulation gave to banks to economize on equity (see Joe Nocera, "Sheila Bair's Bank Shot," *New York Times*, July 24, 2011, and Bair 2012, Chapter 3). We discuss Basel II and III in detail in Chapter 11.

55. See Hellwig (2009), Bair (2012), and the introductory chapter of FCIC (2011), where too little capital is mentioned as a key factor. See note 17 in Chapter 1 for quotes from bankers agreeing with this assessment.

56. See UBS (2008) for the treatment of subprime-mortgage-related securities. The bank's total losses from such securities have been given as more than $50 billion, more than the bank's equity of less than 40 billion Swiss francs. See Susanne Craig, Ben Protess, and Mathew Saltmarsh, "UBS Faces Questions on Oversight after a Trader Lost $2 Billion," *New York Times*, September 14, 2011, as well as "Chronology: UBS in Turmoil," http://www .drs.ch/www/de/drs/nachrichten/wirtschaft/ubs-vom-musterschueler-zum-problemfall/ 72270.218256.chronologie-die-ubs-in-turbulenzen.html, accessed October 14, 2012.

57. See, for example, "Basel III Implementation Delay Looms," *Wall Street Journal*, August 22, 2012, describing delays in Europe, China, and elsewhere. "Europe's Big Bang for Bank Rules Set to Sputter" (Reuters, August 24, 2012) quotes the chair of the EU committee involved in negotiating the banking regulation as saying, "It is likely that dates will be revised" and an accounting consultant as stating, "Banks have a good idea of what might be required but it's a bit of a range at the moment." In Chapter 11 we discuss how banks and the system can be strengthened fairly quickly given the authority that regulators already have under existing rules.

58. Interview, *Süddeutsche Zeitung*, November 20, 2009.

59. For loan rates the forecast was an increase of more than 1 percentage point, for real growth rates a reduction of roughly 0.6 percentage point.

60. Speech by Jamie Dimon, JPMorgan Chase CEO, before Chamber of Commerce, reported by Tom Braithwaite, "Dimon Warns of 'Nail in the Coffin,'" *Financial Times*, March 31, 2011.

61. The first statement is attributed to Steven Bartlett, chair of the Financial Services Roundtable, quoted by Floyd Norris in "A Baby Step toward Rules on Bank Risk," *New York Times*, September 17, 2010. The second is from "A Piece-by-Piece Guide to New Financial Overhaul Law," Associated Press, July 21, 2010. Wayne A. Abernathy of the American Bankers Association wrote in *American Banker* ("Shrinking Banks Will Drag Down the Economy," August 27, 2012), "When used efficiently, a dollar of capital on reserve allows a bank today to put ten dollars to work as expanded economic activity. The new Basel rules would demand that banks maintain more dollars on reserve for the same amount of business, or more capital for no new economic work." Both sentences, and other statements in Abernathy's piece, are false and misleading, implying that capital is the same as cash reserves and that Basel concerns reserve requirements. Alan Greenspan, former chairman of the Federal Reserve, is quoted by the *Financial Times* ("Alan Greenspan, Silently Fade Away, Please," July 27, 2011) as writing that "excess bank equity capital . . .

would constitute a buffer that is not otherwise available to finance productivity-enhancing capital investment." See, in response, Paul Krugman, "The Malevolent Ex-Maestro," *New York Times,* July 30, 2011, and a letter from 20 academics, "Greenspan Reasoning on 'Excess Capital' Is Misleading," *Financial Times,* August 2, 2011. Elsewhere, in fact, Greenspan (2010) has supported higher capital requirements, observing that had banks been funded with more equity prior to 2007, losses from mortgages might not have triggered such a global crisis and taxpayers would have been spared the cost of supporting the banks.

62. As of 2012, one would find small amounts of short-term or "current" liabilities on the balance sheet of Apple; those have to do with day-to-day operations and not with the funding of long-term investments.

63. Capital regulation allows for different so-called tiers of capital. Securities other than common equity, such as preferred equity and even long-term debt, can also be considered "regulatory capital." We discuss this issue in more detail in Chapter 11.

64. Academic Advisory Committee (2010).

SEVEN   *Is Equity Expensive?*

1. See Miller (1995, 483). The incident took place in a conference Mr. Miller had attended fifteen years earlier in Williamsburg, Virginia. Miller's account continues as follows: "At that point, there was a rumbling noise from the audience of bankers, many of whom were selling for even less than 50 percent of book value. And when I looked up I could see through the window a platoon of soldiers in Revolutionary War costumes and muskets marching on the Village Green toward the Town Hall. My God, I thought, they're sending for the firing squad! They did not actually shoot me, needless to say, but they did not let me say anything else either. I never could seem to catch the moderator's eye." Miller discusses in his article some of the issues we cover in this chapter and in Chapter 9.

2. As discussed in Chapter 6, many statements suggesting that capital is costly falsely treat capital as if it were an asset, a kind of idle reserve that is costly because it does not earn interest. When participants in the discussion recognize that, in the context of banking regulation, the word *capital* refers to equity rather than reserves, they still suggest that it is expensive, usually without providing much of an explanation. Terms such as *capital charges* or *capital surcharges* are used to suggest costs. For example, Barry Zubrow, chief risk officer of JPMorgan Chase, has said (2011, 3 and 9) that a "potential surcharge on Globally Systemically Important Financial Institutions (G-SIFIs) . . . creates costs that risk exceeding the diminishing benefits of higher capital requirements above Basel III minimum." We will consider the specifics of this argument in the next chapter.

3. This argument underlies the preparatory studies for Basel III of the Basel Committee on Banking Supervision, for example, the estimates of the impact of increased capital requirements on banks' funding costs and lending rates (BCBS 2010a). We discuss Basel III in Chapter 11.

4. As mentioned in Chapter 4, Weinstein and Yafeh (1998) show that in pre-1990 Japan, the monopoly power of banks was a major factor determining the borrowing costs of Japanese firms.

5. This would be more advantageous to the borrower and disadvantageous to the banks, so the banks might try to engage in price fixing. In the United States, price fixing was outlawed by the Sherman Act of 1890, in the European Union by the antitrust chapter of the Treaty on the Functioning of the European Union (Art. 101). The so-called LIBOR scandal, which we discuss in Chapter 13, may involve some elements of price fixing by traders active in interbank borrowing and lending in London, as well as fraudulent reporting. Such price fixing violates antitrust law.

6. On sovereign debt, see the fundamental work of Reinhart and Rogoff (2009). If the debt is denominated in units over which the government has no control, such as gold or a foreign currency, there is a default risk even for government debt. The relevance of this risk is made all too clear by the data that Reinhart and Rogoff present. The government debt crises in the euro area provide a vivid example. There the debt is denominated in euros. The euro is the currency of the member states of the euro area, but this currency is issued ("printed") by the European Central Bank, a supranational institution that is independent of national governments. If the government can pay its debt by means of money creation, there is no risk of default, but the money creation is likely to cause inflation that will make the money itself lose value in real terms. The risk of inflation might lead investors to prefer real estate or stocks. It will not, however, affect the choice between a government bond and a home mortgage, which are both equally affected by the decline in the value of money. In countries where government finance through money creation and inflation are prevalent, there may arise a demand for so-called indexed debt, that is, debt whose nominal value is adjusted over time so as to keep the real value the same relative to some bundle of goods. Such debt was common in Brazil in the 1970s and is still common in Israel. If inflation is too high, borrowing in the national currency may actually become impossible. We discuss these issues further in Chapter 10.

7. According to http://markets.ft.com/RESEARCH/Markets/Government-Bond-Spreads (accessed October 19, 2012), interest rates for ten-year bonds on October 19, 2012 were 5.37 percent for Spain and 1.60 percent for Germany.

8. Acharya and Steffen (2012) present evidence that this is precisely what European banks are doing, especially weak banks from Southern European countries.

9. Such opportunities might exist temporarily, but investors trying to make use of them would make them disappear by changing the prices at which assets trade. We discuss this issue further in Chapter 8.

10. See "Greece Auction to Settle $3.2 Billion of Credit Default Swaps," Bloomberg, March 18, 2012.

11. This is probably not the only reason for the high interest on credit card debt. The very high rate that we observe probably also involves elements of market power on the side of credit card companies and helplessness on the side of borrowers who are unable to manage their personal finances. See also Chapter 4, note 15.

12. If we were to take account of the possible inefficiencies in the foreclosure process, which might leave the lender with even less than $255,000, the interest rate would have to be even higher. In subprime mortgage lending before the financial crisis, the principles discussed here were often violated—for example, when borrowers got low-interest mort-

gages without making any down payment at all, that is, with zero initial equity. As discussed in Chapter 4, the originating mortgage banks were careless in their assessment of borrowers' creditworthiness and default risk because they expected to sell the mortgages to others for securitization and therefore had no "skin in the game." For references, see note 43 in Chapter 4. We discuss the impact of the cost of default on funding costs in Chapter 9.

13. Top management is also hurt by a price decline if this is taken as a signal of incompetence, leading the corporate board to look for a new management. If management incentives are not linked to the share price, shareholders may become victims of poor corporate governance as the company first raises money from them and then treats them badly. Such behavior has actually been quite prevalent in the past, and in some countries it still is. Thus, in the early 1900s the prominent German banker Carl Fürstenberg coined the much-quoted saying "Shareholders are stupid and impertinent! Stupid because they give their money to somebody else without having any control over what he does with it— impertinent because they ask for dividends to reward their stupidity!" Such governance problems may prevent equity markets from working properly to provide funding for corporations. For a discussion of these issues, see Shleifer and Vishny (1997). We discuss corporate governance issues further in Chapter 8.

14. The same logic applies to bond prices when interest rates change. For example, suppose the market, or "required," interest rate for one-year riskless loans was 4 percent. This means that a bond that promises to pay $100 in a year's time would have a price of about $96.15 (so at 4 percent interest it would pay $100 a year later). If the market rate were higher, say 5 percent, the bond that would pay $100 in one year would have a lower price because, at the price of $96.15, it would not provide the return of 5 percent that investors now require, in the current market with a higher interest rate; the lower price will be about $95.24, so the promise of $100 in one year would pay 5 percent interest. In the case of stock, the notion of required return refers not to the market rate of interest but to an average or expected return that investors require given the risk of the stock (and in view of the riskless rate of interest in the market).

15. The average for large companies' stocks was 11.8 percent and for small capitalization stocks 15.2 percent. These numbers are taken from the *Ibbotson Valuation Yearbook*, 2012, published by Morningstar. The returns are not adjusted for inflation. On corrections for changes in prices, see, for example, "Hedging Inflation," *Forbes*, March 5, 2012, which states that the return on the stock index is 7 percent higher than the increase in the consumer price index.

16. See "Bank of America in $8.5 Billion Settlement," *CNNMoney*, CNN, June 29, 2011. This payment reduced the bank's 2011 earnings. However, we are interested not in the way the loss is reflected in the banks' accounting treatments but in the actual loss of value of shareholders' claims. This will be more immediately reflected in the stock price or the market value of the bank. The impact on the market value will depend on what information investors glean from this settlement for the future earnings of Bank of America. Other banks might be affected if investors learn something about the likelihood and magnitude of such settlements for other banks.

17. By *assets* we mean the so-called operating assets of the company. If the funding mix itself generates tax savings or additional charges, or if it has other indirect effects on the entire balance sheet, the assets will include these effects. We discuss such situations in Chapter 9. This issue is covered in most textbooks on corporate finance. See, for example, Berk and DeMarzo (2011, Chapters 23–25).

18. The original result is in Modigliani and Miller (1958). The material covered in this chapter and in later chapters (including another Modigliani and Miller result that concerns dividends) is covered in every textbook on modern corporate finance (see, e.g., Berk and DeMarzo 2011, Part V).

19. See Berra (1998).

20. For an amusing parable that uses as an analogy a debate on whether the volume formula actually applies to all cylinders, see Pfleiderer (2010). See also David Miles, "Don't Dismiss Modigliani-Miller Logic on Bank Funding," *Financial Times*, November 30, 2010, and Berk and DeMarzo (2011, 456, 470). This column generated some letters essentially saying, "This is just theory," with responses from Miles and the two of us. (David Miles, in "Don't Dismiss Modigliani-Miller Logic on Bank Funding," *Financial Times*, November 30, 2010, states that "the logic of M-M cannot be dismissed so easily. And it also matters hugely why M-M might not exactly hold." Anat Admati, in "Highly Leveraged Lenders Inflict Great Suffering on Society," *Financial Times*, December 2, 2010, concludes that letter writers "must do more than dismiss arguments as theoretical and raise vague and unsubstantiated threats. . . . They must explain precisely what forces should lead society away from imposing high equity requirements on banks and how such an effect comes about." Martin Hellwig, in "Recent Practice Proves Theory That Banks Need to Improve Equity," *Financial Times*, December 2, 2010, says that "the practice of banking in the past few years has certainly taught us many lessons. One of them is that banks' economising on equity is a source of fragility of the financial system and puts all of us at risk. This side of banking practice is overlooked by [the] correspondents.") See Anat Admati, "What Jamie Dimon Won't Tell You," *Huffington Post*, December 5, 2010. (Correction: at the end of this piece, Admati implies that Wal-Mart is larger than JPMorgan Chase. In truth, even by the U.S. accounting rules, JPMorgan Chase is about ten times larger than Wal-Mart.) See also Jenkins (2012b), titled "A Debate Framed by Fallacies."

21. The observation that deposits are special may suggest that we should refrain from regulations that would induce banks to reduce their deposits, but even here the contribution of equity to greater bank safety must not be neglected. With the same amount of deposits and *more* equity, a bank would be in a position to lend more or to engage in other kinds of profitable investments. In this case, the same argument that was given in this chapter shows that the required ROE would be lower because the bank has more equity and the bank would be able to absorb more losses without becoming insolvent.

22. The fallacy in thinking of the required return as constant and independent of the funding mix or in saying that M&M does not apply to banks has been pointed out by many over the past thirty years at least. Here is a partial list of references: King (1990), Schaefer (1990), Miller (1995), Harrison (2004), Brealey (2006), Kashyap et al. (2010), Mehran and Thakor (2010), and Miles et al. (2011).

23. Kashyap et al. (2010), Miles et al. (2011), and Tsatsaronis and Yang (2012) present empirical evidence that banks' average ROE increases with their leverage.

24. The irrelevance of book values can easily be seen by considering nonfinancial companies. For most healthy companies, stock prices or market values are significantly higher than book values reported on balance sheets. For example, on July 31, 2012, Wal-Mart reported a total of about $70 billion in shareholder equity, which translates to a book value of about $21 per share. At the same time, Wal-Mart's stock price was about $75 per share, significantly higher than the book value. According to the banker's logic, it is "cheap" for Wal-Mart to fund investments with equity because its equity is priced so highly in the market. But should this fact matter when Wal-Mart tries to decide whether to make a particular investment? Whatever its book value, Wal-Mart can make good investments or bad investments, and its shareholders will want Wal-Mart's managers to make good investments that will further increase the value of their shares. If Wal-Mart wastes money on a bad acquisition, Wal-Mart's shareholders will not be happy. By contrast, if Wal-Mart makes profitable investments with retained earnings or other funding, its shareholders will be happy. In neither case does it matter to shareholders, or to the managers, that the book value is different from the market value. Our argument does not prejudge whether valuations based on stock market prices are "right." The key point of the discussion is that book values are not relevant to investment decisions. Decisions must be made in the context of all the relevant information at the time that they are made.

25. Bankers might suggest that they have better information about the quality of the bank's assets and the likelihood that the loans might not be paid. If this is true, one wonders why they are unable to communicate this information to investors in a credible way so as to increase the market price of their shares. Most likely, investors are suspicious because, more often than not, book values are inflated due to the unwillingness of bankers to acknowledge losses. For example, there are reasons to suspect that banks' reluctance to proceed with foreclosures or with mortgage restructuring may be affected by the fact that such transactions would force the banks to recognize losses that they could otherwise pretend do not exist. Bankers in the United States have been fighting against local authorities seeking to use eminent domain laws to renegotiate mortgages when they take over properties in the public interest. Many believe that the main motivation for banks is the fact that such action would force them to recognize losses that they are currently not acknowledging. The losses would be particularly severe on second mortgages, which will be repaid only after the first mortgages are paid. See, for example, Rep. Brad Miller, "No Wonder Eminent Domain Mortgage Seizures Scare Wall Street," *American Banker,* July 12, 2012. On the reluctance of banks, sometimes with the collaboration of authorities, to recognize true losses, see also ASC (2012) and BIS (2012). We return to this issue in Chapter 11.

26. Because banks are heavily indebted, any investments they make affect not just their shareholders but also their creditors. This can give rise to a debt overhang effect, which might make shareholders hold back from making investments. The debt overhang effect was introduced in Chapter 3; it is due to the conflicts of interest between borrowers and creditors and creates inefficiencies and possible harm to others. We discuss this issue further in Chapters 9 and 11.

EIGHT   *Paid to Gamble*

1. See Patrick Jenkins and Brooke Masters, "Higher Capital Ratios Talk Cuts Banks' Appeal," *Financial Times*, March 27, 2011. In this piece Jenkins and Masters report that "according to calculations by analysts, banks' current market valuations assume that return on equity—ROE, the traditional measure of bank profitability—will fall to an average of about 11 per cent, way down on the 20 per cent-plus that the best banks racked up in the boom years of the last decade." A hedge fund manager is quoted as saying, "If I can get a higher ROE investing in an utterly safe regulated utility, why on earth would I invest in a bank?" Barry Zubrow, chief risk officer for JPMorgan, stated in testimony that a capital surcharge for global systemically important financial institutions would "diminish investor appetite for large bank equity, which will require large banks to abandon more capital-intensive businesses, increase prices to earn a sufficient return on equity, or push banks to reduce the size of their balance sheets. Any of these options will have impacts on the U.S. economy." The implication is that a capital requirement will make banks less profitable because it will reduce their ROE. See Zubrow (2011).

2. Ackermann (2010, 6). See also statements in the previous note quoted by Jenkins and Masters in "Higher Capital Ratios Talk Cuts Banks' Appeal."

3. Mishkin (2007, 233). Frederic Mishkin was executive vice president and director of research at the Federal Reserve Bank of New York in 1994–1997 and served as a member of the board of governors of the Federal Reserve from 2006 to 2008.

4. This is especially true if problems in their bank are large enough to affect the financial system and the overall economy or the public budget. In this case, shareholders will also be affected as taxpayers and as part of the public.

5. Whereas the magnification of risk can be seen while ignoring the interest expense, the cost of borrowing must be included in the discussion when considering how the funding mix of corporations affects their ROE and how it relates to the return on their assets. The fallacy associated with ROE that we discuss in this chapter is sometimes framed in terms of the impact of corporate borrowing on earnings per share, falsely implying that borrowing benefits shareholders by increasing their earnings per share. See Berk and DeMarzo (2011, 466–468).

6. If there is almost no chance that Kate will default, it is reasonable to assume that the actual rate she is charged will be the same whether she borrows $30,000 or $60,000. If there is a chance of default, Kate might be charged a slightly lower interest rate if she borrows less. If there is a likelihood of default, the rate she is charged may be higher than the average or expected returns that creditors would receive. As discussed in Chapter 7, the required rate would include some compensation for the risk to the lender of making the loan. These observations do not affect any of our conclusions.

7. If the house goes up by exactly 4 percent, the actual ROE will be the same no matter how much Kate borrows. A 4 percent increase in the value of the house means that it will sell for $312,000. With a mortgage of $270,000 and thus a mortgage debt of $280,800, Kate will be left with $31,200 if the house sells for $312,000, which is a 4 percent ROE. If she borrows $240,000 and puts in $60,000 in equity, she will be left with $62,400, again a 4 percent ROE.

8. Anyone who is able to borrow at a particular rate and invest the money in such a way that the debt will be paid for sure would want to borrow as much as possible at this rate and put as much money as possible into this wonderful opportunity. Equity would not even be required if the debt were always paid for sure out of the assets. If such opportunities were readily available, there would be an enormous demand to borrow money and not enough people willing to lend at the low rate offered. The borrowing rate would then have to increase. The observation that banks get away with paying very low interest, if any, on deposits does not refute this argument. For some deposits, the reward to depositors takes the form of ATM and payment services rather than interest; providing such services may generate a surplus because depositors value them more highly than they would value the interest, but even so there is a cost to the bank that must be taken into account. Before the deregulation of the early 1980s, when government regulation prevented banks from using interest rates to compete for deposits, banks actually used their service offers to attract deposits (see Klein 1974). However, as discussed in Chapter 4, when money market funds began to compete with banks and savings institutions by offering higher returns on investments that were almost as convenient as deposits, the latter lobbied for deregulation so they could also compete by offering higher interest. Thus, even for deposits for which depositors are rewarded by the provision of services, interest rates cannot be too far from those of other investment opportunities. On all other forms of debt that banks issue like other corporations, the returns they provide to investors must reflect market conditions, that is, the returns provided by other investments and the risk that investors attribute to such debt. In Chapters 9 and 10 we discuss the incentives and ability of banks and other financial institutions to borrow at favorable rates and under favorable terms. In Chapters 10 and 13 we further consider the impact of money market funds on banking.

9. This observation was made by Sheila Bair, former chair of the FDIC, in a *Washington Post* column on April 13, 2012 titled "Fix Income Inequality Now." Bair whimsically calls on banks to solve the inequality problem by giving everyone a $10 million loan for ten years at an interest rate of zero, which could generate $200,000 a year in interest for a decade. After pointing out that taking $10 million at zero interest and investing at 2 percent would give everyone $200,000 per year as a gift, like a "money machine," she says: "The more adventuresome can buy 10-year Greek debt at 21 percent, for an annual income of $2.1 million. Or if Greece is a little too risky for you, go with Portugal, at about 12 percent, or $1.2 million dollars a year." This recognizes that spreads from so-called carry trades typically come with some risk of loss. Acharya and Steffen (2012) provide evidence that European banks are actually engaging in this sort of gamble; the less equity they have, the more they do so. We discuss subsidized loans and guarantees given to banks in Chapter 9.

10. In an earlier episode, in 1990, when large commercial banks in the United States were on the brink of insolvency, the Federal Reserve lowered short-term interest rates to around 4 percent. With long-term interest rates around 8 percent, banks were then able to make large profits. Between 1990 and 1994, they used this money machine to rebuild their equity. However, when the Federal Reserve raised interest rates again in the spring of 1994, this increase came as quite a shock and created problems for many banks.

11. For example, if the borrowing rate is 4 percent and, on average, the bank is expected to earn a return of 6 percent on its investments, the average ROE will be 24 percent with 10 percent equity and only 14 percent with 20 percent equity relative to the total assets. The logic and intuition is the same as in the preceding section, where we analyzed the various scenarios for Kate. The fact that we are now talking about *average* returns rather than *actual* returns does not make a difference. Having more equity lowers the actual return on equity if the return on assets is larger than the rate paid to borrow, and it raises the actual return on equity if the return on assets is smaller. Intuitively, if the assets produce on average a higher return than the borrowing rate, the outcomes in which the actual ROE is relatively high have a larger weight in the calculation of the average ROE than the outcomes in which the actual ROE is relatively low. Because leverage increases the actual ROE on the upside, the average ROE becomes higher with more leverage (and lower with less leverage). See Berk and DeMarzo (2011, Chapter 14).

12. Even after the turmoil created by the Lehman Brothers bankruptcy, Ackermann still said that "a return on equity of 25% is achievable for the bank, and more than 20% is quite realistic" (William Launder, "Deutsche Bank CEO: 25% RoE Is Achievable for Bank," Dow Jones Newswires, February 5, 2009). When actual returns were lower, Ackermann opined that they would come back soon ("Deutsche Bank CEO: Return to 25% ROE Target in 3 Years," Dow Jones Newswires, December 20, 2010). In March 2011, Ackermann was quoted as saying that "the investment bank's ROE, a key measure of profitability, should be as high as 25 per cent in two years' time" ("Deutsche Targets ROE above 20%," *Financial Times*, March 30, 2011). Later in the year, the targets were lowered (see "Deutsche Bank Eyes 15% Return on Equity," *Wall Street Journal*, December 5, 2011).

13. Patrick Jenkins, "Barclays Chief Ready to Increase Risk Appetite in Search of Profits," *Financial Times*, April 11, 2011.

14. Lewis (2011) mentions the conversion of investment banks from partnerships to corporations as a factor in increased risk taking and leverage, saying specifically that "from that moment, the Wall Street firm [Salomon Brothers, which became a public corporation in 1981] became a black box. The shareholders who financed the risk taking had no real understanding of what the risk takers were doing, and, as the risk taking grew ever more complex, their understanding diminished" (258). Bhide (2010, Chapter 9) and McLean and Nocera (2010, Chapter 11) also mention how the transformation of investment banks in the 1980s and 1990s from privately held partnerships to public corporations led to an increased focus on measures such as ROE, riskier trading strategies, and governance problems. We discuss governance issues later in the chapter.

15. Data for ROE are taken from Deutsche Bank's annual reports (available at https://www.deutsche-bank.de/ir/en/content/reports_2012.htm, accessed October 14, 2012): 9.5 percent in 2003, 4.8 in 2004, 21.7 in 2005, 26.4 in 2006, 24.1 in 2007, −16.5 in 2008, 9.5 in 2009, 15.3 in 2010, and 10.2 in 2011. For the years before 2003, Deutsche Bank's annual reports do not give figures for pre-tax ROE. The after-tax figures given are 41.4 percent for 2000, 2.3 for 2001, and 1.1 for 2002. These figures are dominated by the effects of a change in tax rules. A tax reform that was passed in 2000 eliminated capital gains taxation for corporations holding shares in other corporations. Deutsche Bank, like other German corporations, used the

occasion provided by this change in the law to sell many of its holdings in nonfinancial companies, realizing capital gains that had been accumulating for decades. The numbers given here correspond to U.S. accounting practices. Deutsche Bank also reports what it calls "return on active equity," which adjusts for various effects involving the timing of dividend payments, realization of capital gains and losses, and tax effects. For this index, which is not recognized as a performance measure under official accounting rules but which Deutsche Bank, according to its press releases, treats as the key performance index, the average over the years 2003–2011 was 14.3 percent, somewhat better than for ROE before taxes, but the distance to the target of 25 percent for the average was still huge; peaks were 32.7 percent in 2006 and 29.0 percent in 2007; the trough was –17.7 percent in 2008. Remarkably, it does not seem possible to get this overall picture of how Deutsche Bank fared in the longer run without going back to its annual reports. Publicly available summaries, often giving quarterly returns, such as http://www.wikinvest.com/stock/DEUTSCHE_BANK_AG_(DB)/Data/ROE/2008/Q1 (accessed October 9, 2012), suggest a much smoother course.

16. For example, former Fannie Mae regulator Armando Falcon Jr. told the FCIC (2011, 64), "Fannie began the last decade with an ambitious goal—double earnings in 5 years. . . . A large part of the executives' compensation was tied to meeting this goal. Achieving it brought CEO Franklin Raines $52 out of his $90 million pay from 1993 to 2003. . . . However, the goal turned out to be unachievable without breaking rules and hiding risks. Fannie and Freddie executives worked hard to persuade investors that mortgage-related assets were a riskless investment while at the same time covering up the volatility and risks of their own mortgage portfolios and balance sheets."

17. Barclays' ROE for 2011 was 5.8 percent. The bank's new CEO, Antony Jenkins, announced in August 2012 that his ROE target would be above the bank's stated "cost of capital" of 11.5 percent (see "New Barclays CEO Sets Sights on 'Credible' RoE Plan," Reuters, August 30, 2012). He did not explain how this cost of equity was estimated and whether it could be reduced if the bank had more equity. In fact, Allison (2011, loc. 409) states that megabanks generally fail to generate the risk-adjusted returns that shareholders should expect. Mayo (2011) describes how, as an analyst, he has often been critical of banks' investment decisions.

18. On the flaws of ROE targets, see, for example, Anat Admati, "Beware of Bankers' Flawed ROE Measure," *New York Times,* July 25, 2011, and "Change Bank Pay Now—BoE's Robert Jenkins," Reuters, October 31, 2011, and note 33 of this chapter.

19. Andrew Haldane, the executive director for financial stability at the Bank of England, has argued that the high ROEs banks achieved for a period of time prior to the crisis can be fully explained by increased leverage and risk and cannot be interpreted as an indication of bankers' performance; see Haldane (2010).

20. "Deutsche Bank Doubles Down with a Casino," *Wall Street Journal,* November 17, 2010, and "Cosmopolitan of Las Vegas Loses $58.5M in 3Q," *Bloomberg Business Week,* November 14, 2011.

21. Such skewed incentives are generated by options with very high exercise prices or by compensation schemes with extra bonuses for super-high profits, for example, for reaching and surpassing target ROE when the target has been set at outlandishly high levels.

22. See Acharya et al. (2007) and Acharya and Yorulmazer (2008).

23. See Haldane (2012b) and Daniel Schäfer, "No Stop to Bankers' Pay Rises, Data Reveal," *Financial Times*, June 24, 2012. We discuss governance issues later in the chapter.

24. See Partnoy (2009, 2010) and Bhagat and Bolton (2011). Das (2010, 151) says, "Traders are given every incentive to take risk and generate short term-profits. . . . Calibrated bonus schemes encourage the 'upfronting' and overstatement of earnings."

25. See McLean and Elkind (2004) and Healy and Palepu (2003).

26. This is an example of risk taking in which losses are unlikely but very large when they materialize. Taleb (2001, 2010) emphasizes that neglect of the amount of potential losses is a major source of distortion in financial trading strategies. The problem is analogous to that of car drivers with good mastery of their cars who may be very aggressive in overtaking others, even on narrow roads with poor visibility, enjoying the small reduction in travel time and neglecting the fact that, if the risks they are taking materialize, the consequences can be disastrous.

27. Bhagat and Bolton (2011) show, in contrast to Fahlenbrach and Stulz (2011), that CEOs came out significantly ahead of shareholders by any measure when considering the periods 2000–2008, as well as the subperiods 2002–2008 and 2004–2008. They argue that all evidence is consistent with the hypothesis that managerial incentives to take excessive risk played a role in the run-up to the crisis. Showing that CEOs came out significantly ahead of other shareholders, they refute the suggestion that, because top managers of banks like Bear Stearns or Lehman Brothers lost a lot personally when the values of their shares declined, one can conclude that incentive schemes for CEOs were not important and that the crisis was likely the result of "unforeseen risk." The results are consistent with those of Bebchuk et al. (2010), who also found that incentives generated by executive compensation led to excessive risk taking by banks. Barth et al. (2012, 61 ff) argue that compensation schemes themselves were greatly affected by changes in ownership structures, mergers and acquisitions, and changes in markets and products, all of which were the results of CEO strategies, with huge effects on CEO pay. Mayo (2011, loc. 2909–11) states: "Many executives on Wall Street got tremendously wealthy by taking outsized bets for their companies and then left before those bets went bad. Some losses from the bets got socialized—picked up by the taxpayers." Hayes (2012, 99) refers to "IBGYBG" (I'll be gone, you'll be gone) as a theme that underlies risk-taking incentives.

28. UBS (2008).

29. See McLean and Elkind (2004) and Hayes (2012). Wilmarth (2007) describes how cases such as those of Enron and WorldCom represented a double failure of corporate governance. In addition to the immediate corporate governance failures at the failed firms, banks experienced their own corporate governance failures as they breached their fiduciary duties and exposed themselves to massive legal and reputational risks in their rush to reap short-term profits by servicing the fraudulent schemes of Enron and WorldCom. L. McDonald (2010) gives an insider's account of the fall of Lehman Brothers and how a short-term focus can infuse an organization's corporate culture. Das (2010) and Allison (2011) also discuss how focus on short-term profits in compensation has led to excessive risk taking by large banks. "The Revolution Within" (*The Economist*, May 16, 2009) pre-

dicts changes to practices with respect to risk adjustments, but it does not appear that there have been significant changes.

30. Haldane (2012b) compared the mentality of bankers, the desire to "keep up with the Goldmans," to that of elephant seals who compete, in a "winner-takes-all" manner, to mate with all the females, in the process becoming excessively bloated. Competition between banks to achieve higher returns has led banks to take more risk and to use more leverage.

31. See, for example, "Citi Chief on Buyouts: 'We're Still Dancing,'" *New York Times,* July 10, 2007.

32. For a skeptical view of the shareholder value concept, see Stout (2012). On governance problems, including ineffective boards that often lack expertise, see Pozen (2009, Chapter 11), Smith (2010, Chapter 7), Allison (2011, loc. 474), and Stanton (2012, Chapter 4). Mayo (2011, loc. 3226–29) states, "Boards are typically responsible for three things: (1) hiring a CEO and evaluating that person's compensation and performance; (2) setting an overall risk appetite at the bank; and (3) providing the company with some kind of independent oversight. In all three areas, boards have struck out lately, yet in most cases they remain largely intact and unchanged."

33. For an attempt to approach the JPMorgan board on the issue of capital regulation, see Anat Admati, "An Open Letter to JPMorgan Chase Board," *Huffington Post,* June 14, 2011. See also Robert Jenkins, "A Bank Run for the Benefit of Its Owners? Dream On," *Financial Times,* January 8, 2012, and Jenkins (2012c).

34. Only two major banks have publicly disclosed clawbacks (see "'Likely' JPMorgan Clawbacks Rare on Wall Street," *CNNMoney,* CNN, June 13, 2012). On governance and bonus cultures, see also "Hit Bankers Where It Really Hurts, in Their Bank Accounts," Bloomberg, July 13, 2012, which also mentions a potential role for the Sarbanes-Oxley Act.

35. On possible regulation of compensation structures, see Bebchuk and Spamann (2010), Bebchuk et al. (2010), Wolf (2010), and Bhagat and Bolton (2011). For a proposal that attempts to address different governance issues by creating "liability holding companies," see Admati et al. (2012c). The Dodd-Frank Act includes provisions that mandate the regulation of executive pay that encourages risky behavior, but so far they have not been implemented.

36. Cabiallavetta, who was also in charge of the risk control of the bank, had protected the trader from all interference by risk controllers. In the merger that formed the new UBS, he was almost the only member of the board of the old Union Bank of Switzerland who remained with the new institution—for one year, until the LTCM crisis brought a further loss of $700 million and he had to step down as well. See Schütz (1998, 74–117, esp. 80, 108, and 120).

37. On the lack of importance and resources given to risk management, see UBS (2008). Das (2010), Lewis (2010), and Smith (2010) also describe the relatively low status of risk managers within banks. Stanton (2012, Chapter 5) discusses risk management issues related to the financial crisis.

38. For example, an attempt by shareholders to affect the composition of the risk committee of JPMorgan Chase in 2011 has led to no change. The committee's composition has not changed between 2008 and 2012. It includes three board members with little relevant

experience, one of whom was also on the board of AIG before the financial crisis. See Max Abelson, "JPMorgan Gave Risk Oversight to Museum Head Who Sat on AIG Board," Bloomberg, May 25, 2012. The largest institutional investors, however, may be passive and subject to their own governance problems. Allison (2011, loc. 562), for example, states that "many of the large fund family have an obvious, disturbing motive to avoid confronting megabanks about their business practices and governance; they too have conflicts of interest. The funds' sponsors derive substantial revenues from providing investment services . . . to the megabanks, and many rely on the banks to distribute their funds to the public." He points to governance problems within the funds themselves.

39. See McLean and Elkind (2004). Similar issues arose in other scandals, such as those surrounding Tyco and WorldCom.

40. Francine McKenna, who often contributes to *American Banker,* has pointed to these issues in many pieces. See, for example, "Auditors Are Asleep at the Switch on Banks' Risk Controls," *American Banker,* July 16, 2012, and "Familiar Patterns in Spain's Banking Crisis," *American Banker,* June 27, 2012. The problem of conflicted auditors who are reluctant to challenge models used by banks and their accountants or to alert investors and regulators about risks from off-balance-sheet items adds to the opacity of disclosures and accounting-based valuations, all of which call into question how informative the disclosed valuations are. For example, Das (2010, 221) refers to "the looking glass world of Japanese accounting." In describing it, he states, "This was like giving someone money and then having them give it back to you and calling it income—it did not make any sense."

NINE   *Sweet Subsidies*

1. Mr. Zandi's comment in the epigraph is from Louise Story, "U.S. Program Lends a Hand to Banks, Quietly" (*New York Times,* April 14, 2009), referring to the ability of Goldman Sachs and Morgan Stanley to access loans from the Federal Reserve and guarantees from the FDIC after changing their status from investment banks to bank holding companies in 2008. Mr. Zandi continued by saying, "It's an infinite subsidy." See the section "Banks Have Uncle Sam" in this chapter.

2. Incidents such as this abound in recent history. For example, on November 1, 1986, a huge fire broke out in a dye factory on the Rhine near the Swiss city of Basel. The water used to extinguish the fire mixed with the chemicals and flowed into the river, coloring it red and killing all fish over several hundred miles downstream (see Hernan 2010). The *Exxon Valdez* and, more recently, the BP Gulf of Mexico oil spills are other examples.

3. In the entire discussion we continue to ignore the benefit Kate derived from living in the house. Considering it would not change the discussion, because she lived in the house in all scenarios.

4. To simplify the discussion we are ignoring here again the potential losses if the house had been abandoned or lost value because of lack of maintenance.

5. In the United States before 2007 many people took out second mortgages to finance additional consumption (see "Second Mortgage Misery," *Wall Street Journal,* June 7, 2011).

6. If Kate invests $20,000 in bonds that pay her 3 percent interest for sure instead of investing that amount in the house, she will have $20,600 from this investment no matter what happens subsequently to the value of the house. On the upside, the guarantees do not matter; Kate will be in the same situation as she would be if she was investing all $30,000 in the house (the bottom panel of Table 9.1 and the top panel of Table 9.2). But, on the downside, Kate will be protected from losses. For example, if the house declines to $255,000 in value, Kate will lose only $10,000, whereas she would have lost the entire $30,000 if she had put it all in the down payment. In all cases, Kate is better off with the larger mortgage. The example effectively assumes that the interest rate for riskless investments in the economy is 3 percent. However, the conclusion that Kate prefers the larger mortgage does not depend on what Kate does with the money she does not put in the house; it is based only on the observation that investing less in the house takes more advantage of the guarantees. Because the bank is paid for sure, whatever Kate does not pay, her aunt does; the fact that Claire may pay more and never less implies that Kate benefits more. Of course Kate can make poor investments and take a lot of risk for which she is not fully compensated. She might make less than 3 percent on her $20,000 and therefore possibly lose more than she would by investing it in the house. However, what we have seen is that there is a way for Kate to benefit from the guarantees if she invests the money prudently. As we will see shortly, if Aunt Claire gives Kate blanket guarantees, as long as Claire is not broke, Kate benefits no matter what she does; effectively, blanket guarantees are like money machines.

7. Kate's ROE will be further magnified if she borrows more. First, the gains on her investment in the house will be further magnified in the cases in which she is able to pay her mortgage without the guarantees. For example, if the final house price is $345,000, Kate's ROE will be 123 percent if she invests $30,000 in the house, as seen in Table 9.1; with only $10,000 in equity, the $46,300 Kate will end up with, seen in Table 9.2, represents a 363 percent ROE, much higher indeed. If the house increases in value by "only" 5 percent, to $315,000, Kate will end up with 23 percent ROE if she invests $30,000 in the house, while her final position of $16,300 represents a 63 percent return on her investment of $10,000, again higher. In the unfavorable scenarios, however, with a $10,000 investment Kate's loss per dollar is greater. Comparing Kate's returns from investing $30,000 in the house versus investing $10,000 in the house and $20,000 at a riskless 3 percent, Kate's position is obtained from the bottom panel of Table 9.2 by adding $20,600 in each scenario. Her return will be the same as shown in the bottom panel of Table 9.1 (123 percent, 23 percent, and a loss of 27 percent, respectively) in the scenarios in which the house increases in value by 15 percent and 5 percent and in that in which it stays the same, whereas Kate will lose only 31 percent of her $30,000 thanks to the $20,600 that she will receive on her safe investment even though she will lose the entire $10,000 down payment in the house.

8. Even without guarantees, if lenders believe that housing prices will always increase, as they seem to have believed in the housing bubble before 2006 (or if they believe that the borrowers will always pay their mortgage debts), they might make, and indeed have made, zero-equity loans, requiring no down payment and counting on equity to build as

the value of the house increases. As we have seen, however, housing prices do not always go up.

9. Again, if Kate puts nothing into the house and invests her entire $30,000 safely at 3 percent, she will have $30,900 for sure, plus whatever she might make on the house if its value ends up above $309,000. She is guaranteed an interest rate of at least 3 percent in this case, and her return will be the same as shown in the bottom panel of Table 9.1 if the house value ends up being $315,000 or $345,000. Her return will be 3 percent in the other three scenarios because she does not have to cover the interest or any losses in the value of the house. If Kate makes risky investments with the funds, then of course how she will end up doing depends on how these investments turn out, but clearly, having no money in the house and experiencing only the upside from it is a highly beneficial situation for Kate.

10. This represents a recent increase in the eligible amount. Placing a higher amount under deposit insurance is easy if one divides it across multiple accounts or multiple banks. There are even deposit brokers who would help in this process. Kane (2012b) describes a regulatory arbitrage created by a deposit-swap market in which one can place practically any amount under deposit insurance. Malysheva and Walter (2010) discuss the expansion of the safety net in the United States in recent years.

11. See Acharya et al. (2010) and ASC (2012).

12. For more information on the use of guarantees and recapitalization, see Laeven and Valencia (2010, 2012).

13. On the cost of the bailouts and the recent crisis in the United States, see Better Markets (2012). For detailed descriptions of how bailout funds were used—and sometimes not used, or actually abused—see Bair (2012) and Barofsky (2012).

14. See Phil Kuntz and Bob Ivry, "Fed Once-Secret Loan Crisis Data Compiled by Bloomberg Released to Public," Bloomberg, December 22, 2011. According to this piece, the amount that the Federal Reserve pledged in order to rescue the financial industry was $7.77 trillion, and loan rates were below market rates and provided a large subsidy. Bloomberg News had to fight in the courts to be able to obtain the information about loans. Alan Feurer, in "Appeals Court Rules Fed Must Release Loan Reports" (*New York Times*, March 19, 2010), describes the lengthy legal battle over the information. According to this story, the Federal Reserve, helped by The Clearing House, a consortium of the largest banks, fought to keep the information from becoming public. Barofsky (2012, 88) writes regarding one of the Fed support programs, the so-called Term Asset-Backed Securities Loan Facility (TALF), that "under the terms of one TALF-eligible bond issued by Ford's finance company, an issuer could take out a TALF loan for $100 million that required him to pay the New York Fed 3.0445 percent interest (about $3 million) for a bond that paid out 6.07 percent (about $6 million), allowing the investor to pocket the difference of 3 percent (about $3 million) each year. That's the investor's equivalent of shooting fish in a barrel." In lending to entities formed in the AIG bailout, the New York Fed used LIBOR to determine the interest rate it charged for loans to the entities, knowing the rate was artificially low at the time. See Mark Gongloff, "Tim Geithner Admits Banks Bailed Out with Rigged Libor, Costing Taxpayers Huge Amount," *Huffington Post*, July 25, 2012. See more references in the following notes.

15. See Boyd and Gertler (1994).

16. See Burnside (2011) and Acharya and Steffen (2012). As pointed out by Louise Armitstead, in "ECB's LTRO Plan Flops as Banks Cut Lending" (*The Telegraph*, March 28, 2012), banks seem to have used these funds for lending to their governments rather than private businesses.

17. See Louise Story, "U.S. Program Lends a Hand to Banks, Quietly." (This is the story referred to in the chapter epigraph and in note 1, where Mr. Zandi is quoted as saying that "it's an infinite subsidy.") On Morgan Stanley's use of the Fed lending facility, see Jonathan Weil, "Morgan Stanley's Deep Secret Now Is Revealed," Bloomberg, March 23, 2011.

18. The German Bank Restructuring Act of 2010 follows the same logic. Only the United Kingdom's Banking Act of 2009 acknowledges the possibility that, even though this is undesirable, support from taxpayers may again be needed in a future crisis. For a discussion, see ASC (2012) and Hellwig (2012). See also our discussion and notes at the end of Chapter 5.

19. Victoria McGrane, "Obama Signs Financial Regulation Bill," *Wall Street Journal*, July 21, 2010.

20. According to Curry and Shibut (2000), the total cost was about $153 billion, of which $29 billion was paid by private funds, mostly by means of charges on other institutions in the industry.

21. Rules for interest deductibility on mortgages differ by country. For example, in Switzerland interest on mortgages is deductible up to an "imputed rent" plus 50,000 Swiss francs. In Germany mortgage interest for owner-occupied housing is typically not deductible for individuals.

22. Is there a catch? If instead of investing in a house one invests one's money elsewhere, one will pay taxes on profits from that investment. But if one makes relatively safe investments (also to prevent having to default on the mortgage), one can choose investments that would be taxed at a lower rate than income, for example, taking advantage of the lower tax rate on capital gains. This can make borrowing to buy a house attractive even to those who have enough money to buy it without borrowing.

23. This is based on the analogy between corporations and individuals. For an individual owning a firm, interest expenses are a cost. In computing the individual's income, interest expenses are therefore deducted. For a corporation, interest expenses are also a cost, but so are, in a sense, distributions to shareholders. From the perspective of investors—that is, the individuals ultimately affected—the key question is how taxation affects the returns they earn on the different assets that the corporation is issuing.

24. When income taxation of investors is also taken into account, the picture may change somewhat, because capital gains are often taxed at a lower rate (see Miller 1977).

25. On taxes in general, see Slemrod and Bakija (2008); on correcting the tax advantage of debt, see De Mooij (2011) and Fleischer (2011). Panier et al. (2012) focus on an explicit tax subsidy to equity introduced in Belgium in 2006.

26. There are other ways for corporations to try to avoid paying corporate taxes, such as moving funds and entities to areas with lower tax rates. See, for example, Charles

Duhigg and David Kocieniewski, "How Apple Sidesteps Billions in Taxes," *New York Times,* April 28, 2012.

27. See, for example, Lewis (2011).

28. Allison (2011) argues that the banks are inefficient and have not generated risk-adjusted shareholder value. Clear evidence of subsidized funding through implicit guarantees is the fact that credit rating agencies give large banks "credit bumps" that allow them to borrow on better, cheaper terms. Davies and Tracey (2012), Carbo-Valverde et al. (2011), Noss and Sowerbutts (2012), and Ueda and Weder di Mauro (2012) show that the size of the subsidies for systemically important financial institutions is substantial. Allison (2011), Boot (2011), and Hu (2012) argue that the increasing complexity of banks is problematic for the banks and for regulators and the public. In addition to the complications associated with resolution and bankruptcy, the complexity raises serious concerns about governance and control. Some of these issues were discussed in earlier chapters.

29. Previous authors—for example, Berger et al. (1993)—had suggested that the efficient scale of banks might be quite low, less than $1 billion in total assets. Hughes and Mester (2011) argue that previous estimates were distorted by not paying attention to economies of scale in banks' risk choices, diversification of risks, and information processing. When paying attention to risk choices, they find significant benefits to banks' becoming larger, and the larger the banks, the larger are these benefits. Anderson and Jöeveer (2012) also find significant effects of bank scale; however, these take the form of higher payments to bank managers rather than gains for shareholders. Both Hughes and Mester (2011) and Anderson and Jöeveer (2012) claim that their findings cannot be due to too-big-to-fail policies, but they do not actually take account of the effects of too-big-to-fail status on banks' borrowing costs and on banks' behaviors. In response to Hughes and Mester (2011), Davies and Tracey (2012) provide a study that does take account of the effect of implicit guarantees on banks' funding costs. When adjusting for the value of guarantees, they find that there are no benefits from having banks operate at a larger scale. If anything, they find that large banks are "too big to be efficient"; that is, banks benefiting from government guarantees may well be operating at an inefficiently large scale. In discussing the role of risk choices and the benefits of better diversification of risks in large banks, Hughes and Mester (2011) also fail to allow for the possibility that risk diversification in investors' portfolios might take the place of risk diversification in banks. One might also wonder about their focusing on data from 2007, when banks were recording large profits. Boyd and Heitz (2011) discuss the issue of efficient scale from a *social* perspective, taking account of risks for the financial system from too-big-to-fail banks; they argue that the socially efficient scale of banks is likely to be quite small. Allison (2011, loc. 437) argues that it is a "fallacy that diversification can protect the megabanks during a downturn. Markets and businesses that seemed to have low correlations during good times all converged during the crisis and compounded the banks' losses and liquidity problems."

30. The bank analyst Mike Mayo describes the following incident from 2010 (Mayo 2011, loc. 2677-79): "One of Citigroup's goals . . . was to increase assets on its Citicorp business by 5 percent." He goes on to say (2685-89) that "for a company with assets of $1.4 trillion in the targeted growth area, a 5 percent increase means generating upward of $70 billion

in new business every year, equivalent to half a percent of total U.S. gross domestic product. Citigroup was aiming at that kind of growth during a slumping global economy. . . . Citi's 5 percent goal was like a hitter in baseball saying he's going to go three for four in a particular game before he even knows who's pitching." When he asked the company about this, he reports (2697–99), "Pandit's approach was to say, That's not a goal. It's not something we're reaching for—we're so well positioned that we're merely going to be the passive recipient of that growth. Nice. Like manna from heaven." This is consistent with our suggestion that unlimited guarantees amount to a money machine.

31. Brewer and Jagtiani (2009).

32. See Kelly et al. (2012). Gandhi and Lustig (2012, 5) discuss the impact of guarantees and implicit subsidies on the returns of large and small banks and estimate that the value of the guarantees to the largest commercial banks has been about $4.71 billion per year.

33. Haldane (2011b, Table 1) provides estimates of the value of the guarantees to banks in the United Kingdom and globally. The estimates for the value of the subsidy that he obtains using an options pricing approach are $496 billion in 2007, $1.8 trillion in 2008, about $2.3 trillion in 2009, and $924 billion in 2010, for an average of $1.3 trillion per year for 2007–2010. Haldane obtains lower estimates using uplifts in credit ratings; these are differences between credit ratings for banks assuming government support relative to unsupported ratings.

34. See Haldane (2011b), Davies and Tracey (2012), Gandhi and Lustig (2012), and Noss and Sowerbutts (2012).

35. All numbers here are taken from Chapter 1 of Acharya et al. (2011a), which gives a systematic account of Fannie Mae and Freddie Mac over several decades. The $85 billion and $5.2 trillion in engagements in mortgages and mortgage guarantees in 1980 and in 2008 are composed of $64.8 billion and $1.7 trillion in residential mortgages in 1980 and 2008 and $20.6 billion and $3.5 trillion in mortgage guarantees in 1980 and 2008.

36. Acharya et al. (2011a, 29).

37. If the industry is not very competitive, the effect of government guarantees and subsidies might be different. Subsidies and guarantees increase the value of a bank's license. The fear of losing its license might cause the bank to be more careful about the risks it takes. Keeley (1990) suggests that the increase in banks' risk taking in the 1980s was caused by reductions in banks' franchise values due to increased competition. If the industry is very competitive, the potential positive effect of subsidies and guarantees on the banks' franchise values is usually dissipated by competition. When banks have difficulties earning a profit, their owners and managers may feel that they do not have much to lose, so they gamble—for survival or for resurrection. If depositors and other creditors do not care, the result can be very costly.

38. For an early warning about the S&Ls, see Kareken (1983). An interesting natural experiment was provided by the German Landesbanken. A 2001 agreement between the European Commission and the German government determined that government guarantees to the banks would be discontinued in 2005. Thus the expected benefits from future guarantees were reduced in 2001, but the Landesbanken had four more years to borrow with the help of government guarantees. During those years they engaged in a lot of addi-

tional borrowing and risk taking. The additional risk taking was most pronounced in those Landesbanken that were weakest. See Fischer et al. (2011) and Körner and Schnabel (2012).

39. For TARP, loss estimates now are around $60 billion. See Mark Gongloff, "TARP Profit a Myth, Claims TARP Inspector General Christy Romero," *Huffington Post*, April 25, 2012. For Fannie Mae and Freddie Mac, loss estimates lie between $150 billion and $350 billion (see Acharya et al. 2011, 2). For the assets acquired by the Federal Reserve, predictions are unclear. See also Better Markets (2012) and the list provided at http://projects .propublica.org/bailout/list, accessed October 12, 2012. For some cost estimates in Europe, see Sebastian Dullien, "The Costs of the Financial Crisis 2008–2009: Governments Are Paying the Tab," *Social Europe Journal*, October 19, 2011. The German cost estimates of Kaserer (2010), amounting to €34–52 billion, have been overtaken by developments since 2010, which have added some €20–30 billion to the bill. As noted in Chapter 1, on the basis of actual (rather than projected future) costs so far, Laeven and Valencia (2012) estimate that Germany's bailout costs in the recent crisis were 1.8 percent of GDP. The corresponding figures are 1 percent for France, 6 percent for Belgium, 3 percent for Denmark, 27.3 percent for Greece, 12.7 percent for the Netherlands, 3.8 percent for Spain, and 1.1 percent for Switzerland. Whereas Kaserer's estimates are based on forecasts of future losses that have yet to be confirmed, Laeven and Valencia's assessments are based on actual outlays and losses already incurred, as recorded in the governments' books.

40. This issue will be discussed in Chapter 13.

41. See Holtfrerich (1981), Berger et al. (1995), Alessandri and Haldane (2009), and Carbo-Valverde et al. (2011).

TEN *Must Banks Borrow So Much?*

1. In fact, as we saw in Chapter 6, loans are quite a small part of the assets of global banks. Smaller banks may also make investments that are not much different from those made by other investors rather than making loans. Although banks are set up to make loans, they are not required by regulation to do so, and they choose which loans and investments to make according to their own preferences. The role of regulation in distorting banks' incentives is discussed in Chapter 11, and we return to bank lending in Chapter 13.

2. It is derived from the Italian *banca rotta*, which literally means "broken bench" or "broken table" and is said to refer to a practice in the late Middle Ages of breaking the table of a money changer when he defaulted. This explanation of the origins of the term is given for the Italian word *bancarotta* by Pietro Ottorino Pianigiani in *Dizionario etimologico online* (http://www.etimo.it/?term=bancarotta, accessed October 28, 2012), and for the French word *banqueroute* by François Noël ([1857] 1993). Kluge (1975) also gives this explanation of the origin of the German *Bankrott* but warns that there is no evidence to show that the practice of breaking the tables of defaulting money changers actually existed. According to Kluge, the term *rotta* should be translated as "in default, insolvent," a second meaning that both the Italian word and its Latin ancestor, *ruptus*, broken, took on in the high Middle Ages. Hoad (1986) also refers to the medieval meaning of *ruptus* as "insolvent."

3. Gorton (2010) suggests that the "quiet period" in U.S. banking lasted until 2007, but he neglects the S&L crisis of the 1980s and early 1990s, as well as the hidden crisis of U.S. commercial banks in 1990. On the latter, see Boyd and Gertler (1994). The S&L crisis, discussed in Chapter 4, cost taxpayers $129 billion (see Curry and Shibut 2000).

4. See Goodhart (1996).

5. In this vein, Gorton (2010) calls for an extension of the scope of federally guaranteed insurance from traditional deposits to other forms of short-term lending. Mehrling (2010) calls for the central bank to stand ready as a "dealer of the last resort," buying assets when markets freeze so banks can be sure of always having enough liquidity. Both authors neglect the problem that banks might be insolvent, and they ignore banks' incentives to take excessive risk and to borrow too much; as we saw in previous chapters, distorted incentives and the likelihood of insolvencies are larger if banks and other institutions can rely on guarantees. In focusing on liquidity, these authors fail to pay attention to the deeper problems of insolvency and possibly the need to eliminate excess capacity in banking. We discuss liquidity narratives further in Chapter 13.

6. From 1816 to 1914, a holder of a pound note could ask for a sovereign, a coin containing 1320/5607 troy ounces, or 7.32238 grams, of gold. The right to exchange pound notes in gold was suspended at the beginning of World War I. It was resumed again in 1926 and definitely ended in 1931, during the Great Depression. In 1926–1931, the right to exchange pound notes was limited to bullion rather than coins. Before the twentieth century, conversion of Bank of England notes into gold had been suspended during the wars of the French Revolution and Napoleon, from 1797 to 1816.

7. In England, the use of notes as claims on deposits that could be used for payments is said to have originated with goldsmiths in the middle of the seventeenth century. Merchants who had been used to depositing gold in the Tower of London stopped doing so and deposited their gold with goldsmiths after King Charles I had seized the gold in the Tower in 1640 to finance his war against Parliament. The goldsmiths soon used some of this gold for lending.

8. There is some controversy as to whether the goldsmiths' use of gold deposits for lending violated the deposit contracts. According to some authors, the deposit contract was a safekeeping contract, so lending some of the gold was a breach of trust (see Rothbard 2008, 85 ff). The contrary view suggests that the deposit contract was a lending contract, so the goldsmiths were allowed to use the gold as they saw fit; the key argument for the latter view is that the goldsmiths promised to pay interest on the deposits, which would not have been possible if they had provided just a safekeeping service (see Quinn 1997 and Selgin 2010; Gorton [1985, 1988] discusses analogous issues in U.S. banking history).

9. A general overview of the development of payment systems and central banking is given by Goodhart (1988). In the United Kingdom, the Bank Act of 1844 gave the Bank of England a monopoly on the issue of banknotes. In the United States, the Federal Reserve received such a monopoly when it was created in 1913. Previously, under the National Banking Act of 1863, banknotes could be issued by any nationally chartered bank but had to be backed by debt securities of the federal government.

10. Because of their ready availability and their role in the payment system, deposits are

sometimes considered a kind of money. From the perspective of a buyer in a supermarket that accepts checks as well as cash, a dollar in a bank account may indeed be equivalent to a dollar in cash. In the tradition of Friedman and Schwartz (1963), therefore, demand deposits in banks are treated as part of the "quantity of money" in the economy. In the simplest definition, the quantity of money is said to consist of the cash and demand deposits of private individuals and nonfinancial companies. Because banks hold less than 100 percent reserves against their deposits, the quantity of money by this definition is larger than the quantity of money issued by the central bank, which consists of the cash of private individuals and nonfinancial companies along with the reserves of banks. Therefore, banks are sometimes said to be "creating money." However, there is an important difference: if Kate, say, deposits $1,000 in a bank, the bank owes her $1,000. If she holds $1,000 in cash, nobody owes her anything. A dollar in a bank account is a debt of the bank. A dollar in cash is nobody's debt. The importance of this difference for the functioning of private banks and central banks and, more generally, for the financial system has been stressed by Tobin (1967). Some authors emphasize the role of the government and the central bank in determining what the currency is and how much cash is issued; this is the so-called "cartalist" view of money, which goes back to Knapp (1924). For a recent statement, see Goodhart (1998).

11. Mehrling (2010, 4–5).

12. Ahamed (2009).

13. See, for example, Gorton (2010) and Mehrling (2010). Goodhart (1988) explain how different mechanisms of collective actions were developed in order to mitigate the effects of fluctuations in deposits, withdrawals, and payments on individual banks, clearing houses, clubs, and finally central banks.

14. From a cartalist perspective (see note 10), banknotes can be seen as claims on the government, because the government is committed to accepting them (or claims on them such as checks) as a means of paying taxes (see, e.g., Goodhart 1998). However, beyond that, the issue of banknotes does not commit the government to anything. In particular, the government does not and cannot guarantee the future value of money. This point was driven home in a disastrous manner in the post–World War I inflation in Germany. At the time, the Reichsbank, the German central bank, stood under the influence of Knapp ([1905] 1924) and did not seem to understand that the printing of money was causing the inflation.

15. In many countries, the practice of converting banknotes into gold ended during the Great Depression of the early 1930s—in the United States in 1933, in the United Kingdom in 1931. Thereafter, until 1968 there was a central bank commitment to maintain the price of gold at $35 per ounce. In 1968 this commitment was limited to exchanges between central banks. In 1971, even this was ended. Even before 1968, the commitment to maintain the price of gold at $35 per ounce did not imply any obligation of a central bank to the holders of banknotes. In some countries, central banks promise to convert the notes they issue into a foreign currency. For example, in the 1990s Argentina had a so-called currency board linking the peso to the U.S. dollar; on a currency board the promise of convertibility is supported by a 100 percent reserve requirement. The Baltic states have had currency boards linking their currencies first to the Deutsche Mark and then to the euro.

16. The central bank's money issue does appear as a liability on its balance sheet, but this is a liability that does not impose any real obligation on the central bank. The only practical significance of this balance-sheet entry might be that, if the central bank makes losses on the assets it holds, its equity—the difference between its assets and its liabilities— might have to be written down and could possibly become negative. Because liabilities do not oblige the central bank to anything, this would be economically irrelevant but might draw public attention to the losses incurred on the bank's assets. By saying that central bank money has no default risk we do not mean to imply that central bank money is riskless. There is always a risk that central bank money might lose value. This is, in fact, quite likely if the central bank prints a lot of money. Reinhart and Rogoff (2009) have stressed that money creation's causing inflation—that is, a devaluation of money relative to real goods—can be understood as a form of government default on domestic debt that has been issued in a home currency.

17. Of course the choice between cash and deposits also reflects differences in convenience.

18. This observation underlies proposals for so-called narrow banking, discussed in Chapter 6, note 38.

19. For example, the eighteenth-century runs on the Bank of England occurred in 1745, when investors feared that the Stuart pretender to the English throne might win the war and impound the Bank's assets, and in 1797, when the war against the French was going badly and investors feared that the Bank's loans to the U.K. government might not be repaid (see, e.g., Bowman 1937).

20. As explained in Chapter 6, reserves have the drawback that a bank earns lower returns if it makes fewer loans. With equity, there is no such drawback because, when the bank has more equity, investing in the equity is safer and the required ROE lower.

21. If there is concern about managers' having access to excessive "free cash flow," the equity backing can be put into a separate entity, as proposed by Admati et al. (2012c).

22. This view is most strongly expressed by Gorton (2010). See also Mehrling (2010).

23. The analogy of bank debt to cars, or to printers, iPhones, and iPads, is from a talk Gary Gorton gave at the Twentieth Annual Hyman P. Minsky Conference at the Levi Economic Institute at Bard College on April 14, 2011, available at http://www.levyinstitute .org/news/?event=32 (session 5, audio, at about 19–20 minutes), accessed October 18, 2012. Gorton (2010, 19, 42–43, 135–144) explicitly downplays the role of bank lending, borrower creditworthiness assessments, and monitoring as functions of banks as he emphasizes the importance of "liquidity creation." Gorton ignores the fact that, when banks take risks with the funds that they obtain by "producing debt," this risk can create solvency problems that would threaten the very liquidity that he extols.

24. An asset is said to be liquid if it can easily be converted into cash and used for payments. There are two reasons that an asset would seem to be "liquid." First, the issuer might give the holder the right to a quick repayment. Second, the asset might be traded in a well-functioning market. The first would apply to a demand deposit, the second to a corporate stock or bond that is traded on an organized exchange—or to cash, which serves as a means of payment in every market.

25. This is an underlying theme of Gorton (2010).

26. As discussed in note 16, there is a risk that the purchasing power of money—that is, how much can be bought for central bank banknotes—might be eroded because the government funds itself by printing more money, causing the prices of goods and services to go up. Reinhart and Rogoff (2009) refer to this use of the printing press as a form of default on domestic-currency sovereign debt.

27. Some might view a Treasury bill as safer than the cash one keeps at home, but it is not as convenient as cash for paying a grocery bill.

28. See Floyd Norris, "Buried in Details, a Warning to Investors," *New York Times*, August 3, 2012). Other unpleasant surprises are described by Partnoy (2009, 2010) and Dunbar (2011).

29. In the run-up to the financial crisis, financial institutions invested in mortgage-related securities that were rated AAA by the credit rating agencies and paid a few basis points—that is, a few hundredths of 1 percent, more interest than other AAA-rated securities. The question of why the interest was higher seems not to have been asked. See Hellwig (2009) and the references given there, as well as Acharya et al. (2013).

30. Any potential buyer of the loan would fear that the bank might be selling bad loans while keeping good ones. This is an example of what is known in economics as a "lemons problem," after Akerlof's (1970) Nobel Prize–winning analysis of what he called the *market for "lemons."* Akerlof (1970) shows that markets in which sellers have better information than buyers may work very differently from ordinary markets. For example, in the market for used cars, potential buyers might require large discounts in compensation for the risk that sellers might be hiding important information about their cars and about their reasons for selling them. If these discounts induce owners of good cars to refrain from selling and instead to hold onto their cars a bit longer, the market for used cars might, in fact, work as a market for bad cars, "lemons." The used cars that are actually sold are lemons, and the price reflects this expectation. Akerlof's analysis has been applied and extended to many markets in which participants have different information—not only financial markets but also insurance and labor markets and even markets for slaves in New Orleans before the Civil War. See, for example, Spence (1973), Rothschild and Stiglitz (1976), and Greenwald and Glasspiegel (1983).

31. For example, Pozsar et al. (2010, 1) state, "Credit creation through maturity, credit, and liquidity transformation can significantly reduce the cost of credit relative to direct lending. However, credit intermediaries' reliance on short-term liabilities to fund illiquid long-term assets is an inherently fragile activity and may be prone to runs."

32. This is another example of the lemons problem discussed in note 30. In 2007, hedge fund manager John Paulson earned enormous profits by putting together a portfolio of mortgage-related securities that he thought were going to go down in value and having Goldman Sachs arrange for his fund to sell claims on this portfolio to other investors (see Zuckerman 2009 and Cohan 2012, 11–16). In April 2010, the SEC brought suit against Goldman Sachs for failing to inform buyers that Paulson, the seller, had played a significant role in selecting the securities. According to the SEC, the buyers thought that Goldman Sachs had selected the securities and was acting as a neutral broker; had they suspected

that Paulson, the seller, had selected them, they might have been less ready to buy the claims. The SEC subsequently allowed Goldman Sachs to settle the case for a fine of $550 million (see "Goldman, SEC Discuss Catch-All Settlement," *Wall Street Journal*, July 15, 2010).

33. Demyanyk and Van Hemert (2009), Hellwig (2009), Lewis (2010), McLean and Nocera (2010), Ben-David (2011), and FCIC (2011). Gorton (2010, 138 ff) dismisses the quality problems of the underlying mortgages without considering the empirical evidence.

34. One might wonder, in fact, whether the purported "liquidity" was an illusion that was exposed as such when investors became nervous about the value of the securities.

35. The classical reference on central bank support for private banks is Bagehot ([1873] 1906); see also Goodhart (1988). Whereas Bagehot emphasizes the role of the central bank as a lender of the last resort, Mehrling (2010) suggests that the central bank should act as a dealer of the last resort, standing ready to step in when banks need to sell assets to cover their liquidity needs and there are no buyers in private markets.

36. When Bagehot ([1873] 1906) discusses the role of the central bank as a lender to private banks, he insists that the private banks must provide good collateral and that they should be charged penalty rates to discourage them from looking at borrowing from the central bank as a normal source of funds. In the years since 2007, central banks have often accepted securities of dubious quality as collateral or even purchased such securities. Mehrling (2010) emphasizes the positive effects of these measures on bank liquidity without addressing the risks to central banks, and indirectly to taxpayers, of potential losses from such securities.

37. Strictly speaking, this is to be expected only for money creation in excess of the growth of economic activity in the economy. Moreover, in a time of structural change, central bank money might be created without inflationary consequences. For example, since 2008, interbank borrowing and lending have been much reduced because private banks no longer trust each other; because they cannot rely on short-term borrowing, private banks rely much more on deposits with their central bank to meet unforeseen cash needs. Such deposits have expanded greatly, without inflationary consequences. The effect is reinforced, and inflationary effects further reduced, by central banks' paying interest on private banks' deposits with them. An old argument, which goes back to Friedman (1969), suggests that paying interest on deposits with the central bank may actually be efficient, because deposits with the central bank are a more reliable source of liquidity than interbank borrowing. If no interest is paid on deposits with the central bank, private banks have an incentive to economize on their holding reserves at the central bank and instead turn to riskier sources of liquidity. In the logic of Friedman (1969), this way of arranging for liquidity is inefficient because liquidity through central bank deposits does not impose a cost on society.

38. For example, excessive printing of money may culminate in hyperinflation, which can destroy the monetary system altogether. Reinhart and Rogoff (2009) emphasize the use of the printing press and the inflation it induces as a means by which governments can devalue their domestic debt.

39. Some of these safeguards and rules concern the status of the central bank, others the kinds of securities that central banks are allowed to accept as collateral or to buy. The

most important institutional safeguard is to make the central bank independent of the government (see, e.g., Grilli et al. 1991, and Alesina and Summers 1993). Rules of conduct involve, for example, prohibitions against direct lending to governments, against buying shares in the stock market, or against lending to banks without collateral. The independence of the ECB and of the national central banks that are members of the European System of Central Banks, as well as a prohibition of direct central bank lending to governments, are central elements of the European Monetary Union, laid down in Articles 130 and 123 of the Treaty on the Functioning of the European Union. A major point of discussion in Europe is whether the prohibition of direct central bank lending to governments should be interpreted as implying that purchases of government bonds in the open market are also prohibited or whether these purchases should be treated as normal activities in support of the financial system, that is, private banks. In the United States, the Federal Reserve is in principle independent, but it owes this independence to a simple act of Congress that might be revoked at any time. Historical accounts suggest that in World War II and until 1951, the Federal Reserve was in fact committed to supporting the federal government's issue of debt, pegging the interest on this debt at 2.5 percent. This period was ended by the Treasury–Federal Reserve Accord of 1951, which gave the Federal Reserve the freedom to conduct monetary policy without instructions from the Treasury. See, for example, *Federal Reserve Bank of Richmond Economic Quarterly 2001*, Special Issue on the 50th Anniversary of the Treasury–Federal Reserve Accord, http://www.richmondfed.org/publications/research/special_reports/treasury_fed_accord/eq_special/index.cfm, accessed October 19, 2012.

40. *The Tragedy of Pudd'nhead Wilson and the Comedy of the Extraordinary Twins* (1894).

41. This is the typical funding pattern for covered bonds, as discussed in Chapter 4, notes 47 and 48, where a portfolio of nontradable mortgages serves as collateral for a tradable bond.

42. The risks would have been irrelevant if the mortgage-related securities had been held by pension institutions or life insurance companies, whose liabilities extend over decades and which should actually be happy to acquire long-lasting assets such as mortgages and real estate, so that the question of what to invest in when current assets expire will not arise. According to Hellwig (1994), this practice would actually be efficient if the problem of providing incentives for creditworthiness assessments were brought under control.

43. Gorton (2010).

44. Many contracts actually had very low initial "teaser" rates; after two years, the interest rates would be adjusted upward anyway. Gorton (2010, 79 ff) suggests that because of these clauses, which were bound to be renegotiated, subprime mortgages actually were short-term. Because mortgages had adjustable rates that were bound to be renegotiated, he argues that banks using short-term debt to fund their holdings of mortgage-related securities were not actually engaged in maturity transformation. This argument, however, neglects the possibility that, if the required interest is raised, the borrower might be unable to pay. In this case, the bank might repossess the property, but then it would be stuck with a long-lasting asset that might not be easy to sell. Gorton's analysis neglects the fact that the ultimate assets, namely houses, are long lasting and there are no adjustable-rate clauses

governing the comfort and other services they provide. Assessments of maturity transformation and liquidity transformation that are limited to just one element of the overall chain of transactions are incomplete and potentially misleading. For a proper assessment, the entire chain of transactions must be considered. As explained in Chapter 3, adjustable-rate mortgages led to many defaults in the high-interest phase of the late 1980s, not only in the United Kingdom but also in the United States. Interest rates were much lower in the United States in 2006–2007 than in the late 1980s, but the effects of the increase from 2004 to 2007 on borrowers' defaults were much stronger because the creditworthiness of the mortgage borrowers was much lower. On the extent of borrower insolvency and the role of mortgage banks' laxness in checking creditworthiness, see note 43 in Chapter 4 and the references given there.

45. Gorton (2010, 123 ff) argues that events in the summer of 2007 are more appropriately interpreted as a panic that resulted from the fact that nobody knew which mortgage-related securities were affected and which ones were not. He emphasizes liquidity problems from the breakdown of funding for structured investment vehicles in the summer of 2007, comparing it to a nineteenth-century run. However, the breakdown of funding for structured investment vehicles in the summer of 2007 meant only that the sponsoring banks had to take the mortgage-related securities held by these vehicles onto their own books. These banks typically did not have serious funding problems, but once they moved these assets onto their balance sheets, they did not have enough equity to back them. Because of the price declines, some, like the German Industriekreditbank and Sächsische Landesbank, became insolvent right away and had to be bailed out. Others just found that the price declines squeezed their equity more and more as the contagion effects discussed in Chapter 5 played out. The actual funding problems came later, in March 2008 for Bear Stearns and in September 2008 for Lehman Brothers, when their solvency began to be doubted. Krishnamurthy et al. (2012) show that, except for broker-dealer banks like Bear Stearns or Lehman Brothers, repo lending, which is emphasized by Gorton (2010), played a much smaller role than asset-backed commercial paper; in their account, the breakdown of funding for asset-backed commercial paper in the summer of 2007 had little semblance to a bank run; by contrast, the Bear Stearns and Lehman Brothers episodes did involve repos and did have some elements of a run.

46. Money market mutual funds were first invented in the 1970s to circumvent Regulation Q, which limited the interest paid on demand and savings deposits. It is also useful to recall that the promise of stable net asset value makes shares in mutual funds a strange hybrid: although they are shares, their denomination is such that any one of them is assigned a stable value of $1. The result is that U.S. money market funds have grown dramatically. According to BIS (2012, 68), money market funds controlled about $2.7 trillion in the United States, $1.5 trillion in Europe, and $400 billion elsewhere. Recent discussions refer to $2.6 trillion in the United States (see, e.g., "Reform Still Looms over Money Market Funds," *Financial Times*, August 23, 2012). Money market funds are attractive to investors because they appear safe and liquid and they pay relatively high returns. In fact, they are shifting risks to others, eventually to the government and taxpayers, and at the same time adding to the fragility of the financial system. See Fink (2008) and Goodfriend (2011).

47. See Tett (2009), McLean and Nocera (2010), Dunbar (2011), Morgenson and Rosner (2011), and Thiemann (2012).

48. Similarly, money market funds are sometimes sponsored by regulated banks. This allows them to provide services similar to those of banks without being regulated as banks. Some funds are sponsored by mutual fund families, in which case they allow the funds to offer a broader menu of investments. Some money market funds are held mainly by institutions. See note 46 and Acharya et al. (2013).

49. These risks were vastly underestimated, partly because of the fiction that with adjustable interest rates on the mortgages, there was no significant maturity transformation, partly because of a belief that real estate prices could only go up, and partly because the AAA ratings of these securities suggested that they were perfectly safe. The incentives of investment banks and rating agencies to sell and assess these securities were not much questioned. See Acharya et al. (2010) and Lewis (2010).

50. UBS (2008), Hellwig (2009), Tett (2009), McLean and Nocera (2010), Dunbar (2011), and Morgenson and Rosner (2011).

51. See Admati et al. (2012a).

52. For example, suppose that a bank issues a ten-year bond. If after a year it issues more debt and this debt is given priority over the ten-year bond, the default risk for the ten-year bond will go up. The ten-year creditors might put a condition into the contract saying that any new debt issue must be junior to the ten-year bond. But this condition is meaningless if the new debt comes due earlier, for example, after five years. When the five-year debt comes due, there will be nothing the holders of the ten-year bond can do to prevent it from being repaid, even though the payment may hurt their own prospects. See Brunnermeier and Oehmke (2013).

53. Brunnermeier and Oehmke (2013).

54. By having a loan contract with collateral dressed up as a combination sale and repurchase, the creditor avoids being drawn into bankruptcy proceedings; in fact, he has jumped ahead of all other creditors, including the FDIC-insured depositors (see Bolton and Oehmke 2012 and Skeel and Jackson 2012). According to Gorton (2010), repo lending should be considered a modern version of bank deposits and repo runs as a modern version of bank runs, except that repo lending comes from firms rather than individuals. In his view, the runs were caused by concerns about the value of the collateral and by the lack of precise information about this value. Lack of information might be useful for avoiding "lemons problems" (note 30) in normal times but might be a source of panic when there are doubts about the collateral. Using data from money market funds and securities lending, Krishnamurthy et al. (2012), however, show that the magnitude of the contraction in repos based on private-sector collateral during a crisis is relatively insignificant compared to the contraction in so-called asset-backed commercial paper. In the summer of 2007, the contraction in asset-backed commercial paper lending disrupted the funding of the structured investment vehicles that regulated banks had used to hold mortgage-related securities. Contrary to what a liquidity narrative of the financial crisis would suggest, this disruption caused not a breakdown of funding but an equity squeeze: the sponsoring banks themselves had no funding problems and stepped in, but as they did

so they had to back the investments with equity (see Hellwig 2009 and the references given there). Regarding the contraction in repo lending, Krishnamurthy et al. (2012) show that lenders' concerns about the value of the collateral could be traced to the private-sector issuers, in particular some key dealers such as Bear Stearns and Lehman Brothers. Krishnamurthy et al. (2012, 6) conclude that, in contrast to Gorton's (2010) interpretation, the run on the repo markets "looks less like the analogue of a traditional bank run of depositors and more like a credit crunch in which dealers acted defensively given their own capital and liquidity problems, raising credit terms to their borrowers." Credit crunches are actually due to the effect of debt overhang discussed in Chapter 3, which leads distressed lenders to avoid making loans that they would have made had they been less distressed.

55. As discussed by Skeel and Jackson (2012), rules from 1994 and their expansion in 2005 exempt repos and derivatives from automatic stays in bankruptcy and give them special preference. The use of collateral for so much of bank borrowing exacerbates the fragility of the system because collateralization of some debt makes other debt less safe. These problems are made worse by the practice of rehypothecation, which involves a broker dealer's reusing clients' collateral to back its own trades and borrowings. Singh and Aitken (2010, 7) study the role of rehypothecation in the 2007–2009 crisis, suggesting that "the collapse in overall funding to banks was sizable." Issues related to rehypothecation were again raised in the failure of MF Global in December 2011. For an explanation of the legal issues around the practice, which involve in particular the lax regulation of the practice in the United Kingdom, see Christopher Elias, "MF Global and the Great Wall Street Re-hypothecation Scandal," Thompson Reuters News and Insight, December 7, 2011.

56. There is a large academic literature that builds on this idea (e.g., Calomiris and Kahn, 1991 and Diamond and Rajan, 2000, 2001). French et al. (2010), writing after the financial crisis, state that "the disciplining effect of short-term debt . . . makes management more productive. Capital requirements that lean against short-term debt push banks toward other forms of financing that may allow managers to be more lax." Admati et al. (2011, section 5) provide a detailed discussion of the underlying logic of these models and argue that they are inadequate to guide policy. An example (not discussed by Admati et al.) is given by Dewatripont and Tirole (1994, 2012). In their analysis, debt is needed because debt holders are more conservative than shareholders and therefore more likely to force a bank to be shut down when a continuation of activities would be inefficient. This analysis assumes that debt holders act as a single person and neglects the impact on the rest of the system of shutting the bank down. In fact, the only reason given for banking regulation by Dewatripont and Tirole is the need for someone to act in the collective interest of debt holders and shut the bank down when this is desirable. Debt holders are assumed to be dispersed and unable to shut the bank down. This assumption stands in marked contrast with other academic work on the role of short-term debt in "disciplining" managers, which suggests that a run by depositors serves this very purpose, or with the empirical evidence on banks' being forced to shut down by runs.

57. Geanakoplos (2010) suggests that concerns about the value of collateral are a key driver of leverage and risk in the financial system. These concerns are represented by the "haircuts" that creditors apply to collateral, which measure the amount of collateral they

require to lend a given amount of money and thus are a measure of creditworthiness and are similar to an equity requirement that a creditor requires to be willing to lend. In the run-ups to the Bear Stearns and Lehman Brothers crises, lenders sharply increased the haircuts they applied because of concerns about the collateral as well as the banks. The changes in haircuts precipitated the breakdowns of Bear Stearns and Lehman Brothers.

ELEVEN   *If Not Now, When?*

1. See, for example, "Danger Everywhere: The Debt Crisis in Europe Is Draining Confidence in Banks," *The Economist*, October 8, 2011. Recall also the discussion in Chapters 1 and 6 about the confusion between equity and reserves, the presumption that it is not possible to raise more equity, and the warnings that increased capital requirements would reduce lending and harm growth.

2. As discussed in Chapter 1 (note 22) and Chapter 6, important elements of banking regulation are based on international agreements, the so-called Basel Accords, worked out and negotiated in the Basel Committee on Banking Supervision (BCBS), a body of supervisors from major countries. Banking regulation and supervision itself is in the competence of each country. The Basel Accords become effective by being put into national (or EU) laws. Most national laws comply with (most of) the conditions in these agreements because this is a prerequisite for the application of the so-called home country principle, by which a country's banks can do business in other countries subject to supervision from the home supervisor only. For historical accounts of the BCBS, see Tarullo (2008) and Goodhart (2011).

3. See Mary Winton and Jon Hilsenrath, "Unease Rises over Funds: U.S. Regulators Worried about Exposure of Money-Market Assets to European Banks," *Wall Street Journal*, June 10, 2011; "Concerns Rise on Exposure of Some Money-Market Funds to European Banks," *Wall Street Journal*, June 21, 2011; and "US Money Market Funds Cut European Exposure," *Financial Times*, August 22, 2011. According to Brady et al. (2012), more than sixty prime money market funds had positions in Dexia, the Belgian-French bank that was nationalized later in 2011. Figure 5 in Rosengren (2012) shows the substantial exposure of prime money market funds in the United States to Italy, France, and Spain between December 2010 and early 2012.

4. Central bank support was made possible by an agreement between central banks under which the Federal Reserve made dollars available to, for example, the European Central Bank (ECB), which the latter could then lend to French banks such as BNP Paribas that had lost their dollar funding. Because the funding was in dollars, the ECB could not do it alone but had to borrow dollars from the Federal Reserve. See "ECB Announces Additional US Dollar Liquidity-Providing Operations over Year-End," ECB press release, September 15, 2011, http://www.ecb.int/press/pr/date/2011/html/pr110915.en.html, accessed October 15, 2012, and http://www.federalreserve.gov/monetarypolicy/bst_liquidityswaps.htm, accessed October 14, 2012. The solvency problems of European banks are further discussed in Chapter 12.

5. See Liz Alderman and Jack Ewing, "Largest Greek Banks to Receive Financing," *New York Times*, May 22, 2012, and "Spain Creates Bad Bank, Injects Funds in Bankia," Reuters, August 31, 2012.

6. Specifically, the requirement was that equity be 9 percent of so-called risk-weighted assets (discussed later in this chapter), and many banks had quite a bit less equity at that time. Banks were also required to acknowledge and recognize losses on government debts that they had not previously recognized. See "Statement of EU Heads of State or Government," http://www.consilium.europa.eu/uedocs/cms_data/docs/pressdata/en/ec/125621.pdf, accessed October 14, 2012. Most banks held government bonds in the so-called bank book, treating them as loans that they would hold to maturity. Bonds and loans in the bank book are usually reported at face value, and their values are written down only when the bank and its accountants believe that these debts will not be repaid in full. In the summer and fall of 2011, the market values of some government debts were much below the values at which these debts were carried in the banks' books; although no default had occurred yet, market investors were very pessimistic. For the purposes of determining the required capital, in the fall of 2011, however, banks had to value these holdings at market values. This forced them to recognize losses and to replace the equity that these losses had eaten up. See "EBA Recommendation on the Creation and Supervisory Oversight of Temporary Capital Buffers to Restore Market Confidence" (EBA/REC/2011/1), http://stress-test.eba.europa.eu/capitalexercise/EBA%20BS%202011%20173%20Recommendation%20FINAL.pdf, accessed October 14, 2012.

7. In November 2011, banks aiming to reach the 9 percent target set at the summit were trying to sell assets, causing further price declines in asset markets. The target had been set in terms of a ratio rather than a value, for example, the amount needed to make equity equal to 9 percent of assets in September 2011. See "Fears Rise over Banks' Capital Tinkering," *Financial Times*, November 13, 2011.

8. In particular, the requirement was set in terms of a ratio, 9 percent of risk-weighted assets, which gave banks too much discretion as to how to achieve it. The responses of banks to a requirement in terms of a ratio can be harmful to the economy. See Admati et al. (2012a) and the discussion later in this chapter.

9. In addition to the warnings based on mixing up capital and reserves discussed in Chapters 1 and 6, see, for example, "HSBC Warns of New Credit Crunch from Tough Bank Regulation," *The Guardian*, May 8, 2010; Patrick Jenkins, "For Their Health, Banks Need a Holiday away from Basel," *Financial Times*, August 9, 2011 (which elicited Anat Admati's "Easing Capital Rules Would Lead Banks away from Vital Lending," *Financial Times*, August 23, 2011); "Basel III: Don't We Have Enough Problems?," *Wall Street Journal*, May 6, 2012; "Regulate and Be Damned: Basel III Was Designed to Prevent Another Financial Crisis, but the Unintended Consequences Could Lock Up Global Trade," *Wall Street Journal*, February 7, 2011; "Banks Warn Rule Change Will Hurt Recovery," *Financial Times*, January 29, 2012; "Dimon Tells Bernanke He Fears New Rules Hurt Recovery," Reuters, June 7, 2011; and Steven Davidoff, "A Debt Market's Slow Recovery Is Burdened by New Regulation," *New York Times*, January 21, 2012.

10. This quote and the epigraph to this chapter are taken from Cornford (1908); see Chapter 1, note 11. The title of this chapter is attributed to Rabbi Hillel, one of the most influential scholars in Jewish history. The full quote is "If I am not for myself, then who will be for me? And if I am only for myself, then what am I? And if not now, when?"

11. ASC (2012).

12. Hoshi and Kashyap (2004, 2010). Some say the crisis has not ended.

13. Onaran's book (2011), titled *Zombie Banks*, makes the same point. Among the banks he suspects as being insolvent are Bank of America and Citigroup, as well as several European banks (see note 19). Regarding Bank of America, see also a petition submitted by the nonprofit organization Public Citizen on January 25, 2012, available at http://www.citizen.org/documents/Public-Citizen-Bank-of-America-Petition.pdf, accessed October 14, 2012. Regarding Citigroup, see also Mayo (2011) and Bair (2012).

14. Warnings such as those cited in notes 1 and 9 and discussed earlier in the book provide the background for this fear.

15. Since the aftermath of the Lehman Brothers bankruptcy, governments have refrained from letting large banks fail, but even when they have provided funds for bailouts, they have not tried to restructure banks and banking industries to make them safer.

16. See Caprio and Klingebiel (1996, 1997). In a similar spirit, Laeven and Valencia (2012) observe that advanced economies seem to take much longer than emerging economies to get back to a normal rate of economic development; they suggest that the delay may be due to the fact that public support is not only slowing the downturn but also preventing, or at least delaying, a cleanup of the underlying weaknesses.

17. A typical example of cutthroat competition is provided by the German covered bond sector in the years before the crisis. A 2005 "reform" removed restrictions on entry into this sector. A bank that issues covered bonds—bonds that are secured by a portfolio of mortgages—has an additional need for unsecured funding because the initial value of the portfolio of mortgages must be larger than the value of the covered bonds. With excess capacity in the market before the crisis, competition was intense. To reduce the costs of unsecured funding, banks engaged in maturity transformation for the unsecured part of their funding, relying on deposits or on short-term borrowing in the money market to fund the excess of their holdings over the covered bond issue in order to be competitive. When interbank markets froze in 2008, short-term funding from the money market evaporated, and Hypo Real Estate needed government support. See "Hypo Real Estate Tripped by Funding Strategy," *MarketWatch*, October 6, 2008, as well as Expertenrat (2011).

18. How would one know whether there is excess capacity in the market? In other markets, answering this question is left to market participants who enter or exit as this action appears profitable to them. In banking, the normal market mechanism does not work well because government support enables banks to survive even though they are not profitable. The experience of the German covered bond market, discussed in the previous note, had a lot to do with the fact that the Landesbanken, state-owned and state-guaranteed banks, were active in this market. These banks have been unable to earn reasonable margins even with state guarantees and have been a constant source of financial instability, but the state governments did not want to give them up. We return to this subject in our discussion of the politics of banking in Chapter 12.

19. See Expertenrat (2011), ASC (2012), and BIS (2012, 42, 63, 74). Onaran (2011) asserts that as of June 2011, the following banks were effectively insolvent: four Landesbanken, Commerzbank and Hypo Real Estate in Germany, the Cajas in Spain, and three banks

each in Ireland and Iceland, as well as Citigroup and Bank of America in the United States (see note 13). (He has not examined banks elsewhere, for example, in France.) Spanish banks have run into major problems, and the Spanish banking crisis has been threatening Europe. See "Spain Creates Bad Bank, Injects Funds in Bankia," mentioned in note 5.

20. As already mentioned, in mid-2011 Mayo (2011, 3091–3092) assesses that around $300 billion in losses don't show up because of leeway in accounting rules. This assessment was made before the various scandals and lawsuits of the summer and fall of 2012. BIS (2012, 26) has noted that the observed reduction in the aggregate amount of debt in the United States in 2010 and 2011 reflects a reduction in new mortgages rather than the acceptance of losses on existing loans.

21. This is known as the "pecking order" hypothesis in corporate finance (see Myers and Majluf 1984, Mayer 1988, Hellwig 1991 and 2000, and Berk and DeMarzo 2011, 539).

22. This discussion of payout policies is simplified to make the key points. Indeed, there is another Modigliani and Miller (M&M) result, this one concerning dividends, that is the starting point of the discussion, just as the M&M result for funding discussed in Chapter 7 is the starting point for the discussion of the costs of different funding mixes. For more on this issue see, for example, Berk and DeMarzo (2011, Chapter 17). In the case of nonfinancial companies, there is a concern that investment opportunities might not be good enough to warrant reinvesting most profits. Such companies might have "cash cows," units that earn a lot from past investments, but no good opportunities for the future. An example is oil companies with high earnings from known wells and few prospects of finding comparable wells by drilling more. See, for example, Jensen (1986, 1993). For banks the argument is less convincing because they can always invest their funds in traded securities.

23. If the shares are not traded, shareholders may have more difficulty creating a "homemade dividend," but they might be able to borrow on their own against their assets.

24. If shareholders are concerned that bank managers do not make good investments on their behalf, this indicates a governance problem within the bank. Governance issues arise in every corporation, and some claim that such problems motivate leveraged buyouts or the use of debt. However, as discussed in Chapters 8 and 9, the governance problems of banks are a bit different, and colored by bankers' ability to take and hide risks, and by the conflict of interest between bank managers and shareholders on the one hand, and creditors and taxpayers on the other.

25. See Acharya et al. (2011b) and Rosengren (2010).

26. TARP funds were actually given in exchange not for common equity but for preferred equity, which resembles long-term debt. In that sense, the funds given by the government created something similar to a debt burden on the banks and were not as useful for loss absorption as retained earnings would have been. With the restriction on pay and dividends that came along with TARP, the banks were anxious to pay off the government. The funds were therefore less useful for making loans to the economy. Other countries also used such hybrid securities for bailouts, with similar results. In the case of the German Commerzbank, where government support consisted of €16.4 billion in hybrid debt and €1.8 billion for a 25 percent share in the bank, the repayment of €14 billion in hybrid debt in the first half of 2011 made the bank very vulnerable to the losses from Greek and other

sovereign debts in the second half of 2011. On TARP, see Barofsky (2012); on Germany, see Expertenrat (2011).

27. Banks are required to have a plan by which to reach the Basel III level on time, not earlier. On allowing the dividends, see Anat Admati, "Force Banks to Put America's Needs First," *Financial Times,* January 19, 2011; Anat Admati, "Fed Runs Scared with Boost to Bank Dividends," Bloomberg, February 24, 2011; and a letter by sixteen academics, "Only Recapitalized Banks Should Pay Dividends," *Financial Times,* February 15, 2011. According to Jesse Eisinger ("Fed Shrugged Off Warnings, Let Banks Pay Shareholders Billions," *Pro Publica,* March 2, 2012), the Federal Reserve also ignored warnings by Sheila Bair, chair of the FDIC, and others to delay the payouts, and the large banks paid $33 billion in 2011. Even after the difficulties in Europe in the summer of 2011, payouts were again allowed in 2012. See Anat Admati, "Why the Bank Dividends Are a Bad Idea," Reuters, March 14, 2012.

28. See, for example, Admati et al. (2011, 2012a).

29. This decline is sometimes referred to as a "dilution" of existing shareholders by a new stock issue. As discussed in Chapters 2, 3, and 7, aside from issues of corporate control, the impact of any new stock issue on the value of existing shares depends only on how the money from the stock issue is used and how returns on investments are split between creditors and shareholders. If new equity is raised to fund profitable investments that will benefit shareholders, the stock price will rise to reflect the gain to shareholders from making the investment. In the academic literature, the argument is sometimes given that managers who have better information about a company's assets than shareholders will—and should—resist issuing new shares when they believe that the shareholders undervalue the firm and its assets (see, for example, Myers and Majluf 1984). In the context of banks, the mantra that equity is expensive is sometimes associated with this argument (see, e.g., Bolton and Freixas 2006 and Hanson et al. 2011). However, as explained by Admati et al. (2011, 2012a), the use of this argument against the tighter capital regulation of banks is flawed and represents yet another article of the bankers' new clothes. First, the argument applies only to new share issues in situations in which banks have discretion over the method of funding; if the new shares are issued in response to government regulation, the asserted effects are much weaker and possibly ambiguous. Second, the purported costs are not costs to society but result from a form of redistribution benefiting new shareholders who are given an opportunity to acquire good stocks cheaply. The effect may, in fact, disappear if the new shares are issued through a rights offering. Finally, the effects will be much reduced if banks have more equity to begin with, and thus have less need to replenish their equity.

30. As shown by Admati et al. (2012a), a preference for this form of deleveraging through asset sales over a new equity issue is to be expected if assets can be sold for a good price and if it is mainly junior debt that is repaid. If the bank has lower levels of both assets and junior debt, the outstanding senior debt will be more exposed to the bank's insolvency risk.

31. In the case of the European Union, some of the deleveraging that upset financial markets in November 2011 could have been avoided if the new target ratio of 9 percent had been specified as being in relation to the assets that banks had held on September 30, 2011,

prior to the summit, rather than in relation to the assets held in June 30, 2012. For government debts, capital requirements actually were calibrated to holdings of September 30, 2011, but not for other securities.

32. The current stock price might be positive, reflecting the upside potential that the bank might recover, as well as the value of government subsidies. This does not preclude the possibility that the bank might be insolvent.

33. As indicated in note 16, Laeven and Valencia (2012) suggest that the use of government support as a way of avoiding a cleanup may be a reason that advanced economies take much longer to come out of a crisis than emerging economies.

34. In contrast, since 2007 European countries seem to have had a policy of rescuing every bank without even considering whether the bank was solvent or not. For an extensive discussion of this policy, see ASC (2012). See also Dag Detter, "Swedish Lessons for the New Owners of Spanish Banks," *Financial Times*, October 9, 2012.

35. See notes 17 and 18.

36. This 7 percent consists of a minimum equity requirement of 4.5 percent (up from 2 percent under Basel II) and a newly introduced so-called capital conservation buffer of 2.5 percent of the banks' risk-weighted assets. In addition, banks will be required to have so-called Tier 1 capital of at least 6 percent and Tier 2 capital of at least 8 percent of their risk-weighted assets, to which the capital conservation buffer must be added. Tier 1 capital and Tier 2 capital consist of common equity and, in addition, certain forms of hybrid securities that have some properties of debt and some properties of equity. In December 2011, the Federal Reserve announced that it will require U.S. banks with total assets of $50 billion or more to satisfy the requirements of Basel III (see http://www.federalreserve.gov/newsevents/press/bcreg/20111220a.htm, accessed October 14, 2012).

37. Deutsche Bank itself lists "Tier 1 capital without hybrid securities" as worth €37 billion, or 9.5 percent of its risk-weighted assets. The difference reflects various deductions, such as deductions for expected losses on sovereign debt, mandated by the European Banking Authority, which have not yet entered the bank's balance sheet. The 9.5 percent ratio thus obtained put the bank in compliance with the requirement of the EU summit of October 2011 that was discussed earlier in this chapter.

38. The differences are not as large for U.S. banks, mainly because, as discussed later in this chapter, the United States has not implemented Basel II for commercial banks. However, for U.S. banks as well, the risk-weighted assets are significantly less than their total assets (see Ledo 2012). Capital requirements in the United States have traditionally included required ratios relative to total assets at least for FDIC-insured institutions. See FDIC Law, Regulations, Related Acts—Rules and Regulations, Part 325, http://www.fdic.gov/regulations/laws/rules/2000-4400.html, accessed October 14, 2012, and FDIC Law, Regulations, Related Acts—Bank Holding Company Act, http://www.fdic.gov/regulations/laws/rules/6000-2200.html, accessed October 14, 2012. For proposals of the Office of the Comptroller of the Currency, the Federal Reserve, and the FDIC regarding the U.S. implementation of Basel III, see https://www.federalregister.gov/articles/2012/08/30/2012-16757/regulatory-capital-rules-regulatory-capital-implementation-of-basel-iii-minimum-regulatory-capital#h-10, accessed October 14, 2012.

39. See "The Wait Is Over: The Biggest Sovereign Default in History, and the Most Anticipated," *The Economist*, March 17, 2012.

40. As discussed in Chapter 6, note 56, this was the case for Swiss bank UBS. The Dexia insolvency was due to losses on government debt, in particular Greek government debt. We discuss Dexia in Chapter 12.

41. Bair (2012, Chapter 3) describes her attempts to argue against the Basel II risk weights.

42. Full introduction is to begin in 2015 if a foregoing trial period is deemed to have been successful. Taken literally, the term *leverage ratio* refers to the relation between debt and equity. Requiring that a bank's equity be at least 3 percent of its total assets, that is, the sum of its debt and equity, is equivalent to requiring that the leverage ratio not exceed 97:3, that is, 32.3:1.

43. September 14, 2010. Our discussion of capital regulation in Chapter 6 referred to the regulation of leverage measured in this way.

44. The evolution of bank equity was discussed at the end of Chapter 2, and safety nets were discussed in Chapter 9. See Holtfrerich (1981), Berger et al. (1995), Alessandri and Haldane (2009), Malysheva and Walter (2010), and Haldane (2011b).

45. Some—for example, Eugene Fama, a well-known University of Chicago finance professor—argued in a CNBC interview in May 2010 that equity levels should be even higher, on the order of 40–50 percent. Kotlikoff (2010) proposes, essentially, that no debt be allowed for financial intermediaries except for a narrow bank that essentially invests only in cash. All other financial institutions should be run as mutual funds, with requirements for extensive reporting about activities and investments in order to protect shareholders. These mutual funds would not have any debt at all. Such funds might, however, have serious problems of their own. Investors want fund shares to be liquid so they can get at (some of) their money when they need it. In the case of open-end funds, investors would return their shares and get whatever the shares were worth. If the assets held by a fund were traded daily on a public exchange, determining share values would be easy. If the assets were not traded daily on a public exchange, or perhaps not traded daily at all, share values could at best be estimated. In this case, moreover, the mutual fund could be vulnerable to runs if shareholders fearing asset price declines returned their shares and the fund had to sell assets to get the cash it needed to repay shareholders. Because Germany has had such experiences with open-end mutual funds for real estate investments, the German Federal Ministry of Finance proposed in July 2012 to outlaw open-end mutual funds for real estate investments.

46. Miller (1995, 487).

47. The United States has a tradition of distinguishing institutions on the basis of the activities in which they traditionally engage. With a very literal interpretation of legal terms, this leaves room for new institutions to claim that they are doing something different than banks and therefore should not be subject to the same regulations as banks. Gorton (1994) explains how this arrangement tends to destabilize the financial system by allowing for excessive competition between "banks" and "nonbanks" performing banking services. By contrast to the U.S. law, the German law on banking regulation defines a credit institution (the German legal term for a bank) as any institution engaging in any one of a

number of activities; using this approach, "banks" and "banking" are always the same. By this logic, money market mutual funds that allow customers to participate in the payment process should be treated like banks. In particular, if money market mutual funds promise a stable net asset value, this promise should be treated as a liability and the shares as deposits. Legally, the promise might not be binding, but when a money market fund "breaks the buck"—that is, when the value of its shares falls below \$1—its "depositors" are likely to run in just the same way as the depositors of a bank. Money market funds are not explicitly insured by the deposit insurance system. Sponsoring institutions routinely provide them with backing. In the Lehman crisis, however, money market funds suffered a panic anyway until the federal government provided them with the analog of deposit insurance. Even primary money market funds take nontrivial risks in their investments without the ability to absorb losses on their own. See Acharya et al. (2010, Chapter 10), Brady et al. (2012), and Rosengren (2012). Money market funds in the United States are supervised by the SEC, as investment funds that have little to do with banking. As of October 2012, the SEC has not been able to decide on any reform of money market fund regulation.

48. Examples would be clearinghouses, in particular those designated for derivatives trading; market makers for key securities, that is, dealers who stand ready to trade these securities with anyone wishing to do so; and investment banks that are highly interconnected to other financial institutions.

49. Interestingly, hedge funds were significantly less highly leveraged in the run-up to the financial crisis (see Ang et al. 2011), and although many failed, none created any significant contagion. Nevertheless, to prevent the buildup of systemic risk, hedge funds should be watched—for example, through disclosure requirements—particularly if they become large. On hedge funds, see Mallaby (2010).

50. On clearinghouses, see Levitin (2013). Allison (2011, 426–432), after arguing that the 2007–2009 crisis (which he calls a crash) proved that diversification is a myth, states, "Instead of confirming that megabanks could get by with less capital than the total required to support their businesses on a stand-alone basis, the crash proved the opposite: They must have enough capital to sustain each business through its own highly stressed scenario, as if each were a separate unit. Therefore, in terms of reducing capital requirements, there seems to be no advantage to combining supposedly diversified financial businesses. If the capital base of a subsidiary can be tapped by an affiliate, then that subsidiary must hold additional capital against that contingency."

51. For example, BCBS (2010a) assumes that banks target a particular fixed return on equity even as equity requirements change. Some of the models that were used (so-called dynamic stochastic general equilibrium models, semi-structural models, and reduced-form models) falsely assume that if banks have more equity, it will be costly to society, for example, by increasing lending spreads in a way that creates social costs. A model used in some of the analysis is from Van den Heuvel (2008), in which higher equity forces banks to limit their deposits, although, as we saw, deposits amount to only a fraction of the debts of some banks, and there is no reason to assume that equity cannot be added. (Van den Heuvel 2008, published around the time of the financial crisis, concludes that the Basel II capital requirements are *too high*, something that the crisis proved to be patently false. See

Admati et al. 2011, section 3.2.) Angelini et al. (2011), posted as a Federal Reserve Bank of New York staff report, claims that each additional percentage of capital requirements would reduce GDP by 0.09 percent. The report admits that it ignores the benefits of higher requirements, but its title suggests that it is about the *long-term impact* of higher requirements, and the statement about GDP declines can easily be taken out of context. Bank lobbying groups such as the Institute of International Finance or the Clearing House routinely claim that their "research" has indicated significant declines in growth, jobs, and so on as a result of increased capital requirements. One of the studies justifying the Basel III numbers (BCBS 2010d, 1) states: "The regulatory minimum is the amount of capital needed [by the bank] to be regarded as a viable going concern by creditors and counterparties." By this criterion, however, regulation would not be necessary: if a bank failed to be regarded by creditors and counterparties as a viable entity that they could safely interact with, the bank would, virtually by definition, no longer be viable because creditors and counterparties would refuse to deal with it. The statement fails to recognize that the regulation should reduce the *collateral damage* of high leverage, the impact of banks' distress or insolvency on the system. To achieve this, much more equity is beneficial, particularly because there is no social cost in having more equity. In BCBS (2010a), the benefits from avoiding financial crises and recessions are explicitly taken into account, but in this study the costs of higher capital requirements are assessed based on the assumption that the required rate of ROE is independent of how much equity a bank has, a fallacy we discussed in Chapter 7. (The report recognizes that this overstates the cost of additional equity but chooses this approach to show that even with this assumption, the benefits of additional equity outweigh the costs.) The studies also ignore the distorted incentives generated by the use of risk weights and their consequences for the financial system and the economy, which we discuss later.

52. Hanson et al. (2011), Miles et al. (2011), Buch and Prieto (2012), Cole (2012), and Junge and Kugler (2012) show that there would be little if any negative impact on lending and the cost of loans if banks had much more equity. As noted, Hanson et al. (2011) fails to recognize that banks' paying more taxes or raising new equity do not have social costs. Their concerns with the shadow banking system point to the challenge of enforcement, but it is not a rationale for avoiding beneficial regulation. If there is a governance concern with managers' having access to too much "free cash flow," solutions such as creating a "liability holding company," as suggested by Admati et al. (2012c) should be considered. We discuss governance problems and concerns with shadow banking again in Chapter 13.

53. "Healthy Banking System Is the Goal, Not Profitable Banks," *Financial Times*, November 9, 2010, initiated by the two of us and signed by twenty academics, including John H. Cochrane, Eugene F. Fama, Charles Goodhart, Stewart C. Myers, William F. Sharpe, Stephen A. Ross, and Chester Spatt, criticizes Basel III as flawed and insufficient, calls for at least 15 percent equity relative to total assets, raises concerns with the use of risk weights, and proposes a ban on dividends as the obvious place to start in a transition. (Text and full list available at http://www.gsb.stanford.edu/news/research/admatiopen.html, accessed October 20, 2012.) For additional commentary, see Joseph V. Rizzi, "Case Is Strong for Capital Additions," *American Banker*, February, 16, 2011; Mark J. Perry and Robert Dell,

"More Equity, Less Government: Rethinking Bank Regulation," *The American,* February 24, 2011; Matt Miller, "The Next Bank Crisis Is Coming," *Washington Post,* April 27, 2011; Sebastian Mallaby, "Radicals Are Right to Take on the Banks," *Financial Times,* June 7, 2011; Simon Johnson, "Jamie Dimon's Faulty Capital Requirement Math," Bloomberg, June 9, 2011; Joe Nocera, "Banking's Moment of Truth," *New York Times,* June 20, 2011; Tim Hartford, "More Equity, Less Risk," *Financial Times,* July 2, 2011; David Miles, "Banks Can Raise More Capital," *Wall Street Journal,* Europe edition, July 2, 2011; John Cochrane, "The More Bank Capital, the Safer the Bank," *Wall Street Journal,* July 15, 2011; Clive Crook, "Real Reasons That Bankers Don't Like Basel Rules," Bloomberg, December 20, 2011; Robert Jenkins, "Basel II Proved to Be Inadequate, So Are the New Rules Really 'Too Severe'?," *The Independent,* April 27, 2012; and "Rules for Bank Capital Still Broken after Four Years," Bloomberg editorial, May 6, 2012. Bair (2012) discusses capital requirements extensively and argues for higher requirements than those in Basel III. Jenkins (2011), Haldane (2012c), and Hoenig (2012) also urge higher requirements, and both view risk weights, discussed later, as highly problematic. Senators Sherrod Brown and David Vitter echoed the sentiment in a letter to regulators written in October 2012 (see William Alden, "2 Regulators Call for Greater Bank Capital Requirements," *New York Times,* October 17, 2012).

54. Allan Meltzer, in testimony before the Congressional Oversight Panel, recommended 20 percent equity for the largest banks. See note 120 in the report, available at http://www .gpo.gov/fdsys/pkg/CHRG-112shrg64832/pdf/CHRG-112shrg64832.pdf (accessed October 31, 2012), which also mentions testimony by Simon Johnson agreeing with Eugene Fama's suggestion (see note 45) that banks should have 40–50 percent equity.

55. One could go further to suggest that even the levels of equity that were seen in the past, before the development and growth of the safety nets, have also been inefficiently low. Banks, in other words, may have been chronically inefficient, always taking too much risk given their level of equity or, equivalently, having too little equity for the risks they take. This can be attributed to the fundamental conflicts of interest about risk between borrowers and creditors and to the fact that bank creditors, such as depositors, might be more dispersed than other creditors in the economy. Their ability to withdraw their funds, in fact, gives depositors a sense that they can just withdraw when they fear that the banks are in trouble. In the middle of the nineteenth century, as we noted in Chapter 2, banks had 40–50 percent equity, and their shareholders had unlimited liability. Whereas it is not practical to rely on the personal liability of banks' owners, it should be noted that, relative to the nineteenth century, equity markets are vastly more developed now, and the access of all companies to equity investors is much easier than it was a century or more ago.

56. Admati et al. (2011), first posted in August 2010, concludes with the statement "We have based our analysis of the costs and benefits of increasing equity requirements for banks on what we assess to be the fundamental economic issues involved. We expect that some will disagree with our conclusions. Any discussion of this important topic in public policy should be fully focused on social costs and benefits. Moreover, any assertions that are made should be based on sound arguments and persuasive evidence. Unfortunately, the level of policy debate on this subject that we have seen is not always consistent with these standards."

57. The Federal Reserve has approved the payouts. However, after JPMorgan Chase incurred losses of $5.8 billion in spring 2012, some of the payouts were delayed. See Dan Fitzpatrick and Matthias Rieker, "Whale's Tail Hits Bank on Buyback," *Wall Street Journal*, August 9, 2012.

58. A typical example (reported to Martin Hellwig by several participants) is the following. German savings banks, most of them owned by the cities or the districts in which they operate, have given warning that, if the leverage ratio regulation is put in place, lending to municipalities or districts might be restricted and in any case will become more expensive because, for the first time in history, such lending will have to be backed by 3 percent equity. Because every mayor knows a member of the Bundestag or the European Parliament, these concerns have become the subject of broad discussion in those bodies.

59. Admittedly, this view was shared in Hellwig (1995) and in Hellwig and Staub (1996) as opposed to Hellwig (2009, 2010a). However, in Hellwig and Staub (1996) the issue of how to control the quality of the models used to determine risk weights is already raised.

60. See Tarullo (2008) and Goodhart (2011).

61. See "FDIC: Crisis Validates US Basel II Delay and Leverage Ratio," *Risk Magazine*, August 20, 2009.

62. Under Basel III as well as Basel II, there are three "pillars" of banking supervision. Pillar 1 concerns capital regulation, pillar 2 the professional quality of banking, and pillar 3 "market discipline." Of these three pillars, pillar 1 is most important because it involves hard rules for capital requirements. Pillar 1 distinguishes assets depending on whether they are held in the "banking book" or the "trading book" of the bank; assets in the banking book are meant to be held until they are repaid, whereas assets in the trading book are available for resale at an opportune moment. For each category, banks can choose whether they want to use a "standard approach," with risk weights specified in the regulations, or, for credit risks, an "internal ratings–based" approach and, for assets in the trading book, a model-based approach to determine the capital required. The zero-risk-weights rule for government debt is given in the regulations for the standard approach to credit risk. A major flaw of the entire approach is that it assumes that risks are independent. Correlations are neglected, for example, those due to the fact that mortgage borrowers often are likely to fail together or not at all.

63. Some of the attempts to appear well capitalized are described as "alchemy" by Tom Braithwaite in "Banks Turn to Financial Alchemy in Search for Capital" (*Financial Times*, October 24, 2011). The article quotes Jamie Dimon of JPMorgan Chase as saying that the bank will " 'manage the hell out of RWA [risk-weighted assets]' to reach the higher levels" and concludes by saying that "capital hawks will need to watch both the banks and the national regulators if RWA is not to mean Really Weird Accounting."

64. An example is the risk that if banks use short-term borrowing to fund long-term lending, an increase in the market rates of interest might require them to borrow at rates above those they receive on outstanding loans. As discussed in Chapter 4, this risk caused many U.S. savings banks to become insolvent in the early 1980s. Even so, it is ignored in Basel II and Basel III. By tradition, banks' investments are separated into two groups, those in the so-called banking book and those in the so-called trading book. The banking

book includes loans that the bank plans to hold until they are paid back. For these loans, Basel II and III impose risk weights that depend only on credit risk, that is, the risk that the borrowers might not pay. The risk that funding conditions might change is not considered. Another example is the risk that many debtors might default at the same time. Existing capital regulation, the so-called Pillar 1 of the Basel rules, is based on the assumption that the credit risks of different debtors can be assessed in isolation. This would be appropriate if the risks were independent; in fact, the credit risks of, say, mortgage debtors in Southern California are highly correlated because real estate markets in Southern California depend on how the economy there is doing. Similarly, the credit risks of suppliers to the big auto manufacturers are highly correlated. Both the risk that funding conditions might change and the risk from loans' being correlated should in principle be considered under the so-called Pillar 2 of the Basel rules, which is concerned with the professional quality of the individual banks' management and procedures. However, there are no hard and fast rules as to how to do this, and in practice not much is done.

65. The Bank for International Settlements has been calling for a change in this rule (see, e.g., BIS 2012, 62–63; see also J. Caruana and S. Avdjiev, "Sovereign Creditworthiness and Financial Stability: An International Perspective," *Banque de France, Financial Stability Review* 16 [April 2012]: 71–85). However, such calls meet with resistance from countries that have a long tradition of using banking regulation to ensure that banks pay for government deficits; as discussed in the notes to Chapter 12, zero risk weights for government debt are a key political concern of many governments.

66. First, a 1996 amendment to Basel I allowed banks to use their own risk models to determine how much equity they need for so-called market risks, the risks of changes in the market prices of their investments. In Basel II this approach was extended to credit risk, that is, the risk of default by a borrower or another partner in a contract (see Tarullo 2008, Goodhart 2011, Haldane 2011a and 2012c, and Hoenig 2012). IMF (2008a) and Acharya et al. (2011) show that leverage had increased in the decade before the crisis.

67. Incentive effects of the regulation—in particular, incentive distortions from flawed risk weights—had been discussed in academic research. See, for example, Koehn and Santomero (1980), Kim and Santomero (1988), and Rochet (1992).

68. For a systematic overview and explanation why some of the flaws are fundamental and can hardly be repaired, see Hellwig (2010a). King (2010) also raises concerns about the use of risk weights. In "We Need Much Simpler Rules to Rein in the Banks" (*Financial Times,* August 26, 2012), Nicholas Brady, who chaired the Presidential Task Force on Market Mechanisms after the 1987 crash and subsequently served as U.S. secretary of the Treasury, wrote: "This computer modelling is impressive stuff. However, while these models create the appearance of mathematical certainty about the relationships between markets and the way world events will affect prices, it is essential to recognise that, at their root, these models rely on man-made assumptions about human behaviour—not iron-bound laws of nature. In addition, the behaviour of derivatives markets can be episodic and illiquid at precisely the times we most need greater liquidity and confidence. No matter how sophisticated the maths or how large the data base supporting a model, no one can predict behaviour—human or market—with certainty. Inevitably, this means the formulas break

down at the most critical times." In the same vein, Andrew Haldane of the Bank of England has argued that Basel III is too complex and called for simplifying banking regulations (see Haldane 2011a and 2012c and Jason Zweig, "The Jackson Hole Speech People Should Long Remember," *Wall Street Journal*, August 31, 2012). In a similar vein, Hoenig (2012), from the FDIC, criticized Basel for its failed risk weight approach and low levels of equity requirements (see "Basel III Should Be Scrapped, Hoenig Says," *American Banker*, September 14, 2012). Roubini and Mihm (2010, 203–209 and 214) also criticize the use of risk weights and recommend caps on absolute leverage for banks of all sizes, without allowing any discretion to be given bankers to interpret the requirements.

69. UBS (2008) gives several examples of how, under certain conditions, risks in quantitative models were set equal to zero.

70. Mortgage-related securities would usually be held in the so-called trading book, loans in the bank book. For securities in the trading book, the model-based approach to determining equity requirements provided banks with much greater scope to downplay risks (see FSA 2010). Government bonds, which receive an automatic zero risk weight when they are held in the bank book, are an exception. By contrast, loans to small and medium-sized businesses are treated as fairly risky, partly because they led to large losses in the crises of the early 1990s, but in 2007–2008 they actually were much safer.

71. For a more detailed description, see Chapter 5, note 2 and Chapter 4, note 43. At each stage, a package of junior ("mezzanine") claims, with low credit ratings of BBB or worse, would be formed, and new claims, with different priorities, would be issued against the returns from this package. Under the assumption that credit risks on the different securities in a package of mezzanine mortgage-backed securities (MBS) were independent, the senior MBS collateralized debt obligations (CDOs) would be treated as almost riskless and given ratings of AAA. However, the assumption of independence of credit risks was unwarranted because all of the underlying mortgages depended on the factors driving U.S. real estate markets, such as the overall economy, the interest rate policy of the Federal Reserve, and the real estate bubble itself. McLean and Nocera (2010, 362) sarcastically ask: "Collateralized debt obligation? Synthetic securities? What had been the point of that?" The point was that banks responded to flawed regulations in their own interest; their actions had little to do with efficiency.

72. The regulators require banks to use five years of data. For a boom-and-bust cycle in real estate that extends over a decade, this amounts to less than one full observation. For an assessment of the creditworthiness of a partner like AIG, a lot of the information from four years ago may already be irrelevant.

73. Another criticism is that the model-based approach to equity requirements focuses on probabilities rather than potential losses. Equity requirements for market risk are given by three times the amount needed to cover any losses that might occur with 99 percent probability. The size of losses that might occur with the remaining probability of 1 percent or less is not considered. This approach betrays a remarkable confidence in our ability to assess probabilities, and a remarkable lack of concern for the potentially disastrous consequences that might arise from large losses in one of those so-called tail events that are neglected.

74. See Demirgüç-Kunt et al. (2010) and Brealey et al. (2011).

75. See the Web sites of the EBA, for example, http://www.eba.europa.eu/EU-wide-stress-testing/2011/2011-EU-wide-stress-test-results.aspx, and the Federal Reserve, for example, http://www.federalreserve.gov/newsevents/press/bcreg/20120313a.htm, accessed October 19, 2012.

76. In 2010 this was the experience of the major Irish banks, in the summer of 2011 that of, for example, Dexia. See Admati et al. (2012b) for additional comments on stress tests. Because there is no reason to economize on bank equity, the cost–benefit considerations underlying the stress tests are not clear. To some extent stress tests seem to address problems arising because accounting rules mask the true financial positions of banks.

77. The treatment of these securities is a major issue in Spain. Spanish banks had sold many such securities, such as preferred stocks, to small investors, workers, or pensioners, presenting them as "savings products" without explaining the risks involved. European authorities called on to bail out Spanish banks have asked that holders of such hybrid securities share in the banks' losses. Spanish courts, meanwhile, have judged that these sales were invalid because banks did not properly inform their customers about the risks. See Miles Johnson, Peter Spiegel, and Joshua Chaffin, "Spain Pressed to Inflict Losses on Small Investors," *Financial Times*, July 12, 2012. See also "Unhappy Holidays: A Proposed Hit to Savers Increases the Government's Unpopularity," *The Economist*, August 18, 2012.

78. Following this experience, the Basel Committee on Banking Supervision proposed rules that would ensure that hybrid securities participated in losses before government funds were used for bailouts (see BCBS 2010b). These proposals, however, do not address the problem that governments might be intent on bailing out the very holders of these hybrid securities. See the discussion about triggers later in this chapter and notes 80 and 81, as well as Admati (2010) and Hellwig (2010b). In the United States, the Collins Amendment to the Dodd-Frank Act (see Bair, 2012, Chapter 19) disallows the consideration of so-called trust preferred securities, which are essentially debt, as loss absorbing in capital regulation. (The amendment also requires that the capital standards be imposed on U.S. bank holding companies and systemically important nonbank financial companies.)

79. The success of this lobbying can be seen in Europe. Whereas Basel III insists that, for banks whose shares are traded on stock exchanges, only common equity will be accepted as "core capital," the capital requirements regulation that has been proposed by the European Commission gives a list of only fourteen criteria that must be fulfilled. The list is spelled out in such a way that, in addition to common equity, banks might also use "silent participations," which are popular with public banks in Germany. The details of these funding instruments depend on each contract, but typically the holders are not given any rights of control and the lack of control is compensated for by a debt-like promise to pay a fixed return unless the bank is incurring losses. For the EU proposals, see http://ec.europa.eu/internal_market/bank/regcapital/new_proposals_en.htm, accessed October 21, 2012; for a critique, see Basel Committee on Banking Supervision, Basel III Regulatory Consistency Assessment (Level 2) Preliminary Report: European Union, Basel, October 2012, http://www.bis.org/bcbs/implementation/l2_eu.pdf, accessed October 22, 2012.

80. Contingent capital has been championed by a number of academics (see, for example, Flannery 2005; French et al. 2010, written by fifteen academics; and Calomiris and Herring 2011). In some variations, the trigger for conversion is specified as a condition on the stock price or on measures of equity on the balance sheet. In other variations, the regulation or the contract for this type of debt also specifies conditions indicating a systemic crisis that would allow regulators to convert the debt into equity. The bail-in concept is similar to resolution in many respects, relying on regulators to impose losses and convert some debt to equity. (Some of the issues around resolution mechanisms were discussed at the end of Chapter 5. For comments on BCBS 2010b, see Admati 2010 and Hellwig 2010b.)

81. For example, suppose that significant positions in these securities are held by insurance companies. If events occur that induce the contractually stipulated conversion of contingent capital into common stock, how is the government going to deal with the systemic implications of the conversion? At the conversion point, there is likely to be a discontinuous drop in the stock price. Will insurance companies bear the associated losses, or will the government prefer to preempt the conversion so as to avoid such systemic fallout? Another issue is how the conversion ratio and the degree of dilution of preexisting shareholders should be defined. Because different stakeholders (holders of co cos, existing equity holders and creditors, and bank managers) are likely to have different preferences regarding conversion, a serious concern is that manipulation and instability will occur if the triggers seem to be within reach, with different parties trying to affect accounting measures or stock prices so as to bring about the outcome desirable to them. The use of accounting triggers is further problematic because accounting numbers are often based on historical values and thus may not provide the proper triggers for recapitalization near a crisis. Issues associated with triggers are discussed by R. McDonald (2010), Sundaresan and Wang (2010), and Prescott (2012). In particular, Sundaresan and Wang (2010) and Prescott (2012) show that the use of price triggers can create significant instabilities and difficulties in pricing.

82. Among the reasons that debt-like hybrids such as co cos are more popular in Europe than in the United States is that their interest is considered a tax-deductible expense even though it has an equity-like component. In the United States, co cos do not qualify as a debt for tax purposes because they do not offer "creditor rights." On the other hand, the tax code recognizes payments for so-called trust-preferred securities, which banks have used as part of their regulatory capital even though they are effectively debt securities. This practice has allowed banks to appear better capitalized than they were. The Collins Amendment to the Dodd-Frank Act seeks to stop this practice. On ways banks have tried to use the securities, see Yalman Onaran and Jody Shenn, "Banks in 'Downward Spiral' Buying Capital in CDOs," Bloomberg, June 8, 2010. The use of preferred stock instead of equity is also problematic because it constrains banks in many ways and thus adds a debt overhang that can interfere with lending, as discussed in Chapter 3 and earlier in this chapter.

83. The discussion in Chapter 7 about whether equity is "expensive" also applies to the comparison of equity and co cos. It is false to suggest that using equity is more expensive than using co cos just because equity is riskier and thus has a higher required ROE than

co cos. Although co cos would have a lower required ROE than equity, using co cos instead of equity would make equity more risky and thus increase its risk and its required ROE. French et al. (2010) suggest that short-term debt "disciplines" managers. However, this suggestion does not explain why co cos are superior to equity, because co cos are in fact *long-term* debt. As discussed in Chapter 10 (note 56) and in Admati et al. (2011, section 5), the suggestion that debt disciplines managers is not supported empirically; the models that argue this ignore important features of the real world, such as banks' repeated ability to borrow (the rat race of borrowing) and the distorted incentives of bank managers to increase leverage and risk, discussed in Chapters 8 and 9. If co cos are instead issued as equity from the start, effectively converting immediately, they will automatically be able to absorb the same losses in the same scenarios as do co cos, fixing the banks' investment decisions (see Admati et al. 2011, section 8, and Admati and Hellwig 2011a).

84. Bob Diamond of Barclays admitted as much in 2011, saying the bank would seek to use co cos in an attempt to avoid harming its ROE (see "Barclays Chief Ready to Increase Risk Appetite in Search of Profits," *Financial Times*, April 11, 2011, discussed in Chapter 8; see note 13).

85. See the discussion in note 82 of this chapter.

86. See Patrick Jenkins, "UK Banks to Issue New Equity for Bonuses," *Financial Times*, March 4, 2012. The banks were responding to pressure from the Bank of England to avoid depleting their equity.

87. The range between 20 and 30 percent provides for a so-called conservation buffer where banks must try to conserve their equity and not let it be depleted by payouts such as dividends. Basel III includes this sensible concept, with a range of 4.5–7 percent of Tier 1 capital (primarily equity but often including other securities, such as preferred equity) relative to risk-weighted assets. Basel III also postulates the use of countercyclical buffers meant to contain the credit booms that often lead to credit busts (see BCBS 2010e). Goodhart (2010) also discusses the need for graduated capital standards.

88. As noted in Chapter 6, JPMorgan had 8 percent equity relative to its total assets as measured by U.S. accounting standards in December 2011, but its equity would have been only 4.5 percent of its total assets using the standards that are applied to European banks. See Tucker (2012) for similar observations on consolidating assets on balance sheets. Other areas of concern are the use of collateral to hide indebtedness in contracts such as repos (see Skeel and Jackson 2012) and the practice of rehypothecation. Singh and Aitken (2010, abstract), from the IMF, state that "from a policy angle, supervisors of large banks that report on a global consolidated basis may need to enhance their understanding of the off–balance sheet funding that these banks receive via rehypothecation from other jurisdictions."

89. In the case of Lehman Brothers, so-called repo 105 transactions made the bank appear stronger than it actually was. See Valukas (2010) and Michael J. De La Merced and Julia Werdigier, "The Origins of Lehman's 'Repo 105,'" *New York Times*, March 10, 2010. Haldane (2011c) calls for a reexamination of accounting rules for banks so as to provide better information to regulators.

90. There remains the concern about the governance of banks and whether bankers have incentives to take excessive risks. We will revisit this issue in Chapter 13.

TWELVE   *The Politics of Banking*

1. See Chapter 11, notes 4 and 5.

2. Central banks are prohibited from acquiring equity in other banks, so the only support they can give is in the form of loans against collateral, as "lenders of last resort" (see "Bank State Aid in the Financial Crisis," Center for European Policy Studies Task Force Report, October 29, 2010, http://www.ceps.eu/book/bank-state-aid-financial-crisis-fragmentation-or-level-playing-field, accessed October 15, 2012).

3. On the history of Dexia (already mentioned in Chapter 4; see note 39), from its founding in 1996 to the end in 2011, see Thomas (2012). In the 2011 bailout, €95 billion of toxic assets were split off into a "bad bank" that was guaranteed by the two governments. In addition, the Belgian government paid €4 billion for Dexia's Belgian retail business, which it nationalized. The operations and remaining assets and liabilities of the French part of Dexia were transferred to two government-owned institutions in France. See "Governments to Take Toxic Assets Off Dexia's Hands: Report," *Agence France Presse,* October 9, 2008; "Rescued Bank Dexia Posts 3.3 Billion Euros Losses for 2008," *Agence France Presse,* February 26, 2009; and "France, Belgium Reach Pact on Ailing Dexia," *Wall Street Journal,* October 10, 2011.

4. "Lagarde Calls for Urgent Action on Banks," *Financial Times,* August 27, 2011.

5. Mr. Noyer's remarks are quoted in a piece by David Enrich and David Gauthier-Villars, "Struggling French Banks Fought to Avoid Oversight," *Wall Street Journal,* October 21, 2011. Similar remarks were made by the French finance minister, who said that there was no reason "to question or worry about the French banking system" (see "French Finmin Says Country's Banks Healthy," Reuters, August 31, 2011).

6. See "Paris and Berlin Seek to Dilute Bank Rules," *Financial Times,* January 22, 2012; "French Banks Lobby Politicians over Basel Concerns," Reuters, January 29, 2010; Brian Blackstone and David Enrich, "Germany Holds Out for Better Deal at Basel," *Wall Street Journal,* July 28, 2010; Tom Braithwaite, "FDIC Chief Says Watchdogs 'Succumbing' to Bank Lobby," *Financial Times,* July 20, 2010; "Heavy Lobbying Leads to Easing of Basel III Banking Norms," Reuters, July 27, 2010; and "Feud Deepens over EU Bank Rules; Germany, France Lead Effort to Relax Regulations; U.K. Urges Tougher Approach," *Wall Street Journal,* June 18, 2011. Bair (2012, Chapter 22) describes the negotiations.

7. Kaserer (2010) estimates that the costs of the bailout to the German taxpayers will eventually come to €34–€52 billion. Information that has become available since his estimate—for example, on the sizes of the "bad bank" portfolios of Hypo Real Estate and WestLB and of losses in these portfolios from the sovereign debt crisis in Europe—suggests that this estimate should be raised by some €20–30 billion. The Dexia bailouts in 2008 and 2011 were costly to France as well as Belgium (see note 3). In the mid-1990s, Crédit Lyonnais, then the largest French bank, had losses in excess of €20 billion and required an injection of taxpayer money amounting to €15 billion.

8. As an example, see the discussion of the role of the City of London in ICB (2011, 15), which reads, "The recommendations in this report will be positive for UK competitiveness overall by strengthening financial stability. That should also be good for the City's inter-

national reputation as a place to do business." Andrew Tyrie, chair of the Parliamentary Committee on Banking Standards, wrote that banking is "one of the UK's most important industries and if banks are to be at the heart of our economy, they must be allowed to remain internationally competitive" ("A Mandate to Tackle Our Banks' Failure," *Financial Times*, October 1, 2012). Thiemann (2012) shows how supervisors' concerns about the competitive positions of "their" banks had been responsible for some of the worst lapses of supervision before the crisis. In the context of Basel III, France and Germany not only resisted increases in capital requirements as such; they also wanted to preserve some past rules that allowed securities other than banks' common equity to be treated as "capital"—in the case of France, minority participations in insurance companies owned by the banks, in the case of Germany, so-called silent participations, hybrids between debt and equity, which are debt-like in that they have given nominal claims with priority over payments to shareholders and are equity-like in that these claims are reduced or even voided when the banks are incurring losses. In practice, the banks' shareholders experience mainly the debt-like nature of these hybrids, in particular the burden of debt when the bank is in distress; for an account of problems this can create, see Expertenrat (2011).

9. See Viscusi et al. (2005). A famous example of capture is the transformation of the Interstate Commerce Commission, created in 1887 to protect consumers from railroad companies exploiting monopoly power, into an agency that prevented competition between railroad (and later also trucking) companies and imposed high prices for transportation, in particular long-haul transportation. See Friedman and Friedman (1990, 183 ff) and the references given there. On capture in the financial industry, see Kane (2001), Johnson and Kwak (2010), Wilmarth (2011), and Kwak (2012). See also Lessig (2011) on the increasing effect of lobbying in U.S. politics. Barofsky (2012, Chapter 1) describes the culture in Washington, D.C., as one based on narratives and everyone's thinking about their next job. The book opens by describing a conversation in which Mr. Barofsky is advised that his career would suffer if he challenged those in the system too much.

10. Olson (1982) and Acemoglu and Robinson (2012) discuss the origins of such differences and show how economic and political performance are affected by them.

11. Dimon, interview in the *Financial Times*, September 12, 2011.

12. "German Banks Try to Fend Off Basel III," *Financial Times*, September 6, 2010. See "Behind French Bank Drama, a Relaxed Regulator?" *Wall Street Journal*, September 15, 2011.

13. See "EU Warns US to Speed Up Bank Reform," *Financial Times*, June 1, 2011.

14. See Ronald Orol, "Geithner Urges Global Capital Rules for Swaps," *MarketWatch*, June 6, 2011.

15. See note 6, as well as notes 33–34 in Chapter 1. Clear warnings about the impact of such pressures were expressed by Swiss supervisors in 1995 and 1996; see the statements of Kurt Hauri in Blattner (1995, 826–827) and of Daniel Zuberbühler in Hellwig and Staub (1996, 768–771).

16. We neglect the sequencing of payments. In practice, a business first has to obtain funding through borrowing or raising equity. It can use this funding to pay for inputs, such as labor, machines, or raw materials. When the output is sold, it can use the revenues

to repay its debt and pay the remainder to its owners. If the activity is maintained, the payments to creditors and owners may be limited to interest and dividends; this avoids the need to acquire new funding for input purchases for further activity.

17. See Lewis (2011); "Financial: Iceland: From the Devil to the Deep Blue Sea: After the Banking Collapse, a Stricken Nation Hopes a Return to Fishing Will Save It," *The Guardian*, June 3, 2009; and "Tiny Iceland's Huge Banking Debt Led to Downfall," Reuters, October 7, 2008.

18. This is the essence of the theory of international trade with competitive markets, one of the classics of economics, first developed by David Ricardo (1817, Chapter 7). The argument is independent of any considerations of distributive fairness in the sense that any alternative to the market outcome would involve at least one set of participants who were worse off; moreover, these people's losses would in the aggregate be larger than the gains of people who benefited from the move away from the market outcome.

19. See OECD (2009). The costs may become larger yet. A conflict with the Netherlands and the United Kingdom about some €4 billion for compensation to depositors in Dutch and U.K. branches of Icelandic banks is still pending in European courts. On the 2011 rejection by voters, see "Icelanders Reject Deal to Repay U.K., Netherlands," *Wall Street Journal*, April 11, 2011. Oral arguments began on September 18, 2012 (see Stephanie Bodoni, "Iceland Neglected U.K., Dutch Icesave Clients, Watchdog Says," Bloomberg, September 18, 2012).

20. For an overview of the European assistance package for Ireland, see http://ec.europa .eu/economy_finance/articles/eu_economic_situation/2010-12-01-financial-assistance-ireland_en.htm, accessed October 21, 2012.

21. The conclusion also applies if governments use tariffs and monopoly franchises to provide their "champions" a generous source of profits at home that enables them to "conquer" foreign markets with much lower prices.

22. On corn subsidies, see Lessig (2011, 50). Some have suggested that banks should be taxed to correct the distortion (see Acharya et al. 2010, Chapter 5). However, it is not clear how such a tax should be determined. Measuring the risks and the costs that a bank's actions impose on others is extremely difficult. The arguments that were raised in Chapter 11 against the fine-tuning of capital requirements according to risks apply here as well. High equity requirements would reduce the subsidies, in effect relying more naturally on market forces to determine the funding costs of the bank in a less distortive manner.

23. The assessment of subsidies (and taxes) presumes that markets are competitive and that firms do not have market power. The so-called strategic theory of international trade has shown that if markets are not competitive and have room for only a small number of suppliers, a country can gain by subsidizing firms so that they can be successful in gaining a place in the market, from which they can charge high prices to the rest of the world. The practical relevance of the argument is limited, however, because the political system does not have the information that would be needed to implement such a policy successfully. Moreover, the argument is invalid if the companies in question are foreign owned—that is,

if the profits obtained by exploiting market power accrue to foreign shareholders. For a discussion of the pros and cons of strategic trade policy, see Krugman (1996) and Monopolkommission (2005) and the references given there.

24. See, for example, "U.S. Relief for Steel Expected," *New York Times,* September 30, 1980, and Leonard Silk, "Protectionism: Reagan's View," *New York Times,* November 12, 1980.

25. Jaffe et al. (1995) give an overview of the literature and the issues. They suggest that the effects of environmental regulation on the competitiveness of U.S. manufacturing were actually small. For some of the industries that have dramatically shrunk or even disappeared, one may suppose that changes in unit labor costs, driven by competition from other industries, may have been the most important reasons for the change.

26. For example, French et al. (2010, 69) state: "Capital requirements can also affect the competitiveness of a country's banking sector. If capital requirements in the United States, for example, are too onerous, firms may turn to banks in other countries for financial services. This would undermine an important American industry."

27. Very few countries have investigated the reasons and responsibilities for the crisis, and none had anything like the 1933 Pecora hearings, in which the U.S. Senate Banking and Currency Committee, under the guidance of its chief counsel, Ferdinand Pecora, uncovered much of the recklessness that had characterized bankers' behavior and their treatment of clients in the late 1920s. On the Pecora hearings, see Perino (2010). Only Iceland had substantial criminal proceedings. See "Trial of Iceland Ex-PM Haarde over 2008 Crisis Begins," *BBC News Europe,* BBC, March 5, 2012.

28. Switzerland set capital requirements higher than other countries in what is dubbed a "Swiss finish" (see "Bankers' Group Warns of Overly Tough Swiss Capital Rules," Reuters, January 16, 2012). However, Swiss banks are known for having particularly low levels of risk-weighted assets relative to their total assets, and the requirements are formulated relative to risk-weighted assets (see Chart 5 in Ledo 2012). Regarding Sweden, see Mark Scott, "Sweden Proposes Higher Capital Requirements for Bank," *New York Times,* November 25, 2011. The United Kingdom has balked at attempts to harmonize the requirements (see Alex Barker, "Barnier vs the Brits," *Financial Times,* November 8, 2011). As discussed in Chapter 6, the United Kingdom's ICB (2011) proposed "ring fencing" for retail banking, requiring retail banking to be done by separate legal entities that must satisfy higher capital requirements. A legislative proposal to implement this measure was introduced by the British Government on October 12, 2012 (see http://www.hm-treasury.gov.uk/d/icb_banking_reform_bill.pdf, accessed October 21, 2012).

29. The quotation in the heading of this section is a statement that legend incorrectly attributes to the bank robber Willie Sutton when he was answering a reporter who had asked why he robbed banks (Keys 2006).

30. For accounts of pre-1990 Europe, see Borges (1990), Bruni (1990), and Caminal et al. (1990) for Southern Europe, as well as Englund (1990) for Sweden. For 1987, Bruni (1990, 250) lists the shares of governments' debts in banks' portfolios as 35.4 percent for Italy and 37.4 percent for Spain; Borges (1990, 330) reports 43 percent for Portugal in 1988. Though minimum reserves in fact paid some interest, Bruni (1990, 258) estimates that the

cost to the private sector of this implicit taxation of banking was 0.6–1 percent of GDP in Italy. Borges, though he does not give a numerical estimate, makes clear that the implicit taxation through banking regulation of Portuguese banks in the 1980s was also quite substantial. See also CEC (1988).

31. After the July 2011 stress tests, the European Banking Authority (EBA) published data showing that, out of €98 billion in Greek government debt held by the banks tested, €67 billion was held by Greek banks (see EBA, *2011 EU-wide Stress Test Aggregate Report,* http://stress-test.eba.europa.eu/pdf/EBA_ST_2011_Summary_Report_v6.pdf, accessed October 20, 2012). The March 2012 default and assistance package for Greece therefore included assistance for Greek banks as well as the government.

32. If the U.S. Congress refuses an increase in the debt ceiling, a default might be possible, but even then it is unlikely that the government would end up not paying its debt. The notion that money is printed should be treated as a metaphor. Most money today is created electronically in the form of book entries in certain accounts. From World War II to the 1970s, the Federal Reserve had a long history of buying up federal debt with newly created money, thus "monetizing" the government debt. Before the Treasury Fed Accord of 1951, it was actually mandated by the Treasury to do so—more precisely, to maintain the interest rate at a given low level. After 1951 the Federal Reserve became independent but continued to keep market rates of interest at relatively low levels, which required buying government debt with (newly created) money. Thornton (1984) gives an overview of the historical development. He also questions the intentionality of monetization, at least for the period since the early 1970s when the Federal Reserve began to formulate its policy in terms of monetary aggregates rather than interest rates. In Italy in the 1970s, the central bank was actually obliged to purchase those Treasury securities that had not been taken up by the market. See also Goodhart (2012).

33. The Mexican default of 1982 marked the beginning of the international debt crisis of the 1980s. A few years earlier, in the mid-1970s, New York City avoided bankruptcy only through the intervention of New York State with the Municipal Assistance Corporation to impose fiscal discipline, as well as a restructuring of New York City debt (see, e.g., Dunstan 1995). For a more recent discussion of state bankruptcy issues, see Conti-Brown and Skeel (2012).

34. Reinhart and Rogoff (2009) show that over the centuries, this risk has appeared again and again and has shaped relations between banks and governments. They also warn that the "risklessness" of domestic debt must not be taken too seriously. Printing money to pay for the government leads to inflation, that is, a loss of the real value of government debt. For banks, whose debt is denominated in domestic currency, this devaluation may be less serious than a simple government default, but for investors there is not much of a difference between a loss from default and a loss from inflation.

35. See Directive 2006/48/EC of The European Parliament and of the Council of June 14, 2006, "relating to the taking up and pursuit of the business of credit institutions" (http://eur-lex.europa.eu/LexUriServ/LexUriServ.do?uri=OJ:L:2006:177:0001:0001:EN:PDF, accessed October 21, 2012), Annex VI, item 4; see also Art. 109, Section 4, of the European

Commission's Proposal for a Regulation of the European Parliament and of the Council on prudential requirements for credit institutions and investment firms (http://eur-lex .europa.eu/LexUriServ/LexUriServ.do?uri=COM:2011:0452:FIN:en:PDF, accessed November 25, 2012). Zero risk weights for government debt are not actually required by the Basel agreement, which in principle has a scheme for setting risk weights according to credit ratings, but the agreement permits exceptions to be made for debt that is denominated and funded in the government's home currency. See BCBS (2004) and BCBS (2010e).

36. Dexia (discussed earlier in the chapter, particularly in note 3) was formed in 1996 by the merger of the Crédit Communal de Belgique and the Crédit Local de France, two institutions that had dominated lending to municipalities in Belgium and France. For this type of lending, the zero-risk-weight rule applied because municipalities were effectively guaranteed by the central governments. Fear of disturbing the flow of funds to local governments was a major reason for the 2008 and 2011 bailouts and perhaps also a reason for the toleration of the very low equity that Dexia had. On December 31, 2008, three months after the first bailout, the bank's balance sheet reported that it had equity equal to 2.7 percent of its total assets; in fact, this was possible only because, in conflict with International Financial Reporting Standards, Dexia had not written down the value of certain assets it held as the market values of these assets had gone down. See Thomas (2012), in particular Part 1 on the founding of Dexia and p. 168 on Dexia's equity.

37. See Reinhart and Rogoff (2009) for a history of government borrowing and banking crises over the past 800 years.

38. Some of the development of subprime mortgage lending in the United States in the 1990s and 2000s may be linked to the 1994 changes in the application of the Community Reinvestment Act (CRA) and to political pressure for financial institutions to be more forthcoming with housing finance for low-income families. How much these developments contributed to the crisis has been controversial. The FCIC (2011, executive summary, 27, and Chapter 7) concludes that the CRA "was not a significant factor." Das (2011, 187), an industry insider, concluded, "It was not lending money to poor people that was the problem. The problem was lending money poorly." A dissenting view by FCIC member Peter Wallison (available at http://fcic-static.law.stanford.edu/cdn_media/fcic-reports/fcic_final_report_wallison_dissent.pdf, accessed October 21, 2012) claims that housing policy was the primary cause of the crisis. Empirical investigations by staff of the Board of Governors of the Federal Reserve (available at http://www.federalreserve.gov/newsevents/speech/20081203_analysis.pdf, accessed October 21, 2012) and the BIS (see Ellis 2008) do not support such an interpretation.

39. The system of public banks in Germany involves the local savings banks, owned by municipalities and districts, and the Landesbanken, jointly owned by the Länder, the German analogues of U.S. states, and the regional associations of local savings banks. For an overview, see Krahnen and Schmidt (2003), in particular Chapter 3. Sinn (2010) explains that this structure was partly responsible for the recklessness of certain German banks before the financial crisis and for their vulnerability in the crisis. See also Chapter 11, note 18.

40. Egregious examples are Bayerische Landesbank and Westdeutsche Landesbank. WestLB is said to have cost the taxpayers €18 billion since 2005 alone (see "WestLB-Desaster kommt Steuerzahler teuer zu stehen," *Financial Times Deutschland,* June 20, 2012). In 2008 BayernLB required €10 billion in new equity from the state of Bavaria, in addition to €15 billion in debt guarantees from the federal government. Kaserer (2010) shows that most of the costs of the crisis to taxpayers were due to losses of the Landesbanken.

41. See Chapter 11, notes 17 and 18 and the references given there.

42. In this context it is worth noting that, whereas in the United States the word *public* refers to something that is openly accessible, in France *public* refers to something that is in the domain of the state (see Fourcade 2009). Fourcade also notes that the notion of "state" is not the same in the United States and France.

43. *Enarques* can be translated as "rulers from the ENA," "enarchs."

44. A generation earlier, Jean-Yves Haberer had enjoyed an even more distinguished ministerial career before being appointed CEO of the bank Paribas and, later, CEO of Crédit Lyonnais, then the largest French bank. His tenure ended in 1993, when Crédit Lyonnais needed €15 billion in taxpayer money to avoid bankruptcy. Bad real estate loans, loans to politically connected businessmen, and fraudulent accounting were among the causes of the scandal. Apart from the revolving-door effect, this system also strengthens the home-team effect because the supervisors and the supervised went to the same school and on occasion may even have been classmates (see "Old School Ties," *The Economist,* March 10, 2012).

45. In 2000 the governor of the Bank of France, Jean-Claude Trichet, played a very active role in the merger of Banque Nationale de Paris and Paribas, two of the largest French banks, into BNP Paribas, thus preempting any merger of these banks with a foreign bank. He made it clear that he would have preferred that Société Générale, another large bank, also join in the merger, but the shareholders of that bank refused. See Nicolas Lecaussin, "What's the Matter with the French Banks? Whether the Market's Worst Fears Are Realized or Not, the Financial System Maintains Too Close a Relationship to the State," *Wall Street Journal,* September 13, 2011. See also Thomas (2012) on Dexia.

46. Investment banks spent $169 million on such contributions in 2008, giving 57 percent to Democrats (third-highest amount overall); they spent $104 million in 2010, giving 49 percent to Democrats (fourth-highest overall). In 2012, so far banks have spent $128 million, giving 38 percent to Democrats. There was a notable shift toward the GOP after 2008. See "Wall Street Shifting Political Contributions to Republicans," *Washington Post,* February 24, 2010. Mian et al. (2010) show that the amount of campaign contributions from the financial sector is a strong predictor of voting on the Economic Emergency Stabilization Act of 2008, which provided the Treasury up to $700 billion in bailout funds that could be used to support the financial industry. Stiglitz (2010, 42) states that the political contributions might be the most profitable investments of banks in recent years. Ross (2011, 75) also makes the connection between favorable legislation and political contributions. Lessig (2011, 83) reports, "From 1999 to 2008, the financial sector expended $2.7 billion in reported federal lobbying expenses; individuals and political action committees in the sector made more than $1 billion in campaign contributions. . . . Comparing the cam-

paign contributions of the one hundred biggest contributing firms since 1989, we find contributions from firms in the financial sector total more than the contributions of energy, health care, defense and telecoms combined."

47. For example, German savings banks have mounted a strong campaign against the introduction of a leverage ratio, requiring banks to have equity equal to at least 3 percent of their total assets. The campaign has been joined by their owners, the municipalities, which have so far benefited from the fact that lending to government institutions requires no capital at all. See "Basel Bank Plans Eased after Heavy Lobbying," Reuters, July 26, 2010.

48. Ryan Grim, "Dick Durbin: Banks 'Frankly Own the Place,'" *Huffington Post,* May 30, 2009. Lessig (2011) calls such relations "corruptive dependencies." The impact of money on politics has been identified and discussed more generally by many others recently, particularly Johnson and Kwak (2010), Ferguson (2012), and Hayes (2012).

49. Johnson and Kwak (2010), Lessig (2011), Morgenson and Rosner (2011), Ferguson (2012), Hayes (2012), and Kwak (2012).

50. Johnson and Kwak (2010, Chapters 6 and 13), Kane (2012c), and Barth et al. (2012).

51. Johnson and Kwak (2010, Chapter 5) and other accounts describe how the initial proposal by Brookley Born, chair of the Commodity Futures Trading Commission, to regulate derivatives trading, made in 1998, was dismissed and followed by the Commodity Futures Modernization Act, passed in December 2000, exempting most over-the-counter derivatives from regulation. This Act is seen as a major reason that significant risk could build up and go unchecked in the derivatives markets.

52. William Cohan, in "How We Got the Crash Wrong" (*Atlantic,* June 2012), suggests that, contrary to what others have written, this decision actually tightened capital regulation for investment banks. The fact remains that the ruling allowed them to have much less equity than U.S. commercial banks, on the order of 3 percent of their total assets or less. In addition, the regulators allowed investment banks to keep many securities off their own balance sheets in special-purpose vehicles.

53. See Patrick Jenkins and Brooke Masters, "Finance: London's Precarious Position," *Financial Times,* July 29, 2012. However, because the United Kingdom has been particularly hard hit by the financial crisis, U.K. authorities have taken the lead in the debate on tightening banking regulation. The Independent Commission on Banking proposed the imposition of significantly stricter regulation than the Basel Committee on Banking Supervision, and Adair Turner, head of the Financial Services Authority, has been a strong advocate for the type of reform we propose in this book (see, e.g., Turner 2010, 2012). Many calls for higher capital requirements have also come from the Bank of England (e.g., Miles et al. 2011, Haldane 2012a,c, and Jenkins 2012a,b).

54. Johnson and Kwak (2010), Dunbar (2011), Barth et al. (2012), and Kane (2012a).

55. These entities had practically no equity. They were funded by short-term borrowing and held various asset-backed securities. An extreme example is Sächsische Landesbank, with more than €40 billion in guarantees to conduits and SIVs when its equity was less than €4 billion. See Acharya et al. (2013).

56. On revolving doors, see Kristina Cooke, Pedro da Costa, and Emily Flitter, "The Ties That Bind at the Federal Reserve," Reuters, September 30, 2010, and Brooke Masters,

"Enter the Revolving Regulators," *Financial Times*, April 23, 2012. The phenomenon is pervasive (see Suzy Khimm, "How JPMorgan Exploits Washington's Revolving Door; the Project on Government Oversight Points out That JPMorgan Frequently Dispatches Former Government Officials to Lobby Current Regulators Who Are Writing the Rules for Wall Street Reform," *Washington Post*, June 22, 2012; "Why Can't Obama Bring Wall Street to Justice? Maybe the Banks Are Too Big to Jail. Or Maybe Washington's Revolving Door Is at Work," *Newsweek*, May 14, 2012; and Nicolas Lecaussin, "What's the Matter with the French Banks? Whether the Market's Worst Fears Are Realized or Not, the Financial System Maintains Too Close a Relationship to the State." *Wall Street Journal*, September 13, 2011. Lessig (2011, 123) states that in 2009 the financial sector had seventy former members of Congress lobbying on its behalf. He further describes the revolving door with staffers (222–223). Zingales (2012, 277–278) argues that capture is more likely when regulators need to have highly specific skills.

57. See, for example, Annalyn Censky, "Why Is Jamie Dimon on a Federal Reserve Board?" *CNNMoney*, CNN, May 21, 2012.

58. In March 2008, when Mr. Dimon was on the board of the New York Fed, JPMorgan Chase acquired the failing investment bank Bear Stearns, with guarantees from the New York Fed. Johnson and Kwak (2010, 159) state that "this was a coup for JPMorgan, which was paying for Bear Stearns approximately what its *building* was worth." Richard Fuld, CEO of Lehman Brothers, served on the board of the New York Fed from 2005 and had just started his second three-year term when Lehman Brothers went into bankruptcy. See Huma Khan, "Federal Reserve Board Rife with Conflict of Interest, GAO Report," *ABC News*, ABC, October 19, 2011. On the perception of investors that having a director on the board of the local Federal Reserve Bank is beneficial, see Adams (2011).

59. Empirical research has shown that in sports in which referees' judgment calls are important, these judgment calls tend to favor the home teams. Referees seem to be subconsciously influenced by the watching crowds' sympathies for the home team. See Barth et al. (2012), who use the analogy in discussing capture in banking, and references therein.

60. This insight is originally due to Olson (1965), Stigler (1971), and Peltzman (1976). According to the Center for Responsive Politics (information available at http://www.opensecrets.org/lobby/top.php?showYear=a&indexType=c, accessed October 21, 2012), the financial industry spent $479,237,675 on lobbying in 2011, an increase of about 13.9 percent relative to 2007. (Total inflation during this period was roughly 8 percent.) Lessig (2011, 147) notes that "in October 2009, around the time the Dodd-Frank Act was debated, there were 1,537 lobbyists representing financial institutions registered in D.C. . . . twenty-five times the number registered to support consumer groups unions and other proponents of strong reform." This does not take into account the direct connection between politicians and prominent bankers who make substantial campaign contributions.

61. See Jackie Calmes and Louise Story, "In Washington, One Bank Chief Still Holds Sway," *New York Times*, July 18, 2009.

62. An example is the intense battle in the United States over the Financial Consumer Protection Bureau (see Wilmarth 2012a,b; Nathan Kopel, "Consumer Protection Bureau Mired in Politics," *Wall Street Journal*, June 15, 2011; and Michelle Singletary, "Consumer

Financial Protection Bureau Got Off to a Good Start in Its Inaugural Year," *Washington Post,* July 10, 2012). Bair (2012, 342) states that "industry lobbyists have found that the best way to harass the SEC and the CFTC [Commodity Futures Trading Commission] and block efforts at financial reform is through convincing appropriation committees to restrict how these agencies can use their money." She describes efforts to "prohibit the CFTC from using its funds to implement rules forcing more derivatives into public trading facilities and other measures."

63. For example, the old monopolies in telecommunications were lifted when would-be new suppliers managed to convince judges and politicians that they had legitimate reasons for wanting to enter those markets and that there was much to be gained from competition and innovation (see Crandall 1991, Waverman and Sirel 1997, and Viscusi et al. 2005).

64. The National Transportation Safety Board is dedicated to investigating causes of major accidents in transportation systems; a similar agency that might prevent financial "accidents" is lacking (see Fielding et al. 2011). The Financial Stability Oversight Council established by the Dodd-Frank Act is made up of existing regulators; so far there is little evidence that it has been useful for this purpose (see, e.g., Bair, 2012, 337–339). Similarly, the Dodd-Frank Act established the Office of Financial Research, but this agency has been slow to develop, and its potential impact is unclear as of this writing.

65. An exception that proves the rule is that Nikolaus von Bomhard, CEO of the world's largest reinsurer, Munich Re, called for banking reform. At the same time he stated that the insurance sector does not add systemic risk and thus should not receive as much attention from regulators. See "Munich Re CEO Says Europe Needs to Push Forward Structural Reforms," *Wall Street Journal,* July 16, 2012. In the United States, Paul Singer, a hedge fund manager, called for financial reform (see "Donor Urges Romney Shift on Banks," *Financial Times,* August 15, 2012). However, as Eric Rosengren, president of the Federal Reserve Bank of Boston, said, "Financial stability has no constituency" (see "Money-Market Funds Still Need Reform," *Wall Street Journal,* April 26, 2012, and Rosengren 2012).

66. There are a number of organizations dedicated to improving financial regulation for the public, such as Better Markets and Americans for Financial Reform in the United States and Finance-Watch in Europe. In "Facing Down the Bankers" (*New York Times,* May 20, 2012), Annie Lowrey describes Dennis Kelleher from Better Markets as "battling against Wall Street and its lobbies to regulate the banking system" and quotes former senator Byron Dorgan as saying, "It's David versus Goliath, but at least David's there." See also Scott Patterson, Serena Ng, and Victoria McGrane, "Boo, and Backers, for 'Volcker Rule,'" *Wall Street Journal,* February 14, 2012, and Simon Johnson, "Opening up the Fed," *New York Times,* Economix blog, February 23, 2012. Lessig (2011) describes the excessive impact of money on policy in the United States. In the broader context, Ross (2011, 68) states that "it is not clear that contemporary political institutions, whether national or international, do in fact successfully give sufficient attention to the common interests of humanity. Instead, it's increasingly evident that these institutions instead [*sic*] elevate the interests of the most powerful interest groups over collective interests, and neglect long-term primary needs."

67. See Norimitsu Onishi and Ken Belson, "Culture of Complicity Tied to Stricken Nuclear Plant," *New York Times,* April 26, 2011.

THIRTEEN   *Other People's Money*

1. For the full letter, see http://www.bbc.co.uk/news/business-18678731, accessed October 15, 2012.

2. LIBOR, the "London interbank offered rate," is not actually quoted in any market but is based on interest rates reported by participating banks. If traders manipulate their reports, this can change the interest on all LIBOR-related debts—for example, on any debt with interest specified at a variable rate equal to "LIBOR + 1 percent." The traders themselves profited from the way the lower rates affected their own positions in derivatives or the costs attributed to the funds they were employing. In addition to alleged manipulations of this sort by individual traders who, according to released e-mails, may have helped each other, there seems to have been a more coordinated effort by banks to report lower figures so as to avoid alerting investors to their financial difficulties. Regulators seemed aware of manipulations at least after 2007.

3. See "Diamond Cuts Up Rough as He Quits Barclays," *The Guardian,* July 4, 2012, and "MPs Slam Barclays and Bank of England over Libor Scandal," *The Guardian,* August 18, 2012.

4. Within the industry, the manipulation seems to have been well known since at least the early 1990s. In the *Financial Times* of July 27, 2012, Douglas Keenan, a former trader for Morgan Stanley, reports that, in one of his first experiences as a trader in 1991, he lost money because, due to the manipulation of reporting by traders at other banks, the value at which LIBOR was fixed differed from the interest rates that he had actually seen on his screen. Morgan Stanley itself was not among the banks reporting their LIBOR quotes, but, as Keenan reports, the practice of misreporting was well known to his colleagues, who smiled at his naïveté. At the time, the head of interest rate trading at Morgan Stanley was Mr. Diamond, who is now surprised that such practices should have been engaged in at Barclays. According to an investigation by the Financial Services Authority (FSA) in the United Kingdom, LIBOR manipulation by traders was common; the FSA mentions 257 e-mails pointing to manipulation between 2005 and 2009. Separately, in 2007–2008 there was a more coordinated effort by banks to shave down their reported borrowing rate so as to appear healthier and less distressed than they actually were. It seems that regulators were aware of this. See "Timeline: Barclays' Widening Libor-Fixing Scandal," *BBC News* business, BBC, July 17, 2012. On issues related to the setting of LIBOR, see Peter Eavis and Nathaniel Popper, "Libor Scandal Shows Many Flaws in Rate-Setting," *New York Times,* July 19, 2012. See also "Libor's Trillion-Dollar Question," editorial, Bloomberg, August 27, 2012.

5. Such questions are asked in a *Financial Times* editorial titled "Shaming the Banks into Better Ways," June 28, 2012. Hayes (2012, 100) discusses the "culture of lying" on Wall Street. Das (2010, 53) describes derivatives as the world of "beautiful lies." See also Smith (2010).

6. The summer of 2012 saw many scandals, from the loss by JPMorgan Chase of close to $6 billion in derivatives trading in London to banks being charged with manipulating municipalities and energy prices and with defrauding clients. Also, two hedge funds went

into bankruptcy in the United States, and in both cases customer accounts were compromised. Over the centuries, a willingness to cut corners and bend the law in the pursuit of wealth has often characterized behavior in financial markets. See, for example, Perino (2010) on the late 1920s or, for a more general overview, Kindleberger and Aliber (2005). However, from the 1930s to the 1970s, the stakes for individual traders were much smaller, and there seems to have been less scope for abusing trust. For developments since the 1980s, see Lewis (1990, 2010, 2011), Partnoy (2009, 2010), Das (2010), and Dunbar (2011). See also Greg Smith, "Why I'm Leaving Goldman Sachs," *New York Times*, March 14, 2012. For a response that puts the issue in perspective, see Frank Partnoy, "Goldman's 'Muppets' Need Treating Like True Clients," *Financial Times*, March 15, 2012. Mr. Partnoy says, "No one should expect derivatives salespeople to be honourable, any more than we should expect a zebra to scrub off its stripes. Nor should we be sympathetic to municipal treasurers and pension fund managers who succumb to their own animal instincts and sit at the poker table when they should not." He goes on to insist on the need to regulate derivatives markets.

7. The vast majority of the traders are males (see, for example, "Women Sue Goldman, Claiming Pay and Jobs Bias," *New York Times*, September 15, 2010; see also "Keep Taking the Testosterone," *Financial Times*, February 10, 2012).

8. See, for example, Lewis (1990), Partnoy (2009, Chapter 8), Das (2010, Chapter 7), Rohatyn (2010), and Morgenson and Rosner (2011). Some of the unethical behavior in banking is not illegal, but it involves taking advantage of people's ignorance, leading them to take risks that they are not aware of and that they might not be able to bear. When investing money, many people are particularly vulnerable because they are not in a position to assess the risks. They often fail to realize that, if something sounds too good to be true, such as earning high returns at little or no risk, it is most likely not true. Moreover, if an investment adviser is shading the truth just slightly or neglecting to mention some relevant information, the fraud may be difficult to detect. An example in which even some of the bankers involved may not have understood the risk is given in an article by Floyd Norris, "Buried in Details, a Warning to Investors" (*New York Times*, August 2, 2012). The first paragraph states: "The bank that put together the unusual security did well. The customers who bought it suffered large losses. No one—at least no one who traded the security —seems to have understood the risks that were hidden deep in the prospectus."

9. According to Barofsky (2012, 8), " 'adopting a narrative' was a tried-and-true tactic in Washington: define the status quo as a success, and then ignore all evidence that suggests otherwise."

10. According to the "profit" narrative, authorities supported the markets by buying assets at low prices when market participants had lost confidence, and they ended up making money when confidence returned. See, for example, "New York Fed Sells Last of Its Bonds from AIG Bailouts," *New York Times*, August 24, 2012. This account leaves out the cost of the support that was given to Fannie Mae and Freddie Mac. The cost of taking over Fannie and Freddie is estimated at $151 billion (see, e.g., "U.S. Nets $25 Billion on Mortgage Debt," *Wall Street Journal*, March 19, 2012). As of April 2012 it was estimated that taxpayers were still owed $119 billion on TARP investments (see "Billions in Loans Still in

Doubt," *Wall Street Journal,* April 25, 2012). The inspector general of TARP estimated that close to $10 billion written off by the Treasury will not be returned. The supposed profits also do not account for the risks to which taxpayers were exposed. As discussed in Chapter 9, providing guarantees and loans at below-market rates is also a form of subsidy.

11. The enormous cost of the crisis was discussed in Chapter 1, note 19. For society, one has to distinguish between the direct cost of providing subsidies through underpriced and implicit guarantees that may be called on in bailouts and supports (discussed in Chapter 9) and the collateral damage to society of a financial crisis or of having distressed or insolvent banks, impacted by the inefficiencies of the dark side of borrowing that we discussed in Chapter 3.

12. As discussed in Chapter 10, Gorton (2010) focuses on describing the crisis as resulting from runs similar to earlier runs by depositors. The liquidity narrative was used in the lobbying that beat back efforts to reform the U.S. money market fund industry in 2012 (see James Stewart, "Influence of Money Market Funds Ended Overhaul," *New York Times,* September 7, 2012). The article states that "Vanguard has also argued that the 2008 crisis set off by the Reserve Fund was a liquidity crisis."

13. According to this interpretation, the breakdown of liquidity caused by the runs disrupted the flow of money through the economy, and the central bank had to step in and provide money when and where it was needed. Not surprisingly, Chairman Bernanke is fond of the liquidity narrative (see David Ignatius, "Ben Bernanke, Quiet Tiger at the Fed," *Washington Post,* May 28, 2009).

14. See, for example, Mehrling (2010) and Duffie (2012); Gorton (2010) compares liquidity provision by the financial system to electricity.

15. On extensions of government guarantees, see Gorton (2010), on the role of the central bank Mehrling (2010).

16. See Calomiris and Mason (1997) and Schnabel (2004).

17. The first models of runs in economic theory have focused on the case in which an institution will be solvent if nobody runs, and everybody knows that this is the case. In this setting, a run is necessarily due to coordination failure. If the solvency of the institution is in doubt, however, the question is how the information possessed by different investors might be put together to permit a better assessment of the institution's solvency. Letting investors withdraw when they lose confidence is one way to do so (see Calomiris and Kahn 1991, Morris and Shin 1998, Goldstein and Pauzner 2005, Hellwig 2005, and Admati et al. 2011, section 5).

18. See Hellwig (2009), and Krishnamurthy et al. (2012). As discussed in Chapter 10, notes 45 and 54, the results of Krishnamurthy et al. (2012) show that the most popular version of the liquidity narrative of the crisis does not quite fit the facts. The "panic of 2007," as Gorton (2010) calls it, involved asset-backed commercial paper rather than repo (repurchase agreement) markets, and it damaged the financial system because the commercial banks that were involved became squeezed for equity rather than for liquidity. It should also be noted that boom-and-bust developments in Irish and Spanish real estate markets were similar to the real estate bubble in the United States. In Ireland and Spain, the real estate bubbles were also fueled by excessively easy bank lending, but the mortgages were

held by the issuing banks rather than securitized. See the dissenting statement of Hennessey, Holtz-Eakin, and Thomas to the Financial Crisis Inquiry Report, available at http://fcic-static.law.stanford.edu/cdn_media/fcic-reports/fcic_final_report_hennessey_holtz-eakin_thomas_dissent.pdf, accessed October 18, 2012. In both countries, government support preempted any runs. This support did not, however, eliminate the underlying solvency problems. In both countries the banks' losses and the resulting solvency problems were so large that the governments had to apply for assistance from the IMF and the other members of the European Union.

19. This is a clear conclusion from the analysis of the history of financial crises by Reinhart and Rogoff (2009), who conclude their book by saying, "We have come full circle to the concept of financial fragility in economies with massive indebtedness. . . . Highly leveraged economies . . . seldom survive forever, particularly if leverage continues to grow unchecked. . . . Encouragingly, history does point to warning signs that policy makers can look at to assess risk—if only they do not become too drunk with their credit bubble–fueled success." Similarly, Lawrence Summers, the U.S. Treasury secretary from 1999 to 2001, refers to "the increasing salience of long-standing financial-sector weaknesses, arising from some combination of insufficient capitalization and supervision of banks and excessive leverage and guarantee—the combination that, along with directed lending, has been captured in the term 'crony capitalism,'" as a root cause of most crises (Summers 2000, 5). Turning to runs, Summers (2000, 7) states that "they are not driven by sunspots: their likelihood is driven and determined by the extent of fundamental weaknesses" and concludes that "preventing crises is heavily an issue of avoiding situations where the bank run psychology takes hold, and that will depend heavily on strengthening core institutions and other fundamentals." See also King (2010) and Schularick and Taylor (2012).

20. The risks are described by Tett (2009), Lewis (2010, 2011), McLean and Nocera (2010), Morgenson and Rosner (2011), Dunbar (2011), and the FCIC (2011). Barth et al. (2012) focus particularly on the regulatory failures.

21. See Tett (2009), Mclean and Nocera (2010), Dunbar (2011), FCIC (2011), and Barth et al. (2012). We discussed many of the issues related to the design and enforcement of capital regulation in Chapter 11.

22. The FCIC (2011, page ix) concludes that "a combination of excessive borrowing, risky investments and lack of transparency put the financial system at a collision course with crisis." Acharya and Richardson (2009, Chapter 1) also describe the crisis as a result of high leverage and a credit boom that led to insolvencies. Blundell-Wignall and Atkinson (2009) argue that the crisis was a solvency crisis that was exacerbated by liquidity problems. See also notes 18 and 19 of this chapter as well as note 47 of Chapter 1.

23. See, for example, "Bernanke: Banking System Stronger, but Mortgage Credit Still Tight," *Dow Jones Business News,* May 10, 2012.

24. See the discussion in the first part of Chapter 11.

25. This argument was originally developed by Olson (1965, 1982). Stigler (1971) and Peltzman (1976) applied it to the politics of regulation of an industry, Grossman and Helpman (1994) to the politics of protection from foreign competition. See also Wilson (1980) and Lessig (2011).

26. See the discussion and references in Chapter 12 regarding regulatory capture.

27. On the accounting debate and its conclusion, see Carruth (2003) and Farber et al. (2007). See also "High Anxiety: Accounting Proposal Stirs Unusual Uproar in Executive Suites," *Wall Street Journal*, March 7, 1994; "Stock Options Are Not a Free Lunch," *Forbes*, May 18, 1998; and the concluding remarks of Admati et al. (2011) on "the political economy of fallacious arguments." On flawed arguments in bank lobbying. see Jenkins (2011, 2012b).

28. In 2009 Nicholas Brady, the U.S. Treasury secretary under George H. W. Bush, who chaired the Presidential Task Force on Market Mechanisms following the stock market crash of 1987, stated that President Obama had "wasted" the crisis and criticized reform proposals as "incoherent" (see Edward Luce, "Obama 'Wasted' Reform Chances," *Financial Times*, June 29, 2009). The sentiment is expressed in a number of books about the crisis, for example, McLean and Nocera (2010), Dunbar (2011), Morgenson and Rosner (2011), and Ferguson (2012). Mayo (2011, 2928–2932) writes, "The truly outrageous thing about the financial crisis is not that it happened. . . . No, the truly outrageous thing about Citi is that all the factors that led to the problems over its long history and especially over the past decade—questionable accounting, the separation of risk from reward, outsized executive pay—are *still* happening. It's like we've learned nothing."

29. The statement in the heading of this section is a paraphrase of the last paragraph of an April 26, 2013, column in the *Wall Street Journal* by Eric Rosengren, president and CEO of the Federal Reserve Bank of Boston, titled "Money-Market Funds Still Need Reform." Rosengren concluded by stating, "While it often seems that financial stability has no natural constituency, that constituency is actually all of us who want to avoid another autumn of 2008 and its aftermath."

30. On the erosion of Glass-Steagall, see, for example, Fink (2008), Partnoy (2009), and Johnson and Kwak (2010, Chapter 3).

31. Simon Johnson, "The Federal Reserve and the Libor Scandal," *New York Times*, July 19, 2012, and Sudeep Reddy, "Congress Joins Libor Probes; Focus Includes U.S. Regulators Who Knew about Problem as Early as 2007," *Wall Street Journal*, July 10, 2012. See also "The Federal Reserve and the Libor Scandal," *New York Times*, July 19, 2012. On the United Kingdom, see the BBC timeline, http://www.bbc.co.uk/news/business-18671255, accessed October 15, 2012.

32. "Financial Crimes Bedevil Prosecutors," *Wall Street Journal*, December 6, 2011; "Federal Prosecution of Financial Fraud Falls to 20-Year Low, New Report Shows," *Huffington Post*, November 11, 2011; Matt Taibi, "Why Isn't Wall Street in Jail?" *Rolling Stone*, February 16, 2011; and Hayes (2012, 72).

33. Mr. Madoff's being sentenced to 150 years in prison for defrauding thousands of people of large amounts of money over many years is an extreme and rare exception.

34. Daniel Kaufman, "Judge Rakoff Challenge to the S.E.C.: Can Regulatory Capture Be Reversed?" Brookings Institution research opinion, December 2, 2011, http://www.brookings.edu/research/opinions/2011/12/02-rakoff-challenge-kaufmann, accessed October 15, 2012.

35. Lessig (2011) uses the term "corruptive dependencies" to describe relationships such as those between lobbyists or wealthy individuals and policymakers. On accountability looked at in a historical perspective, see Adrian R. Bell's somewhat whimsical "Libor Scandal

Is No Match for Its Medieval Precedent," Bloomberg, July 27, 2012, and "Should Crimes of Capital Get Capital Punishment?," *Wall Street Journal,* July 27, 2012.

36. Brandeis ([1914] 2009), whose book title is "Other People's Money and What Bankers Do with It," was mainly concerned with the power bankers derived from their control over money. In contrast, we are concerned with the risks inherent in their dealing with other people's money.

37. See Cochrane (2005) and Korteweg and Sorensen (2010).

38. For a discussion of the need to focus on this objective without allowing other concerns to interfere, see Admati and Hellwig (2011b).

39. In the 1990s, Argentina had a currency board that required the issue of pesos to be fully backed by dollars. Because the government could not use the central bank's printing press, it borrowed from private banks. In 2000–2001, when it had become clear that government borrowing was unsustainable, there was a run on the banks because people wanted to withdraw pesos to convert them into dollars before the currency regime was changed. The run precipitated a severe financial and economic crisis. The standard of living dropped drastically.

40. See, for example, Johnson and Kwak (2010), Allison (2011), and Hoenig and Morris (2011). The Federal Reserve Bank of Dallas (2012) dedicated its 2011 annual report to a call to "end too big to fail now." Many other colorful expressions are used to describe these banks. For example, see Thomas Hoenig, "Too Big to Succeed," *New York Times,* December 1, 2010; Sebastian Mallaby, "Woodrow Wilson Knew How to Beard Behemoths," *Financial Times,* July 5, 2012; Patrick Jenkins, "Too Big to Be Trusted: Banks' Balance Shifts towards the Historical and Ethical," *Financial Times,* July 17, 2012; Jim Wells, "Too Big to Behave, Not Too Big to Be Punished," *American Banker,* July 20, 2012; and George Will, "Too Big to Maintain?" *Washington Post,* October 12, 2012. Hu (2012) discusses the problem of banks' being "too complex to be depicted." Referring to Haldane (2012b), see "Bank of England Official Likens Banks to Overgrown Elephant Seals," *Financial Times,* April 25, 2012.

41. The risk is greater when many banks choose similar strategies. If they expect supervisors and central banks to pursue a too-many-to-fail policy, they may actually want to choose lending strategies so that, if the loans do badly, they will all fail at the same time and the authorities will have to clean up the mess (see, for example, Acharya et al. 2007, Acharya and Yorulmazer 2008, and Farhi and Tirole 2011). The S&L crisis of the 1980s in the United States, the Japanese banking crisis in the 1990s, and the recent crisis of the Spanish *cajas* (local or regional savings banks) all involved many banks' failing. These crises show that bailouts may also be difficult to avoid if many banks are in trouble at the same time. Not only are such bailout policies costly; they can also distort the banks' incentives so that they become motivated to take risks so that different failures will occur at the same time.

42. In the first round, the damage involved short-term creditors, such as money market funds and hedge funds, as well as participants in derivatives markets who had expected Lehman Brothers to serve as market maker. The first-round effects had further repercussions through runs on other investment banks and on money market funds and through price declines in many asset markets.

43. Paradoxically, Bear Stearns and Lehman Brothers were more lightly regulated than commercial banks, and this contributed to their downfall. As pure investment banks, they were regulated by the Securities and Exchange Commission (SEC), which allowed them to apply the Basel II approach to determining their equity requirements, as do European banks. As a result, these banks' indebtedness and risk taking grew to such levels that they could not absorb their large losses in 2007 and 2008. The Lehman bankruptcy was discussed at the end of Chapter 5.

44. The CDS contracts were structured so that AIG would have to post cash collaterals if the insured mortgage securities were downgraded. These were the commitments that AIG could not fulfill and that were paid in full by the U.S. government. See Barofsky (2012).

45. Interconnectedness will actually be increased if the breakup means that some institutions must borrow from others, whereas previously the two had been under the same corporate roof. For example, under the McFadden and Glass-Steagall Acts in the United States, some depositors' funds would be lent from local commercials banks to the large money center banks, and some depositors' funds would be lent from commercial banks to investment banks. In European universal banks with large branch networks, all of these would be in-house transactions. The ultimate problem of controlling what risks are taken with the money is the same in both regimes. However, in a regime in which the commercial banking units have a say as to where the funds from depositors go, control of these risks is likely to be more effective than in a regime in which investment banking units rule the roost and can ask for any funds they like at the prevailing "price" that the parent organization is setting. For an example of how the control of investment banking by senior management in a universal bank can fail, see UBS (2008). One might think that control of investment bankers would be stricter if they had to obtain funding through an arm's-length relation with another party. However, as discussed in Chapter 10, arm's-length funding of investment banks such as Bear Stearns or Lehman Brothers by money market funds and other institutions did not provide much discipline, either. Structural arrangements between complete integration of the UBS type and complete separation of the Glass-Steagall type—for example, an organization of deposit taking and investment banking in separate subsidiaries of the same parent corporation—might give rise to fake arm's-length relations between the different subsidiaries. An example of such fake arm's-length relations is provided by the system of German public banks, in which local savings banks, which are active in retail banking, collect more funds from depositors than they can use themselves and automatically invest large parts of their surplus funds with the Landesbanken, which are active in investment banking. In any arrangement, the key question is how to ensure proper governance for the funding of risky investment banking activities.

46. Attempts to form central clearinghouses for derivatives might actually create new and particularly dangerous systemically important institutions. Being owned by the participating banks would make the clearinghouses highly connected. It is essential that they have sufficient ability to absorb losses without needing any support from banks or from the government. Regulating them effectively would be critical. If more derivatives were

traded on exchanges, this might increase financial stability without much harm to the economy. See Levitin (2013) for a discussion of clearinghouses.

47. See Admati and Hellwig (2011b).

48. As discussed in Chapter 11, it is misleading to use the existing sizes of banks or the banking industry as a base from which to calculate the astronomical amounts of new equity that such requirements would supposedly entail. It may well be the case that the industry or individual banks ought to shrink because their current size is inefficiently large for society; in this case, much less equity needs to be raised. As we argued in Chapters 11 and 12, we cannot tell what the size of the industry should be because of the existing distortions brought about by subsidies and the harmful fragility of the system. Banks have a significant amount of debt that is not part of their business and that seems underpriced. With more equity, the funding costs of banks would be brought in line with the overall economy, and the sizes of banks and the industry would be determined in a less distorted market.

49. The quotes are from Turner (2010, 5 and 57 respectively). In a similar vein, Haldane et al. (2010), provocatively titled "What Is the Contribution of the Financial Sector: Miracle or Mirage?," focuses on the need for bank performance measures to be adjusted for risk, as we discussed in Chapter 8. Both Turner and Andrew Haldane, executive director of financial stability at the Bank of England, call for higher equity requirements as a key element of financial reform. See also Haldane (2012a,c).

50. As discussed in Chapter 11 and in Admati et al. (2012a), capital requirements that are specified in terms of equity ratios relative to risk-weighted assets can lead to inefficient reductions in lending. The transition to higher equity requirements, therefore, must be managed by regulators to avoid this effect.

51. This issue was discussed in the last part of Chapter 8.

52. For example, Kashyap et al. (2010) warn that increased capital requirements will lead to a migration of risk out of the regulated system and will increase the overall fragility. Patrick Jenkins et al., in "New Forces Emerge from the Shadows" (*Financial Times,* April 10, 2012), quotes bank CEOs warning that tighter regulation will drive activity to the shadow banking system. In Chapter 10 we debunked the notion that the existing shadow banking system is efficient. Rather, the system has been developed primarily to evade regulation, and the buildup of fragility in this system reflects distorted incentives and a rat race of borrowing that are inefficient.

53. For an overview of the shadow banking system, which includes hedge funds, special-purpose vehicles, and other entities, see Poszar et al. (2010), Acharya et al. (2010, Part III), and FCIC (2011, Chapter 2), and FSB (2012). As discussed in Chapter 4 (see note 27) and Chapter 10 (see note 46), money market mutual funds were developed in the 1970s in order to get around the regulation of commercial banks and savings banks. These funds are regulated by the SEC, which means that they are very lightly regulated relative to banks and operate with few restrictions. The concern with shadow banking and so-called regulatory arbitrage can be traced to the establishment of money market funds. Since that time, regulators have feared that regulating banks might lead to the displacement of regulated

banks with new unregulated institutions. The problem of enforcement is particularly challenging in the United States because the regulatory system is highly fragmented. Under
the Dodd-Frank Act, the Financial Stability Oversight Council is authorized to provide
"comprehensive monitoring to ensure the stability" of the U.S. financial system, with the
idea of closing regulatory gaps (see http://www.treasury.gov/initiatives/fsoc/Pages/default
.aspx, accessed October 22, 2012).

54. FCIC (2011, xviii). See also Tett (2009), McLean and Nocera (2010), Morgenson and
Rosner (2011), and especially Dunbar (2011) and Barth et al. (2012). Thiemann (2012) discusses the politics underlying the passivity of supervisors in different countries.

55. See Hellwig (2009), FCIC (2011, Chapter 10), and Acharya et al. (2013). Sometimes
the affiliations were indirect—for example, money market funds holding SIVs, which had
to be supported by large banks, as described by the FCIC (2011, Chapter 13). See also
Jonathan Weil, "Citigroup SIV Accounting Looks Tough to Defend," Bloomberg, October
24, 2007. Ang et al. (2011) show that the leverage of independent hedge funds during the
crisis was low relative to that of other entities in the shadow banking system that were affiliated with regulated banks.

56. See the references in the previous two notes. Supervisors could have invoked rules that
forbid banks from taking large risks with a single partner in order to limit the guarantees that
banks give to their SIVs. That would have drastically limited funding for these vehicles.

57. This refers to derivatives and so-called repos. The laws regarding rehypothecation
can also create problems (see note 55 in Chapter 10 and note 88 in Chapter 11).

58. See Chapter 12.

59. Or they might be directly under orders from the government, as is the case in many
European countries.

60. In this context it is important to find ways to improve the incentives of supervisors
and regulators and to combat the effects of regulatory capture. Kane (2012a, 2012c) and
Barth et al. (2012) propose some useful approaches.

61. Peter Lattman, "A Jury's Message for Wall Street," *New York Times*, August 4, 2012.
The manager was found not guilty, but the defense and the jurors wondered why higher-
up officials were not charged.

FOURTEEN   *Too Fragile Still*

1. King (2016, 335).

2. Technically, the closure of SVB on March 10, 2023 was done by the California
Department of Financial Protection and Innovation (DFPI) since the Bank is incorporated in California. The DFPI appointed the FDIC as the receiver to deal with the bank's
assets and liabilities after its closure.

3. The Financial Stability Board, a body of bank supervisors around the world, publishes a list of 30 *global systemically important banks* each year. The Swiss bank UBS figures
prominently on this list, and so did Credit Suisse until its disappearance. The 2022 list is
available at https://www.fsb.org/2022/11/2022-list-of-global-systemically-important-banks
-g-sibs/, accessed April 4, 2023.

4. Also, on March 15, a representative of Saudi National Bank, which had purchased 9.9 percent of CS equity for 1.5 billion Swiss francs in December 2022, announced that Saudi National Bank would not provide any more equity.

5. The guarantee sets in after UBS has borne 5 billion Swiss francs' worth of losses. It is limited to 9 billion Swiss francs.

6. See "A Running Tab on Bank Deposits," May 4, 2023, https://www.calcbench.com /blog/post/716394887408386048/a-running-tab-on-bank-deposits, accessed May 22, 2023. Stephan Luck, Matthew Plosser, and Josh Younger, "Bank Funding During the Current Monetary Policy Tightening Cycle," May 11, 2023, Federal Reserve Bank of New York, https://libertystreeteconomics.newyorkfed.org/2023/05/bank-funding-during-the-current-monetary-policy-tightening-cycle/, accessed May 30, 2023, describe trends of bank deposit and other funding between early 2022 and the end of April 2023.

7. See, for example, Rachel Louise Ensign and Ben Eisen, "First Republic Bank Is Seized, Sold to JPMorgan in Second-Largest U.S. Bank Failure," *Wall Street Journal*, May 1, 2023.

8. See Hakyung Kim, "Stocks Close Lower for a Fourth Day on Renewed Bank Worries, Dow Goes Negative for 2023," CNBC, May 4, 2023.

9. Jiang et al. (2023a), Drechsler et al. (2023).

10. For a short analysis of the events of spring 2023 in Switzerland and the United States, which we discuss in more detail in this chapter and the next one, see the two short pieces by Anat Admati, Martin Hellwig, and Richard Portes, both at VoxEU. The first is "Credit Suisse: Too Big to Manage, Too Big to Resolve, or Simply too Big?," May 8, 2023, https://cepr.org/voxeu/columns/credit-suisse-too-big-manage-too-big-resolve-or-simply -too-big, accessed May 23, 2023; and the second, "When Will They Ever Learn? The US Banking Crisis of 2023," May 18, 2023, https://cepr.org/voxeu/columns/when-will-they -ever-learn-us-banking-crisis-2023, accessed May 23, 2023.

11. Agreements of the Basel Committee on Banking Supervision are not by themselves binding. Their implementation requires legislation or administrative action in the participating jurisdictions. In the United States, much of the regulation is in the hands of regulators such as the Federal Reserve, the FDIC, and the Securities and Exchange Commission (SEC). In the member states of the EU, financial regulation is based on European and national legislation. Some European legislation takes the form of a regulation, which is directly binding, and some takes the form of a directive, which must be transposed into national law and thereby becomes binding. The implementation of Basel III involved both forms. The so-called Capital Requirements Regulation (CRR) contains the most important equity requirements. The so-called Capital Requirements Directive (CRD IV, because it was the fourth version) contains the softer parts of the requirements, such as the authorities' oversight over banks' professional practices as well as potential add-ons to equity requirements. Both CRR and CRD IV were passed in 2013 and took effect in January 2014. Until Brexit in early 2020, EU legislation also applied in the U.K. It remains in force there until new U.K. legislation supersedes it.

12. Dodd-Frank was a massive 2,300-page legislation that required hundreds of rules to be written by different regulatory agencies, sometimes in coordination with one another.

Wilmarth (2013) noted that, by mid-2013, U.S. regulators had missed deadlines for 60 percent of implementing rules required by the Dodd-Frank Act. He suggests that this slowness was largely in response to industry efforts trying to emasculate or even rescind the law at the level of regulatory implementation. The leader of a bank industry trading group explained that "when the president signed the financial reform law, that was half-time. . . . The legislators left the field and now it's time for the regulators to take over." (See Scott Horseley, "Can an Ex Prosecutor Make the SEC Tougher on Wall Street?" NPR, January 24, 2013.) See also the comment of SEC Commissioner Paredes, cited in note 3 to Chapter 6, that, although Congress had passed the law, the SEC still had to study whether to implement it. See also notes 20, 24, and 27 below.

13. European legislation for dealing with failing banks consisted of the so-called Bank Recovery and Resolution Directive of 2014, available at https://eur-lex.europa.eu/legal-content/DE/TXT/?uri=CELEX:32014L0059, accessed March 23, 2023. European legislation creating banking union consisted of two regulations, the Single Supervisory Mechanism Regulation (SSM Regulation) dealing with the unification of supervision, available at https://eur-lex.europa.eu/legal-content/EN/TXT/?uri=celex%3A32013R1024, accessed March 23, 2023, and the Single Resolution Mechanism Regulation (SRM Regulation) dealing with the unification of bank resolution procedures, available at https://eur-lex.europa.eu/legal-content/EN/TXT/?uri=celex%3A32014R0806, accessed March 23. 2023. The SSM Regulation took effect in late 2014, the SRM Regulation in 2015. On the difference between regulations and directives, see note 11. Before the SSM Regulation took effect and responsibility for bank supervision shifted to the ECB, the ECB and the national authorities conducted a comprehensive assessment of banks consisting of *asset quality reviews* and *stress tests* for all institutions that came under the umbrella of the SSM. There is no European Deposit Insurance System; see ASC (2012) and Hellwig (2020a).

14. Treasury Secretary Mnuchin and Federal Reserve Chair Powell came from investment banking, and Randal Quarles, Federal Reserve Vice Chair for Supervision, came from a private equity firm. We are not saying that all of those who move to the public sector from industry are biased in favor of the industry. However, the Trump administration chose people who would be so biased. Among the industry veterans we have met, many have been highly dedicated to the public interest when serving in public positions.

15. Andrew Haldane, executive director for Financial Stability and one of the leading analysts of the causes of the financial crisis whose work is cited extensively in this book, was moved to the position of chief economist and became silent on matters of financial stability. Robert Jenkins, who had decades of experience in the banking sector and was a member of the interim Financial Policy Committee that was charged with banking regulations between July 2011 and March 2013, was not appointed to the permanent committee. On his successor, see Jill Treanor, "Dame Clara Furse: Being Bailed Out Is No Bar to Serving on FPC," *The Guardian*, June 5, 2013, with the statement "it is a mystery why the government failed to select Jenkins for service on the FPC in its full form." The mystery might have something to do with speeches cited in this book and the headlines they generated that strongly challenged bankers' claims and even their ethics. In addition to Jenkins (2011, 2012a, 2012b,

2012c), see also these opinion pieces by Robert Jenkins, in *Financial Times*: "Has JPMorgan Become an Argument for Breaking up the Banks?" October 6, 2013, "How HSBC Chairman Flint Can Restore Accountability at His Bank," March 10, 2015.

16. The ousted head of the Financial Conduct Authority was Martin Wheatley. His successor, now the governor of the Bank of England, became known for inactivity and poor performance, which contributed to substantial losses for savers, investors, and pensioners. See Kalyeena Makortoff, "Andrew Bailey to Be Quizzed on Regulator's Role in LC&F Scandal," *The Guardian*, January 23, 2020, and Josephine Cumbo, "Ex-FCA Chief Bailey 'Fell Asleep' in Pensions Mis-Selling Meeting," *Financial Times*, March 17, 2022.

17. Legislative proposals by the Commission must be accepted by the European Parliament and the Council, in which the member states are represented. In cases of disagreement, the European Commission manages the so-called trilogue in which the three bodies negotiate an acceptable text.

18. Thus, in January 2023, a joint letter from the French and German Finance Ministers asked the European Commission to initiate deregulation of asset-backed securities. The text of the letter was taken almost word for word from a letter that the industry associations of four countries had sent to the German Finance Ministry in May 2022. For documentation, see https://www.finanzwende.de/themen/finanzlobbyismus/was-das-lobbyregister-ueber-die -finanzlobby-verraet/wie-sich-die-bankenlobby-gegen-strengere-regeln-wehrt/christian -lindner-und-der-naechste-coup-der-bankenlobby/, accessed May 18, 2023. Finanzwende, the German anti-finance-lobby organization, had obtained the letters under the German Freedom-of-Information Act. The proposals themselves went counter to a fact-finding report "On the functioning of the securitization legislation" that the European Commission had submitted to the European Parliament and the Council in October 2022. See https://eur-lex .europa.eu/legal-content/EN/TXT/PDF/?uri=CELEX:52022DC0517, accessed May 18, 2023.

19. Michael Corkery, "Citigroup Becomes the Fall Guy in the Spending Bill Battle," *New York Times*, December 12, 2014, describes the heavy involvement by Citigroup lobbyists. According to Freeman and McKinley (2018), Citigroup had routinely used its bank (Citibank) to engage in risky trading and to provide guarantees to off-balance-sheet entities such as those issuing mortgage securities. As a result, Citibank incurred tens of billions in losses during the financial crisis. See also Bair (2012). On Mr. Dimon's intervention, see Steven Mufson and Tom Hamburger, "Jamie Dimon Himself Called to Urge Support for the Derivatives Rule in the Spending Bill," *Washington Post*, December 11, 2014.

20. See Steele (2022). When President Trump took office in January 2017, the implementation process for the Dodd-Frank Act stopped entirely. The law firm Davis and Polk, which had released periodic progress reports about the implementation of the Dodd-Frank Act, issued their last report on July 19, 2016. See https://www.davispolk.com/insights/resource -centers/dodd-frank-resource-center, accessed March 27, 2023.

21. Steele (2022) provides a comprehensive treatment of the Trump-era changes in bank regulation and the "tailoring agenda."

22. See Rebecca Burns, David Sirota, Julia Rock, and Andrew Perez, "SVB Chief Pressed Lawmakers to Weaken Bank Risk Regs," *The Lever*, March 15, 2023, https://www.levernews .com/svb-chief-pressed-lawmakers-to-weaken-bank-risk-regs/, accessed May 30, 2023.

23. The reductions concerned ratios involving risk-weighted assets as well as leverage ratios.

24. In this context, it is also noteworthy that the Federal Reserve never implemented a countercyclical capital buffer, which would allow equity requirements to be increased during a boom and relaxed in a time of stress. However, many jurisdictions that have such a regime were slow to increase equity requirements in the late 2010s and very quick to relax them in the spring of 2020, some with additional forms of forbearance as well. For example, in Germany, regulators decided in mid-2019 to impose these requirements to take effect on July 1, 2020, and voided the decision even before it was to take effect.

25. See note 53 to Chapter 11. The legislative proposal would have required institutions with assets above $500 billion to have at least 15 percent of their total assets funded with equity, and those with assets between $50 billion and $500 billion to have at least 8 percent equity relative to total assets. For details, see https://www.brown.senate.gov /newsroom/press/release/brown-vitter-unveil-legislation-that-would-end-too-big-to -fail-policies, accessed February 23, 2023. In some of the news coverage, e.g., Danielle Douglas, "Brown-Vitter Bill Seeks to End 'Too Big to Fail,'" *Washington Post*, April 24, 2013, the proposal was characterized as asking banks to "sock away" more capital, again confusing equity funding with cash reserve like a "rainy day fund." The proposed bill did not get much past the proposal stage. See M. J. Lee, "Brown-Vitter Struggling for Support," *Politico*, June 2, 2013.

26. The statement is early in this press conference, https://www.youtube.com/watch?v =wn2GFslBso4, accessed February 23, 2023.

27. Wilmarth (2013) suggests that, quite generally, the Federal Reserve and other regulators have procrastinated on the implementation of the Dodd-Frank Act. He attributes their failures to industry lobbying, regulators' fears of banks' moving to other jurisdictions, and a mindset that promotes deregulation and opposes effective supervision of large institutions.

28. In the United States, leftovers from the financial crisis involved the continued impact of housing foreclosures, in Europe, the low profitability of banks and the inability or unwillingness to deal with losses incurred in the crises. The problems of certain German and Italian banks reflected these difficulties.

29. In early 2012, Greek banks had become insolvent from the default on Greek government debt, but, after that, they had been recapitalized and had become much more cautious. In the spring of 2015, their holdings of Greek sovereign debt were no more than €23 billion, about one-tenth of their total assets, and it remained unchanged throughout the conflict. Stress tests performed by the European supervisor in the summer of 2015 on the four major Greek banks showed that all four were solvent and would remain solvent after a small shock, but two would become insolvent after a large shock. The need for additional equity to ensure that even after a large shock, equity requirements would be fulfilled was assessed to be €14 billion.

30. The fear that Greece might leave the euro caused a run on "Greek euros," euro-denominated claims under Greek jurisdiction, such as deposits at Greek banks that would become claims in Greek drachmas if the currency were to change. The Greek central bank

tried to neutralize the effects of the run by providing emergency liquidity assistance to the commercial banks. The crisis culminated when the Greek government called a referendum on the negotiations with the Eurogroup, the European Central Bank vetoed any further provision of emergency liquidity assistance by the Greek central bank, the commercial banks had to be closed, and the Greek government caved in.

31. The strength of banks during the COVID crisis has been vaunted in research conducted at the Federal Reserve; see Abboud et al. (2022). This research overlooks the fact that this strength was due to the support that the Federal Reserve and the federal government provided to the financial system and to the banks' borrowers. In research done at the Federal Reserve Bank of Minneapolis, Feldman and Schmidt (2021) estimated that banks received about $300 billion of indirect support during COVID. Feldman and Schmidt (2022) argue that "large banks' strength during Covid is not all it was purported to be." See also Steele (2022) on this topic.

32. These programs differed across countries. In the United States, the so-called Payment Protection Program (PPP) meant to support small businesses gave a windfall to the banks, through fees and an interest rate differential between the interest rate they earned (1%) and the interest they paid (0.25%), with no risk of default because the loans were forgivable and guaranteed, and with not much cost for checking creditworthiness. Ash et al. (2020) calculated that PPP lending provided more than $21 billion to the banking sector, including $3.6 billion to the ten largest U.S. banks. Banks also benefited from a windfall of investment banking fees helping corporations issue debt to take advantage of the Federal Reserve's willingness to buy corporate debt. See Paula Seligson and Lisa Lee, "Wall Street Reaps a Bonanza on Fed's Support for Corporate Debt," *Bloomberg News*, July 13, 2020. In Germany, banks benefited from being in partnership with the government-owned KfW (Kreditanstalt für Wiederaufbau, i.e., Bank for Reconstruction) in channeling government loans to nonfinancial businesses.

33. See, for example, Robert Burgess, "Banking's Next Threat? It Might Be Commercial Real Estate," *Bloomberg*, March 13, 2023.

34. Unless there are clear defaults, banks tend to procrastinate in their reactions to nonperformance of loans. Treating the borrowers' problems as temporary, they delay taking losses. See ASC (2012). In 2017, Andrea Enria, then chair of the European Banking Authority, reported that banks in the European Union had over €1 trillion in nonperforming loans. See Enria (2017), Hellwig (2017a). By 2018, this number had been much reduced, partly by shifting these loans to separate institutions, with support from governments. However, for banks in Cyprus, Greece, Portugal, and Italy, the levels were still unusually high. See EBA (2019).

35. By "excess capacity" we mean a situation in which competition is so intense that many institutions cannot survive without public support, directly or through guarantees. In banking, such intense competition causes banks to take excessive risks, gambling for survival, perhaps even for resurrection.

36. The ECB's purchases of long-term debt, in competition to with private banks, reduced interest rates on long-term debt. For safe debt securities, these interest rates even became negative. For institutions with market power in retail deposits, the effect on profitability was particularly strong because their long-standing practice of paying zero interest

on deposits suddenly no longer provided a margin. Negative interest rates on deposits were contentious; they also induced customers to shift into cash.

37. For several years after 2009, there also was procrastination in the United States. For example, in its 2012 Annual Report, the Bank for International Settlements noted that aggregate deleveraging after the crisis in the United States "did not come about through write-downs of unsustainable debt. Rather, it was driven by . . . a reduction in new mortgage borrowing"; see BIS (2012, 26, 42, 65, 74).

38. For details of this episode, see Steele (2022, 1027ff, 1049ff). According to Smialek (2023), Vice Chair Quarles, in charge of supervision, opposed restrictions on payouts and considered it sufficient to ask for voluntary payout suspensions. Other central banks, such as the Bank of England and the ECB, did impose restrictions on payouts in 2020 and 2021.

39. See Abboud et al. (2022).

40. Vissing-Jorgensen (2021) documents massive withdrawals by households, mutual funds, and money market funds (in response to redemption requests) as well as foreigners.

41. A December 2019 report from Bank of International Settlement (Avalos et al. 2019) suggests that actions by highly indebted institutions such as hedge funds exacerbated instabilities in the markets for U.S. Treasury securities in September 2019. The events of March 2020 showed again that such concerns are valid. See Sonali Basak, Liz McCormick, Donal Griffin, and Hema Parmar, "Before Fed Acted, Leverage Burned Hedge Funds in Treasury Market," *Bloomberg News*, March 19, 2020.

42. In addition to U.S. Treasuries, the Federal Reserve purchased significant amounts of mortgage-related securities, commercial paper, and corporate bonds. For a summary, see Eric Milstein and David Wessel, "What Did the Fed Do in Response to the Covid Crisis?," Brookings Institution, December 17, 2021, available at https://www.brookings.edu/research/fed-response-to-covid19/. Smialek (2023) gives a more detailed account. We discuss central banks in more detail in Chapter 15.

43. In particular, the Money Market Mutual Fund Liquidity Facility (MMLF) provided loans to banks purchasing assets from money market funds.

44. For early discussions of this concept, see Anne Sibert and Willem Buiter, "The Central Bank as the Market Maker of Last Resort: From Lender of Last Resort to Market Maker of Last Resort," VoxEU, August 13, 2007, https://cepr.org/voxeu/columns/central-bank-market-maker-last-resort-lender-last-resort-market-maker-last-resort, accessed May 29, 2023, and Mehrling (2010). For recent discussions and warnings, see Hauser (2021) and ESRB (2022).

45. In practice, the line between buying assets for market making purposes and buying assets for investment purposes is difficult to draw. Because the Dodd-Frank Act's version of the Volcker rule prohibiting proprietary trading by commercial banks has an exemption for market making, this difficulty has played an important role in the regulators' discussions about the implementation of the Volcker rule in the Dodd-Frank Act and has hampered the effectiveness of the law.

46. The various support operations in the United States led to the sense expressed in the headline in Matt Phillips, "Too Big to Fail: The Entire Private Sector," *New York Times*, May 19, 2020. Notes 31, 32, and 42 above discuss the impact of the Federal Reserve buying

corporate bonds in enabling more corporate borrowing and benefiting the investment banks. The stock market thrived during the COVID pandemic. See Emily Stewart, "Why Stocks Soared while America Struggled," *Vox*, May 20, 2021.

47. On mortgage-related securities and covered bonds, see notes 47 and 48 to Chapter 4. During the COVID crisis, as mentioned, banks benefited from central banks buying corporate bonds because they could facilitate more debt issuance for corporations and for various off-balance-sheet entities. See notes 31 and 32. We discuss central bank actions in more detail in the next chapter.

48. The ECB ended net increases of securities holdings in July 2022 and began to reduce renewals of maturing securities in March 2023. The Federal Reserve had begun to reduce its holdings slightly in 2018 but increased them dramatically again in 2020 by even larger amounts.

49. In the United States, the regulation of money market funds is in the domain of the SEC, which however dragged its feet and in 2010 tried to get by with restrictions on risk taking and asset maturities and a requirement to hold liquidity buffers, without addressing the problems posed by promises of "stable net asset values" (SNAV) and the associated risks of a fund's "breaking the buck," which had triggered the post-Lehman run. Following criticisms from the President's Working Group on Financial Markets and from the Financial Stability Oversight Council and following an extended period of discussion, the SEC issued a new regulation in 2014. Key innovations were a prohibition of SNAV funds holding nongovernment debt and catering to institutional investors as well as *fees* and *gates*, charges and delays on redemptions in situations in which certain thresholds were crossed. In the European Union, in 2012, the European Systemic Risk Board proposed a wholesale prohibition of SNAV funds; see ESRB (2012). The European Commission's legislative proposal followed this recommendation but met with strong resistance from member states. The Regulation on Money Market Funds that was finally passed, Regulation (EU) 2017/1131, restricts SNAV funds to holding government debt. This regulation does not have *fees* and *gates* or other devices for dealing with runs.

50. The SEC proposed rules in December 2021 and asked for comments; see https://www.sec.gov/news/press-release/2021-258 accessed May 30, 2023. The rule has not been finalized as of this writing in May 2023. ESRB (2022) also proposed new rules but the European Commission has not yet acted.

51. The Liquidity Coverage Ratio (LCR) requirement was reduced from 100 percent of payment needs over the next thirty days to 85 percent of payment needs over the next thirty days. See Steele (2022).

52. Steele (2022, 1049), estimates that Trump-era deregulation "lowered minimum capital by $150 billion and leverage requirements by $1.8 trillion at the holding company level

53. Even if one accepts the reliance on risk-weighted assets, the comparison to pre-crisis figures recalls Martin Wolf's quip, cited on p. 178, that "tripling almost nothing does not give one very much."

54. ASC (2014).

55. See Chapter 11 on how the precise implications of these numbers depend on what is included in the balance sheet, how assets are valued, and how the regulators can respond

to capital shortfalls before distress and insolvency set in. Of course, asset valuations are often tricky, making it very difficult to assess banks' health, but to the extent possible, they should reflect the relevant amounts that are usable to pay debt, and measured liabilities should include a proper count of commitments made off-balance-sheet. Contingent commitments and assets and liabilities related to the trading of derivatives must also be incorporated into the assessments.

56. A 20 percent equity requirement would also have restrained the bank's growth with a tripling of deposits between late 2019 and early 2022 unless the bank had raised more equity. Given that the bank used most of its deposit growth to buy securities in the open market, such restraint would have been helpful.

57. Wilmarth (2013).

58. See Tom Braithwaite, Michael Mackenzie, and Kara Scannell, "Deutsche Bank: Show of Strength or a Fiction?," *Financial Times*, December 5, 2012. The unsatisfactory resolution of this case is discussed, for example, in this column by one of the whistleblowers, Eric Ben Artzi, "We Must Protect Shareholders from Executive Wrongdoing," *Financial Times*, August 16, 2016, and Michael Skapinker, "Lessons from the Deutsche Bank Whistleblower Eric Ben-Artzi," *Financial Times*, August 24, 2016. For more on the history as well as events related to this accounting fraud, see Enrich (2020). See also the discussion of whistleblowers in Chapter 17.

59. Reported equity ratios were between 4 percent and 5 percent, but the "fully charged CRR/CRDIV" ratio was reported as 3.5 percent throughout (the term CRR/CRD IV refers to the European legislation implementing Basel III). The difference concerns subordinated debt liabilities that were treated as "Tier 2 Equity" under pre–Basel III rules and would no longer be included after the 2018 end of the transition period for Basel III. The asset side included intangible assets such as the fair value of future claims for tax reductions from using past losses to offset future profits. Without such intangible assets, the "fully charged" tangible equity would have been below 3 percent of total assets.

60. In total, U.S. fines for Deutsche Bank have added up to more than $18 billion since 2000; see https://violationtracker.goodjobsfirst.org/parent/deutsche-bank, accessed March 8, 2023. For CS, fines in the United States added up to more than $11 billion, see https://violationtracker.goodjobsfirst.org/parent/credit-suisse. European authorities refrained from imposing fines of this magnitude. In public discussion in Europe, there sometimes was a sense that U.S. authorities were going after the foreigners. In fact, they also went after U.S. institutions, perhaps even more so. Bank of America, Citigroup, and JPMorgan Chase had to pay more in fines than any of the large European banks. The organization Better Markets keeps track of the fines and penalties of the largest U.S. banks, available at https://bettermarkets.org/analysis/the-rap-sheets-for-wall-streets-six-biggest-banks-continue-to-grow-as-they-rack-up-another-1-billion-in-fines/, accessed May 30, 2023. We discuss fines and other law enforcement issues in Chapter 17.

61. There was another €1.3 billion loss in 2016. According to Hetzer (2015), the bank was involved in some 7,000 lawsuits in 2015. Chapter 1 of Enrich (2020), another book about Deutsche Bank, is entitled "A Criminal Organization."

62. Rumors in the press reports stated that the German government had refused to give the bank some reassurance about a possible bailout. These rumors were quickly denied, by the government as well as the bank, but their very existence indicates the atmosphere of those weeks. Other media reported that information from the German Ministry of Finance showed that people there were making sure they were well prepared in case of a crisis. This report may have been meant to reassure the markets, but markets did not regard the fact of preparations taking place as reassuring.

63. IMF (2016, 29 ff). The IMF's warning even made it into the tabloids. *BILD*, the German mass circulation daily, carried the headline: "The Most Dangerous Bank in the World!".

64. The market price was under €9 per share, the book value over €38 per share.

65. Throughout the decade, the market value of Deutsche Bank's equity was much lower than the book value. After the fall of 2016, market value recovered a bit, but reached another low in 2019, at barely €14 billion, with book value equal to €54 billion. Since 2019, the market value of equity has risen again, reaching €24 billion at the end of 2021, still less than half the book value (€58 billion at the end of 2021).

66. There is a question to what extent the results of 2020 and 2021 were due to indirect government support during the pandemic.

67. See Chapter 3 on the distinction between default and insolvency and on the difficulties involved in assessing insolvency. One criterion mentioned concerns the question whether the value of the bank's assets exceeds the bank's liabilities or not.

68. Onaran (2011) suggests that, in the financial crisis of 2007–2009, government supports kept many "Zombie Banks" alive.

69. In the 1980s, U.S. savings and loans institutions failed to account for the fact that, with market rates of interest above 12 percent, the 6 percent fixed-rate mortgages that they had held from the 1960s were worth much less than their nominal values indicated. In the 1990s, the large Japanese banks preserved a kind of make-believe solvency by not depreciating the loans they had made to large nonfinancial firms. See ASC (2012), as well as Chapter 4 and note 70 to Chapter 5.

70. See, e.g., Onaran (2011). Not properly accounting for nonperforming loans was a major issue with Italian banks and some German banks in the second half of the 2010s. In 2017, Andrea Enria, the chair of the European Banking Authority, suggested that European banks had €1 trillion of nonperforming loans in their books and proposed to handle the problem by splitting these loans off into one or several asset management companies, whose risks would ultimately be borne by taxpayers. For an analysis of the proposal, see Hellwig (2017a).

71. Regulators distinguish between Level 1 assets, which are regularly traded in markets, Level 2 assets, which are not regularly traded in markets, but can be valued on the basis of observed market data, such as interest rates, and finally, Level 3 assets, whose values cannot be clearly inferred from such market information. Many derivatives, including many asset-backed securities, are Level 3 assets and can only be "marked to model." For a more extensive explanation, see https://www.sec.gov/Archives/edgar/data/1739940/000173994020000012/R21.htm, accessed March 12, 2023.

72. For Deutsche Bank, from June 30 to December 31, 2016, these numbers declined to €485 billion in assets and €463 billion in liabilities. Over these six months, the bank's

balance sheet shrank from just over €1.8 trillion to just under €1.6 trillion, with most of the contraction occurring in financial assets and liabilities, including derivatives. This diminution of activities was the most marked reaction to the turmoil, but it is not clear to what extent it was due to counterparties' loss of trust and to what extent to the bank's own defensive reactions.

73. One example, which we discuss in the Chapter 17, is JPMorgan Chase's experience with the "London Whale," a trader in London whose misconceptions ended up costing the bank about $6 billion in losses, plus $1 billion in fines.

74. Sometimes there also is a discussion about the so-called notional values of derivatives, which for the merged UBS/CS in Switzerland amounts to CHF35 trillion. These notional values, however, do not form the basis of legal claims. For example, in an interest rate swap, the notional value would be the value of the principal on which interest is calculated, but a legal claim from the contract would consist of the difference between the fixed rate mentioned in the contract and the realized value of the variable rate in the contract. For an overview in the context of the Swiss discussion about CS, see Hansueli Schöchli, "35000 Milliarden Franken, eine UBS Zahl, die Politiker verstört" (CHF 35 trillion, a UBS number that disturbs politicians), *Neue Zürcher Zeitung*, May 16, 2023. In the United States, the OCC publishes quarterly reports on derivatives positions. There are four major banks that are particularly active in these markets (JPMorgan Chase Bank, Citibank, Bank of America, and Goldman Sachs). The notional amounts are in the hundreds of trillions, and the exposure to actual risk is still enormous. See https://www.occ.gov/publications-and-resources/publications/quarterly-report-on-bank-trading-and-derivatives-activities/index-quarterly-report-on-bank-trading-and-derivatives-activities.html, accessed May 30, 2023.

75. This was David Einhorn, manager of the hedge fund Greenlight Capital, who made large profits by selling Lehman shares short, betting that the stock price would go down.

76. Valukas (2010).

77. Haldane (2011a). In the European Union, a number of insolvencies were hidden by allowing banks to take mortgage-related securities out of their trading books and into their loan books, so that they no longer had to apply mark-to-market accounting (see Onaran 2011). Fraser (2013) reports that at the time, Royal Bank of Scotland used fictitious marks on some of its securities to prop up its equity.

78. See Haldane (2011c) and our discussion of accounting issues in Chapters 8 and 11 and below in Chapter 17. Former Federal Reserve governor Kevin Warsh said in 2012 that "disclosure practices by the largest financial firms remain lacking, and the periodic reporting . . . tends to obfuscate as much as inform." (See Gretchen Morgenson, "Telling Strength From Weakness, *New York Times*, April 28, 2012.) In Frank Partnoy and Jesse Eisinger, "What's Inside America's Banks?," *Atlantic*, January 2013, a law academic who previously worked in investment banking and an investigative reporter expose how little information there is in the disclosures of Wells Fargo Bank when it comes to "off-balance-sheet" items. For banks that are active in derivatives trading, the situation is much worse. Paul Singer, a well-known hedge fund investor, said in the World Economic Forum meetings in Davos in January 2014, that "the leverage in the system, especially in derivatives—has to be meaningfully reduced: that he does not believe markets are safer or safe or that banks "unques-

tionably understand" the potential risks on their balance sheets, and that derivatives are "net negative" for society. See, e.g., Matt Clinch, "Derivatives Get Damning Verdict at Davos," CNBC, January 22, 2014; "Bankers Insist They've Changed, But Davos Skeptics Unconvinced," MarketWatch, January 22, 2014. The full debate is available here, at https://www.youtube.com/watch?v=tV7NOEdBvf4, accessed February 17, 2023. According to Singh and Alam (2018), off-balance-sheet funding for many banks was greater in 2016 than in 2007. More recently, there is rising concern with hidden leverage across the system; see Neil Callanan and Silas Brown, "Banking Crisis Raises Concerns about Hidden Leverage in the System," *Bloomberg News*, March 27, 2023.

79. See Ball (2018) for the claim that the bank was fundamentally solvent and Chari (2022, 1504) for a rebuttal of this claim.

80. Since the accounts are presented in Swiss francs, we list numbers in that currency, as we did for Deutsche Bank in euros. Exchange rates vary over time, but a rough estimate is obtained by equating 1 Swiss franc to 1.1 dollar and one euro to one dollar.

81. Most of the third-quarter loss of over 4 billion Swiss francs announced in late September 2022 was due to a write-down on deferred tax assets, as the new management acknowledged, or was forced by authorities to acknowledge, that CS would not be able to earn enough profits to realize these tax assets. The remaining losses throughout the year were due to write-downs on long-term debt and to shrinking operating revenues.

82. See Myriam Balezou, "Credit Suisse Raises $4.3 Billion Capital After Wild Ride," *Bloomberg News*, December 8, 2022. The equity increase was announced in October and approved November 23. It came in two parts. The first part was a direct sale to selected investors, completed on November 25, which resulted in proceeds of 1.8 billion Swiss francs, of which 1.5 billion was provided by Saudi National Bank, for a share of 9.9 percent of CS. The second part was a rights offering, completed on December 9, which resulted in proceeds of 2.2 billion Swiss Francs. See p. 119 of the 2022 Annual Report. On the Saudi investment, see Lee Ying Shan, "Credit Suisse Shares Are a 'Steal,' Say New Saudi Backers after Taking 9.9% Stake," CNBC, October 31, 2022. See also Natasha Turak, "Saudi National Bank Loses Over $1 billion on Credit Suisse Investment," CNBC, March 22, 2023.

83. As of September 2022, while the book value of the bank's equity was reported as 43 billion Swiss francs, the market value was about 10 billion, less than a quarter of the book value. The December recapitalization helped a bit, but not much. All along, investors seem to have been wondering how many more skeletons there might be in the bank's books. The 2021 Annual Report devoted an unusually large amount of space to legal proceedings in which the bank is involved. Over the past decade, the bank had already been forced to pay more than $10 billion in penalties for rule infringements.

84. According to newspaper reports, after the announcement of the new equity issue, CS lost more than 80 billion francs' worth of funds in wealth management for clients, about 6 percent of the total. See "Wieder ein Milliardenverlust für die Credit Suisse: Kunden ziehen weiterhin Gelder ab" (A multi-billion loss for Credit Suisse: Clients continue to remove their funds), *Neue Zürcher Zeitung*, November 23, 2022. Whereas the September 2022 balance sheet still has total assets above 700 billion Swiss francs, the December 2022 balance sheet has total assets well below 600 billion Swiss francs.

85. Other causes mentioned in public discussion are (i) a contagion effect from the failure of Silicon Valley Bank a few days earlier, (ii) an announcement a few days earlier that U.S. authorities had asked for a delay in publishing the 2022 report, and (iii) an announcement by a representative of Saudi National Bank on March 15 that they would not acquire further shares of Credit Suisse, in addition to the 9.9 percent they had acquired in December.

86. The more pessimistic numbers appear in the accounts of the CS Group Holding Company, the parent company of the CS Group, which involve the values assessed for the parent's holdings of equity and debt securities of the different subsidiaries. The large reported loss in these accounts is due to large reductions in the values assigned to the different subsidiaries. The more optimistic numbers appear in the consolidated accounts of CS Group, which involve the assets and liabilities of the subsidiaries as well as the parent, while netting out any intra-group claims and liabilities. The accounts of the holding company are prepared under Swiss law, the consolidated group accounts under International Financial Reporting Standards (IFRS). One explanation for the difference may be that under Swiss law accounts are to be prepared with caution in the interest of the creditors, under IFRS, they are meant to inform investors about future prospects. The holding company's accounts under Swiss law matter for the assessment of solvency. Moreover, the auditors can be made liable for damages from negligence.

87. This statement is on page 50 of the Annual Report. According to outside reports, this statement as well as the auditors' warning were inserted in response to a request from the U.S. Securities and Exchange Commission (SEC). The SEC raised the issue of errors in Credit Suisse's annual reports as early as mid-2022, but the bank and its auditors had resisted taking action, arguing that material errors in valuations were unimportant. The conflict came to a head in early March 2023 and seems to have been the reason for a delay in the publication of the report that was announced on March 9. The conflict concerned certain valuations in the 2020 and 2021 reports, but the warnings in the 2022 report are formulated in general terms, which contributed to unsettling investors. See Anika Sidhika, "Credit Suisse and SEC Dispute over Accounting Errors," *Private Banker International*, April 12, 2023, https://www.privatebankerinternational.com/news/credit-suisse-and-sec -dispute-over-reporting-errors/, accessed May 26, 2023. See also Francine McKenna, "Anatomy of a Failure: Credit Suisse, PwC, and KPMG, Too," *The Dig*, May 28, 2023, https://thedig.substack.com/p/anatomy-of-a-failure-credit-suisse, accessed May 29, 2023.

88. The 3 billion Swiss francs paid by UBS for CS equity is criticized by many as being much too low. See Stephen Wilmot and Telis Demos, "Credit Suisse's Death Gives Birth to New Type of Bank Crisis," *Wall Street Journal*, March 20, 2023, with the assessment that 7 percent of Credit Suisse's reported "tangible equity" was a low number. Whether the 3 billion Swiss francs are an appropriate price depends on the quality of the CS's assets, which UBS is currently finding out. According to other media reports, CS may have vastly overstated its assets in the accounts. Supposedly, the bank had treated all IT expenditures, including spending on consulting services, as investments, so these expenditures would not be treated as costs and would instead magnify the bank's assets. Supposedly also, the bank had a history of selling profitable assets that had been carried at cost in the books, so

the excess of the selling price over the previous accounting value would contribute to current profits, hiding weaknesses in the actual operations. See Arthur Rutishauser, Beatrice Bösiger, "Der letzte Abzocker der Credit Suisse" (The Last Gambler of CS), *Tages-Anzeiger Sonntagszeitung*, May 20, 2023, https://www.tagesanzeiger.ch/der-letzte-abzocker-der -credit-suisse-210271011048?utm_source=sfmc&utm_medium=email&utm_campaign =TA_ED_9_ENG_EM_NL_XX_DERMORGEN_XX_2023-05-23&utm_term=2023-05 -22&utm_content=3705088_, accessed May 26, 2023. Ramanna (2015) describes how the process of rule setting in accounting has become distorted against the public interest, including in the treatment of some costs as investments.

89. Deposits shrank from 371 billion Swiss francs to 233 billion Swiss francs, customers' assets under management from 1.6 trillion Swiss francs to 1.3 trillion Swiss francs. Whereas revenues shrank from 22 billion Swiss francs to 15 billion Swiss francs, costs declined only by one billion, from 19 billion Swiss francs to 18 billion Swiss francs. A plan to reduce costs by 15 percent was announced, but no concrete actions seem to have been taken, and no provisions seem to have been made yet for the costs attached to a restructuring of the bank's activities. Such restructuring costs would involve for example payoffs to people who are laid off. In the case of Deutsche Bank mentioned above, the large loss in 2019 was mainly due to such costs.

90. Remarkably, this debt was written down to zero even though shareholders did not lose everything. See Editorial Board, "A Very Swiss Bank Rescue," *Financial Times*, March 20, 2023. According to Finma, the Swiss supervisor, the debt contracts provided for the possibility of a write-down if the bank was to have a "viability event." See "FINMA Provides Information About the Basis for Writing Down AT1 Capital Instruments," https://www .finma.ch/en/news/2023/03/20230323-mm-at1-kapitalinstrumente/, accessed March 27, 2023. This write-down is likely to be contested in court. To eliminate the need for approval by the shareholders of CS and UBS, the Swiss government rushed through a special law. For a summary, see Sam Jones and Oliver Ralph, "Swiss Regulator Defends $17bn Wipeout of AT1 Bonds in Credit Suisse Deal," *Financial Times*, March 23, 2023.

91. See, e.g., Jiang et al. (2020), showing that nonbank lenders have twice as much equity as banks.

92. In the case of Deutsche Bank before the strategy turnaround after 2017, people used to joke that this was really a huge hedge fund with a side business in lending and deposit taking that was useful because it enabled the institution to get away with much less equity funding than banks required from hedge funds to which they lent.

93. See notes 19 to Chapter 5 and 30 to Chapter 9, as well as Lewis (2011, 67). The two banks were Industriekreditbank, which cost taxpayers some €9 billion, and WestLB, which was said to cost taxpayers some €18 billion. Other German banks were also heavily affected. Total costs of the bailouts for German taxpayers exceeded €70 billion. See Hellwig (2018c).

94. In addition to discussion in Chapters 4, 5, and 10, see also Grind (2012) and Taub (2014).

95. Since this book was first published, publications about Citigroup have provided much evidence of recklessness there, leading to the near demise of the bank in the crisis and three massive separate bailouts that kept it alive despite serious doubts about its

solvency. In note 28 to Chapter 13, we quoted the analyst Mayo as saying in 2011: "the truly outrageous thing about Citi is that all the factors that led to the problems . . . are still happening."

96. Technically, Archegos was a "family office," investing just the money of its owner, Bill Hwang. As such it had minimal disclosure requirements. On the regulatory void regarding family offices, see Katie Martin, Robin Wigglesworth, and Laurence Fletcher, 'They Can Do What They Want': Archegos and the $6tn World of the Family Office," *Financial Times*, April 2, 2021. Archegos also used "total return swaps," contracts with banks under which the bank would buy shares and promise to pay Archegos the returns on these shares in return for Archegos promising to pay the bank a fee. In terms of the returns they generate, the swaps are equivalent to Archegos borrowing from the bank to buy the shares. However, Archegos would not become the owner of the shares and would therefore avoid legal requirements from ownership such as having to report any holding of more than 5 percent of the equity of a corporation publicly. See Quentin Webb, Alexander Osipovich, and Peter Santilli, "What Is a Total Return Swap and How Did Archegos Capital Use It?," *Wall Street Journal*, March 30, 2021.

97. The price decline in ViacomCBS was triggered by the company's announcing on March 22 that it would raise about $3 billion in additional equity on March 22, 2021, which was followed by an analyst's report that the shares were drastically overvalued.

98. Credit Suisse Group Special Committee of the Board of Directors Report on Archegos Capital Management, July 29, 2021, https://www.credit-suisse.com/about-us/en /reports-research/archegos-info-kit.html, accessed March 27, 2023. For a summary, see Jack Ewing, "Credit Suisse Finds Incompetence but No Criminal Conduct in Archegos Debacle," *New York Times*, July 29, 2021.

99. So-called supply-chain finance, factoring, and reverse factoring activities.

100. See Finma, "FINMA Concludes "Greensill" Proceedings against Credit Suisse," https://www.finma.ch/en/~/media/finma/dokumente/dokumentencenter/8news /medienmitteilungen/2023/02/20230228-mm-greensill.pdf?sc_lang=en&hash=4B2C2D0 9A4369C7957F1999F61CE23F1, accessed March 27, 2023. For a summary, see Eliot Smith, "Credit Suisse 'Seriously Breached' Obligations in Greensill Case, Swiss Regulator Says," CNBC, February 28, 2023.

101. Numbers are taken from either the bank's own 10-K/10-Q filings with the SEC or from Marc Rubinstein, "The Demise of Silicon Valley Bank," *Net Interest*, https:// www.netinterest.co/p/the-demise-of-silicon-valley-bank, accessed March 16, 2023. See also Jiang et al. (2023a) on the extent of uninsured deposit funding at SVB and elsewhere.

102. Loans did grow, from $33 billion in late 2019 to $69 billion in March 2022, but this growth was much smaller than the growth in deposit funding and in securities held.

103. According to Stephen G. Cecchetti and Kermit Schoenholtz, "The Extraordinary Failures Exposed by Silicon Valley Bank's Collapse," Money and Banking blog, March 20, 2023, SVB and other U.S. banks were already insolvent in the spring of 2022. https://www .moneyandbanking.com/commentary/2023/3/20/the-extraordinary-failures-exposed-by -silicon-valley-banks-collapse, accessed May 23, 2023.

104. If a bank declares that it wants to hold a debt security until it is fully repaid ("hold to maturity"), it can ignore changes in market value of the security and show losses only if the debtor fails to pay in time (such as when a loan the bank has made becomes "nonperforming").

105. The total equity reported by the bank was $16 billion, but this includes around $3.5 billion in preferred stock, a security that has certain debt-like features. Acknowledging the loss on "held-to-maturity" securities would have set total reported equity to approximately zero, as well as making a default on the debt-like promises for preferred stock unavoidable. If the effects of interest rate increases on the fair value of SVB's loans were also taken into account, total reported equity would have been strongly negative.

106. See Daniel Gilbert, Todd C. Frankel and Joseph Menn, "Silicon Valley Bank's Risk Model Flashed Red. So Its Executives Changed It," *Washington Post*, April 2, 2023.

107. On the effort to raise equity, see Craig Coben, "Dissecting Goldman's Gory $2.25bn SVB Equity Issue," *Financial Times*, March 13, 2023. The speed and magnitude of withdrawals was partly due to the rise of mobile banking and social media. See Jonathan Yerushalmy, "'The First Twitter-Fuelled Bank Run': How Social Media Compounded SVB's Collapse," *The Guardian*, March 16, 2023.

108. The $21 billion of securities sold had been classified as "available for sale" (AFS) and had been marked to market. After the sale, the bank did not have many AFS securities left. The deposit withdrawals on March 9 necessitated sales of securities classified as "held to maturity," whose accounting valuations did not reflect losses in market value. Had these securities been sold, *all* HTM securities had to be reclassified as AFS and marked to market. See Maureen Farrell, "Inside the Collapse of Silicon Valley Bank," *New York Times*, March 14, 2023. SVB ended March 9 with a negative cash balance and it became clear that it could not meet its obligation. See the regulator's statement on March 10, describing the situation, https://dfpi.ca.gov/wp-content/uploads/sites/337/2023/03/DFPI-Orders-Silicon-Valley-Bank-03102023.pdf, accessed May 21, 2023.

109. Rather than investing as much in Treasury securities, First Republic Bank made numerous large mortgage loans at very low interest such as 2 percent or even less, and many were structured as "interest only" loans, thus making very small payments for years even as the short-term funding costs of the bank increased to 5 percent or more. See Noah Buhayar, Jennifer Surane, Max Reyes, and Ann Choi, "First Republic Worked Hard to Woo Rich Clients. It Was the Bank's Undoing," *Bloomberg News*, April 16, 2023.

110. See Jiang et al. (2023a). Drechsler et al. (2023) arrive at a similar figure.

111. See Antoine Gara and Brooke Masters, "Asset Management: BlackRock's Risk Control Warnings to SVB," *Financial Times*, March 19, 2023.

112. See Marc Rubinstein, "The Demise of Silicon Valley Bank," mentioned in note 101 above. According to the FDIC, the ten largest deposit accounts at SVB held a total of $13.3 billion in deposits, of which only $2.5 million (0.02%) was guaranteed by deposit insurance. See "Recent Bank Failures and the Federal Regulatory Response," March 28, 2023, available at https://www.banking.senate.gov/hearings/recent-bank-failures-and-the-federal-regulatory-response, accessed March 27, 2023.

113. See Ben Eisen and Andrew Ackerman, "Where Were the Regulators as SVB Crashed?" *Wall Street Journal*, March 11, 2023, and Jeanna Smialek, "Before Collapse of Silicon Valley Bank, the Fed Spotted Big Problems," *New York Times*, March 19, 2023. It appears that some supervisors saw problems and pointed them out to management, but little was actually done to address them. See Hannah Levitt, Sridhar Natarajan, and Saleha Mohsin, "The Fed Was Too Late on SVB Even Though It Saw Problem After Problem," *Bloomberg News*, March 17, 2023. Jesse Eisinger, "Regulatory Failure 101: What the Collapse of Silicon Valley Bank Reveals," *ProPublica*, March 17, 2023, wonders whether we should question the ability and will of the Federal Reserve to undertake effective supervision.

114. Federal Reserve (2023).

115. See GAO (2023). Prompt corrective action had already been recommended by the GAO in 2011.

116. See Wilmarth (2013) and Isaac Chotiner, "The Regulatory Breakdown Behind the Collapse of Silicon Valley Bank," *New Yorker*, March 19, 2023. The latter includes an interview with Peter Conti-Brown, who notes that one of the problems with evaluating bank supervision at the Federal Reserve is the fact that the process is entirely opaque, and the Federal Reserve does not allow any researchers to study it.

117. The word "solvency" appears just once in the report, in contrast to "liquidity," which appears 332 times. Similarly, the report of the State of California's Department of Financial Protection and Innovation on SVB has 103 mentions of liquidity and only one of solvency concerns. See https://dfpi.ca.gov/wp-content/uploads/sites/337/2023/05/Review -of-DFPIs-Oversight-and-Regulation-of-Silicon-Valley-Bank.pdf, accessed May 23, 2023.

118. At this writing (May 2023), the Federal Reserve is charging more than 5 percent in its discount window. For the latest rates see https://www.frbdiscountwindow.org/. On March 12 it opened a new Bank Term Funding Program that makes loans of up to a year at similar interest rate. Both programs value bank collateral at par, which is often much higher than the fair or market value. In addition, many U.S. banks borrow from the Federal Home Loan Bank (FHLB) system, which generally lends with harsher terms. Both Silicon Valley Bank and First Republic Bank borrowed from the San Francisco FHLB, and many more are taking such "advances." See, for example, Lorenzo Migliorato, "Schwab Turns to Costly FHLB Advances as Deposits Drop," Risk.net, April 19, 2023, available at https:// www.risk.net/risk-quantum/7956520/schwab-turns-to-costly-fhlb-advances-as-deposits -drop, accessed May 30, 2023.

119. As we discussed in Chapter 4, around 1980, U.S. savings institutions were holding mortgages from the past that paid, say, 6 percent per year and still had many years to go. When market rate of interest soared to 15 percent, savings institutions lobbied for deregulation of interest rates on deposits because they were losing customers to money market funds, but when they paid depositors 15 percent themselves, after deregulation, they found that they had to pay more interest than they received from their mortgage debtors. At that time, about two-thirds of U.S. savings institutions were technically insolvent, but the insolvencies were hidden. The substantial worsening of the situation from the increase in the cost of funding was not recognized in the accounting. Regulators and supervisors failed to step in and prevent the gambling for resurrection and effective looting of the institutions.

Remarkably, regulators and supervisors seem to have forgotten the 1980s' lesson about the danger of failing to recognize losses. See Chapter 4, p. 54, including notes 30–32.

120. Jiang et al. (2023b).

121. The 2022 Nobel Memorial Prize in economics was awarded "for research on banks and financial crises," showing "why avoiding bank collapses is vital." See https://www .nobelprize.org/prizes/economic-sciences/2022/press-release/, accessed May 30, 2023. The article by Diamond and Dybvig (1983) that was so honored presents a theoretical model of demand deposits as a device that provides investors with insurance against uncertainty about the timing of their cash needs. In this model, runs can occur merely because of self-fulfilling prophecies of depositors about each other. Diamond and Dybvig (1983) propose government-backed deposit insurance as a remedy. In the model, however, a run could also be prevented by private contracts that allow the bank to stop payouts temporarily after a certain threshold of withdrawals had been reached. In a more complicated model in which the individual depositors' cash needs are not subject to a law of large numbers, this device does not work, so Diamond and Dybvig (1983) suggest that only deposit insurance works to prevent a run. Wallace (1988) shows that this claim rests on an implicit assumption that the deposit insurer is able to observe aggregate cash needs, and market participants are not.

122. See the references given in note 20 to Chapter 4, particularly Calomiris and Gorton (1981). In the analysis of Diamond and Dybvig (1983) discussed in the previous note, there is no room for bad news of the sort considered in Calomiris and Gorton (1981) and other references, because asset returns are not subject to any risk.

123. There have also been discussions about applying fair value accounting to liabilities. Such an application would be problematic because assessments of solvency and default depend on the nominal (or "face") value of liabilities, not on their market values.

124. For a long time, banks only needed to recognize impairments of creditworthiness when there was an actual credit event such as a default or exorbitant delay in a borrower's payment. A 2018 change in International Financial Reporting Standards requires them to articulate expectations about forthcoming payment flows and to recognize impairments when they expect problems with future payments, even though no delinquency in debt service has occurred yet.

125. Particularly the Federal Deposit Insurance Corporation Improvement Act (FDICIA) of 1991.

126. Some commentators suggest that had regulators conducted stress tests for SVB they would have been able to do more to prevent its failure. However, during the relevant period, stress tests in the United States did not consider the full effects of interest rate increases on banks, so it is not clear how much they would have helped. See Joseph R. Mason and Kris James Mitchener, "Stress Testing Wouldn't Have Saved Silicon Valley Bank," *Wall Street Journal*, March 15, 2023. In the euro area, the results of stress tests, even when they consider interest rate changes, are not very reliable: First, in stress tests as in ordinary accounting, the effects of interest rate increases on fair values of securities classified as "held to maturity" are neglected. Second, at least the 2014 stress test was carried out under the presumption that funding structures would remain unchanged, so banks

that borrowed large amounts from the ECB did not have much of a funding cost increase because the assumed interest rate increase did not encompass the lending rate of the ECB. For more on flaws in stress tests, see Chapter 11 as well as note 32 to Chapter 16 and the references given there.

127. The exchange took place at the 42nd Economics Conference of the Austrian National Bank, Vienna May 12–13, 2014. The first question was a response to another former central banker's asking why we were so dissatisfied with the reforms that had taken place.

128. The first statement was made at a conference at George Washington University marking four years since the Dodd-Frank Act and discussing financial stability and the "too big to fail" issue. See a summary at https://www.sifma.org/resources/general/gwu -school-of-law-presents-financial-stability-after-dodd-frank-have-we-ended-too-big-to -fail/, accessed May 29, 2023. The second statement was during a talk at the Stanford Institute for Economic Policy Research on February 26, 2018, at around minute 14:50, at https://www.youtube.com/watch?v=BINr1JZJKC0, accessed March 12, 2023.

129. In the United States, the report of the Financial Crisis Inquiry Commission (FCIC 2011) came out *after* the passage of the Dodd-Frank Act. In Europe, apart from the United Kingdom, neither the member states nor the European Union engaged in such an analysis at all. In the United Kingdom, the report of the Independent Commission on Banking (ICB 2011) appeared after the European legislation had already been introduced; therefore, its scope was fairly limited and even then its recommendations were only partly followed by the U.K. government. Exceptions to this pattern were Iceland and Switzerland, small countries where the crisis brought an awareness that the financial sector posed existential threats to the overall population.

130. The 2010 reports of the Basel Committee on Banking Supervision contain many assertions but hardly any evidence about causation (BCBS 2010 a–d).

131. See Haselmann et al. (2022).

132. On the watering down of money market reform in the United States, see note 49. In the European Union, member state governments also played an important role in killing the European Commission's attempt to introduce a version of the Volcker rule prohibiting securities trading by commercial banks. The Commission's 2014 Proposal for a Regulation on structural measures improving the resilience of EU credit institutions was very much watered down by the Council. The Council's version was then rejected by the European Parliament. In 2017, the Commission withdrew its proposal.

133. The Basel Accord has a scheme of risk weights, discussed in Chapter 11, which for government debt depends on the assessments that rating agencies give to the country. However, the accord also has a clause whereby bank regulators in a country are free to choose lower risk weights for the debt of central governments and central banks that is denominated in the currency of the jurisdiction in question. Regulators have routinely used this clause to set the risk weight for government debt equal to zero. They even apply this practice to the debt of regional and municipal governments in cases where this debt is not guaranteed by the central government.

134. ESRB (2015). As vice chair of the Advisory Scientific Committee of the ESRB, Martin Hellwig had initiated and then co-chaired the work of the expert group that

wrote this report. One major finding was that, in good times, zero risk weights for government debt do not matter much for equity requirements because rating agencies are optimistic, so risk weights based on ratings are favorable anyway. What really matters is the exemption of government debt from large-exposure rules requiring that a bank's holdings of securities from any one issuer may amount to no more than 25 percent of its equity.

135. BCBS (2021).

136. Far from acknowledging risks attached to government debt, some of the participants want to take the system in reverse and exempt government debt from leverage ratio regulation. Basel III introduced the leverage ratio regulation because abuses of risk weighting in determining required equity had caused some institutions to have so little equity that, except for government support, they would have been insolvent in late 2008. Some of the problems concerned institutions like Dexia and Hypo Real Estate that had specialized in holding government debt and mortgages. They were hard hit by strong declines in market prices of government debt after the Lehman bankruptcy. By year-end 2008, Hypo Real Estate reported negative equity, due to €5.5 billion in losses. A large part of these losses involved the Dublin-based bank Depfa, acquired in 2007, which had mainly invested in government debt. The French-Belgian Bank Dexia had pursued a similar strategy as Hypo Real Estate and would also have shown negative equity at the end of 2008, except that it has taken advantage of a crisis rule allowing banks to stop marking the values of their investments to the market. The fiction that government debt is riskless is convenient for governments, but it is a fiction.

137. For much of the decade, the Basel Committee was headed by Stefan Ingves, governor of the Swedish central bank, previously an official of the Swedish finance ministry in charge of cleaning up the Swedish banks after the 1992 crisis. The 1992 experience had strongly influenced his understanding of the problem of financial stability.

138. Another reaction of regulators and supervisors was to extend the scope of supervision by asking for additional reporting on ongoing activities and even asking banks to submit their business models for evaluation by the regulators. For an overview, see Coelho et al. (2022). Such interventions of regulators are problematic and can even be counterproductive because the regulators are not always competent to assess business models. They would be superfluous if the banks had much more equity funding, so that there is no need to worry much about bank insolvencies.

139. See BCBS (2016a), as well as Behn et al. (2022). Chapter 11 explains how risk weights are used and gives our own criticism. Mayra Rodríguez Valladares, "Signs for Hope in Basel's Bank Regulation Agenda," *New York Times*, January 28, 2015, is an early expression of hope about Basel Committee's work.

140. Specifically, there is a so-called output floor such that equity must not be less than 72.5 percent of what would be required under the coarser, model-independent "standard approach." See BCBS (2017).

141. The Basel Committee referred to the new agreement as "finalizing Basel III." For a summary of the issues and a reaction to this debate, including a flawed study by the Bank of England, see Admati (2016).

142. For an overview of the Commission's legislative proposal, see European Commission Press Release, "Banking Package 2021: New European Rules to Strengthen Banks' Resilience and Better Prepare for the Future," available at https://ec.europa.eu /commission/presscorner/detail/en/ip_21_5401, accessed May 30, 2023. The different parts of the legislative proposal itself are available at https://finance.ec.europa.eu /publications/banking-package_en#documents, accessed May 30, 2023.

143. For a detailed discussion see Chapter 11, especially note 68. Thomas Hoenig, as vice chair of FDIC between 2012 and 2018, continued to criticize the approach. See, e.g., Michael R. Crittenden, "FDIC's Hoenig: Basel III Is Well-Intended Illusion," *Wall Street Journal*, April 9, 2013, and Leonard (2022). Behn et al. (2022) show that banks "optimized" model-based regulation to lower their capital requirements.

144. See Duffie (2016), who does note the problem of zero risk weights and suggests a possible floor on all weights. For a summary of flaws in the Basel approach, see Admati (2016).

145. FSA (2010).

146. As we explain in Chapter 11, in a transition phase, a higher equity requirement might be applied to asset levels from before the reform, so the banks must actually build up equity funding, e.g., by retaining earnings, rather than merely sell assets. In this chapter and in other writing we urged regulators, given the extremely high indebtedness in banking, to ban payouts to shareholders such as dividends and issue more equity. See note 27 to Chapter 11. Admati et al. (2018) show that if banks adjust investments and/or funding choices to improve their ratio of equity relative to assets, they have incentives to sell assets or reduce investments inefficiently rather than replace debt with equity or issue new equity. Inability to raise equity at any price is a clear sign of likely insolvency, and as we discuss and will revisit in the next chapters, bailouts can maintain insolvent "zombie" institutions that do not help the economy.

147. For example, the Stakeholder Group of the European Banking Authority that was mentioned in the introduction is dominated by industry representatives. See also Ben Protess, "Wall Street Lobbyist Aims to 'Reform the Reform,'" *Dealbook New York Times*, July 14, 2011.

148. Wilmarth (2013) emphasizes the role of cognitive capture, involving (i) a view that large banks are safe, (ii) a view that globally systemic banks are needed to ensure that the country's export industries are globally competitive, and (iii) a view that regulation harms the competitiveness of banks. In connection with Deutsche Bank, we pointed out that (i) is false. (ii) has been raised since the discussion about the Edge Act of 1919, which allowed U.S. banks to establish foreign subsidiaries outside the U.S. regulatory domain. In fact, as shown by Steele (2023), there is no empirical basis for this claim. Finally, (iii) is contradicted by the fact that, in the 2010s, U.S. banks and the U.S. economy did better than European banks and the European economy, to some extent because, from 2013 on, U.S. authorities were stricter in enforcing regulation and forcing banks to clean up their balance sheets than European banks. For a long time, Swiss banks used to have strong equity positions as a marketing argument. On cognitive capture, see also Johnson and Kwak (2010) and Kwak (2013).

149. The legal profession also plays a role. Legal expertise is useful in formulating laws and regulations. Big law firms stand ready to provide advice, not only to banks but also to

governments. In Germany, for example, the laws enabling government interventions in 2008–2010 were drafted by members of leading law firms. Since these law firms are also active in advising and even litigating for banks, particularly large banks, there was a clear conflict of interest.

150. As discussed by Steele (2022), in the COVID crisis, the Federal Reserve was alone among major central banks allowing payouts to shareholders, dividends, and share repurchases, to proceed almost without restrictions. Attempts to impose such restrictions in 2022 met with an outcry from the lobbyists. See Hugh Son, "Dimon Rips Fed Stress Test As 'Terrible Way To Run' Financial System After His Bank Halts Buybacks," CNBC, July 14, 2022; Shubham Saharan, "US Banks Passed the Latest Stress Test, But Are Still Unhappy," *Bloomberg/Business Week*, July 29, 2022; Joshua Franklin, "Jamie Dimon Warns Capital Rules Pose 'Significant Economic Risk,'" *Financial Times*, September 20, 2022.

151. The discussions in Chapter 6, Chapter 9, and Chapter 12 explain the distinction between private and social costs and benefits and the distortions that can arise from misplaced subsidies.

152. Steele (2022)

153. See Connaughton (2012).

154. For an empirical analysis, see Cecchetti (2015). Acharya and Steffen (2012) showed that, among the banks that benefited from the ECB's 2011/12 Long Term Refinancing Operation, those that had relatively little equity used the funds they borrowed from the ECB in order to invest in their own governments' debts, in preference to lending to nonfinancial companies, while those that had more equity took advantage of higher returns from lending to nonfinancial companies.

155. This document, which we have updated periodically, provides a list of flawed claims that people continued to make, with short texts explaining what is wrong with each of them. The current version is Admati and Hellwig (2023).

156. Tom Braithwaite, "Wells Chief Warns Fed over Debt Proposal," *Financial Times*, June 2, 2013. Mr. Stumpf was objecting to a proposed requirement that banks issue "loss absorbing debt," whose bearers would share in losses if the bank became insolvent, unlike deposits with guarantees from the FDIC.

157. We are referring to Frederic Mishkin of Columbia University; see note 3 to Chapter 8 and the debunking throughout the chapter. Remarkably, recent editions still contain the same false statements we debunked.

158. For a systematic empirical analysis of funding costs, see IMF (2014). One finding there shows that the introduction of a leverage ratio requirement preventing banks from funding more than 97 percent of their assets with debt *lowered* the interest rates at which they could borrow, presumably because this requirement reduced default risks.

159. In Chapter 3, we explained that borrowing is addictive. In Admati et al. (2018), we showed that this addictiveness creates what we called a leverage ratchet effect, meaning that, in the absence of prior commitments, over time and in response to new information, leverage can ratchet up without ever declining again. In DeMarzo and He (2021), a study of leverage dynamics without commitment in a particular formal model, the effect of a commitment never to borrow again on the interest rate on initial borrowing provides

benefits that fully compensate for the foregone tax savings under a policy of unconstrained ever-increasing debt.

160. In Admati and Hellwig (2019), we argue that because of the fragmentation of the banks' creditors, in space and time, private contracting is unable to discipline debt overhang and leverage ratchet effects. Lenders may use covenants and collateral requirements to constrain these effects, but such constraints are often not very effective, and moreover, they harm the banks' ability to react to changing circumstances. For an analysis involving collateral requirements see Donaldson et al. (2020).

161. Some of this work is discussed in Chapter 10, some in Admati and Hellwig (2013), which had originally been written for this book but then was left out because people with experience in banking told us that the material we criticized, also covered in Section 5 of Admati et al. (2011, 2013), was too far removed from the real world to be taken seriously. A banking practitioner, upon reading this section, wondered why it is there, asking "is this some academic thing?" Current discussions about the "endgame of Basel" repeat the arguments that we refuted in earlier writings.

162. For a more elaborate formulation of this criticism, see the previous note and Admati and Hellwig (2019).

163. On the misuse of models, see Pfleiderer (2018), and Anat Admati, "Political Economy, Blind Spots, and a Challenge to Academics," *ProMarket*, November 15, 2019, https://www .promarket.org/2019/11/15/political-economy-blind-spots-and-a-challenge-to-academics/, accessed May 30, 2023. See also Admati (2017). In private conversations, a number of people in regulatory bodies have told us that some research is written entirely for political reasons to justify what policymakers want to do and that inconvenient research is suppressed or self-censored. In many organizations, including IMF, research papers must undergo review by the communication department. In the context of central bank policy, Fabo et al. (2021) indicate that research done within central banks shows more positive impact for so-called Quantitative Easing than research done in academic departments.

164. Cechetti (2015).

165. It is certainly possible to target housing subsidies so that they reach those who need them most, such as first-time buyers, without necessarily subsidizing debt. (An example would be a tax credit to be used for a down payment.) In the United States, housing tax subsidies ultimately benefit wealthy people more than those with low income and renters. See, e.g., Katie Orton, "Federal Government Spends More Subsidizing Homeowners Than It Does Helping People Avoid Homelessness," *Washington Post*, October 11, 2017. The evolution of the student debt crisis in the United States bears similarities to the housing crisis that led to the 2007–2009 crisis as it pertains to misguided policies related to household debt. See Mitchell (2021).

166. On the addictiveness of borrowing, see Chapters 3 and 10 as well as Admati et al. (2018), who show how the tax effect leads corporations acting on behalf of shareholders to always wish to increase indebtedness (and never reduce it) if possible, no matter how indebted they already are, in contrast to the notion that corporations have a static "trade-off" that creates an optimal funding mix. The effect is particularly powerful for banks because many of their creditors feel secured by deposit guarantees and do not counter the

addictiveness of borrowing by either increasing the interest rate they demand, putting stringent conditions, such as seniority and collateral requirements, on the debt, or refusing to lend altogether. As discussed in Admati and Hellwig (2019) and Brunnermeier and Oehmke (2013), the difficulty of making commitments to creditors not to harm them in the future makes regulation of banks' indebtedness particularly important.

167. There have been persistent calls to re-examine debt tax subsidies. See "A Senseless Subsidy," and "The Great Distortion," both in *The Economist*, May 16, 2015, which say that debt subsidies are "a vast distortion in the world economy [that is] is wholly man-made," discuss some of the many harms, and call for ending these subsidies and the "debt addiction" they create. Also see a *Bloomberg View* editorial from October 15, 2018, entitled "Stop Subsidizing Debt." In the years before 2020, some had warned of the risks from large, heavy corporate indebtedness. See, for example, Daniel Bergstresser, "Is the Rise in U.S. Corporate Debt Cause for Concern?" *EconFact* and *PBS Newshour*, September 8, 2019, discussing in particular the rise in loans to heavily indebted corporations, so-called leveraged loans with few covenants, i.e., conditions to constrain risk taking. See also John Plender, "The Seeds of the Next Debt Crisis," *Financial Times*, March 3, 2020. On a previous occasion, excessive corporate indebtedness had greatly contributed to the recession of 1990–1991 and to the credit crunch that delayed the recovery. See Bernanke and Campbell (1988), Warshawsky (1991), and Bernanke and Lown (1991).

168. Schön (2012) explains some of the differences in the way corporate law and tax law see the issues and notes the challenges of drawing distinctions between debt and equity. Schön et al. (2014) review relevant policies around the world.

169. Such an arrangement has been strongly promoted by Wilmarth (2011) and Lubben and Wilmarth (2017). Roe and Troege (2018), written by a legal scholar and an economist, makes specific proposals to change the tax code to avoid encouraging banks to borrow excessively and argues against the subsidy, particularly for banks. The same authors advocate more broadly; see "Ending Tax Law's Subsidy for Corporate Debt" *Bloomberg Tax*, December 23, 2021.

FIFTEEN   *Bailouts and Central Banks*

1. The quote in the epigraph is from a senior London-based banker. See Chris Giles, Emma Dunkley, George Parker, Owen Walker, Peter Foster, Josephine Cumbo, Jim Pickard, and Harriet Agnew, "Bank of England Launches £65bn Move to Calm Markets," *Financial Times*, September 28, 2022. The context was the Bank of England's stepping in with massive purchases of long-term government bonds (gilts) in order to save U.K. pension funds from default. The warning "This might be a Lehman moment" was already prominent in May 2010, in the first phase of the Greek sovereign debt crisis (potential contagion from Greece to Italy), and in the fall of 2011, when European financial institutions and markets were strongly affected by solvency concerns, withdrawals of funds, and asset price declines. More recently, since the fall of 2022, the expression has also been used in the context of Credit Suisse and the collapse of crypto exchange FTX, e.g., Kevin Roose, "Is This Crypto's Lehman Moment?," *New York Times*, November 9, 2022.

2. See Mary Williams Walsh, "A.I.G. Lists Banks It Paid with U.S. Bailout Funds," *New York Times*, March 15, 2009. Multibillion-dollar payments went to Goldman Sachs ($12.9 billion), Merrill Lynch ($6.8 billion), Bank of America ($5.2 billion), Citigroup ($2.3 billion), and Wachovia ($1.5 billion), Société Générale of France and Deutsche Bank of Germany (nearly $12 billion each), Barclays of Britain ($8.5 billion), and UBS of Switzerland ($5 billion). See also Gretchen Morgenson, "An A.I.G. Failure Would Have Cost Goldman Sachs, Documents Show," *New York Times*, July 23, 2010. Cities and municipalities, and retail customers of AIG also benefited.

3. The FDIC has sold SVB to First–Citizens Bank, NC, and Signature Bank to Flagstar Bank, NY. See FDIC Press Releases of March 26 and May 19, 2023, https://www.fdic.gov /news/press-releases/2023/pr23023.html, accessed March 27, 2023, and https://www.fdic .gov/news/press-releases/2023/pr23021.html, accessed May 24, 2023. On May 11, 2023, the FDIC announced a proposed rule for special assessment to 113 banks to cover the cost of uninsured deposit guarantees in these two banks. 95 percent of the fees are to be charged to banks with over $50 billion in assets. The losses were originally estimated to be $20 billion for SVB and $2.5 billion for Signature but have since been revised downward. See https:// www.fdic.gov/news/financial-institution-letters/2023/fil23024.html, accessed May 23, 2023. In the case of First Republic Bank, which was closed and sold to JPMorgan Chase on May 1, 2023, the loss to the FDIC of an estimated $13 billion results from sharing losses with JPMorgan Chase under the agreement between the FDIC, as the receiver of the bank, and JPMorgan Chase when the latter bought the bank. See "JPMorgan Chase Bank, National Association, Columbus, Ohio Assumes All the Deposits of First Republic Bank, San Francisco, California," FDIC press release, https://www.fdic.gov/news/press-releases /2023/pr23034.html, accessed May 23, 2023.

4. If the Deposit Insurance Fund is exhausted, an additional levy is charged. Some banks will pay an additional levy for losses of the fund from paying the uninsured depositors of SVB and Signature Bank. The exact plans, proposed on May 11, 2023 may be revised. In addition to the previous note, see, e.g., Katanga Johnson, "Big Banks Face Billions in Extra FDIC Fees After SVB Failure," *Bloomberg News*, May 11, 2023.

5. The guarantee sets in if losses exceed 5 billion Swiss francs. The amount promised is limited to 9 billion francs.

6. For example, Royal Bank of Scotland (U.K.), Commerzbank, Hypo Real Estate, and West LB (Germany), UBS (Switzerland) received direct equity participations from their governments. U.S. support of large banks, as well as the larger part of the German support of Commerzbank, involved purchases of preferred stocks and "silent participation," debt-like securities whose claims could be written down if the bank earned no profits and made no payments to shareholders. In the United States, the government provided direct investments in numerous banks and also took ownership stake in insurance company AIG, in a process managed by the Federal Reserve Bank of New York, and took into receivership, and still controls, the mortgage companies Fannie Mae and Freddie Mac.

7. See also Chapter 10.

8. On the bailouts, see, in particular, Barofsky (2012) and Bair (2012).

NOTES TO PAGES 272–273 **485**

9. See https://obamawhitehouse.archives.gov/economy/middle-class/dodd-frank-wall
-street-reform, accessed February 18, 2023.

10. See Bobby Allyn, "The White House Is Avoiding One Word When It Comes to Silicon
Valley Bank: Bailout," NPR, March 14, 2014. Some in the media accepted the narrative that
an intervention is not a bailout if taxpayers do not pay for it, e.g., Caitlin Reilly, "Regulators
to Protect SVB, Signature Depositors, but No Bailout," Roll Call, March 13, 2023.

11. See for example Brierley (2009) on this principle in the U.K. Banking Act of 2009.

12. In the first edition, we did not focus much on central banks but treated support
from central banks and governments as parts of a common package. Since then, the difference between them has become important, politically because central banks are free to
intervene more flexibly than governments, and economically because the distinction
between central bank loans that do not affect the solvency of an institution and government injections of funds has taken on great importance.

13. Jevons (1910) presents a vivid and picturesque account of the difficulties attached to
multilateral exchange of goods and services when there is no generally accepted medium
of exchange.

14. Coins also serve this purpose, but in terms of total value, their role is quite small,
about $28 billion in coins in the United States, versus $2.3 trillion in banknotes. In the U.S.
and the euro area, the issue of coins is in the competence of governments, rather than the
central banks.

15. In the United States, this status of banknotes as legal claims was abolished in 1933.
The term "fiat money," which is sometimes used for paper money with banknotes that are
not legal claims, contains a reference to the designation of this money as a means of payment by government "fiat." Latin "fiat" here means "so be it." See also notes 10 and 14 to
Chapter 10.

16. Some argue that the acceptability of banknotes in transactions is due to the governments designing them as a legal means of payment, particularly for taxes. Episodes like the
German hyperinflation of the early 1920s, however, show that this legal status is not sufficient to ensure that banknotes have real value and that they are widely accepted.

17. For information about the declining use of cash and the issues involved, see the conference volume of Beer et al. (2016). In some parts of the world, the decline in the use of
cash proceeds so dramatically that laws are used to mandate the acceptability of cash as a
means of payment. By contrast, Rogoff (2016) proposes to even accelerate the process, particularly in order to enable central banks to make interest rates negative. Academic
Advisory Committee (2017), in a report to the German Ministry for Economic Affairs,
criticized this proposal because, among other things, negative interest rates would push
the financial sector into uncharted territory where fundamental values of many long-lived
assets would be unbounded and appropriate criteria for investment choices would be lacking. See also Prasad (2021) on the topic of cash.

18. In the United States, these banks are often referred to as "commercial banks," as distinct from "investment banks" that engage in many activities; see Chapters 4 and 5. It is
tempting to use the term "private banks," but then, in some countries, there are institutions

such as the Landesbanken and savings banks in Germany that are owned by governments while engaging in ordinary banking business, subject to the same regulations as private banks. On the varied meanings of the terms "public" and "private" in different languages and cultures, see Fourcade (2009).

19. The idea of central banks offering digital currency has come up in recent years, and digital technology can help improve the efficiency of payment systems and help law enforcement, but it need not be the same as abolishing cash. See Prasad (2021).

20. For the much-discussed transition to an economy with digital central bank money, in which Kate and Aunt Claire might both have accounts with the central bank, this observation raises the question of what legal claims Kate would have in such an economy.

21. Of course, we are assuming that the banks involved are not bankrupted or that these deposits are insured.

22. If Kate sends a check to Aunt Claire, Aunt Claire submits the check to her bank, the bank submits the check to Kate's bank, this bank charges Kate and at the same time asks the central bank to transfer $100 from its own account to the account of Aunt Claire's bank. These payment mechanisms could also be handled by interbank clearing mechanism, but, for any differences that remain at the end of the day, such mechanisms would ultimately require a use of an extraneous means of payment such as gold (in past centuries) or central bank money.

23. The Federal Reserve has been paying interest on reserves since October 2008. The ECB had put the interest rate on reserves somewhat below the so-called main refinancing rate for its lending to banks, so when the latter rate was zero, from 2014 to 2022, it had "negative interest" on reserves, i.e., banks were required to pay for having reserves with the ECB.

24. More precisely: un-borrowed reserves.

25. In the euro area, there are multiple central banks. Besides the ECB, the euro area also has the National Central Banks (NCBs) of a previous era. The NCBs are the shareholders of the ECB, but in matters of monetary policy, they act as agents for the ECB, under the ECB's orders.

26. The image of helicopters serving for the distribution of banknotes comes from Friedman (1969). Friedman used the image because he wanted to abstract from the details of how money gets into the economy. Alas, he did not consider the effects of the "helicopter money" regime on the uses and the value of land.

27. For a basic explanation, see https://www.federalreserve.gov/regreform/discount-window.htm, accessed March 20, 2023. Note that there are three slightly different programs. During normal times, banks do not borrow much from the discount window, partly because the rate at which banks lend to each other overnight, the federal funds rate, is slightly lower than the discount rate, partly because borrowing from the discount window may convey the impression that one cannot borrow elsewhere (stigma effect). Borrowing from the discount window can, however, be massive in times of crisis. See note 14 to Chapter 9 about the Federal Reserve programs during the 2007–2009 crisis.

28. Together with the discount rate, the Federal Reserve announces a target interval for the federal funds rate, as of March 24, 2023, from 4.75 percent per year to 5 percent per year, so small downward deviations are possible. In the years of the pandemic, the target

interval for the federal funds rate went all the way down to zero, and for extended periods of time, the federal funds rate was actually close to zero, below 0.05 percent.

29. See https://www.frbdiscountwindow.org/, accessed May 30, 2023. Of course, these rates change, and the website has historical information as well.

30. For much of the following discussion, see Hellwig (2014a), and Hellwig (2015).

31. Banknotes are treated as valueless paper until they leave the central bank in payment of a claim presented by a depositor.

32. The U.S. Federal Reserve is different in that it does not hold much if any foreign currency.

33. Under the so-called Bretton Woods regime, from the mid 1940s until 1973, most central banks were committed to stabilize the exchange rates of their currencies relative to the dollar.

34. Central bank profits are sometimes referred to as "seigniorage," income of a ruler ("seigneur") from exploiting the right to issue money. If banks' reserves with the central bank bear negative interest, this charge on the banks adds to the central bank's profits.

35. A notable exception is the Swiss National Bank, which is organized as a joint-stock corporation. Between 50 percent and 60 percent of its shares are owned by the cantons, the rest by private shareholders. The Swiss federal government holds no shares.

36. These banks are entitled to dividends that are fixed by law at 6 percent of the amount they actually invested in the regional Federal Reserve Bank, which is half of the amount they are committed to have available to the Federal Reserve Bank. (The other half is "on call.") The dividend rate does not vary with interest even though it is in effect equivalent to a mandatory investment in a riskless government bond. Any excess of the Federal Reserve System's profits over these dividends is paid to the U.S. Treasury. For a detailed discussion of the history and governance of the Federal Reserve System, see Conti-Brown (2016).

37. See Chapter 10, particularly note 16.

38. The first central bank was the Swedish Riksbank, founded in 1668, the second the Bank of England, founded in 1694. At that time, banknotes could also be issued by other banks—as claims to payments in gold. The central bank monopoly on issuing notes was created later. On the history of central banks, see Goodhart (1988).

39. As observed in note 15 above, the United States, the right of individuals to ask for gold in return for dollars was abolished in 1933. The right of other countries (or their central banks) to ask for gold in return for dollars was abolished in 1971.

40. If the banks receive positive interest on these deposits, as they do in the United States, the present value of that interest is a kind of debt because the bank cannot merely fulfill this obligation by printing money, at least if it wants to avoid inflation. If the banks "receive" negative interest on these deposits, as they did for several years in the euro area, the reserves are a source of income to the central bank, so the present value of this income is a kind of asset. For the implications of positive interest on central bank money, see Pesek and Saving (1967), Johnson (1969), and, more recently, Reis (2015) and Hall and Reis (2015).

41. The fact that, with a paper currency, banknotes are not really a debt of the central bank plays a central role in the early macroeconomic literature about wealth effects associated

with money. See, in particular, Patinkin (1965, Chapter 12), Gurley and Shaw (1960), Pesek and Saving (1967), and Johnson (1969).

42. "Federal Reserve Saw Fall in Profits in 2022," Central Banking Newsdesk, January 16, 2023, https://www.centralbanking.com/central-banks/governance/financial-reporting/7954210/federal-reserve-saw-fall-in-profits-in-2022, accessed May 30, 2023; "Annual Loss for Swiss National Bank Precludes Profit Distribution," Ad hoc announcement of the Swiss National Bank, January 9, 2023; "Financial Statements of the ECB for 2022," Press release of the European Central Bank, February 23, 2023.

43. Bell et al. (2023), and "The Fed's Operating Losses Become Taxpayer Losses," The Federalist Society, February 13, 2023, https://fedsoc.org/commentary/fedsoc-blog/the-fed-s-operating-losses-become-taxpayer-losses, accessed May 20, 2023.

44. Tom Braithwaite, "Wells Chief Warns Fed over Debt Proposal," *Financial Times*, June 2, 2013. Mr. Stumpf was objecting to a proposed requirement that banks issue "loss absorbing debt," whose bearers would share in losses if the bank became insolvent, unlike deposits with guarantees from the FDIC.

45. For example, this was a major objection that the president of the Bundesbank brought against the European Central Bank's starting huge asset purchases in 2015. Jens Weidmann, "Für die Verluste haften die Steuerzahler (Taxpayers are liable for losses)," *Frankfurter Allgemeine Sonntagszeitung*, December 28, 2014.

46. See announcement on March 12, 2023 entitled "Federal Reserve Board announces it will make available additional funding to eligible depository institutions to help assure banks have the ability to meet the needs of all their depositors," available at https://www.federalreserve.gov/newsevents/pressreleases/monetary20230312a.htm, accessed March 24, 2023.

47. See Jeanna Smialek and Joe Rennison, "Banks Are Borrowing More from the Fed: What to Know," *New York Times*, March 23, 2023.

48. The Federal Reserve generally has recourse to the assets of the borrowing bank beyond the collateral. In an event of a bank failure handled by the FDIC, if the bank's assets are not enough, this recourse by the Federal Reserve may increase the cost to the FDIC of covering the deposits of the bank. The term sheet of the new program is available at https://www.federalreserve.gov/newsevents/pressreleases/files/monetary20230312a1.pdf, accessed March 24, 2023.

49. There has also been record borrowing by banks from institutions called Federal Home Loan Banks, which are considered "lender of next-to-last resort." The Federal Home Loan Bank (FHLB) system was established in 1932 "as a government-sponsored enterprise to support lending and related community investment activity." (See https://www.fdic.gov/resources/bankers/affordable-mortgage-lending-center/guide/part-3-docs/federal-home-loan-bank-system.pdf, accessed March 26, 2023.) Loans from FHLB are also made against collateral and they tend to have somewhat higher interest rates than Federal Reserve programs, but longer maturities, starting in one year. In the week after the SVB collapse, the FHLB issued $304 billion in loans to banks, almost twice the total loans from the combined Federal Reserve programs that week and bringing its total loans to an estimated $1.1 trillion. See Austin Weinstein and Max Reyes, "FHLB Issues $304 Billion in a Week as Banks Boost Liquidity," *Bloomberg News*, March 20, 2023.

50. Bagehot (1873).

51. The Bank of England had been founded in 1694 to serve as a bank for the government, particularly as a lender to the government. According to Goodhart (1988), its refraining from competing with other banks provided the basis for its becoming a bank of banks.

52. Goodhart (1988) also suggests that private solutions for such problems were not working because the stronger participating banks would have an interest in seeing competitors disappear through bankruptcy.

53. Such fear already played an important role in the debates about the founding of the First Bank of the United States in 1791, even though this did not yet have the functions and the powers of a central bank. After twenty years, in 1811, the charter of this bank expired. The founding of the Second Bank of the United States in 1816 seems to have been less controversial, but controversy rose again in the 1830s, when its charter came up for renewal. President Jackson's veto of the renewal and the subsequent "bank war" took the topic off the political agenda for a long time.

54. On the National Banking System, see Friedman and Schwartz (1963) and Gorton (1988). On legal and governance issues related to the Federal Reserve from its founding through after the 2007–2009 financial crisis, including the peculiar structure of the regional Federal Reserve Banks, see Conti-Brown (2016).

55. See Friedman and Schwartz (1963). In addition to the banking crises in October 1930, March 1931, and March 1933, in which the Federal Reserve did not intervene, they observe that, in the ultimate crisis in early 1933, the Federal Reserve actually contributed to the difficulties of banks by raising interest rates.

56. In addition to Friedman and Schwartz (1963), see also Bernanke (1983).

57. See Friedman and Schwartz (1963) and Eichengreen (1992). Bernanke (1995) shows that the depth of the depression depended on whether and when a country abandoned the gold standard, as the United Kingdom did in 1931, causing an immediate 25 percent decline in the value of the pound relative to the dollar.

58. Friedman and Schwartz (1963) note that, in 1932, an attempt by the Federal Reserve to ease the crisis by purchasing government bonds and thereby lowering interest rates did not last very long. The lower interest rates caused investors to move their funds abroad, so the Federal Reserve was afraid of losing gold reserves. The interest rate increase in early 1933 was also motivated by this fear.

59. Between World War II and 1973, international currency relations were governed by the so-called Bretton Woods agreement, named after the New Hampshire village where it had been negotiated in 1944. The agreement aimed at re-establishing the stability of exchange rates experienced under the gold standard without the problems that had emerged in the Great Depression. This regime still imposed constraints on central banks, but as we wrote in Chapter 4, between the 1930s and the 1970s, there was no large bank insolvency and no banking crisis in the countries involved, so there was no call on a central bank to act as a lender of last resort in the Bagehot tradition.

60. The first prominent example was Continental Illinois in 1984. This bank had made large losses on bad loans. Uninsured depositors and other short-term creditors began a

run. To avert a panic, federal regulators provided a guarantee for depositors and even bond holders. The FDIC infused new equity, altogether some $5.5 billion, the Federal Reserve provided emergency lending. The case established the notion of "too big to fail" in the United States. As we described in Chapters 5 and 9, in the crisis of 2007–2009, central banks in the United States and many European jurisdictions made enormous loans to financial institutions, sometimes below market rates. The Federal Reserve offered loans to other central banks and it was also involved in the sale of investment bank Bear Stearns to JPMorgan Chase in March 2008, where it provided guarantees, as well as arranged the government bailout of insurance company AIG. See, in particular, notes 13 and 14 of Chapter 5 and notes 14 and 16 of Chapter 9.

61. See Andrew Ross Sorkin, Ravi Mattu, Bernhard Warner, Sarah Kessler, Michael J. de la Merced, Lauren Hirsch, and Ephrat Livni, "Why Did Silicon Valley Bank Collapse?," *New York Times*, March 11, 2023, which declared that "the failure of Silicon Valley Bank was caused by a run on the bank. The company was not, at least until clients started rushing for the exits, insolvent or even close to insolvent." A law academic suggested the Federal Reserve should have supported SVB because it was solvent according to the allowed accounting standards. See Hal Scott, "Fed Action Could Have Prevented SVB's Collapse," *Wall Street Journal*, March 16, 2023.

62. Kane (1985, 1989).

63. See Kane (1989), White (1991), Akerlof and Romer (1993), Dewatripont and Tirole (1994).

64. See Hockett (2023), and Ramishah Maruf, "Why Some Lawmakers Want to Raise the FDIC Insurance Limit for Your Savings," CNN, March 22, 2023.

65. Jiang et al. (2023a). More precisely, 190 banks would have to sell assets and realize losses so large that even the insured deposits would be impaired. If, in addition to the effect of higher market rates of interest, there were also a fire sale effect on asset prices, the number of affected banks would be even larger.

66. This valuation of the collateral deviates from the normal way the Federal Reserve values collateral, which is at "fair market value." To the value of the collateral, the Federal Reserve applies "haircuts" that depend greatly on the quality and risk of the asset. See https://www.frbdiscountwindow.org/Pages/Collateral/collateral_valuation, accessed March 24, 2023. The haircut likely still applies in the new regime, but it starts not from a fair market value but with a potentially inflated "par" value. For example, if the Federal Reserve only lends the bank 95 percent of the nominal or par value but the market value is 20 percent below the nominal value, a haircut of 5 percent on the nominal value corresponds to a "negative haircut" of more than 15 percent relative to the market value. In the words of Martin Wolf in "Banks Are Designed to Fail—and They Do," *Financial Times*, March 14, 2023, the haircut became a "hair graft."

67. In 1990, under the chairmanship of Alan Greenspan, the Federal Reserve did execute such a policy shift, lowering short-term interest rates to 4 percent when large money center banks were on the brink of insolvency. Since long-term rates stayed around 8 percent, banks were able to earn large profits from borrowing short and investing long, thereby rebuilding equity. See Boyd and Gertler (1994). Such policy shifts came to be

known—and criticized—as Greenspan "puts," an assurance that, if the financial sector got into trouble, the Greenspan Fed would help.

68. See the references in note 64 above as well as the discussion in Admati, Anat, Martin Hellwig, and Richard Portes, "When Will They Ever Learn? The US Banking Crisis of 2023," VoxEU, May 18, 2023, mentioned in note 10 of Chapter 14.

69. For example, Banco Popular Español in Spain had deposits from regional governments that exceeded the limit for deposit insurance, so in May 2017 these depositors ran when the bank seemed to be on the way to insolvency, and the bank was sold overnight to Banco Santander.

70. Some banks were absorbed into others, like Fortis into BNP Paribas, or Dresdner Bank into Commerzbank. WestLB in Germany disappeared only because the state aid control unit of the European Commission insisted on closing the bank. We discuss the European Commission's role in such proceedings in Chapter 16, particularly note 23 to that chapter.

71. Hellwig (2018c), ASC (2014).

72. See note 1 and, for more context, Richard Partington, "The Mini-Budget That Broke Britain—and Liz Truss," *The Guardian*, October 20, 2022.

73. Following this turmoil, the government's plan was reversed and Prime Minister Liz Truss resigned after only forty-five days in office.

74. See note 29 to Chapter 5 and page 67 of Lewis (2010). Some might argue that there is no moral hazard because the protection is only available when there are economy-wide problems. This argument overlooks the fact that risks taken by banks tend to be correlated so, if they run into problems, they tend to do so together. There are two reasons for this. First, rates of return tend to be highest for risks that affect the entire economy, and such risks tend to be correlated and non-diversifiable. Second, there is safety in numbers, so different banks may choose the same kinds of assets because they like to be members of a herd that the authorities will want to rescue. On these issues, see Acharya and Yorulmazer (2008), Acharya et al. (2007), Farhi and Tirole (2011).

SIXTEEN   *Bailouts Forever*

1. See "Dass viele eine Wut im Bauch haben, verstehe ich gut" ("I Understand Very Well That Many Are Angry"), Interview with Swiss Finance Minister Karin Keller-Sutter, *Neue Zürcher Zeitung*, March 25, 2023, quoted in the CNN article cited in note 7 below.

2. The quote is from the website of Deutsche Bundesbank, https://www.bundesbank.de /en/tasks/banking-supervision/individual-aspects/recovery-and-resolution/recovery-and -resolution-623118, accessed February 17, 2023.

3. Jill Treanor, "Mark Carney Hails New Deal for 'Too Big to Fail' Banks," *The Guardian*, November 10, 2014. Most headlines at the time hailed the accomplishment. An exception was Laurence Arnold and C. Thompson, "Carney Underwhelms Admati with His Plan for Banks: Opening Line," *Bloomberg News*, November 11, 2014, citing skepticism expressed by Anat Admati on Twitter.

4. For example, in an interview discussing the case of Archegos, (mentioned in Chapter 14), where CS incurred a large loss, the moderator stated that the "too-big-to-fail"

problem has been solved. See "Why Regulators May Have Missed Archegos Excessive Risk Warning Signs," CNBC, March 20, 2021.

5. See Finma, "Recovery and Resolution," https://www.finma.ch/en/enforcement/recovery-and-resolution/too-big-to-fail-and-financial-stability/, accessed March 24, 2023.

6. The guarantee can only be called upon when UBS losses from the takeover exceed 5 billion Swiss francs, but even so the taxpayer is put at risk. Shareholders of CS are compensated with UBS shares worth 3 billion Swiss francs. Some of CS's bonds (the so-called co cos, contingent-convertible bonds we discussed in Chapter 11) will not be paid at all. See note 90 to Chapter 14.

7. See Hanna Zlady and Julia Horowitz, "Post-2008 Reforms Didn't Solve the Problem of 'Too Big to Fail' Banks," CNN, March 31, 2023.

8. In addition to the interview by Keller-Sutter cited in note 1, see "Die CS hatte ein kulturelles Problem, das sich in fehlenden Verantwortlichkeiten niederschlug" ("CS Had a Cultural Problem that Was Reflected in Unclear Responsibilities"), Interview with Marlene Amstad, *Neue Zürcher Zeitung*, March 25, 2023, also quoted in the CNN article cited in the previous note.

9. IMF (2014) attaches numbers to this advantage, $50 billion for banks in the United States and in Switzerland, $110 billion for banks in Japan and the United Kingdom, and $300 billion for banks in the euro area. In addition to presenting the results of its own analysis, FSB (2021) provides an extensive overview of the literature. The FSB's own analysis suggests that the funding advantage of globally systemic institutions rose dramatically in the global financial crisis, stayed high until around 2014, and then declined, without however going down to pre-crisis levels. The post-2014 decline is also attributed to a decline in perceived risks in a period of calm and to a decline in risk premia in a period of low interest rates. In the COVID crisis, the funding advantage rose again.

10. See https://www.fsb.org/work-of-the-fsb/market-and-institutional-resilience/crisis-management-and-resolution/, accessed March 25, 2023. As we discuss later, the recommendations are a wish list and unlikely to become reality.

11. Lubben and Wilmarth (2017).

12. The details of the agreement are given in FSB (2015).

13. The idea had actually been introduced earlier, in the so-called Liikanen Report (2012) that an expert group under the leadership of Erkki Liikanen, the Governor of the Bank of Finland, had produced for the European Commission in 2012. The expert group had been asked to report on desirable additions to banking regulation beyond Basel III. Given that legislation about equity requirements, the implementation of Basel III, was on the way, tighter equity requirements were not on the agenda. Instead, the report recommended a minimum requirement on funding by "eligible liabilities" (MREL), equity and debt that would be available to absorb losses in a resolution or bankruptcy procedure. The report also recommended that holdings of such liabilities be restricted to individuals and institutions that could bear losses without a risk of contagion. In the process of legislation, the latter recommendation was much watered down, but the Bank Recovery and Resolution

Directive of 2014 does require banks to fund at least 8 percent of total assets with equity or loss-absorbing debt.

14. See FSB (2015), as well as BCBS (2016b), which integrates TLAC requirements into Basel III.

15. The EU's Bank Recovery and Resolution Directive (BRRD) contains a long list of liabilities that are exempt from bail-in. It leaves open what should happen if losses exhaust the loss absorption capacity of equity and the other liabilities. Such a list is also problematic because, as discussed earlier in the book, e.g., on pp. 164 and 227, it introduces further distortions into investment and funding decisions. For example, the BRRD has an exemption for short-term debt with initial maturities of seven days or less. Such a rule biases funding away from, say, initial maturities of thirty days and toward initial maturities of seven days. For a discussion of such biases in the U.S. context, see Lubben and Wilmarth (2017). Admati (2019) gives an overview of the issues.

16. In Chapter 11, we also discussed proposals to fund banks with contingent-convertible debt, so-called co cos. Co cos start out as debt, but in certain contingencies that are specified in advance, they may be converted into equity, or they may be required to absorb losses, like equity. According to their proponents, co cos would be a panacea for all problems of financial distress. Most important, in an ideal world, loss absorption by co cos would not require anyone—politician, regulator, or banker—to pull a trigger. As yet we have seen no argument why this kind of equity-like debt would be any less likely to give rise to fears of systemic risk than the kinds that had been issued before 2008, where the authorities were careful to provide bailouts before any trigger points would be reached. See Wang (2023) on the debate regarding loss absorbing contingent capital and the debate about whether they are debt or equity. Interestingly, co cos are popular in Europe because tax authorities treat them as debt and allow interest to be deducted from taxable corporate income, so using them rather than equity lowers funding costs net of taxes. In the United States, by contrast, tax authorities do not treat co cos as debt because co cos do not gives their holders "creditors' rights" in default. This difference explains why European banks have been more eager to try co cos than American banks.

17. In many cases, the bailouts occurred as governments prevented banks from failing without asking the holders of subordinate debt, or even shareholders, to bear some of the losses. In some countries, governments simply put up cash to provide banks with additional equity. For example, the U.K. government provided Royal Bank of Scotland with 37 billion pounds in new equity. The German government provided Commerzbank with €1.8 billion in new equity and €16.4 billion in a silent participation that counted as equity (subordinated debt with contingency clauses allowing a discontinuation of payments, or even a write-down of the debt, in case the bank incurred losses).

In the United States, in the financial crisis, the FDIC provided guarantees to all bank debt, not just deposits. This program, which eventually guaranteed over $600 billion of debt by banks and related institutions, is the one that the expert quoted in the epigraph of Chapter 9 referred to as "invaluable" and "an infinite subsidy" that many banks, including investment banks such as Goldman Sachs, benefited from. See Louise Story, "US Program

Lends a Hand to Banks, Quietly," New York Times, April 14, 2009, already quoted in note 1 to Chapter 9. The "helping hand" of the government was largely invisible to the public. FDIC also offered significant loss sharing to investors who bought the assets of the almost 500 small banks that failed between 2008 and 2013, which private equity companies and hedge funds took advantage of. For details on the various expanded guarantee programs of the FDIC in and after the crisis, see https://www.fdic.gov/bank/historical/crisis/overview .pdf accessed May 30, 2023.

18. For a critique of debt bail-ins in a systemic crisis, see Persaud (2014) and Avgouleas and Goodhart (2015). Persaud refers to bail-in-able liabilities as "fool's gold." In the case of Washington Mutual, in September 2008, the bail-in of unsecured debt was highly controversial; many suggested that this decision enhanced market apprehensions about the treatment of debt; see FCIC (2011, 366), Geithner (2014, 213 ff).

19. See our discussion in Chapter 11 on "Anything But Equity!" (pp. 187–189). Bankers' preference for loss-absorbing debt over equity is likely motivated by considerations of Return on equity (ROE) that are driven by tax and debt overhang (or leverage ratchet) effects. See Admati et al. (2018) and Admati and Hellwig (2019).

20. In this context, the role of lawyers must also be mentioned. In discussions with lawyers about the efforts to address the too-big-to-fail problem, one of us suggested that TLACs were more popular with them than equity because the writing of the contracts and the legal issues around imposing losses on the holders of such securities provide a lot of business for lawyers, much more so than equity. The suggestion was not contested. We have also observed that specialists in traditional insolvency law tend to be quite hostile to any deviation of rules and procedures for bank resolution from traditional practices.

21. The six banks were located in Germany, Italy, and Spain. We are leaving out the Greek banks because they fall into a different category: Following the write-down of Greek government debt in March 2012, the major Greek banks (four banks with total assets between €70 billion and €110 billion) had been insolvent and were recapitalized by the Hellenic Financial Stability Fund, an offshoot of the European Financial Stability Fund. In 2015, they became victims of conflict between Greece and the European institutions, with a bank run and a deep recession. After that, they again had to be recapitalized. Recently, more government support was granted in the form of guarantees for the Hellenic Financial Stability Fund's Hercules scheme for dealing with nonperforming loans. We are also leaving out two small banks in Latvia that were closed down under national law in 2017 and 2019, as well as the subsidiary Sberbank Europe of the Russian Sberbank and the Slovenian and Croatian subsidiaries of Sberbank Europe. Following the sanctions imposed after the Russian invasion of Ukraine, Sberbank Europe, with total assets just below €14 bilion, was liquidated by the Austrian authorities and its Slovenian and Croatian subsidiaries, with total assets below €7 billion, were sold by the national authorities to banks in those countries.

22. These were HSH Nordbank and Nord LB, two of the German Landesbanken, and Banca Monte dei Paschi di Siena in Italy, all with total assets between €100 billion and €200 billion. The two Landesbanken received support from the governments that owned them, HSH Nordbank through a second-loss guarantee of €10 billion and a takeover of bad assets, Nord LB through a recapitalization from the regional government of Niedersachsen. Monte

dei Paschi received a "precautionary recapitalization" from the Italian government. On precautionary recapitalizations, see Hellwig (2017b).

23. These were Banca Popolare di Vicenza and Veneto Banca in Italy with total assets between €10 and €100 billion. After the European Commission had disallowed precautionary recapitalizations of these two banks, the supervisor declared them as likely to fail, the EU's Single Resolution Board declared that they were not systemically important and left them to the Italian authorities for liquidation. The authorities sold parts of them for one euro to Banca Intesa and transferred the remainder for liquidation by an asset management company owned by Banca Intesa, all the while providing Banca Intesa with certain guarantees against losses.

24. Banco Popular Español in Spain, with total assets between €100 billion and €200 billion, was sold to Banco Santander for one euro.

25. The Treaty on the Functioning of the European Union gives the European Commission some control over public subsidies (state aid) over commercial enterprises. In the context of banking, under the Bank Recovery and Resolution Directive of 2014, this control concerns any *precautionary recapitalization* that a government might provide to forestall a resolution procedure. In the cases of Monte dei Paschi di Siena, Banca Popolare di Vicenza, and Veneto Banca, the Commission insisted that equity and any subordinate debt that counted toward equity requirements be written down to zero. In the case of Banco Popular Español in Spain, the Single Resolution Board, presumably in accord with the Commission, applied the same bail-in condition. The Spanish authorities do not seem to have interfered. Their main concern may have been to make sure that the purchaser of Banco Popular would again be a Spanish bank. In the case of HSH Nordbank, the Commission required that the bank be either liquidated or sold to a private owner. It deemed the willingness of a private buyer to step in to be sufficient proof of the bank's viability; see also note 28 to this chapter. In the case of Nord LB, surprisingly, the Commission raised no concerns. HSH Nordbank and Nord LB are somewhat different from the other cases because support came from the regional governments that were or are also the owners of these banks. Since 2001, however, the European Commission has established the principle that support provided by public owners is also a form of state aid, which must accord with the Treaty's ban on unwarranted government subsidies. An overview of the Commission's treatment of state aid in banking is given in Hellwig (2018a).

26. See our discussion of this point in Chapter 12, particularly with respect to the German Landesbanken. In addition to the banks listed in note 40 to Chapter 12, HSH Nordbank has cost the regional governments owning it close to €15 billion, more than €8 billion in lost equity investments and more than €7 billion for a $10 billion second-loss guarantee on a portfolio of loans minus $3 billion in fees for this guarantee. The final sales price was around $1 billion.

27. In the case of the German bank Hypo Real Estate, mentioned in Chapters 1 and 4, reference had been made to Deutsche Bank and Allianz, but newspaper interviews by Hannes Rehm, the president of Soffin, the government institution administering the public support, suggested the bailout was needed to protect the established churches, social security and pension institutions, and even public television. See for example *Frankfurter*

Allgemeine Sonntagszeitung, March 15, 2009. https://www.faz.net/aktuell/wirtschaft /unternehmen/im-gespraech-hannes-rehm-schlimmer-als-die-pleite-von-lehman -brothers-1923302.html, accessed May 30, 2023. In the cases of the Italian banks, bail-ins of subordinated debt contributed to the government's losing the subsequent election in 2018.

28. Both banks had made large losses from loans to shipping companies that were affected by the deep shipping crisis 2008–2020. Nord LB was recapitalized by the government of Lower Saxony in 2019. HSH Nordbank was recapitalized in 2008. It was also provided with guarantees against losses. In 2013, the regional governments proposed to increase the guarantees. The European Commission's unit in charge of state aid control agreed to this proposal on condition that the bank be privatized. The privatization proceeded after the bank had transferred a portfolio of bad shipping loans to the regional governments owning it; the transfer price involved a 50 percent write-down on the loans. The write-down was covered by the governments' loss guarantees.

29. We discussed contagion in Chapter 5. For the U.S. authorities' announcement concerning "systemic exception," see the March 12, 2023 statement from the Federal Reserve, the FDIC, and the Department of Treasury at https://www.federalreserve.gov/newsevents /pressreleases/monetary20230312b.htm, accessed April 3, 2023.

30. On the Venetian banks, see https://www.bruegel.org/blog-post/tangled-tale-bank -liquidation-venice, accessed May 30, 2023 and Hellwig (2017b).

31. In Cyprus, in 2013, the two largest banks, Laiki and Bank of Cyprus, were insolvent from losses on Greek sovereign debt that they had acquired in the years before the write-down of March 2012. Laiki was liquidated, its good assets and deposits up to €100,000 were transferred to Bank of Cyprus. Any excess of deposits above €100,000 was written down as was any other unsecured debt, for total write-offs above €4 billion. In Bank of Cyprus, deposits up to €100,000 were bailed out. For investors with deposits above €100,000, 47.5 percent were converted into equity of the bank.

32. See David Sirota and Julia Rock, "Fed Insisted SVB Posed No Serious Risk to Financial System," *The Lever*, March 15, 2023, https://www.levernews.com/powell-approved -svb-merger-insisting-bank-posed-no-systemic-risk/, accessed April 3, 2023.

33. See Lily Jamali, "Regulators Designated SVB and Signature Bank as Systemic Risks. But Are They Really?," NPR Marketplace, March 13, 2023.

34. This attitude prevailed even in so-called stress tests. In Chapter 11, we discussed stress tests and expressed skepticism about their reliability, especially since the 2010 and 2011 stress tests in Europe were shortly followed by failures of banks that had done well on the tests; see note 76 to Chapter 11. For critical assessments of the European Banking Authority's 2011 stress test, see Vestergaard and Retana (2013). The stress tests in the comprehensive assessment of banks before the creation of the European Banking Union in 2014 involved assumptions that, among other things, treated the dependence of banks on funding by the European Central Bank (ECB) as a source of strength rather than weakness. Goldstein (2017) provides a systematic and critical evaluation of stress tests in the EU and the United States. A major problem involves the reliance of stress tests on book values of equity rather than market values; see John Vickers, "The Case for Market-Based Stress Tests," VoxEU, June 14, 2019, https://cepr.org/voxeu/columns/case-market-based-stress

-tests, accessed May 29, 2023, as well as Vickers (2019). Kevin Dowd of Durham University has maintained a website where he assesses the stress tests run by the Bank of England. His reports are entitled "No Stress" and are generally very critical; see https://www.kevindowd .org/central-bank-stress-tests/, accessed March 8, 2023. Stress tests in the United States have been considered a key tool for regulators and they use specific scenarios and models to predict regulatory ratios, but the exercise is not well suited to predict real-world stresses and contagion mechanisms. In particular, stress tests consider the effects of adverse developments on banks' balance sheets, but usually do not take account of second-round effects from price changes that occur as institutions react to the developments, such as the implosion of stock prices that occurred in the weeks after the Lehman Brothers bankruptcy.

35. Acharya and Steffen (2012). This mechanism was reinforced by the 2008 weakening of quality requirements for collateral to receive loans from the ECB; see Nyborg (2017).

36. The subsequent cleanup seems to have been fairly thorough, but, like Ireland in 2010, Spain needed help from the European Stability Mechanism, i.e., the other member states. Reluctance to invoke such help was probably one reason for their resistance to an earlier cleanup.

37. Before 2008, German investors and German banks had played a key role in financing shipping companies worldwide. The shipping industry was in crisis from 2008 to 2020.

38. The president of the ECB had been a leading promoter of the European banking union, partly because this would expand the power of the ECB and partly because the existence of "zombie" banks was an encumbrance to an effective monetary policy. On the discussion about procrastination of supervisors and the creation of the European banking union, see ASC (2012) and Hellwig (2014b).

39. The case of Banco Popular Español was different in that news of losses triggered a run by large depositors, which was accelerated by actual or purported leaks. The ultimate result, an overnight sale to Banco Santander, preempted an auction that might have involved foreign as well as Spanish bidders. The fact that Banco Popular Español was not acquired by a foreign bank may not have been unwelcome to the authorities.

40. The role of the European Commission is discussed in note 25 above. In the case of Monte dei Paschi di Siena, the Commission agreed to a recapitalization by the government on condition that equity and any subordinate debt that counted toward the statutory equity requirements be written down to zero. The write-downs on subordinated debt counted as "private investor participation." In the cases of Banca Popolare di Vicenza and Veneto Banca, the European Commission vetoed any recapitalization. Some of the operations of these banks were sold to Banca Intesa, the rest were put into a "bad bank" managed by Banca Intesa with a government guarantee against losses. In these banks, equity and subordinate debt that counted toward the statutory equity requirements were also written down to zero.

41. In the case of Monte dei Paschi di Siena, the supervisors had determined that there was an equity shortfall of more than €8 billion. The Italian government provided a "precautionary recapitalization" of roughly €4 billion. Previous shareholders lost their investments. In addition, holders of subordinated debt securities amounting to roughly €4 billion also had to abandon their claims to the bank, but, with permission from the European Commission, the

Italian government compensated investors in these securities for about half of their losses, so the overall subsidy from the Italian government amounted to more than €6 billion.

42. For an extensive discussion of the issue, see Lubben and Wilmarth (2017).

43. The living will of Credit Suisse mentions one year as a period over which important assets and activities might be disposed of without extensive losses. The Chapter 11 bankruptcy of Lehman Brothers in the United States, filed on September 15, 2008, has still not been concluded fourteen years later. See dockets, available at https://dm.epiq11.com/case /lbh/dockets, accessed January 7, 2023.

44. Curry and Shibut (2000) report $153 billion in losses, of which $124 billion were borne by taxpayers and $29 billion by the industry. Around 1990, by contrast, there was talk of $600 to $800 billion of losses.

45. Englund (1999).

46. On September 25, 2008, the bank's supervisor, the Office of Thrift Supervision, seized its banking operations and placed them under the receivership of the FDIC. The price of $1.9 billion that JPMorgan Chase paid was widely regarded as very low; this came at the expense of shareholders and unsecured debt holders. The effect on unsecured debt holders was criticized because it exacerbated systemic risk in the month after the Lehman bankruptcy. There also was criticism that the unsecured debt holders of Washington Mutual did not get the same treatment as the unsecured debt holders of Bear Stearns in March 2008. See Geithner (2014, 213 ff) and Grind (2012). Ball (2018) and Chari (2022) have also argued that the authorities' treatment of Lehman Brothers involved undue discrimination.

47. U.K. and German banks in 2008, Irish banks in 2010, Spanish banks in 2012, Greek banks in 2012 and 2015, three Italian banks in 2017.

48. Such a conflict induced the German government to force a squeeze out of external shareholders of Hypo Real Estate (HRE) in 2009. In Commerzbank, the German government had limited its equity participation to 25 percent plus one share and given the bulk of its support in the form of subordinate hybrid debt because it wanted to avoid the influence and the responsibility from a larger equity participation. The subordinate debt was subsequently paid back, but the German government still holds the shares it purchased in 2008 (now only 15% of outstanding shares). The burden of the subordinate debt contributed substantially to the bank's difficulties in 2011 and 2012 and to the overall losses of the government from the intervention, which amount to more than €4 billion.

49. Germany initially tried to have the banks themselves indicate which assets should be transferred to a government-owned *bad bank*. To protect itself against abuses by the banks' managers, the German government set strict rules for the valuation of these assets. As a result, the banks that did not come under government control did not make use of this arrangement. For an overview and assessment, see Hellwig (2017a). In such operations, one needs to distinguish between assets according to their tradability. The Swiss National Bank could easily exit its 2008 bailout of UBS (at a profit) because the impaired assets it had taken over consisted mainly of securities and derivatives, so once markets were functioning again, many of these assets were easily liquidated. In contrast, Spain's Sareb fund and Germany's FMS Wertmanagement (bad bank for HypoReal Estate) needed—and still need—a lot of patience because their assets involved a lot of real estate

and real estate loans, which were not easily tradable even after markets had recovered from the crises. Ireland's NAMA comes somewhere in between.

50. In the United Kingdom, the Banking Act of 2009 puts the Bank of England in charge of bank resolution with a primary mandate to ensure financial stability in the United Kingdom. It also specifies a set of powers of the Bank of England in resolution. The powers include the creation and administration of a "bridge bank" for addressing the relevant assets and operations and the use of funds from the Bank of England or the U.K. Treasury subject to a set of detailed rules. The U.K. Treasury must be involved whenever the bank in question is deemed to be insolvent, rather than merely illiquid. In the United States, Title 2 of the Dodd-Frank Act gives the FDIC similar powers. Funding comes from the FDIC's own resolution fund and, if necessary, borrowing from the U.S. Treasury. Treasury loans must be repaid, possibly with clawbacks from the bank's creditors or a levy on the industry. The law is silent on the possibility that clawbacks from the bank's creditors or a levy on the industry might not yield enough to cover the shortfall, as happened in the S&L crisis.

51. In the case of Banco Popular Español, the accountants complained that they had only had thirteen days for the valuation, rather than the six weeks needed to do the job properly; see Hellwig (2018b).

52. In the euro area, the Single Resolution Board has no resources worth speaking about. In the case of Banco Popular Español in Spain, it made the fire sale to Santander even before there had been a full valuation of BPE. The cases of Banca Popolare di Vicenza and Veneto Banca are dealt with under Italian law, outside the European rules, through a special asset management company that oversees winding down the nonperforming assets, probably over a period of ten years or more. The asset management company, SGA (Società per la Gestione di Attività) had been created by the Italian government in 1997 and had previously managed the bad assets of Banca di Napoli and, over almost twenty years, achieved a windfall of some €6 billion. It is now managed by Intesa, to which the Italian government sold it in 2016. For the management and liquidation of the bad assets of Banca Popolare di Vicenza and Veneto Banca, the Italian government has paid Intesa some €5 billion in cash, but it has a senior claim for this amount on the proceeds of the liquidation. In addition, it has provided Intesa with guarantees against losses.

53. See FSB (2014).

54. With institutions such as BNP Paribas or Deutsche Bank, the funding needs for a bridge bank might amount to more than €1 trillion. Such a number was politically unpalatable, even if governments were only to provide guarantees rather than the funds as such. The target for Single Resolution Fund in the euro area amounts to less than €100 billion. The European Stabilisation Mechanism (ESM) can provide a backstop, but that would not bring the total above €200 billion. This sum may be enough to cover ultimate losses, but is far from enough to cover ongoing liquidity needs when the institutions in question are large.

55. See Grund et al. (2020). In the United States, Federal Reserve chair Bernanke has argued that the Fed could not bail out Lehman Brothers because the bank was insolvent.

56. In March 2020, this fear induced governments and central banks to provide massive support not only to private households and nonfinancial businesses affected by the COVID pandemic, but also to financial markets and financial institutions. The warning

"This might be a Lehman moment" was also prominent in May 2010, in the first phase of the Greek sovereign debt crisis, and in the fall of 2011, when European financial institutions and markets were strongly affected by solvency concerns, withdrawals of funds, and asset price declines.

57. Complexity and loss of control are already problems for the bank's own management. In Chapter 17, we discuss cases where recklessness on the side of individual traders caused huge losses for their banks.

58. In the United States, this is mandated by the Dodd-Frank Act, in the EU by the Bank Recovery and Resolution Directive. The living wills are submitted to the relevant regulators, in the United States the Federal Reserve and the FDIC and only a very small portion is made public. See https://www.federalreserve.gov/supervisionreg/resolution-plans .htm, accessed March 26, 2023.

59. For example, in 2014, the Federal Reserve and FDIC rejected the living wills of eleven institutions, U.S. and foreign, on the grounds that they were based on implausible assumptions and that the organizations were still too complex. In 2016, they rejected the living wills of five U.S. institutions, in 2018, the living wills of four foreign institutions. In December 2022, they again rejected the living will of Credit Suisse on grounds of poor governance and insufficient planning to ensure the liquidity of the U.S. subsidiary in resolution. As a member of the FDIC Systemic Resolution Advisory Committee from 2011 until 2018, Anat Admati asked questions about how institutions could possibly know enough to have satisfactory living wills, since there are many failure scenarios and the outcome in each scenario would depend on actions by many counterparties, market participants, and authorities that would be difficult for anybody to predict. The issues were acknowledged but with no satisfactory response. See minutes from meetings such as April 14, 2016, all available here https://www.fdic.gov/about/advisory-committees/systemic-resolutions/agenda/2016-04 -14-agenda.html, accessed April 3, 2023. In November 2022, Rohit Chopra, chair of the Consumer Financial Protection Bureau and member of the board of the FDIC, responded to the living wills submitted in 2021 with the assessment: "It is highly unlikely that any of these institutions, as currently constituted, could be resolved in a rapid and orderly manner under the bankruptcy code." See his statement at https://business.cch.com/BFLD/Chopra-Statement -Resolution-Plan-Feedback-Letter-11222022.pdf, accessed May 30, 2023.

60. Only small portions are made public, but several sources told us about their length, in one case reportedly more than 30,000 pages. See also note 43 above.

61. In 2019, the Federal Reserve proposed to move from a requirement to submit living wills annually to a requirement that globally systemic banks submit living wills every two years and mid-size banks submit living wills once every three years. It also allowed banks to submit shortened versions of living wills in every other submission. Steele (2022, n. 254) notes estimates of the costs of producing the living wills properly as a total of 1.14 million hours and nearly $40 million in wages. These figure do not include the cost to taxpayers of the personnel needed to evaluate the documents at the regulatory agencies.

62. In the United States in 2012, the recently created Financial Stability Oversight Council (FSOC) designated clearinghouses as "systemic institutions." The financial institutions who are "members" of a CCP are themselves exposed to risk from the CCP becom-

ing distressed or defaulting on obligations. Paddrik and Young (2021) attempt to assess the safety of CCPs using mostly public data. However, the "stress" scenarios considered in such studies and in other efforts to ensure the resilience of CCPs are problematic because the deep interconnectedness of the participants means that stress scenarios might involve some institutions having other problems of their own, which makes any prediction of the likely outcome difficult. Anat Admati served on a Market Risk Advisory Committee to the Commodities and Futures Trading Commission (CFTC) the main supervisor of CCPs, for over three years between 2015 and 2018 and observed many blind spots on the issues.

63. See Skeel (2017).

64. The COVID-19 pandemic exposed the fragility and systemic importance of central clearinghouses and the years-long debates between large global institutions that are "members" of the clearinghouses and trade through them and the clearinghouses themselves about who among them create risks for others. See Hugh Jones, "Clearing Houses Face Tougher Crisis Management Scrutiny," Reuters, November 16, 2020. To Anat Admati on the CFTC Market Risk Advisory Committee mentioned in note 62 above, the tensions between major banks and clearinghouses were evident. The stress test and disaster planning of the institutions envision defaults by one or two members, but the scenario being envisioned does not consider the potential context of such defaults, such as who is the defaulter, whether they are in bankruptcy or resolution, and whether, in at least some of these scenarios, contagion effects like the dominos discussed in Chapter 5 would create cascading effects with more defaults.

65. As discussed in Chapter 5, Lehman Brothers had integrated cash management of its subsidiaries around the world. At the close of business in London, reserves of central bank money would be sent to New York; subsequently, reserves would be sent from New York to Asia and later again from Asia back to London. On the critical weekend in September 2008, money had left the U.K. subsidiary on the preceding Friday, but no money came back before the opening on Monday. When U.K. authorities entered the bank that Monday, there was literally no money with which to do business. Even more critical are integrated IT systems. If different authorities enter different units independently, there may be no legal basis for continued joint use and continued joint maintenance of such integrated systems. Interestingly, however, the London arm of Lehman Brothers did have significant assets in the United Kingdom and by 2013, it was able to pay many of its customers in full with interest. See James Mackintosh, "The Short View," *Financial Times*, June 27, 2013, and *Financial Times* video "Lehman Lock-in Beats Hedge Funds," https://www.ft.com/video/908884d2-4589-36e4-ae2c-e44139f40fdb, accessed May 23, 2023.

66. FSB (2021, 4).

67. Antoine Gara, Kadhim Shubber, and Joshua Oliver, "FTX Held Less than $1bn in Liquid Assets against $9bn in Liabilities," *Financial Times*, November 12, 2022; Samuel Wilkes, "FTX's Mifid License Exposes Europe's Regulatory Gaps," Risk.net, December 15, 2022. FTX subsidiaries appear to be, in addition to the United States and Bahamas, operating at least in Europe, Canada, Singapore, Hong Kong, Japan, Turkey, and Switzerland, and customers are likely to be spread beyond. The list of the 134 subsidiaries is available at https://www.gizmotimes.com/blockchain/cryptocurrency/ftx-bankruptcy-filing-list-ofcompanies/45029, accessed February 19, 2023.

68. See FSB (2013, 2014).

69. When at a policy panel in Frankfurt in late 2013, Martin Hellwig pointed to the unresolved problem of cross-border resolution, he was answered by Mr. Fitschen, then the co-CEO of Deutsche Bank, that all these problems were addressed in Deutsche Bank's living will ("But of course you have not read that!"). Mr. Fitschen also asserted, and was seconded by Ms. Lautenschläger, then a vice-president of the Bundesbank in charge of bank supervision, that all of this was the subject of friendly and effective coordination between all the supervisors involved, U.S. and European. According to the short version of Deutsche Bank's living will that is publicly available, Deutsche Bank was proposing to have a single-point-of-entry system of resolution, putting the German authorities fully in charge. Funding of all operations was supposed to come through the Frankfurt headquarters of the bank, as before. This plan met with a point-blank veto from U.S. authorities, who did not want to be at the mercy of someone in Germany for continued funding of Deutsche Bank's U.S. operations. Whereas the FDIC, which is in charge of "systemic resolution" according to Title 2 of the Dodd-Frank Act, has been in discussions with other jurisdictions, to the best of our knowledge no U.S. official, including in meetings of the Systemic Resolution Advisory Committee that Anat Admati participated in between 2011 and 2018 where such questions were raised, has ever promised that the United States will allow another nation to lead a resolution process of a bank with significant U.S. presence. Even if there was such intention, it would be politically difficult to follow through should an institution like Deutsche Bank actually fail.

70. This approach refers to so-called internal TLAC ("total loss absorbing capacity"), whereby the parent company provides equity or bail-in-able debt to a subsidiary. See Tucker (2018).

71. Issues of loss distribution also concern the scope of government guarantee schemes such as deposit insurance. In the Icelandic crisis of 2008, the authorities of Iceland provided compensation only for depositors in Iceland. British and Dutch depositors did not receive compensation from the Icelandic government, even though the banks' branches in the United Kingdom and Netherlands had operated under European rules requiring nondiscrimination, in providing Icelandic banks with access to EU depositors and in dealing with people from different member states. On Iceland, see note 51 to Chapter 1. Iceland is a member of the European Economic Area (EEA), which comprises the member states of the European Union (EU) and other countries that signed up to participate in the EU's Internal Market, many of them formerly members of the European Free Trade Area (EFTA). U.K. and Dutch depositors did receive compensation in their own countries, and their governments sued Iceland for compensation in the EFTA court, which is in charge of European law pertaining to countries in the European Economic Area that are not in the EU. Since the first edition of this book, the EFTA court has ruled that Iceland's discrimination between domestic depositors and depositors in other member states of the EEA was lawful. However, the U.K. and Dutch institutions that had paid for compensation of U.K. and Dutch depositors did get first-priority claims against the Icelandic banks, and these claims eventually paid off. Switzerland, which is not part of the EEA, provides a protection scheme for deposits in Switzerland, but all other depositors only receive a first-priority claim in bankruptcy.

72. Darrell Duffie of Stanford University shares the Federal Reserve optimism about the ease with which TLAC can make bank resolution easy and smooth. He described bail-in as analogous to regulators pressing "red buttons" on their desks, without discussing the difficulties involved in valuing assets and operations of subsidiaries. (See https://www.gsb.stanford.edu/insights/us-banking-sector-better accessed May 30, 2023.) For a devastating critique of the single-point-of-entry and TLAC approach, see Lubben and Wilmarth (2017). As they present it, the industry supports this approach as a step on the way to a kind of prepackaged Chapter 11 approach, in which the corporation's management would present a package for restructuring activities and debts, a judge would ratify the plan, and corporate management would proceed as it wishes.

73. It is perhaps not a coincidence that the resolution agenda and in particular the single-point-of-entry approach have been most strongly promoted by representatives of the Bank of England, who were prominently positioned at the Financial Stability Board (Governors King and Carney, Deputy Governor Tucker, and Andrew Gracie, executive director for Resolution). The City of London is a major beneficiary of the system we currently have, with large financial institutions all having important activities in London, and the global derivatives business centered in London as well. If we were to return to a world in which regulation forces the institutions to organize themselves so that all subsidiaries could be handled on a stand-alone basis, the City of London would probably suffer. Other parts of the United Kingdom might benefit, however, because distortions favoring the financial sector have contributed to the decline of other industries in the United Kingdom.

74. For an early warning that "too big to fail" might quickly become "too big to be rescued," see Hellwig (1999).

75. According to an IMF study (Singh and Alam 2018), off-balance-sheet funding for many banks was greater in 2016 than in 2007.

76. Over this period, the French bank BNP Paribas, the U.K. bank HSBC, and Citigroup also experienced significant growth. In particular, the reported total assets of BNP Paribas grew from €1.7 trillion at the end of 2007 to €2.6 trillion, or 113 percent of French GDP, at the end of 2021.

77. See Chapter 15 in FCIC (2011).

78. Andrew Ross Sorkin, "JPMorgan Raises Bid for Bear Stearns to $10 a Share," *New York Times*, March 24, 2008, describes Mr. Dimon as anxious to make the deal, originally at $2 a share, which the Federal Reserve preferred in order to draw less attention to the extent to which it was subsidizing the transaction. When realizing that the deal might be at risk by Bear Stearns shareholders voting it down because of the low price, Mr. Dimon initiated renegotiation. Private conversations with people involved in the transaction suggested that the deal was rushed ahead of the next financial disclosures of Bear Stearns that would have exposed more of its weaknesses, in part because JPMorgan Chase stood to lose significantly in a Bear Stearns bankruptcy. See also note 58 to Chapter 12.

79. See David Lynch, "Big Banks May Get Bigger as Crisis Swamps 'Too Big to Fail' Worries," *Washington Post*, March 19, 2023. Eleven banks combined to make an uninsured deposit of $30 billion in First Republic Bank on March 16, 2023. See David Hollerith, "Inside the $30 Billion Rescue of First Republic Bank," *Yahoo Finance*, March 16, 2023. The

amount includes $5 billion each from JPMorgan Chase, Citigroup, Bank of America, and Wells Fargo.

80. For example, BB&T/SunTrust becoming Truist, and the mergers of U.S. Bank/ MUSG Union Bank, Goldman Sachs/GE Capital and Morgan Stanley/E*Trade.

81. Zimmer (2010) suggests that too-big-to-fail considerations should be added to the criteria for merger control. Hellwig (2018a) discusses the proposal in the context of European competition policy.

82. The list is available at https://www.fsb.org/work-of-the-fsb/market-and-institutional -resilience/global-systemically-important-financial-institutions-g-sifis/, accessed March 12, 2023.

83. Since 2008, both banks have shrunk significantly, but right after the acquisition of CS the assets of the new UBS amount to some 1.8 trillion Swiss francs, more than twice the Swiss Confederacy's 2022 GDP of 771 billion Swiss francs and more than twice the total assets of the Swiss National Bank, which amount to about 881 billion Swiss francs.

84. The Spanish government would have preferred that the ESM put money directly into the banks. This is why it agreed to the European Banking Union, with supervisory powers shifting from Spain to the ECB. However, the legislation for the Banking Union took two years, and the cleanup of the banks had become urgent.

85. The Irish government had actually wanted to apply existing Irish law and bail-in the holders of senior unsecured debt. This intention was revoked when the ECB threatened to withdraw its permission for emergency liquidity assistance from the Irish central bank to the Irish banks.

86. Tooze (2018).

87. For comparison, in Chapter 6 we saw that at the end of 2011, deposits amounted to $1.13 trillion, about 54 percent of $2.08 trillion in reported total liabilities.

88. As stated in Jiang et al. (2023a), in early 2023, all U.S. banks combined had $10 trillion in insured deposits and $8 trillion in uninsured deposits. For the figures on JPMorgan Chase deposits, see its 2022 annual report (the deposit amounts are on p. 44 and the uninsured deposit figures on p. 100).

89. On deposits moving to larger banks see, for example, see Nathaniel Popper and Jessica Silver-Greenberg, "Big Depositors Seek a New Safety Net," *New York Times*, December 30, 2012, describing some of the strategies. A bank analyst notes that these strategies "make the F.D.I.C.'s limits toothless and exposes the government to more risk if banks fail in the future," and the analyst states, "If I were on the F.D.I.C. board, I would be concerned about this." This problem persists. See, e.g., Marcie Geffner, "How Do You Insure Funds More Than the FDIC Limit?," *USA Today*, July 21, 2020.

90. On the deposit guarantees, see https://www.fdic.gov/regulations/resources/TLGP /index.html, accessed March 12, 2023. In Chapter 9, the epigraph about "infinite subsidies" refers to an FDIC program guaranteeing all bank debt, including newly issued debt that is not in the form of deposits. See note 1 to Chapter 9. Note 14 to Chapter 9 describes the many other supports offered to banks by the Federal Reserve.

91. This number does not yet include deposits obtained with the purchase of First Republic Bank on May 1.

92. Since the beginning of 2023, total deposits have declined slightly from the $18 bil-
lion in Jiang et al. (2023a) after SVB failure; see Joshua Walker, "US Commercial Bank
Deposits See Biggest Drop in 50 Years," Risk.net, May 9, 2023. As of May 10, the total is
about $17.2 trillion; see https://fred.stlouisfed.org/series/DPSACBW027SBOG, accessed
May 23, 2023. The decline is primarily in uninsured deposits. Some of the decline is likely
a reaction to the recent turbulence, some of it a reaction to the increases in market rates of
interest that have no counterparts in deposit rates. As yet, total deposits in the United
States are substantially above the level of $13.3 trillion of February 2020, before the COVID
pandemic. For a recent analysis of deposit flows, see Caglio et al. (2023).

93. The Federal Deposit Insurance Fund is less than $100 billion. As early as 2009, there
were concerns that if one of the major banks were to fail, the FDIC would need to borrow
from the Treasury. See Louise Story, "US Program Lends a Hand to Banks, Quietly," *New
York Times*, April 14, 2009. This article, which describes one of the guarantee programs the
FDIC ran after the crisis discussed in note 1 of Chapter 9, also quotes William Isaac, FDIC
chair in the early 1980s, as saying: "The banking industry has funded the FDIC for 75 years.
That is why the FDIC has the ability" to guarantee large amounts of bonds. Isaac's reference
to past industry contributions overlooked the fact that industry contributions in any one
year depend on assessed needs (risks) for that year and that there have been many years,
including just before the financial crisis, with hardly any contributions at all. To be sure, if
the FDIC does not have enough money to cover its obligations, it can increase its levy on
the industry. However, if the industry is in a crisis, there are limits to this levy. In the case
of the S&L crisis, the industry contributed no more than $29 billion to covering the losses
of $153 billion. The remaining $124 billion had to come from the government. See Curry
and Shibut (2000).

94. One may suspect that the interventions of March 2020 were already driven by such
concerns. Above we pointed to exposure of regulated banks to downturns in asset prices
and problems in money market funds. If this exposure had caused one or more large
banks to fail, the FDIC would already have been in trouble for funds. See Steele (2022).

95. The bailouts are discussed in some detail in Bair (2012) and Barofsky (2012).
According to Freeman and McKinley (2018), in 2008 the FDIC assessed that Citibank was
deeply insolvent and had incurred tens of billions in losses, partly from guarantees to off-
balance-sheet entities. Had the bank been taken over by the FDIC, the resulting commitments of the FDIC would have been much larger than its available funds. In this situation,
Mr. Geithner, first as CEO of the Federal Reserve Bank of New York, Citigroup's main regulator, and then as Treasury Secretary, wanted to "save Citigroup at all costs" (the title of
Chapter 21 in Freeman and McKinley 2018). In repeated operations, the Federal Reserve,
the Treasury, and the FDIC provided Citigroup with injections of funds and with guarantees on a massive scale. Even after all the bailouts, Onaran (2011) assessed that Citigroup
was a "zombie bank," i.e., insolvent. He said the same about other banks in Europe as well
as Bank of America.

96. Jill Treanor, "King Calls for Banks to Be Cut Down to Size," *The Guardian*, June 17,
2009. The same story quotes a Treasury spokesperson saying, "The Concept of Private
Banks Being 'Too Big to Fail' Is an Economic and Democratic Outrage."

97. See Thomas Hoenig, "Too Big to Succeed," *New York Times*, December 1, 2010; Menand (2018) on "too big to supervise"; and a U.S. banking regulator expressed concerns in January 2023 about "too big to manage" institutions. See Acting Comptroller Michael J. Hsu remarks on "Detecting, Preventing, and Addressing Too Big to Manage," January 17, 2023, at https://www.occ.gov/news-issuances/speeches/2023/pub-speech-2023-7.pdf accessed May 30, 2023. See Kress (2019), and Anna Hrushka, "'Too-Big-to-Manage' Banks Could Be Broken Up, OCC Says," Banking Dive, January 18, 2023. Wilmarth (2013) describes in detail the political dynamics that have led Washington to turn a blind eye to the problems plaguing the largest financial institutions. This dynamics has not changed much.

98. For an extensive analysis of Edge Act Corporations, see Steele (2023).

99. See Joris Luyendijk, "How the Banks Ignored the Lessons of the Crash," *The Guardian*, September 30, 2017, and Luyendijk (2015).

SEVENTEEN   *Above the Law?*

1. Eucken (1940, 489). Just before the quoted sentence, Eucken explains that everyday life in the economy is full of power struggles. The essay from which the quote is taken discusses Gustav Schmoller, the leader of the German Historical School. In a famous lecture in 1905, Schmoller had extolled the leaders of industry as "men of the greatest foresight, . . . tact, and sense of the common good." The text in the epigraph, which in 1940 took some courage to publish, was meant to defuse Schmoller's hero worship. Responsibility for translation, in the epigraph and in this note, rests with us.

2. The major exception was Iceland, whose banks imploded shortly after the Lehman Brothers bankruptcy. The banks had taken unconscionable risks and, moreover, provided cheap loans to builders related to their owners. The collapse of the banks caused a deep depression, which only came to an end after the 2010 eruption of a volcano and the television series *Game of Thrones* (beginning in early 2011) turned the country into a tourist attraction. Iceland created a Special Prosecutor to investigate criminal behavior in the run-up to the crisis. The prosecutor brought several leading bankers and government officials to trial, and some of them ended up serving prison sentences. For accounts of the Icelandic crisis, see Johnsen (2014), Baldursson and Portes (2013). These references rely largely on the report of the special investigation commission that Iceland had installed in December 2008, which had direct access to individuals and institutions in Iceland. For English summaries of the main findings see https://www.rna.is/eldri-nefndir/addragandi-og-orsakir-falls-islensku-bankanna-2008/skyrsla-nefndarinnar/english/, accessed May 26, 2023. For a recent account, see Bibler (2021).

3. Below we discuss the cum-ex tax fraud in Europe. We also discuss Deutsche Bank's involvement in the LIBOR scandal concerning manipulated reports on interest rates. (On this issue, see also Chapter 13 and the detailed account in Enrich 2017.) Many banks were involved in manipulations of interest rate and exchange rate manipulations. The 2016 fine for Deutsche Bank that was mentioned in Chapter 14 concerned deception in selling mortgage-related securities. Since 2017, there have been recurrent instances of large-scale money laun-

dering by Deutsche Bank, with money from Russia, Azerbeidjan, Syria, and others. Money laundering from Russia was also the cause of two bank closures in Latvia and a large fine for the Danish bank Danske, for activities of its Estonian subsidiary. At Wells Fargo Bank, employees were pressured into creating as many accounts as possible. The scandal first came to light in 2013 with a number of lawsuits filed in California; see E. Scott Reckard, "Wells Fargo's Pressure-Cooker Sales Culture Comes at a Cost," *Los Angeles Times,* December 21, 2013, and became national news in the fall of 2016 when the Consumer Financial Protection Bureau (CFPB) hit the bank with a large fine. See Emily Glazer, "Wells Fargo's Year of Scandal Stretches On," *Wall Street Journal,* September 8, 2017. For civil and criminal cases against financial institutions that resulted in fines in the United States, see https://violationtracker .goodjobsfirst.org/prog.php?major_industry_sum=financial+services (accessed February 22, 2023) for a list of cases and their resolution in the United States. Brandon Garrett, author of Garrett (2016), maintains a Corporate Prosecution registry that covers actions by the Department of Justice in the United States only, see https://corporate-prosecution-registry .com/browse/, accessed February 22, 2023. In the United Kingdom, a major consumer fraud scandal involved so-called Payment Protection Insurance (PPI). See Isabel Togoh, "PPI in Numbers: A Look at the Scale of Britain's $59 Billion Consumer Scandal," *Forbes,* August 29, 2019. Another scandal involved interest rate hedging, with mis-selling by nine banks, including Royal Bank of Scotland, Bank of Ireland, Barclays, HSBC, Lloyds, Allied Irish Banks, Clydesdale & Yorkshire Banks, Co-operative Bank, and Santander U.K. See Jennifer Thompson and Chris Tighe, "Lenders Seek to Cap Latest Scandal," *Financial Times,* January 31 2013, and more recently, revelations about the failure of regulators to handle the scandal, see Laura Noonan, "UK Financial Regulator Rebuked for Handling of Banks' Mis-Selling Scandal," *Financial Times,* December 14 2021.

4. Such is the case in Germany, but the corporation can face a (modest) regulatory fine if anyone committed a crime or an offense on its behalf. In the United Kingdom, there must be a "controlling mind" with criminal intent if a corporation is to be liable, and such a condition is impossible for any large corporation. For an overview of issues around corporate criminal liability in different countries, see https://www.justice.gc.ca/eng/rp-pr /other-autre/jhr-jdp/dp-dt/iss-ques.html, accessed March 6, 2023.

5. See Garrett (2016), Eisinger (2017), Coffee (2020), and Rakoff (2021).

6. Atkinson (2023) shows that concerns about collateral damage to the organization play a key role in assessments of fines by most U.S. agencies.

7. See the full session and transcript here: https://www.c-span.org/video/?311311-1/justice -department-oversight, accessed February 22, 2023.

8. A number of books, including Eisinger (2017), Rakoff (2021), and Coffee (2020), discuss in detail why corporate enforcement is weak in the United States and why executives are hardly ever prosecuted. The overall conclusion is that bringing cases against high-level individuals is judged to be too costly for the prosecutors themselves and for the governments, with the result that they choose the easy path of extracting as high a settlement as they can and proudly claim success, even if the outcomes deliver little in the way of justice, accountability, or deterrence. A broader problem is the lack of resources for white-collar

enforcement, particularly since the attacks of September 11, 2001, when priorities shifted toward fighting terrorism.

9. The same problem arises in the context of terrorist organizations or of organized crime. To deal with this problem in those contexts, Germany introduced the concept of a criminal association, as one whose objectives or activities are directed toward criminal offenses, and made membership in such an association a criminal offense. A book by a former department head at the European Anti-Fraud Office suggested provocatively that Deutsche Bank might satisfy the criteria for such an association; see Hetzer (2015).

10. In a few narrow situations, strict liability rules that do not require intent apply to "responsible officers" in the United States. See, e.g., Michael W. Peregrine, "The 'Responsible Corporate Officer Doctrine' Survives to Perplex Corporate Boards," Harvard Law School Forum on Corporate Governance blog, July 5, 2017, https://corpgov.law.harvard.edu/2017/07/05/the-responsible-corporate-officer-doctrine-survives-to-perplex-corporate-boards/, accessed May 30, 2023. The notion of "willful blindness" or "conscious avoidance" may enable a person who refuses to confirm something they know is likely to be true as knowing the fact. However, it has not been applied frequently to pursue executives in large corporations for conduct that they have not been directly involved in. In order to prove "criminal intent" of an individual, prosecutors must find evidence and/or credible witnesses. However, it is extremely costly for individuals within organizations to blow the whistle or testify against higher ups, and they often pay a high upfront price and depend on the willingness of authorities to proceed. See the discussion below of settlements and whistleblowers.

11. See Carreyrou (2018). In 2022, both the ex-CEO Elizabeth Holmes and President "Sunny" Balwani were convicted separately for fraud and sentenced to prison. Both are appealing as of this writing, but had to start serving their prison time. Although patients, doctors, and even employees were harmed, and harm to potential future patients was the most dangerous part of the misconduct, Ms. Holmes was only found guilty of defrauding investors.

12. Brady and Kent (2022) give an overview of the erosion of trust in past decades. In their account, the erosion was strongest for Wall Street, followed by TV News, Congress, and banks.

13. Tooze (2018) emphasizes the political ramifications of the crisis of 2007–2009 and subsequent European crises. Wolf (2023) laments the crisis in democratic capitalism, placing the global financial crisis as a key triggering event.

14. On cum-ex, see Deutscher Bundestag (2017), Spengel (2016, 2017, 2021), Correctiv (2018, 2021), Schröm (2021), Bognanni (2022), and ESMA (2019). The term "cum-ex" refers to the fact that the first transaction (sale from B to C) involves the share with a right to the dividend ("cum" is Latin for "with"), and the second transaction (purchase by B from A) involves the share after the dividend has been paid ("ex" meaning here "without"). Deutscher Bundestag (2017) is the report of the parliamentary investigation committee on cum-ex. The later publications draw on this report for developments up to 2017.

15. See Schröm (2021) and Bognanni (2022).

16. These schemes involved exempt investors buying shares from short sellers. (Short sellers are people who sell shares that they do not actually own but intend to acquire later.) Timed to enable the duplication, the buyer's bank would see a record that its client has acquired the shares, pay the dividend, and provide the associated tax certificate even though the shares were not actually there yet. The buyer would actually receive the shares after the seller had purchased them from a third party. If this later transaction took place after the dividend payment, the original owner of the shares would also have received a dividend payment and a tax certificate. If both certificates led to "tax reimbursements," there would be a windfall for the seller, the buyer, or the bank, most likely for all three. The fact that the tax has only been paid once is overlooked if there is no mechanism ensuring that the certificates provided by banks match the tax withholdings of the corporation. The absence of such a mechanism, however, does not exculpate the fraud involved in claiming reimbursements for taxes that have not been paid. To make the fraud work, the parties involved, including the bank, must coordinate precisely so that the short sale takes place just before the dividend comes due, the short sale is reversed just after the dividend is paid, and the prices for both transactions are fixed in such a way that the seller, the buyer, and the bank receive satisfactory shares of the spoils.

17. Deutscher Bundestag (2017), Spengel (2016, 2017, 2021), Schröm (2021), Bognanni (2022), Correctiv (2018). The numbers become much larger if one includes the so-called cum-cum cases. These are cases in which a shareholding person or institution that is not exempt from income taxes on the dividends sells the shares just before the dividend payment to someone who is exempt and buys them back immediately after the dividend payment. The initial sales price would take account of the right to receive dividends in the immediate future, and the subsequent repurchase price would be correspondingly lower. Such transactions do not involve fraud and as such are not illegal. However, there are rules against the exploitation of transactions that have no real economic purpose *except* to reduce taxes. Such rules would seem to apply in cases where the initial sale and subsequent repurchase involve the same parties and the terms of the repurchase are fixed from the beginning. For cum-ex and cum-cum together, Correctiv (2018) estimates total taxpayer losses worldwide to amount to $150 billion, including $5 billion in the United States.

18. Schröm (2021).

19. After cum-ex deals involving shares had been explicitly outlawed, perpetrators switched to using American Depository Receipts (ADRs) instead, claims on foreign shares held by banks or by the Depository Trust Company in the United States. ADRs were created to reduce transactions costs of investors in the United States trading shares of foreign corporations. The German politician Gerhard Schick coined the term "cum-fake" for the use of ADRs in cum-ex deals. See Schröm (2021) and Bognanni (2022).

20. A 2007 law prohibited banks in Germany from issuing certificates of tax payments without verifying that the tax had actually been paid. This left a loophole for banks outside of Germany, which was used extensively. See Schröm (2021) and Bognanni (2022).

21. The first one, in 2007, involved WestLB, the second one, in 2013, HVB. In the second case, the head of the bank's tax department, who had alerted BaFin, was dismissed. See Bognanni (2022, 78, 153–158).

22. At that point, they sent questionnaires to banks asking to what extent they might also be exposed to such a risk.

23. Deutscher Bundestag (2017).

24. Schröm (2021, 182).

25. The legal proceedings have not yet been concluded. The prosecutor's investigation had begun in 2014 with a six-month imprisonment of the former head of compliance at the bank. Proceedings before the lower court in Zürich took place in the spring of 2019, with a judgment imposing a prison sentence for economic espionage on the former head of compliance and fines for violations of bank secrecy on the other two accused, the difference being that the former head of compliance had also given the information to a journalist. In January 2022, the appeals court in Zürich voided the lower court's judgment because the prosecutor had been biased and the evidence he had produced was unusable. In September 2022, the Swiss Federal Court voided the appeals court's judgment and demanded that the appeals court consider the case without disregarding the evidence brought by the prosecutor. Meanwhile, the bank had lost in two rounds in German courts and chose to pay €45 million in damages rather than try another round in the German Federal Court. In Schröm (2021), one of the journalists involved in uncovering the cum-ex fraud gives an account of these developments, except for the last two stages in Swiss courts.

26. Parliamentary committees in Hamburg and Berlin have been trying to find out what role the then Mayor of Hamburg Olaf Scholz played in these decisions. He initially claimed that he never met the relevant banker in private, but this claim has been disproved by the banker's diaries. Now, while acknowledging that the meetings took place, he cannot remember anything about them.

27. For the significance of LIBOR, see note 2 to Chapter 13.

28. An example would be an interest rate swap between a fixed rate claim of y percent and a variable claim of LIBOR plus x percent. Despite the manipulation scandal and much discussion about ending the use of such indices, the use of LIBOR as a base rate has persisted and, as of early 2021, included around $225 trillion of derivatives, consumer loans, corporate loans, and cash investments. Authorities have been discussing potential replacements for years, but a full agreement has not yet been reached. As of this writing, some partial replacements seem to be on the way. See press release from December 16, 2022, at https://www.federalreserve.gov/newsevents/pressreleases/bcreg20221216a.htm, accessed May 30, 2023.

29. Whether one classifies these manipulations as fraud depends on how narrowly one defines "fraud." If criminal law uses the term fraud only if the people who were lied to were also the victims, then the LIBOR manipulations were not fraud. However, from the victims' perspective, the difference was irrelevant.

30. There also were EURIBOR manipulations involving interest rate indices for lending in euros, and similar exchange rate index manipulations involving the "closing" exchange rates at which different currencies were traded between banks. Large fines were paid by Barclays, Citigroup, Credit Suisse, Deutsche Bank, JPMorgan Chase, NatWest, Royal Bank of Scotland, Société Générale, UBS.

latter function, he had played a leading role in the disastrous 2001 takeover of Dresdner Bank, which subsequently, in 2008, was sold to Commerzbank in a fire sale.

42. At the 2015 shareholders' meeting, some 39 percent of shareholders voted not to discharge the executive board, i.e., not to relieve the board from liability for the preceding year's activities. This was less than a majority, but such a large opposition was deemed very alarming.

43. In 2013, Achleitner himself had recruited the lawyer Georg Thoma, from the law firm of Shearman and Sterling, to join the supervisory board of Deutsche Bank as head of the bank's integrity committee. He seems to have gotten more than he bargained for. The arguments in the text are taken from interviews that Alfred Herling, Mr. Achleitner's deputy on the Supervisory Board, gave at the time.

44. In connection with the 2018 leadership change, Mr. Achleitner publicly declared that Mr. Cryan, Mr. Jain's successor as CEO, had to leave because he had not moved fast enough on reducing investment banking; in the interim, however, there had been many reports to the effects that Mr. Achleitner himself was resisting Mr. Cryan's attempts to reduce the scale of the bank's investment banking. The subsequent appointment of an insider with no affiliation to investment banking came after media leaks had revealed that two attempts by Mr. Achleitner to recruit a new CEO from outside had been rebuffed.

45. Partnoy (2009) contains much material on Bankers Trust in this period, with an expression of dismay that, despite "a mountain of damning evidence," no one "did any jail time" and "the principal actors were not even charged with crimes." One quote from taped conversations had an employee saying about the information given to a client: "We told him 8.1 million when the real number was $14 million" (Partnoy 2009, 161). Civil litigation was more effective, causing Bankers Trust to pay what were then large sums in settlements. See also Enrich (2020).

46. Even before the 1998 merger, Citicorp had long been a poster child for risk taking by banks and for government bailouts. On the history of Citi and the people involved, see Freeman and McKinley (2018).

47. See note 39 to Chapter 5.

48. See our discussion in Chapter 14 and Credit Suisse Group Special Committee of the Board of Directors Report on Archegos Capital Management, July 29, 2021, https://www.credit-suisse.com/about-us/en/reports-research/archegos-info-kit.html, accessed March 27, 2023. For a summary, see Jack Ewing, "Credit Suisse Finds Incompetence But No Criminal Conduct in Archegos Debacle," New York Times, July 29, 2021. On Archegos overall, see Kalyeena Makortoff, "Bank Losses Linked to Archegos Top $10bn After Latest Results," The Guardian, April 27, 2021.

49. We referred to this episode briefly in note 57 to Chapter 11 and stated the loss as $5.8 billion, the figure reported at the time of our writing in fall 2012. Recall as well that we went through JPMorgan Chase financial disclosures in January 2012 regarding what CEO Dimon called the "fortress balance sheet," noting that the bank hides much risk off-balance-sheet and particularly in derivatives trading. In 2014, the Federal Reserve raised slightly the "leverage ratio" requirement that does not rely on risk weights, leading to the

story by Matt Phillips, "The Fed Was Not Impressed with Jamie Dimon's 'Fortress Balance Sheet'," *QZ*, April 9, 2014.

50. See Jessica Silver-Greenberg, "JPMorgan Cuts Dimon's Pay, Even as Profit Surges," *New York Times*, January 16, 2013, which also includes the report of the task force and mentions a second report of the board of directors. Both reports are difficult to find online at this writing. (Links in other news stories, such as within Nick Summers, "JPMorgan Halves CEO Dimon's Pay Over 'Whale' Losses," *Bloomberg News*, January 16, 2013, do not work.)

51. The full text is available at https://www.govinfo.gov/content/pkg/CHRG-113shrg80222/pdf/CHRG-113shrg80222.pdf, accessed March 5, 2023.

52. See Dan Fitzpatrick, "Senate Slams Bank on 'Whale'," *Wall Street Journal*, March 14, 2013. The senate report included information about the compensation of the traders in 2010 and 2011. Two individuals, including Ina Drew, were paid around $30 million each. Yet, the bank's own task force report was not critical of the compensation practices of the bank.

53. The figure consists of $920 million to authorities in the United States and United Kingdom for securities laws violation, including $200 million to settle a suit from the SEC in which the bank admitted to wrongdoing, See Chris Isidore and James O'Toole, "JPMorgan Fined $920 Million in 'London Whale' Trading Loss," CNN, September 19, 2013, and another $100 million in October 2013, to settle a suit by the Commodities Futures Trading Commission (CFTC) connected to manipulation charges, see https://www.cftc.gov/PressRoom/PressReleases/6737-13, accessed May 23, 2023. In addition, the bank settled a private lawsuit by investors for $150 million, see Ben McLannahan, "JPMorgan Pays $150m to Settle 'London Whale' Class Action," *Financial Times*, December 21, 2015.

54. Although neither Mr. Iksil nor any senior managers faced criminal charges, U.S. prosecutors tried to indict two lower level individuals for hiding losses from the bank's managers. See Patricia Hurtado, "The London Whale," *Bloomberg*, February 23, 2016.

55. On the issue of willful blindness more generally, see Heffernan (2012).

56. See Credit Suisse Group Special Committee of the Board of Directors Report on Archegos Capital Management, July 29, 2021, https://www.credit-suisse.com/about-us/en/reports-research/archegos-info-kit.html, accessed March 27, 2023.

57. Das (2010, 54–55, 139). See also note 43 to Chapter 5.

58. One of the interviews that provided the basis for Luyendijk (2015) is Joris Luyendijk, "Voices of Finance: Risk and Compliance Consultant at a Major Bank," *The Guardian*, November 3, 2011.

59. As we discussed earlier in this chapter, in dealing with this conflict, UBS under Axel Weber chose one alternative and became a world leader in wealth management; Deutsche Bank under Achleitner and Jain chose the other and stumbled from one piece of bad news to the next.

60. The criticism of the Office of the Comptroller of the Currency (OCC) appears on pages 5–6 of the Senate report linked in note 51, and the report includes numerous documents

related to failures of the supervision of JPMorgan Chase by the OCC. (See also the timeline on pp. 519–521 of the report.)

61. See Victoria McGrane and Ryan Tracy, "Full Report on 'London Whale' Incident Sheds More Light on New York Fed Role," *Wall Street Journal*, January 9, 2015.

62. An example is given by the reactions of the French and German governments and the European Commission, discussed in Chapter 14, to the Basel Committee's proposals to limit the banks' scope for reducing equity requirements by abusing the right to base risk assessments on their own risk models. In 2020, these very proposals were also the subject of a parliamentary intervention by the Free Democratic Party, which at the time was in opposition but today is in charge of the Federal Ministry of Finance. As discussed in Hellwig (2020b), the text of the intervention looked as though it had been dictated by the Bankers' Association. See also note 18 to Chapter 14 on the new French-German initiative to weaken restrictions on securitization.

63. The argument neglects the fact that an outright subsidy to down payments on the first home purchase might be more effective than the subsidy to borrowing that is implicit in the tax deductibility of interest on homeowners' and the banks' debt (which we discussed earlier, in Chapters 9 and 14). It also neglects the fact that, for some risky loans, high rates of interest may be called for as appropriate risk premia. In the early 1990s, Martin Hellwig was once involved in a discussion with people from a large Swiss bank about banks' losses in the Latin American debt crisis of the 1980s. A researcher in his group had used World Bank data on international lending to compute aggregate rates of return on the banks' lending to Latin American countries. For the years 1970–1992, using 1992 secondary-market prices as exit values, he had found that, on average, these rates of return were 1.5 percentage points below LIBOR. The bankers in this discussion challenged the interpretation that the losses were relatively small when considering the panic that had dominated the discussion in the 1980s. Rates 1.5 percentage points below LIBOR translated to a lot of money, they claimed. The researcher asked how that amount compared to the losses on Swiss mortgages, given that Swiss mortgage rates had been much lower than LIBOR and much below the effective rates of return in country lending. The answer was that Swiss mortgages are funded with Swiss savings accounts and the interest rates on those are lower than LIBOR. For an economist, such compartmentalizations of different parts of the business do not make much sense. They do make sense, however, if one realizes that low mortgage rates help the banks find good friends in the political arena and the media. For an updated version of the research under discussion, see Klingen et al. (2004).

64. For more on the problem of capture, see Johnson and Kwak (2010), Carpenter and Moss (2013), and Igan and Lambert (2019). The term "regulatory capture" is associated with George Stigler, who recognized that the issue of rules and enforcement is a matter of politics in a democracy. See Anat Admati, "George Stigler and the Challenge of Democracy," *ProMarket*, June 3, 2021. Studies of the revolving doors phenomenon tend to support a "regulatory schooling" of "human capital" hypothesis rather than "quid pro quo" of regulatory capture where regulators are lax in order to curry favors with regulated institutions. Lewis (2014) describes career concerns of young specialists at the SEC as a major

reason why the SEC closed its eyes to the fact that, in the late 2000s, high frequency trading was a tool to damage investors by front-running their orders, causing prices to move against investors before their orders even reached the market. See also Lucca et al. (2014) about banking regulations and deHaan et al. (2015) about accounting-related enforcement at the SEC, mostly involving lawyers. Of course, those with financial sector background might be highly effective regulators, as the cases of Robert Jenkins in the Bank of England, discussed in note 15 of Chapter 14, and Gary Gensler, who transitioned to policy positions after a career in Goldman Sachs, show.

65. In private conversations with people within regulatory bodies in the United States, there is a definite sense that regulators present themselves as constrained even though they have clear authority to act more forcefully against imprudent behavior.

66. Pillar 2 of the Basel Accord asks supervisors to consider the professionalism of bankers, and U.S. basic banking laws give supervisors extensive powers to demand that banks "cease and desist: in pursuing imprudent and unprofessional actions." The German regulators and supervisors, BaFin and Bundesbank, however, referred to legal concerns to explain their inactivity in the years before the financial crisis of 2007–2009. See Hellwig (2017c). On inactivity of the Federal Reserve as a regulator and supervisor see Wilmarth (2013), Taub (2014), Steele (2022), and Isaac Chotiner, "The Regulatory Breakdown Behind the Collapse of Silicon Valley Bank," *The New Yorker*, March 19, 2023, mentioned in note 116 of Chapter 14. The various reports on SVB and Signature Bank, including FDIC (2023), Federal Reserve (2023), GAO (2023), and DFPI (2023), portray supervisors as being too passive for too long. Interestingly, in response to Federal Reserve (2023), the Bank Policy Institute (BPI), a trade and lobbying organization for banks, published a critique of the report about SVB supervision, complaining that the report and the supervisors had paid too little attention to the fundamental weaknesses in SVB's risk profile that led to its failure, that "examiners were far too focused on management processes and procedures and not on actual risk," that "regulators failed to enforce several key requirements," and that supervisory ratings "are not focused on actual risk and financial conditions." Perhaps not surprisingly, BPI treats the problems as mostly having to do with liquidity rather than solvency. See https://bpi.com/a-failure-of-self-examination-a-thorough-review-of-svbs-exam-reports-yields-conclusions-very-different-from-those-in-the-feds-self-assessment/, accessed May 23, 2023.

67. Grind (2012) describes the anger of Washington Mutual shareholders with FDIC chair Sheila Bair for wiping out the shareholders of the bank, which many assessed as insolvent, to protect the deposit insurance fund. Shareholders believed the bank was solvent and, as well, were upset that Citigroup was bailed out because it was deemed "systemic," as discussed in Chapter 16.

68. See the discussion in Chapter 14 and particularly note 103.

69. See "CS schraubte per September 2022 an ihrem CET1" ("per September 2022, CS manipulated ist CET1"), Lukas Hässig, *Inside Paradeplatz*, March 17, 2023, https://insideparadeplatz.ch/2023/03/17/cs-schraubte-per-september-2022-an-ihrem-cet1/, accessed May 30, 2023. The article points out that, on p. 116 of the bank's 2022 report, there is a figure "Capital Frameworks for Credit Suisse" showing a buffer component of equity

under Swiss regulation equal to 4.78 percent of risk-weighted assets when previously the regulation had asked for 5.5 percent (and UBS continued to show 5.5 percent). The number is accompanied by the statement, "Reflects the updated capital and leverage requirements, effective September 30, 2022, resulting from the assessment of surcharges."

70. Bichsel and Blum (2005), Blum (2008).

71. Switzerland imposed the leverage ratio requirement at the peak of the crisis in 2008, but even then, despite the public outcry against UBS's being supported by the government and the central bank, the measure was highly controversial.

72. Above, we cited criticism of the Federal Reserve Bank of New York's supervision of the trading that led to the London Whale losses at JPMorgan Chase. The article mentioned in note 61 quotes Michael Gibson, the director of supervision at the Federal Reserve arguing that the problem was due to lack of resources, and the report is said to provide "further detail about the ways in which the New York Fed was overwhelmed with new responsibilities during and after the crisis," which may have led to it neglecting the Chief Investment Officer unit involved in the trading. Mr. Gibson also noted the work associated with running stress tests for JPMorgan Chase. This case illustrates also the fragmented structure of U.S. regulation, discussed again below.

73. 2005 was the year when the leading German tabloid wrote: "We are Pope!" on the occasion of the election of Cardinal Ratzinger to the Holy See. "Wir sind Papst!," *Bild-Zeitung*, April 20, 2005.

74. For an extensive account of the Wirecard scandal, see Deutscher Bundestag (2021), the report of the parliamentary investigation committee on the scandal. Hellwig and Schick (2022) sketch a few salient points.

75. The Wirecard fraud bears some similarity to of the massive Ponzi scheme of Bernie Madoff, which went on from the early 1990s until the 2008 crisis. For years, U,S, regulators refused to follow whistleblower accounts of Madoff's scheme. The fraud only came to light in the financial crisis in 2008, when investors withdrew their funds and Mr. Madoff could not raise enough additional funds to pay them. See Henriques (2017) and the documentary series "Madoff: the Monster of Wall Street."

76. See McCrum (2022). The attitude of the public prosecutor in this case was not unlike that of the Swiss prosecutor in the cum-ex case.

77. For a damning account of the transaction, see Bericht (2014), the report of the Austrian investigation committee on the disaster of Hypo Group Alpe Adria.

78. BaFin had supervised a bank subsidiary of Wirecard without however appreciating the role of the bank as a basis for funding the fraudulent scheme of the parent. In refusing to examine the parent, the supervisor violated the Basel Committee's Core Principles for Effective Banking Supervision, and even, after June 2019, European law. The Basel Committee's Core Principles for Effective Banking Supervision call for supervising bank subsidiaries of larger groups by examining the group as a whole and the role of the bank subsidiary in the group See BCBS (2012b), Principle 12 EC (wider group) in combination with Principle 8 EC 1a. As for European law, Art. 4 (1) #20 of a revised version of the EU's Capital Requirements Regulation, which came into force on June 7, 2019, gives a definition of a financial holding company that covers Wirecard, so from that date at the latest, BaFin

should have treated Wirecard as such and supervised the entire corporation, not just the bank subsidiary.

79. For an overview and general criticism, see GAO (2016). Banks in the United States can be either a federal or a state charter, and state banks can choose whether to become members of the Federal Reserve. They are assigned primary and secondary supervisors, which sometimes alternate supervisions between the state and the federal authorities. Agrawal et al. (2014) show that state regulators tend to be more lenient than federal regulators when such turn-taking is in place. The tension between FDIC and other regulators, for example with the Office of Thrift Supervision around Washington Mutual and the Federal Reserve in the context of Citigroup in 2007–2009, is described in Bair (2012) and Grind (2012). Bair (2012) and Freeman and McKinley (2018) also describe tensions between the FDIC and the Federal Reserve in the context of Citigroup. Recall also the tension between the OCC and the Federal Reserve Bank of New York over the supervision of JPMorgan Chase in the context of the London Whale episode in this chapter. Silicon Valley Bank was supervised not only by the Federal Reserve Bank of San Francisco, with instruction from the Federal Reserve Board, but also by the Department of Financial Protection and Innovation of California (DFPI). See Federal Reserve (2023) and DFPI (2023). FDIC was the main supervisor of both Signature Bank and First Republic Bank, both of which were so-called state nonmember banks. On Signature, see FDIC (2023).

80. In 2009, Martin Hellwig chaired a committee advising the German government on large applications for government loans or loan guarantees from nonfinancial companies in the crisis. In one case, the company was active in a declining service industry, had produced losses for a few years and, by ordinary accounting rules, had been insolvent for more than a year. None of this prevented the auditors from accepting the company's accounts or a prestigious consulting firm from presenting the narrative behind the company's rescue plans as credible. Creative writing courses seemed to have been a prerequisite for doing these reports.

81. Auditors' failings ahead of the financial crisis of 2007–2009 were extensively documented in the United States despite the existence of an auditor regulator since the scandals of the early 2000s. Little has changed since the financial crisis. Among the most spectacular failures were Carillion in the United Kingdom in 2018 (see Wylie 2020), which led to a series of articles about auditing and an editorial in the *Financial Times* on August 1, 2018 ("Reform Accounting Rules to Restore Trust in Audit"), which included the statement "Bad audits and beleaguered auditors are symptoms of a cancer in the body corporate." Plans for future reforms in the United Kingdom were announced in May 2022 but are not in place as of this writing (May 2023). In Germany, the Wirecard scandal, described in detail in McCrum (2022), engulfed regulators, politicians, and the media who cheered for the company and blamed short sellers and even a *Financial Times* reporter for manipulation, while refusing to consider their concerns until the company collapsed in July 2020. See "Timeline: The Rise and Fall of Wirecard, a German Tech Champion," Reuters, March 16, 2021, and Ben Taub, "How the Biggest Fraud in German History Unravelled," *New Yorker*, February 27, 2023.

82. See Deutscher Bundestag (2021) and McCrum (2022) on the massive accounting frauds. For its handling of Wirecard, auditor Ernst & Young has been sanctioned by APAS, the auditors' supervisor (which itself had been scandalously inactive). Ernst & Young must pay a €500,000 fine and for two years is banned from auditing listed corporations. See René Bender, Bert Fröndhoff, Martin Greive, and Volker Votsmeier, "Wirecard: Aufsicht Apas sanktioniert EY mit historisch hohen Strafen" [Supervisor APAS imposes historically high sanctions on EY]. *Handelsblatt*, April 6, 2023. Accessed May 30, 2023. The auditors also face lawsuits that may end up holding them liable for investors' losses.

83. See Bognanni (2022, 136). The bank was Hamburg-based Varengold Bank, and the auditor KPMG, one of the major auditors worldwide.

84. See Stephen Foley, "Three Failed US Banks Had One Thing in Common: KPMG," *Financial Times*, May 2, 2023. Francine McKenna, who publishes a blog on auditing called The Dig, provides a detailed description of the actions by KPMG related to the failed banks, in "Part 1: Where Was KPMG While Silicon Valley Bank, and the Rest, Were Teetering?," May 13, 2023, at https://thedig.substack.com/p/where-was-kpmg-while-silicon -valley, accessed May 23, 2023. KPMG has a long history of troubles with the auditing regulators related to its bank auditing, see "Part 2: What Is KPMG's Bank Audit Quality History with the PCAOB and SEC?," May 21, 2023, at https://thedig.substack.com/p/part-2 -what-is-kpmgs-bank-audit-quality, accessed May 23, 2023.

85. Partnoy (2017) provides a thorough discussion of all the developments in this area.

86. Lee (2022).

87. German law actually treats the lawyer as an institution of the legal system, with obligations to the law that may transcend obligations to the client. See H.-J. Hellwig (2008).

88. See https://www.globalwitness.org/shadyinc/, accessed May 26, 2023, and Alley (2022). The highly disturbing investigation is described in Louise Story, "Report Describes Lawyers' Advice on Moving Suspect Funds Into U.S," *New York Times*, January 31, 2016, and was the subject of an episode of *60 Minutes* on CBS entitled "Anonymous, Inc.," August 28, 2016, available at https://www.cbsnews.com/news/hidden-camera-investigation -money-laundering-60-minutes/, accessed May 23, 2023. The same lawyer who said that lawyers run the country admitted that lawyers belong to "a privileged class" and quoted the quip "a good lawyer knows the law, a great lawyer knows the judge." Pistor (2019) also suggests that private law, particularly in the United States and United Kingdom, has an outsized influence on market and political outcomes not only in those jurisdictions but around the globe.

89. See Kalyeena Makortoff, "Three Former Barclays Executives Found Not Guilty of Fraud," *The Guardian*, February 28, 2020. These cases highlighted the fact that in the United Kingdom, corporate crime requires that there is a "directing mind" behind the corporate action, which in a large corporation with diffuse responsibility is hardly ever true. See also Dave Michaels, "All U.S. Trial Convictions in Crisis-Era LIBOR Rigging Have Now Been Overturned," *Wall Street Journal*, January 27, 2022.

90. See Garrett (2016), Eisinger (2017), Rakoff (2021), Taub (2020), and Coffee (2020).

91. Corporations are loath to admitting wrongdoing primarily because doing so would subject them to many private lawsuits, which can be extremely costly, but also to "save

face." See Sonary Glinto, "Why Companies and CEOs Rarely Admit to Wrongdoing," NPR, September 20, 2013, discussing the admission by JPMorgan Chase in the case of the losses associated with the London Whale reckless trading in 2012 that led to $6 billion in losses. Authorities have been able to insist on such admissions because of public pressure, but it is not clear that it adds much to the deterrence effect of the settlements, as long as individuals are effectively immune.

92. See the announcement and "statement of facts" at https://www.justice.gov/opa/pr /justice-department-federal-and-state-partners-secure-record-13-billion-global -settlement, accessed February 22, 2023. In reference to the largely vague information made available with the announcement, one commentator wrote, "although it took the Justice Department more than five years to pursue a major bank for its role in the mortgage mania, the investigation seems to have unearthed material that, by and large, could have been dug up with a spoon," and a legal scholar says, "The facts here are all stuff we knew years ago." See Gretchen Morgenson, "$13 Billion, Yes, but What Took So Long?," *New York Times*, November 23, 2013.

93. See the press release, at https://www.justice.gov/opa/pr/bank-america-pay-1665 -billion-historic-justice-department-settlement-financial-fraud-leading.

94. See "JPMorgan CEO Dimon says government cases were 'unfair,'" Reuters, January 23, 2014. For a cynical view on the settlement and narratives in parts of the financial media, see these two segments of the *Jon Stewart Daily Show* from October 23, 2013, https://www.cc.com/video/g4lysm/the-daily-show-with-jon-stewart-a-nightmare-on -wall-street and https://www.cc.com/video/x4swvg/the-daily-show-with-jon-stewart-a -nightmare-on-wall-street-jpmorgan-chase, accessed May 20, 2023.

95. Sarah N. Lynch and Aruna Viswanatha, "Better Markets Sues Justice Department over JP Morgan Settlement," Reuters, February 10, 2014, and "Fact Sheet" posted on Better Market website, at https://bettermarkets.org/newsroom/fact-sheet-better-markets-files -lawsuit-challenging-record-setting-13-billion-settlement/, accessed March 5, 2023.

96. Lindsay Dunsmuir, "U.S. Judge Dismisses Lawsuit Over $13 Billion JPMorgan Chase Settlement," Reuters, March 19, 2015. The Department of Justice submitted a motion asking the judge to dismiss the case in May 2014.

97. See Ben Protess and Jessica Silver-Greenberg, "In Extracting Deal From JPMorgan, U.S. Aimed for Bottom Line," *New York Times*, November 19, 2013.

98. See William Cohan, "Jamie Dimon's $13 Billion Secret," *The Nation*, August 13, 2014, which did not reveal the name of the witness but focused on the process that led to the settlement, and which was followed in late 2014 by Matt Taibbi, "The $9 Billion Witness: Meet JPMorgan Chase's Worst Nightmare," *Rolling Stone*, November 6, 2014, and Kevin McCoy, "Ex-JPMorgan Lawyer Tells Tale of Wrongdoing," *USA Today*, November 8, 2014. A video interview with the whistleblower, Alayne Fleischmann, and Matt Taibbi is available here https://www.democracynow.org/2015/1/1/matt_taibbi_and_the_9_billion, accessed February 23, 2022. Ms. Fleischman was the anonymous individual mentioned in the "statement of fact" by the Department of Justice said to have informed her superiors and the banks' executives of the extremely poor quality of the mortgages that had been sold to investors with false representations. Clearly it would have been difficult for JPMorgan

Chase executives to claim that they were not aware of the problem given the information she provided and potential testimony. In her interviews, Ms. Fleischman provided a bit more information about the culture in the bank, including a manager who instituted a strict "no-email" rule, and the many red flags around the quality of the mortgages that had been sold. Parts of the civil lawsuit were eventually released. See William Cohan, "Jamie Dimon's $13 Billion Secret—Revealed," *Vanity Fair*, September 6, 2017.

99. See Edward Wyatt, "Judge Blocks Citigroup Settlement with S.E.C.," *New York Times*, November 28, 2011; James Downie, "Judge Jed Rakoff Courageously Rejects SEC-Citigroup Settlement," *Washington Post*, November 28, 2011.

100. See Joseph Ax, "U.S. Judge Reluctantly Approves SEC-Citigroup $285 Million Deal," Reuters, August 5, 2014.

101. Outside the United States, the only unit imposing large fines seems to be the European Commission's competition unit, which is used to such fines from competition cases. As mentioned in note 31 above, the LIBOR case was treated as an infringement against the prohibition of agreements under competition law.

102. In the United States, Attorney General Eric Holder said that regulators have to consider the systemic impact of fines, with the clear interpretation that the fines will be limited. See notes 6 and 7 to this chapter. As a member of the General Board of the European Systemic Risk Board (ESRB), in 2015, Martin Hellwig participated in a discussion about a proposal to issue an official warning by the ESRB concerning the threat to financial stability from large fines. The observation that any such warning would be incomplete if it failed to take account of the threats to financial stability from the misbehavior that the fines were punishing ended the discussion.

103. "Carney Hints Era of Big Fines Is Over," *Financial Times*, April 21, 2017.

104. Dyck et al. (2010) examine many incidences where fraud was detected and show that indeed, detection more often comes from outsiders rather than standard corporate governance and law enforcement channels. It requires more resources and legal power to investigate small corporations, often with anonymous beneficial owners. Banks are required to abide by "know your customer" rules and report "suspicious transactions" to authorities to fight money laundering. However, banks often report such transactions and still process them, and authorities cannot seem to keep up and act on the information in a timely manner. The "FinCen files," posted by the International Consortium of Investigative Journalists (ICIJ), "reveals the role of global banks in industrial-scale money laundering— and the bloodshed and suffering that flow in its wake." See https://www.icij.org/investigations/fincen-files/, accessed March 28, 2023. See also the next note.

105. An unknown number of the 1.8 million corporations listed in the state of Delaware that operate entirely in the dark may well hide crime that is uncovered rarely, and often accidentally. On Delaware, see Weitzman (2022). Shell corporations are hardly scrutinized, and that is likely "Why Manafort and Cohen Thought They'd Get Away With It," Jesse Eisinger, *ProPublica*, August 24, 2018. In addition to the discussion of lawyers earlier in chapter, secrecy jurisdictions, money laundering, and the role of people and institutions, particularly banks in the developed world in enabling corruption and kleptocracy, is described in investigations. See Alley (2022), Baker (2023), Bullough (2018),

Michel (2021), and Vogl (2021) describe how the United States handles the problem of money laundering and kleptocracy and the enabling role of western governments, banks, and laws. The 2016 Panama Papers (see https://www.icij.org/investigations/panama-papers/, accessed May 27, 2023) and 2021 Pandora Papers (see https://www.icij.org/investigations/pandora-papers/, accessed May 27, 2023) show that the challenge of abolishing financial secrecy is that people with power even in democracy are benefiting personally from them. A new Corporate Transparency Act, which will take effect in the United States starting January 2024, requires corporations to file with federal authorities the names of key beneficial owners and those in control of all corporations in the United States, to be used only by law authorities. Public disclosure of beneficial owners is not proposed in the United States and was recently reversed by courts in Europe. See this statement from Transparency International: https://www.transparency.org/en/press/eu-court-of-justice-delivers-blow-to-beneficial-ownership-transparency, accessed May 30, 2023.

106. In the United States, some laws allow witnesses of wrongdoings also to go to court under some conditions. For example, a provision refers to as *qui tam* in the False Claims Act allows those who witnessed fraud against the government to pursue legal action even if the Department of Justice fails to do so. Of course, such legal action requires legal representation and there are private lawyers who specialize in bringing such claims to court. See https://www.justice.gov/civil/false-claims-act, accessed May 20, 2023.

107. In the cum-ex tax fraud, some victims preferred not to sue in order to hush up the fact that they had been taken for a ride. See Schröm (2021).

108. On lack of resources of government, see Taub (2020), as well as references in note 8. See a recent summary in "Catholic Church Child Sexual Abuse Scandal," BBC, October 5, 2021, https://www.bbc.com/news/world-44209971, accessed March 2, 2023.

109. See Jed S. Rakoff, "Why You Won't Get Your Day in Court," *New York Review of Books*, November 24, 2016, and Rakoff (2021). Another highly regarded judge, Richard Posner, became increasingly alarmed by the injustice associated with the courts' hostility toward people without lawyers, so-called pro-se. His effort to address the problem through a nonprofit center was overwhelmed and had to close. See Posner (2018), and Jenna Green, "The Short and Sorry Tale of Judge Posner's Center of Justice for Pro Se's," Law.com, September 10, 2019.

110. One case outside finance that involved intimidation of a whistleblower was that of Theranos, where low-level employees were tracked and threatened for revealing information that would harm the company's reputation and business success to a *Wall Street Journal* reporter. See Carreyrou (2018).

111. See note 98.

112. See William Cohan, "Was This Whistle-Blower Muzzled?," *New York Times*, September 21, 2013. The whistleblower, Richard Bowen, maintains an active blog on the issues. See https://richardmbowen.com/blog/, accessed May 30, 2023.

113. Bognanni (2022). This was the head of HVB's tax division. We do not know what happened to the earlier whistleblower at WestLB.

114. For details on this case, see note 58 to Chapter 14 and references there.

115. A new post-crisis program at the SEC and a few other regulatory agencies that pay whistleblowers offered two whistleblowers $8.25 million each, also meant to cover the legal fees they incurred. Mr. Ben Artzi declined to take his part in the award because the fine would be paid by shareholders rather than the managers who actually committed the fraud. See Tom Braithwaite, Kara Scannell, and Michael Mackenzie, "Deutsche Bank Whistleblower Spurns Share of $16.5m SEC Award," *Financial Times*, August 16, 2016.

116. The example of cum-ex discussed above illustrated the problem. In 2019, the European Union passed a directive "on the protection of persons that report breaches of Union law." See https://eur-lex.europa.eu/legal-content/EN/TXT/PDF/?uri=CELEX :32019L1937, accessed May 30, 2023. Member states should have transposed this directive into national law by December 17, 2021, but several of them failed to do so. According to Transparency International, Europe is still failing whistleblowers; see https://www .transparency.org/en/blog/eu-countries-continue-to-fail-whistleblowers, accessed March 7, 2023.

117. Other laws in the United States have a variety of programs, the strongest being associated with the False Claims Act discussed in note 106 above.

118. Hollywood producer Harvey Weinstein exploited his position to engage in sexual abuse for decades, using many techniques to intimidate victims and to prevent media investigations into his conduct. He had many enablers, including in the media. See Farrow (2019). For another example of many enablers of wrongdoings in Los Angeles, see Pringle (2022).

119. This was the inspiration for Admati's (2017) title, "It Takes a Village to Maintain a Dangerous Financial System," and speaks of the many enablers of the system that we discuss in this chapter.

120. The importance of spin in public discourse as a means of domination is the subject of Guriev and Treisman (2022) entitled *Spin Dictators*.

121. See Jack Ewing, "Bringing Bank Regulation to the Masses," *New York Times*, July 12, 2013. Indeed, some of our motivation in writing this book was to be able to help the media understand the issues better. Nevertheless, in many of our interactions with banking reporters, our impression was that they must quote the industry even knowing that the content is false and misleading. In one case, a reporter asked Anat Admati to write a letter to the editor challenging a piece of flawed commentary he wrote, seemingly wishing to show his sources in the industry that he is facing criticism to help them get their message out.

122. Mr. Dimon specifically complained that the rules would treat covered bonds, but not mortgage-backed securities, as liquid, i.e., saleable without loss at short notice. Covered bonds were prevalent in Europe and mortgage-backed securities in the United States, hence he viewed the rules as harming U.S. banks. See Kate Mackenzie, "Basel III Is 'Anti-American', Says Dimon," *Financial Times*, September 11, 2011.

123. As we discussed, Mr. Dimon conveniently overlooked the fact that, in August 2007, the markets for mortgage-backed securities had suddenly broken down, and the securities were not saleable at all. He also neglected that with mortgage-backed securities, unlike covered bonds, the issuing bank usually has no liability for paying the investors' claims

and therefore also has no incentive to check on the quality of the mortgages that stand behind the securities. As we discussed in Chapters 4 and 5, the lack of such incentives played a major role in the 2007–2009 crisis.

124. An editor of a major publication told Anat Admati privately that if a bank CEO submits an opinion piece, it is always published. We know of a number of incidents, relayed privately to us by journalists, where quotes that would be challenging to bankers or policymakers are omitted from stories. We also had such experiences ourselves. The links to pieces that challenge the banking industry, including a number of opinion pieces and letters to the editor we wrote in 2010–2013, have vanished from some media websites, even as almost all of those by the industry and its lobbies during the same period are still available. PDFs of all opinion pieces and letters by Anat Admati are posted at https://gsb-faculty .stanford.edu/anat-r-admati/opinion-pieces/. Luyendijk (2015), which we quoted at the end of Chapter 16, describes the relations between reporters and bankers or regulators as cozy. As we were finalizing the text for this book, journalists of a major Swiss newspaper mangled Martin Hellwig's answers to repeated questions about the "costs of equity." When he corrected the draft answers, they decided to cut the material from the interview, upon which he refused to have the interview published at all.

125. See Peter Osborne, "Why I Have Resigned from the Telegraph," *Open Democracy*, February 17, 2015, available at https://www.opendemocracy.net/en/opendemocracyuk /why-i-have-resigned-from-telegraph/, accessed March 1, 2023.

126. See Luigi Zingales, "Are Newspapers Captured by Banks? Evidence From Italy," *ProMarket*, May 12, 2016 https://www.promarket.org/2016/05/12/are-newspapers-captured -by-banks/accessed May 30, 2023.

127. For an analysis of the effects of Basel III that takes the IIF forecast apart, see Cecchetti (2015).

128. See Eric Lipton and Brooke Williams, "How Think Tanks Amplify Corporate America's Influence," *New York Times*, August 7, 2016.

129. A banking organization provided some support and its CEO moderated one of the panels. For a report on this conference by an industry self-regulatory institution, see https://www.sifma.org/resources/general/gwu-school-of-law-presents-financial-stability -after-dodd-frank-have-we-ended-too-big-to-fail/, accessed March 2, 2023.

130. Among the many instances discussed in the movie, as well as in Ferguson (2010), academic reports stating that the large Icelandic banks had sound and profitable business models figure prominently. As discussed in Baldursson and Portes (2013), these academic reports themselves were based on audited statements and regulatory reports that were entirely untrustworthy as they rested on untruthful information from the bankers. Like Johnsen (2014), Baldursson and Portes (2013) is based on the report of the Icelandic special investigation commission that was mentioned in note 2. This commission could access unfiltered information from every relevant institution and person in Iceland.

131. See Zingales (2013) regarding the general problem of bias by economists as well as the failure of the profession to acknowledge the possibility of such biases. See also Anat Admati, "Political Economy, Blind Spots, and a Challenge to Academics," *ProMarket*, November 15, 2015, mentioned in note 163 to Chapter 14. Kwak (2013) refers to "economism"

as a sort of religious belief that what we see must be efficient. This issue is discussed in Admati et al. (2013), Admati and Hellwig (2013) (the omitted chapter from this book; see note 161 to Chapter 14), and Pfleiderer (2018). Rodrik (2017) offers a balanced view on how economics can help and harm. Berman (2022), written by a sociologist, laments that economists have become influential and their focus on efficiency overwhelms other policy considerations.

132. See Admati and Hellwig (2013) and note 161 to Chapter 14.

133. Some referred to benefits from the liquidity of bank deposits and other short-term debt, some to the purported "discipline" that short-term debt imposes on managers afraid of runs, and some simply to the availability of cheap loans to nonfinancial firms; see French et al. (2010), Gorton (2010), as well as Raghu Rajan, "Did the Bankers Do It?" Project Syndicate, December 12, 2012, available at https://www.project-syndicate.org/commentary/why-blaming-bankers-for-the-crisis-is-bad-policy-by-raghuram-rajan?barrier=accesspaylog, accessed May 30, 2023. For criticisms, see Admati et al. (2013, Sections 5–7), Admati and Hellwig (2013, 2019) and Pfleiderer (2018).

134. Pfleiderer (2018) discusses the methodological issues in great detail.

135. Lancieri et al. (2022) argue that economists focusing on efficiency and using contrived arguments have greatly undermined the practice of competition law.

136. The theoretical analysis goes back to Baumol et al. (1982) and the markets to which it applies are called "contestable." A crucial assumption is that there be no *sunk costs*, i.e., fixed costs that a competitor must pay upfront, such as costs of advertising to reach potential clients. The obvious failure of this assumption in the real world has not prevented economists affiliated with network utilities from arguing that after market liberalization, markets for services that relied on the network were perfectly competitive and therefore no regulation was needed. As chair of the German Monopolies Commission in the early 2000s, Martin Hellwig had to rebut such arguments on numerous occasions.

137. Zingales (2015) asks whether finance benefits society.

138. Eucken (1940, 489). The paragraph is ostensibly concerned with cartels and monopolies around 1900, but contemporary readers might also have interpreted it as a comment on the Nazi economy.

139. Smith (1776).

140. Chandler (1990) suggests that cartel-based protection from competition in home markets provided German steel producers with a basis for conquering markets in other countries.

141. Bork (1978) interprets the formulation "in restraint of trade" as referring to the fact that price fixing usually leads to smaller quantities being sold. Posner (1976) points to the inefficiency involved when cartel participants invest resources to protect their cartels against deviators and outsiders, and against interference from politicians and authorities. Lancieri and Zingales, "Towards a Democratic Antitrust," *Truth on the Market*, 2019, available at https://truthonthemarket.com/author/zingalesandlancieri/, accessed May 29, 2023, and Lancieri et al. (2022) complain that the focus on efficiency considerations has diverted attention away from the distributive concerns of the law. In their view, the school founded

by Bork and Posner has contributed to a significant decline in antitrust thinking and antitrust enforcement.

142. As chair of the German Monopolies Commission in the early 2000s, Martin Hellwig experienced many monopolists or ex-monopolists parading this theme, usually with some outrage that they even had to appear before the Monopolies Commission.

143. See Tariq Fancy, "The Secret Diaries of a Sustainable Investor, Part 3," *Medium*, August 20, 2021 https://medium.com/@sosofancy/the-secret-diary-of-a-sustainable-investor-part-3-3c238cbodcbf accessed May 30, 2023. In the four-part series, Mr. Fancy discusses why he views the focus on metrics meant to capture "Environmental, Social, and Governance" as a dangerous diversion.

144. For an unpacking of the terminology and the issues, see Admati (2021) and Hellwig (2021), two contributions to a symposium on the question: "Capitalism: What Has Gone Wrong, What Needs to Change and How Can It Be Fixed?" Admati's article is available at https://gsb-faculty.stanford.edu/anat-r-admati/publications/capitalism-laws-and-the-need-for-trustworthy-institutions/ accessed May 30, 2023. For Hellwig's text, see https://academic.oup.com/oxrep/article/37/4/664/6423494 accessed May 30, 2023.

145. On anti-government and pro "free market" propaganda in the United States, see Oreskes and Conway (2023).

146. Wolf (2023).

147. Desmond (2023) describes how badly designed, poorly enforced and wasteful policies contribute to extreme inequality in the United States, where the poor are routinely deprived even of what they are entitled to while the rich use the system to their own advantage. Slobodian (2023) describes the actions of powerful people who seek to take control from democratic governments using narratives by which everything, including nation-states and the law, are for sale in "free markets."

148. Pistor (2019) ends her book on the role of law and lawyers in creating and exacerbating inequality by expressing concern that "naked power may prevail and we will be all worse for it." Scheidel (2017) expresses similar concerns about the symbiosis of political power and wealth generating ever more concentration of both—and exploitation of the rest of us.

149. Postman (1985) was re-published in 2006 with a new preface by Andrew Postman.

150. By now, we are bombarded with entertainment and nonsense even more than back in the 1980s or even the 2000s. See Andrew Postman, "My Dad Predicted Trump in 1985—It's Not Orwell, He Warned, It's Brave New World," *The Guardian*, February 2, 2017.

151. The term "alternative facts" was used by Kellyanne Conway, counselor to President Donald Trump who, in response to a question on NBC program *Meet the Press* about why White House Press Secretary Sean Spicer would "utter a provable falsehood" regarding the inauguration event of President Trump, particularly about the size of the crowd in the event, said "Our press secretary . . . gave alternative facts." Interviewer Chris Todd retorted that "alternative facts are not facts. They're falsehoods." See Alexandra Jaffe, "Kellyanne Conway: WH Spokesman Gave 'Alternative Facts' on Inauguration Crowd," NBC News, January 22, 2017.

152. Manipulation of information, deceptive practices, and the intentional creation of ignorance and confusion occur in many domains, not only banks and banking regulation. Typical examples involve damage from smoking, climate change, and gun control. See Oreskes and Conway (2012), with the telling title *Merchants of Doubt*. Historians Proctor and Schiebinger (2005) coined the term *agnotology* for the study of the strategic creation of ignorance in others.

REFERENCES

Abboud, Alice, Elizabeth Duncan, Akos Horvath, Diana Iercosan, Bert Loudis, Francis Martinez, Timothy Mooney, Ben Ranish, Ke Wang, Missaka Warusawitharana, and Carlo Wix. 2022. "COVID-19 as a Stress Test: Assessing the Bank Regulatory Framework." *Journal of Financial Stability* 61: 1–21.

Academic Advisory Committee. 2010. "Reform der Bankenregulierung und Bankenaufsicht nach der Finanzkrise" (Reforming Banking Regulation and Banking Supervision after the Financial Crisis). Report to the German Federal Ministry of Economic Affairs and Technology, Berlin. May.

———. 2017. "Zur Diskussion um Bargeld und die Null-Zins-Politik der Zentralbank" (A Contribution to the Discussion about Cash and about the Central Bank's Zero-Interest-Rate Policy). Report to the German Federal Ministry for Economic Affairs and Energy, Berlin. February.

Acemoglu, Daron, and James Robinson. 2012. *Why Nations Fail: The Origins of Power, Prosperity, and Poverty.* New York: Crown Publishers.

Acharya, Viral V., and Matthew Richardson. 2009. *Restoring Financial Stability.* New York: John Wiley and Sons.

Acharya, Viral V., and Sascha Steffen. 2012. "The 'Greatest' Carry Trade Ever? Understanding Eurozone Bank Risks." Working paper. Stern School of Business, New York University, New York, and European School of Management and Technology, Berlin. Subsequently published in 2015 *Journal of Financial Economics* 115 (2): 215–236.

Acharya, Viral V., and Tanju Yorulmazer. 2008. "Information Contagion and Bank Herding." *Journal of Money, Credit, and Banking* 40: 215–231.

Acharya, Viral V., Demos Gromb, and Tanju Yorulmazer. 2007. "Too Many to Fail—An Analysis of Time-Inconsistency in Bank Closure Policies." *Journal of Financial Intermediation* 16 (1): 1–31.

Acharya, Viral V., Thomas F. Cooley, Matthew P. Richardson, and Ingo Walter, eds. 2010. *Regulating Wall Street: The Dodd-Frank Act and the New Architecture of Global Finance.* New York: John Wiley and Sons.

Acharya, Viral V., Matthew Richardson, Stijn van Nieuwerburgh, and Lawrence J. White. 2011a. *Guaranteed to Fail: Fannie Mae, Freddie Mac, and the Debacle of Mortgage Finance*. Princeton, NJ: Princeton University Press.

Acharya, Viral V., Irvind Gujral, Nirupama Kulkarni, and Hyun Song Shin. 2011b. "Dividends and Bank Capital in the Financial Crisis of 2007–2009." NBER Working Paper 16896. National Bureau of Economic Research, Cambridge, MA.

Acharya, Viral V., Philipp Schnabl, and Gustavo Suarez. 2013. "Securitization without Risk Transfer." *Journal of Financial Economics* 107(3): 515–536.

Acheson, Greame G., Charles R. Hickson, and John D. Turner. 2010. "Does Limited Liability Matter? Evidence from Nineteenth-Century British Banking." *Review of Law and Economics* 6 (2): 247–273.

Ackermann, Josef. 2010. "The New Architecture of Financial Regulation: Will It Prevent Another Crisis?" LSE Special Discussion Paper 194. London School of Economics, London.

Adams, Renee. 2011. "Who Directs the Fed?" Working paper. Business School, University of Queensland, Australia.

Admati, Anat. 2010. "Comments on Proposal to Ensure the Loss Absorbency of Regulatory Capital at the Point of Non-viability: Consultative Document of the Basel Committee on Banking Supervision, August 2010." Stanford Graduate School of Business, Stanford, CA. October 1. https://www.gsb.stanford.edu/sites/gsb/files/stanfordunivers.pdf. Accessed May 30, 2023.

———. 2016. "The Missed Opportunity and Challenge of Capital Regulation." *National Institute Economic Review* 235 (1): R4–R14.

———. 2017. "It Takes a Village to Maintain a Dangerous Financial System." In *Just Financial Market? Finance in a Just Society*, ed. Lisa Herzog. Oxford: Oxford University Press.

———. 2019. "Towards a Better Financial System." Policy Brief, Economists for Inclusive Prosperity, https://econfip.org/policy-briefs/towards-a-better-financial-system/. Accessed April 4, 2023.

———. 2021. "Capitalism, Laws, and the Need for Trustworthy Institutions." *Oxford Review of Economic Policy* 37 (4): 678–689.

Admati, Anat R., and Martin F. Hellwig. 2011a. "Comments to the UK Independent Commission on Banking." July 4. https://gsb-faculty.stanford.edu/anat-r-admati/files/2022/04/admati-hellwig_icb-comments.pdf. Accessed May 30, 2023.

———. 2011b. "Good Banking Regulation Needs Clear Focus, Sensible Tools, and Political Will." Working paper. Stanford Graduate School of Business, Stanford, CA, and International Center for Financial Regulation, London. https://gsb-faculty.stanford.edu/anat-r-admati/files/2022/04/admati-hellwig_good_regulation.pdf. Accessed May 30, 2023.

———. 2013. "Does Debt Discipline Bankers? An Academic Myth about Bank Indebtedness." Rock Center for Corporate Governance at Stanford University Working Paper 132. Stanford University, Stanford, CA.

———. 2019. "Bank Leverage, Welfare and Regulation." In *Systemic Risk in the Financial Sector: Ten Years after the Great Crash*, ed. Douglas Arner et al., 217–233. Centre for International Governance Innovation, Waterloo, ON, Canada.

———. 2023. "The Parade of Bankers' New Clothes Continues: 38 Flawed Claims Debunked." Working Paper. Stanford University, Stanford, CA.

Admati, Anat R., Peter M. DeMarzo, Martin F. Hellwig, and Paul Pfleiderer. 2011. "Fallacies, Irrelevant Facts, and Myths in the Discussion of Capital Regulation: Why Bank Equity Is *Not* Expensive." Working Paper 86. Rock Center for Corporate Governance at Stanford University, and Research Paper 2065. Stanford Graduate School of Business, Stanford, CA; Preprint 2010/42, Max Planck Institute for Research on Collective Goods, Bonn, Germany.

———. 2012a. "Debt Overhang and Capital Regulation." Working paper, Rock Center for Corporate Governance at Stanford University; and research paper, Stanford Graduate School of Business, Stanford, CA; Preprint 2012/05, Max Planck Institute for Research on Collective Goods, Bonn, Germany.

———. 2012b. "Comments to the Federal Reserve on Sections 165 and 166 of the Dodd-Frank Act." Submitted to the Federal Reserve, April 30. https://www.federalreserve.gov /SECRS/2012/May/20120507/R-1438/R-1438_050312_107297_334689900548_1.pdf. Accessed May 30, 2023.

———. 2013. "Fallacies, Irrelevant Facts, and Myths in the Discussion of Capital Regulation: Why Bank Equity Is Not *Socially* Expensive." Working Paper. Stanford Graduate School of Business, Stanford, CA.

———. 2018. "The Leverage Ratchet Effect." *Journal of Finance* 73 (1): 145–198.

Admati, Anat, Peter Conti-Brown, and Paul Pfleiderer. 2012c. "Liability Holding Companies." *UCLA Law Review* 852: 852–913.

Agarwal, Sumit, Gene Amromin, Itzhak Ben-David, Souphala Chomsisengphet, and Douglas Evanoff. 2011. "The Role of Securitization in Mortgage Renegotiation." *Journal of Financial Economics* 102 (3): 559–578.

Agarwal, Sumit, David Lucca, Amit Seru, and Francesco Trebbi. 2014. "Inconsistent Regulators: Evidence from Banking." *The Quarterly Journal of Economics* 129(2): 889–938.

Ahamed, Liaquat. 2009. *Lords of Finance*. New York: Penguin.

Aiyar, Shekhar, Charles W. Calomiris, and Tomasz Wieladek. 2012. "Does Macro-Pru Leak? Evidence from a UK Policy Experiment." NBER Working Paper 17822. National Bureau of Economic Research, Cambridge, MA.

Akerlof, George A. 1970. "The Market for 'Lemons': Quality Uncertainty and the Market Mechanism." *Quarterly Journal of Economics* 84 (3): 488–500.

Akerlof, George A., and Paul M. Romer. 1993. "Looting: The Economic Underworld of Bankruptcy for Profit." *Brookings Papers on Economic Activity* 1993 (2): 1–73.

Alesina, Alberto, and Lawrence J. Summers. 1993. "Central Bank Independence and Macroeconomic Performance: Some Comparative Evidence." *Journal of Money, Credit, and Banking* 25 (2): 151–162.

Alessandri, Piergiorgio, and Andrew G. Haldane. 2009. "Banking on the State." Paper presented at the Federal Reserve Bank of Chicago's 12th Annual International Banking Conference, September 25.

Allen, William, Reinier Kraakman, and Guhan Subramanian. 2009. *Commentaries and Cases on the Law of Business Organization*, 3rd ed. Richland Hills, TX: Aspen.

Alley, Patrick. 2022. *Very Bad People: The Inside Story of Our Fight Against the World's Network of Corruption.* London: Monoray.

Allison, Herbert M. 2011. *The Megabanks Mess.* Kindle Single. Seattle: Amazon Digital Services.

Anderson, Ronald W., and Karin Jöeveer. 2012. "Bankers and Bank Investors: Reconsidering the Economies of Scale in Banking." Financial Markets Group Discussion Paper 712. London School of Economics.

Ang, Andrew, Sergey Gorovyy, and Gregory B. van Inwegen. 2011. "Hedge Fund Leverage." NBER Working Paper 16801. National Bureau of Economic Research, Cambridge, MA.

Angelini, Paolo, Laurent Clerc, Vasco Cúrdia, Leonardo Gambacorta, Andrea Gerali, Alberto Locarno, Roberto Motto, Werner Roeger, Skander Van den Heuvel, and Jan Vlček. 2011. "Basel III: Long-Term Impact on Economic Performance and Fluctuation." Staff Report 485. Federal Reserve Bank of New York, New York.

Aron, Janine, and John Muellbauer. 2010. "The Second UK Mortgage Crisis: Modelling and Forecasting Mortgage Arrears and Possessions." Oxford Housing Seminar. Nuffield College, Oxford University, Oxford, England. February 26.

ASC (Advisory Scientific Committee of the European Systemic Risk Board). 2012. "Forbearance, Resolution and Deposit Insurance." Report 1. Frankfurt, Germany, July.

———. 2014. "Is Europe Overbanked?" Report 4. Frankfurt, Germany, June.

Ash, Michael, Zeke Ash, and Rich Puchalsky. 2020. "The Bank's Take on the Paycheck Protection Program." University of Massachusetts Amherst: Political Economy Research Institute Research Brief.

Atkinson, Nathan. 2023. "Corporate Liability, Collateral Consequences, and Capital Structure." *Columbia Business Law Review* 2023 (1): 1–68.

Avalos, Fernando, Torsten Ehlers, and Egemen Eren. 2019. "September Stress in Dollar Repo Markets: Passing or Structural?" *BIS Quarterly Review*, December 12–14.

Avgouleas, Emilios, and Charles Goodhart. 2015. "Critical Reflections on Bank Bail-ins." *Journal of Financial Regulation* 1 (1): 3–29.

Bagehot, Walter. [1873] 1906. *Lombard Street: A Description of the Money Market.* New York: Charles Scribner's Sons.

Bair, Sheila. 2012. *Bull by the Horns: Fighting to Save Main Street from Wall Street and Wall Street from Itself.* New York: Free Press.

Baker, Raymond W. 2023. *Invisible Trillions: How Financial Secrecy Is Imperiling Capitalism and Democracy and the Way to Renew Our Broken System.* San Francisco, CA: Berrett-Koehler Publishers.

Baldursson, Fridrik, and Richard Portes. 2013. "Gambling for Resurrection in Iceland: The Rise and Fall of the Banks." Centre for Economic Policy Research. CEPR Discussion Paper No. 9664.

Ball, Laurence H. 2018. *The Fed and Lehman Brothers: Setting the Record Straight on a Financial Disaster.* Cambridge, UK: Cambridge University Press.

Baltensperger, E., and Jean Dermine. 1987. "Banking Deregulation in Europe." *Economic Policy* 2 (4): 63–109.

Bancel, Franck, Nalinaksha Bhattacharyya, Usha R. Mittoo. 2009. "Cross-Country Determinants of Payout Policy: European Firms." In *Dividends and Dividend Policy*, ed. H. Kent Baker. Hoboken, NJ: John Wiley and Sons.

Barofsky, Neil. 2012. *Bailout: An Inside Account of How Washington Abandoned Main Street while Rescuing Wall Street.* New York: Free Press.

Barth, James R., and Martin A. Regalia. 1988. "The Evolving Role of Regulation in the Savings and Loan Industry." In *The Financial Services Revolution: Policy Directions for the Future*, ed. Catherine England and Thomas Huertas. Boston: Kluwer. 113–161.

Barth, James R., Gerard Caprio, Jr., and Ross Levine. 2012. *Guardians of Finance: Making Regulators Work for Us.* Cambridge, MA: MIT Press.

Barth, Mary E., and Wayne R. Landsman. 2010. "How Did Financial Reporting Contribute to the Financial Crisis?" *European Accounting Review* 19 (3): 1–25.

Baumol, William J., John C. Panzar, and Robert D. Willig. 1982. *Contestable Markets and the Theory of Industry Structure.* New York: Harcourt, Brace, Jovanovich.

BCBS (Basel Committee on Banking Supervision). 2004. "International Convergence of Capital Measurement and Capital Standards: A Revised Framework." Discussion Paper 107. Bank for International Settlements, Basel. June.

———. 2010a. "An Assessment of the Long-Term Economic Impact of Stronger Capital and Liquidity Requirements." Discussion Paper 173. Bank for International Settlements, Basel. August.

———. 2010b. "Proposal to Ensure the Loss Absorbency of Regulatory Capital at the Point of Non-viability." Consultative Document 174. Bank for International Settlements, Basel.

———. 2010c. "The Basel Committee's Response to the Financial Crisis: Report to the G20." Discussion Paper 179. Bank for International Settlements, Basel.

———. 2010d. "Calibrating Regulatory Minimum Capital Requirements and Capital Buffers: A Top-Down Approach." Discussion Paper 180. Bank for International Settlements, Basel.

———. 2010e. "Basel III: A Global Regulatory Framework for More Resilient Banks and Banking Systems." Discussion Paper 189. Bank for International Settlements, Basel.

———. 2011a. "Resolution Policies and Frameworks—Progress So Far." Discussion Paper 200. Bank for International Settlements, Basel.

———. 2011b. "Global Systemically Important Banks: Assessment Methodology and the Additional Loss Absorbency Requirement." Discussion Paper 201. Bank for International Settlements, Basel.

———. 2011c. "Important Banks: Assessment Methodology and the Additional Loss Absorbency Requirement." Discussion Paper 207. Bank for International Settlements, Basel.

———. 2012a. "A Framework for Dealing with Domestic Systemically Important Banks." Discussion Paper 233. Bank for International Settlements, Basel.

———. 2012b. "Core Principles of Effective Banking Supervision." Bank for International Settlements, Basel. September.

———. 2016a. "Reducing Variation in Credit Risk-Weighted Assets—Constraints on the Use of Internal Model Approaches." Discussion Paper 362. Bank for International Settlements, Basel. March.

———. 2016b. "Standard TLAC Holdings: Amendments to the Basel III standard on the definition of Capital." Bank for International Settlements, Basel. October.

———. 2017. "Basel III: Finalising Post-Crisis Reforms." Discussion Paper 424. Bank for International Settlements, Basel. December.

———. 2021. "Voluntary Disclosures of Sovereign Exposures." Bank for International Settlements, Basel. November.

Beattie, Vivien, Charles Sutcliffe, Richard Dale, Peter Casson, and George McKenzie. 1995. *Banks and Bad Debts: Accounting for Loan Losses in International Banking.* London: John Wiley.

Beaver, William H., and Ellen E. Engel. 1996. "Discretionary Behavior with Respect to Allowance for Loan Losses and the Behavior of Securities Prices." *Journal of Accounting and Economics* 22: 177–206.

Bebchuk, Lucian A., and Holger Spamann. 2010. "Regulating Bankers' Pay." *Georgetown Law Journal* 98 (2): 247–287.

Bebchuk, Lucian A., Alma Cohen, and Holger Spamann. 2010. "The Wages of Failure: Executive Compensation at Bear Stearns and Lehman 2000–2008." *Yale Journal of Regulation* 27: 257–282.

Beer, Christian, Ernest Gnan, and Urs W. Birchler, eds. 2016. *Cash on Trial, SUERF Conference Proceedings 2016/1*, Wien und Zürich. https://www.suerf.org/docx/SUERF _Conference_Proceedings_2016_1.pdf. Accessed April 5, 2023.

Behn, Markus, Rainer Haselmann, and Vikrant Vig. 2022. "The Limits of Model-Based Regulation." *Journal of Finance* 77 (3): 1635–1684.

Bell, Sarah, Michael Chui, Tamara Gomes, and Paul Moser-Boehm. 2023. "Why Are Central Banks Reporting Losses? Does It Matter?" *BIS Bulletin* 68. Bank for International Settlements, Basel.

Ben-David, Itzhak. 2011. "Financial Constraints and Inflated Home Prices during the Real-Estate Boom." *American Economic Journal: Applied Economics* 3 (3): 55–78.

Benston, George J., Mike Carhill, and Brian Olasov. 1991. "The Failure and Survival of Thrifts: Evidence from the Southeast." In *Financial Markets and Financial Crises*, ed. R. Glenn Hubbard. Chicago: University of Chicago Press.

Berger, Allen N., William C. Hunter, and Stephen G. Timme. 1993. "The Efficiency of Financial Institutions: A Review and Preview of Research Past, Present, and Future." *Journal of Banking and Finance* 17: 221–249.

Berger, Allen N., Richard J. Herring, and Giorgio P. Szegö. 1995. "The Role of Capital in Financial Institutions." *Journal of Banking and Finance* 19: 393–430.

Berglöf, Erik, and H. Sjögren. 1998. "Combining Control-Oriented and Arm's-Length Finance—Evidence from Main Bank Relationships in Sweden." In *Comparative Corporate Governance: The State of the Art and Emerging Research*, ed. Klaus J. Hopt,

Hideki Kanda, Mark J. Roe, Eddy Wymeersh, and Stefan Progge. Oxford, England: Oxford University Press.

Bericht. 2014. *Bericht der unabhängigen Untersuchungskommission zur transparenten Aufklärung der Vorkommnisse rund um die Hypo Alpe-Adria.* [Report of the independent committee charged with investigating the case of Hypo Group Alpe-Adria]. December 2, 2014. Vienna, Austria.

Berk, Jonathan, and Peter DeMarzo. 2011. *Corporate Finance,* 2nd ed. Englewood Cliffs, NJ: Prentice Hall.

Berman, Elizabeth Popp. 2022. *Thinking Like an Economist: How Efficiency Replaced Equality in U.S. Public Policy.* Princeton, NJ: Princeton University Press.

Bernanke, Ben S. 1983. "Nonmonetary Effects of the Financial Crisis in Propagation of the Great Depression." *American Economic Review* 73 (3): 257–276.

———. 1995. "The Macroeconomics of the Great Depression: A Comparative Approach." *Journal of Money, Credit, and Banking* 27 (1): 1–28.

Bernanke, Ben S., and John Y. Campbell. 1988. "Is There a Corporate Debt Crisis?" *Brookings Papers on Economic Activity* 19 (1): 83–140.

Bernanke, Ben S., and Cara S. Lown. 1991. "The Credit Crunch." *Brookings Papers on Economic Activity* 22 (2): 205–248.

Bernanke, Ben, Mark Gertler, and Simon Gilchrist. 1996. "The Financial Accelerator and the Flight to Quality." *Review of Economics and Statistics* 78 (1): 1–15.

Berra, Yogi. 1998. *The Yogi Book: "I Really Didn't Say Everything I Said!"* United Kingdom: Workman Pub.

Better Markets. 2012. "The Costs of the Financial Crisis." Available at http://bettermarkets .com/sites/default/files/Cost%20Of%20The%20Crisis_1.pdf. Accessed September 22, 2012.

Bhagat, Sanjai, and Brian Bolton. 2011. "Bank Executive Compensation and Capital Requirements Reform." Working paper. University of Colorado, Boulder.

Bhide, Amar. 2010. *Call for Judgment: Sensible Finance for a Dynamic Economy.* Oxford, England: Oxford University Press.

Bibler, Jared. 2021. *Iceland's Secret: The Untold Story of the World's Biggest Con.* Petersfield, UK: Harriman House.

Bichsel, Robert, and Jürg Blum. 2005. "Capital Regulation of Banks: Where Do We Stand and Where Are We Going." *Quarterly Bulletin of the Swiss National Bank* 4: 42–51.

BIS (Bank for International Settlements). 2008. *78th Annual Report, 1 April 2007–31 March 2008.* Basel.

———. 2009. *79th Annual Report, 1 April 2008–31 March 2009.* Basel.

———. 2012. 82nd Annual Report, April 2011–March 2012. Basel.

Black, Fischer, and Myron S. Scholes. 1973. "The Pricing of Options and Corporate Liabilities." *Journal of Political Economy* 81 (3): 637–654.

Blattner, Niklaus. 1995. "Panel Discussion—Statements and Comments." *Swiss Journal of Economics and Statistics* 131: 819–830.

Blum, Jürg. 2008. "Why 'Basel II' May Need a Leverage Ratio Restriction." *Journal of Banking and Finance* 32: 1699–1707.

Blundell-Wignall, Adrian, and Paul Atkinson. 2009. "Origins of the Financial Crisis and Requirements for Reform." *Journal of Asian Economics* 20 (5): 536–548.

Bognanni, Massimo. 2022. *Unter den Augen des Staates: Der größte Steuerraub in der Geschichte der Bundesrepublik.* [Under the eyes of the state: organized crime and the failure of the state in the cum-ex scandal]. Munich: dtv Verlagsgesellschaft.

Bolton, Patrick, and Xavier Freixas. 2006. "Corporate Finance and the Monetary Transmission Mechanism." *Review of Financial Studies* 19: 829–870.

Bolton, Patrick, and Martin Oehmke. 2012. "Should Derivatives Be Privileged in Bankruptcy?" Working paper. Columbia University, New York. July 3.

Boot, Arnoud. 2011. "Banking at the Cross Roads: How to Deal with Marketability and Complexity?" Amsterdam Business School, University of Amsterdam; Centre for Economic Policy Research (CEPR); and Tinbergen Institute, Amsterdam.

Borges, Antonio. 1990. "Portuguese Banking in the Single European Market." In *European Banking in the 1990s,* ed. Jean Dermine. Oxford, England: Blackwell. 325–343.

Bork, Robert H. 1978. *The Antitrust Paradox: A Policy at War with Itself.* Bork Publishing.

Bowman, William D. 1937. *The Story of the Bank of England.* London: Jenkins.

Boyd, John H., and Gianni De Nicolò. 2005. "The Theory of Bank Risk Taking and Competition Revisited." *Journal of Finance* 60 (3): 1329–1343.

Boyd, John H., and Mark Gertler. 1994. "The Role of Large Banks in the Recent US Banking Crisis." *Federal Reserve Bank of Minneapolis Quarterly Review* 18 (1): 2–21.

Boyd, John H., and Amanda Heitz. 2011. "The Social Costs and Benefits of Too-Big- to-Fail Banks: A Bounding Exercise." Working paper. University of Minnesota, Minneapolis.

Brady, Henry E., and Thomas B. Kent. 2022. "Fifty Years of Declining Confidence & Increasing Polarization in Trust in American Institutions." *Dædalus* 151 (4): 43–66.

Brady, Stephanie A., Ken E. Anadu, and Nathaniel R. Cooper. 2012. "The Stability of Prime Money Market Funds: Sponsor Support from 2007 to 2011." Working Paper RPA12-3. Federal Reserve Bank of Boston, Boston. August.

Brandeis, Louis Dembitz. [1914] 2010. *Other People's Money, and How the Bankers Use It.* New York: Fredrick A. Stokes. Reprint Seattle: Amazon Digital Services.

Brealey, Richard A. 2006. "Basel II: The Route Ahead or Cul-de-Sac?" *Journal of Applied Corporate Finance* 4: 34–43.

Brealey, Richard A., Ian A. Cooper, and Evi Kaplanis. 2011. "International Propagation of the Credit Crisis." Mimeo. London Business School, London.

Brewer, Elijah, and Julapa A. Jagtiani. 2009. "How Much Did Banks Pay to Become Too-Big-to-Fail and to Become Systemically Important?" Working Paper 09-34. Federal Reserve Bank of Philadelphia, Philadelphia.

Brierley, Peter. 2009. "The UK Special Resolution Regime for Failing Banks in an International Context." Financial Stability Paper No. 5. Bank of England, London.

Bruni, Franco. 1990. "Banking and Financial Reregulation: The Italian Case." In *European Banking in the 1990s,* ed. Jean Dermine. Oxford, England: Blackwell. 241–267.

Brunnermeier, Markus. 2009. "Deciphering the Liquidity and Credit Crunch, 2007–08." *Journal of Economic Perspectives* 23 (1): 77–100.

Brunnermeier, Markus, and Martin Oehmke. 2013. "The Maturity Rat Race." *Journal of Finance* 68 (2): 483–521.

Bryant, John. 1980. "A Model of Reserves, Bank Runs, and Deposit Insurance." *Journal of Banking and Finance* 4: 335–344.

Buch, Claudia M., and Esteban Prieto. 2012. "Do Better Capitalized Banks Lend Less? Long-Run Panel Evidence from Germany." Working Papers in Economics and Finance 37. Faculty of Economics and Social Sciences, University of Tübingen, Tübingen, Germany.

Bullough, Oliver. 2018. *Moneyland: Why Thieves and Crooks Now Rule the World and How to Take It Back*. London: Profile Books.

Burnside, Craig. 2011. "Carry Trades and Risk." NBER Working Paper 17278. National Bureau of Economic Research, Cambridge, MA.

Caglio, Cecilia, Jennifer Dlugosz, and Marcelo Rezende. 2023. "Flight to Safety in the Regional Bank Crisis of 2023." Working Paper. Washington, DC: Board of Governors of the Federal Reserve.

Calomiris, Charles W., and Gary Gorton. 1991. "The Origins of Banking Panics: Models, Facts and Bank Regulation." In *Financial Markets and Financial Crises*, ed. R. Glenn Hubbard. Chicago: University of Chicago Press. 109–173.

Calomiris, Charles W., and Richard J. Herring. 2011. "Why and How to Design a Contingent Convertible Debt Requirement." Working paper. Finance Department, University of Pennsylvania, Philadelphia, and Columbia Business School, Columbia University, New York.

Calomiris, Charles W., and Charles M. Kahn. 1991. "The Role of Demandable Debt in Structuring Optimal Banking Arrangements." *American Economic Review* 81: 497–513.

Calomiris, Charles W., and Joseph R. Mason. 1997. "Contagion and Bank Failures during the Great Depression: The June 1932 Chicago Banking Panic." *American Economic Review* 87 (5): 863–883.

Caminal, Ramon, Jordi Gual, and Xavier Vives. 1990. "Competition in Spanish Banking." In *European Banking in the 1990s*, ed. Jean Dermine. Oxford, England: Blackwell. 271–321.

Campbell, John J., Stefano Giglio, and Parag Pathak. 2011. "Forced Sales and House Prices." *American Economic Review* 101 (5): 2108–2131.

Caprio, Gerald, and Daniela Klingebiel. 1996. "Bank Insolvencies, Cross-Country Experiences." Policy Research Working Paper 1620. World Bank, Washington, DC.

———. 1997. "Bank Insolvency: Bad Luck, Bad Policy, or Bad Banking?" Paper written for the Annual World Bank Conference on Development Economics, April 25–26, 1996.

Carbo-Valverde, Santiago, Edward J. Kane, and Francisco Rodriguez-Fernandez. 2011. "Safety-Net Benefit Conferred on Difficult-to-Fail-and-Unwind Banks in the US and EU before and during the Great Recession." Working paper. Department of Finance, Boston College, Boston.

Carpenter, Daniel, and David Moss, eds. 2013. *Preventing Regulatory Capture: Special Interest Influence and How to Limit It*. New York: Cambridge University Press.

Carreyrou, John. 2018. *Bad Blood: Secrets and Lies in a Silicon Valley Startup.* New York: Alfred A. Knopf.

Carruth, Paul J. 2003. "Accounting for Stock Options: A Historical Perspective." *Journal of Business and Economics Research* 1 (5): 9–14.

CEC (Commission of the European Communities). 1988. *Research on the Costs of Non-Europe: Basic Findings.* Vol. 9. Luxembourg City.

Cecchetti, Stephen G. 2009. "Crisis and Responses: The Federal Reserve in the Early Stages of the Financial Crisis." *Journal of Economic Perspectives* 23 (1): 51–75.

———. 2015. "The Jury Is In." In *The New International Financial System: Analyzing the Cumulative Impact of Regulatory Reform,* ed. Douglas D. Evanoff, Andrew G. Haldane, and George G. Kaufman, 407–423. World Scientific Publishing.

Chandler, Alfred. 1990. *Scale and Scope: The Dynamics of Industrial Capitalism.* Cambridge, MA: Harvard University Press.

Chari, V. V. 2022. "Larry Ball's *The Fed and Lehman Brothers*: A Review Essay." *Journal of Economic Literature* 60 (4): 1503–1508.

Cochrane, John H. 2005. "The Risk and Return of Venture Capital." *Journal of Financial Economics* 75: 3–52.

Coelho, Rodrigo, Amélie Monteil, Vasily Pozdyshev, and Jean-Philippe Svoronos. 2022. "Supervisory Practices for Assessing the Sustainability of Banks' Business Models." FSI Insights on Policy Implementation No. 40, Financial Stability Institute: Basel.

Coffee, John. 2020. *Corporate Crime and Punishment: The Crisis of Underenforcement.* Oakland, CA: Berrett-Koehler Publishers.

Cohan, William D. 2012. *Money and Power: How Goldman Sachs Came to Rule the World.* New York: Anchor.

Cole, Rebel A. 2012. "How Did the Financial Crisis Affect Small-Business Lending in the U.S.?" Research study. U.S. Small Business Administration, Washington, DC.

Connaughton, Jeff. 2012. *Payoff: Why Wall Street Always Wins.* Westport, CT: Prospecta Press.

Conti-Brown, Peter. 2016. *The Power and Independence of the Federal Reserve.* Princeton, NJ: Princeton University Press.

Conti-Brown, Peter, and David Skeel, eds. 2012. *When States Go Broke: The Origins, Context, and Solutions for the American States in Fiscal Crisis.* New York: Cambridge University Press.

Copeland, Adam, Antoine Martin, and Michael Walker. 2012. "Repo Runs: Evidence from the Tri-Party Repo Market." Staff Report 506. Federal Reserve Bank of New York, New York.

Cornford, F. M. 1908. *Microcosmographia Academica.* Cambridge, England: Bowes & Bowes.

Correctiv. 2018. "The Cum-Ex Files: A Cross-Border Investigation." https://correctiv.org/top-stories/2018/10/18/cumex-files/. Accessed April 6, 2023.

———. 2021. "Cum-Ex Files 2.0." https://correctiv.org/en/latest-stories/2021/10/21/cumex-files-2/. Accessed April 6, 2023.

Crandall, Robert W. 1991. *After the Breakup: U.S. Telecommunications in a More Competitive Era.* Washington, DC: Brookings Institution.

Cumming, Christine, and Robert A. Eisenbeis. 2010. "Resolving Troubled Systemically Important Cross-Border Financial Institutions: Is a New Corporate Organizational Form Required?" Staff Report 457. Federal Reserve Bank of New York.

Curry, Timothy, and Lynn Shibut. 2000. "The Costs of the Savings and Loan Crisis: Truth and Consequences." *FDIC Banking Review* 13: 26–35.

Das, Satyajit. 2010. *Traders, Guns and Money: Knowns and Unknowns in the Dazzling World of Derivatives.* Rev. ed. Financial Times Series. Englewood Cliffs, NJ: Prentice Hall.

———. 2011. *Extreme Money: Masters of the Universe and the Cult of Risk.* Upper Saddle River, NJ: FT Press.

Davies, Richard, and Belinda Tracey. 2012. "Too Big to Be Efficient? The Impact of Implicit Funding Subsidies on Scale Economies in Banking." Working paper. Bank of England, London.

Davydenko, Sergei A., Ilya A. Strebulaev, and Xiaofei Zhao. 2012. "A Market-Based Study of the Cost of Default." *Review of Financial Studies* 25 (10): 2599–2999.

deHaan, Ed, Simi Kedia, Kevin Koh, and Shivaram Rajgopal. 2015. "The Revolving Door and the SEC's Enforcement Outcomes: Initial Evidence from Civil Litigation." *Journal of Accounting and Economics* 60 (2–3): 65–96.

Dell'Ariccia, Giovanni, Luc Laeven, and Deniz Igan. 2008. "Credit Booms and Lending Standards: Evidence from the Subprime Mortgage Market." IMF Working Paper 08/106. International Monetary Fund, Washington, DC.

DeMarzo, Peter, and Zhiguo He. 2021. "Leverage Dynamics without Commitment." *Journal of Finance* 76 (3): 1195–1250.

Demirgüç-Kunt, Asli, Edward J. Kane, and Luc Laeven. 2008. "Determinants of Deposit-Insurance Adoption and Design." *Journal of Financial Intermediation* 17 (3): 407–438.

Demirgüç-Kunt, Asli, Enrica Detragiache, and Ouarda Merrouche. 2010. "Bank Capital: Lessons from the Financial Crisis." Policy Research Working Paper 5473. World Bank, Washington, DC.

De Mooij, Ruud A. 2011. "Tax Biases to Debt Finance: Assessing the Problem, Finding Solutions." IMF staff discussion note. International Monetary Fund, Washington, DC. May 3.

Demyanyk, Yuliya, and Otto Van Hemert. 2009. "Understanding the Subprime Mortgage Crisis." *Review of Financial Studies* 24 (6): 1848–1880.

Dermine, Jean. 1990. *European Banking in the 1990s.* Oxford, England: Blackwell.

Desmond, Matthew. 2023. *Poverty, by America.* New York: Crown Publishing Group.

Deutscher Bundestag. 2017. *Bericht des 4. Untersuchungsausschusses nach Artikel 44 des Grundgesetzes* [Report of the 4th Investigation Committee according to Art. 44 of the Basic Law]. https://dserver.bundestag.de/btd/18/127/1812700.pdf. Accessed March 28, 2023.

———. 2021. *Bericht des 3. Untersuchungsausschusses nach Artikel 44 des Grundgesetzes* [Report of the 3rd Investigation Committee according to Art. 44 of the Basic Law]. https://dserver.bundestag.de/btd/19/309/1930900.pdf. Accessed April 5, 2023.

Dewatripont, Mathias, and Jean Tirole. 1994. *The Prudential Regulation of Banks.* Cambridge, MA: MIT Press.

———. 2012. "Macroeconomic Shocks and Banking Regulation." *Journal of Money, Credit, and Banking* 44(2): 237–254.

DFPI (Department of Financial Protection and Innovation). 2023. "Review of DFPI's Oversight and Regulation of Silicon Valley Bank." State of California, May 8.

Diamond, Douglas W. 1984. "Financial Intermediation and Delegated Monitoring." *Review of Economic Studies* 51: 193–414.

———. 1991. "Monitoring and Reputation: The Choice between Bank Loans and Directly Placed Debt." *Journal of Political Economy* 99 (4): 689–721.

Diamond, Douglas W., and Phillip H. Dybvig. 1983. "Bank Runs, Deposit Insurance, and Liquidity." *Journal of Political Economy* 91: 401–419.

Diamond, Douglas W., and Raghuram G. Rajan. 2000. "A Theory of Bank Capital." *Journal of Finance* 55: 2431–2465.

———. 2001. "Liquidity Risk, Liquidity Creation and Financial Fragility." *Journal of Political Economy* 109: 287–327.

Donaldson, Jason R., Denis Gromb, and Giorgia Piacentino. 2020. "The paradox of pledgeability." *Journal of Financial Economics* 137(3): 591–605.

Douglas, Paul H., Irving Fisher, Frank D. Graham, Earl J. Hamilton, Willford I. King, and Charles D. Whittlesay. 1939. "A Program for Monetary Reform." Mimeo. July.

Duffie, Darrell. 2012. "Re-plumbing Our Financial System: Uneven Progress." Working paper. Stanford University, Stanford, CA.

———. 2016. "Financial Regulatory Reform after the Crisis: An Assessment." ECB Forum on Central Banking, June 27–29.

Dunbar, Nicholas. 2011. *The Devil's Derivatives: The Untold Story of the Slick Traders and Hapless Regulators Who Almost Blew Up Wall Street . . . and Are Ready to Do It Again.* Cambridge, MA: Harvard Business Review Press.

Dunstan, Roger. 1995. "Overview of New York City's Fiscal Crisis." Sacramento, CA: California Research Bureau. March 1.

Dyck, Alexander, Adair Morse, and Luigi Zingales. 2010. "Who Blows the Whistle on Corporate Fraud?" *Journal of Finance* 65 (6): 2213–2253.

EBA (European Banking Authority). 2019. *EBA Report on NPLs: Progress Made and Challenges Ahead.*

Eichengreen, Barry J. 1992. *Golden Fetters: The Gold Standard and the Great Depression, 1919–1939.* Oxford, England: Oxford University Press.

Eisinger, Jesse. 2017. *The Chickenshit Club: Why the Justice Department Fails to Prosecute Executives.* New York: Simon & Schuster.

Ellis, Luci. 2008. "The Housing Meltdown: Why Did It Happen in the United States?" Working Paper 259. Bank for International Settlements, Basel.

Englund, Peter. 1990. "Financial Deregulation in Sweden." *European Economic Review* 34: 385–393.

———. 1999. "The Swedish Banking Crisis—Roots and Consequences." *Oxford Review of Economic Policy* 15 (3): 80–97.

Enria, Andrea. 2017. "The EU Banking Sector—Risks and Recovery: A Single Market Perspective." Presentation at the ESM Seminar, Luxembourg, January 30.

Enrich, David. 2017. *The Spider Network: The Wild Story of a Math Genius, a Gang of Backstabbing Bankers, and One of the Greatest Scams in Financial History.* New York: Custom House.

———. 2020. *Dark Towers: Deutsche Bank, Donald Trump, and an Epic Trail of Destruction.* New York: Custom House.

ESMA (European Securities and Markets Authority). 2019. "Preliminary Findings on Multiple Withholding Tax Reclaim Schemes." Report of the European Securities and Markets Authority 70-154-1193, Paris, July 2.

ESRB (European Systemic Risk Board). 2012. "Recommendation of the European Systemic Risk Board of 20 December 2012 on Money Market Funds. (ESRB/2012/1)." *Official Journal of the European Union* C146/1 of May 25, 2013.

———. 2015. "ESRB Report on the Regulatory Treatment of Sovereign Exposures." March. Frankfurt.

———. 2022. "Recommendation of the European Systemic Risk Board of 2 December 2021 on reform of Money Market Funds. (ESRB/2021/9)." *Official Journal of the European Union* C129/1 of March 3, 2022.

Esty, Benjamin C. 1998. "The Impact of Contingent Liability on Commercial Bank Risk Taking." *Journal of Financial Economics* 47: 189–218.

Eucken, Walter. 1940. "Wissenschaft im Stile Schmollers" [Scholarship in the Style of Schmoller]. *Weltwirtschaftliches Archiv* 52: 468–506.

European Policy Studies Task Force. 2010. "Bank State Aid in the Financial Crisis—Fragmentation or Level Playing Field?" CEPS Task Force Report. Centre for European Policy Studies, Brussels.

Expertenrat (Expert group of the German federal government). 2011. "Strategien für den Ausstieg des Bundes aus krisenbedingten Beteiligungen an Banken: Gutachten des von der Bundesregierung eingesetzten Expertenrats" (Strategies for an exit of the federal government from its crisis-induced participations in banks: Report to the federal government). https://www.coll.mpg.de/34666/gutachten-bankenbeteiligung.pdf. Accessed May 30, 2023.

Fabo, Brian, Martina Jancokova, Elisabeth Kempf, and Lubos Pastor. 2021. "Fifty Shades of QE: Comparing Findings of Central Bankers and Academics." *Journal of Monetary Economics* 120: 1–20.

Fahlenbrach, Rüdiger, and René Stulz. 2011. "Bank CEO Incentives and the Credit Crisis." *Journal of Financial Economics* 99: 11–26.

Farber, David B., Marilyn F. Johnson, and Kathy R. Petroni. 2007. "Congressional Intervention in the Standard-Setting Process: An Analysis of the Stock Option Accounting Reform Act of 2004." *Accounting Horizons* 21 (1): 1–22.

Farhi, Emmanuel, and Jean Tirole. 2012. "Collective Moral Hazard, Maturity Mismatch, and Systemic Bailouts." *American Economic Review* 102 (1): 60–93.

Farrow, Ronan. 2019. *Catch and Kill: Lies, Spies, and a Conspiracy to Protect Predators.* Boston: Little, Brown and Company.

FCIC (Financial Crisis Inquiry Commission). 2011. *The Financial Crisis Inquiry Report.* Washington, DC: U.S. Government Printing Office.

FDIC (Federal Deposit Insurance Corporation). 2023. "FDIC Supervision of Signature Bank."

Federal Reserve. 2023. "Review of the Federal Reserve's Supervision and Regulation of Silicon Valley Bank."

Federal Reserve Bank of Dallas. 2012. "Choosing the Road to Prosperity: Why We Must End Too Big to Fail Now." 2011 annual report. Dallas.

Feldman, Ron J., and Jason Schmidt. 2021. "Government Fiscal Support Protected Banks from Huge Losses During the COVID-19 Crisis." Federal Reserve Bank of Minneapolis, Minneapolis, MN.

———. 2022. "Large Bank Strength During the COVID Financial Shock: Not All It Was Purported to Be." Federal Reserve Bank of Minneapolis, Minneapolis, MN.

Ferguson, Charles H. 2012. *Predator Nation: Corporate Criminals, Political Corruption, and the Hijacking of America*. New York: Crown Business.

Ferguson, Thomas, and Peter Temin. 2003. "Made in Germany: The German Currency Crisis of July 1931." *Research in Economic History* 21: 1–53.

———. 2004. "Comment on 'The German Twin Crisis of 1931,'{~?~thinspace}" *Journal of Economic History* 64 (3): 872–876.

Fielding, Eric, Andrew W. Lo, and Jian Helen. 2011. "The National Transportation Safety Board: A Model for Systemic Risk Management." *Journal of Investment Management* 9 (1): 17–49.

Fink, Matthew P. 2008. *The Rise of Mutual Funds*. Oxford, England: Oxford University Press.

Fischer, Markus J., Christa Hainz, Jörg Rocholl, and Sascha Steffen. 2011. "Government Guarantees and Bank Risk Taking Incentives." AFA 2012 Chicago Meetings paper. American Finance Association, Berkeley, CA.

Flannery, Mark J. 2005. "No Pain, No Gain? Effecting Market Discipline via Reverse Convertible Debentures." In *Capital Adequacy Beyond Basel: Banking Securities and Insurance*, ed. Hall S. Scott. Oxford, England: Oxford University Press. Chapter 5.

Fleischer, Victor. 2011. "Tax Reform and the Tax Treatment of Debt and Equity." Testimony before Joint Congressional Committee on Ways and Means, Senate Committee on Finance, July 13.

Fohlin, Caroline. 2007. *Finance Capitalism and Germany's Rise to Industrial Power*. Cambridge, England: Cambridge University Press.

Ford, Richard. 1926. "Imprisonment for Debt." *Michigan Law Review* 25 (1): 24–49.

Fourcade, Marion. 2009. *Economists and Societies: Discipline and Profession in the United States, Britain, and France, 1890s to 1990s*. Princeton, NJ: Princeton University Press.

Fraser, Ian. 2013. *Shredded: Inside RBS, the Bank That Broke Britain*. Edinburgh: Birlinn Publishing.

Freeman, James, and Vern McKinley. 2018. *Borrowed Time: Two Centuries of Booms, Busts, and Bailouts at Citi*. New York: Harper Business.

Freedman, Abraham L. 1928. "Imprisonment for Debt." *Temple Law Quarterly* 2: 336.

French, Kenneth, Martin N. Baily, John Y. Campbell, John H. Cochrane, Douglas W. Diamond, Darrell Duffie, Anil K. Kashyap, Frederic S. Mishkin, Raghuram G. Rajan,

David S. Scharfstein, Robert J. Shiller, Hyun Song Shin, Matthew J. Slaughter, Jeremy C. Stein, and René M. Stulz. 2010. *The Squam Lake Report: Fixing the Financial System*. Princeton, NJ: Princeton University Press.

Friedman, Milton. 1960. *A Program for Monetary Stability*. New York: Fordham University Press.

———. 1969. *The Optimum Quantity of Money and Other Essays*. Chicago: University of Chicago Press.

Friedman, Milton, and Rose Friedman. 1990. *Free to Choose: A Personal Statement*. New York: Harcourt.

Friedman, Milton, and Anna Schwartz. 1963. *A Monetary History of the United States, 1867–1960*. Princeton, NJ: Princeton University Press.

Frydman, Roman, and Michael D. Goldberg. 2011. *Beyond Mechanical Markets: Asset Price Swings, Risk, and the Role of the State*. Princeton, NJ: Princeton University Press.

FSA (Financial Services Authority). 2010. "The Prudential Regime for Trading Activities: A Fundamental Review." Discussion Paper 10/4. Financial Services Authority, London.

FSB (Financial Stability Board). 2011a. "Effective Resolution of Systemically Important Financial Institutions: Recommendations and Timelines."

———. 2011b. "Key Attributes of Effective Resolution Procedures for Financial Institutions." October.

———. 2012. "Strengthening the Oversight and Regulation of Shadow Banking." Progress Report to G20 Ministers and Governors. London.

———. 2013. "Recovery and Resolution Planning for Systemically Important Financial Institutions: Guidance on Developing Effective Resolution Strategies."

———. 2014. "Key Attributes of Effective Resolution Regimes for Financial Institutions."

———. 2015. "Principles on Loss-absorbing and Recapitalisation Capacity of G-SIBs in Resolution and Total Loss-absorbing Capacity (TLAC) Term Sheet."

———. 2021. *Evaluation of the Effects of Too-Big-To-Fail Reforms: Final Report*.

Gandhi, Priyank, and Hanno Lustig. 2012. "Size Anomalies in U.S. Bank Stock Returns: A Fiscal Explanation." NBER Working Paper w16553. National Bureau of Economic Research, Cambridge, MA.

GAO (U.S. Government Accountability Office). 2016. *Financial Regulation: Complex and Fragmented Structure Could Be Streamlined to Improve Effectiveness*.

———. 2023. "Preliminary Review of Agency Actions Related to March 2023 Bank Failures."

Garrett, Brandon L. 2016. *Too Big to Jail: How Prosecutors Compromise with Corporations*. Cambridge, MA: Harvard University Press.

Geanakoplos, John. 2010. "Solving the Present Crisis and Managing the Leverage Cycle." *Economic Policy Review* (Federal Reserve Bank of New York), August, 101–131.

Geithner, Timothy F. 2014. *Stress Test: Reflections on Financial Crises*. New York: Crown Publishers.

Gerschenkron, Alexander. 1962. *Economic Backwardness in Historical Perspective*. Cambridge, MA: Harvard University Press.

Ghent, Andra C., and Mariana Kudlyak. 2009. "Recourse and Residential Mortgage Default: Evidence from U.S. States." Working Paper 09-10R. Federal Reserve Bank of Richmond, Richmond, VA.

Gilbert, R. Alton. 1986. "Requiem for Regulation Q: What It Did and Why It Passed Away." *Federal Reserve Bank of St. Louis Review* (February): 22–37.

Goldstein, Itay, and Adi Pauzner. 2005. "Demand Deposit Contracts and the Probability of a Bank Run." *Journal of Finance* 60 (3): 1293–1327.

Goldstein, Morris. 2017. *Banking's Final Exam: Stress Testing and Bank-Capital Reform*. Washington, DC: Peterson Institute for International Economics.

Goodfriend, Marvin. 2011. "Money Markets." *Annual Review of Financial Economics* 3 (1): 19–37.

Goodhart, Charles A. E. 1988. *The Evolution of Central Banks*. Cambridge, MA: MIT Press.

———. 1996. "Has Financial Risk Really Worsened?" In *Risk Management in Volatile Financial Markets*, ed. Franco Bruni, Donald F. Fair, and Richard O'Brien. Dordrecht, The Netherlands: Kluwer.

———. 1998. "The Two Concepts of Money: Implications for the Analysis of Optimal Currency Areas." *European Journal of Political Economy* 14: 407–432.

———. 2010. "How Should We Regulate the Financial Sector?" *The Future of Finance*. LSE Report. London School of Economics and Political Science, London. Chapter 5.

———. 2011. *The Basel Committee on Banking Supervision: A History of the Early Years, 1974–1997*. Cambridge, England: Cambridge University Press.

———. 2012. "Sovereign Ratings When Default Can Come Explicitly or via Inflation." VoxEU, London. February 2.

Gorton, Gary. 1985. "Clearinghouses and the Origin of Central Banking in the United States." *Journal of Economic History* 45 (2): 277–283.

———. 1988. "Banking Panics and Business Cycles." *Oxford Economic Papers* 40 (4): 751–781.

———. 1994. "Bank Regulation When 'Banks' and 'Banking' Are Not the Same." *Oxford Review of Economic Policy* 10: 106–119.

———. 2010. *Slapped by the Invisible Hand: The Panic of 2007*. Oxford, England: Oxford University Press.

Gorton, Gary, and Andrew Metrick. 2010. "Regulating the Shadow Banking System." *Brookings Papers on Economic Activity* 41 (2): 261–312.

Greenspan, Alan. 2010. "The Crisis." *Brookings Papers on Economic Activity*, Spring, 201–246.

Greenwald, Bruce C., and Robert R. Glasspiegel. 1983. "Adverse Selection in the Market for Slaves: New Orleans, 1830–1860." *Quarterly Journal of Economics* 98 (3): 479–499.

Grilli, Vittorio, Donato Masciandaro, and Guido Tabellini. 1991. "Institutions and Policies." *Economic Policy* 6 (13): 341–392.

Grind, Kristen. 2012. *The Lost Bank: The Story of Washington Mutual—The Biggest Bank Failure in American History*. New York: Simon & Schuster.

Grossman, Gene M., and Elhanan Helpman. 1994. "Protection for Sale." *American Economic Review* 84: 833–850.

Grossman, Richard S. 2001. "Double Liability and Bank Risk Taking." *Journal of Money, Credit and Banking* 33 (2, pt. 1): 143–159.

———. 2007. "Fear and Greed: The Evolution of Double Liability in American Banking, 1865–1930." *Explorations in Economic History* 44 (1): 59–80.

———. 2010. *Unsettled Account: The Evolution of Banking in the Industrialized World since 1800*. Princeton, NJ: Princeton University Press.

Grossman, Richard S., and Masami Imai. 2011. "Contingent Capital and Bank Risk-Taking among British Banks before World War I." Wesleyan Economics Working Paper 2011-003. Department of Economics, Wesleyan University, Middletown, CT.

Grund, Sebastian, Nele Nomm, and Florian Walch. 2020. "Liquidity in Resolution: Comparing Frameworks for Liquidity Provision Across Jurisdictions." ECB Occasional Paper No. 251. European Central Bank.

Guriev, Sergei, and Daniel Treisman. 2022. *Spin Dictators: The Changing Face of Tyranny in the 21st Century*. Princeton, NJ: Princeton University Press.

Gurley, John E., and Edward S. Shaw. 1960. *Money in a Theory of Finance*. Washington, DC: Brookings Institution.

Haldane, Andrew G. 2010. "Regulation or Prohibition: The $100 Billion Question." *Journal of Regulation and Risk North Asia* 2 (2–3): 101–122.

———. 2011a. "Capital Discipline." Speech delivered at the American Economic Association, Denver, January 9.

———. 2011b. "Control Rights (and Wrongs)." Wincott Annual Memorial Lecture, Westminster, London, October 24.

———. 2011c. "Accounting for Banks' Uncertainty." Speech delivered at the Institute of Chartered Accountants in England and Wales, London, December 19.

———. 2012a. "The Doom Loop." *London Review of Books* 34 (4): 21–22.

———. 2012b. "Creating a Socially Useful Financial System." Speech delivered at the Institute of New Economic Thinking's "Paradigm Lost" conference in Berlin.

———. 2012c. "The Dog and the Frisbee." Speech delivered at the Federal Reserve Bank of Kansas City's 366th economic policy symposium, Jackson Hole, Wyoming, August 31.

Haldane, Andrew, Simon Brennan, and Vasileios Madouros. 2010. "What Is the Contribution of the Financial Sector: Miracle or Mirage?" In *The Future of Finance*. London: London School of Economics. Chapter 2.

Hall, Robert E., and Ricardo Reis. 2015. "Maintaining Central-Bank Financial Stability under New-Style Central Banking." Economics Working Paper No. 15109, Hoover Institution, Stanford University, Stanford, CA.

Hanson, Samuel, Anil K. Kashyap, and Jeremy C. Stein. 2011. "A Macroprudential Approach to Financial Regulation." *Journal of Economic Perspectives* 25: (1): 3–28.

Harding, John P., Eric Rosenblatt, and Vincent W. Yao. 2009. "The Contagion Effect of Foreclosed Properties." *Journal of Urban Economics* 66 (3): 164–178.

Harrison, Ian. 2004. "Banks, Capital and Regulation: Towards an Optimal Capital Regime for a Small Open Economy." Working paper. Reserve Bank of New Zealand, Wellington.

Haselmann, Rainer, Arkodipta Sarkar, Shikhar Singla, and Vikrant Vig. 2022. "The Political Economy of Financial Regulation." LawFin Working Paper No. 45, University of Frankfurt.

Hauser, Andrew. 2021. "From Lender of Last Resort to Market Maker of Last Resort via the Dash for Cash: Why Central Banks Need New Tools for Dealing with Market Dysfunction." Bank of England, London.

Hayes, Christopher. 2012. *The Twilight of the Elites: America after Meritocracy.* New York: Crown.

Healy, Paul M., and Krishna G. Palepu. 2003. "The Fall of Enron." *Journal of Economic Perspectives* 17 (2): 3–26.

Heffernan, Margaret. 2012. *Willful Blindness: Why We Ignore the Obvious at Our Peril.* New York: Bloomsbury Publishing.

Hellwig, Hans-Jürgen. 2008. "At the Intersection of Legal Ethics and Globalization: International Conflicts of Law in Lawyer Regulation." *Penn State International Law Review* 27: 395–401.

Hellwig, Martin F. 1991. "Banking, Financial Intermediation, and Corporate Finance." In *European Financial Integration*, ed. A. Giovannini and C. Mayer. Cambridge, England: Cambridge University Press. 35–63.

———. 1994. "Liquidity Provision, Banking, and the Allocation of Interest Rate Risk." *European Economic Review* 38: 1363–1389.

———. 1995. "Systemic Aspects of Risk Management in Banking and Finance." *Swiss Journal of Economics and Statistics* 131: 723–737.

———. 1998. "Banks, Markets, and the Allocation of Risks." *Journal of Institutional and Theoretical Economics* 154: 328–351.

———. 1999. "Zur 'Volkswirtschaftlichen Verantwortung' der Banken." [On the 'economic responsibility' of banks]. In *Die volkswirtschaftliche Verantwortung der Banken*, ed. Franz Jaeger and Winfried Stier, 9–57. Chur and Zürich: Verlag Rüegger.

———. 2000. "On the Economics and Politics of Corporate Finance and Corporate Control." In *Corporate Governance*, ed. X. Vives. Cambridge, England: Cambridge University Press. 95–134.

———. 2005. "Market Discipline, Information Processing, and Corporate Governance." In *Corporate Governance in Context: Corporations, States, and Markets in Europe, Japan, and the US*, ed. K. J. Hopt, E. Wymeersch, H. Kanda, and H. Baum. Oxford, England: Oxford University Press. 379–402.

———. 2009. "Systemic Risk in the Financial Sector: An Analysis of the Subprime-Mortgage Financial Crisis." *The Economist* 157: 129–207.

———. 2010a. "Capital Regulation after the Crisis: Business as Usual?" Max Planck Institute for Research on Collective Goods, Bonn, Preprint 2010-31.

———. 2010b. "Comments on Proposal to Ensure the Loss Absorbency of Regulatory Capital at the Point of Non-viability." Max Planck Institute for Research on Collective Goods, Bonn. October 1.

———. 2012. "The Problem of Bank Resolution Remains Unsolved: A Critique of the German Bank Restructuring Law." In *Too big to fail—Brauchen wir ein Sonderinsolvenzrecht für Banken?*, ed. Patrick S. Kenadjian. Boston: De Gruyter. 35–62.

———. 2014a. "Financial Stability, Monetary Policy, Banking Supervision, and Central Banking." In *ECB Forum on Central Banking: Conference Proceedings.* European Central Bank, Frankfurt/Main, 21–54.

———. 2014b. "Yes, Virginia, There Is a European Banking Union! But It May Not Make Your Wishes Come True." *Proceedings of the 42nd Economics Conference*, Austrian National Bank, Vienna, 157–181.

———. 2015. "Financial Stability and Monetary Policy." Paper prepared for the Federal Reserve Bank of Atlanta Conference on Central Banking in the Shadows: Monetary Policy and Financial Stability Postcrisis, March 30–April 1. Discussion Paper 10/2015, Max Planck Institute for Research on Collective Goods, Bonn.

———. 2017a. "Carving Out Legacy Assets: A Successful Tool for Bank Restructuring?" Report to the European Parliament's Economic and Monetary Affairs Committee, March. https://www.europarl.europa.eu/RegData/etudes/IDAN/2017/587399/IPOL_IDA(2017)587399_EN.pdf. Accessed March 13, 2023.

———. 2017b. "Precautionary Recapitalisations: Time for a Review." Report to the European Parliament's Economic and Monetary Affairs Committee, July. https://www.europarl.europa.eu/RegData/etudes/IDAN/2017/602089/IPOL_IDA(2017)602089_EN.pdf. Accessed March 13, 2023.

———. 2018a. "Competition Policy and Sector-Specific Regulation in the Financial Sector." Paper prepared for the 64th meeting of OECD Working Party No. 2 on Competition and Regulation, Paris, December 4. Discussion Paper 2018/7 of the Max Planck Institute for Research on Collective Goods, Bonn.

———. 2018b. "Valuation Reports in the Context of Banking Resolution: What Are the Challenges?" Report to the European Parliament's Economic and Monetary Affairs Committee, June. https://www.europarl.europa.eu/RegData/etudes/IDAN/2018/624417/IPOL_IDA(2018)624417_EN.pdf. Accessed March 13, 2023.

———. 2018c. "Germany and the Financial Crises since 2007." Paper prepared for the Fourth Annual Macroprudential Conference of the Sveriges Riksbank, the Nederlandsche Bank and the Deutsche Bundesbank, June 15–16. https://www.riksbank.se/en-gb/press-and-published/conferences/2018/annual-macroprudential-conference-15-16-june-2018/. Accessed April 5, 2023.

———. 2020a. "How Important Is a European Deposit Insurance System?" In Institute for Law and Finance series, ed. Andreas Dombret and Patrick S. Kenadjian, 7–19. Berlin: De Gruyter.

———. 2020b. "Stellungnahme für den Finanzausschuss des Deutschen Bundestags zum Antrag der FDP 'Basel III Finalisierung—Kreditversorgung Deutschlands erhalten' vom 10. März 2020" [Report to the Finance Committee of the German parliament on a resolution proposed by the Liberal Party on preventing the finalization of Basel III from endangering credit supply in Germany]. https://www.bundestag.de/resource/blob/703722/4a56 4c6d1f10788301237511854047ea/05-Hellwig-data.pdf. Accessed May 30, 2023.

———. 2021. "'Capitalism: What Has Gone Wrong?' Who Went Wrong? Capitalism? The Market Economy? Governments? 'Neoliberal' Economics?" *Oxford Review of Economic Policy* 37 (4): 664–677.

Hellwig, Martin F., and Gerhard Schick. 2022. "Versagen und Reformbedarf der deutschen Finanzaufsicht." [Failure and the need for reform of the German financial supervision]. Working Paper 02/2022. Forum for a New Economy, Berlin.

Hellwig, Martin F., and Markus Staub. 1996. "Capital Requirements for Market Risks Based on Inhouse Models—Aspects of Quality Assessment." *Swiss Journal of Economics and Statistics* 132: 755–776.

Hendershott, Patric C., and James D. Shilling. 1991. "The Continued Interest Rate Vulnerability of Thrifts." In *Financial Markets and Financial Crises*, ed. R. Glenn Hubbard. Chicago: University of Chicago Press. 259–282.

Henriques, Diana B. 2017. *The Wizard of Lies: Bernie Madoff and the Death of Trust*. New York: St. Martin's Griffin.

Hernan, Robert. 2010. *This Borrowed Earth: Lessons from the Fifteen Worst Environmental Disasters around the World*. Houndmills, Basingstoke, Hampshire, England: Palgrave McMillan.

Herring, Richard, and Jacopo Carmassi. 2010. "The Corporate Structure of International Financial Conglomerates: Complexity and Its Implications for Safety and Soundness." In *The Oxford Handbook of Banking*, ed. A. Berger, P. Molyneux, and J. Wilson. Oxford, England: Oxford University Press.

Hesse, Heiko, Nathaniel Frank, and Brenda González-Hermosillo. 2008. "Transmission of Liquidity Shocks: Evidence from the 2007 Subprime Crisis." IMF Working Paper 08/200. International Monetary Fund, Washington, DC.

Hetzer, Wolfgang. 2015. *Ist die Deutsche Bank eine kriminelle Vereinigung?* [Is Deutsche Bank a criminal organization?]. Frankfurt: Westend Verlag.

Hoad, T. F. 1986. *Concise Oxford Dictionary of English Etymology*. Oxford, England: Oxford University Press.

Hockett, Robert. 2023. "Universal Deposit Insurance." Working Paper.

Hoenig, Thomas M. 2012. "Back to Basics: A Better Alternative to Basel Capital Rules." Speech delivered to the American Banker Regulatory Symposium, Washington, DC, September 14.

Hoenig, Thomas M., and Charles S. Morris. 2011. "Restructuring the Banking System to Improve Safety and Soundness." Federal Reserve of Kansas City, Kansas City, MO.

Holtfrerich, Carl-Ludwig. 1981. "Die Eigenkapitalausstattung deutscher Kreditinstitute 1871–1945." (Equity of German Banks 1871–1945). *Bankhistorisches Archiv* 5: 15–29.

Horngren, Charles, Walter T. Harrison, and M. Suzanne Oliver. 2012. *Accounting*. 9th ed. Upper Saddle River, NJ: Pearson Education.

Hoshi, Takao, and Anil Kashyap. 2004. "Japan's Financial Crisis and Economic Stagnation." *Journal of Economic Perspectives* 18 (Winter): 3–26.

———. 2010. "Why Did Japan Stop Growing?" NBER working paper. National Bureau of Economic Research, Cambridge, MA.

Hoshi, Takeo, Anil Kashyap, and David Scharfstein. 1990. "The Role of Banks in Reducing the Costs of Financial Distress in Japan." *Journal of Financial Economics* 27 (1): 67–88.

———. 1991. "Corporate Structure, Liquidity, and Investment: Evidence from Japanese Industrial Groups." *Quarterly Journal of Economics* 106 (1): 33–60.

Hu, Henry T. C. 2012. "Too Complex to Depict? Innovation, 'Pure Information' and the SEC Disclosure Paradigm." *Texas Law Review* 90: 1601–1715.

Huertas, Thomas F. 2010. *Crisis: Cause, Containment and Cure.* Houndmills, Basingstoke, Hampshire, England: Palgrave Macmillan.

Hughes, Joseph P., and Loretta J. Mester. 2011. "Who Said Large Banks Don't Experience Scale Economies? Evidence from a Risk-Return Driven Cost Function." Financial Institutions Center, Wharton School, University of Pennsylvania, Philadelphia.

Hull, John. 2007. *Risk Management and Financial Institutions.* Upper Saddle River, NJ: Pearson Prentice Hall.

Huxley, Aldous. 1932. *Brave New World.* London: Chatto & Windus.

Hyman, Louis. 2012. *Borrow: The American Way of Debt.* New York: Vintage.

ICB (Independent Commission on Banking). 2011. "Final Report: Recommendation." London.

Igan, Deniz O., and Thomas Lambert. 2019. "Bank Lobbying: Regulatory Capture and Beyond." IMF Working Paper 171. International Monetary Fund, Washington, DC.

IIF (Institute of International Finance). 2010. "Interim Report on the Cumulative Impact on the Global Economy of Changes in the Banking Regulatory Framework." Washington, DC. June.

IMF (International Monetary Fund). 2007. "Market Developments and Issues." *Global Financial Stability Report.* Washington, DC. April.

———. 2008a. "Containing Systemic Risks and Restoring Financial Soundness." *Global Financial Stability Report.* Washington, DC. April.

———. 2008b. "Financial Stress and Deleveraging: Macro-Financial Implications and Policy." *Global Financial Stability Report.* Washington, DC. October.

———. 2009. "Sustaining the Recovery." *World Economic Outlook.* Washington, DC. October.

———. 2010a. "Rebalancing Growth." *World Economic Outlook.* Washington, DC. April.

———. 2010b. "Sovereigns, Funding, and Systemic Liquidity." *Global Financial Stability Report.* Washington, DC. October.

———. 2014. "How Big Is the Implicit Subsidy for Banks Considered too Important to Fail?" *Global Financial Stability Report*, April. Washington, DC, 101–132.

———. 2016. "Financial System Stability Assessment: Germany." IMF Country Report No. 16/189. Independent Evaluation Group. 2012. *The World Bank Group's Response to the Global Economic Crisis—Phase II.* Washington, DC: World Bank Group.

ISDA (International Swaps and Derivatives Association). 2012. "Netting and Offsetting: Reporting Derivatives under GAAP and under IFRS." Working paper.

Ivashina, Victoria, and David Scharfstein. 2010. "Bank Lending during the Financial Crisis of 2008." *Journal of Financial Economics* 97 (3): 319–338.

Jaffe, Adam B., Steven R. Peterson, Paul R. Portney, and Robert N. Stavins. 1995. "Environmental Regulation and the Competitiveness of U.S. Manufacturing: What Does the Evidence Tell Us?" *Journal of Economic Literature* 33 (1): 132–163.

Jenkins, Robert. 2011. "Lessons in Lobbying." Speech delivered at the third Gordon Midgley Memorial Debate, London.

———. 2012a. "Let's Make a Deal." Speech delivered at the Worshipful Company of Actuaries, Haberdasher's Hall, London.

———. 2012b. "A Debate Framed by Fallacies." Speech delivered at the International Centre for Financial Regulation's 3rd Annual Regulatory Summit, London.

———. 2012c. "Investors: Speak Now or Forever Hold Your Peace." Speech delivered at the CFA UK Annual Chairman's Dinner, London.

Jensen, Michael C. 1986. "Agency Costs of Free Cash Flow, Corporate Finance, and Takeovers." *American Economic Review* 76 (2): 323–329.

———. 1993. "The Modern Industrial Revolution, Exit, and the Failure of Internal Control Systems." *Journal of Finance* 48: 831–880.

Jevons, William Stanley. 1910. "Barter." In *Monetary Theory*, ed. Robert W. Clower. Harmondsworth: Penguin Books 1969, 25–29; reprinted from William Stanley Jevons. 1910. *Money and the Mechanism of Exchange*, 23rd ed. London: Kegan Paul, 1–7.

Jiang, Erica, Gregor Matvos, Tomasz Piskorski, and Amit Seru. 2023a. "Monetary Tightening and the U.S. Bank Fragility in 2023: Mark-to-Market Losses and Uninsured Depositor Runs?" Working Paper.

———. 2023b. "Limited Hedging and Gambling for Resurrection by U.S. Banks During the 2022 Monetary Tightening?" Working Paper.

Jiang, Erica, Tomasz Piskorski, Amit Seru, and Gregor Matvos. 2020. "Banking Without Deposits: Evidence from Shadow Bank Call Reports." Working Paper.

Johnsen, Gudrun. 2014. *Bringing Down the Banking System: Lessons from Iceland.* New York: Palgrave Macmillan. Text available at https://link.springer.com/book/10.1057/9781137347350. Accessed May 30, 2023.

Johnson, Gordon. 1994. *University Politics: F. M. Cornford's Cambridge and His Advice to the Young Academic Politician.* Cambridge, England: Cambridge University Press.

Johnson, Harry G. 1969. "Inside Money, Outside Money, Income, Wealth, and Welfare in Monetary Theory." *Journal of Money, Credit, and Banking* 1: 30–45.

Johnson, Simon, and James Kwak. 2010. *13 Bankers: The Wall Street Takeover and the Next Financial Meltdown.* New York: Pantheon.

———. 2012. "Is Financial Innovation Good for the Economy?" In *Innovation Policy and the Economy*, ed. Josh Lerner and Scott Stem. Cambridge, MA: National Bureau of Economic Research.

Jordà, Oscar, Moritz Schularick, and Alan Taylor. 2011. "When Credit Bites Back: Leverage, Business Cycles, and Crises." Working Paper 2011-27. Federal Reserve Bank of San Francisco.

Jostarndt, Philipp, and Stefan Wagner. 2006. "Kapitalstrukturen börsennotierter Aktiengesellschaften–Deutschland und die USA im Vergleich." Discussion Paper 2006-17. Munich School of Management, University of Munich, Munich.

Junge, Georg, and Peter Kugler. 2012. "Quantifying the Impact of Higher Capital Requirements on the Swiss Economy." Mimeo. University of Basel, Basel.

Kane, Edward. 1985. *The Gathering Crisis in Federal Deposit Insurance.* Cambridge, MA: MIT Press.

———. 1989. *The S & L Insurance Mess: How Did It Happen?* Washington, DC: Urban Institute Press.

———. 2001. "Dynamic Inconsistency of Capital Forbearance: Long-Run vs. Short-Run Effects of Too-Big-to-Fail Policymaking." *Pacific-Basin Finance Journal* 9 (4): 281–299.

———. 2012a. "Bankers and Brokers First: Loose Ends in the Theory of Central-Bank Policymaking." Working paper, Boston College.

———. 2012b. "The Inevitability of Shadowy Banking," Working paper. Boston College.

———. 2012c. "Missing Elements in U.S. Financial Reform: A Kübler-Ross Interpretation of the Inadequacy of the Dodd-Frank Act." *Journal of Banking and Finance* 36: 654–661.

Kareken, John H. 1983. "Deposit Insurance Reform or Deregulation Is the Cart, Not the Horse." *Federal Reserve Bank of Minneapolis Quarterly Review* 7: 1–9.

Kaserer, Christoph. 2010. "Staatliche Hilfen für Banken und ihre Kosten–Notwendigkeit und Merkmale einer Ausstiegsstrategie" (Government support for banks and its costs—Necessity and characteristics of an exit strategy). Working paper. Technical University of Munich, Munich.

Kashyap, Anil K., Jeremy C. Stein, and Samuel Hanson. 2010. "An Analysis of the Impact of 'Substantially Heightened' Capital Requirements on Large Financial Institutions." Working paper. University of Chicago, Chicago, and Harvard University, Cambridge, MA.

Kay, John. 2010. "Should We Have 'Narrow Banking'?" *The Future of Finance.* LSE Report. London School of Economics and Political Science, London. Chapter 8.

Keeley, Michael C. 1990. "Deposit Insurance, Risk, and Market Power in Banking." *American Economic Review* 80: 1183–1200.

Kelly, Brian, Hanno Lustig, and Stijn Van Nieuwerburgh. 2012. "Too-Systemic-to-Fail: What Option Markets Imply about Sector-Wide Government Guarantees." NBER Working Paper 17615. National Bureau of Economic Research, Cambridge, MA.

Keys, Benjamin J., Tanmoy Mukherjee, Amit Seru, and Vikrant Vig. 2010. "Did Securitization Lead to Lax Screening? Evidence from Subprime Loans." *Quarterly Journal of Economics* 125 (1): 307–362.

Keys, Ralph. 2006. *The Quote Verifier.* New York: St. Martin's Griffin.

Kim, Daesik, and Anthony M. Santomero. 1988. "Risk in Banking and Capital Regulation." *Journal of Finance* 43: 1219–1233.

Kindleberger, Charles P. 1984. *A Financial History of Western Europe.* Allen and Unwin.

Kindleberger, Charles P., and Robert Aliber. 2005. *Manias, Panics, and Crashes: A History of Financial Crises.* New York: Palgrave Macmillan.

King, Mervyn. 1990. "International Harmonisation of the Regulation of Capital Markets: An Introduction." *European Economic Review* 34: 569–577.

———. 2010. "Banking from Bagehot to Basel and Back Again." Second Bagehot Lecture, Buttenwood Gathering, New York, October 25.

———. 2016. *The End of Alchemy: Money, Banking and the Future of the Global Economy.* London: Abacus.

Klein, Benjamin. 1974. "Competitive Interest Payments on Bank Deposits and the Long-Run Demand for Money." *American Economic Review* 64: 931–949.

Klingen, Christoph, Beatrice Weder, and Jeromin Zettelmeyer. 2004. "How Private Creditors Fared in Emerging Debt Markets, 1970–2000." Working Paper WP/04/13. International Monetary Fund.

Kluge, Friedrich. 1975. *Etymologisches Wörterbuch der deutschen Sprache*, 21st ed. Berlin: De Gruyter.

Knapp, Georg Friedrich. [1905] 1924. *Staatliche Theorie des Geldes.* Trans. as *The State Theory of Money.* London: Macmillan.

Koehn, Michael, and Anthony M. Santomero. 1980. "Regulation of Bank Capital and Portfolio Risk." *Journal of Finance* 35: 1235–1244.

Körner, Tobias, and Isabel Schnabel. 2012. "Abolishing Public Guarantees in the Absence of Market Discipline." Working paper. University of Mainz, Mainz, Germany.

Korteweg, Arthur. 2010. "The Net Benefit to Leverage." *Journal of Finance* 55 (6): 2137–2170.

Korteweg, Arthur, and Morten Sorensen. 2010. "Risk and Return Characteristics of Venture Capital–Backed Entrepreneurial Companies." *Review of Financial Studies* 23 (10): 3738–3772.

Kotlikoff, Laurence J. 2010. *Jimmy Stewart Is Dead: Ending the World's Financial Plague before It Strikes Again.* Hoboken, NJ: John Wiley and Sons.

Krahnen, Jan P., and Reinhard H. Schmidt. 2003. *The German Financial System.* Oxford, England: Oxford University Press.

Kress, Jeremy C. 2019. "Solving Banking's 'Too Big to Manage' Problem." *Minnesota Law Review* 104: 171–241.

Krishnamurthy, Arvind, Stefan Nagel, and Dmitri Orlov. 2012. "Sizing Up Repo." Working Paper, Stanford University.

Krugman, Paul. 1996. *Pop Internationalism.* Cambridge, MA: MIT Press.

Kwak, James. 2012. "Cultural Capture and the Financial Crisis." In *Preventing Capture: Special Interest Influence in Legislation and How to Limit It*, ed. Daniel Carpenter, Steve Croley, and David Moss. Cambridge, England: Cambridge University Press. Chapter 7.

———. 2013. "Cultural Capture and the Financial Crisis." In *Preventing Regulatory Capture: Special Interest Influence and How to Limit it*, ed. Dan Carpenter and David Moss. Cambridge, UK: Cambridge University Press.

Laeven, Luc, and Fabian Valencia. 2009. "Systemic Banking Crises: A New Database." IMF Working Paper 08/224. International Monetary Fund, Washington, DC.

———. 2010. "Resolution of Banking Crises: The Good, the Bad and the Ugly." IMF Working Paper 10/146. International Monetary Fund, Washington, DC.

———. 2012. "Systemic Banking Crisis Database: An Update." IMF Working Paper 163. International Monetary Fund, Washington, DC.

Lancieri, Filippo Maria, Eric A. Posner, and Luigi Zingales. 2022. "The Political Economy and the Decline of Antitrust Enforcement in the United States." Becker Friedman Institute Working Paper 2022–104. University of Chicago, Chicago, IL.

La Porta, Rafael, Florencio Lopez-de-Silanes, and Andrei Shleifer. 1999. "Corporate Owner-ship around the World." *Journal of Finance* 54: 471–517.

La Porta, Rafael, Florencio Lopez-de-Silanes, Andrei Shleifer, and Robert W. Vishny. 1997. "Legal Determinants of External Finance." *Journal of Finance* 52: 1131–1150.

———. 1998. "Law and Finance." *Journal of Political Economy* 106: 1113–1155.

———. 2000a. "Agency Problems and Dividend Policies around the World." *Journal of Finance* 55 (1): 1–33.

———. 2000b. "Investor Protection and Corporate Governance." *Journal of Financial Economics* 58 (1–2): 3–27.

Laux, Christian, and Christian Leuz. 2010. "Did Fair-Value Accounting Contribute to the Financial Crisis?," *Journal of Economic Perspectives* 24: 93–118.

Ledo, Mayte. 2012. "Towards More Consistent, Albeit Diverse, Risk-Weighted Assets Across Banks." Bank of Spain, Madrid.

Lee, Allison Herren. 2022. "Send Lawyers, Guns and Money: (Over-) Zealous Representation by Corporate Lawyers." Remarks at PLI's Corporate Governance—A Master Class 2022.

Leonard, Christopher. 2022. *The Lords of Easy Money: How the Federal Reserve Broke the American Economy*. New York: Simon & Schuster.

Lessig, Lawrence. 2011. *Republic, Lost: How Money Corrupts Congress—and a Plan to Stop It*. New York: Twelve.

Levitin, Adam J. 2013. "The Tenuous Case for Derivatives Clearinghouses." *Georgetown Law Journal* 101; Georgetown Law and Economics Research Paper 12-032; Georgetown Public Law Research Paper 12-124, Georgetown University, Washington, DC.

Lewis, Michael. 1990. *Liar's Poker: Rising through the Wreckage on Wall Street*. Ontario City, Canada: Penguin.

———. 2010. *The Big Short: Inside the Doomsday Machine*. New York: W. W. Norton.

———. 2011. *Boomerang: Travels in the New Third World*. New York: W. W. Norton.

———. 2014. *Flash Boys: A Wall Street Revolt*. New York: W.W. Norton.

Liikanen Report. 2012. *Final Report of the High Level Expert Group on Reforming the Structure of the EU Banking Sector*.

London Economics and Achim Dübel (Finpolconsult) in association with the Institut für Finanzdienstleistungen e.V. (iff). 2009. "Study on the Costs and Benefits of the Differ-ent Policy Options for Mortgage Credit: Final Report." Report prepared for the European Commission, Internal Markets and Services DG.

Lopez, Robert S. 1976. *The Commercial Revolution of the Middle Ages, 950–1350*. New York: Cambridge University Press.

LoPucki, Lynn. 2005. *Courting Failure*. Ann Arbor: University of Michigan Press.

Lowenstein, Roger. 2001. *When Genius Failed*. New York: Random House.

Lubben, Stephen J., and Arthur E. Wilmarth. 2017. "Too Big and Unable to Fail." *Florida Law Review* 69 (5): 1205–1249.

Lucca, David, Amit Seru, and Francesco Trebbi. 2014. "The Revolving Door and Worker Flows in Banking Regulation." *Journal of Monetary Economics* 65: 17–32.

Lütge, Friedrich. 1966. *Deutsche Sozial- und Wirtschaftsgeschichte* (German social and eco-nomic history), 3rd ed. Berlin: Springer.

Luyendijk, Joris. 2015. *Swimming with Sharks: My Journey into the World of the Bankers.* London: Faber & Faber.

Macey, Jonathan R., and Geoffrey P. Miller. 1992. "Double Liability of Bank Shareholders: History and Implications." *Wake Forest Law Review* 27: 31–62.

Mallaby, Sebastian. 2010. *More Money than God: Hedge Funds and the Making of a New Elite.* London: Penguin.

Malysheva, Nadezhda, and John R. Walter. 2010. "How Large Has the Federal Financial Safety Net Become?" Working paper. Federal Reserve of Richmond, Richmond, VA.

Markham, Jerry W. 2002. *A Financial History of the United States.* Armonk, NY: M. E. Sharpe.

Mayer, Colin. 1988. "New Issues in Corporate Finance." *European Economic Review* 32: 1167–1188.

Mayo, Mike. 2011. *Exile on Wall Street: One Analyst's Fight to Save the Big Banks from Themselves.* Hoboken, NJ: John Wiley and Sons.

McCrum, Dan. 2022. *Money Men: A Hot Startup, A Billion Dollar Fraud, A Fight for the Truth.* London: Transworld Publishers.

McDonald, Lawrence G. 2010. *A Colossal Failure of Common Sense: The Inside Story of the Collapse of Lehman Brothers.* New York: Three Rivers.

McDonald, Robert L. 2010. "Contingent Capital with a Dual Price Trigger." Working paper. Kellogg School of Management, Northwestern University.

McLean, Bethany, and Peter Elkind. 2004. *The Smartest Guys in the Room: The Amazing Rise and Scandalous Fall of Enron.* New York: Portfolio Trade.

McLean, Bethany, and Joe Nocera. 2010. *All the Devils Are Here: The Hidden History of the Financial Crisis.* New York: Portfolio Trade.

Mehran, Hamid, and Anjan Thakor. 2010. "Bank Capital and Value in the Cross Section." *Review of Financial Studies* 24 (4): 1019–1067.

Mehrling, Perry. 2010. *The New Lombard Street.* Princeton, NJ: Princeton University Press.

Meltzer, Allan. 2012. *Why Capitalism?* New York: Oxford University Press.

Melzer, Brian T. 2012. "Mortgage Debt Overhang: Reduced Investment by Homeowners with Negative Equity." Working paper. Northwestern University, Chicago.

Menand, Lev. 2018. "Too Big to Supervise: The Rise of Financial Conglomerates and the Decline of Discretionary Oversight in Banking." *Cornell Law Review* 103 (6): 1527–1588.

Merkley, Jeff, and Carl Levin. 2011. "The Dodd-Frank Act Restrictions on Proprietary Trading and Conflicts of Interest: New Tools to Address Evolving Threats." *Harvard Law and Policy Review* 48: 515–553.

Merton, Robert C. 1973. "Theory of Rational Option Pricing." *Bell Journal of Economics* 4 (1): 141–183.

Merton, Robert K. 1957. "The Self-Fulfilling Prophecy." In *Social Theory and Social Structure*, rev. and enl. ed. New York: Free Press of Glencoe. 421–436.

Mian, Atif, Amir Sufi, and Francesco Trebbi. 2010. "The Political Economy of the US Mortgage Default Crisis." *American Economic Review* 100 (5): 1967–1998.

Michel, Casey. 2021. *American Kleptocracy: How the U.S. Created the World's Greatest Money Laundering Scheme in History.* New York: St. Martin's Press.

Miles, David, Jing Yang. and Gilberto Marcheggiano. 2011. "Optimal Bank Capital." Discussion paper. Bank of England, London.

Miller, Merton H. 1977. "Debt and Taxes." *Journal of Finance* 32: 261–275.

——. 1995. "Does the M&M Proposition Apply to Banks?" *Journal of Banking and Finance* 19: 483–489.

Mills, Lillian F., and Kaye J. Newberry. 2005. "Firms' Off Balance Sheet and Hybrid Debt Financing: Evidence from Their Book–Tax Reporting Differences." *Journal of Accounting Research* 43 (2): 251–282.

Mishkin, Frederic S. 2007. *The Economics of Money, Banking and Financial Institutions.* 8th ed. Upper Saddle River, NJ: Pearson Addison Wesley.

Mitchell, Josh. 2021. *The Debt Trap: How Student Loans Became a National Catastrophe.* New York: Simon & Schuster.

Modigliani, Franco, and Merton H. Miller. 1958. "The Cost of Capital, Corporation Finance, and the Theory of Investment." *American Economic Review* 48: 261–297.

Monopolkommission. 2005. *Wettbewerbspolitik im Schatten "nationaler Champions": XV. Hauptgutachten 2002/2003* (Competition policy in the shadow of "national champions": XVth Biennial Report 2002/2003). Baden-Baden, Germany: Nomos. German text with English summary.

Morgenson, Gretchen, and Joshua Rosner. 2011. *Reckless Endangerment: How Outsized Ambition, Greed, and Corruption Led to Economic Armageddon.* New York: Times Books.

Morris, Stephen, and Hyun Song Shin. 1998. "Unique Equilibrium in a Model of Self-Fulfilling Currency Attacks." *American Economic Review* 88: 587–597.

Muellbauer, John, and Anthony Murphy. 1997. "Booms and Busts in the UK Housing Market." CEPR Discussion Paper 1615. Centre for Economic and Policy Research, London.

Myers, Stewart C. 1977. "Determinants of Corporate Borrowing." *Journal of Financial Economics* 5: 147–175.

Myers, Stewart C., and Nicholas S. Majluf. 1984. "Corporate Financing and Investment Decisions when Firms Have Information That Investors Do Not Have." *Journal of Financial Economics* 13: 187–222.

Noël, François. [1857] 1993. *Dictionnaire étymologique et historique du français.* Nouvelle edition. Paris: Références Larousse.

Noss, Joseph, and Rihannon Sowerbutts. 2012. "The Implicit Subsidy of Banks." Financial Stability Paper 15. Bank of England, London.

Nyborg, Kjell. 2017. *Collateral Frameworks: The Open Secret of Central Banks.* Cambridge, UK: Cambridge University Press.

OECD (Organisation for Economic Cooperation and Development). 2009. *Economic Surveys: Iceland.* Paris.

O'Keffee, John. 2009. "The Effects of Underwriting Practices on Loan Losses: Evidence from the FDIC Survey of Bank Lending Practices." *International Finance Review* 11: 273–314.

Olson, Mancur. 1965. *The Logic of Collective Action: Public Goods and the Theory of Groups.* Cambridge, MA: Harvard University Press.

———. 1982. *The Rise and Decline of Nations*. New Haven, CT: Yale University Press.

Onaran, Yalman. 2011. *Zombie Banks: How Broken Banks and Debtor Nations Are Crippling the Global Economy*. Hoboken, NJ: Bloomberg.

Oreskes, Naomi, and Erik M. Conway. 2012. *Merchants of Doubt*. London: Bloomsbury Press.

———. 2023. *The Big Myth: How American Business Taught Us to Loathe Government and Love the Free Market*. New York: Bloomsbury Publishing.

Oxford Economics. 2012. "The Aggregate Mortgage Repossessions Outlook." *Economic Outlook* 36: 20–32.

Paddrik, Mark, and H. Peyton Young. 2021. "Assessing the Safety of Central Counterparties." OFR Working Paper 21–02. Office of Financial Research, Washington, DC.

Panier, Frédéric, Francisco Pérez-González, and Pablo Villanueva. 2012. "Capital Structure and Taxes: What Happens When You (Also) Subsidize Equity?" Working paper. Stanford University, Stanford, CA.

Paredes, Troy. 2010. "Corporate Governance and the New Financial Regulation: Complements or Substitutes?" Speech delivered at the Transatlantic Corporate Governance Dialogue, Brussels, October 25.

Partnoy, Frank. 2009. *Infectious Greed: How Deceit and Risk Corrupted the Financial Markets*. New York: PublicAffairs.

———. 2010. *F.I.A.S.C.O.* New York: Penguin, New York: W. W. Norton.

———. 2017. "What's (Still) Wrong with Credit Ratings?" *Washington Law Review* 92 (3): 1407–1472.

Patinkin, Don. 1965. *Money, Interest, and Prices: An Integration of Monetary and Value Theory*, 2nd ed. New York: Harper & Row.

Peltzman, Sam. 1975. "The Effects of Automobile Safety Regulation." *Journal of Political Economy* 83 (4): 677–725.

———. 1976. "Towards a More General Theory of Regulation." *Bell Journal of Economics* 19 (2): 211–240.

Perino, Michael. 2010. *The Hellhound of Wall Street: How Ferdinand Pecora's Investigation of the Great Crash Forever Changed American Finance*. New York: Penguin.

Persaud, Avinash. 2014. "Why Bail-In Securities Are Fool's Gold." Policy Brief PB14–23. Peterson Institute for International Economics, Washington, DC.

Pesek, Boris P., and Thomas R. Saving. 1967. *Money, Wealth, and Economic Theory*. New York: Collier Macmillan.

Petersen, Mitchell A., and Raghuram G. Rajan. 2002. "Does Distance Still Matter? The Information Revolution in Small Business Lending." *Journal of Finance* 57 (6): 2533–2570.

Pfleiderer, Paul. 2010. "On the Relevancy of Modigliani and Miller to Banking: A Parable and Some Observations." Working Paper 93. Rock Center for Corporate Governance, Stanford University, Stanford, CA.

———. 2018. "Chameleons: The Misuse of Theoretical Models in Finance and Economics." *Economica* 87: 81–107.

Pistor, Katharina. 2019. *The Code of Capital: How the Law Creates Wealth and Inequality*. Princeton, NJ: Princeton University Press.

Plantin, Guillaume. 2012. "Shadow Banking and Bank Capital Regulation." Working paper. Toulouse School of Economics and CEPR, Toulouse, France. May 27.

Posner, Richard A. 1976. *Antitrust Law: An Economic Perspective*. Chicago: University of Chicago Press.

———. 2018. *Justice for Pro Se's*. Scotts Valley, CA: CreateSpace.

Postman, Neil. 1985. *Amusing Ourselves to Death: Public Discourse in the Age of Show Business*. New York: Penguin.

Pozen, Robert C. 2009. *Too Big to Save? How to Fix the U.S. Financial System*. Hoboken, NJ: John Wiley and Sons.

Pozsar, Zoltan, Tobias Adrian, Adam B. Ashcraft, and Haley Boeskey. 2010. "Shadow Banking." Staff Report 458. Federal Reserve Bank of New York, New York.

Prasad, Eswar. 2021. *The Future of Money: How the Digital Transformation Is Transforming Currencies and Finance*. Cambridge, MA: Belknap Press.

Prescott, Edward S. 2012. "Contingent Capital: The Trigger Problem." *Federal Reserve Bank of Richmond Economic Quarterly* 98 (1): 33–50.

President's Working Group on Financial Markets. 1999. "Hedge Funds, Leverage, and the Lessons of Long-Term Capital Management."

Pringle, Paul. 2022. *Bad City: Peril and Power in the City of Angels*. New York: Celadon Books.

Proctor, Robert N., and Londa Schiebinger, eds. 2008. *Agnotology: The Making and Unmaking of Ignorance*. Stanford, CA: Stanford University Press.

Quinn, Stephen. 1997. "Goldsmith-Banking: Mutual Acceptance and Interbank Clearing in Restoration London." *Explorations in Economic History* 34: 411–432.

Rajan, Raghuram G. 1992. "Insiders and Outsiders: The Choice between Informed and Arm's-Length Debt." *Journal of Finance* 47 (4): 1367–1400.

———. 1994. "Why Bank Credit Policies Fluctuate: A Theory and Some Evidence." *Quarterly Journal of Economics* 109 (2): 399–441.

Rajan, Raghuram, and Luigi Zingales. 1995. "What Do We Know about Capital Structure? Evidence from International Data." *Journal of Finance* 50 (5): 1421–1460.

———. 1998. "Debt Folklore and Cross-Country Differences in Financial Structure." *Journal of Applied Corporate Finance* 10: 102–107.

Rajan, Uday, Amit Seru, and Vikrant Vig. 2010. "The Failure of Models to Predict Models." Working paper. University of Chicago, Chicago.

Rakoff, Jed S. 2021. *Why the Innocent Plead Guilty and the Guilty Go Free: And Other Paradoxes of Our Broken Legal System*. New York: Farrar, Straus, and Giroux.

Ramanna, Karthik. 2015. *Political Standards: Corporate Interest, Ideology, and Leadership in the Shaping of Accounting Rules for the Market Economy*. Chicago: University of Chicago Press.

Reinhart, Carmen M., and Kenneth Rogoff. 2009. *This Time Is Different: Eight Centuries of Financial Folly*. Princeton, NJ: Princeton University Press.

———. 2010. "Growth in a Time of Debt." *American Economic Review* 100 (2): 573–578.

Reis, Ricardo. 2015. "Different Types of Central Bank Insolvency and the Central Role of Seignorage." *Journal of Monetary Economics* 73: 20–25.

Reiss, Peter. 1990. "Economic and Financial Determinants of Oil and Gas Exploration Activity." In *Asymmetric Information, Corporate Finance and Investment*, ed. R. Glenn Hubbard. Chicago: University of Chicago Press.

Ricardo, David. 1817. "The Principles of Political Economy and Taxation." London. Full text available at http://www.econlib.org/library/Ricardo/ricP.html. Accessed October 21, 2012.

Riesser, Jakob. [1912] 1971. *Die deutschen Großbanken und ihre Konzentration* (The large banks in Germany and their concentration), 4th ed. Jena, Germany: Gustav Fischer. Reprint Glashütten, Germany: Detlev Auvermann KG.

Rochet, Jean Charles. 1992. "Capital Requirements and the Behaviour of Commercial Banks." *European Economic Review* 36: 1137–1170.

Rodrik, Dani. 2017. *Economic Rules*. New York: W.W. Norton.

Roe, Mark, and Michael Troege. 2018. "Containing Systemic Risk by Taxing Banks Properly." *Yale Journal on Regulation* 35 (181): 181–231.

Rogoff, Kenneth. 2016. *The Curse of Cash*. Princeton, NJ: Princeton University Press.

Rohatyn, Felix G. 2010. *Dealings: A Political and Financial Life*. New York: Simon and Schuster.

Rosengren, Eric S. 2010. "Dividend Policy and Capital Retention: A Systemic 'First Response.'{~?~thinspace}" Speech delivered at the "Rethinking Central Banking" conference. Washington, DC. October 10.

———. 2012. "Money Market Mutual Funds and Financial Stability." Speech delivered at the Federal Reserve Bank of Atlanta's 2012 Financial Markets Conference. April.

Ross, Carne. 2011. *The Leaderless Revolution: How Ordinary People Can Take Power and Change Politics in the 21st Century*. New York: Blue Rider.

Rothbard, Murray N. 2008. *The Mystery of Banking*, 2nd ed. Auburn, AL: Ludwig von Mises Institute.

Rothschild, Michael, and Joseph Stiglitz. 1976. "Equilibrium in Competitive Insurance Markets: An Essay on the Economics of Imperfect Information." *Quarterly Journal of Economics* 90 (4): 629–649.

Roubini, Nouriel, and Stephen Mihm. 2010. *Crisis Economics: A Crash Course in the Future of Finance*. London: Penguin.

Satchell, Stephen. 2011. "Stress and Scenario Testing for UK Residential Mortgage-Backed Securities: A Methodology for Loan-by-Loan Testing." MIAC Acadametrics, London. September 26.

Schaefer, Stephen M. 1990. "The Regulation of Banks and Securities Firms." *European Economic Review* 34 (2–3): 587–597.

Scheidel, Walter. 2017. *The Great Leveler: Violence and the History of Inequality from the Stone Age to the Twenty-First Century*. Princeton, NJ: Princeton University Press.

Schnabel, Isabel. 2004. "The German Twin Crisis of 1931." *Journal of Economic History* 64: 822–871.

———. 2009. "The Role of Liquidity and Implicit Guarantees in the German Twin Crisis of 1931." *Journal of International Money and Finance* 28: 1–25.

Schnabel, Isabel, and Hyun Song Shin. 2004. "Liquidity and Contagion: The Crisis of 1763." *Journal of the European Economic Association* 2: 929–968.

Schoenmaker, Dirk. 2010. "Burden Sharing: From Theory to Practice." DSF Policy Paper 6. Duisenberg School of Finance, Amsterdam. October.

Schön, Wolfgang. 2012. "The Distinct Equity of the Debt-Equity Distinction." *Bulletin for International Taxation* 66 (9): 490–502.

Schön, Wolfgang, Andreas Bakrozis, Johannes Becker, Tobias Beuchert, Martin Boer, Nadja Dwenger, Andreas Gerten, Maximilian Haag, Sabine Heidenbauer, Carsten Hohmann, Alexander Jehlin, Karin E.M. Kopp, Daniel Kornack, Nadia Lagdali, Christian Marquart, Lukas Müller, Marta Oliveros Castelon, Christine Osterloh-Konrad, Natalia Paxinou, Carlo Pohlhausen, Philipp Redeker, Erik Röder, Astrid Roesener. 2014. "Debt and Equity in International Tax Law—A Comparative Policy Analysis." *British Tax Review (BTR)* 2: 146–217.

Schröm, Oliver. 2021. *Die Cum-Ex-Files: Der Raubzug der Banker, Anwälte und Superreichen— und wie ich ihnen auf die Spur kam.* [The cum-ex files: the raid of the bankers, lawyers, and super rich—and how I tracked them down]. Berlin: Christoph-Links-Verlag.

Schularick, Moritz, and Alan Taylor. 2012. "Credit Boom Gone Bust: Monetary Policy, Credit Cycles, and Financial Crises, 1870–2008." *American Economic Review* 102 (2): 1029–1061.

Schütz, D. 1998. *Der Fall der UBS.* Zürich: Weltwoche-Verlag.

Schwartz, Eduardo S., and Walter N. Torous. 1991. "Caps on Adjustable Rate Mortgages: Calcuation, Insurance, and Hedging." In *Financial Markets and Financial Crises*, ed. R. Glenn Hubbard. Chicago: University of Chicago Press. 283–303.

Selgin, George. 2010. "Those Dishonest GoldSmiths." Mimeo. Terry College of Business, University of Georgia, Athens.

Sengupta, Rajdeep, and Yu Man Tam. 2008. "The Libor–OIS Spread as a Summary Indicator." Federal Reserve Bank of St. Louis, St. Louis, MO.

Shiller, Robert. 2008. *The Subprime Solution: How Today's Financial Crisis Happened and What to Do about It.* Princeton, NJ: Princeton University Press.

Shleifer, Andrei, and Robert Vishny. 1997. "A Survey of Corporate Governance." *Journal of Finance* 52: 737–783.

Silva, John. 1973. *An Introduction to Crime and Justice.* New York: MSS Information.

Singh, Manmohan, and James Aitken. 2010. "The (Sizeable) Role of Rehypothecation in the Shadow Banking System." IMF discussion paper. International Monetary Fund, Washington, DC. July.

Singh, Manmohan, and Zohar Alam. 2018. "Leverage—A Broader View." Working Paper No. 2018/062. International Monetary Fund. Washington, DC.

Sinn, Hans-Werner. 2010. *Casino Capitalism: How the Financial Crisis Came About and What Needs to Be Done Now.* Oxford, England: Oxford University Press.

Skeel, David A., Jr. 2010. *The New Financial Deal: Understanding the Dodd-Frank Act and Its (Unintended) Consequences.* Hoboken, NJ: John Wiley and Sons.

———. 2017. "What If a Clearinghouse Fails?" Brookings Center on Regulation and Markets, June 6.

Skeel, David A., Jr., and Thomas H. Jackson. 2012. "Transaction Consistency and the New Finance in Bankruptcy." *Columbia Law Review* 112: 152–202.

Slemrod, Joel, and Jon Bakija. 2008. *Taxing Ourselves: A Citizen's Guide to the Great Debate over Taxes*. 4th ed. Cambridge, MA: MIT Press.

Slobodian, Quinn. 2023. *Crack-Up Capitalism: Market Radicals and the Dream of a World Without Democracy*. London, UK: McMillan.

Smialek, Jeanna. 2023. *Limitless: The Federal Reserve Takes on a New Age of Crisis*. New York: Alfred A. Knopf.

Smith, Adam. 1776. *Wealth of Nations*. London: W. Strahan and T. Cadell.

Smith, Yves. 2010. *Econned: How Unenlightened Self Interest Undermined Democracy and Corrupted Capitalism*. New York: Palgrave Macmillan.

Sorkin, Andrew Ross. 2009. *Too Big to Fail: The Inside Story of How Wall Street and Washington Fought to Save the Financial System—and Themselves*. New York: Penguin.

Spence, Michael. 1973. "Job Market Signaling." *Quarterly Journal of Economics* 87 (3): 355–374.

Spengel, Christopher. 2016. "Darlegung der tatsächlichen und rechtlichen Gegebenheiten, welche bei sogenannten Cum/Ex-Geschäften mit Leerverkäufen zur mehrfachen Erstattung bzw. Anrechnung von tatsächlich nur einmal einbehaltener und abge-führter Kapitalertragsteuer bzw. bis zur Abschaffung des körperschaftsteuerlichen Anrechnungsverfahrens nur einmal gezahlter Körperschaftsteuer führten." (Explanation of factual and legal conditions that enabled multiple reimbursements of capital income or corporate income taxes in connection with so-called cum-ex transactions and short sales.) Report to the German Parliament, July 7.

———. 2017. "Kollektivversagen: Cum/Cum, Cum/Ex und Hopp!" [Collective Failure: cum/cum, cum/ex and Hopp!]. *Wirtschaftsdienst (WD)* 97 (7): 454–455.

———. 2021. "Statement for the Public Hearing of the Subcommittee on Tax Matters of the European Parliament on the Cum-Ex/Cum-Cum Scandal." February 24, Mannheim.

Stanton, Thomas H. 2012. *Why Some Firms Thrive while Others Fail: Governance and Management Lessons from the Crisis*. Oxford, England: Oxford University Press.

Staub, Markus. 1998. "The Term Structure of Interest Rates and the Swiss Regional Bank Crisis—Empirical Evidence and Its Limits." *Swiss Journal of Economics and Statistics* 134 (4): 655–684.

Steele, Graham. 2022. "The Tailors of Wall Street." *University of Colorado Law Review* 93 (4): 993–1060.

———. 2023. "Banking on the Edge." *University of Chicago Business Law Review* 2 (1): 171–254.

Stigler, George J. 1971. "The Theory of Economic Regulation." *Bell Journal of Economics and Management Science* 2 (Spring): 3–21.

Stiglitz, Joseph E. 2010. *Freefall: America, Free Markets, and the Sinking of the World Economy*. New York: W. W. Norton.

Stout, Lynn. 2012. *The Shareholder Value Myth: How Putting Shareholders First Harms Investors, Corporations, and the Public*. San Francisco: Berrett-Koehler.

Summers, Lawrence H. 2000. "International Financial Crises: Causes, Prevention, and Cure." Richard T. Ely Lecture. *American Economic Review* 90 (2): 1–16.

Sundaresan, Suresh, and Zhenyu Wang. 2010. "Design of Contingent Capital with Stock Price Trigger for Conversion." Staff Report 448. Federal Reserve Bank of New York, New York. April 23.

Taleb, Nassim N. 2001. *Fooled by Randomness: The Hidden Role of Chance in the Markets and in Life.* New York: W. W. Norton.

———. 2010. *The Black Swan, Second Edition: The Impact of the Highly Improbable, with a New Section: On Robustness and Fragility.* New York: Random House.

Tarullo, Daniel K. 2008. *Banking on Basel: The Future of International Financial Regulation.* Washington, DC: Peter G. Peterson Institute of International Economics.

Taub, Jennifer. 2014. *Other People's Houses: How Decades of Bailouts, Captive Regulators, and Toxic Bankers Made Home Mortgages a Thrilling Business.* New Haven, CT: Yale University Press.

———. 2020. *Big Dirty Money: The Shocking Injustice and Unseen Cost of White Collar Crime.* New York: Viking Press.

Tett, Gillian. 2009. *Fool's Gold: How the Bold Dreams of a Small Tribe at J. P. Morgan Was Corrupted by Wall Street Greed and Unleashed a Catastrophe.* New York: Free Press.

Thiemann, Matthias. 2012. "Out of the Shadow? Accounting for Special Purpose Entities in European Banking Systems." *Competition and Change* 16: 37–55.

Thomas, Pierre-Henri. 2012. *Dexia: Vie et mort d'un monstre bancaire* (Dexia: Life and death of a banking monster). Paris: Les Petits Matins.

Thornton, Daniel. 1984. "Monetizing the Debt." *Federal Reserve Bank of St. Louis Review* (December): 30–43.

Tilly, Richard H. 1989. "Banking Institutions in Historical and Comparative Perspective: Germany, Great Britain and the United States in the Nineteenth and Early Twentieth Century." *Journal of Institutional and Theoretical Economics* 145: 189–249.

Tobin, James. 1967. "Commercial Banks as Creators of 'Money.'{~?~thinspace}" In *Financial Markets and Economic Activity*, ed. Donald D. Hester and James Tobin. Cowles Foundation Monograph 21. New Haven, CT: Yale University Press.

Tooze, Adam. 2018. *Crashed: How a Decade of Financial Crises Changed the World.* New York: Viking.

Tsatsaronis, Kostas, and Jing Yang. 2012. "Bank Stock Returns, Leverage, and the Business Cycle." *BIS Quarterly Review* (March): 43–59.

Tucker, Paul. 2012. "Shadow Banking: Thoughts for a Possible Policy Agenda." Bank of England. Speech delivered at the European Commission High-Level Conference, Brussels.

———. 2018. "Resolution Policy and Resolvability at the Centre of Financial Stability Regimes?" Paper prepared for the joint conference of the International Association of Deposit Insurers (IADI), the Bank for International Settlements (BIS), and the Financial Stability Institute (FSI). Basel. February 1.

Turner, Adair. 2010. "What Do Banks Do? Why Do Credit Booms and Busts Occur and What Can Public Policy Do about It?" In *The Future of Finance.* London: London School of Economics. Chapter 1.

————. 2012. *Economics after the Crisis: Objectives and Means.* Cambridge, MA: MIT Press.

Turner, Adair, Andrew Haldane, and Paul Woolley. 2010. *The Future of Finance.* LSE Report. London: London School of Economics and Political Science.

UBS. 2008. "Shareholder Report on UBS's Writedowns." Zurich, April 18. http://maths-fi .com/ubs-shareholder-report.pdf. Accessed May 30, 2023.

————. 2011. "Annual Report."

Ueda, Kenichi, and Beatrice Weder di Mauro. 2012. "Quantifying Structural Subsidy Values for Systemically Important Financial Institutions." IMF Working paper 128. International Monetary Fund, Washington, DC.

UNDESA (United Nations Department of Economic and Social Affairs). 2011. *The Global Social Crisis: Report on the World Social Situation 2011.* United Nations publication ST/ ESA/334. New York.

Valukas, Anton R. 2010. *Report of Anton R. Valukas, Examiner, In re Lehman Bros. Holding Inc.* Chapter 11, Case No. 08-13555 (JMP). U.S. Bankruptcy Court, Southern District of New York, New York.

Van den Heuvel, Skander J. 2008. "The Welfare Cost of Bank Capital Requirements." *Journal of Monetary Economics* 55: 298–320.

Vestergaard, Jakob, and María Retana. 2013. "Behind Smoke and Mirrors: On the Alleged Recapitalization of Europe's Banks." DIIS (Danish Institute of International Studies) Report 2013: 10.

Vickers, John. 2019. "The Case for Market-Based Stress Tests." *Journal of Financial Regulation* 5 (2): 239–248.

Viscusi, W. Kip, Joseph E. Harrington, and John M. Vernon. 2005. *Economics of Regulation and Antitrust,* 4th ed. Cambridge, MA: MIT Press.

Vissing-Jorgensen, Annette. 2021. "The Treasury Market in Spring 2020 and the Response of the Federal Reserve." *Journal of Monetary Economics* 124: 19–47.

Vogl, Frank. 2021. *The Enablers: How the West Supports Kleptocrats and Corruption— Endangering Our Democracy.* Washington, DC: Rowman & Littlefield.

Wallace, Neil. 1988. "Another Attempt to Explain an Illiquid Banking System: The Diamond and Dybvig Model with Sequential Service Taken Seriously." *Federal Reserve Bank of Minneapolis Quarterly Review* 12 (Fall): 3–16.

Warshawsky, Mark. 1991. "Is There a Corporate Debt Crisis? Another Look." In *Financial Markets and Financial Crisis, A National Bureau of Economic Research Project Report,* ed. R. Glenn Hubbard, 207–230. Chicago: University of Chicago Press.

Waverman, Leonard, and Esen Sirel. 1997. "European Telecommunications Markets on the Verge of Full Liberalization." *Journal of Economic Perspectives* 11 (4): 113–126. doi:10.1257/ jep.11.4.113.

Weinberg, John A. 1995. "Cycles in Lending Standards?" *Economic Quarterly* 81 (3): 1–18.

Weinstein, David, and Yishay Yafeh. 1998. "On the Costs of a Bank Centered Financial System: Evidence from the Changing Main Bank Relations in Japan." *Journal of Finance* 53: 635–672.

Weitzman, Hal. 2022. *What's the Matter with Delaware? How the First State Has Favored the Rich, Powerful, and Criminal—and How It Costs Us All*. Princeton, NJ, and Oxford, UK: Princeton University Press.

Wheelan, Charles. 2003. *Naked Economics: Understanding the Dismal Science*. New York: W. W. Norton.

Whitaker, Stephan, and Thomas J. Fitzpatrick IV. 2012. "The Impact of Vacant, Tax-Delinquent, and Foreclosed Property on Sales Prices of Neighboring Homes." Working Paper 1123. Federal Reserve Bank of Cleveland, Cleveland, OH.

White, Lawrence J. 1991. *The S&L Debacle: Public Policy Lessons for Bank and Thrift Regulation*. Oxford, England: Oxford University Press.

———. 2004. "The Savings and Loans Debacle: A Perspective from the Early Twenty-First Century." In *The Savings and Loan Crisis: Lessons from a Regulatory Failure*, ed. J. Barth, S. Trimbaugh, and G. Yago. Dordrecht, The Netherlands: Kluwer.

Wilmarth, Arthur E., Jr. 2007. "Conflicts of Interest and Corporate Governance Failures at Universal Banks during the Stock Market Boom of the 1990s: The Cases of Enron and Worldcom." In *Corporate Governance in Banking: A Global Perspective*, ed. Benton E. Gup. Northampton, MA: Edward Elgar.

———. 2011. "The Dodd-Frank Act: A Flawed and Inadequate Response to the Too-Big-to-Fail Problem." *Oregon Law Review* 89: 951–1057.

———. 2012a. "The Financial Services Industry's Misguided Quest to Undermine the Consumer Financial Protection Bureau." Public Law Research Paper 2012-4. George Washington University Law School, George Washington University, Washington, DC.

———. 2012b. "The Dodd-Frank Act's Expansion of State Authority to Protect Consumers of Financial Services." *Journal of Corporation Law* 36 (4): 893–954.

———. 2013. "Turning a Blind Eye. Why Washington Keeps Giving in to Wall Street." *University of Cincinnati Law Review* 81 (4): 1283–1446.

Wilson, James Q., ed. 1980. *The Politics of Regulation*. New York: Basic Books.

Wolf, Martin. 2010. "Why and How Should We Regulate Pay in the Financial Sector?" In *The Future of Finance*. The LSE Report. London: London School of Economics and Political Science. Chapter 9.

———. 2023. *The Crisis of Democratic Capitalism*. New York: Penguin Press.

Wuffli, Peter. 1995. "Comment on the Paper by Professor Hellwig, 'Systemic Aspects of Risk Management in Banking and Finance.'" *Swiss Journal of Economics and Statistics* 131: 139–140.

Wylie, Bob. 2020. *Bandit Capitalism: Carillion and the Corruption of the British State*. Edinburgh: Birlinn Publishing.

Zimmer, Daniel. 2010. "Finanzmarktregulierung—Welche Regelungen empfehlen sich für den deutschen und europäischen Finanzsektor?" [Financial Regulation—Which Rules for the German and European Financial Sector?]. Report G for the 68th German Lawyers' Reunion. Munich: Verlag C.H. Beck.

Zingales, Luigi. 2012. *A Capitalism for the People: Recapturing the Lost Genius of American Prosperity*. New York: Basic Books.

————. 2013. "Preventing Economists' Capture." In *Preventing Regulatory Capture: Special Interest Influence and How to Limit It*, ed. Daniel Carpenter and David Moss. Cambridge, UK: Cambridge University Press.

————. 2015. "Presidential Address: Does Finance Benefit Society?" *Journal of Finance* 70 (4): 1327–1363.

Zubrow, Barry. 2011. Testimony given at a hearing before the House Financial Services Committee, Washington, DC, June 16.

Zuckerman, Gregory. 2009. *The Greatest Trade Ever: The Behind-the-Scenes Story of How John Paulson Defied Wall Street and Made Financial History*. New York: Crown Business.

INDEX

This index includes entries for the main subjects of this book, including institutions and individuals in positions of responsibility. With a few exceptions, it does not include references to authors and works that we cite. Page numbers for entries occurring in notes are followed by an *n*; those for entries in figures are followed by an *f*; those for entries in tables are followed by a *t*.

29–30; in TARP, 429n26; usefulness of
a ban on, 172–176, 190, 223, 238, 241,
172–176, 434n53, 480n146, 481n150
Dodd-Frank Act of 2010 (U.S.), 234,
235, 236, 272, 461–461n12, 478n29,
523n129; bailouts forbidden by, 138, 272,
290; Collins Amendment to, 439n78,
440n82; Consumer Financial Protection
Bureau under, 373n13; on costs of bank
failures, 76; on credit limits, 392n24; on
credit rating agencies regulations, 334;
delayed implementation of, 234, 236,
356n16, 389n3, 462n12, 463n20, 464n27,
478n128; Financial Stability Oversight
Council under, 395n37, 451n64, 460n53;
on living wills, 77, 387–388n65, 500n59;
lobbyists' influence on, 3, 235, 355n13,
393n24, 394n34, 450n60; Office of Financial Research under, 451n64; on regulation of compensation, 409n35; repeal
of part of, 235; on resolution authority,
76, 77, 138–139, 387n63, 499n50,
500nn58–59, 502n69; on single counterparty credit limit, 392–393n24; on systemically important financial institutions,
235, 290, 296–297, 360n36, 363n53,
395n37, 478n128; whistleblower program
established by, 341. *See also* Volcker Rule
domino effects, 61; from credit default
swaps, 68–69; in financial crisis of
2007–2009, 61, 66. *See also* contagion
dot-com bubble of 1990s, 60, 61, 379n3,
380n6
down payments, home, 18–24, 22t
downturns. *See* recessions
"dumb banks," 78, 388n67
Durbin, Dick (U.S. senator), 449n48
Düsseldorf (Germany), banks located in,
as willing buyers of mortgage-related
securities, 248, 383n29, 473n93

earthquakes: as analogues to financial cri-
ses, 206–207; preparing for, 78
EBA. *See* European Banking Authority
ECB. *See* European Central Bank
École Nationale d'Administration (ENA),
203, 448n43

economic downturns. *See* recessions
Economic Emergency Stabilization Act of
2008 (U.S.), 448n46
economic growth. *See* growth
Economic Growth, Regulatory Reform, and
Consumer Protection Act of 2018, 235
economic nationalism, 193–194, 199
economic recessions. *See* recessions
economy, benefits provided to, by banks, 3,
49–51, 148, 355n14
Edge Act, 312, 480n148
efficiency, economic, 345–346
efficient scale, for banks, 50–51, 89, 144,
394n31, 414n29
Ellison, Keith (Congressman), 394n33
embezzlement, 330
eminent domain, 369n10, 403n25
Emperor's New Clothes (Andersen), 1–2, 9,
97, 262, 351
employees: bonuses for (*see* compensation);
career concerns of, 127, 228, 443n9
employment, in financial crisis of 2007–2009,
357n20, 361n42
ENA. *See* École Nationale d'Administration
enablers of abuse and fraud, 342–347
Enarques, 203, 448n43
enforcement of rules and regulations,
214–217, 314–315, 348, 350; in institutions, 324–327; by public authorities,
171–172, 225–228, 327–331, 459–460n53,
507n8, 514–515n64
England, history of banking in, 149–150,
151, 374n16, 417nn6–9. *See also* United
Kingdom
Enria, Andrea (President, European Banking Authority), 465n34, 469n70
Enron: bankruptcy of, 61, 333, 369n13;
culture of ROE at, 125, 408n29; governance problems at, 127; off-balance-sheet
commitments of, 83, 124
environmental pollution analogies, 13, 82,
97, 130, 197
environmental regulation, 82, 199, 445n25
equity, 6, 18–26, 100–114, 364n9. *See also*
capital (equity); capital regulation (minimum capital requirements); corporate
equity; return on equity; share(s) of equity

Florida, nonrecourse mortgage clauses in, 364n5

FMS Wertmanagement ("bad bank" of Hypo Real Estate), 360n38

foreclosure: impact of on home prices, 369n10; inefficiencies of, 364n6, 400n12; in nonrecourse mortgages, 21

foreign currency reserves, 276

"fortress balance sheet," 83–87, 390n6

forward contracts, 69–70

fragility of banking system: backlash on regulatory reform and, 233–238; bankers' claims about, 83, 148–149, 212; ban on cash payouts to shareholders and, 172–176, 223; central bank supports and, 239–241; COVID pandemic and, 237–241; current status of, xvii–xviii, 4, 172, 212; failures of regulation and supervision and, 253–256, 327–331; flawed regulation as cause of, 170, 185; "fortress balance sheet" and, 83–87; high indebtedness and, 241–243; incompetence and recklessness and, 248–253, 324–327; interconnectedness and, 66–69; opaqueness and, 243–248, 441n48, 470–471n78, 503n75; parade of bankers' new clothes and, 261–265; payment systems and, 149–153; persisting in 2023, 231–233; potential for reducing, 78; reforming accounting rules and equity requirements and, 257–258; regulation of capital and, 94–99; regulation of investment risks and, 87–92; regulation of liquidity risks and, 92–94; regulatory reform and politics and, 258–261; said to be a byproduct of benefit of banking, 3, 148–149; strategies for preventing bank failures and, 218–224

fragmentation of authorities, 331, 517n79

France: bank bailouts by, 11, 57, 192, 361n38, 377n39, 416n39, 442n3, 442n7, 447n36; bank debt as percentage of GDP of, 362n50; bank failures in, 55–56, 376n37; bank mergers in, 447n36, 448n45; banks as providers of positions for *Enarques*, 203, 448nn44–45; banks as public institutions in, 203; costs of

bailouts in, 416n39, 442n7; effectiveness of lobbying by, 3, 355n12; implicit guarantees in, 137; opposition to banking reform by, 3, 192–193, 203, 355n12, 443n8, 463n18; reception of Basel III in, 194

Franklin National, 382n23

fraud, 348, 453n8, 508n11, 509n16; in bankruptcy delays, 370n19; cum-ex tax fraud scandal, 315–318, 506n3, 508n14, 509n17, 509n19, 521n107, 522n116; enablers and spin of, 342–347; in mortgage loans, 58; prosecution of, 208, 215, 228, 456n33

Freddie Mac: cost of bailout of, 145, 209, 416n39, 453n10; debt as percentage of assets of, 8, 358n27; government control of, 484n6; guarantees in credit rating of, 360n32; history of growth of, 144–145, 415n35; implicit guarantees for, 137, 144–145; mortgage securitization by, 377n43

free-market capitalism, 350

free markets, 349–350

FSA. *See* Financial Services Authority

FSB. *See* Financial Stability Board

FSLIC. *See* Federal Savings and Loan Insurance Corporation

FSOC. *See* Financial Stability Oversight Council

FTX, 232, 305, 483n1, 501n67

Fuld, Richard, 450n58

full reserve banking, 359n38. *See also* narrow banking

funding costs: costs of borrowing to banks, 7–9, 100–101; costs of borrowing to society, 8–9, 10, 33; costs of capital (equity) to banks, 7–8, 100–102, 111–112; impact of bankruptcy prospects on, 141; impact of change in funding mix on, 109–110; impact of guarantees on, 130

funding mix, debt-equity, 107–13; of banks, 94, 101, 111–12, 146; change in, effects on funding costs, 109–10; of corporations, 18, 29, 101, 105, 108–110, 112, 140; costs of, to society, 146; impact of tax code on, 140, 188, 226–227; and required return on equity, 107–110, 112–113, 116, 120

funding source(s), of banks: borrowing as,
49; deposits as, 48–49, 51–52, 111, 150,
402n21; equity as, 4–5, 48f, 94, 97–99,
100, 105–112, 152–153; retained earnings
as, 172–176, 182, 189
Fürstenberg, Carl (German banker), 401n13

GAAP. *See* Generally Accepted Accounting
Principles
gambling: in casinos, 123; with derivatives,
70–71, 73, 123; for resurrection, 33,
54–55, 255, 261, 271, 465n35, 476n119
Garn–St. Germain Depository Institutions
Act of 1982 (U.S.), 375n28
GDP. *See* gross domestic product
Geithner, Timothy F., 360n34, 370n16,
412n14, 505n95
gender, of traders, 453n7
Generally Accepted Accounting Principles
(GAAP), 84f, 85–86, 390n11, 391n15,
391n18
General Motors Acceptance Corporation
(GMAC), 359n29, 364n2
geographic restrictions: on bank activities,
88, 202; on bank branches, 393n25
Germany: bailouts of individual banks in
2007–2009 crisis, 11, 360n38, 370n14,
377n39, 380n12, 382n27, 415–416n38,
428–429n19, 429–430n26, 485–486n18,
491n70, 494n17, 495n26; banking crisis of
1931, 380n8, 396–397n45; banking system
of, 91, 362n50, 395n40, 432–433n47,
447n39, 458n45; bankruptcy, insolvency,
resolution, and restructuring of banks,
77, 364n53, 368n8, 369n11, 370–371n19,
413n18, 494–495nn21–22; competition
policy in, 347, 348, 524n149; corporations
and criminal law in, 507n4, 508n9; covered
bonds and mortgages in, 378–379n48,
394–395n36, 428nn17–18; crisis interventions in 2007–2009, general features of,
57,91, 137, 416n39, 442n7, 484n6, 495n27,
498nn47–49; cum-ex tax fraud scandal in,
315, 509nn19–20, 510n25; excess capacity and competition in banking in, 202,
428nn17–18, 464n28; failure of Herstatt
Bank (1974), 376n36, 382n23; great infla-

tion in, 419n14, 485n16; history of banking
in, 366nn20–21, 372n8; nonperforming
loans of banks in, 464n28,469n70, 496n28,
497n37; open-end mutual funds in,
432n45; public banks (Landesbanken and
savings banks) in, 94, 202, 359n32, 415n38,
429–430n19, 436n58, 447n39, 449n47,
463n18, 458n45, 485–486n18; resistance
against stricter regulation, 193, 194, 203,
260, 355n12, 436n58, 442n6, 442n8,
449n47, 463n18, 514n62, 463n18, 464n24;
tax treatment of interest paid, 140, 413n21.
See also BaFin; Deutsche Bank; "Düsseldorf"; European crises of 2010–2015;
Landesbanken
GFG Alliance Group, 249
Glass-Steagall Act (U.S.): balance sheets
under, 47–49, 48f; bank activity restrictions in, 46, 47; erosion and demise
of (1999), 46, 372n3, 377n41, 456n30;
interconnectedness under, 458n45; interest rates on deposits under, 53, 372n6,
375n26
global crisis, financial crisis of 2007–2009
as, 65–70
global economy, impact of subprime mortgage crisis on, 60
globalization, and interconnectedness of
institutions, 66
global systematically important banks
(GSIBs), 305, 308, 395n37, 399n2, 404n1,
460n3
Global Witness, 335–336
GMAC. *See* General Motors Acceptance
Corporation
gold: and banknotes, 374n16, 417nn7–8,
418n15; reserves, 276, 278, 280, 283,
489n58
Goldman Sachs: bailouts, benefits of, 410n1,
484n2, 493–494n17; change in status to
bank holding company, 93, 138, 410n1;
conflicts of interest in mortgage securities
and SEC settlement of, 322, 420–421n32;
culture of, 453n7; size and opacity of,
470n74, 504n80; mistakes admitted by,
354n8; on single-counterparty credit
limit proposal, 393n24

implicit guarantees and subsidies (*continued*)
and credit ratings, 359n31, 415n33; in
financial crisis of 2007–2009, 137–138;
funding costs affected by, 9, 137–138,
140–142, 414n29; Jamie Dimon's denial
of, 359n30; perverse incentives from, 130,
139, 142–145, 198, 283–285, 289, 291;
as unlimited, 129, 137; value to banks
of, 145, 393n22, 415nn32–33. *See also*
explicit guarantees and subsidies; guarantees, government
inaction of authorities, 169–176, 253–256,
297–298, 327–331. *See also* enforcement of rules and regulations, by public
authorities
incentives and moral hazard: in bank borrowing, 129, 130, 142–145, 220; for becoming
too big to fail, 130, 142–145, 218; in bonuses, 162; in capital regulation, 95; career
concerns and, 127, 228, 443n9; in compensation, 116, 122–127, 407n21, 408n24,
408n27 (*see also* compensation, corporations); in creditworthiness assessments, 56,
58; in dealing with internal rules of banks
and with public regulations, 324–330; in
debt overhang, 130, 162–163; in evaluation
of insolvency, 41; gambling for resurrection, 33, 54–55; induced by guarantees,
130, 139, 142–145, 198; for lending versus
trading assets, 391n19; in mergers, 89; and
need for banking regulation, 81; and securitization, 58; in tax code, 139–140
income: corporate, definition of, 140;
per capita, impact of financial crisis of
2007–2009 on, 361n42
incompetence and recklessness, 248–250
Independent Commission on Banking
(ICB), 90, 218n8, 445n28, 449n53,
478n179
indexed debt, 400n6
India, banking crisis in, 382n22
Industriekreditbank, 382n27, 383n29,
390n9, 423n45
inflation: in Germany (1923), 418n14;
money creation in, 157–158, 400n6,
418n14, 419n16, 420n26, 421n37, 446n34;
of 1970s, 53

information contagion. *See* contagion
innovation, role of risk taking in, 216
innovations, financial: and interconnectedness, 66–69; of 1980s and 1990s, 57–59;
risk management through, 68–74; and
safety of banking system, 70–74. *See also*
specific types
Inside Job (book and movie), 345
insolvency. *See* solvency problems
Insolvency Act of 1986 (UK), 245
Institute of International Finance (IIF), 97,
356n18, 357n22, 358n25, 434n51
insurance. *See* credit insurance; deposit
insurance
insurance companies: capital requirements
for, 179; contingent convertible bonds
and, 440n81
insured deposits, 252, 269, 271, 285–286,
293, 490n65, 504n88. *See also* deposit
insurance; explicit guarantees and subsidies; uninsured deposits
interbank clearing, 486n22
interbank lending. *See* LIBOR
interconnectedness of financial institutions:
capital requirements and, 181; contagion
and, 61, 66, 161, 219; from dependence
on money market funds, 66–67; in derivatives, 501n62; of Deutsche Bank, 243; in
financial crisis of 2007–2009, 61, 65–69,
185; in new risk management techniques,
68–69; after a potential breakup of largest banks, 219, 458n45; and resolution,
challenges of, 303–307, 388n66. *See also*
fragility; systemically important financial
institutions; systemic risk
interest-bearing assets, versus cash,
153–155
interest margins, 50, 54, 250, 255, 272, 285,
465n32, 465–466n36
interest payments: by corporations, 140,
413n23; on mortgages, 18–19, 21,
117–119, 140, 364n8, 413nn21–22
interest rate risk and volatility, 34, 47, 57,
96; adjustable-rate mortgages and, 34,
368n2, 422–423, 44; derivatives and,
71–72, 73, 125, 384n37, 384n40; lack
of understanding of, 253, 422–423n44,

424n49, 438n71; largely ignored in capital regulation, 258, 260; maturity transformation and, 159, 160; neglect of, before 2022, 237, 239, 241, 253; prepayment risk on mortgages and, 378nn47–48. *See also* interest rates

interest rates: affected by central bank policy, 53–55, 72, 88, 133, 233, 238, 251–252, 276, 279, 283, 375n25, 380, 405n10, 446n32, 446n36, 475n118, 489n53, 489n58, 490n67; affected by government regulation, 54, 375n25, 375n28, 405n8, 475n119; affected by properties of loan contracts and borrowers (default risk, equity, government guarantees), 103, 104, 105, 109, 111, 120–122, 131–133, 141–143, 283, 400n7, 401n11, 404n6, 481nn158–159, 492n9; on banks' reserves, 200, 465–466n36, 485n17, 486n23; on deposits, 54, 111, 375n25, 375n28; effects of increases in, on asset values, 401n14, 475n105; effects of increases in, on asset values ignored by accounting rules for held-to-maturity securities, 256, 257, 284; effects of increases in, on debtors' borrowing costs, 102, 125, 129, 155, 213; in stress tests, 477–78n126. *See also* LIBOR

International Accounting Standards Board (IASB), 390n13

international competition: Basel rules and, 194; environmental regulations and, 199, 445n25; home-team bias of regulators in, 195, 205; "level playing field" rhetoric in, 10, 194–199; in national politics, 193, 194–199, 442n8; subsidies and guarantees in, 197–199

International Financial Reporting Standard (IFRS), 84f, 85–86, 390n11, 390n13, 391n15, 391n18, 472n86, 477n124

International Monetary Fund (IMF), 12, 57, 60, 192, 243, 269, 357n19, 361n42, 362n46, 363nn51–52, 367n2, 379nn2–3, 379n5, 381nn18–19, 382n26, 437n66; central bank liabilities to, 277; on crossborder resolution, 305

International Swaps and Derivatives Association (ISDA), 390n11, 391nn15–16, 391n18

international trade: Ricardian theory of, 444n18; strategic theory of, 444n23

Interstate Commerce Commission, U.S., 443n9

investment(s): of banks, controlling risks from, 87–92; distortions due to financial distress, 41–43, 370n18; of individuals and businesses, borrowing for, 17–18

investment bankers, 248, 289, 321–323, 326, 330, 458n45

investment banks: approaches to regulation of, 90; versus bank holding companies, 93, 138, 410n1; campaign contributions by, 448n46; capital regulation of, 180, 204, 449n52; COVID supports helping, 466–467n46; debt as percentage of assets of, 8; Glass-Steagall Act restrictions on, 46; guarantees for, 90; money market fund runs and, 380n12; mortgage securitization by, 58; need for tighter regulation of, 218–219, 458n43; regulatory capture and, 204, 449n52; versus retail banks, risks of, 90–91; ring fencing and, 90; services offered by, 390n14; transformation from partnerships to corporations, 406n14. *See also specific banks*

Ireland: cost of bailouts in, 197, 309; EU support of banks in, 12, 363n52; failure of banks of, 12, 89, 143, 362n45, 362n51, 504n85; mortgage debt in, 364n4; real estate bubble in, 56, 454n18; solvency problems in, 429n19, 455n18

ISDA. *See* International Swaps and Derivatives Association

Israel, indexed debt in, 400n6

Italy: aversion to resolution, bail-ins and closures, 295, 296, 298, 299; bailout of Monte dei Paschi di Siena, 494n22, 495n25, 497nn40–41; banks as source of government funding in, 445n30, 446n32; closures of Banca Popolare di Vicenza and Veneto Banca, 495n23, 495n25, 496n30, 497n41, 499n52; firms of, pressured by competition in global markets, 345; media coverage of banks in, 523n126; problems of banks with nonperforming loans in mid-2010s, 464n28, 465n34, 469n70

media: bias in favor of "national champions," 195, 329, 343–344, 517n81; conflicts of interest and capture of, 343–344; confusion about capital in, 6, 98, 358n23, 522n121; confusion on return on equity in, 126, 404n1, 406n12, 407nn17–18, 441n84; as enablers of distortions in banking, 1, 55–56, 290, 299, 329, 337–338, 341–344, 519n94; impact on political discourse, 351; role of investigative, 330, 338–342, 470n78, 520–521nn104–105; role in SVB case of, 250, 286, 351, 475n107, 485n10, 490n61; role in Wirecard case of, 330, 517n81; and whistleblowers, 339–340, 342, 468n58
megabanks. *See* systemically important financial institutions
Menke, Frauke (banking supervision at BaFin, the German supervisor), 320, 321, 322, 326
mergers, bank: BNP Paribas, 393n28, 448n45; deregulation of, 375n28; Dexia, 393n28, 447n36; growth in number of, 89, 393n28; incentives for, 89, 144; UBS, 127, 393n28, 409n36; in United States since 2015, 308. *See also* concentration
Merkley, Jeff (U.S. senator), 355n13, 383n32
Merrill Lynch: acquired by Bank of America, 308; cum-ex tax fraud scandal and, 316; money market fund of, 375n27
Mexico, sovereign default by, 446n33
MF Global, failure of, 425n55
Middle Ages: default in, 36; early banking in, 373n16; guilds in, 347–349
Miller, Brad (U.S. congressman), 394n33, 403n25
Miller, Merton (academic), 100, 102, 109, 112, 113, 179, 432n46. *See also* Modigliani-Miller (M&M)
Mishkin, Frederic (academic), 115, 374n17, 404n3, 481n157. *See also* banking textbooks
Mnuchin, Steve (U.S. Treasury secretary), 262, 462n14
models: in capital regulation, 184, 186–187, 191, 259–260; in mark-to-model

accounting, 392n21; risk (*see* risk models); in stress testing, 186–187
Modigliani-Miller (M&M), 109, 402n18; applicability to banks, 110–111; for dividends and payouts, 429n22
monetary policy, U.S., 422n39
monetization of government debt, 446n32. *See also* central bank money
money (means of payment): banknotes (*see* banknotes); bank reserves (*see* reserves); cartalist view of, 418n10, 418n14; of central banks (*see* central bank money); deposits treated as, 150, 417n10; digital, 446n32, 486n19–20; fiat, 485n15; history of, 149–150, 374n18, 417nn6–9; liquidity of, 153; political impact of, 203, 449n48; purchasing power of, 157, 420n26, 421n37; quantity of, definitions of, 418n10; as a source of power, 200
money laundering, 507n3, 520–521nn104–105
money-like debt, 154–156, 160; excessive production of, 165
money machine, 119, 405nn9–10; arbitrage opportunity as, 103, 400n9; bank borrowing from central banks as, 138; blanket guarantees as, 411n6, 415n30; zero-equity mortgages as, 136
money market, definition of, 48
money market funds (mutual funds), 48, 53–54, 67, 375n27, 423n46, 459n53; contagion in, 62–63; during the COVID crisis, 239, 288; versus deposit institutions, 67, 433n47; deposit insurance for, lack of, 67, 93, 433n47; European sovereign debt and, 170, 426n3; in financial crisis of 2007–2009, 62–63, 66, 138, 161; and French banks, 192; as funding source for banks, 48, 62–63, 67; guarantees for, 161; interconnectedness and, 66–67; interest rates of, 53–54, 67, 284–285; legal definition of banks and, 433n47; Lehman bankruptcy and, 62–63, 66, 380n9, 433n47; liquidity narrative and, 454n12; mechanisms of, 67; as off-balance-sheet entities, 84; reductions in lending by, 62–63; regulation of, 54, 67, 161,

240–241, 259, 356n16, 375n27, 383n30, 424n48, 433n47, 459n53; rise of, 66–67, 423n46; risks of, 423n46; runs on, 62–63, 67, 93, 161; safety of, 232, 250; in securitization of mortgages, 159–160; as shadow banking institutions, 225, 459n53; stable net asset value (SNAV), 433n47, 467n49

money view of banking, 149–151, 374n18

Moody's, downgrade of Bank of America and Citigroup, 359n31

moral hazard. *See* incentives and moral hazard

Morgan Stanley: bailouts benefit of, 410n1, 484n2, 493–494n17; change in status to bank holding company, 93, 138, 410n1; and knowledge about LIBOR scandal, 452n4; large trading losses of, 384n39; mistakes admitted by, 356n17

mortgage(s), 18–24; adjustable-rate, 34, 160, 367n2, 422n44; in covered bonds, 378nn47–48, 422n41; creditworthiness assessments for, 56, 58, 372n9, 401n12; default on (*see* mortgage default); down payments and, 18–24, 22t; in financial crisis of 2007–2009, 59, 60–61, 65–66; financial distress and, 42–43, 370n18; guarantees on, impact of, 130–136, 132t, 134t, 142–143, 145–146, 411nn6–8; in homeowner balance sheets, 18, 19, 20f, 23; interest only, 475n109; interest payments on, 18–19, 21, 117–119, 140, 364n8, 413nn21–22; interest rates on, 34, 104, 105, 117, 160, 327, 400n12, 404n6, 514n63; homeowners trying to sue banks, 340; leverage effect in, 19, 21–22, 107–108, 118–119, 466n37; in liquidity transformation, 158–159; for low income, 447n38; in maturity transformation, 158–159, 475n109, 476–477n119; nonrecourse clauses in, 21, 23, 364n5; politics of, 327, 447n38, 514n63; prime, 378n43; problems caused by burden of, 33–34; return on equity in, 117–119, 118t, 135, 404n7, 411n7; risks of, 18–24, 102–103; second, 34, 44, 364n5, 371nn21–22, 410n5; securitization of (*see* securitization); solvency problems for banks in 2023, 255,

475n109; solvency problems of S&Ls from, 54, 159, 376n32; subprime (*see* subprime mortgage[s]); tax subsidies for, 140, 265; underwater, 20–21, 42, 95, 133, 370n18; zero-equity, 135–136, 287–288nn8–9

mortgage-backed securities (MBS) and mortgage-related securities: 58, 159, 379n2; in the banking crisis of 2023, 251; breakdown of markets for, 58–59; as collateral for central banks, 157; in collateralized debt obligations, 379n2; contagion in markets for, 63–64, 381n17; versus covered bonds, 378nn47–48, 522–523nn122–123; credit ratings for, 156–157, 185, 334; deception and fraud in selling of, 242, 313, 322, 337–338, 340–341, 348, 519n92; German banks' purchase of, 66, 248, 383n29; in global impact of financial crisis of 2007–2009, 65–66; held by central banks, 240, 271, 288–289, 466n42; held by off-balance-sheet entities, 83–84, 330, 463n19; interconnectedness in, 68; as liquid assets, 396n44, liquidity problems with, 156–157, 421n34; losses from, in financial crisis of 2007–2009, 60, 96, 245–245, 379nn2–3, 398n56, 470n77, 479n136; and maturity transformation, 159–160; panic in 2007 over, 423n45; risks of, 73, 162, 424n49; in risk-weighting approach, 185, 438n70, 522–523nn122–123; in structured investment vehicles, 161–162, 423n45

mortgage default, 34, 367nn1–2; adjustable rates and, 34, 160, 367n2, 422n44; in financial crisis of 2007–2009, 211, 367n2; risk of, in costs of borrowing, 103, 105; securitization and, 58, 68, 378n43; in United Kingdom, 34, 367n1; in United States, 34. *See also* foreclosure

Moynihan, Brian (Bank of America CEO), 354n8, 356n17. *See also* Bank of America

Munich Re, 451n65

municipalities: borrowing by, 201, 446n33; banks' involvement in bonds of, 452–453n6; debt of in risk weights, 447n36, 478n 133; as savings bank owners in Germany, 447n39, 449n47